New Society

SOCIOLOGY FOR THE 21ST CENTURY

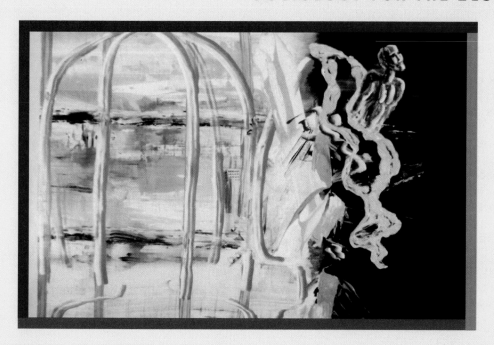

ABOUT THE COVER ART

THE GREAT GERMAN SOCIOLOGIST MAX WEBER LIKENED THE MODERN ERA TO AN "IRON CAGE." SOCIOLOGY PROMISES TO TEACH US BOTH THE DIMENSIONS OF THAT CAGE AND THE POSSIBILITIES FOR RELEASE. SPECIFICALLY, THE SOCIOLOGICAL IMAGINATION ENABLES THE INDIVIDUAL TO CRITICALLY ASSESS AND RISE ABOVE HIS OR HER SUBJECTIVE EXPERIENCE BY VIEWING IT AS PART OF A LARGER, SOCIOHISTORICAL REALITY.

SOURCE: CAROL WAINIO, UNTITLED (1985). ACRYLIC ON CANVAS, 33" x 50". IMAGE COURTESY OF THE S.L. SIMPSON GALLERY, TORONTO. REPRODUCED WITH PERMISSION OF THE ARTIST.

New Society

SOCIOLOGY FOR THE 21ST CENTURY

SECOND EDITION

ROBERT J. BRYM
University of Toronto

HARCOURT
BRACE
CANADA

Harcourt Brace & Company, Canada

Toronto Montreal Fort Worth New York Orlando
Philadelphia San Diego London Sydney Tokyo

Canadian Cataloguing in Publication Data

Brym, Robert J., 1951–
          New society : sociology for the 21st century

2nd ed.
Includes bibliographical references and index.
ISBN 0-7747-3568-6

1. Sociology. I. Title.

HM51.B897 1998   301   C97-930749-X

Senior Acquisitions Editor: Ken Nauss
New Editions Editor: Megan Mueller
Supervising Editor: Semareh Al-Hillal
Production Co-ordinator: Sheila Barry

Copy Editor: Jim Lyons
Proofreader: Anne Norman/West Coast Editorial Associates
Permissions Editor: Andrea Holden-Boone
Cover and Interior Design: Sonya V. Thursby/Opus House Incorporated
Typesetting and Assembly: Brian Lehen • Graphic Design Ltd.
Printing and Binding: RR Donnelley & Sons Company

Art on Part Openers: PART ONE: Glenn Priestley, *Monster Donuts* (1992). Oil and tempera on board, 36″ x 30″. Image courtesy of the Mira Godard Gallery, Toronto. Reproduced with permission of the artist. PART TWO: Joanne Tod, *Two Perspectives* (1986). Oil on canvas, 152.4 x 312.4 cm. Private collection, Toronto. Image provided courtesy of the artist and the Sable-Castelli Gallery, Toronto. Reproduced with permission of the artist. PART THREE: Paraskeva Clark, *Parachute Riggers* (1946–7). Oil on linen canvas, 101.7 x 81.4 cm. Image provided by Canadian War Museum, Ottawa. Reproduced with permission of Clive Clark, Toronto. PART FOUR: Marion Dale Scott, *Tenants* (c. 1940). Oil on canvas, 63.5 x 38.1 cm. Image courtesy of the Art Gallery of Ontario, Toronto. Gift from the J.S. MacLean Collection, by Canada Packers Inc., 1990. Reproduced with permission of the Art Gallery of Ontario. PART FIVE: Paraskeva Clark, *Petroushka* (1937). Oil on canvas, 121.9 x 81.3 cm. Image provided by the National Gallery of Canada, Ottawa. Reproduced with permission of Clive Clark, Toronto. PART SIX: Carol Wainio, *We Can Be Certain* (1982). Acrylic on masonite, 48″ x 96″. Image courtesy of the S.L. Simpson Gallery, Toronto. Reproduced with permission of the artist.

This book was printed in the United States of America.

1 2 3 4 5   02 01 00 99 98

For my mother, Sophie, אֵשֶׁת־חַיִל
and
my father, Albert, אִישׁ נֶאֱמָן

— RJB

PREFACE

The job of figuring out what to do with one's life and how to act in the world is more difficult than ever before. Sociology contributes to the task of clarification; sociologists are in the business of analyzing the pressing social issues of the day, showing how those issues affect all of us, and setting out options for dealing with them. Moreover, as you will learn in the following pages, sociology views social issues from a unique disciplinary perspective. All in all, it is a controversial and exciting business. Social problems are typically complex. The various options for action often involve different benefits and disadvantages for different groups. Sociologists usually see things differently from other social and natural scientists. It is not surprising, then, that sociology, like any vibrant academic discipline, involves a lot of heated debate.

Unfortunately, you are unlikely to get much of a feel for the excitement of sociology from reading most introductory textbooks, which tend to resemble encyclopedias full of definitions and presumably undeniable facts. They make sociological knowledge seem like the tablets some people say were brought down by Moses from Mount Sinai: abstract principles carved in stone, eternal truths that most people agree with but that tell us little about the way life is actually lived.

In preparing this book, I tried to overcome this deficiency in two ways. First, when I recruited authors to write chapters, I asked them to focus as much as possible on social issues that are likely to be of real, everyday concern to Canadian undergraduates on the verge of entering the twenty-first century. To that end I also commissioned chapters on sexuality, globalization, the environment, and postmodern culture — hot topics not covered extensively in most introductory texts. Second, I asked the authors to highlight the controversies in the field, not the tired clichés. There is no sense in keeping secret what any good scientist knows: Advances in knowledge usually result from intellectual conflict, not consensus.

■ ORGANIZATION OF THE TEXT

Chapter 1 of *New Society* reflects the focus sketched out above and sets the tone for the rest of the book. Instead of sermonizing on the arid question, "What is sociology?" as countless other textbooks do, I ask, "Why sociology?" That is, why does an undergraduate in this particular time and place need to know what sociology has to offer? My aim in Chapter 1 is not to trace intellectual pedigrees, outline theories, and introduce methods whose relevance to the life of the reader is still unclear. Instead, I show how sociological thinking can clarify and perhaps even help resolve the real-life social issues that confront all of us, here and now. Enticement, not didacticism, is the task I set myself in Chapter 1.

The remainder of the book is divided into five parts. Part 2, "Culture," could be subtitled "Becoming Human." In Chapter 2, Jack Haas and William Shaffir thoroughly discuss the mechanisms through which we learn beliefs, symbols, values, and self-identities throughout the life cycle and in various institutions, including, most recently, the Internet. David Cheal is more concerned with the actual content of culture and its variety in Chapter 3. He makes a clear, strong case for the view that ours is an increasingly fragmented and globalized "postmodern" culture. Mariana Valverde then devotes Chapter 4 to a spirited, in-depth analysis of what might seem to be the most intimate and biologically determined aspect of our identity — our sexuality — and demonstrates that in fact it has deep roots in culture and society. There follows a comprehensive examination of two of the most important cultural institutions in our society. In Chapter 5, Graham Knight traces the lineaments and analyzes the impact of the pervasive and highly influential mass media, while in Chapter 6 Reginald Bibby assesses the social origins, consequences, and future of religion, relying heavily on his own fundamentally important survey research to argue his case. In sum, the analyses of Part 2 will give the reader a solid appreciation of how we become part of society and how society becomes part of us through the transmission of culture from generation to generation.

Part 3 is about how people become and remain unequal. Harvey Krahn shows in Chapter 7 that, despite recent assertions of the demise of social classes, stratification persists and continues to structure our life-chances in profound ways. In Chapter 8, Monica Boyd convincingly demonstrates that gender is an equally important basis of social inequality, in both economic and political spheres. Vic Satzewich devotes Chapter 9 to highlighting the deficiencies of biological and purely cultural approaches to understanding the bases of ethnic and racial inequality. Finally, in Chapter 10, Gordon Laxer incisively criticizes modernization and other theories of economic underdevelopment and global inequality, offering a compelling argument for the analytical benefits of a modified dependency approach to the problem. The reader will complete Part 3 with a firm understanding that, though we are all human, we are highly differentiated and differently rewarded depending on our structural location.

Part 4 shifts the reader's attention to some of society's fundamental institutions. A virtue of Bonnie Fox's analysis of families in Chapter 11 is that she usefully draws on a broad historical and anthropological literature to supplement her sociological overview, providing a clear sense of how families have developed and where they may be headed. Sandy Welsh devotes Chapter 12 to tracing the development and future shape of work and shows, among other things, that steady, well-paying jobs may soon be as rare as traditional nuclear families. And in Chapter 13, Jane Gaskell dissects our educational system, demonstrating that, paradoxically, it is as much a cause of the persistence of inequality as it is an avenue for upward mobility.

Change and conflict is the subject of Part 5. Here the reader is introduced to the main forces of turbulence in our society. John Hannigan's analysis of urbanization in Chapter 14 is a novel and revealing look at how cities have developed from preindustrial to industrial to postmodern forms. He then devotes Chapter 15 to one of the most pressing issues of the day — the environment — and analyzes such problems as the scope and social roots of the environmental movement and the process by which environmental issues are socially constructed. In Chapter 16, Roderic Beaujot clearly and meticulously surveys the sociological study of population, emphasizing the immediacy and significance of such issues as the global population explosion and the aging of the Canadian population. Globalization is the theme of Chapter 17, by Martin Albrow. Culturally, politically, and economically, Albrow shows, the world is becoming a single place and its inhabitants are developing a global consciousness. This does not imply that we are becoming one big happy family. On the contrary, conflict has persisted and even intensified at the end of the twentieth century, as the last two chapters of this part demonstrate. In Chapter 18, Rosemary Gartner elegantly analyzes one form of social conflict — deviant and criminal behaviour — undermining a number of common misconceptions in the process. In Chapter 19, I survey the evolution of social movements and politics, showing how various forms of conflict emerge and change our lives and how change gets institutionalized.

Part 6 takes a step back from society and focusses on sociology itself. In a somewhat more abstract manner than the previous chapters, it shows how sociologists actually do sociology. The primacy of theory in the sociological enterprise is emphasized by Ken Menzies in Chapter 20. Not only does Menzies review the basics of conflict theory, functionalism, feminism, and symbolic interactionism/ethnomethodology, he also makes a sensible and appealing case for a multivariate approach to theory that is capable of tying together the "grand narratives." Finally, in Chapter 21, Neil Guppy reviews the many methods that sociologists employ to test their ideas. He leaves the reader with the firm sense that, for all the intellectual liveliness and controversy displayed in Chapters 1–20, sociology can be and is disciplined by the judicious use of logic and evidence.

■ FEATURES AND ANCILLARIES

Each chapter of the book opens with a concise list of key learning objectives. A chapter introduction provides a further brief overview of the subject matter, and a chapter summary offers a numbered, point-by-point review of the central themes discussed. End-of-chapter discussion questions assist in self-directed review, a glossary provides definitions of all key terms and concepts used in the chapter, and a short list of suggested reading is provided for further research.

The text is further enriched by the use of thought-provoking boxes featuring contemporary newspaper and magazine articles and relevant materials from books and journals. Extensive use of full-colour photographs, cartoons, figures, tables, and graphs enhances both the meaning and visual impact of the book. The index at the end of the book is divided into name and subject listings, and it is preceded by a complete list of references cited in the book, organized by chapter.

For the instructor, a full range of innovative ancillaries is available to augment teaching and learning inside and outside the classroom and to facilitate testing. Contact your local Harcourt Brace Canada representative for further information about these ancillaries.

▲ COMPUTERIZED TEST BANK

The test bank contains approximately 1000 multiple-choice and true-or-false questions. The computerized format allows instructors to generate a wide variety of customized tests and to edit, delete, or add to the existing bank of test items.

▲ INSTRUCTOR'S MANUAL

This chapter-by-chapter outline helps instructors make the most of *New Society*. It summarizes each chapter in the form of lecture notes, describes how best to integrate each chapter with all of the ancillary products, and provides suggestions on how to create the most effective lectures possible.

▲ STUDENT LEARNING GUIDE

This concise guide helps students to check their progress with sample quizzes. Critical-thinking questions encourage them to use their imagination to develop a richer sociological perspective.

▲ THE HARCOURT BRACE SOCIOLOGY VIDEO COLLECTION

This seven-hour set of 31 video segments, each 5–23 minutes in length, was created to stimulate discussion of topics raised in the book. Produced in conjunction with Face to Face Media (Vancouver), the Jesuit Communication Project (Toronto), and the National Film Board of Canada, the selections have been edited to optimize their impact in the classroom. Many of the selections are taken from films that have won national and international awards. Six of the selections are from the celebrated work of Gwynne Dyer, one of Canada's leading media intellectuals.

▲ PRESENTING NEW SOCIETY POWERPOINT® SOFTWARE

Presenting New Society has been created using Microsoft's PowerPoint® software. Over 400 full-colour slides offer a detailed summary of each chapter of the book along with supplementary graphs, tables, and diagrams to illustrate key points. The slides can be easily output from a computer in several formats. The PowerPoint® Viewer that is packaged with the slides enables them to be (1) viewed on a computer; or (2) projected from a computer to a viewing screen in a classroom. If you have the entire Microsoft PowerPoint® package, the slides can also be (3) printed out as full-colour transparencies for use with an overhead projector; or (4) printed out as black-and-white handouts for students.

▲ NEW SOCIETY ON THE WORLD WIDE WEB

The *New Society* Web site contains standard features, such as chapter-by-chapter "Current Events" and related "Web Links." In addition, it boasts three features that are available on no other sociology site in the world: interactive exercises, online research projects, and a focus on Canada in a global context. This is not a U.S. Web site that has been quickly "adapted" to the Canadian market. These exciting features make the *New Society* Web site unique and useful to Canadian instructors and students. It allows students to *do* sociology and better understand their place in the world.

■ ACKNOWLEDGEMENTS

For the past year I was privileged to work closely with many people who contributed heavily to the successful completion of this project. Dan Brooks, formerly senior acquisitions editor at Harcourt Brace Canada, foresaw the need for many of the innovative ancillaries that accompany the second edition of *New Society* and began mobilizing the resources necessary to do the job. Dan worked with great purpose, clarity of vision, and unceasing humour in laying the groundwork for this book and became my friend in the process. Ken Nauss picked up where Dan left off and proved to be a worthy successor. He worked with extraordinary efficiency and diligence on a complex project, always keenly mindful of the needs of instructors and students. Megan Mueller, new editions editor at Harcourt Brace Canada, shepherded the book through the developmental process. Her firm but always friendly hand helped to turn this into a polished work. Semareh Al-Hillal, supervising editor, oversaw the final edit of the manuscript and worked with vigour, meticulousness, and high spirits from beginning to end.

Handling the development of the ancillaries was a daunting job, especially given the complexity of the Web site and the PowerPoint® series. It required Kelly Nakamura's meticulousness and industry to get the job done smoothly and flawlessly. For Gary Marcuse and John Pungente, videography is a labour of love. Combining their passion with their vast knowledge and resources resulted in a video series second to none. Stephen Jordan, at the time a senior acquisitions editor at Harcourt Brace in Fort Worth, Texas, ran the bureaucratic gauntlet with agility. He made it possible for us to prepare a Web site that is a rarity — a truly useful pedagogical resource of which we can all be proud. Renae Bent of Archipelago in Monterey, California, and the staff of Media 9 in Montreal provided the technical know-how, and Cathy Richard exercised the exemplary organizational skills needed to make the Web site come alive.

And overseeing the entire show, forsaking a career in Canada's diplomatic service in the interest of textbook publishing, was Heather McWhinney, formerly director of product development at Harcourt Brace Canada. Only Heather knows as well as I do the name of every bump on the road to publication day; only Heather knew how to overcome every difficulty and make this the best introductory sociology textbook in Canada.

But, of course, *New Society* could not become that without the authors of the following chapters, who include some of the very best sociologists in Canada. I believe that while concentrating on the exposition of their own subfields they have conveyed to the novice a real sense of the excitment and promise of sociology. I am deeply indebted to them, as tens of thousands of introductory sociology students and their instructors inevitably will be.

Robert J. Brym
University of Toronto

▲ A NOTE FROM THE PUBLISHER

Thank you for selecting *New Society: Sociology for the 21st Century,* Second Edition, by Robert J. Brym. The author and the publisher have devoted considerable time to the careful development of this book. We appreciate your recognition of this effort and accomplishment.

We want to hear what you think about this edition of *New Society.* Please take a few minutes to complete the stamped reader reply card at the back of the book. Your comments and suggestions will be valuable to us in the preparation of new editions and other books.

CONTRIBUTORS

Martin Albrow, *Roehampton Institute,
University of Surrey*

Roderic Beaujot, *University of Western Ontario*

Reginald W. Bibby, *University of Lethbridge*

Monica Boyd, *Florida State University*

Robert J. Brym, *University of Toronto*

David Cheal, *University of Winnipeg*

Bonnie J. Fox, *University of Toronto*

Rosemary Gartner, *University of Toronto*

Jane Gaskell, *University of British Columbia*

Neil Guppy, *University of British Columbia*

Jack Haas, *McMaster University*

John Hannigan, *University of Toronto*

Graham Knight, *McMaster University*

Harvey Krahn, *University of Alberta*

Gordon Laxer, *University of Alberta*

Ken S. Menzies, *University of Guelph*

Vic Satzewich, *McMaster University*

William Shaffir, *McMaster University*

Mariana Valverde, *University of Toronto*

Sandy Welsh, *University of Toronto*

BRIEF CONTENTS

CONTENTS

Part Three INEQUALITY

Part Five CHANGE AND CONFLICT

■ *Part Six* THEORY AND METHOD

YOUNG PEOPLE TODAY ARE OFTEN PROMISED
A GLORIOUS AND EXCITING FUTURE, BUT
THEIR REALITY IS OFTEN MORE DRAB. THE
BOOK'S FIRST CHAPTER DEVELOPS THIS
THEME BY ARGUING THAT SOCIOLOGY CAN
HELP TO SORT OUT THE DIFFERENCES
BETWEEN SOCIAL MYTH AND SOCIAL REALITY
AND ENLIGHTEN US BY REVEALING OUR OWN
AND OUR SOCIETY'S POSSIBILITIES.

Part One **INTRODUCTION**

INTRODUCTION

Chicken Little was right. The sky is falling. On second thought, maybe Chicken Little didn't go far enough. The ground is also slipping out from under our feet. That, at any rate, is what life today often feels like. You can get up in the morning and discover that your parents — or your country — have split up. You can go to work and find that your job has been redefined, requiring you to learn radically new skills — or that you no longer have a job. You can adhere to a religion that was founded 2000 years ago, or you can change your mind and choose one that was founded last week — or you can decide not to worship at all. If you go out expecting to relax and have fun on a date with someone you recently met, you may find yourself embroiled in a debate about what constitutes appropriate sexual behaviour. If you go out expecting to take a long walk on a hot summer day in the big city, you may find that your lungs begin to ache because of the pollutants in the air. Instability reigns in the environment, sex, religion, work, politics, and family life. It is a defining characteristic of our new society.

ROBERT J. BRYM
University of Toronto

Life used to be much more regular, orderly, and predictable. Indeed, three or four hundred years ago, people of European origin thought that everything in the universe fit together like the parts of a mechanical clock. The clock might not always run smoothly. There were, after all, war and thunder, premature death and sudden good fortune. Nonetheless, it was God who wound the clock up, and its movements — even when they were erratic — were understandable. Everthing had meaning. Even the most horrifying events were thought to have their place in the order of things.

Examine the early-seventeenth-century English engraving reproduced in Figure I.1. It shows how most educated Europeans pictured the universe in Shakespeare's time. Three things are noteworthy about the engraving:

- It suggests that everything that happens is ultimately determined by God. Thus, at the top of the circle, in a bright cloud, is the hand of God holding a chain. The chain is attached to a woman representing Nature. Nature also holds a chain in her hand. It is attached to "the ape of Nature," which represents humankind. The symbolism is clear: Human actions are shaped by God and his intermediary, Nature.
- Second, the engraving places humans at the centre of the universe. It suggests that the universe was created chiefly for human benefit.
- Third, the engraving arranges everything in an interlinked hierarchy that includes the mineral, vegetable, and animal kingdoms, the elements, mobile heavenly objects, fallen angels, angels, and so forth. Each level of the hierarchy corresponds to, and in some cases controls, some aspect of the one below it. For example, the archangels were believed to regulate the movements of the planet Mercury, and the movements of Mercury were thought to affect human commercial activities. Similarly, in the medieval world view, God ordained a hierarchy of people. The richest people were the closest to God and therefore enjoyed the privilege of ruling. A medieval English verse reflects this view:

The rich man at his castle,
The poor man at his gate.
God made them high or lowly
And ordered their estate.[1]

It is impossible to know exactly when the medieval world view began to crumble, but the year 1609 is a good candidate. It was then that the Italian astronomer Galileo pointed his newly invented telescope at the heavens and proved that the earth revolves around the sun. With that discovery, it became increasingly difficult to believe that humankind stands at the centre of the universe and is the main reason for its existence.

The universe continued to be viewed as a sort of huge mechanical clock. But even that belief began to change about 100 years ago. Twentieth-century physics demonstrated that the universe is an uncertain, paradoxical, and chaotic place. We used to think that the amount of time that elapses between two events is the same for any two observers; we now know that that is false. We used to think that space is flat; we now know it is curved. We used to think that light is either a particle or a wave; we now know it is both. We used to think that it was possible, at least in principle, to know all physical states and mathematical systems; we now realize that there are definite limits to our ability to measure and to know. We used to think that natural laws would keep all physical systems, including the solar system, operating smoothly for eternity; we now know that the very operation of orderly laws can cause systems to blow apart. Is it any wonder that one of the most important innovations in contemporary science is known as chaos theory? For that matter, is it any wonder that the medieval artist's realistic paintings of lords, ladies, and neatly ordered landscapes have given way to canvases portraying everyday objects, abstract forms, and figures that appear to be seen simultaneously from many angles? Or that some schools of modern philosophy arose to declare the death of God and underline the anxiety and meaninglessness pervading contemporary life? Or that most people now believe they are free to replace their rules if they are dissatisfied with them, and to get rich if they are sufficiently talented and industrious? In short, what's new is that our society — our universe — is less orderly, less predictable, and less meaningful than it was in the past.

In the nineteenth century, most people in the West believed that the collapse of the medieval social order and world view signalled progress. They thought that humanity was becoming more enlightened, guided less by tradition, passion, and superstition than by science and reason. Progress, it was widely held, was both inevitable and desirable.

By the beginning of the twentieth century, doubts began to creep in. Increasingly, progress came to seem like a mixed blessing. Consider the ambivalence of the celebrated German sociologist Max Weber. He was far from enthusiastic about modern times. True, Weber admired the relentless drive to achieve greater efficiency in industry, commerce, the

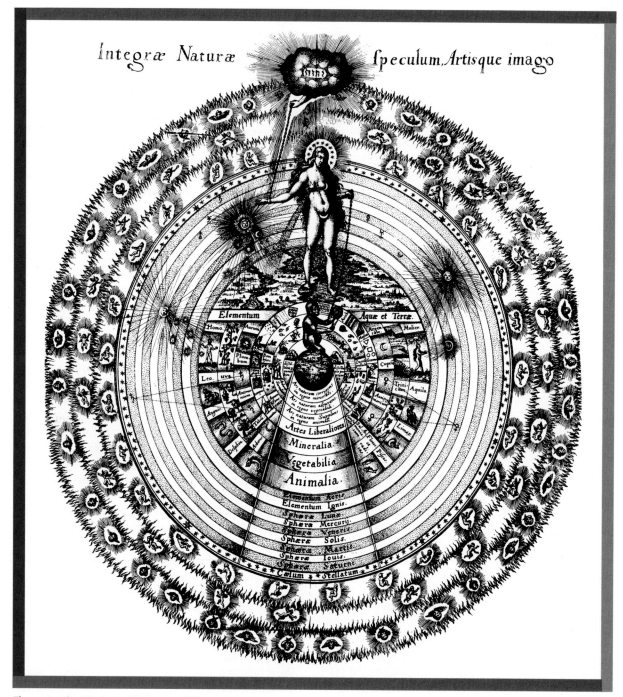

Figure I.1 The Mechnical Universe of Premodern Europe. SOURCE: From Robert Fludd's *Utriusque Cosmi Historia* (1617–19). Reprinted with permission of the Harvard College Library.

military, law, education, and politics. Everywhere, he wrote, people are encouraging the growth of bureaucracies because, more than any other form of social organization, bureaucracy enables the precise calculation of the best means available to achieve a given end: "Precision, speed, unambiguity, knowledge of the files, continuity, discretion, unity, strict sub-ordination, reduction of friction and of material and personal costs — these are raised to the optimum point in the strictly bureaucratic organization" (Weber, 1946 [1922]: 214).

But Weber also saw two dark aspects of these developments. First, modern bureaucracies are tremendously influential organizations, and they are composed of unelected officials. Consequently, they concentrate power and threaten democracy. Second, bureaucracies discourage officeholders from considering what the goals of their organization ought to be; bureaucrats are encouraged only to determine the best way to achieve the goals defined by their superiors. Officeholders thus lose their spontaneity, their inventiveness, and all opportunity to act heroically. It is "horrible to think," wrote Weber, "that the world could one day be filled with nothing but those little cogs, little men clinging to little jobs and striving towards bigger ones" (quoted in Mayer, 1944: 127).

It is only in the past 50 years that the full negative implications of Weber's observations have become clear. An example that drives the point home is the extermination of the Jews, Gypsies, communists, homosexuals, and mentally disabled people of Europe by the Nazi bureaucracy during World War II. How, one might ask, was it possible for thousands of ordinary men and women — products of what many people regarded as the most advanced civilization in the world — to systematically murder millions of defenceless and innocent people, including many small children? Part of the answer is that the Nazi genocide machine was bureaucratically organized. As in all efficient bureaucracies, the overall goal — in this case, killing Jews and other undesirables — was broken up into many small tasks. Most officials performed only one function — checking train schedules, organizing entertainment for camp guards, ordering Zyklon B gas, arranging for the removal of ashes, and so forth. The full horror of what was happening eluded many officials, or at least could be conveniently ignored as they concentrated on their little jobs, most of them far removed from the gas chambers themselves. Like bureaucrats everywhere, Nazi officials were trained not to question the ultimate goal of their organization, but to treat it as a given. Thus, bureaucratic organization, the fruit of modernity and progress, ensured that Jews, for example, were killed in their proportionately greatest numbers not where the hatred of Jews was most intense (e.g., Romania),

but where the Nazi bureaucracy was best organized (e.g., Holland) (Bauman, 1991).

We are now aware that, like bureaucracy, most elements of progress have a dark underside. For all the marvellous benefits that science, industry, and urbanization have brought us, few people now believe that they are an unqualified good. "The future," as one French writer said, "is not what it used to be"; or, in the words of American poet E.E. Cummings, "nothing recedes like progress."

We thus arrive at the main dilemma of the contemporary era: Spectacular opportunities to enhance the quality of life open up before us, but the openings often rupture, only to become dangerous chasms. Are we to plunge blindly, passively allowing things to happen to us? Or should we use reason to attempt to identify authentic opportunities and avoid pitfalls? As you will learn in this book, good sociology, like good natural and social science in general, is on the side of reason. In the following pages, you will encounter some of the burning social problems facing humankind today. You will grapple with the fact that solutions are rarely clear-cut. But you will also see that sociology offers a unique perspective that contributes significantly to identifying the dimensions of social problems as well as their causes, their consequences, and their possible solutions.

NOTES

1. These lines were originally incorporated in the Anglican hymn "All Things Bright and Beautiful" and removed only in the twentieth century. The idea that social inequality is ordained by God and that the rich are closest to God is a universal premodern theme. In Russian and other Slavic languages, for example, the words for "rich" (bogati) and "God" (bog) have the same root. In the Hindu scriptures, it is said that the highest caste sprang from the lips of the supreme creator, the next highest from his shoulders, the next from his thighs, and the lowest from his feet. And in the Koran, it is said that social inequality exists by virtue of the will of Allah. See Ossowski, 1963: 19–20.

CHAPTER ONE
Why Sociology?

IN THIS CHAPTER YOU WILL LEARN THAT

■ the causes of human behaviour lie not just in the psychological and biological make-up of people but also in the patterns of social interaction and culture that constitute society

■ sociologists analyze how patterns of social interaction and culture affect human behaviour and how those patterns change historically

■ although sociologists employ scientific research methods, their analyses are also influenced by the social settings in which research takes place

■ today we are experiencing a series of revolutionary changes in patterns of social interaction and culture; among the most important of these are transformations in the relations between men and women and in the structure of industry and work

■ the chief value of sociology is that it can help clarify the scope, direction, and significance of such revolutionary changes and suggest ways of managing them

ROBERT J. BRYM
University of Toronto

■ INTRODUCTION

▲ WHY I ALMOST DECIDED *NOT* TO STUDY SOCIOLOGY

When I first entered university at the age of 18, I was bewildered by the wide variety of courses from which I could choose. Having now taught sociology for nearly twenty years, and having met a couple of thousand undergraduates in the process, I am quite sure that most students today feel as I did then.

One source of confusion for me — and, I expect, a common source of frustration for students today — was uncertainty about why I was in university in the first place. Like you, I knew that higher education could improve one's chances of finding good work. But, like most students, I also had a sense that university was meant to provide something more than just the training needed to embark on an interesting and relatively well-paying profession. I had heard ambiguous rumblings from various high school teachers and guidance counsellors about how university was also supposed to "broaden my horizons" and teach me to "think critically." Whatever that meant, it sounded mildly enticing, and so I wanted to know more. Thus, although I decided, in my first year, to take mainly "practical" courses that might prepare me for a law degree (economics, political science, psychology), I also enrolled in a couple of other courses to indulge my "intellectual" side (philosophy, theatre). One thing I knew for sure was that I did not want to study sociology.

Sociology, I had come to believe, was thin broth with uncertain ingredients. When I asked a second-year student what sociology was, he told me that it dealt mainly with the reasons why people are unequal — why some are rich and others poor, some powerful and others weak. Judging by that definition, it appeared that sociology could teach me something about my own life, since I came from a poor immigrant family in an economically depressed region of the country. But it also seemed that sociology must be a lot like what I imagined economics and political science to be about. What, then, was unique about sociology? My growing sense that sociology had nothing special to offer was confirmed when another second-year student informed me that sociologists try to describe the ideal society and figure out how to make the world a better place. That characterization certainly appealed to my youthful sense of the world's injustice, but it also sounded an awful lot like philosophy. A third-year student explained that sociology analyzes how and why people assume different roles in their lives, making it sound close to the province of theatre. Finally, one student reported that, in her sociology class, she was learning why people commit suicide, homicide, and other deviant acts — which seemed a lot like abnormal psychology to me. I concluded that sociology had no distinct flavour of its own. Accordingly, I decided to forgo it for more savoury courses.

▲ YORICK'S DILEMMA

Despite the opinion I'd formed, I unexpectedly found myself taking no fewer than four sociology courses a year after starting university. That revolution in my life was attributable in part to the influence of an extraordinary professor I happened to meet just before I began my second year. He set me thinking in an altogether new way about what I could and should do with my life. He shattered some of my deepest beliefs. He started me thinking sociologically.

Specifically, he first put Yorick's dilemma to me in striking terms. Yorick is a character — in a sense — in Shakespeare's *Hamlet*. Toward the end of the play, Hamlet finds two gravediggers at work. They unearth the remains of the former court jester, Yorick, who, laments Hamlet, was "a fellow of infinite jest, of most excellent fancy: he hath borne me on his back a thousand times" (*Hamlet,* 4.7). Holding high his old friend's skull, Hamlet then reflects on what we must all come to. Even the remains of Alexander the Great, he says, turned to dust, and in that form may have been used to make the loam that fills a hole in a barrel.

This incident implies Yorick's dilemma and, indeed, the dilemma of all thinking people: Life is finite, and if we wish to make the most of it, we must determine how best to live. That is no easy task. It requires study, reflection, and the selection of values and goals. Ideally, a liberal arts education is supposed to supply students with precisely that opportunity. Finally, I was beginning to understand what I could expect from university apart from job training.

I am grateful to numerous introductory sociology students and to Rhonda Lenton and Jim Richardson for helpful comments on earlier versions of this chapter.

Sociology offers no easy solutions as to how life's goals can be accomplished or how life's meaning can be deciphered, but it does offer a useful perspective for understanding our current predicament and seeing possible ways of dealing with it.

Sociology in particular, I discovered, could open up a new and superior way for me to comprehend my world, my place in it, how I might manoeuvre through it, and perhaps even how I might contribute to improving it, however modestly. Before I began my study of sociology, I had always taken for granted that things happened in the world — and to me — because physical and emotional forces caused them. Famine, I thought, is caused by drought, war by territorial greed, material success by hard work, marriage by love, suicide by bottomless depression, and rape by depraved lust. But now, evidence contradicting my easy formulas was repeatedly thrown in my face. If drought causes famine, why is it that so many famines have occurred in perfectly normal weather conditions or have involved some groups' hoarding or destroying food so that others would starve? If love leads to marriage, then why are so many families the site of violence against women and children, and why is it that, throughout most of recorded history and in most **cultures,** marriages have been arranged by people other than the couple themselves? And so the questions multiplied.

As if it were not enough that the evidence seemed to upset many of my assumptions about the way the world worked, I was now also being asked to believe that there existed an entirely different order of causation, a different way of explaining social life. Quite distinct from the physical and the emotional is the *social,* which helps explain famine, marriage, and the rest. In public school, I was taught that people are free to do what they want with their lives. It now became apparent that, in fact, the organization of the social world opens up some opportunities and closes off others, thus constraining our freedom and helping to make us what we are. By examining the operation of these powerful social forces, I was told, sociology can help us know ourselves. I was hooked. And so, of course, I hope you will be too.

▲ THE GOALS OF THE CHAPTER

My aim in this chapter is to achieve the following three goals:

1. I will illustrate the power of sociology to dispel foggy assumptions and to help us see the operation of the social world more clearly. To that end, I will examine two phenomena that at first glance appear to be the outcome of breakdowns in *individual* functioning — woman abuse and suicide — and show how *social* relations help to shape them. This exercise will introduce you to what is unique about the sociological perspective.

2. I will outline two recent social transformations of major significance: the arrival of postindustrialism and the rise of feminism. My discussion of these topics will suggest some of the features that the twenty-first century — your century — is likely to take on. Here, I will also begin to demonstrate that sociology is not just an arid academic exercise, but rather that it can help you to understand how society is likely to affect your own life.

3. I will examine how we can acquire sociological knowledge and what we can do with it. We will see that the discipline is full of controversy about what constitutes valid knowledge. I will suggest that, despite such fundamental challenges, sociology can help you come to grips with your century, just as it helped the founders of sociology to deal with theirs.

My second and third points need to be explained. The main founders of sociology — Karl Marx, Émile Durkheim, and Max Weber — lived in the period 1820–1920. They witnessed various phases of Europe's wrenching transition to industrial **capitalism**. They wanted desperately to understand the human suffering they observed as people moved from countryside to city, worked agonizingly long hours in crowded and dangerous factories, lost faith in their religions, confronted faceless bureaucracies, and reacted to the conditions of their existence by means of strikes, crime, revolution, and war. They also wanted to chart a better course for their societies. The ideas they developed are therefore not just diagnostic tools from which we can still learn much, but also, like many sociological ideas, prescriptions for combatting social ills.

Today, we are also witnessing massive and disorienting social changes. Entire countries are coming unglued. Women are demanding equality with men in all spheres of life. New religions are emerging and old ones are being revived. People's wants are increasingly governed by the mass media. Computers are radically altering the way people work. There are fewer good jobs to go around. Crime rates are reaching record levels for the century. Environmental ruin threatens us all. As was the case 100 years ago, sociologists today try to understand these phenomena and to suggest credible ways of improving their societies. This chapter should therefore be viewed as an open invitation to participate in that sociological challenge.

But first things first. Before showing how sociology may be able to help us comprehend and better our world, I want briefly to examine the two social problems just mentioned — woman abuse and suicide. That will help illustrate how the sociological perspective can clarify and sometimes overturn common-sense beliefs.

▲ WOMAN ABUSE

The Frequency of Woman Abuse

How common is the physical and sexual abuse of women? In a survey conducted in Toronto in 1987, more than 11 percent of 604 women who at one time lived with a man reported that they had been *severely* abused: kicked, bitten, punched, hit with an object, beaten, choked, or threatened with a knife or a gun. More than 11 percent of 304 undergraduate men in southern Ontario universities reported in another

1987 survey that they had similarly abused the women they had dated. According to a 1984 Canada-wide survey, more than half of all Canadian women had been raped, otherwise sexually assaulted, or threatened with sexual assault at least once in their lives (DeKeseredy and Hinch, 1991: 22, 45, 69). And a 1993 Canada-wide survey of 12 300 women found that 51 percent of them had been physically or sexually assaulted at least once in their lives — 9 percent of them violently enough to be physically injured (Johnson, 1996: 53). These rates are so high that even women who have never been personally threatened with sexual abuse are often anxious about the possibility of being molested. Thus, many daily experiences that are unremarkable for men — walking alone down a dimly lit street or fetching one's car from an underground parking lot — are fearful experiences for most women. A 1992 survey of 1007 Canadians, for example, showed that only 17 percent of men, but fully 54 percent of women, were afraid to walk in their neighbourhoods at night. The figure for women in British Columbia was 62 percent; for women in Montreal, it reached 68 percent (*The Toronto Star*, Nov. 28, 1992).[1]

The Sociological Explanation of Woman Abuse

Common sense tells us that woman abuse results from some sort of *individual* breakdown either in a person's psychological functioning or in the nature of two people's interpersonal communication. Consider sexual assaults against women, which may range from unwanted touching to rape.[2] Offenders are often viewed as men who suffer from some form of psychological disorder that compels them to achieve immediate sexual gratification even if violence is required. Alternatively, the sexual assault of women is sometimes explained as the result of flawed communication — that is, some women who are sexually assaulted may appear to be giving mixed signals to their assailants by, for example, getting drunk and flirting with them.

Such individualistic explanations are not entirely invalid. Interviews with victims and perpetrators of sexual assault show that some offenders do suffer from psychological disorders. Other offenders do misinterpret signals in what they regard as sexually ambiguous situations. But interviews also show that such cases account for only a small proportion of the total. Men who sexually assault women are rarely mentally disturbed and it is abundantly clear to most abusers during the assault that they are doing something that their victims oppose.

What, then, accounts for the widespread problem of sexual assault against women? One sociological answer is suggested by the repeated finding that rape is often not about sexual gratification at all. Many rapists cannot ejaculate or even achieve an erection. Significantly, however, all rape involves domination and humiliation as principal motives.

Correspondingly, many sociologists agree that sexual assault in general is encouraged by a lesson most of us learn at home, in school, and in the mass media — that it is natural and right for men to dominate women. To be sure, recent decades have witnessed important changes in the way women's and men's roles are often defined. Nonetheless, in the world of paid work, in the household, in government, and in all other spheres of life, men still tend to command substantially more **power** than women, which is to say that they have a greater capacity to influence and control. Men typically have more **authority** than women as well, which means that their greater power is generally considered valid or acceptable. Daily patterns of gender domination, viewed as legitimate by most people, can and do spill over into the realm of sex. They are built into our sexual and courtship rules. From this point of view, most sexual assault is simply an expression of male authority by other means.

This does not mean that all men endorse the principle of male dominance, much less that all men are inclined to assault women sexually. Clearly, some men oppose male dominance and very far from all men have ever engaged in sexual assault. What the sociological argument does mean is that some aspects of our culture legitimize male dominance or make it seem proper. For instance, pornography, jokes at the expense of women, and whistling and leering at women might be seen at a superficial level as merely examples of harmless play. At a more subtle, sociological level, however, they are assertions of the appropriateness of women's submission to men. Such frequent and routine reinforcements of male authority increase the likelihood that some men will view it as their right to assault women sexually if the opportunity to do so exists or can be created. Stated differently, the frequent and routine reinforcement of male authority allows some men to think that, by interpreting "no" to mean "maybe," they are merely expressing their "natural" manliness.

My argument may be stated as a testable research hypothesis: *Rates of sexual assault and other forms of woman abuse vary inversely with the ratio of women's to men's power.* In other words, if my argument is correct, one would expect research to demonstrate lower levels of woman abuse where the ratio of women's to men's power (or the level of gender equality) is higher.

Some research data supporting my hypothesis will be found in Figure 1.1. The data come from official U.S. government sources and a nationwide survey conducted in the United States in 1975. The graph plots the rate of severe wife abuse against an index of gender equality. The index of gender equality measures the economic, educational, political, and legal status of women. Where the value of the index is high, the level of gender equality is high (the ratio of women's to men's power is high). The rate of severe wife abuse is the percentage of couples who indicated in the nationwide survey that the husbands had used any of the following conflict tactics against their wives in the year preceding the interview: kicked, bit, or hit with a fist; hit or tried to hit with something; beat up; threatened with a knife or a gun; or used a knife or a gun. As one would expect on the basis of my argument, it turns out that the rate of severe wife abuse does indeed fall as the index of gender equality increases — at least up to a certain point. Said differently, wives are in fact less likely to be severely abused where the ratio of women's to men's power is higher.

But why is this true only "up to a certain point"? Why, at the extreme right of the graph — at the very highest level of gender equality, precisely in the U.S. states where women have gained most relative to men — is there a sudden jump in the rate of severe wife abuse? One plausible explanation that has been offered for this finding is the "male backlash" theory. It seems that, after the relative power of women increases beyond a certain point, some men react violently to the erosion of their authority and engage in levels of abusive behaviour comparable to those in settings where the ratio of power between women and men is relatively low. Presumably, when and if the culture changes and men learn to accept high levels of gender equality, there will be no such backlash. But in the absence of such cultural change, I conclude on the basis of research that the relationship between woman abuse and the female/male power ratio is actually more complex than I originally stated: Rates of woman abuse are highest where the female/male power ratio is highest and where the female/male power ratio is lowest.

The implications of this argument are profound and, especially for men, unsettling. Sociology teaches us that sexual assault and other forms of woman abuse are rooted in the structure of social relations between men and women. In particular, men have considerably more power and authority than women, and that imbalance is expressed in myriad cultural forms. It follows that, although policies to punish and rehabilitate rapists and other woman abusers are desirable, the problem of woman abuse cannot be solved comprehensively unless power and authority between men and women are more evenly distributed in society and unless our culture comes to reflect that redistribution. Until then, the everyday practices of most men will continue to contribute to the high incidence of woman abuse (Ball-Rokeach, 1980).

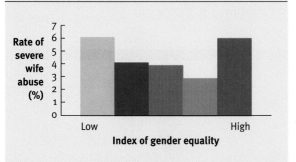

◆ **Figure 1.1** Severe Wife Abuse and Gender Equality in 36 U.S. States, 1975

SOURCE: Adapted from Kersti A. Yllo and Murray A. Smith, "Patriarchy and Violence Against Wives: The Impact of Structural and Normative Factors," in Murray A. Straus and Richard J. Gelles with the assistance of Christine Smith, eds., *Physical Violence in American Families: Risk Factors and Adaptations to Violence in 8,145 Families* (New Brunswick, NJ: Transaction Publishers, 1990), p. 393. Copyright © 1990 by Kersti A. Yllo and Murray A. Smith; All rights reserved. Used by permission of Transaction Publishers.

▲ SUICIDE

Is Suicide an Antisocial Act?

Like woman abuse, the taking of one's own life is a phenomenon that seems, at first, to result solely from an individual's state of mind, and not from social conditions. Indeed, suicide seems to be the supreme example of a nonsocial and antisocial act. It is, in the first place, committed in solitude. It is also comparatively rare: in Canada in 1993, there were about thirteen suicides for every 100 000 people (Statistics Canada, 1995: 266, 332). And each suicide eradicates all of society, at least for one person.

The Sociological Explanation of Suicide

At the end of the last century, Émile Durkheim (1951 [1897]) demonstrated that suicide is much more than just an individual act of desperation that results from psychological disorder, as was commonly believed at the time. Suicide rates, Durkheim showed, are strongly influenced by social forces.

Durkheim made his case by examining the association between rates of suicide and rates of psychological disorder for different groups. The idea that psychological disorder causes suicide would be supported, he reasoned, by evidence that suicide rates tend to be high where rates of psychological disorder are high, and low where rates of psychological disorder are low. But his analysis of European government statistics, hospital records, and other sources revealed nothing of the kind. He discovered, for example, that there were slightly more women than men in insane asylums, but there were four male suicides for every female suicide. Jews had the highest rate of psychological disorder among the major religious groups in France, but they also had the lowest suicide rate. Psychological disorders were most common among people who had just reached maturity, but suicide rates increased steadily with advancing age.

Clearly, suicide rates and rates of psychological disorder did not vary directly; in fact, they often appeared to vary inversely. Why? Durkheim argued that, in modern societies, suicide rates vary with the degree of **social solidarity** in different categories of the population. According to Durkheim, the more a group's members share beliefs and values, and the more frequently and intensely they interact, the more social solidarity there is in the group. He expected groups with a high degree of solidarity to have lower suicide rates than groups with a low degree of solidarity. Durkheim showed that married adults are half as likely as unmarried adults to commit suicide, since marriage creates social ties and a sort of moral cement that bind the individual to society. In the absence of those conditions, there is a higher probability of suicide. In general, he wrote, "suicide varies with the degree of integration of the social groups of which the individual forms a part" (Durkheim, 1951 [1897]: 209). Of course, this generalization tells us nothing about why any particular individual might take his or her own life. But it does tell us that the likelihood of a person's committing suicide decreases with the degree to which he or she is anchored in society. And it says something uniquely sociological about how and why the suicide rate varies from group to group.

Durkheim's theory is not just a historical curiosity. It sheds light on the factors that account for variations in suicide rates here and now. In Canada, suicide rates have nearly doubled since the early 1960s, but they have increased even more among people between the ages of 15 and 39. Thirty-five years ago, the older you were, the more likely you were to commit suicide. Today, men 90 years of age and older are still about twice as likely to commit suicide as men under the age of 90. But for all women and for men under 90, it is no longer true that aging is accompanied by an increased tendency to commit suicide (see Figure 1.2).

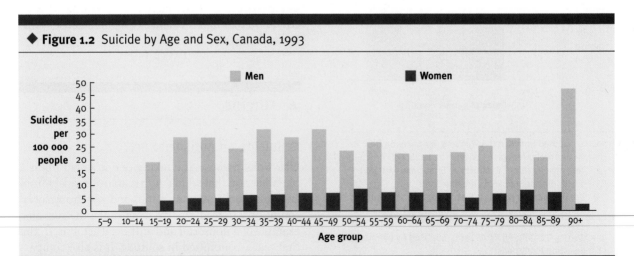

◆ **Figure 1.2** Suicide by Age and Sex, Canada, 1993

SOURCE: Statistics Canada, *Causes of Death 1993*, Cat. no. 84-208. Reproduced by authority of the Minister of Industry, 1997.

Why has the suicide rate gone up? Why has it gone up especially quickly among younger people? Following Durkheim, I believe that these changes are caused mainly by the erosion of shared moral principles and strong social ties since the early 1960s, as reflected in the following statistics: In 1965, unemployment stood at just over 3 percent; by 1994, it had reached over 11 percent. In 1965, there were about 200 divorces for every 100 000 married women; by 1986, there were 1255 divorces for every 100 000 married women — a more than six-fold increase in 31 years. Fifty-five percent of Canadians attended church or synagogue in any given week in 1965; the figure for 1988 was only 33 percent. These figures suggest that social solidarity, as indicated by the stability of families, jobs, and moral codes, is now lower than it was just a few decades ago. As a result, suicide is more common. Moreover, shared moral beliefs and the hope of steady work have faded most dramatically for young people, who are also the group most affected by divorce. The unemployment rate, for example, is more than twice as high for Canadians aged 15–24 as for Canadians aged 25 and older. In part, that is why the suicide rate has increased most dramatically among young people, reaching 24 cases per 100 000 Canadian males aged 15–24 in 1993. When we shift attention from Canadian youth in general to young aboriginal Canadians, the situation changes from serious to alarming. As Box 1.1 illustrates, social solidarity has plummeted in Native communities over the past few decades. Suicide has consequently become a catastrophic problem among Native youth, reaching 112 cases per 100 000 males in the period 1987–91 (see Figure 1.3).

■ TWO REVOLUTIONS

The conclusions described in the preceding section may surprise you. You may even have difficulty accepting them. Upon reflection, however, you may agree that they have deepened your understanding of woman abuse and suicide. If so, then I have succeeded in my first goal. Good sociologists characteristically reach surprising conclusions that are initially hard to accept but then yield new insight into how the social world works. Thinking about woman abuse as a function of the balance of power between women and men, and of suicide as a function of social solidarity, ought to give you a small taste of sociology's capabilities.

But the main course is even tastier than the appetizer. So far, we have seen that sociologists try to show how individual troubles are related to social issues. At their best, sociologists go a step further. They try to connect social problems to broad changes that characterize entire eras. C. Wright Mills, a famous American sociologist, put it this way nearly 40 years ago (1959: 129):

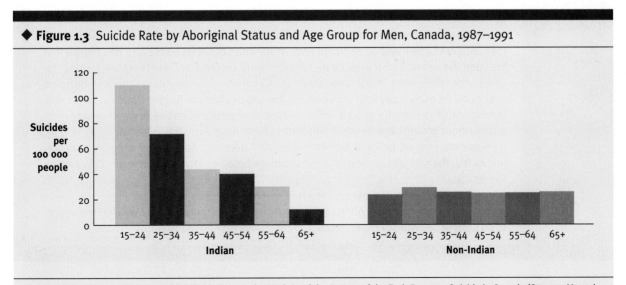

◆ **Figure 1.3** Suicide Rate by Aboriginal Status and Age Group for Men, Canada, 1987–1991

SOURCE: Adapted from Health Canada, *Suicide in Canada: Update of the Report of the Task Force on Suicide in Canada* (Ottawa: Mental Health Division, Health Services Directorate, Health Programs and Services Branch, Health Canada, 1994), p. 56. Reproduced with the permission of the Minister of Public Works and Government Services Canada, 1997.

Box 1.1
Death In, and the Death Of, Grassy Narrows

Imagine a village of 490 souls in which three out of four deaths can be attributed to alcohol- or drug-related acts of violence. In a single year, over a third of all children between the ages of 5 and 14 are removed from the community by a welfare agency because they are physically abused or severely neglected. Over the same twelve months, nearly a fifth of all children between the ages of 11 and 19 try to commit suicide. Two-thirds of the population between the ages of 16 and 64 are heavy or very heavy consumers of alcohol. In Grassy Narrows, an Indian reserve near Kenora, Ontario, these and other similarly appalling statistics summarize the conditions of social existence in 1978.

It was not always that way. Before the mid-1960s, only a small minority of deaths on the reserve were due to violence. Alcohol was used almost exclusively for ceremonial occasions and drunkenness was rare. Suicide and child abuse were unknown. There were strong and effective taboos against incest and promiscuity. People earned their livelihoods in traditional ways, migrating to their traplines in winter, hunting in autumn and spring, guiding and gardening on the reserve in spring and summer, fishing whenever possible. The community, although poor, was hardworking, self-sufficient, and relatively free. Its members had little contact with white society, and Ojibwa culture served as a sound guide to daily life.

Then, in the summer of 1963, the regional Indian Affairs office, an arm of the federal government, initiated a process of relocating the community to a new site. Government officials felt that relocation would make it easier to modernize the community and assimilate its members into white society by providing them with a road to town, new houses, an on-reserve school, better medical facilities, government-sponsored jobs, social welfare services, and more frequent contacts with nonaboriginal peoples. Community members were threatened with financial reprisals if they did not move, and they were promised jobs and welfare payments if they did. They moved reluctantly: the last family relocated only in 1972.

Largely because the move suddenly replaced traditional ways of earning a livelihood with dependence on government handouts, the social fabric of the reserve was soon lacerated beyond recognition. Establishing a school on the reserve and creating a year-round sedentary community prevented winter migration to the traplines. In the area of the new reserve, there was less game and more competition from white hunters. Gardening was impossible because the soil was poor and the new houses were placed too close together. Fishing became impossible when it was announced in 1970 that a pulp and paper mill had dumped over 9000 kg of mercury into the river 100 km upstream from Grassy Narrows, poisoning the entire river system for at least half a century. Moreover, as families began receiving cash income from government employment and welfare programs, the incentive to hunt, fish, grow one's own food, and trap fur-bearing animals declined. As the level of community solidarity fell, the rate of suicide and other social pathologies skyrocketed, especially among the young.

SOURCE: Based on a reading of Anastasia Shkilnyk, *A Poison Stronger than Love: The Destruction of an Ojibwa Community* (New Haven, CT: Yale University Press, 1985).

In the class tradition of social science, problems are formulated in such a way that their very statement incorporates a number of specific milieux and the private troubles encountered there by a variety of individuals; these milieux, in turn, are located in terms of larger historical and social structures.

In the next section, I will illustrate Mills's point. As we enter the twenty-first century, we are caught up in sociohistorical changes so vast that they necessarily and profoundly affect us all. Among the numerous contemporary revolutions that sociologists have identified, two of the most influential are postindustrialism and feminism. They are the focus of my attention here. **Postindustrialism** refers to the shift in modern economies from manufacturing to service industries, and to the consequences of that shift for work and leisure, the distribution of wealth, the control of corporations, and the nature of conflict between different classes of people. **Feminism** refers to the "liberation" of women as a result of their entry in large numbers into the system of higher education and the paid labour force, and to the consequences of that movement for the organization of family life, male–female relations, politics, sexuality, and gender inequality. Let us consider these two revolutions in turn.

▲ POSTINDUSTRIALISM

Industrialization

The **Industrial Revolution** is commonly regarded as the most important event in world history since the invention of agriculture about 10 000 years ago. It began in Britain in the 1780s, developed at a breathtaking quick pace, and soon involved many of the world's societies.

Coal mining, railway construction, and textile manufacturing were the early engines of industrial growth. Britain was transformed as tens of thousands of men, women, and children began to work sixteen-hour days in dangerous and filthy conditions in Manchester, Leeds, and other manufacturing centres.

Over the next century, industrial capitalism spread to Belgium and France, then to Germany and the United States, and finally, by the late 1800s, to Japan, Russia, Italy, Sweden, and Canada. Gas and oil and electricity fuelled engines and electric motors. Steel became the latest industrial material. The automobile reshaped much of the world.

Wherever it took root, industrial capitalism created so-called smokestack industries, usually in or near big cities, along with a large class of "blue-collar" **workers**. Typically, labour in these industries was manual, dirty, and physically demanding, even when it involved machinery. Often it required little skill. When skills were needed, they could learned in a relatively short time on the job.

Workers soon protested the long work days, low pay, and dangerous working conditions. They went on strike, formed trade unions, and joined political parties in order to improve their lives. Karl Marx, a great German social thinker of the mid-nineteenth century, felt that workers would ultimately take control of industry and government themselves and create prosperity and equality for all (see Box 1.2). But capitalism did not develop that way. For example, in Western Europe and, to a somewhat lesser degree, in North America, workers forced employers to limit the length of the working day, improve working conditions, and raise wages. Governments were compelled to tax citizens and provide at least minimal protection against ill health, unemployment, and poverty. As a result, workers became less interested in trying to overthrow the capitalist system. Employers, for their part, were forced to rely less on brutal exploitation and more on technological innovation to earn profits.

The Postindustrial Revolution

Collecting taxes, providing social services, and investing heavily in technological change required the growth of government and business offices, hospitals, schools, universities, and research laboratories. Thus, the new "service sector" was born. Its employees came to be known as "white-collar" workers. At its apex were highly trained professionals; near its base were secretaries and clerks. White-collar workers differed from blue-collar workers in several ways. They did cleaner, nonmanual work, often requiring years of formal education. Their earnings tended to be higher, and they were usually paid a set monthly or semimonthly salary rather than weekly wages based on the number of hours spent on the job. More prestige was attached to their occupations. And employees at the top of the service-sector hierarchy received more fringe benefits (vacation and sick leave, pension plans, medical and dental insurance, etc.) and enjoyed more authority and greater job security.

By 1980, 52 percent of all people working in Canada's paid labour force were in nonmanual occupations.[3] In the United States, the comparable figure was 51 percent; in West Germany and Japan, it was 46 percent (Ornstein, 1983: 252). The shift

Box 1.2
Karl Marx on the Rise and Fall of Capitalism

In about 1850, Marx proposed a sweeping theory of the development of human societies. In his theory, class structure and technology are the sources of societal change.

Marx noted that, in medieval Europe, peasants worked small plots of land that were owned by landlords. Peasants were legally bound to the land, obliged to give their landlords a set part of their harvest and to continue working for them under any circumstance. In turn, landowners were obliged to protect peasants against marauders and poor economic conditions.

By the late 1400s, certain processes had been set in motion that began to transform these feudal arrangements into a capitalist system. Most important was the growth of exploration and trade, which increased the demand for many goods and services in commerce, navigation, and industry. By the 1600s and 1700s, some urban craftsmen and merchants had opened small manufacturing enterprises and had saved enough capital to expand production greatly. But in order to increase profits, they also needed legally free workers, who could be hired in periods of high demand and fired during slack times. It was therefore necessary to force peasants off the soil and turn them into workers who would work for wages.

In Marx's view, the relations between wage labourers and capitalists at first encouraged rapid technological innovation and economic growth. Capitalists were eager to improve the way work was organized and to adopt new tools, new machines, and new production methods. These changes allowed them to produce more efficiently, earn higher profits, and drive less efficient competitors out of business.

Marx argued that the drive for profits caused capitalists to concentrate workers in larger and larger factories, keep wages as low as possible, and invest as little as possible in improving working conditions. This in turn helped to create a large and growing class of poor workers who would come to oppose a small and shrinking class of wealthy owners.

Marx felt that the workers would ultimately become aware of belonging to the same exploited class. Their "class consciousness" would, he wrote, encourage the growth of working-class organizations, such as trade unions and political parties. These organizations would seek to put an end to the private ownership of property, and to replace it with a system in which property, and therefore wealth, would be shared by everyone.

According to Marx, this revolutionary change was bound to occur during a "crisis of overproduction." The ability of capitalism to produce goods, he said, would eventually far exceed the ability of workers to purchase those goods. In order to sell their products, capitalists would be forced to lower their prices. Profits would then fall, the less efficient capitalists would go bankrupt, and massive unemployment of workers would result. In Marx's view, whereas the capitalist class system had originally encouraged economic growth, recurring and worsening crises of overproduction would ultimately hinder that growth. Then, wrote Marx, the workers would overthrow capitalism and replace it with a classless society. He called that new society "communist."

SOURCE: Based on readings of Karl Marx, *A Contribution to the Critique of Political Economy*, trans. N. Stone (Chicago: Charles H. Kerr, 1904 [1859]), and Karl Marx and Friedrich Engels, "Manifesto of the Communist Party," in R. Tucker, ed., *The Marx–Engels Reader* (New York: W.W. Norton, 1972), pp. 331–62.

from manual to nonmanual work prompted some commentators to argue that the era of postindustrialism was at hand (Bell, 1976; Toffler, 1990). Although emphases vary from one writer to the next, postindustrialists tend to argue that this new era involves five main developments:

- Power is changing hands. Domination by business owners is giving way to domination by scientifically trained managers and professionals.
- Greater prosperity can be expected since nonmanual jobs pay better.
- Work is becoming more enjoyable. Not only are hours on the job reduced, thus giving people more leisure time, but work in the service sector is more interesting and more creative.
- Service industries pollute less than manufacturing industries do, making "sustainable development" possible.
- Class conflict is subsiding. Strikes and political revolts, which characterized the industrial era, are now less frequent and less intense. That is because work is less arduous and more rewarding, and the manual working class now forms only a minority of the labour force.

Criticisms of the Theory of Postindustrialism

Each of the points listed above has been hotly contested. Consider first the question of corporate control. Modern corporations often raise money by selling shares on the stock market. Purchasing a share makes one a part-owner of the company. But ownership is not the same thing as control — that is, the capacity to set basic policy and to hire and fire top officials. Who controls the modern corporation? There are two possibilities. First, a single shareholder or a small group of shareholders may own so many shares that they have the power to decide on matters of policy and personnel. Alternatively, share ownership may be so widely dispersed that control is left in the hands of professional managers, many of whom hold postgraduate degrees in business administration and/or the sciences.

Postindustrialists tend to argue that control by managers and scientists is becoming more common. How accurate is that argument? Studies of decision making in corporations show that shareholder control still predominates. Indeed, in large Canadian corporations, shareholder control *by members of the same family* is actually increasing. In 1985, for example, nearly 70 percent of the 170 largest Canadian-owned nonfinancial corporations were controlled by family groups of shareholders — up 3 percent from

1978. In 1987, of the 17 largest nonfinancial enterprises in the country, 12 were controlled by family groups of shareholders. That figure was up from 11 in 1985 and 7 in 1978. Although there is no denying that scientists and professional managers play increasingly important roles in the business world today, the Canadian experience shows that shareholders in general, and family groups of shareholders in particular, are becoming *more* powerful, not less (Richardson, 1990: 345–46; Bottomore and Brym, 1989).

What of the postindustrialists' argument that the growth of the service sector has brought us more prosperity? Canadian sociologists have analyzed the growth of new jobs in Canada, and have found that, from the 1950s to the present, the great majority of new jobs have been created in the service sector. They have also examined the proportions of jobs that are high-paying, medium-paying, and low-paying, establishing that, in recent years, more high-paying and low-paying jobs have been created, but many jobs in the middle range have disappeared. The fastest-growing job categories are for relatively low-paying jobs, such as secretary, bookkeeper, teller, clerk, and waiter.[4] Moreover, such jobs are often part-time. Partly for that reason, average after-tax income, measured in terms of what it can purchase, has been *falling* in Canada since the early 1970s (Myles, Picot, and Wannell, 1993). Although the reasons for these developments are too complex to consider here, they do not support the view that growth in the service sector necessarily results in increased prosperity overall.

Consider now the third part of the postindustrialist theory — the view that work is becoming more interesting and less onerous while leisure time is increasing. That claim can also be disputed. First, as we have just seen, most new jobs are low-paying service positions. They involve the performance of closely supervised, routine tasks. As you may have experienced firsthand, creativity and independence are not prized in such occupations. Second, as far as leisure is concerned, surveys conducted to determine how people use their time show that leisure time is slowly increasing — for example, in Finland, it increased by an average of an hour a week between 1979 and 1987. But the sources of this change are not what the postindustrialists led us to expect. In Canada and other wealthy countries, there is more leisure time on average largely because there are more retired and unemployed people; not surprisingly, such people have more free time on their hands. But some groups are experiencing the opposite trend. Notably, an increasingly large number of women now work outside the home, and they enjoy *less* leisure time, especially if they have small children. This is so because, when women enter the paid labour force, they often continue to do most of the domestic work, thus assuming a double burden (Harvey, Marshall, and Frederick, 1991: 73; Meissner, 1988). Third, work-related stress and depression are increasing overall. One national survey found that nearly half of Canadians feel "really stressed" from several times a week to nearly all the time and one-third felt "really depressed" at least once a month. More than half of the respondents attributed stress to work and financial problems. People aged 25–54 experienced the most stress (*The Globe and Mail*, Dec. 19, 1992). Such evidence allows us to conclude that the postindustrialist vision of more interesting work and increased leisure time is at best a distant dream, at least for most Canadians employed in the paid labour force, and especially for women with small children.

The postindustrialist theory fares little better with respect to its environmental claim. The growth of service industries has not led to a decline in the consumption of goods and an attendant decline in pollution. On the contrary, service industries from advertising to the programming of robots in factories help *increase* the production and consumption of goods. In addition, most service industries have turned out to be big polluters. In the early 1980s, some analysts forecast that the widespread use of computers would save valuable forest resources by creating the "paperless office." As things turned out, computers (as well as fax machines) greatly increased paper use in offices — specifically, at twice the rate of economic growth since World War II. Heightened demand for paper has stimulated investment in environmentally dangerous pulp and paper megaprojects in northern Manitoba and elsewhere (Novek and Kampen, 1992). "Sustainable development" may be possible, but, as this example shows, the expansion of service industries is not enough to make it happen.

The postindustrialists appear to be on somewhat safer ground when it comes to the question of class conflict. Before World War II, many trade unions and political parties in Western Europe and North America had revolutionary ambitions, inspired by Marx's ideas. Now such goals are much less common. Furthermore, since the late 1970s, Canada and other rich industrialized countries have witnessed a sharp decline in strike activity and a modest decline in the proportion of employees organized in trade unions (Shalev, 1992).

This does not, however, signal the death of class conflict. New possibilities exist for unionization among lower-level white-collar workers. Strike waves continue to occur, especially during periods of relative prosperity, when workers have less to risk and employers have more to lose from work stoppages. Political parties supported by trade unions have often won elections in Western Europe and Australia, and gradually gained popularity in Canada between the early 1960s and the early 1990s. These parties tend to promote the redistribution of wealth to lower-income earners as well as the growth of state-run programs for health care, pensions, worker training, unemployment insurance, and industrial investment. The working class is certainly not the revolutionary power that Marx once envisaged, but workers continue to act as an important force for change.

What, then, in the final analysis, can one say about the postindustrialist theory? Informed sociological opinion is divided, but in the light of available evidence it seems to me that, on balance, we may agree on several points. The theory of postindustrialism draws our attention to some important social changes in the modern world. The rise of the service sector has altered the nature of work for many people. Professional managers and scientists in modern corporations are highly influential, and are becoming increasingly so. The proportion of jobs at the upper end of the white-collar wage scale has increased, and professionals are able to exercise more creativity and autonomy at work than are other people. Overall, class conflict is less intense. That said, one must immediately recognize the serious flaw in the theory of postindustrialism. It generalizes too hastily from changes at the top of the service sector to the whole society. Postindustrialism's sunny prognosis ignores what is happening to most people in the paid labour force: They earn less money, continue to perform routine tasks, enjoy little if any additional leisure time, are still massively affected by the decisions of powerful shareholders, and keep trying to improve their lives by organizing, striking, and supporting political parties that seem to be willing to further their interests. Postindustrialism is a form of capitalism. Thus, although much has changed, much remains the same.

▲ FEMINISM

The "Liberation" of Women

Industrialization was largely responsible for the second great transformation I want to consider here:

the rise of feminism. Two hundred years ago, virtually all women worked at home without pay. They prepared food, made clothing, raised children, and cleaned. One hundred years ago, as a result of the spread of manufacturing, a growing number of women, especially those living in cities, began to work in factories, schools, hospitals, and offices, and, consequently, to buy household services outside the home.

As their economic independence grew, women began to see the world differently. Increasingly, they came to regard the unchallenged authority of men in the family as oppressive. They also saw that they earned far less than men in the paid workforce and sometimes had to endure inferior working conditions. Their sharpened sense of domestic and market inequality cause them to demand social reform. The feminist movement was born (Strong-Boag, 1986).

Today, the sociological arm of feminism is concerned with analyzing the domination of men over women in the household, in the paid labour force, and in the realms of politics, law, and culture. Sociological feminists also study policies for overcoming male–female inequalities. To introduce this area of research, I will focus on inequality in domestic and paid work.

Inequality in the Labour Market and in the Home

Here are the plain facts of labour-market inequality. About two-thirds of adult women now work in the paid labour force, but most of them are segregated in a sort of "pink-collar" ghetto. About three-quarters of all female employees work in just five occupational groups: clerical, sales, medicine and health (mostly nursing and technical services), and teaching (Armstrong and Armstrong, 1988: 163). On average, women working full-time in the paid labour force earned just under 70 percent of what men earned in 1991, up 10 percent from 1974 (*The Globe and Mail,* Jan. 15, 1993). That figure drops to roughly 60 percent if we include part-time workers, since a larger proportion of women than of men work part-time (Fox and Fox, 1986: 7), but it increases to 91.1 percent if we examine only full-time, single, never-married workers (*The Globe and Mail,* Jan. 15, 1993). The latter finding hints at a fact that I will discuss at greater length below: Given present arrangements for day care and parental leave, having children is perhaps the single biggest deterrent to gender equality in wages.

Here are the similarly plain facts of inequality in the sphere of domestic work. On average, Canadian women spend 150 percent more time on domestic work than men do. Women and men also do different kinds of domestic work. Women spent 350 percent more time preparing meals, 300 percent more time cleaning up after meals, 250 percent more time doing indoor cleaning, and 30 percent more time taking care of children. Women do virtually all the laundry. Men, in contrast, do 300 percent more home repairs and outdoor cleaning than women. In general, women do domestic work that is more menial and has deadlines, whereas men do domestic work that is more fun, more creative, and less pressing. For example, the only child-care activities that men spend slightly more time on than women include playing with, helping, and teaching children (Harvey, Marshall, and Frederick, 1991: 50, 59).

Overcoming Gender Inequality

These few statistics instantly raise the question of how inequalities between women and men might be overcome. Sociologists have suggested many means, two of which I will consider here: equal pay for work of equal value and a publicly funded system of family support.

Part of the pay differential between women and men derives from the fact that women tend to be segregated in certain kinds of jobs, and those jobs tend to be undervalued and underpaid. Take kindergarten teachers, almost all of whom are women. One might reasonably argue that they perform one of the most important jobs in society — after all, they provide children with knowledge and values that serve as the foundation for all subsequent learning. Yet kindergarten teachers earn relatively low incomes — certainly much lower than do, say, truck drivers, most of whom are men.

Feminists argue that incomes should be modified to take into account the value to society of the work being performed.[5] That is what is meant by **equal pay for work of equal value**. If kindergarten teaching and other occupations in which women are concentrated were paid according to the value of the work done in those jobs relative to the value of the work done in the jobs in which men predominate, then much of the income difference between women and men would be eliminated.

Feminists know that it is hard to define "value to society" in terms that are generally acceptable. A major international research effort has therefore been mounted to establish criteria that will enable fair comparisons of the value of different jobs. In Canada and elsewhere, these criteria have begun to be applied in deciding how much people should be paid. In the public service and in large corporations, occupations in which women are overwhelmingly concentrated are now assessed in terms of their value. If they are found to be undervalued, salaries for those occupations are raised. However, only a minority of women employed in Canada's paid labour force are affected by the laws governing these practices, which apply only to occupations in which a very large proportion of the employees are women and to sizable companies.

In addition to emphasizing the merits of equal pay for work of equal value, feminists argue that a publicly funded family support system is needed to lessen the economic inequality between women and men. Such a system would include universally available day-care facilities and substantially more paid parental leave than is now available.

Women are penalized in the job market for bearing and raising children. As one feminist sociologist writes, "child care . . . responsibility is what

Women normally shoulder the burden of dual responsibility — for child care as well as for wage earning. Feminists argue for institutional relief through a publicly funded family-support system. SOURCE: Photo courtesy of Talia Lenton-Brym.

makes women's lives so different from men's, and represents the crucial handicap in the labour market" (Fox, 1986: 42). Many employers prefer not to promote or even hire women because they have or may decide to have children. Bosses often feel that the unpredictable and heavy demands of pregnancy, breast feeding, and child care simply do not fit the routines of the paid labour force. It follows that if affordable child-care facilities were more widely available, and if employers were required by law to grant longer parental leave with full pay, then women would not be so heavily penalized for having children, and the level of economic inequality between women and men would drop. This is precisely the outcome that research has confirmed (Reed, 1986). In countries with well-developed family-support systems, such as Sweden and France, women's earnings are closer to those of men; in countries with poorly developed family-support systems, such as Canada and the United States, women's earnings are far below men's.

A program of equal pay for work of equal value and a generous family-support system are very expensive policies. Moreover, they involve the redistribution of wealth from the more to the less affluent and from men to women. Not surprisingly, therefore, such policies have become political hot potatoes.

Women did not express their sense of injustice 200 years ago, when they were nearly powerless. In order to protest, they needed resources, such as education and a measure of economic independence, and it was only in the course of the twentieth century that they gained access to those resources. The intense political controversy that now surrounds such policies as equal pay for work of equal value and the strengthening of the family-support system is attributable, in part, to these improvements in women's status. It is also partly attributable to the fact that privileged groups rarely give up their advantages without a fight. It seems that many men oppose the adoption of policies favoured by feminists because those policies would, in effect, redistribute privileges from men to women. It seems that most men do not want to pay higher taxes to support policies that benefit mainly women. Nor do they wish to do more housework. Some analysts feel that growing resentment against the erosion of male privilege has fuelled an antiwoman backlash, expressed in part by increased violence against women. It has certainly ensured that the issues raised here, and many others related to them, will be the subject of much political controversy — and sociological research — well into the next century.

■ SOCIOLOGY AND THE NEW SOCIETY

Let me summarize what I hope to have accomplished and where I am now headed. I first argued that sociological knowledge differs from our common-sense understanding of human action. Sociology is concerned mainly with how *patterned relations* among people affect behaviour, not just with how individuals choose to act. I illustrated this point by showing how the distribution of power between men and women influences the rate of woman abuse, and how levels of social solidarity influence suicide rates.

I next pointed out that the best sociologists are not content to discover links between individual action and social circumstances. They also try to place their analyses in the broader context of social change. Stated otherwise, good sociology gives us a sense of how our personal concerns are shaped by social forces — *and* of how those social forces develop historically. I illustrated this point by examining in detail two of the most important social transformations we face today: the coming of postindustrialism and the rise of feminism.

I must now confess that things are actually more complicated than I first made them appear, since, for any given phenomenon, there may be half a dozen or more **theories,** or tentative explanations. How do we know which theory is best? Indeed, what does "best" mean? Sociologists seem to know. They often engage in heated disputes trying to establish which theory is most valid; they are specialists in the art of blackening an opponent's eye. Sociology is not, however, an intellectual free-for-all. Guidelines regulate sociological controversy. What then are the rules of sociological debate? That is the issue we will examine next.

▲ TWO RULES OF SOCIOLOGICAL DEBATE

The Scientific Rule

It is recorded that medieval monks pondered the question, "How many angels can dance on the head of a pin?" They consulted ancient authoritative books written in Hebrew, Greek, and Latin. They thought long and hard. They employed all their rhetorical skills in debating the issue. It is not recorded that the monks ever resolved their dispute. We may be assured, however, that they never con-

sidered inspecting the head of a pin, and counting. Any such suggestion would have been considered heresy. We, in contrast, would call it science.

Religious devotion, political zeal, and scientific commitment all involve the pursuit of some form of truth, but only science requires that we carefully observe and count, that our theories be systematically and publicly tested against evidence. When I say "systematic," I refer to the many research methods that have been developed to help avoid biased results. In sociology, for example, we experiment, conduct surveys, observe social interaction in a controlled manner, select representative samples of historical documents for analysis, and so forth. When I say "public," I refer to the fact that research is conducted and published so that it can be checked and replicated by other trained analysts.

In order better to understand how scientific knowledge differs from the nonscientific variety, consider the following ten statements, each of which represents a commonly accepted basis for knowing that something is "true" in our everyday lives (Babbie, 1986: 6–16):

- *"Everybody knows that's true; it's common knowledge."* This statement represents knowledge rooted in *tradition.* The trouble with this basis for knowledge is that while some traditional knowledge is valid (sugar *will* rot our teeth), some is not (masturbation will *not* blind us). Science is required to sort out valid from invalid knowledge.

- *"I know it's true because my professor (minister, mother, etc.) told me so."* This statement represents knowledge based on *authority.* We often think that something is true because we hear it from an expert. But experts can be wrong. For example, nineteenth-century Western physicians commonly "bled" their patients using leeches or some other device, in the belief that "poisons" would thus be eliminated from their patients' bodies. This practice often did more harm than good — which is why the first real advance in modern Western medicine took place when doctors *stopped* treating their patients. As this example suggests, in science, authority must always be questioned in order to arrive at more valid knowledge.

- *"Of course it's true. I saw it."* In our personal lives, we often gain knowledge through *casual observation.* However, we are usually pretty careless observers. That is why good lawyers can often trip up eyewitnesses in courtrooms; eyewitnesses are rarely certain about what they saw. In general, uncertainty can be reduced by observing in a conscious and deliberate manner and by recording observations. That is just what scientists do.

- *"I'm sure I'm right because I know several such cases."* People often *overgeneralize*. For instance, if you know a few people who started off poor, worked hard, and became rich, you may assume that anyone who is poor may become rich simply by working hard enough. You may not know about the far more numerous cases of poor people who work hard but, for a variety of reasons over which they have no control, remain poor. Scientists, however, have techniques for taking samples that are representative of the entire population. These are among the most powerful techniques available for overcoming the danger of overgeneralization. Overgeneralization may also be avoided by repeating research. Replication ensures that research findings are not idiosyncratic.

- *"I'm right because there are no contrary cases."* Sometimes we engage in *selective observation*, choosing to ignore evidence that challenges our firmly held beliefs. To extend the preceding example, you may know some people who work hard but remain poor. In order to maintain your belief that hard work results in wealth, you will have to explain away those annoying cases, perhaps by asserting that hard workers who remain poor do not work hard enough or that they are rare and therefore irrelevant exceptions to the general rule. As we have seen, however, in science, hypotheses must be tested against evidence drawn from samples that are representative of the population. And because science is a public enterprise, other researchers will always be on the lookout for evidence that contradicts one's research findings. These aspects of scientific research minimize the possibility of bias arising from selective observation.

- *"That's a special case. My generalization still holds."* In the preceding example, the argument that hard workers who remain poor just aren't working hard enough is a *qualification* of the original argument that hard workers get rich. Qualifications are often made in everyday life, and in science, too. The difference is that, in everyday life, qualifications are often and easily accepted as valid, whereas in scientific inquiry they are typically treated as hypotheses that have to be tested as rigorously as the original hypothesis.

- *"Because it has happened so many times before, it's likely to happen next time, too."* There is reasonable cause to expect many events to recur. For instance, we expect the sun to rise tomorrow because no cat-

astrophe has disturbed the structure of the solar system. But in everyday life, we may expect the recurrence of events without reasonable cause. Say the Toronto Blue Jays win 50 percent of all their games over a period of two months, and 80 percent of their Thursday games during the same period. Some fans may conclude that the good luck is likely to recur next Thursday, even though there is no apparent reason why the Jays should be more successful on Thursdays. This is an example of *illogical reasoning*.

Consider the following experiment: Take a coin, flip it, and record whether it comes up heads or tails. Flip the coin and record the result nine more times. Most often, you will wind up with five heads and five tails. Fairly often, you will get six heads and four tails. You will seldom get seven heads and three tails. In extremely rare cases, you will get ten heads. If you do ten coin flips enough times, however, you are sure to get ten heads in a row eventually, because extremely rare sequences of events do occur. The Jays' winning 80 percent of their Thursday games is a rare sequence of events. In the absence of any apparent reason for the sequence, it is also merely coincidental. It is illogical to believe otherwise, and scientists refrain from such illogical reasoning.

To be sure, there are many cases in which logic alone cannot distinguish between chance and nonchance events. A sociologist might speculate, for example, that a range of particular factors may lead people to vote for one political party or another. She may conduct a survey among a representative sample of the population to measure both party choice and the strength of those possible causes. She will then use certain statistical techniques that allow her to distinguish possible causes that occur by chance from those that are predictable. Most people in their everyday lives have neither the time nor the training, neither the resources nor the interest to use research methods and statistics to reach sound conclusions.

- *"I must be right."* Small children often refuse to accept responsibility for their behaviour, typically blaming their parents or older siblings for things that go wrong. Most adults are more responsible; they are less subject to *ego-defence* in understanding their world. Still, many scientists are passionately committed to the conclusions they reach in their research because they have invested much time and energy in them. It is other scientists — more accurately, the whole institution of science, with its commitment to publishing research results and critically scrutinizing findings — who put strict limits on ego-defence in scientific understanding.

- *"The matter is settled."* In our personal lives, we may engage in the *premature closure of inquiry,* deciding that all the relevant evidence has been gathered on a particular subject. Science, however, is committed to the idea that all theories are only temporarily true, valid only "until further notice." In science, inquiry is always open. Matters are never settled.
- *"There must be supernatural forces at work here."* When we can find no rational explanation for a phenomenon, we may engage in *mystification,* attributing the phenomenon to forces that cannot be observed or fully understood. Although such forces may exist, scientists remain sceptical. They are committed to discovering real, observable causes of real, observable effects. Without a scientific bent of mind, we might still believe that fire is a gift from the gods and that the sun revolves around the earth.

We may conclude that scientists, including the sociologists among them, tend to avoid the ten pitfalls just listed. In the course of their education, they learn — and learn to believe in — the rules or norms of science. Moreover, science is equipped with certain institutionalized safeguards against making the errors discussed above. Scientists are therefore less likely than nonscientists to commit them. Scientists treat traditional and authoritative opinion with scepticism. They develop special techniques and instruments to facilitate accurate observation. They are careful to take samples that are representative of the populations about which they wish to generalize. They purposely look for disconfirming evidence, and when such evidence accumulates, they discard or reformulate theories. They avoid illogic. In sum, it is only a modest exaggeration to say that, in science, seeing is believing, whereas in everyday life, believing is seeing.

We can now state one of the rules sociologists typically follow when they decide that one theory is better than another: Superior theories are those that withstand attempts to disprove them with evidence that has been systematically collected by means of publicly scrutinizable methods.

The Value Rule

That, however, is only half the story. In order to be regarded by a sociologist as valid, a theory must also correspond to the pertinent values of that so-

ciologist (Edel, 1965). Like everyone else, sociologists are members of society. The way they think about the social world is therefore influenced by the conditions of their existence. People who become sociologists are born into various classes, ethnic groups, religions, and countries; they have different upbringings, educations, career patterns, and temperaments; they are men or women; they are raised in different historical periods. Such circumstances leave an imprint on the way a sociologist thinks, and influence the kinds of theories he or she will favour. Someone once told Émile Durkheim that the facts contradicted his theories; his blunt reply: "The facts are wrong" (quoted in Lukes, 1973: 52). Durkheim's attitude may seem more than a little headstrong, but all sociologists (and other scientists, too) are inclined to favour one theory over another to some degree, independent of what the evidence shows.[6]

Values influence sociological thought in three main ways. First, values help sociologists pick theoretical favourites by leading them to study problems and formulate questions that they consider important. As Max Weber emphasized, we choose to study "only those segments of reality which have become significant to us because of their value-relevance" (Weber, 1964 [1949]: 76). For example, a sociologist who, as a child, was exiled from her country of birth because a revolutionary upheaval led to her family's expulsion might develop a lifelong interest in the conditions underlying political harmony and change. Another sociologist, prone to religious experiences, may become fascinated with the social conditions that encourage or discourage belief in God. A third sociologist, one who had an unusually strict upbringing, may develop an avid interest in prostitution. In general, topics and questions become "value-relevant" either because they somehow resonate with the sociologist's personal experiences or because they are viewed as meaningful by the groups to which the sociologist belongs and with which he or she identifies.

Second, once the sociologist has selected a topic and posed research questions, and as he or she chooses or formulates a theory to be tested against the evidence, certain untested (and often unconscious) assumptions come into play. For example, the personal experiences and group affiliations of one sociologist may lead him to assume that societies naturally tend toward a state of equilibrium and that social institutions such as the family and the political system all contribute to maintaining social order. The experiences and associations of a second sociologist may lead her to assume that societies are in a state of constant change and that institutions promote social transformation, not social stability. Completely different concepts and hypotheses may be (and have been) suggested by these two sets of assumptions. It should thus be clear that the very constitution of a theory — what it purports to explain, the problems it raises, and the concepts and hypotheses it involves — is necessarily influenced by values.

Third, sociologists' values influence the uses to which their work is put. For sociology is not just a pure intellectual exercise; it is also an applied science, with practical, everyday uses, as Table 1.1 suggests. The table lists the jobs that are commonly held by Canadians with B.A.s in sociology.[7] Most of these jobs involve working with people to solve social problems of one sort or another. Sociology is thus used in a variety of practical ways, including the evaluation and recommendation of policies

for governments and a whole host of organizations ranging from hospitals and schools to trade unions and armies.[8] And just as a laser may be used both to heal and to kill, so sociological training and the results of sociological research may suggest both how to ease racial tensions in a school and how to prevent factory workers from unionizing, or how to further peace negotiations between warring parties and how best to select and organize personnel for nuclear bomber squadrons. Whether a sociologist feels comfortable having his or her research used in a particular way will depend heavily on his or her values and will influence his or her job choices.

In sum, values influence the selection of research problems that the sociologist considers important; they are embedded in many of the unconscious assumptions and testable hypotheses contained in

---

◆ Table 1.1 Jobs Commonly Held by Canadian Sociology Graduates

Government	Research	Corrections
Community affairs officer	Social-research specialist	Corrections officer
Urban/regional planner	Consumer researcher	Criminology assistant
Legislative aide	Data analyst	Police officer
Affirmative action worker	Market researcher	Rehabilitation counsellor
Foreign service officer	Survey researcher	Criminal investigator
Human rights officer	Census officer/analyst	Juvenile court worker
Personnel coordinator˙	Demographer/population analyst	Parole officer
	Systems analyst	

Community affairs	Teaching	Business
Occupational/career counsellor	Public health educator	Advertising officer
Homeless/housing worker	Teacher	Sales manager
Public health/hospital administrator	Admissions counsellor	Project manager
Child development technician	College placement worker	Sales representative
Public administration assistant		Market analyst
Social assistance advocate		Real estate agent
Resident planning aide		Journalist
Group-home worker		Public relations officer
Rehabilitation program worker		Actuary
Rural health outreach worker		Insurance agent
Housing coordinator		Human resources manager
Fund-raising director/assistant		Production manager
Caseworker/aide		Labour relations officer
Community organizer		Administrative assistant
Youth outreach worker		Quality control manager
		Merchandiser/purchaser
		Computer analyst
		Data entry manager
		Publishing officer

SOURCE: Adapted from Neil Guppy and R. Alan Hedley, *Opportunities in Sociology* (Montreal: Canadian Sociology and Anthropology Association, 1993), p. 8. Used with permission.

favoured theories; and they are put to uses favoured by the sociologist. Hence the second rule sociologists apply when deciding that one theory is better than another: Theories regarded as superior tend to correspond to sociologists' values.

Balancing the Two Rules

The proper balance between the pursuit of values and the quest for scientific truth can be a source of tremendous creativity. Sensitivity to human values can lead sociologists to conduct research that really matters to many people. Values can also lead sociologists in new and exciting theoretical directions. Research based on the scientific method can require that theories be modified so that they correspond more closely to perceived reality. Rigorous theory testing can also suggest new and fruitful lines of inquiry.

It is, of course, always possible that one may lose the balance between the pursuit of values and adherence to scientific method. Doing so can have serious negative consequences: it can result in one of the two extremes of "ideologism" or "scientism."

Ideologism refers to an exaggerated concern with the issue of whom sociology serves — the rich or the poor, businesses or unions, women or men, whites or visible minorities — combined with a low regard for the need to test theory empirically and rigorously. It results in a form of sociology that is both highly argumentative and of questionable validity. Reading ideological sociology, one is often confronted by a vexing question: "This may raise important issues, but is it true?"

Scientism, on the other hand, refers to an exaggerated concern with research techniques, combined with a denial of the role of values in science.

With the collapse of the USSR, the rise of nationalism in Europe, ethnic violence, and global economic insecurity, many people have reacted with despair and apathy. This Scottish artist has become fascinated with and horrified by the terrors of contemporary Europe. Many of his paintings illustrate the dead souls and misanthropes who occupy and "survive" today's war zones. SOURCE: Ken Currie, *The Troubled City* (1991). Oil on canvas, 274 x 335 cm. Slide courtesy of Boukamel Contemporary Art, London. Reproduced with permission of the artist.

It results in a form of sociology that is not much concerned with searching out, explaining, and proposing solutions to the main human problems of the era. Indeed, in some cases, it leads to research that is of little interest to anybody except the researcher. The reader of scientistic sociology is also confronted by a troubling question: "This may be true, but is it important?"[9]

▲ THE ROLE OF SOCIOLOGY TODAY

Perhaps more than ever before, it is vital that sociological research be both true and important. For, as renowned English sociologist Anthony Giddens is fond of saying, we live "in an era suspended between extraordinary opportunity . . . and global catastrophe" (1982: 166). With the collapse of the USSR in 1991, nuclear devastation became less likely than it had been just a few years before. But a whole range of environmental issues, profound inequalities in the wealth of nations and of classes, racial and ethnic violence, and unsolved problems in the relations between women and men continue to stare us in the face and profoundly affect the quality of our everyday lives.

Despair and apathy are two possible responses to these complex issues, but these are not responses that humans have often favoured. If it were in our nature to give up hope or not to care, we would still be sitting around, half-naked, in the mud outside a cave.

People are more inclined to look for ways of improving their lives, and this period of human history is full of opportunities to do so. We have, for example, advanced to the point at which, for the first time, we have the means to feed and educate everyone in the world. Similarly, it now seems possible to erode some of the inequalities that have always been with us and have always been the major source of human conflict.

Sociology offers no easy solutions as to how these goals might be accomplished. It does, however, promise a useful way of understanding our current predicament and seeing possible ways of dealing with it, of leading us a little farther away from the mud outside the cave. You sampled sociology's inclination to tie personal troubles to public issues when you read the material on woman abuse and suicide in this chapter. You saw the discipline's tendency to provide a historical and critical understanding of where we are and where we might be heading when you read about the half-fulfilled promises of postindustrialism and feminism. You were introduced to some of the dilemmas inherent in this particular intellectual pursuit when you learned about the scientific and value dimensions of the discipline.

I frankly admit that the questions I have raised here are tough to answer. Sharp controversy surrounds them all. But I am quite sure that, if you try to grapple with them, you will enhance your understanding of your society's, and your own, possibilities. That is "Why sociology." ■

● SUMMARY

1. The sociological perspective urges us to recognize that the mainsprings of human action are found in the patterns of social interaction and culture that constitute society. Human action is constrained by physical and biological realities, individuals have particular psychological constitutions, but some portion of human action is shaped by uniquely social causes.

2. For example, sociologists commonly regard the rate of woman abuse as a function of the distribution of power between men and women in society. Rates of woman abuse are highest where the female/male power ratio is highest and where the female/male power ratio is lowest. In the latter case, men are much more powerful than women and one expression of male domination is a high level of woman abuse. In the former case, gender equality is greatest and some men react violently to the erosion of their authority by engaging in high levels of woman abuse.

3. Another example of sociological thinking may be found in the analysis of suicide. Following Durkheim, many sociologists agree that suicide rates vary with levels of social solidarity. When individuals are best anchored in society, they are least likely to take their own lives. The forces that bind people to society include the frequency and intensity of interaction with others and the moral cement that shared values create.

4. Contemporary social revolutions are taking place in the realm of gender inequality and in the structure of industry. Gender inequality is evident in the labour market (where women earn considerably less than men) and in the home (where women do considerably more unpaid domestic work than men). Labour-market inequality between men and women has been decreasing in recent decades. Historical data on domestic labour

inequality are fragmentary but suggest a similar though less rapid trend. Further advances in both spheres depend on the passing of laws requiring equal pay for work of equal value and the growth of publicly funded day-care and family-support systems.

5. A second contemporary social revolution is that of postindustrialism. Postindustrialism refers to the shift from manufacturing to service industries and the consequences of that shift for work and leisure, the distribution of wealth, the control of corporations, and the nature of conflict between different classes of people. Although evidence suggests that there is some truth to the claims of the postindustrialists, many of them exaggerate the degree to which society has moved toward better jobs, more affluence and leisure, the control of corporations by managers and scientists, and the lessening of class conflict.

6. Like other scientists, sociologists (a) are committed to testing theories publicly through the use of systematically collected evidence, and (b) find that values enter into the scientific process when they select problems for analysis, formulate theories, and decide how they want the results of their research to be used.

7. Sociology promises increased understanding of (a) why we act the way we do, (b) the possibilities and limitations of human action, and (c) the courses of action that are necessary in order to achieve given goals.

QUESTIONS TO CONSIDER

1. Do you think it is likely that the postindustrialists' promise of an affluent "leisure society" will be realized in the next century? Why or why not?
2. Do you think it is likely that the promises of feminism will be realized in the next century? Why or why not?
3. In this chapter, you learned how variations in the distribution of power affect the rate of woman abuse and how variations in the level of social solidarity affect the rate of suicide. How do you think variations in power distribution and social solidarity affect other areas of social life, such as criminal behaviour and political protest?
4. Is a science of society possible? If you believe that such a science is possible, what are its advantages over common sense? What are its limitations?

GLOSSARY

authority Power that is considered legitimate.

capitalism An economic system in which workers are legally free to sell their labour to owners of capital, and owners of capital are legally free to invest their capital so as to maximize profits.

culture Patterns of beliefs, symbols, and values that develop over time among groups of people. Culture helps people adapt to their environment and usually facilitates group survival.

equal pay for work of equal value A wage system in which pay is based on the value to society of the work being performed.

feminism In sociology, a school of thought concerned with analyzing the domination of men over women in the household, in the paid labour force, and in the realms of politics, law, and culture. Sociological feminists also study policies for overcoming male–female inequalities.

ideologism An exaggerated concern with the question of whom sociology serves, combined with a low regard for testing theory empirically and rigorously.

Industrial Revolution The rapid economic transformation that began in Britain in the 1780s; often regarded as the most important event in world history since the development of agriculture and cities. It involved the large-scale application of science and technology to industrial processes, the creation of factories, and the formation of a working class.

postindustrialism The theory that a shrinking manufacturing sector and an expanding service sector have resulted in the decline of working-class conflict, greater prosperity, more interesting work, more leisure time, and a shift in the locus of ultimate power from capitalists to professionals.

power The capacity to influence and control others.

scientism An exaggerated concern with research techniques, combined with a denial of the role of values in science.

social solidarity The degree to which group members share beliefs and values, and the intensity and frequency of their interaction.

theories Tentative explanations of some aspect of social life.

workers People who sell their labour to employers. There are different categories of workers, including *blue-collar* (manual), *white-collar* (service), and *pink-collar* (women ghettoized in low-paying service occupations).

SUGGESTED READING

Becker, Howard S., and William C. Rau. (1992). "Sociology in the 1990s." *Social Science and Modern Society, 30,* 70–74. A well-written and accurate assessment of sociology's current predicament.

Berger, Peter. (1992). "Sociology: A Disinvitation?" *Social Science and Modern Society, 30,* 12–18. A sober analysis of some of the false turns taken by sociology over the past three decades.

Brym, Robert J. (1997). "Canadian Sociology." *Contemporary Sociology, 26,* 543–46. An update of the following item.

Brym, Robert J., with Bonnie J. Fox. (1989). *From Culture to Power: The Sociology of English Canada.* Toronto: Oxford University Press. An overview of theoretical controversies and empirical findings in several of the main fields of sociological research in Canada outside Quebec.

Guppy, Neil, and R. Alan Hedley. (1993). *Opportunities in Sociology.* Montreal: Canadian Sociology and Anthropology Association. A useful booklet on the job prospects for students who graduate with a B.A. in sociology.

NOTES

1. Note, however, that (a) men are more frequently victims of violence than women and (b) in the abuse of both women and men, it is mainly men who initiate violence and who cause most injury. This suggests that women are far from the only victims of violence and that woman abuse is part of the larger problem of male violence.

2. The law defines *any* intentional physical contact that is unwanted as assault. My overview of theories is necessarily sketchy. For a comprehensive treatment, see Johnson (1996).

3. "Lower-middle-class" occupations (mainly sales and clerical) accounted for 28 percent of the Canadian workforce; "upper-middle-class" positions (mainly professional and technical) accounted for about 16 percent; and "upper-class" positions (mainly administrative and management) accounted for 8 percent.

4. The situation is much the same in the United States, but proportionately more high-paying jobs have been created in Germany, Sweden, and other Western European countries, because those countries follow different economic policies. See Myles, 1988.

5. Some feminists also argue that domestic work should be paid. The estimated dollar value of domestic work in Canada in 1981 was nearly 36 percent of the gross national product (GNP) — that is, more than a third of the dollar value of all goods and services produced for money. See Swinamer, 1990.

6. Some people naïvely believe that values and beliefs contribute to the determination of theoretical validity only in the social sciences. In fact, they can hinder or promote the acceptance of theories in the natural sciences as well. For example, in 1906, when a colleague's experimental evidence appeared to challenge Albert Einstein's special theory of relativity, Einstein's reaction, according to his biographer, was something like "tant pis pour les faits" ("so much the worse for the facts") — a reaction not unlike Durkheim's (Clark, 1971: 144).

7. Incidentally, a 1988 study found that 70 percent of the 2500 Canadians who received B.A.s in sociology in 1986 held full-time jobs, compared with 61 percent of all other social science graduates. (The remainder were still studying in university, employed part-time, or unemployed.) They had a median income of $23 000 per year, compared with $24 000 for all other social science graduates. About 60 percent of the jobs held by sociology graduates required high qualification levels. These figures all refer to sociology graduates who were in the labour force for only two years; comparable figures for graduates with longer labour-force experience rise significantly. See Guppy and Hedley, 1993.

8. Less apparently, pure sociology has been used as raw material for various *ideologies,* or sets of ideas that justify particular group interests.

9. In the worst case, practitioners of scientism become "hired guns," willing to sell themselves to the highest bidder and to remain blind to the larger goals that their work may be helping to achieve (Brym and Myles, 1989).

Part Two CULTURE

CULTURE SURROUNDS US, BECOMING OUR
"SECOND NATURE" AS WE LEARN AND CONTRIBUTE
TO IT. HOWEVER, WE CAN ALSO LEARN TO STAND
ASIDE AND OBSERVE CULTURE AND ITS EFFECTS
ANALYTICALLY AND SOCIOLOGICALLY, AS THE
FIGURE IN THE CENTRE OF THIS PAINTING
SUGGESTS.

CHAPTER TWO
Socialization

IN THIS CHAPTER YOU WILL LEARN THAT

■ socialization refers to the learning of knowledge, skills, motivations, and identities as our genetic potential interacts with our social environment

■ socialization takes place at all stages of the life cycle and in a variety of settings: families, schools, peer groups, the mass media, and occupational groups

■ among the major contributors to socialization theory are Sigmund Freud (who regarded adult personality as the result of childhood repression), Jean Piaget (who saw cognitive development as the result of interaction between the child's physical maturation and his or her social environment), and George Herbert Mead and other *symbolic interactionists* (who focussed on the way we actively create and negotiate our roles and self-concepts, partly by imagining ourselves in the roles of others)

■ socialization continues into adulthood: as people work, marry, divorce, raise children, retire, and so on, they enter new relationships with others, encounter new guidelines for behaviour, and adopt new roles

■ sometimes our self-concept undergoes abrupt change as we quickly learn new role identities and negotiate a new self-image; this process of resocialization occurs when we abandon, or are forced to abandon, our way of life and self-concept for a radically different one — it is most evident in jails, mental hospitals, boot camps, and in religious and political conversions

JACK HAAS AND WILLIAM SHAFFIR
McMaster University

■ INTRODUCTION

This chapter focusses on socialization, the social learning of beliefs and behaviour. One conception of socialization, typified by the *structural-functionalist* perspective, focusses on the individual's adaptation and conformity — how we learn the ways of society in order to be able to function in it (Elkin and Handel, 1972). This conception views socialization from the viewpoint of the group to which the individual belongs. It refers to the learning of expectations, habits, values, motives, skills, beliefs, and other requirements necessary for effective participation in social groups.

An alternative conception, **symbolic interactionism,** uses the individual rather than the group as the frame of reference: emphasis is placed on the development of the person. According to this view, socialization refers to the process of development or change that the person experiences as a consequence of social influences. "Its focus tends to be the development of self-concept, identity and various attitudes, dispositions, and behaviours of the individual" (Gecas, 1981: 165). It is an approach in which socialization is viewed as a continuous process of negotiating identities and the shaping of self-concepts.

The process of becoming socialized occurs in a cultural context. As such, we must expect that the content of socialization differs greatly from one society to another. People in different societies learn different norms, values, and lifestyles and are likely to approach their environment from different perspectives. At the same time, however, within every society, each person is different. These differences are also the product of socialization. Our unique personal history permits us to share not only in the larger society, but also in a specific part of it. As such, we are influenced by distinctive **subcultures** of family, friends, class, and religion. We see, then, that the socialization process helps to explain similarities and differences between people in a particular society.

■ NATURE AND NURTURE

There is a continuing dispute among sociologists and other social scientists about the relative importance of biological inheritance and of the social

One of the fundamental debates in social science concerns the relative weight of "nature" (biological inheritance) versus "nurture" (the social environment) in shaping beliefs and behaviours. SOURCE: Don Smetzer/Tony Stone.

environment in shaping our beliefs and behaviour. One of the most controversial areas of debate is the relationship between race and IQ test scores.

Early in this century, social scientists, including major figures such as Sigmund Freud, claimed that human behaviour is caused by inherited, or inborn, features of human biology. According to this view, behaviour occurs in all members of a species without having to be learned; the social environment has little impact.

Controversy has arisen over the extent to which race and intelligence — or, more generally, heredity and environment — affect individual behaviour and aptitude. For example, hereditarians argue that intelligence differences among racial groups are attributable to genetic factors, whereas environmentalists contend that social variables such as class and family structure are the most important causes.

Hereditarianism was given a dramatic impetus when educational psychologist Arthur Jensen concluded in 1969 that genes affecting IQ differ in blacks and whites, causing the average black to have a lower IQ than the average white. A strong counterargument was made by Thomas Sowell (1978).

Sowell argued that black–white IQ differences resulted from social and cultural factors rather than genetic differences. By comparing the IQ results for blacks with those for white immigrants from deprived backgrounds shortly after they arrived in the United States, Sowell proved the power of social and cultural forces to modify heredity. Beginning from the observation that the situation of most American blacks resembled that of recent immigrants more than that of groups long resident in the United States, and that until recent times most blacks lived in the rural South under laws and customs of segregation, Sowell showed that there was nothing unusual about lower black IQ scores. Sowell's data revealed that the average black IQ scores in the 1970s were above those of many white ethnic groups in the 1920s.

But the controversy by no means ended there. For instance, in the late 1980s J. Phillipe Rushton of the University of Western Ontario created an uproar in Canada when he claimed to have found evidence that a racial hierarchy exists, with "Orientals" at the top, "Africans" at the bottom, and "Caucasoids" in the middle. Rushton purportedly used over 50 different measures, including brain size, IQ, and sexual and personal restraint. His research led him to predict that Orientals would overtake Caucasoids economically and scientifically.

Numerous studies have challenged the racist assumption that individual and group differences are due to genetic differences and have demonstrated the significance of social–cultural influences and context. One of the best known studies focussed on the power of teachers to affect IQ test results. Rosenthal and Jacobson (1968) demonstrated the power of the self-fulfilling prophecy — when an expectation leads to behaviour that causes the expectation to become a reality.

In their study, Rosenthal and Jacobson administered a standard IQ test to all the children in a school from grades one to six. The teachers were told that this was a special test that would predict intellectual "blooming." The teachers were told to expect that certain students, who had in fact been randomly selected, would be higher achievers. At the end of the year, the researchers found that this randomly selected group of children scored significantly higher on the same intelligence test they had taken at the beginning of the year. Their classmates, as a group, did not. The test results demonstrated that those children whom the teachers expected to bloom actually did bloom. According to Rosenthal and Jacobson, teachers treated these students as if they were special, thus causing the students to believe they were special and then to become high academic achievers.

None of this is to deny that both biological and environmental factors interact in shaping human beings. However, these examples do show that a child's inherited characteristics are channelled, developed, or repressed through the process of socialization. Let us consider some biological–environmental interactions.

Human babies have both a biological and emotional need to cling to and interact with a warm, sheltering figure. Verbal communication may not be part of this contact, but some form of communication is — whether smiles, laughs, or pats. Without this attachment, socialization is impaired and irreversible damage may be done to the person's sense of self. Evidence for this view comes from several sources: reports of so-called feral (untamed) children who were allegedly raised by wild animals; studies of children who were deliberately raised in isolation by their own families; and studies of children in institutions.

Although the evidence relating to children raised in the wild is dramatic, it is also quite unreliable. In the late nineteenth and early twentieth centuries, a few cases were reported, from India and elsewhere, of the discovery of children whose behaviour seemed more like that of animals than human beings (Singh and Zingg, 1942). Efforts to socialize the children were said to have met with little success, and all the children died at a young age.

More convincing evidence comes from studies of children raised in isolation by their families. The case of Anna is the best-known instance of the long-term social isolation of an infant. Anna was an illegitimate child hidden away in a room until she was nearly 6 years old. Her mother gave her only enough care to be kept alive. When she was discovered, her clothing and bedding were filthy and she was emaciated and was unable to walk, talk, feed herself, or respond to others. She was thought to be both blind and deaf. Anna made slow but steady progress as she became human through the process of socialization, but five years of social isolation had left her permanently damaged. At the age of 8, Anna's mental and social development was still less than that of a 2-year-old. Not until she was 10 did she show the first signs of using language.

For ethical reasons, researchers cannot conduct experiments on humans to investigate further the consequences of human isolation. They have, however, studied the effects of social isolation on animals. Harry and Margaret Harlow (1962) placed rhesus monkeys, whose genetic makeup and behaviour are in some ways similar to those of humans, in various conditions of isolation. The Harlows found that complete isolation for a period of six months seriously disturbed the monkeys' development. When these isolated monkeys subsequently encountered others, they were fearful and unable to defend themselves. Later, they were unable to have sexual relations. These research results suggest that lack of socialization, on a wide enough scale, spells species death.

When the Harlows isolated infant monkeys in cages but provided them with an artificial mother made of wire mesh, a wooden head, and the nipple of a feeding tube for a breast, the monkeys were subsequently found to be incapable of interacting with others. However, when the artificial mother was covered with soft terry cloth, the infant monkeys clung to it in comfort and later revealed less emotional distress. Infant monkeys preferred the cloth

In the early 1960s, researchers Harry and Margaret Harlow placed baby rhesus monkeys in various conditions of isolation, with artificial mothers made of wire mesh and terry cloth, in order to witness and study the animals' reactions. Among other things, they discovered that baby monkeys fail to develop normal social skills if reared in isolation. SOURCE: Martin Rogers/Tony Stone.

mother even when it gave less milk than the wire mother. The Harlows concluded that emotional development requires affectionate cradling as part of the mother–infant relationship.

The Harlows' research also demonstrated that the absence of the mother was less significant when other monkeys were present, thus suggesting that it is social isolation rather than maternal deprivation that has serious, long-term consequences. Moreover, short-term isolation of three months or so was much less harmful to emotional health than longer-term isolation, which created irreversible emotional and behavioural effects.

The importance of social contact in the development of human infants has also been demonstrated. In 1945, R.A. Spitz compared infants in an orphanage with those in a women's prison nursery. The infants in the prison nursery interacted with their own mothers for the first year of their lives, whereas infants raised in the foundling home were attended by nurses and spent their days lying on their backs, seeing and hearing very few people, and lacking social stimulation. Although in the beginning the foundling children were as healthy as those in the nursery, after two years some of the children in the orphanage were "retarded" and all were psychologically and socially undeveloped for their age, and by age 4 a third of them had died. No such problems were observed among the prison nursery infants. Socialization, we may safely conclude, is often a matter of life and death.

■ THE SELF AND SOCIALIZATION THEORIES OF DEVELOPMENT

In the course of parent–child interaction, children learn to define themselves as social creatures. They develop a **personality,** the core of which is the **self**. One may view the self as a reference centre for planning and orientation, for sorting and assessing life's situations in terms of their relative importance. The self refers to one's awareness of ideas and attitudes about one's own personal and social identity.

The development of a sense of self, or self-image, greatly depends on social interaction. For instance, the newborn does not differentiate himself or herself from the mother. Such differentiation occurs gradually as the newborn learns to see his or her mother as a separate person. Over time, through social interaction, the young child acquires the ability to see himself or herself reflected in the eyes of others and to sense his or her own identity. It is precisely this ability that children who have been reared in isolation lack.

To understand the process of self-growth, we will examine the theories of four scholars — Sigmund Freud, Jean Piaget, Charles Horton Cooley, and George H. Mead — whose contributions, while different in detail, emphasize that the self emerges through social interaction with others. Freud (1962 [1930]) developed a model of personality with three main parts: **id, ego,** and **superego**. For Freud, the id represents the basic drives or **instincts** for food, sex, and so forth, drives that require gratification but that are unconscious. The id is present from birth; hence right from the beginning, the infant is a package of needs demanding attention. The child's caretakers, however, are not entirely responsive to the needs of the child's id. To adapt to the resulting frustration, the child's ego develops and comes into play. The ego, Freud believed, emerges from the id and represents an attempt to balance the child's innate drives with the realities of life — in particular, the fact that we can't have everything we want.

The third component of personality, the superego, is the individual's learning of and internalization of the culture of the groups in which he or she participates. The superego, therefore, involves the development of personal conscience. As a consequence of socialization, the child moves from demanding the satisfaction of basic needs to developing a moral sense of right and wrong, a sense of appropriateness and guilt, depending on the cultural guidelines learned with others.

In the well-adjusted personality, according to Freud, the ego successfully manages the opposing forces of the id and the superego. When the ego cannot successfully manage these conflicts, the individual develops some form of personality disorder. Because childhood is so critical to personality formation, unresolved childhood conflicts are a source of unconscious personality problems in adult life. We see, then, that Freud pictured the individual as being constantly in conflict. The id, the ego, and the superego are best thought of as interacting and conflicting processes within the mind.

In contrast to theories that concern personality development as a whole, the work of Jean Piaget is more limited in focus. It concerns cognitive development, or the way we learn to think. Piaget was the first to show that cognitive development is as much a social as a psychological process. His research demonstrated that children's conceptions of how the world works change with age. He identified four stages of cognitive development, each being a result of increased social experience and age (Piaget, 1950; Piaget and Inhelder, 1969).

The first stage Piaget calls *sensorimotor*. During this stage, which extends from birth to about age 2, the baby sucks, touches, looks, and listens. The child is without thought, knowing the world only as a consequence of direct experience.

The second phase of development, spanning ages 2–7, is the *preoperational* stage. Children experience the world mentally by using and understanding symbolic communication. They are capable of thinking about things they are not experiencing directly. However, they continue to perceive the world only from their own point of view and are not yet able to see things from others' perspectives.

The next stage, the *concrete operational,* typically develops between the ages of 7 and 11. During this phase, children become able to think in terms of cause and effect. Gradually, children move beyond their earlier egocentrism and develop the ability to perceive a situation from other people's points of view.

The fourth stage of development, the *formal operational* stage, is reached when the child is able to use highly abstract thought and to imagine alternatives to reality. The child develops an imagination that allows thinking and fantasizing beyond the immediate situation or reality.

In contrast to Freud, who emphasized the conflict between the opposing forces of biology and society, Piaget believed that people possess considerable ability to shape their own social world. He contributed greatly to our sense of the human mind as an active and creative source and interpreter of reality. He enlarged our understanding of the developmental capacity of the human mind as resulting directly from an interactive process of biological maturation and social experience.

George H. Mead contributed to a still more sociological conception of the development of self. According to Mead (1934), the self is not biological and does not exist at birth but develops only as a consequence of social experience.

In Mead's view, the social experiences responsible for the development of the self are rooted in the communication of symbols. By using symbols, people create and share meanings about their situation. Humans, Mead argued, understand the actions of others by interpreting the meaning of their actions. And understanding the meaning of others' actions in a particular situation requires imagining the situation from the others' points of view. The uniquely human ability to use and manipulate symbols allows us imaginatively to take the role of others, empathize with others' points of view, and imagine how others see and respond to us. Moreover, Mead thought, this human ability to interpret situations from others' points of view allows us to anticipate the reactions of others even before acting. Thus, humans can consider alternative lines of action, review the possible consequences of reactions to their actions, and check and align their behaviour accordingly.

Mead argued that, because we can imagine ourselves from the perspectives of other people, we are first aware of ourselves as social objects. This objective element of the self he called the *me*. Accompanying the me is the subjective or active part of the self, which he called the *I*. All social experience involves an interaction of the I and the me, with the I initiating action and the me reflectively taking the role of the other.

Mead thought the self develops as a consequence of social experience. As a child learns to use language and other symbols, the self develops and the child moves from an egocentric reality to a reality in which he or she is able to take the role of others. Gradually, the child learns to take the role of several others simultaneously. A final stage in the development of the self involves acquiring the ability to conceptualize a view of society in general. Mead used the term the **generalized other** to refer to the widespread and shared set of cultural norms and values used in self-evaluation and in developing concepts of the self.

Socialization, according to Mead, continues as long as the individual has social experiences. Changing contexts and contacts produce new opportunities for learning. But Mead also believed that humans affect others. In other words, they help shape their situations and lives.

Like Freud and Mead, Charles Horton Cooley believed that the self was essentially a social product. But, unlike Freud, he felt that the structure and contents of the self are derived from the society that is represented by the groups and significant others surrounding the individual; self-image emerges as a product of group involvement and communication with others.

Focussing on the process of self-realization, Cooley (1902) used the image of a looking glass to explain how others influence the way we see ourselves. Cooley argued that the gestures and reactions of others are a mirror or "looking glass" in which we see ourselves. We look to others to see a reflection of our psychological self, just as we look in a mirror to see a reflection of our physical body. Our conceptions about ourselves — our feelings about who

and what we are — are organized around our evaluation of how we see ourselves judged by others.

The self, for Cooley, has three major elements: our imagination of how our physical appearance, friends, manners, goals, and self-presentation are seen in the minds of other people whose opinions we value; our perception of other people's judgements about us; and a self-feeling, or reaction, about the judgements, such as pride or embarrassment. In this manner, we develop a set of beliefs and evaluations about ourselves. In Cooley's view, a person's self-image and self-esteem are directly related to the feedback received from others. Without the social mirror, there can be no sense of self. The first images of the self are received from *significant others* — for example, parents. Later, however, other images both complement and supplant those first images, especially as the child's interaction network expands and influences who and what he or she believes himself or herself to be. In time, people engage in role taking, which allows them assume the perspective of specific others and also of a generalized other. Through this repeated process of imagination and identification, the self-concept is built and organized.

Almost all of us have experienced situations in which we felt an acutely heightened sense of self; that is, we were extremely conscious of our existence and appearance. Before presenting your assignment orally to your sociology class, for instance, you may feel tense and you may perspire. Before being called on, you may be preoccupied by such concerns as, "What will they think of me?" and "What kind of impression will I make?" It is this connection between self-awareness and imagining what one looks like to others that Cooley had in mind when he coined the phrase "the **looking-glass self**."

■ SOCIALIZATION THROUGH THE LIFE COURSE

Most discussions of socialization focus on childhood and adolescence. Without a doubt, socialization during our pre-adult years lays a foundation that influences our self-concept and involvement in social life for as long as we live. But socialization continues throughout life. Since we have discussed the dynamics of self-development during childhood, we now focus on adolescence and youth, adulthood, and old age. First, however, it is important to recognize the core significance of gender in any discussion of socialization and identity.

▲ GENDER

What does it mean to be male and what does it mean to be female in our society? How are these definitions changing? In the past, the words *sex* and **gender** were often used interchangeably. Now, however, sex is used to refer to a person's biological maleness or femaleness; gender refers to the non-physiological aspects of sex — the cultural expectations of femininity and masculinity (Archer, 1988). Gender is now seen as the establishment of differences and domination by means of the distinctions drawn between women and men. This distinction between sex and gender reminds us of the fact that many male–female differences have little or nothing to do with biological differences between the sexes.

Although certain biological facts are self-evident, it has become increasingly clear that most of the differences between the sexes in most societies are cultural, not biological (O'Kelly and Carney, 1986). Research into the social construction of masculinity and femininity has shown that, like other social **norms,** masculinity and femininity embody shared expectations of how men and women should or ought to act. In focussing on gender role socialization, researchers have argued that "individuals acquire a gender identity as well as ways of acting, feeling, and thinking that are appropriate to the gender expectations of their society" (Robinson and Salamon, 1987: 123). Thus, for example, research by Lewis (1972) indicates that boys receive more physical contact during the first six months of life and less nonphysical contact than girls, which helps explain their greater motor development (Greenglass, 1982: 38).

Yet, to most members of society, sex roles are not viewed as optional or rooted in culture. To the extent that a culture defines gender roles as distinctly different, parents raise boys and girls so that they *will* be different. Moreover, these boys and girls will grow up *wanting* to be different, believing that these differences in sex roles are both normal and necessary. If, for example, a society believes that men are supposed to be aggressive and women are supposed to be gentle, that is how most men and women in that society will be.

Patterns of sex role socialization reveal that, from the earliest days of life, an infant is not simply a child but, rather, is a boy or a girl. Infant boys are usually addressed differently from infant girls, the blankets in which they are covered are usually differently coloured, and the rooms in which they sleep are usually decorated to reflect their gender. Indeed, one of the first things that a child learns is whether he or she is a "he" or a "she." And from a very early age, children show marked gender-specific preferences, such as for certain toys and activities (Huston, 1983). How does this happen? Do little boys arrive already programmed by their biology to prefer playing with toy guns and dump trucks, while little girls have a biological propensity for dolls, dress-up, and tea parties? Of course not. These are things they learn.

The impact of gender roles and rules on a child's social world begins very early, and one big part of that impact is that males learn to expect more choices, more power, and more control over their lives than females do. Children learn quickly that gender categories are important and pervasive, and they learn to process information according to those categories. Certain activities, clothes, and toys are found to be appropriate only for girls or boys, and they are duly assigned to "masculine" or "feminine" categories. The child's efforts to categorize things correctly are helped along by modelling, reinforcement, and explicit instruction.

Parents are usually the first source of children's gender learning, and indications are that parents both hold and communicate different expectations for males and females. An early study (Rubin, Provenzano, and Luria, 1974) showed that, within 24 hours of childbirth, first-time parents saw their daughters as softer, finer featured, and more delicate than did those with sons, while first-time parents saw their sons as firmer, stronger, better coordinated, hardier, and more alert. In a study of children's assigned household tasks, White and Brinkerhoff (1981) found a clear division of labour: while the boys were mowing the lawn, shovelling snow, taking out the garbage, and doing other yard work, the girls were cleaning the house, washing dishes, cooking, and babysitting for younger children.

The role of parents in gender socialization has also been examined in the context of parents reading gender-free books to young children. DeLoache, Cassidy, and Carpenter (1987) recruited mothers with young children to participate in an observational study. The mothers were informed that the researchers were interested in mother–child interaction in two situations: playing with toys and looking at books together. In the first phase of the study, the mothers were given three widely known books and were asked to read the books as they normally would at home. The mothers were not informed that the researchers were interested in their assignment of gender to the characters in the books. Each of the books included gender-neutral characters who did not have male or female names, did not wear any gender-specific clothing, and were not engaged in any sex-typed activities. How did mothers refer to these characters? Overwhelmingly as males. The mothers used a total of 104 gender-specific labels, of which 102 were masculine. The importance of this finding is related to prior studies, which have shown that characters depicted in children's books are overwhelmingly assumed to be male and that, as a consequence, children learn it is a man's world in which women are subordinate and less important.

Perhaps the most important impact of socialization and the presence of gender stereotypes is seen in the way females and males react to their own achievements. Opportunities for women and men to lead a full life vary from country to country (see Figure 2.1). But a general finding is that gender-differentiated patterns of self-confidence in achievement are transmitted by teachers: teachers interact differently with boys and girls in the classroom, and the differences produce more feelings of control among boys and more feelings of helplessness among girls. Boys typically have higher expectations than girls at the beginning of a given school year, even if the girls performed better the previous school year. Girls' lower expectations are linked to their poorer self-perception (Dweck, Goetz, and Strauss, 1980). This helps to account for the often-observed sex difference in mathematical and verbal achievement. In elementary school, girls equal boys in mathematical achievement and surpass them in verbal achieve-

ment, but eventually fall behind them in math (Maccoby and Jacklin, 1974). A related explanation for this phenomenon is that, as children progress through the educational institutions, they realize that certain subjects (English, art, music, history) are "girls' subjects" and others (math, physics, chemistry, computer science) are "boys' subjects." In a study of 300 school counsellors and teachers, Donahue and Costar (1977) showed that this informal knowledge is conveyed by educational authority figures.

Gender stereotyping is equally critical in the streaming of males and females into traditional careers. More often than not, teachers and guidance counsellors unwittingly encourage boys and girls to pursue occupational goals that are perceived as appropriate to and benefiting the particular sex. The dynamics of the self-fulfilling prophecy cannot be overemphasized: girls develop a self-image consistent with others' perceptions of them. Along this line, one interview study of 150 Canadian teenagers found a tendency for girls to make traditionally feminine occupational choices and to express less confidence than boys that they would realize their occupational goals (Baker, 1985). About three-quarters of the girls planned to hold paying jobs as adults. However, they tended to see the responsibility for household and child care as primarily theirs, and to assume that paid work must fit in with these other duties. This expectation about the future fits clearly with the actual division of household tasks.

Although the social environment strongly affects the way we act as women and men, everyday explanations for social roles still tend to rely exclusively on explanations of biology or individual character: "He's all boy" or "She finally got her head together." Undoubtedly, psychological and biological considerations do affect behaviour. However, in a sociological analysis, we must emphasize the importance of the social context for an understanding of the behaviour and attitudes of individuals and groups. Children and adults are socialized to respond to their social world by developing certain potentials and inhibiting others. It is not innate qualities but differences in the socialization of males and females that affect the assumption of "masculine" and "feminine" characteristics.

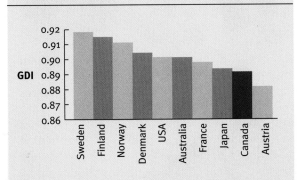

◆ **Figure 2.1** Countries with Highest Scores on 1995 Gender-Related Development Index (GDI)

Note: A GDI score of 1.0 indicates equality of opportunity for women and men in terms of life expectancy, educational attainment, and per capita income.

SOURCE: Adapted from World Bank, *Human Development Report, 1995* (New York: Oxford University Press, 1995), pp. 76–78. Copyright © 1995 by World Bank. Used by permission of Oxford University Press, Inc.

▲ ADOLESCENCE AND YOUTH

Adolescence, the period between childhood and adulthood, was not perceived as a life stage until the late nineteenth century. G. Stanley Hall (1904) was the first to describe this stage as a kind of "second birth," marked by a rise of "moral idealism, chivalry, and religious enthusiasm." In the twentieth century, the development of mass education and compulsory school attendance altered the concept of adolescence. For the first time in history, because of the length of time that people were required to remain in school, they were not expected to assume economic responsibility as soon as they reached sexual maturity.

We generally associate adolescence with emotional and social turmoil: Young people experience conflict with their parents as they attempt to develop identities in adult society. Though much of the social turmoil at this stage is often attributed to physiological changes linked to the onset of puberty, a more sociological way of thinking focusses on inconsistencies in the socialization process. Sexuality serves as an excellent case in point: Adolescents receive messages of encouragement from the mass media and simultaneous messages of restraint from parents.

As they must do in other life stages, adolescents must learn to fill new **statuses** and roles. Simultaneously, however, they are less likely to be under the immediate influence of their families and more subject to the influences of peers. For those who are unable to reconcile the demands of the new and the old, adolescence may be a time of considerable confusion and turmoil (Hogan and Astone, 1986). And yet, for all the turbulence and rebellion generally associated with adolescence, evidence suggests that most teenagers have good experiences of adolescence and have positive relationships with their parents (Coleman and Hendry, 1990).

In Canada and other modern societies, adolescents often tend to be regarded and treated as children. In contrast, premodern societies did not regard adolescence as a separate and prolonged stage of the life cycle. Indeed, as Burgess and Richardson (1984: 120) note, adolescence as a distinct period of life is a product of industrialization. Before industrialization, adult occupational and social roles were less specialized and the family could effectively manage the tasks of socializing children. Burgess and Richardson trace the distinctiveness of adolescence to the modern high school, where students became educated in skills and bodies of knowledge that the family was not equipped to impart.

Friendships initiated at school strongly influence the adolescent's values. The adolescent's values are also influenced by his or her peer group, which consists of people of similar age and status, regardless of whether they are friends. SOURCE: Dick Hemingway.

Adolescence is generally accompanied by the development of a sense of autonomy and independence as young persons prepare for adult responsibilities. In a classic and compelling study, Friedenberg (1959) addressed the conflict encountered by the adolescent during this transitional period. As our society emphasizes co-operation and group adjustment, it interferes with the central developmental task of adolescence — self-definition. "Adolescence," Friedenberg wrote (1959: 29),

> is a period during which the young person learns who he is, and what he really feels. It is a time during which he differentiates himself from his culture.... It is the age at which, by becoming a person in his own right, he becomes capable of deeply felt relationships to other individuals.

In Friedenberg's view, our society places a series of obstacles in the adolescent's path. As society displays anxiety and resentment toward the adolescent's capacity for intense and highly subjective experiences, his or her process of emotional development becomes frustrated.

Finally, it must be noted that adolescence is also a period of **anticipatory socialization,** "the process by which aspirants to a particular social role begin to discern what it will be like to function in that position" (Stebbins, 1990: 99). Through interaction with role incumbents, and by observing how roles are portrayed in the media, adolescents gradually learn to incorporate the perspectives and expectations of the larger society and imagine what it would be like to enact the roles to which they may aspire (Stryker, 1980: 63). Ahead lie an uncertain future and the responsibilities of adulthood.

▲ ADULT SOCIALIZATION

By the time adulthood is reached, the mastery of the basic information and skills required of members of a society, or **primary socialization,** has been almost completed. For the most part, adults have accepted the basic norms and values of their culture and learned to pattern their behaviour in terms of these norms and values. Despite having acquired a culturally appropriate social identity, there is potentially still much to learn. To participate effectively in their society, adults must continue to undergo socialization (Clausen, 1986; Hogan and Astone, 1986).

Adult socialization is the process by which adults take on new statuses and acquire new and different social identities. It differs from primary socialization in two important respects (Brim, 1968). First, adults are much more aware of their socialization. In contrast to young children and adolescents, who have little choice but to participate in various activities, adults usually engage in socializing programs and activities voluntarily, such as enrolling in remedial education or joining a church. Second, adults often exercise more control over the content and direction of their socialization and can better understand and articulate their motives for new undertakings. As a result, adults can often choose roles of their own free will.

Marriage constitutes one of the most important adult responsibilities. Although many of the traditional role expectations of marriage, and marriage itself, are no longer accepted uncritically, most people still choose to get married. In contrast to an earlier period when tradition largely determined the choices new couples would make, newlyweds and live-in partners now chart their own courses. This independence may involve an unwillingness to accept advice offered by parents and relatives.

One of the more significant decisions during adulthood is whether to become parents. Becoming a parent involves the acquisition of new skills and statuses. While the new statuses are conferred automatically, the roles and expectations accompanying them must be learned. As parents inevitably discover, relationships with children require active negotiation and adjustment. As well, the nature of these relationships requires an ability to adapt to and accommodate changing circumstances and situations.

Socialization during adulthood also may involve the development of an occupational career. As college and university graduates are discovering painfully, the difficulty of meeting this challenge successfully is exacerbated by an economy in which employment prospects are dim. Assessing the emerging economy confronting students in the 1990s, David Lawson (1996), a career counsellor at the Career Planning and Employment Centre at McMaster University, identifies a new group of "bad words" serving as signposts of the enormous changes taking place in the workplace: restructuring, reorganization, rationalizing, and re-engineering — the "r" words that strike fear into the hearts of employees and postsecondary students. In practical terms, these changes have resulted in fewer employers visiting universities to hire new graduates. As well, the type of employment offered to graduates is in flux. In contrast to the 1980s, when full-time, permanent employment opportunities were readily available, more and more positions are now contractual, making employment less secure and stable (see Chapter 12).

Although any job may involve an unfamiliar series of tasks, the new employee usually must also fit into a new social context with its own demands. Occupations typically include a subculture of members who develop distinctive ways of perceiving and responding to their social environment, and the members of this subculture generally share a system of norms and values related to their work. Once a subculture is formed, novices who enter the group are confronted with a set of norms and values to which they are expected to conform.

In their studies of work and occupations, sociologists have documented the dynamics in which neophytes learn both the formal and the informal demands and expectations of their work. For example, our research into the professional socialization of medical students offers the example of students recognizing the importance of mastering artful performances of **impression management** and role distancing in order to mask their ignorance and subdue their real feelings. Medical students also discover that their idealism about medicine's place in society, and about how doctors should relate to patients, is considered irrelevant and unprofessional by their evaluators (Haas and Shaffir, 1987).

▲ SOCIALIZATION DURING OLD AGE

Scholars such as Erik Erikson (1982) contend that some of the most difficult changes in adult attitudes and behaviour occur in the last years of life. It is during this period that the individual is most starkly confronted by lower prestige, decreased physical ability, and the prospects of chronic illness and death. Ours is a society that extends little dignity to aging. Medical advances have prolonged lives, but they have not added to dignity and self-esteem for the aged. Through the media especially, we view the elderly in stereotypical terms and old age as a period of increasing helplessness and dependence. The achieving of the status of "senior citizen" is accompanied by the loss of roles and statuses such as those of worker and spouse.

Retirement from the labour force, which, for most Canadians, occurs at age 65, may create an identity problem for the retiree. Although older people are often mandated to retire, there is little preparation for retired life. Cut off from work at an arbitrary age, they are forced to assume what has been called a "roleless status" (Shanas et al., 1972). Hendricks and Hendricks (1986: 332) observe how the transition from work to retirement typically carries negative consequences:

An individual may actually apprehend the processes of compulsory retirement policies and yet be emotionally unable to accept them as beyond control. If the older worker incorporates the negative societal stereotypes, a gradual shift in self-image will occur. ... When the negative appraisal summarized in "We see you as a bumbling fool" becomes internalized to "I am a bumbling fool," a downward spiral is set in motion that is difficult to break.

Many older people, particularly women, must also face the loss of a spouse. Widowhood, like retirement, is an roleless status for which there is little preparation and little guidance offered by society. There are few defined norms that govern when normal functioning should be resumed or how this should come about. This period also involves much stress, as the widowed person seeks to accommodate a new status, a new identity, and a new set of problems.

Finally, socialization in old age also involves facing death and dying. Philippe Aries (1981) observes that Western society attempts to deny death and to remove all traces of it from everyday life. We are not taught to talk about death, particularly to the dying. Relatives often attempt to keep the dying person from knowing that he or she is dying, and dying people sometimes keep their own prognosis secret (Glaser and Strauss, 1967). As Shepard (1993: 153) has said: "The status of a dying person is, like retirement and widowhood, a status almost devoid of roles."

■ AGENTS OF SOCIALIZATION

Socialization evolves through interaction with various *agents of socialization*. The relevance of these agents, and their influence, depends on our place in the life cycle.

Although the family usually constitutes the young person's chief agent of socialization for the first several years of life, socialization is influenced by many other groups and institutions. Here, we consider some of the most important agents of socialization in North American society: the family, the school, the peer group, and the mass media. You will note that socializing agents such as the family and the school receive a mandate from society to "train" the next generation of members — to transmit to them the society's cultural heritage so that they may become full-fledged participants. In contrast, such socializing agents as the peer group and the mass media do much of their "teaching" less formally and directly. Nonetheless, they influence how the individual perceives and responds to the environment.

▲ THE FAMILY

For young children in most societies, the family is virtually the entire world for the first few years of life. The child's first contact with the social world is experienced through the parents. Through close interaction with a small number of people, the child learns to think and speak; internalizes norms, beliefs, and values; forms some basic attitudes; develops some capacity for intimate and personal relationships; and begins to develop a self-image (Handel, 1990). Later experiences may lead to a modification of what was learned within the family, but it is not unusual for people to bring into adult life habits and expectations that characterized their childhood. We are often amused by and take note of the young woman who assumes many of the characteristics and mannerisms of her mother, or the son who closely imitates his father.

The family is well suited to the task of socialization. First, it is a small group in which all of the members can have constant face-to-face contact with one another; this means that the child's progress can be closely observed and individual adjustments made as necessary. Second, parents are usually well motivated; they have a strong emotional tie to their children. As studies have shown, the most meaningful and effective kind of social interaction for the purpose of socialization is that which is fused with emotion.

However, the family is not always an effective or efficient socializer. Parents sometimes have little understanding of parenting; they may be unprepared emotionally and their dedication and commitment to the task may be offset by competing considerations. Newspapers often report on parents who neglect, abuse, or even abandon their children. As well, much evidence indicates that parents may reproduce in their children the negative modelling they experienced in their own upbringing.

The family exists within subcultures of the larger society: it belongs to a geographical region, a social class, one or more ethnic groups, and possibly a religious group and/or other groupings. Families differ with regard to how important these influences are in determining their lifestyle and child-rearing practices (Harrison et al., 1990).

Families also bestow upon us statuses that may significantly affect our lives and sense of self — what we think of ourselves and how others respond to us. These social facts may place constraints on the opportunities that we are afforded. Thus, the impact of social class usually extends into adulthood (Kohn et al., 1990). Occupational attainment is conditioned

by educational achievement, which depends significantly on the family's class membership (Blau and Duncan, 1967: 30).

Arlene Skolnick (1991) describes three macrosocial changes over the past century that have strained the institution of the family in contemporary society. First, the shift from an industrial to an information and service economy drew women into the labour force and thus set the stage for a feminist revival and adolescent rebellion. Second, a demographic change has shortened the active parenting stage and extended old age and living alone as expected parts of the life course. Finally, Skolnick believes there is a growing preoccupation with the quality of intimate relationships, which has contributed to rising divorce rates (see Figure 2.2). Other social changes have also contributed to the reversal of past family trends. These changes include increasing age at marriage, lower rates of marriage, increasing rates of cohabitation outside of marriage, and more single-parent households and "latch-key" children (Baker, 1989).

Although the family is often a critically important agent of socialization, the actual content of what is transmitted and the manner in which the transmission occurs vary across families differentiated by ethnicity, religion, social class, as well as the presence or absence of either parent. It should also be noted, however, that one can easily exaggerate recent changes in the family institution. As one

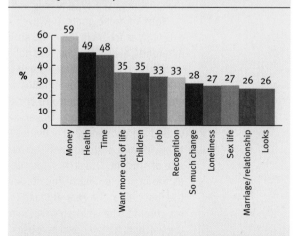

◆ **Figure 2.2** Top Twelve Concerns of Canadians, 1995 (Percentage Concerned "a Great Deal" or "Quite a Bit")

SOURCE: Adapted from Reginald W. Bibby, *The Bibby Report: Social Trends Canadian Style* (Toronto: Stoddart, 1995), p. 82. Used with the permission of Stoddart Publishing Co. Limited, Canada.

commentator has put it: "Things aren't the way they used to be, and they never were." In other words: "Historically, families have been much more disorderly, women much more engaged in productive and wage labor, children less protected, and women and children as poor as they are now, or poorer" (Coontz, 1992: 5).

▲ SCHOOLS

In school, children are supervised by adults who are not relatives or friends of the family. Children move from an environment of personal and intimate relationships to one that is impersonal. For instance, whereas parents may praise their children regardless of the talent they actually display, teachers must evaluate all students by a set of standards; students who

are found lacking are required to meet certain generalized expectations. As a place where children are taught indirectly to be less emotionally dependent, the school serves as a model of much of the secularized adult world. Although some interpersonal relationships may be based on love and affection, others are impersonal and defined by the society with little regard for the particular individuals who enter them. Of all the functions of the school, children's adjustment to its social order — which offers a preview of what will be expected of them as they mature and negotiate their way into and among the institutions of adult society — may be the most important (see Box 2.1).

Schools are organized to impart the technical and intellectual heritage of a society's culture. In technologically advanced societies, such instruction is a prolonged undertaking. Accompanying the more formal curriculum of the school is a "hidden curriculum" — the informal teaching that helps ensure the stu-

Box 2.1
Kindergarten as Academic Boot Camp

Kindergarten is generally conceived by educators as a year of preparation for school. It is thought of as a year in which small children, five or six years old, are prepared socially and emotionally for the academic learning which will take place over the next twelve years. It is expected that a foundation of behavior and attitudes will be laid in kindergarten on which the children can acquire the skills and knowledge they will be taught in the grades. . . . The kindergarten teachers in one . . . elementary [school, which] we shall call the Wilbur Wright School, said their goals were to see that the children "grew" in all ways: physically, of course, emotionally, socially, and academically. They said they wanted children to like school as a result of their kindergarten experiences and that they wanted them to learn to get along with others.

None of these goals, however, is unique to kindergarten; each of them is held to some extent by teachers in the other six grades at the Wright School. And growth would occur, but differently, even if the child did not attend school. The children already know how to get along with others, in their families and their play groups. The unique job of the kindergarten in the educational division of labor seems rather to be teaching children the student role. The student role is the repertoire of behavior and attitudes regarded by educators as appropriate to children in school. Observation in the kindergartens of the Wilbur Wright School revealed a great variety of activities through which children are shown and then drilled in the behavior and attitudes defined as appropriate for school and thereby induced to learn the role of student. Observers both pointed to the teaching and learning of classroom routines as the main element of the student role. The teachers expended most of their efforts, for the first half of the year at least, in training the children to follow the routines which teachers created. The children were, in a very real sense, *drilled* in tasks and activities created by the teachers for their own purposes and beginning and ending quite arbitrarily (from the child's point of view) at the command of the teacher. One teacher remarked that she hated September, because during the first month "everything has to be done rigidly, and repeatedly,

(continued)

CHAPTER TWO • SOCIALIZATION

Box 2.1
(continued)

until they know exactly what they're supposed to do." However, "by January," she said, "they know exactly what to do [during the day] and I don't have to be after them all the time." Classroom routines were introduced gradually from the beginning of the year in all the kindergartens, and the children were drilled in them as long as was necessary to achieve regular compliance. By the end of the school year, the successful kindergarten teacher has a well-organized group of children. They follow classroom routines automatically, having learned all the command signals and the expected responses to them. They have, in our terms, learned the student role.

The kindergarten has been conceived of here as the year in which children are prepared for their schooling by learning the role of student. In the classrooms of the rest of the school grades, the children will be asked to submit to systems and routines imposed by the teachers and the curriculum. The days will be much like those of kindergarten, except that academic subjects will be substituted for the activities of the kindergarten. Once out of the school system, young adults will more than likely find themselves working in large-scale bureaucratic organizations, perhaps on the assembly line in the factory, perhaps in the paper routines of the white-collar occupations, where they will be required to submit to rigid routines imposed by "the company" which may make little sense to them. Those who can operate well in this situation will be successful bureaucratic functionaries. Kindergarten, therefore, can be seen as preparing children not only for participation in the bureaucratic organization of large modern school systems, but also for the large-scale occupational bureaucracies of modern society.

SOURCE: Harry L. Gracey, "Learning the Student Role: Kindergarten as Academic Boot Camp," in Dennis H. Wrong and Harry L. Gracey, eds., *Readings in Introductory Sociology,* 3rd ed. (New York: Macmillan, 1976), pp. 289, 290, 299. © 1976. Reprinted with permission of Allyn and Bacon.

dent's integration into society (Richer, 1988). Students are exposed to, and rewarded for, the acquisition and display of such features as good discipline, conformity, respect for authority structures, and co-operation.

In some instances, the family's values and beliefs run contrary to those of the dominant culture, and socialization in the school is perceived as effectively modifying or reversing the socialization received in the family. It is for this reason that religious groups such as the Hasidic Jews, the Hutterites, and the Amish establish their own schools — so they may better control both the formal and the informal educational content to which their children are exposed. For example, in his study of secular education in Hasidic-Jewish ultra-observant communities, Shaffir (1987) observed that administrators devoted meticulous attention to the range of subject matter to be excluded from the curriculum and to the screening of the curriculum to ensure that its contents did not depart markedly from the group's religious beliefs.

▲ PEER GROUPS

As we know, friendships initiated at school can affect and shape a person's perspective and values. In childhood, *peer groups,* consisting of people usually of a similar age and of equal social status, are formed largely by accident of association, and members of the same peer group are not necessarily friends. For instance, all children in a given Grade 2 class constitute a peer group, but by no means are they all friends. Later in life, however, one *chooses* peer groups on the basis of such criteria as common interests and activities and similar income level or occupation.

The peer group is the only agent of childhood socialization that is not controlled mainly by adults (Corsaro, 1992). Parents typically play the initial leading roles in the inculcation of basic values, but peers seem to have the greatest influence in lifestyle issues such as appearance, social activities, and dating (Sebald, 1986).

In a classic study focussing on the relation between social character and society, David Riesman (1950) offered a critical analysis of the role of the peer group in the adolescent's character formation. He described three very different types of personality structure that result from distinctive patterns of socialization. In what he termed traditional and primitive societies, the culture and stable patterns of social organization usually result in a "tradition-directed" person, one who looks to the accepted ways of society for guidance in matters of personal conduct. In contrast, for the "inner-directed" person, found most often in societies experiencing rapid normative change, such guidance comes mainly from within, as the external codes fail to provide stable guides for personal conduct. The third type of personality structure, that of the "other-directed" person, is characteristic of modern society.

In modern society, according to Riesman, contemporaries — that is, other people known directly or indirectly — are the source of direction for the individual. In an era dominated by other-direction, parents lose their once undisputed role. With neither deeply institutionalized norms nor a strong set of internal convictions to serve as a guide, individuals now look to their peers for ideas as to how they should behave. In Riesman's words: "The peer-group becomes the measure of all things; the individual has few defenses the group cannot batter down" (1950: 82). We can all relate to the uncertainties encountered in gauging the approval and disapproval of our peers. This uncertainty is exacerbated as peer groups change or multiply.

Several studies have documented the increasing significance of peer group socialization in North America. How might this be understood? One possibility is that parents' life experiences and accumulated wisdom may not be very conducive to preparing young people to meet the requirements of life in a society that is in the throes of rapid technological change. Not infrequently, adolescents are better informed than their parents about such things as sex, drugs, and technology. As well, the greater saliency of peer groups can be understood in the context of the organization of everyday life: As parents spend more of their time away from home — commuting to work, working shifts, and meeting work-related obligations — adolescents are likely to spend more time with their peers. In short, the peer group fills a vacuum created by parents who are too overburdened to spend time with their children or who are perceived by their children as too ignorant of current realities, fads, and fashions to serve as a reliable source of guidance.

▲ THE MASS MEDIA

Sociologists agree that the mass media are powerful socializing influences but that it is difficult to measure their effects. The mass media are an impersonal means of transmitting information. For the most part, the communication is one way, creating an audience conditioned to receive passively what is sometimes called "mass culture," consisting of whatever news, messages, programs, or events are brought to them. Television, radio, newspapers, videos, magazines, movies, records, tapes, and books constitute the major forms of mass communication media.

By choosing and emphasizing certain topics, stressing particular views or interpretations, and concentrating on specific themes, the media create, manage, and control impressions of what is important and real. Since the mass media are analyzed comprehensively in Chapter 5, we forgo further discussion of the topic here.

■ RESOCIALIZATION

The influence and power of the socialization process are perhaps best observed in **resocialization**. Resocialization is a remedial attempt to correct or instill particular values and behaviours. It differs from adult socialization. Adult socialization is lifelong, as old ways get discarded or fall into disuse and new perceptions, priorities, objectives, contacts, and affiliations lead to new possibilities. Sociologists generally restrict the idea of resocialization to those contexts where there are *deliberate* efforts to change the individual or group.

For most people, socialization is experienced in familiar settings. For some people, however, socialization is experienced against their will — for example, in prisons or in mental institutions where they are confined. This is the special world of total institutions, analyzed in Erving Goffman's famous work, *Asylums* (1961). According to Goffman, total institutions impose regimented routines with the goal of resocialization. The total institution attempts to achieve this objective by completely controlling and manipulating the environment, thus depriving its charges of contrary sources of social experience.

Resocialization in total institutions is a two-part process. First, the staff attempts to erode the new inmate's established identity. This is accompanied by a series of experiences that include abasements, degradations, and humiliations. Second, efforts are made to reconstitute the inmate's sense of being self-compliant, co-operative, and trustworthy. This process is often painful.

Resocialization usually occurs in an environment where there is a powerful socializing agent that metes out rewards and punishments to encourage a change in the individual. Such change is exemplified by the process of conversion, where there is a radical shift in the individual's value system, or "brainwashing," which involves a breakdown of resistance to previously alien values.

Typically, in order for individuals or groups of individuals to undergo radical changes to moral status and personality, institutions organize a *ritual ordeal,* an initiation ceremony involving status degradation and mortification (Garfinkel, 1956; Haas, 1989). Degradation and mortification are processes whereby the "chosen" (or the "damned") are prepared for their new status through the stripping of their old identities. The self is mortified as part of the process of creating a new identity. The old self and identity are discarded and candidates' ties to lay culture are severed as part of the identity conversion.

In this childlike condition of heightened ambiguity and stress, the person is ripe for conversion to the expectations of the more powerful group. The desire for security and acceptance often leads to imitation or adoption of the behaviour of authority figures (Light, 1980). The resocialized person effectively undergoes a ritual death and rebirth, shedding the old identity and taking on a new one. "Death," or near-death, must precede the rebirth and transformation of the individual into a new being (Eliade, 1963).

Another example of resocialization is basic training in the military, the primary goal of which is to modify the recruit's civilian self-image and to replace it with a military one. Recruits are typically removed from their civilian environment and confined to a military base where they are required to submit to a vast range of stresses, disciplinary measures, and indoctrination to a new set of role expectations. A less dramatic but often equally anxiety-provoking resocialization occurs when newcomers are inducted to prestigious professions such as law, the ministry, and medicine. Several accounts detail how medical students are resocialized to temper their idealism with the professionally defined realities of medicine (Becker et al., 1961; Haas and Shaffir, 1987).

■ DRAMATURGY AND EVERYDAY LIFE

In what came to be known as his **dramaturgical approach,** Canadian-born sociologist Erving Goffman analyzed social interaction using the analogy of life as theatre and of people as actors putting on performances for one another. People play roles called for by society's script, and their performances are judged by an audience alert for slips that might reveal the actors' true characters and intentions (Goffman, 1959; 1963; 1971).

Goffman distinguished between **role** and *role performance.* Role refers to how a person would act if he or she responded to the norms attached to a particular status or position. Role performance refers to the person's actual conduct. Goffman emphasized that while roles greatly shape our behaviour, we rarely organize our behaviour strictly according to the script. He claimed that most of the time we are not completely confined to a role; instead, we display glimpses of our real selves, or an individual "behind" or "inside" the role. In other words, Goffman suggested that roles in life, like those in the theatre, are performed on a "front stage," which implies the existence of a "back stage" where actors can step out of their roles. Behaviour changes as it is managed to suit various settings. The actions intended for strangers or casual friends are designated as "front stage" behaviour, while only those on more intimate terms are permitted to see what goes on "back stage" — that is, to learn the actor's real feelings.

In the dramaturgical view of human behaviour and social interaction, individuals present their selves in a calculated and often contrived way. They do this both to provide a favourable impression of themselves and to establish a particular **definition of the situation,** thereby achieving greater control over others (see Box 2.2). This may be viewed as a manipulative component of human interactions.

Goffman suggests that individuals use specific types of strategies to attempt to control and manage social encounters, as well as to project a desired definition of the situation to others. These strategies include *dramatic realization* and *misrepresentation.* Dramatic realization refers to the successful expression, during interaction, of qualities and attributes claimed by the performer — in short, the actor's ability to convey a sense of sincerity. Misrepresentation, on the other hand, entails the cre-

Box 2.2
The Cloak of Competence

Medical students during clerkship believe they are expected to act as if they are in the know, not in ways which might put their developing competence into question. The pressure to be seen as competent by faculty, fellow students, hospital personnel, and patients narrows the range of alternative roles students can assume. Students recognize their low status in the hospital hierarchy and on hospital rotations. They realize that the extent of their medical knowledge can easily be called into question by fellow students, tutors, interns, residents, and faculty. To reduce the possibility of embarrassment and humiliation, which, at this stage in their medical career, is easily their fate, students attempt to reduce the unpredictability of their situation by manipulating an impression of themselves as enthusiastic, interested, and eager to learn. At the same time, students seize opportunities which allow them to impress others, particularly faculty and fellow students, with their growing competence and confidence.

. . . A [strategy] shared by students to manage an appearance of competence is to limit their initiatives to those situations which will be convincing demonstrations of their competence. Some students decide, for example, to ask questions in areas with which they are already familiar, to cultivate an impression of competence.

The general strategy that the students adopt is to mask their uncertainty and anxiety with an image of self-confidence. Image making becomes recognized as being as important as technical competence. As one student remarks: "We have to be good actors, put across the image of self-confidence, that you know it all. . . . "

. . . Referring to the importance of creating the right impression, [one student said,]

Dr. Jones, who was my adviser or boss for medicine, he always came and did rounds on Wednesday mornings. Well, he didn't have very many patients on the service, but we always knew that his interest was in endocrinology, and . . . if he had an endocrine patient . . . we knew . . . that he was going to pick that endocrine patient to talk about. And so, of course, . . . any dummy can read up Tuesday night like hell on the new American Diabetic Association standards for diabetes or hyperglycemia . . . and you can handle general medicine. So the next day you seem fairly knowledgeable. . . . That afternoon you forget about it because you figure Thursday morning hematology people make their rounds and, of course, you have to read up on hematology. . . .

. . . Students realize that to be a good student-physician is either to be or appear to be competent. They observe that others react to their role-playing. A student describes the self-fulfilling nature of this process when he says:

To be a good GP, you've got to be a good actor, you've got to respond to a situation. You have to be quick, pick up the dynamics of what is going on at the time and try to make the person leave the office thinking that you know something. And a lot of people, the way they handle that is by letting the patient know that they know it all, and only letting out a little bit at a time, and as little as possible. I think that they eventually reach a plateau where they start thinking themselves they are really great and they know it all, because they have these people who are worshipping at their feet.

The process of adopting the cloak of competence is justified by students as helpful to the patient. A student summarizes the relationship between acting competently and patients responding to such a performance by getting well when he says:

(continued)

Box 2.2
(continued)

You know the patients put pressure on you to act as if you are in the know. If you know anything about the placebo effect, you know that a lot of the healing and curing of patients does not involve doing anything that will really help them, but rather creating confidence in the patient that things are being done and will be done. We know that the placebo effect for example has even cured cancer patients. If they have the confidence in the doctor . . . and what treatment they are undergoing, they are much more likely to get well, irrespective of the objective effects of the treatment.

SOURCE: Excerpted from J. Haas and W. Shaffir, "The Cloak of Competence," *Symbolic Interaction*, Vol. 1 (Greenwich, CT: JAI Press, 1978). Reprinted with permission of JAI Press Inc.

ation of a false impression through impersonation, innuendo, strategic ambiguity, crucial omissions, and lies, white or otherwise. Misrepresentation is probably the most widely practised form of manipulation, and some degree of it is inevitable in interaction. Misrepresentation protects the individual from potential danger and provides a wide range of social masks to assist in the management of a person's definition of the situation.

Goffman's basic assumption, then, is that humans are constantly seeking control over others. Individuals seek to manipulate situations, impressions, and information in order to sustain a self that they can cherish. Power is crucial; actors who have it can make claims about themselves and be reasonably sure that their claims will be validated. Thus, every person — every actor — struggles to maintain a valued self, a creation as fragile and tentative as the situations that have engendered it. A central feature of human interaction, then, is the attempt to present ourselves to others so that they will see us as we wish to be seen.

■ IDENTITY AND SOCIAL CHANGE

It has long been recognized that the social conditions of life in the modern era powerfully influence identity formation. That is because industrialization, urbanization, and other sources of social change weaken the relatively cohesive communities in which people find solidarity and meaning, expand the range of personal choice, and permit a greater diversity of beliefs. Thus, modernization emancipates people from the tyranny of tradition. At the same time, however, it leaves people without the comfort and security of heritage and roots. Although **primary groups** limit the range of personal experience, they confer a strong sense of identity, belonging, and purpose. Modern societies, in general, offer far more autonomy but less sense of purpose and fewer enduring social ties than societies in the past. Thus, many people have difficulty in establishing a stable and coherent sense of who they are.

Many people shuttle from one identity to another, changing their lifestyle in search of an elusive "true self." They may join various social groups in search of purpose and belonging, and even experiment with various religions in the hope of finding a system of beliefs that "fits" them. In sociological terms, the difficulty in developing a stable and coherent identity is rooted in the individual's social surroundings. The problem of answering the question "Who am I?" reflects not only a personal crisis but also the complexity and instability of modern mass society. Some analysts refer to this difficulty as the "postmodern" condition (see Chapter 3). Postmodernity exacerbates the identity problem. The individual is confronted by a "meaning vacuum," analogous to placing one's foot into the mud at the bottom of a lake and not finding a firm place to stand (Klapp, 1969: 14).

6. The major premise of symbolic interactionism is that people are actively involved in creating and negotiating their roles and self-concept. The most important figure in this school of thought is George H. Mead, who emphasized how people assume roles by imagining themselves in the roles of others. Charles Horton Cooley is noteworthy for his concept of the "looking-glass self," which stresses that we view ourselves as we think others view us. Erving Goffman used the term "impression management" to describe how we try to present ourselves in favourable ways when interacting with others.

7. Gender socialization is the learning of masculine and feminine behaviour and roles. From birth, and in every area of social life, the socialization of the sexes in terms of content and expectations makes the socially constructed gender role more significant than the biological role of male or female. Assumptions about appropriate male and female attributes limit the range of acceptable behaviour and options for both sexes.

8. The most important agent of socialization is the family. As the examples of child neglect and the monkey experiments demonstrate, initial warmth and nurturing are essential to healthy development. The self-concept formed during childhood has lasting consequences.

9. The central function of schools in industrial society is the teaching of skills and knowledge, but they also transmit society's central cultural values and ideologies. Schools expose children to situations in which the same rules, regulations, and authority patterns apply to everyone.

10. Peer groups provide young people with a looking glass unclouded by love or duty, and an opportunity to learn roles and values that adults do not teach.

11. The mass media are impersonal and large-scale socializers.

12. During adulthood, individuals go through adult socialization as they get jobs, marry, divorce, raise children, retire, etc. These many roles involve new and different relationships with others and guidelines for behaviour.

13. Sometimes there are abrupt changes in our self-concept, and we must learn new role identities and negotiate a new self-image. Resocialization occurs when we abandon or are forced to abandon our way of life and self-concept for a radically different one. This is most efficiently done in total institutions — for example, jails, mental hospitals, and boot camps — or in religious or political conversions.

14. In recent years, social scientists have examined the consequences for identity construction that occurs in the networked virtual worlds on the Internet.

● QUESTIONS TO CONSIDER

1. Discuss the changing relevance of family, school, media, peer group, and occupational group to personal identity as we grow up and as the social influences of each of these institutions intensifies or wanes.

2. Is "all the world a stage" and all of us merely "players" attempting to convince important audiences that we are more than what we know ourselves to be? Does Goffman's dramaturgical analysis lead to a realistic or a cynical assessment of human behaviour?

3. Prisons and mental hospitals are socialization institutions organized to change, test, or "correct" people. How effective are they and why are they not more successful in meeting their goals?

4. In what ways are you an accident of birth in terms of your life chances? What is the relevance of social class to success, achievement, and self-image?

5. What, if any, are the possible effects on personal identity in the use of the Internet? Could the consequences be greater separation and alienation from reality, others and onself, or might the outcome for the user be a heightened sense of belonging, integration, and shared understandings? Are both extremes possible?

● GLOSSARY

adolescence A period of life running from approximately age 12 to age 20.

adult socialization The process of socialization that occurs after childhood to prepare people for adult roles.

anticipatory socialization A process by which aspirants to a particular role begin to discern what it would be like to function in that role.

definition of the situation The meaning people ascribe to the immediate setting.

dramaturgical approach Erving Goffman's approach to social interaction, in which he emphasizes that we are all actors and also audiences for one another.

ego In Freudian theory, the reactional, conscious part of personality.

gender One's awareness of one's self as a sexual being and one's thinking of oneself as behaving in a masculine or a feminine way.

generalized other The organized attitude of social groups.

id In Freudian theory, the instinctual, undisciplined part of personality.

impression management The attempt by an individual to influence others' impression of him or her.

instincts Inborn patterns of behaviour in animals, such as mating, catching food, etc.

looking-glass self A theory developed by Charles Horton Cooley to explain how individuals develop a sense of self through interaction with others.

norms Rules that define appropriate and inappropriate ways of how people are supposed to act, think, or feel in specific situations.

personality The relatively orderly and predictable attitudes and patterns of behaviour associated with an individual.

primary group A relatively small group in which people are emotionally close and where interaction is intimate.

primary socialization The process by which children are prepared for the various roles required of members of society.

resocialization A deliberate effort to change an individual or group, leading to the acquisition of new values and behaviour, particularly in prisons, military training camps, etc.

role The behaviour expected of someone occupying a given status in a group or society.

self One's awareness of ideas and attitudes about one's own personal and social identity.

status A culturally and socially defined position that a person occupies in a group.

subculture A group that, while part of the dominant culture, holds distinctive values, norms, and beliefs.

superego In Freudian theory, the conscience containing all of the ideas of what is right and wrong.

symbolic interactionism The type of interactionism stressing the centrality of symbols and meaning people place on their own and others' behaviour.

● SUGGESTED READING

Erikson, Erik. (1964). *Childhood and Society,* rev. ed. New York: W.W. Norton. This classic work examines the crisis of identity that people encounter during the course of socialization.

Freud, Sigmund. (1962 [1930]). *Civilization and Its Discontents.* Trans. James Strachey. New York: W.W. Norton. In this book, Freud presents his views on the conflict between a person's inborn drives and the demands exerted by society during socialization.

Handel, Gerald, ed. (1988). *Childhood Socialization.* Hawthorne, NY: Aldine de Gruyter. This collection of studies examines the ways in which dominant agencies of socialization turn infants into participants in social life.

Olesen, Virginia L., and Elvi W. Whittaker. (1968). *The Silent Dialogue: A Study in the Social Psychology of Professional Socialization.* San Francisco: Jossey-Bass. This study examines the professional socialization of student nurses. The study offers excellent insights into how professionals socialize their recruits, and adds to a general understanding of the processes of adult socialization in the institutional context.

Rosenberg, Morris. (1979). *Conceiving the Self.* New York: Basic Books. This book presents a general theory of how the self-concept is developed in a variety of settings, and examines the consequences of having one kind of self emerge rather than another.

Williams, Thomas R. (1983). *Socialization.* Englewood Cliffs, NJ: Prentice Hall. Based on research in various societies, this book offers an excellent summary of the major issues and components involved in socialization.

CHAPTER THREE
Culture and the Postmodern

IN THIS CHAPTER YOU WILL LEARN THAT

- in sociology, culture does not refer just to specialized spheres of the arts but to the whole symbolic order of rituals, conversations, mass media, and texts; it exists at every level of social life, from the global diffusion of ideas, to the national discussion of collective values and policies, to the local level of small subcultures, to the face-to-face level of everyday interactions

- variations in the content of culture are evident in the power structures of class, race, and gender; in the unequal distribution of rationalized and professional knowledge; in the silencing and distortion of the voices of people who are excluded from dominant discourses; and in ideologies that advance the interests of one group rather than another

- culture can contribute to the integration of societies by emphasizing values of unity and solidarity, and by constructing a sense of the inevitability of the existing social order, but it can also contribute to social disintegration and the breakup of nations by highlighting issues that cannot be resolved within the discourse of culture itself

DAVID CHEAL
University of Winnipeg

■ INTRODUCTION

Have you ever joined a new group of people and found that you did not know what they were talking about? Perhaps they were talking about individuals whom you had never met or places that you had never visited. Or maybe they were discussing the technical details of a new job that you were about to start, or a game that you had never played before, or the latest movie, which you had not yet seen. Most of us have had this kind of experience at one time or another. These common experiences show just how our life is affected by culture. If we ask our new acquaintances for explanations, and if we persevere in attempting to understand what they tell us, then a whole new world of thinking and doing may be opened up for us. On the other hand, we may feel that these people's ideas and interests are so alien to us that we could never belong to this group. If they constantly change topics of conversation so that we can never catch up to what they are saying, or if they talk about their experiences in ways that make them look superior, we soon get the message: we drop out of their circle. This is culture at work. It can open doors in our minds that we did not know existed, or it can cut us off from other people by creating closed social worlds.

Contrasting features of culture are most evident at the "micro" level, in our relations with small groups. Other aspects of culture are more visible at the "macro" level, in our relations with larger communities. The celebration of Christmas is a major cultural event in our society that illustrates this point. Regardless of our individual feelings about the event and of the state of our finances at the time, as we get closer to Christmas, it becomes harder and harder not to get caught up in the process of buying gifts and preparing food. Few people want to be left out of celebrations with family and friends at the appointed time. Although Christmas was originally a Christian festival, many non-Christians participate in selected activities of the festive season as well. When everybody else is demonstrating support for one another by unusual acts of generosity and sociability, it is difficult not to join in without affecting how others feel about us. In addition, the constant stimulus of advertising prompts us to buy the right things for the right people — and, in so doing, to show others that we have the resources and the skills to be successful members of a "consumer society."[1]

The celebration of Christmas demonstrates vividly how large groups and societies create major ritual occasions on the basis of which the social integration of their members is confirmed. It also shows very clearly the strength of the pressures exerted by the messages conveyed, on the one hand, in mass-media advertising and, on the other hand, in the gestures that individuals make to one another. Our involvement in the festivities at the end of every year reminds us of the extent to which our social life is shaped by the culture of the society to which we belong.

In this chapter, we will examine what culture is and how it is used in contemporary social life. We will also see how theorizing about contemporary social systems as postindustrial "consumer societies" helps us to understand the significance of culture today. Finally, we will consider whether we are justified in looking at contemporary cultures in a new way, as aspects of *postmodernity*.

■ THE SIGNIFICANCE OF CULTURE

Culture is one of the most fundamental properties of social interaction. It is the symbolic order through which individuals communicate with one another and organize their collective life. In any social situation, we want other people to understand our goals and reasons for action in order to gain their co-operation. When we communicate our purposes to them, they may question what we are doing, thus forcing us to think more carefully about what to say next. It is out of this back-and-forth process of communication and reflection that culture emerges. **Culture** consists of the total system of actions and products of action that have meaning for both the actors and their audience (that is, their listeners, readers, or observers).

▲ SYMBOLIC ORDER

In cultural systems, actions such as saying hello or waving goodbye, as well as certain things that we produce (for example, gifts, a white cane, or a cross), are **symbols** that assign a particular meaning to a situation or an event. Often, the most important symbols are those that serve as **signs** within a cultural code. Signs are contrasting symbols, which derive part or all of their meaning from their opposition to one another. Saying hello versus saying goodbye is an example of this. As sociologist Erving Goffman pointed out, saying hello is an "opening" that begins a social encounter, whereas saying goodbye is a "closing" that signifies that an encounter is coming to an end.

Cultural Distinctions

The classical sociologist Émile Durkheim was one of the first people to note the social significance of pairs of contrasting signs. He observed that a general feature of religion is the way in which a distinction is made between the things that are sacred and things that are profane (Durkheim, 1947 [1915]). This distinction is fundamental to religious institutions, Durkheim thought, because people behave differently toward sacred objects from the way they behave toward profane objects. Profane things, such as the food we eat for lunch, are a part of everyday life and are treated in a casual, matter-of-fact way. Sacred objects, on the other hand, such as the holy bread and wine of communion, are treated with great respect. As Durkheim put it, they are set apart and forbidden, by being restricted to certain places and certain times and by having clear limits set on who has access to them.

Cultural distinctions between categories of things, like the sacred and the profane, are the basis for organizing all of life. The effects of cultural distinctions on our lives are often so pervasive that we do not recognize them; they seem natural to us. Nevertheless, they define how we experience the most basic conditions of our existence. Box 3.1 considers the most "natural" distinction of all — that between nature and civilization itself.

Box 3.1
Nature Is a Cultural Phenomenon

Nature is so important to many Canadians that we devote a lot of time and other resources to caring for it. Love of nature flourishes in cultures that have highly developed technologies. With rare exceptions, we are no longer afraid of the forces of nature. We believe that nature can be controlled, so we see it in a benevolent way, as something to be enjoyed. Nature is a source of fantasies about a way of life different from urban civilization; it is a source of entertainment in nature programs on television; and it provides a retreat from alienating work. We tour through nature, hike, mountain-bike, and cross-country ski.

So many people visit our national parks and other nature reserves in the summer that we must control how we use them. In a period of drought, we may have to accept restrictions on where we light campfires. We also accept restrictions on carrying and using firearms, in order to ensure that there is no shooting of wildlife in protected areas. Foreign visitors are sometimes surprised to learn that we voluntarily disarm ourselves before entering places where bears can, and occasionally do, kill us.

In our love of nature, we not only act to conserve it, we also actively manage it. We may have to work hard to restore the "balance of nature" that was disturbed when a park was created. Most provincial parks are too small to support a population of wolves, but, without predators, moose, deer, and elk can multiply to the point where they damage the vegetation. Parks managers may then decide to reduce their numbers by culling the herds, through planned hunting.

Outside the boundaries of national and provincial parks, wildlife management is intended to ensure that there are abundant animals, birds, and fish for people who like to hunt and fish. Organizations such as Ducks Unlimited build dikes around marshes in order to regulate the water level. They do this so that marshes will produce more plants, on which more ducks and geese can feed. The logic behind all this activity is essentially the same as the logic of industrial production. In societies that have large populations and many hunters, the only way that the demand for hunting can be met is by increasing the productivity of nature.

(continued)

Box 3.1
(continued)

Finally, in one of the most puzzling roles that human beings play in nature, we may assist nature by protecting it from itself. If a fire is set naturally, by lightning, for example, should we let it burn, with potentially devastating consequences that will last for years? Or do we fight the fire, so that people can continue to enjoy the forest and the creatures that live in it? The tendency has been to fight all forest fires, thus protecting nature from the forces of nature. The forests whose "natural" beauty we enjoy are therefore really products of human activity. We thus see that nature is not a natural phenomenon after all. It is a cultural phenomenon.

SOURCE: Based on A. Wilson, *The Culture of Nature* (Cambridge, MA: Blackwell, 1992).

▲ RITUAL

Cultural distinctions are constantly communicated by individuals and groups as they strive to influence how the world is defined and, therefore, how it is organized. One fundamental means of communication is **ritual**. Rituals are highly standardized acts through which individuals express the conventional value (positive or negative) that they attach to something or someone. Religious rituals, such as church weddings, are well-known examples of this. The participants are often very conscious of the fact that the care with which they dress (in their best clothes) and speak (in quiet voices) are ways of demonstrating the sacredness of the occasion and the importance of the people who are the centre of attention.

Erving Goffman (1967) stressed that "interaction rituals," such as shaking hands, are found everywhere as standardized means of expressing the value assigned to a particular person on a particular occasion. For example, when university graduates receive their degrees, a senior university official, such as the dean of the faculty or the chancellor of the university, usually shakes hands with them. Interaction rituals can also be observed when people avoid sitting next to someone who belongs to a group that they think of as inferior or unclean. Here, a cultural distinction is marked by physical separation — in other words, by segregation.

Cultural Reproduction

Interaction rituals are practised extensively in many kinds of social situations, and their cumulative impact on social life can be considerable. This is par-

ticularly the case in traditional societies — that is, in societies that place a strong emphasis on reproducing patterns inherited from the past. In rituals, the repetition of the same actions conveys the same fixed meanings over and over again.

Interaction rituals thus help to maintain the traditional social order, by constantly reproducing it. Because rituals often express important economic and social patterns, they contribute to the **cultural integration** of societies. The messages that people receive about themselves from their various social experiences are consistent and, hence, reinforce each other. One result is that there may be little opportunity for subordinated groups to even think about challenging their position. For instance, in societies where women are systematically segregated from puberty onward, they may come to believe in their own inferiority.[2]

▲ LANGUAGE

Rituals are important in countries such as Canada on occasions such as Christmas (Cheal, 1988), but they are not the primary means of communication. The most important medium for interaction is language. Habermas (1987) has pointed out that language is much more flexible than ritual gestures, and more easily changed to produce new messages for new situations. Since modern societies are constantly changing, we rely heavily on language to provide the information we need in order to adapt. Social interaction everywhere tends to be shaped by an established discourse, which evolves as people feel the need to discuss new ideas.

The most important medium for interaction is language. Language is much more flexible than ritual gestures and more easily changed to produce new messages for new situations. SOURCE: Kathy Ruttenberg, *Glass Table One; Saturday 10:30 PM* (1992). Oil on linen, 80 x 48 inches. Slide provided courtesy of Gallery Henoch, New York. Reproduced with permission of the artist.

National Culture and Subcultures

A **discourse** is a set of topics for discussion and a way of talking about those topics that is continued over time by a number of people who have certain interests in common. Through discourse, the participants come to have a shared **knowledge** about the world.

At different times, we all engage in many different discourses, depending on the group we are with and what we are doing. Some discourses are shared by very large numbers of people, as happens when a popular interest is supported and moulded by the mass media. Hockey is a good example of this in Canada, especially among men (Gruneau and Whitson, 1993). After the televised hockey games on Saturday night, the same topics are discussed in similar ways from the Atlantic coast to the Pacific. The discourse of hockey is so widely shared that we may think of it as being part of our common national culture.

Most discourses, however, are not shared very widely, because they reflect the particular interests and experiences that people discuss within particular social networks. Some discourses are so highly specialized that they seem peculiar, even foreign, to outsiders. The conversation of computer "nerds" is a well-known example. Discourses of this sort may be so different that we can think of them as constituting distinctive **subcultures**.

Some subcultures include attempts to create new rituals, which will confirm the changes that people have experienced. For example, as people are living longer, there is more discussion about the kinds of lives we want to have when we are older. In the New Age subculture, this includes an attempt to create a new ritual for menopausal women, which will help them adjust to their changing biology (see Box 3.2).

The Discourse of Gender

Through the many discourses in which we participate, we collaborate with others in defining what our interests are and which experiences are most relevant to us. In Canada today, for example, the position of women is more likely to be limited by the effects of discourse than by interaction rituals (Smith, 1990). The popular Harlequin Romance books thus portray an image of women as submitting to the powerful masculinity of older, richer men. In these stories, the emotional and physical independence of the heroine is typically overwhelmed by the sudden intervention of love or sexual passion, and she becomes dependent on the warm, safe embrace of her protective lover. Brought to her senses (or her knees) by a combination of accidents and coincidences that are beyond her will, the heroine realizes that she cannot deny the mysterious attraction of this magnetic male. Geraldine

Box 3.2
New Age Celebrates the Change

As the baby boomers who were born after World War II hit menopause, they are chang-ing the stereotypes of aging, just as they have changed other norms. New Age spiritu-ality attempts to connect this rethinking to the invention of "severance rituals," which mark the passage from one status in life to another. Here is one such ritual.

Severance rituals are important for grieving the losses experienced in menopause. This is a ritual to honor grief.

1. Prepare the ritual space with candles, flowers, or incense.
2. Invoke the presence of the Sacred through words, music, the lighting of a candle, or the ringing of a bell.
3. Bring to heart the three biggest losses connected with your menopausal rite of pas-sage. Write them down, or draw symbols for them, on three slips of paper; or use pho-tographs.
4. Set fire to each paper or picture and place it in a fireproof bowl or fireplace. Stay with your body, your feelings, your soul as the paper turns to ashes. (After the ritual you might scatter the ashes around a favorite plant as fertilizer, as a reminder that the dying of the old leads to life in new forms.)
5. Thank the Sacred.
6. Mark the end of the ritual by ringing a bell, saying a prayer, or extinguishing candles.

SOURCE: Excerpted from Melissa West, "Celebrating the Change," *New Age Journal*, 13 (Novem-ber/December 1996), pp. 94–99, 166. Copyright Melissa West. Reprinted with permission.

Finn (1988) argues that the Harlequin Romances provide an acceptable interpretation for many women of how the independence, innocence, and freedom of girlhood come to be replaced by the constricting routines of married life. In an ironic twist that is characteristic of postmodern culture (discussed later in this chapter), the discourse of romance novels itself has become the subject of playful social commentary in various media, such as the cartoons on the next page.

The importance of novels such as the Harlequin Romances as an element of contemporary culture is often overlooked because they are so familiar to us, yet their influence is great because they are part of the mass media. Together with the other print media, such as newspapers and magazines, they affect the way in which many people view the world. They are thus very influential in defining the positions of women in our culture.

▲ THE MASS MEDIA

The mass media are means of communicating messages to very large numbers of people. They depend on a variety of technologies for recording and copying sym-bols, and for sending them across great distances. Books, newspapers, and magazines, as well as movies and radio and television programs, are distributed to large numbers of individuals, who are thereby ex-posed to identical messages from the same source. As a result, the mass media have contributed greatly to increased cultural diffusion in this century.

Cultural Diffusion

Cultural diffusion is the spreading of ideas from their original source to other places, which may be very remote.

SOURCE: Reprinted with special permission of King Features Syndicate.

Television is a particularly powerful instrument of cultural diffusion. This fact is evident in the recent history of the Native peoples in Canada. During the last three decades, geographically isolated communities in Canada's North have been increasingly exposed to the culture of the cities in the South. *Hockey Night in Canada,* the latest agonies of soap opera stars, and advertisements for products that support an urban lifestyle have all become familiar experiences among people who previously shared a self-contained hunting-and-gathering way of life. Maintaining a sense of the reality of local meanings is more difficult under these conditions, and cultural integration around a traditional way of life consequently tends to give way to cultural ambiguity and personal confusion.

Global Culture

The replacement of a traditional culture by the imported culture of a dominant group that controls the mass media is sometimes referred to as **cultural imperialism**. For example, despite concerns about the effects of television on children, Native peoples living on reserves in northern Canada have not always been given a choice about the introduction of television transmissions into their communities (Granzberg, 1979). Traditional elites in many Third World countries, as well as some Canadians, are especially likely to think about cultural imperialism in terms of the power of large American television, movie, and publishing corporations. However, in the late twentieth century, Americans, too, have experienced the effects of cultural diffusion. British rock music, Japanese business practices, and Latino tastes have been absorbed into American culture. Perhaps we are all moving toward a unified global culture in the twenty-first century. In any event, the **globalization of culture** is likely to be a significant influence on our lives in the foreseeable future (Featherstone, 1990).

▲ TEXTS

In contemporary social environments, a great deal of communication goes on through the mass media and in other ways that do not involve face-to-face interaction. Dorothy Smith (1990) refers to this kind of communication as **textual discourse**. Textual discourse involves communicating by means of records of symbols that are available for use by many readers or viewers. The symbols may be recorded on paper, on film, on computer disk, in a painting or sculpture, and so on. Regardless of the technology or medium that is used, each of these records is a **text** insofar as it preserves a set of symbols that can be used by many people at different times.

In Canada today, bureaucracies of all kinds are continuously generating texts that have profound effects on our lives. Some of the most important texts are documents, such as birth certificates and high-school and university transcripts, by which bureaucrats measure the passage of life from birth to death. As every student knows, having "the right piece of paper" is essential for gaining access to the career of your choice. Here, official knowledge of our intelligence is so dependent upon certain texts that they become the standard according to which people judge what is real and what is not.

Sociologists are especially interested in the words that are used to describe social problems in official reports. That is because the way a problem is defined has a big influence on the steps that will be taken to solve it. For example, the phrases "wife battering" and "family violence" may seem to be just different ways of talking about the same problem, but they are not. The former term focusses attention on assaults by men on women; the latter term implies that women may also assault men and, furthermore, that both mothers and fathers may assault their children. There is much at stake in whether a social program is called a program against wife battering or a program against family violence. Not surprisingly, there are often struggles between different groups over which term will be used to define social reality (Walker, 1995).

Sociology of Knowledge

The process of defining what is real is referred to by sociologists as the **social construction of reality** (Berger and Luckmann, 1966). The social construction of reality takes place in decisions made by officials in bureaucracies, but it occurs in many other contexts as well.

Sociologists of knowledge have been most interested in the role played by certain occupational groups, such as scientists and doctors, who define the things that we believe to be true. In the modern world, we often look to these groups for guidance because they possess specialized forms of knowledge that the majority of us do not have. Yet we are sometimes uneasy about our dependence on these experts and about the influence that they have on our lives. Troubling questions can arise about the relationship between expert knowledge and practical experience. For example, women have sometimes questioned the value of the medical knowledge of (mainly male) physicians compared with the intimate knowledge of the female body that midwives possess.

More fundamentally, there are important questions concerning the manner in which expert knowledge is used to define the nature of our problems. Typically, it is the very experts who have told us what the problem really is who then tell us that we need their expertise in order to solve that problem. How objective can such knowledge be? These are serious issues, as we see in current discussions about knowledge of childhood sexual abuse in Canada (see Box 3.3). If memories of abuse can sometimes be shaped, and perhaps even created, by the ways in which human-service professionals ask questions, how can we have any official knowledge that is independent of the preconceived ideas held by experts?

■ CULTURAL CONSTRAINTS

In the examples presented above, we have seen that culture is an integral part of social life in everyday interaction, in the functioning of large organizations, and in professional expertise. Cultural codes are used in many different ways, and they produce many kinds of social effects. The effects that are often of greatest interest to sociologists arise from connections between culture and social hierarchies — in other words, from social stratification. How exactly does culture open up greater opportunities for some people than for others, and how does culture constrain some people more than others? In fact, we have already touched on one way in which this can occur — in the use of knowledge by specialized groups whose social position gives them influence over other people's lives. The general point that concerns us here is unequal control over the production and distribution of ideas about oneself (Breton, 1984).

▲ KNOWLEDGE

In a famous series of studies, Michel Foucault argued that there is a close relationship between knowledge

Box 3.3
Remembering Childhood Sexual Abuse: The Social Construction of Memory?

How much of your childhood can you remember? Can you remember feeling the pain when your adult teeth began to push their way through your gums? Do you remember feeling happy or frustrated when your mother or father held you tight? Can you remember how you felt on the day you first started going to school? Do you remember being abused as a child? If so, is that something you have always known, or have you only recently remembered it?

There are two principal views on the nature and extent of our memories of childhood. Let us call one the "recording and recovery approach," and the other the "dispersal and construction approach."

The recording and recovery approach holds that the brain records everything important that has ever happened to us. How much of this material we actually recover into consciousness at any given time depends on a number of factors. One of those factors is the tendency of the mind to suppress all memories of things that are very disturbing emotionally. This view of memory is held by many mental health specialists.

According to the dispersal and construction approach, we quickly forget most of what we experience. We remember only those things that are kept alive by some discourse in ongoing social interaction. Since memory depends on discourse, it is influenced by the forms that interactions take. Memories may change as discourses change. It may even be possible to create memories, through emotion-laden suggestions from trusted sources. This view of memory is held by many people involved in the deprogramming of cult members.

These different views of memory have practical applications today with respect to the treatment of claims made by people who begin to remember childhood sexual abuse. The recording and recovery viewpoint is the basis for the work of many mental health counsellors, who encourage troubled individuals to recover memories of painful childhood experiences. The dispersal and construction viewpoint is the basis for the work of groups such as the False Memory Syndrome Foundation. Because they believe that memories of abuse are often created by therapists and popular psychologists, members of the foundation attempt to protect certain parents and people who work with children against accusations of abuse.

Journalist Kirk Makin states that, remarkably, about one in five cases of abuse recalled later in life feature allegations of Satanism. Yet, intensive investigations by police typically fail to turn up enough corroborating evidence for a successful court case. Supporters of women and children who have made these claims say that it is unrealistic to expect independent confirmations of accounts of ritual abuse, because of the extreme lengths to which perpetrators go to keep people quiet. What do you think?

SOURCE: Based on Kirk Makin, "Memories of Abuse: Real or Imagined?" *The Globe and Mail*, July 3, 1993, pp. A1, A5.

and power (Foucault, 1980). He thought that this was most evident in the ways in which the psychological professions collect and use information about individuals and in the ways in which governments collect and use information about the populations of entire countries. It is also evident in the content of education, and in the ways in which those who provide that content gain power over those who learn.

In Canada's Native population, education was traditionally provided informally by elders, often through story telling. With the coming of Christian missions and schools, the role of elders as transmitters of information began to break down; by the 1960s, it had virtually disappeared (Vanderburgh, 1995). Missionaries and schoolteachers controlled the knowledge now perceived as vital to survival in the larger Canadian society. Traditional knowledge was looked down on by the new educators, as they transmitted Christian values, literacy and mathematics, and modern work skills and domestic science. As the elders' role was taken over by the newcomers, the prestige of the elders also declined. Once seen as vital, contributing members of Native society, the elders were often reduced to the status of a liability and they lost their traditional place of respect in family life.

The educational system has thus displaced and marginalized traditional Native knowledge, and has also had wider effect in shaping the dominant culture's views of Native society. Thomas Dunk (1991) has described how the discourse of working-class men in Thunder Bay, in northwest Ontario, is based on a division between whites and Native peoples. Here, the Native stands for negative personal traits and pathological behaviours. An unattractive white person is described as someone whom only a Native would find interesting. Behaviour that is considered antisocial is referred to as "going Indian." This situation is an example of **ethnocentrism,** in which the world tends to be seen from the point of view of only one ethnic tradition (in this case, that of European immigrants and their descendants), whereas the perspectives of other ethnic groups are perceived as misleading or less useful. The unusual story of Grey Owl offers insight into the close relationship between power and knowledge in ethnocentrism (see Box 3.4).

Moral Panics

The relationship between knowledge and power is often most important when it comes to the way in which social problems are defined. Social change in modern societies creates conditions that many people find disturbing, and sometimes alarming. We are worried by news reports about threatening behaviours that we do not understand, such as serial killing, men stalking women who reject them, abductions of children, and so forth. We hope that such things can be controlled before they spread too far and affect us. Also, we want to know that they can be explained. We demand that someone should understand the problem and do something about it. We have panicked. And when people panic, they often look for simple moral solutions.

The more unusual the behaviour to be explained, the less we can rely on our own everyday knowledge. We are more likely to believe that fantastic forces are at work, such as Satan (see Box 3.3). Of course, not everyone in Canada believes that Satanism is a real danger. Those who do hold the belief have a certain view of the world. Sociologists refer to this kind of world view as an ideology.

▲ IDEOLOGY

An **ideology** is any system of ideas that describes and explains the experiences of certain people, and either justifies their situation or proposes alternatives to it. It identifies appropriate lines of action for them to follow and suggests strategies by which they can achieve their goals. Political parties that seek radical change often have well-developed ideologies that describe how they plan to gain political power and how they intend to use it. The Parti Québécois is a good current example. Its ideology claims that the Canadian federal state is broken and cannot be mended, and so it is best for Quebec to separate from the rest of Canada.

One of the most important ideologies in Canada often receives little attention, because it has temporarily disappeared and reappeared in different forms throughout Canadian history. That ideology is "populism." Today, the Reform Party is the clearest expression of populist ideology, especially in Western Canada. According to Trevor Harrison (1995), populism constitutes an attempt to create a mass political movement around symbols and traditions drawn from popular culture. The movement's followers believe that the "real people" have been betrayed by small, powerful groups, who are thought to be overprivileged and overprotected, such as economic elites, government bureaucrats, and unassimilated minorities. The Reform Party today is a populist movement, which seeks to restore earlier, and simpler, forms of government and social order in Canada.

Another example of a conservative ideology is the conservative, fundamentalist Christian world view that underlies belief in Satanism. It describes social change in terms of a moral struggle between good and evil. It explains current problems as attributable to the increased power of evil, because religion is in crisis and the churches have lost their traditional control, especially over children. The ideology proposes solutions to this situation, by identifying the need to counteract the subversive influence of

Box 3.4
The Imaginary Indian: The Story of Grey Owl

In 1931, a spokesperson for the Native Indian emerged from the Canadian bush. His name was Grey Owl. He said he was an adopted Ojibway trapper from northern Ontario and that he had given up trapping, under the influence of his Iroquois wife, to become a conservationist. Grey Owl's first book, *Men of the Last Frontier,* was a tribute to the life of the wilderness man and, at the same time, a warning that Canada's wild spaces were fast disappearing before industrial civilization. The book struck a chord with the public on both sides of the Atlantic, and Grey Owl became a popular speaker on the lecture circuit. Dressed in buckskin jacket and moccasins, his black hair hanging in two long braids, he appeared to his audiences to be the epitome of the North American Indian. Lloyd Roberts, son of Sir Charles G.D. Roberts, called him "the first Indian that really looked like an Indian."

Grey Owl's success as an author in Canada was followed by a lecture tour of the United Kingdom, where he spoke to nearly a quarter of a million people at more than 200 meetings. The Canadian government decided to take advantage of his sudden fame. In 1931, the Parks Branch hired him to be "caretaker of park animals" at Riding Mountain National Park in Manitoba. After six months, he moved to Prince Albert National Park in Saskatchewan, where he continued his work with wildlife, wrote books, and welcomed a steady stream of visitors.

Grey Owl kept up an exhausting schedule of writing, touring, and lecturing. In the fall of 1937, he began a gruelling speaking tour of Britain. In four months, he made 138 speeches, including a command performance for the royal family at Buckingham Palace. At the end of March 1938, he returned to his home and was hospitalized in Prince Albert for a combination of fatigue and pneumonia. He died on April 13, at age 59.

Grey Owl's many supporters around the world were shocked by the news of his sudden death, but then they were stunned by an even bigger surprise. The man who had impressed his audiences as being the very epitome of an Indian turned out to be a white man: Grey Owl was, in reality, Archie Belaney, an Englishman.

Whites, almost without exception, had believed in Grey Owl's Indian identity. He looked so much like what they thought an Indian should look like. With his long braids (dyed black), dark skin (tinted with henna), and glowering stare (practised in front of a mirror), he impressed everyone. Even his drinking problem was seen as confirmation of his Native identity. "I am sorry to hear that Grey Owl has been indulging too freely in liquor," wrote a senior official in the Parks Branch on one occasion. "As a matter of fact, with so much Indian blood in his veins, I suppose it is inevitable that from time to time he will break out in this connection." There is something ironic about the racial stereotype of the drunken Indian being used to explain away the conduct of an Englishman!

After the revelation of Grey Owl's true identity, the general opinion seemed to be that what he stood for was more important than who he was. But while he lived, being Indian—or, rather, conforming to the white stereotype of an Indian—was crucial to his success.

Grey Owl with two admirers, Sir William Mullock (left), Chief Justice of Ontario, and Sir Charles G.D. Roberts, in 1936.
SOURCE: Reproduced by permission of the City of Toronto Archives, Globe and Mail Collection, SC266-41837.

SOURCE: Adapted from Daniel Francis, *The Imaginary Indian: The Image of the Indian in Canadian Culture* (Vancouver: Arsenal Pulp Press,1992), pp. 131–38. Used with permission.

Satanists. And it suggests concrete strategies for identifying the Satanists among us and for preventing their work.

By comparison with its far greater influence in the United States, conservative Christian fundamentalism is not a very important ideology in most parts of Canada today. Seymour Martin Lipset (1990) notes that ideologies in America are often intensely moralistic. They are the bases for recurring movements to eliminate evil. The tendency to see the "other" as an agent of Satan has deep roots in American history. It has been expressed in a variety of confrontations with "evil empires," a term applied to the former Soviet Union in the context of the anticommunist zeal of the post–World War II period. In contrast, Canadians have generally been more willing to tolerate a measure of human imperfection and to accept that opponents are not necessarily completely evil. Box 3.5 illustrates this point.

Ruling Ideas

Despite their ideological differences in certain areas, Canadians and Americans have similar interests in the ideology of the free market economy. This is one of the most powerful ideologies in the world today. For example, it provides the theoretical underpinning for policies to increase trade between countries through treaties such as the North American Free Trade Agreement (NAFTA).

The ideology of the free market describes social change in terms of a struggle for survival among individuals, companies, and countries as they compete with one another for scarce resources. It explains current problems as the result of interference by governments, because they tend to drive up the cost of doing business and so make industries in certain places uncompetitive. The market ideology proposes solutions to this situation by reducing government intervention in the management of trade and by cutting expensive government programs. Finally, the market ideology suggests concrete strategies, such as negotiated agreements between governments of different countries which stipulate that each is to stop subsidizing certain industries domestically and is to reduce duties on imported goods. Although the ideology of the free market economy has been very influential in recent years, it is by no means new. It has been around for well over two centuries, although the extent of its influence has fluctuated over the years.

Box 3.5
Core Values in Canadian Culture

Between November 1, 1990, and July 1, 1991, some 400 000 Canadians participated in an unprecedented process of national consultation. That process was known as the Citizens' Forum on Canada's Future. Citizens who spoke to the forum focussed on what it meant to them to be Canadians. They expressed their sense of a distinct Canadian identity that sets Canadians apart from Americans and from people in other countries. The final report from the forum presented the following list of core values that emerged strongly from participants in all regions of Canada:

- Belief in equality and fairness in a democratic society
- Belief in consultation and dialogue
- Importance of accommodation and tolerance
- Support for diversity
- Compassion and generosity
- Attachment to Canada's natural beauty
- Commitment to freedom, peace, and nonviolent change in world affairs

SOURCE: Based on Citizens' Forum on Canada's Future, *Citizens' Forum on Canada's Future: Report to the People and Government of Canada* (Ottawa: Supply and Services Canada, 1991).

In 1848, a German writer living in England gave a speech in Brussels that went almost unnoticed. In it, he outlined the sociology of the market ideology. He argued that this system of ideas was created and communicated by people who stood to gain the most from it. He thought that industrial workers would benefit very little because their wages would fall, but that the owners of industry would make bigger profits as a result of their lower manufacturing costs. Therefore, he argued, workers and owners could not relate identically to the free market ideology. The speaker insisted that, although the people who argued for free trade claimed it to be in the general interest of everybody, in reality it served the particular interests of those capitalists who had invested their money in manufacturing. The speaker was Karl Marx (1976).

Marxist sociologists view ideologies such as that of the free market as forms of **hegemony**. What they mean by this is that the most influential ideas, the "ruling ideas," are the ones that benefit the wealthiest economic class. The class of wealthy owners, or the ruling class, is generally successful in making its ideas appear to be the only plausible or feasible ideas. People who are not as well off therefore accept their lesser economic fortune because they believe what they have is the best deal they can get, or because they believe it is the outcome of a system that is basically just.

Legitimation

Karl Marx was not the only classical sociologist who was concerned with the question of why people accept unequal conditions. Max Weber also thought it was an important issue. Weber was especially concerned with the stability of hierarchies of authority in large organizations. Leaders in any large organization face a practical problem, he believed. They can easily give directions to large numbers of followers, but they cannot as easily verify whether their subordinates are all doing what they have been told to do. In practice, leaders rely heavily on the willingness of people to accept controls because they believe that the leaders have the right to impose them. Here we see culture at work again, in the **legitimation** of social control, which is referred to as authority.

Weber stated that there are three types of legitimate domination: traditional authority, charismatic authority, and rational-legal authority (Weber, 1968). In traditional authority, the position of the leader is justified on the basis of his or her connection with sacred symbols from the past. Hereditary monarchy is the classic example of this type of authority. Charismatic leaders, on the other hand, are often followed for the opposite reason, because they promise to bring about radical change. Their charisma, or extraordinary personal quality, persuades people that they have unique insights and powers to do things that are beyond the limits of ordinary achievement. Finally, rational-legal authority is founded on the idea that leaders are rationally selected for important positions on the basis of their qualifications and experience for the particular job that has to be done. Weber thought that this last type of authority was the most prevalent in modern societies, in which complex tasks requiring large numbers of people are typically carried out by bureaucratic organizations. Authority in those organizations is distributed according to fixed rules.

Weber believed that, as the power of large organizations increased, our lives would become increasingly confined within the "iron cage" of bureaucracy. To some extent, that prediction has proved to be true. However, it is also the case today that people in countries such as Canada often express a cynicism and even a lack of respect toward bureaucrats and politicians. Critical attitudes toward governments and big business are often reflected in popular songs and movies, which celebrate the activities of rebels who break the rules and get away with it. In popular culture, the legitimation of authority is usually less obvious than its delegitimation.

▲ CLASS DIVISIONS

Delegitimation of authority is a common theme in certain forms of popular music. It is a common theme in rap and hiphop music, for instance. Those forms of music were invented by blacks in American ghettos, and they give expression to the struggles that blacks regularly face against racial oppression and the problems of an urban underclass. Nevertheless, many young whites also enjoy listening to rap. That is because they, too, may have problems with authority at school, or problems finding work in a depressed economy, where all the good jobs have been taken by older people. Consequently, they relate to the themes of anger and resistance in the songs. Here we see how forms of popular culture can reflect a variety of social divisions that have their origins in experiences of social inequality.

Popular Culture and High Culture

The term **popular culture** refers in a broad sense to any meaningful activity or object that is widely distributed in a population. Watching television, listening to rock music on the radio, eating hamburgers at McDonald's, shopping, or going to the cottage on the weekend are all forms of popular culture. Popular culture is contrasted with high culture, which appeals to a narrow section of the population that considers its tastes to be socially superior. Listening to classical music, viewing paintings in an art gallery, or visiting museums are forms of high culture.

The difference between popular culture and high culture does not lie simply in the number of people who enjoy one or the other. It is also a matter of social distinction. Individuals who occupy higher positions in the class structure generally consider their activities to be socially superior. They justify this assessment on the grounds that appreciating high culture involves specialized knowledge and fine aesthetic judgement, both of which require training. Enjoying classical music is judged to require greater intellectual skill than listening to rap music.

Cultural preferences are shaped by upbringing and education. They are therefore often related to family and class background. Bourdieu (1984) argues that tastes are markers of social class. They are "read" by individuals to distinguish members of one class from those of another, and to make claims for themselves about the class to which they belong. Because trained tastes are passed from one generation to the next by means of childhood socialization, they constitute **cultural capital,** which serves to maintain class membership (Bourdieu, 1977).

Interestingly, social distinction can often be achieved simply by acquiring the symbols of cultural capital without actually learning anything. In a study of tourists who visited one of British Columbia's museums, Kelly (1994) found that nearly a third of the tourists did not even bother to enter the exhibit areas on their one and only visit to the museum! These people were seeking symbolic rather than educational benefits. Their relationship to the cultural capital stored in the museum was expressed through the acquisition and display of some item, such as a T-shirt or a reproduction of an object in the museum, which showed that they had been there.

The social distinctions that higher-class people make between their tastes and the tastes of lower-class people are expressed in negative evaluations of the latter. For example, lawn ornaments that are sometimes found in the front yards of working-class households are criticized as being in bad taste.

Conversely, lower-class individuals sometimes criticize the cultural forms preferred by the higher classes. Ballet dancing, for example, is seen by most working-class males as a highly artificial and pretentious activity that can appeal only to effeminate men and rich women who have nothing better to do. The social hierarchy of the arts is often resisted by working-class people. Their cultural resistance reflects a larger social resistance to class structures of domination and subordination. Such resistance demonstrates that the hegemony of the ruling class is never complete.

Working-Class Culture

In an influential study of nonacademic working-class boys in England, Paul Willis (1977) describes how the boys' culture reinforces their class position as manual workers. He suggests that there is a culture of manual work that runs counter to the school culture of mental work. This counterschool culture is expressed in an opposition to authority, particularly to its immediate representatives, teachers.

Thomas Dunk's (1991) study of working-class men in northwestern Ontario extends and deepens Willis's analysis of working-class culture. The men Dunk observed contrast their own practical, common-sense thought to the "book learning" acquired through formal education.

The working-class preference for common-sense thought that is derived from hard experience often leads to the delegitimation of persons in authority, who are seen as incompetent. A common topic of conversation is the ignorance of managers and other "educated types" who ignore the local knowledge of working men. Professional groups that monopolize bodies of abstract knowledge, such as lawyers and university professors, are believed to contribute little to solving the practical problems of ordinary people, while extracting high incomes and privileges because of their status as professionals.

University students from working-class backgrounds often feel this way as well. They may demand that their professors teach courses that are more practical and more relevant to the achievement of occupational success. Their resistance is rarely successful, however, because knowledge in modern educational institutions is highly rationalized. In the final section of this chapter, we will examine the cultures of modern institutions in more detail, and we will consider how they are related to some fundamental process of cultural change.

■ CHANGING CULTURES

Unlike the traditional societies mentioned earlier in this chapter, contemporary societies do not place a special emphasis on reproducing patterns inherited from the past. The expectation that present conditions will not stay the same forever but that they should, in fact, change is a special characteristic of those societies that we refer to as modern. At the heart of all modern societies is a distinctive process of cultural change known as **modernity** (Baudrillard, 1987).

▲ MODERNITY

In modernity, change is accepted and it is legitimated insofar as it is thought to contribute to the improvement of the human condition. Furthermore, it is believed that useful change is not only possible, but normal as well. People in modern societies believe that useful change is normal because a discourse of progress tells them that progressive changes lay the foundation for future progressive changes, and so on, without end. In this sense, modern cultures are optimistic cultures. They are based on a faith that things are getting better every day in every way, or that technical means exist to make them better in the near future.

In sociology, one of the strongest exponents of the modernist point of view was Talcott Parsons. Parsons thought that societies could be described in evolutionary terms as undergoing "adaptive upgrading." What he meant by this was that, in modern societies, specific procedures are developed to solve well-defined problems within highly specialized institutions. Parsons believed, as other modernists believe, that things can be improved by using reason to calculate the most efficient means to achieve a given end. When followed in a systematic way, this method gives rise to a process of **rationalization,** which consists of drawing general principles from observations and then applying those principles to solve new problems. Parsons (1966) believed that it was mainly because of their thoroughly rationalized legal systems that modern societies had the cultural basis required for growth.

Most of the "book learning" that takes place in modern law schools and universities generally consists of learning broad principles, which it is hoped will later be applied in a variety of specialized activities. The use of scientific principles to improve the design of machines such as computers is a generally accepted phenomenon. However, the same process of rationalization is also at work in the broader application of legal principles, as well as principles of business management, accountancy, social-welfare administration, and so on. Rationalization is in fact one of the broadest forces for change in modern societies (Whimster and Lash, 1987). It is part of that complex of changes that we refer to as modernization.

Modernization and Cultural Assimilation

Modernization is the deliberate attempt by powerful elites to bring about rapid and progressive change. Modernization can occur in a variety of ways, but the greatest transformations are often the result of actions undertaken by governments. Using the extensive powers of the nation-state, modernizing elites attempt to create a cultural revolution by reforming educational institutions and by investing heavily in new ways of producing and distributing knowledge.

In Canada, the best recent example of modernization is the emergence of Quebec, over the past four decades, as a dynamic, progressive province. Quebec sociologist Hubert Guindon (1988) has described how elites in his province became committed to a nationalistic program of modernization. They first removed education and other public institutions from the control of the Catholic clergy, and later sought more extensive powers that would enable them to steer the economic and social development of Quebec.

Throughout the process of modernization in Quebec, cultural issues of language and education were at the centre of political debates. Many of those issues arose from the view that, to unify Quebeckers behind policies for economic and social advancement, immigrants had to assimilate into the French-speaking majority. In Quebec, as in the rest of Canada, pressures for the cultural assimilation of immigrant minorities have often been justified on the grounds of administrative efficiency and political unity. However, such pressures have not always been accepted.

Cultural assimilation is the process whereby ethnic and linguistic minorities are deterred from maintaining distinctive subcultures. They are pressured to conform to the national culture, which is transmitted by the dominant social institutions. Contrary to the respect that many Canadians have for existing cultural diversity (see Box 3.5), there is a great deal of popular support for the cultural assimilation of new immigrant groups. That conclusion emerged from an opinion poll conducted in late 1992 by *Maclean's* magazine in conjunction with CTV (*Maclean's*, Jan. 6, 1993: 26–27). Only 34 percent of respondents said that new immigrants to Canada should be encouraged to maintain their distinctive culture and ways of life, whereas 63 percent stated that immigrants should change their culture and ways to blend with the larger society.

▲ CULTURAL CONTRADICTIONS

There appears to be something contradictory about the way in which people in Canada embrace the idea of respect for existing cultural diversity and yet are reluctant to accept the increased diversity that the newest immigrants bring. However, such lack of consistency is not unusual. Sociologists often point out that we live in a time of deep and widespread **cultural contradictions** (Cheal, 1979). For example, the globalization of the economy and the migration of populations underlie the continuing diversification of advanced industrial societies, but these cultural phenomena create in reaction the desire to surround oneself with familiar, smaller, and more meaningful communities (Berry and Laponce, 1994).

Daniel Bell (1976) was one of the first sociologists to analyze the cultural contradictions of modernity. According to Bell, the main underlying cause of all our cultural contradictions is the division between a political economy that emphasizes efficiency, rationality, bureaucracy, and hierarchy, and a value system that emphasizes self-development, individual freedom, and the pursuit of pleasure as the main goals in life. The inevitable outcome of that situation is cultural pluralism.

Cultural Pluralism

Cultural pluralism is a social context in which many different cultural codes exist side by side. Cultural pluralism is found almost everywhere in Canada today. However, it has not always been recognized in the national institutions that define our national culture. Symbols such as the British monarch in our political system and the Crown in our legal system persist, reminding us of the dominant role that particular ethnic groups have played in the process of nation building and of the imperial ideology that once supported them (Cheal, 1981).

A major factor leading to greater pluralism in Canada is immigration (Tepper, 1994). Federal immigration policy contains fewer racial biases today, and recent changes in less-developed countries have produced new groups who want to come to Canada. As a result, newcomers are increasingly different from the existing population.

One way in which cultural pluralism is clearly recognized today is in the support given by the federal government to multiculturalism programs. They provide funding for activities by a wide range of ethnic groups, to help them preserve their unique cultural heritages. Raymond Breton (1988) argues that the main driving force for the introduction of a multiculturalism policy in Canada in the 1970s was the strongly felt need to restructure the symbolic order of Canadian society. Symbolic restructuring was necessary to ensure the continued loyalty of the population to the Canadian state.

In order for people to feel that they belong to a society, they must be able to find their personal identities reflected in the collective identity projected in public rituals and in the textual discourse of state institutions. Canada's multiculturalism policy was intended to recognize the contributions made by all the "other" ethnic groups — that is, other than the British, the French, and Native groups. Political demands from the French in Quebec and from Native groups had received increased attention in the 1960s, with the result that the tendency for individuals to compare their place in society with that of others in terms of their ethnicity was accentuated. Groups such as the Ukrainians felt excluded from official definitions of Canada. The multicultural ideology attempted to appease them by publicizing the value of cultural pluralism in the Canadian symbolic order.

The success of Canada's multiculturalism policy is reflected today in events such as Folklorama, in Winnipeg, which celebrate the diversity of ethnic heritages. At such events, dancers in traditional costumes visibly affirm the place of ethnic identities in the Canadian mosaic. Nevertheless, exclusionary discourses have been reconstructed in the politics of language in Quebec and in the tendency for ethnic minorities to be identified as "immigrants," regardless of their length of residence in Canada (Karim, 1993). Furthermore, there is often considerable unease over how a balance is to be struck in the future between an evolving multicultural Canada and the need that many people feel for a specifically Canadian identity (Citizens' Forum on Canada's Future, 1991). In sociology, Reginald Bibby (1990) has strongly emphasized the point that a pluralistic country in which there is little consensus on basic values and beliefs is likely to have some difficulty in finding the collective will for concerted action. That is not the only cultural limit that our governing elites must face.

Marketing of Culture

Cultural elites have often used the taxation powers of the state to foster certain forms of high culture that have only limited audiences, such as classical music played by symphony orchestras. Grants and other subsidies are justified on the grounds that they contribute to cultural development, which is implicitly understood from a modern point of view as a linear path of progress toward higher artistic standards. That elitist view of culture was made largely irrelevant, and has been threatened and subverted, by a broad democratization of cultural consumption after World War II. The principal force for change here is the **commodification of culture**.

Commodification is the general process by which things are produced and made available for sale in market exchange as commodities. The commodification of culture is specifically the process by which symbols, such as paintings, are produced and sold, through art galleries and art dealers, department stores, and street vendors. The cultural significance of the commodification process lies in the fact that market economies, such as the "art market," play a major role in facilitating and shaping both the supply of and the demand for cultural goods.

Within the small worlds of cultural elites, criteria of artistic judgement can be ordered into hierarchies of good taste and social distinction. But in the mass markets of consumer societies, that kind of social control over cultural standards is not possible. In markets, the production and distribution of cultural goods, like any other commercial activity, is driven by the need for sales. Recognizing that economic dimension, Adorno (1975) called the deliberate manufacturing of cultural products for consumption by the masses the **culture industry**.

The commodification of cultural phenomena, in professional hockey for instance, has become a subject of great interest to Canadian social scientists (e.g., Gruneau and Whitson, 1993). Stephen Kline (1993) has argued that "children's culture industries" of television cartoons, manufactured toys, and toy advertising are vital agencies of socialization that engineer children's imaginations. His greatest concern is with the limited nature of the "scripts" for character toys, such as Barbie. Gendered stories of combat and fashion define the rules of play and eliminate the need for children to create their own rules through their own discourse. Observers such as Kline think that the expansion of the culture industry in postindustrial societies is helping to create a new kind of symbolic order, known as postmodernity (Crook, Pakulski, and Waters, 1992).

▲ POSTMODERNITY

As the term *postmodern* implies, **postmodernity** is the culture that comes after modernity. It is an era of intensified change, but one in which definite signs of progress are hard to find. Postmodern change is often ambiguous, chaotic, and fragmented.

The idea of postmodernity is controversial in sociology, and not all sociologists accept that a new and distinctive form of culture is emerging.[3] The reason for hesitation and disagreement over how to interpret contemporary cultural change is that many of the cultural traits identified as features of postmodernity are extensions of trends in modernity. The following discussion will try to clarify what is new about postmodernity. It will also illustrate how postmodernity has, in part, grown out of the processes of pluralism and commodification, which were described above.

Creating Differences

One of the most distinctive characteristics of postmodernity is its eclectic mixing of elements from different cultural codes in order to create something new and different. It was this feature that first brought postmodernism in architecture to the attention of most people. In postmodernist architecture, one finds free-standing reproductions of classical Greek or Roman columns placed in front of an angular steel and glass office building. The juxtaposition of different shapes, materials, and time periods creates a new kind of environment, one that is produced neither by a logic of rational functionality (the columns do not actually support anything) nor by a desire for progressive innovation (the columns are not original works of art; they are copies). What is at work here is the Disney ethos — a sense of fun produced by combining elements that are not usually found together. (For another example, who would have believed that the "Mighty Ducks of Anaheim" could ever be the name of an NHL team!)

Postmodern culture is sometimes fun and sometimes serious. Either way, it almost always involves some combination of elements that do not fit together in a developmental or functional manner. The ideology of multiculturalism is a good sociological example of this point. No attempt is made to justify the continued presence of diverse cultural traditions in Canada on the grounds that they produce a more efficient society. And it would be considered politically incorrect to suggest that one ethnocultural tradition should be given a higher or lower standing than another on the basis of the aesthetic standards achieved by their artists. Instead, every cultural tradition stands beside every other cultural tradition, on an equal footing and on the same flat plane. In a postmodern symbolic order, difference is the only justification needed for existence.

There is a similarity here between ethnic multiculturalism and certain consequences of the commodification of culture. In order to maximize the profits made from the sale of cultural goods, such as recorded music, a large number of new products made by different artists are released in quick succession. Since it is difficult to predict which ones will be really successful, the only way for a company to ensure a constant string of "hits" is to have a rapid turnover of different styles. Furthermore, since every company follows the same marketing strategy, consumers are bombarded with an excess of similar products. Only things that are "really different" stand out and catch the consumer's attention (Featherstone, 1991).

The strategy of being obviously different in order to be recognized is also used by individuals to attract attention to themselves. The classical sociologist Georg Simmel (1971) pointed out that, in order to make themselves noticed in cities, people must express their individuality in some way. This can lead to eccentric forms of behaviour that have no intrinsic meaning but that are important only because they are different. Today, this can lead to extreme behaviour, because our cities are much larger and more diverse, and because the media provide the opportunity to capture audiences of millions. This is often seen in musicians and actors, as well as among athletes in today's entertainment-driven sports business. Hair dyes, earrings, noserings, tattoos, and original clothes styles are all used to make the individual stand out from the crowd. Look at Dennis Rodman. His skill in basketball was just the beginning of a career as a celebrity, famous for decorating and displaying his body in visually compelling and outrageous ways. Rodman is almost as well known in Canada as he is in the United States, which illustrates once again the impact that the American media have upon Canadians.

■ CONCLUSION: THE FUTURE IS NOT WHAT IT WAS

Canadian culture today is not that of a traditional society that reproduces all inherited patterns from the past. Nor is it that of a modern society, which confidently claims that the future will be better than the present and which believes it knows how to make the collective changes needed to get there. Culture in Canada today is postmodern. On the one hand, there is widespread preparedness of progressive change. On the other hand, the changes that occur usually involve less unity rather than more, and often involve the delegitimation of elites and institutions rather than respect for authority. The result is a cultural environment of great complexity, and some instability.

In retrospect, one of the most remarkable achievements of modernity was the idea that unified national cultures were based on distinct hierarchies of values. That ideal of cultural unity is still expressed today in the belief, or hope, that every society has, or should have, a set of "core values" (as was illustrated in Box 3.5). For modernizing elites, core values provide principles of social organization in the present, and they identify the direction of progress along which the society should develop in the future. As the Citizens' Forum on Canada's Future concluded, "Canada is a nation because it shares values and strives to preserve and advance common purposes and objectives" (1991: 132).

In postmodern societies, however, values have multiplied and become more international. In practice, national core values exist largely in the rhetoric of public forums, while their application in formal organizations and everyday life is contradicted by other forces. As a result, there is little overarching cultural unity for society as a whole. Consider the case of hockey, which has sometimes been described as Canada's national "religion."

Gruneau and Whitson (1993) suggest that hockey helped to define a sense of national identity among white Canadian males who grew up between the 1940s and the 1980s. However, they think that hockey is less and less able to act as a symbol of nationhood under contemporary conditions. They argue that the mythic Canadianness of hockey is becoming increasingly fragile as a result of a variety of factors, including the following: commercial domination of the NHL by American corporations; internationalization and the importing of European players; the presence in Canada of new immigrants with different cultural traditions, who have little interest in hockey; and the greater public involvement of women, who did not form close emotional bonds with hockey when they were girls. Gruneau and Whitson suspect that the new politics of gender and ethnic differences will make it difficult to sustain communal sports traditions and rituals, and the visions of national culture, that were promoted by white, middle-class males over the last century and in which hockey often had pride of place.

Change in postmodern societies clearly does not take the form of universal progress toward a well-defined set of common goals. Rather, it is experienced as a series of abrupt shifts and chaotic reversals of fortune and changes of direction. The history of the debate over Canada's constitution in the late 1980s and early 1990s is a perfect example of what can happen under such conditions. After years of failure to agree upon a new constitution, a referendum was held in Quebec on October 30, 1995, on whether Quebec should become a sovereign nation. The outcome was a narrow victory for federalism — 50.6 percent of Quebec voters said no to sovereignty. Because the margin of victory was so narrow, the Parti Québécois vowed to continue its fight for independence. The result was dissatisfaction on all sides. Some Quebeckers felt that their political destiny had been frustrated by special-interest groups. On the other hand, many Canadians were anxious about the future, fearing the eventual breakup of their country. The one thing that everyone agreed on was that prolonged debate over constitutional issues was unhealthy. Some people began to call it the "neverendum."

The fragmentation of contemporary cultures makes consensus building in the democratic political process increasingly difficult. At the same time, however, it is liberating for many groups, such as gays and lesbians, who claim that there is no longer only one right way to live.

Today, there are many public voices communicating many different points of view, from the traditional faiths of religious leaders to the anything-goes-that-entertains morality of talk-show hosts. It is possible to find ideas among the multiple meanings of contemporary cultures to justify almost any decision that we care to make — to marry or to remain single, to have children or to be childless, to take an opposite-sex partner or to take a same-sex partner.

Finally, it is worth reminding ourselves that contemporary cultural changes have implications for education as well. Although many university professors continue to see their role as transmitting the received wisdom of scientific or artistic elites, their views are increasingly open to challenge from the multiple perspectives of current scholarship. One of the most challenging issues today is how to reconstruct education in order to reflect local meanings *and* the globalization of culture. That is just one of many postmodern paradoxes that will continue to affect all our lives into the next century. ■

SUMMARY

1. Culture consists of a symbolic order of rituals, conversations, mass media, and texts.
2. Culture exists at every level of social life. It can be seen at the global level, in the international diffusion of ideas; at the national level, in collective values and in textual discourses about national culture and state policies; and at the local level, in small subcultures. It also occurs at the face-to-face level of everyday interactions.
3. Culture consists not only of a specialized sphere of the arts that reflects a self-conscious, high culture, but also of the popular culture of mass consumption and commodified leisure and of the knowledge that is employed in professional and managerial expertise.
4. Culture is implicated in the structures of power of class, race, and gender; in the unequal distribution of rationalized knowledge; in the silencing and distortion of the voices of people who are excluded from dominant discourses; and in ideologies that advance the interests of one group over those of another.
5. Culture can contribute to the integration of societies by emphasizing values of unity and solidarity, and by constructing a sense of the inevitability of the existing social order. It can also contribute to social disintegration and the breakup of nations through cultural contradictions that cannot be resolved within the discourse of culture itself.
6. Culture produces social stability by reproducing traditional practices. It also produces social change by fostering commitment to progressive institutions or, conversely, by delegitimating leaders and established procedures.
7. Finally, cultural changes raise important questions not only about the present but also about the future of Canada as a late modern or postmodern society.

QUESTIONS TO CONSIDER

1. Many of our most important cultural distinctions involve dual categories, such as day or night, black or white, the work week or the weekend. How many of these dual categories can you think of? What effects do they have on people and practices that are ambiguous because they fall across category boundaries?
2. Choose any subculture with which you have some personal experience and define five words that are characteristic of its discourse. What do those words tell you about that subculture?
3. What evidence is there to support the idea that Canadians are victims of cultural imperialism? What evidence is there that Canadians themselves are cultural imperialists?
4. Do you think that there are any significant cultural differences between Canadians and Americans, or are we all homogenized by the hegemonic ideologies of capitalism?
5. Using concepts learned in this chapter, take any field of the arts with which you are familiar and write a sociological account of some recent developments.

GLOSSARY

commodification of culture The process by which symbols become available for sale in market exchange.

cultural assimilation The process whereby ethnic and linguistic minorities in modern nation-states are subjected to pressures to conform to the majority culture.

cultural capital Knowledge and tastes that are transmitted within families and in schools, and that mark those who possess them as socially superior to those who do not.

cultural contradictions Opposed systems of ideas that are held by the same group of people, causing them to act in inconsistent and sometimes unpredictable ways.

cultural diffusion The spreading of ideas from their original source to other groups in different places.

cultural imperialism The replacement of a traditional culture by the imported culture of a dominant group or society that controls the means of communication.

cultural integration The tendency for the various elements in a culture to fit together, and to reinforce the same meanings.

cultural pluralism A social environment in which many different cultural codes co-exist without being organized into a hierarchical or functional system.

culture The symbolic order through which individuals communicate with one another and organize their social life. It is the total system of actions and products of action that have meaning for both the actors and their audience.

culture industry The deliberate manufacturing of cultural products for mass consumption.

discourse A set of topics for discussion and a way of talking about those topics that is continued over time by a number of participants.

ethnocentrism The tendency to view the world from the point of view of one's own ethnic group and to devalue the perspectives of members of other ethnic groups.

globalization of culture The process by which all parts of the world are affected by the same cultural influences, as a result of the existence of international institutions such as the world economy and multinational media corporations.

hegemony The ideologial domination of one class by another.

ideology A system of ideas that describes, explains, and justifies or proposes alternatives to existing social arrangements, and that identifies appropriate lines of action for people to follow.

knowledge The set of procedures by which facts are observed and verified, and their possible uses interpreted.

legitimation The justification of a social practice, which is accepted because it is believed to be right.

modernity A culture that is committed to the invention of dynamic social structures believed to bring about continuous improvements in human existence.

popular culture All meaningful activities and objects that are widely distributed in a population.

postmodernity The culture that comes after modernity. It is an era of intensified change and is often chaotic, ambiguous, and fragmented.

rationalization The deliberate calculation of the most efficient means of achieving given ends, by drawing general principles from observations and then applying those principles to solving particular problems.

ritual A highly standardized, repetitive act through which individuals express the conventional value (positive or negative) that they attach to a particular class of persons or things.

signs Symbols that derive part or all of their meaning from their contrast with other signs within a cultural code.

social construction of reality The process by which judgements about what is real and what is not real are shaped by social interactions among people.

subcultures Distinctive discourses about specialized interests and experiences shared by a network of individuals whose way of life is different from that of the majority of people in their society.

symbols Any actions or products of action that are used to assign a meaning to a situation.

text A record of a set of symbols that is available for interpretation by many readers, viewers, listeners, and so on.

textual discourse Discourse that occurs through "reading" and "writing" texts, not through the face-to-face interaction of ritual gestures or spoken conversation.

● SUGGESTED READING

Denzin, N. (1991). *Images of Postmodern Society.* Newbury Park, CA: Sage. What do sociologists see when they go to the movies? Norman Denzin sees ideologies of class, race, and gender in our obsessions with money, crime, love, beauty, and sex. Read this book and try analyzing the next movie you see.

Elias, N. (1978). *The Civilizing Process.* New York: Urizen Books. Here is a contemporary classic in the sociology of culture that is both educational and entertaining. You will learn things that you never expected about the history of attitudes toward table manners, the "natural functions," blowing your nose, and spitting. Avoid reading this book while eating.

Goffman, E. (1979). *Gender Advertisements.* London: Macmillan. Erving Goffman was noted for the clarity and wit of his writing, as well as for the durability of his sociological analyses. His study of expressions of femininity and masculinity in commercial advertising is enlightening, thought provoking, and amusing.

Griswold, W. (1992). "The Sociology of Culture." *Acta Sociologica*, 35, 323–28. In only six pages, this article expertly reviews five major debates in the sociology of culture today, which deal with meaning, power, action, hegemony, and methods of analysis.

Hall, S., D. Held, and T. McGrew, eds. (1992). *Modernity and Its Futures.* Cambridge, UK: Polity Press. In Chapters 5 and 6, Kenneth Thompson and Stuart Hall discuss current issues in modernity and postmodernity, with special reference to culture and society. Together, these chapters constitute an excellent introduction for students to the latest work in the sociology of culture.

Livingstone, D., and J.M. Mangan, eds. (1996). *Recast Dreams: Class and Gender Consciousness in Steeltown.* Toronto: Garamond. The political economy of ideology in southern Ontario is the subject of this book. A team of researchers shows how to use sociological surveys to answer questions about the social distribution of ideas.

Nelson, C., and L. Grossberg, eds. (1988). *Marxism and the Interpretation of Culture.* Urbana, IL: University of Illinois Press. This book is packed with important ideas from a galaxy of academic stars who shaped the emergence of left-wing cultural studies and who continue to influence much current work in sociology.

Wernick, A. (1991). *Promotional Culture.* London: Sage. Andrew Wernick is one of Canada's most active sociological analysts of culture. In this book, he draws together his conclusions about the commodification of culture in capitalism. Wernick extends the analysis of advertising beyond a focus on goods to include people (such as politicians) and institutions (such as universities).

NOTES

1. This phenomenon has affected other religious groups as well. For example, Chanukah is a minor Jewish holiday, celebrated at about the same time as Christmas. Traditionally, gift giving played no part in Chanukah celebrations. Under the influence of the pervasive and highly commercialized celebration of Christmas in North America, however, Chanukah has become a major gift-giving holiday for many Jews.

2. This was demonstrated in the sociological study of a traditional village in India conducted by V. Dhruvarajan (1989).

3. The approach taken in this chapter is similar to the classical anthropological and sociological concept of culture as a whole way of thinking, feeling, and acting — but with one important difference. In postmodernity, there is no whole.

CHAPTER FOUR
Sexuality

IN THIS CHAPTER YOU WILL LEARN THAT

- although sexual behaviour may appear to be determined by nature and biology, it is actually a cultural product; this is evident from a consideration of the difference between social gender roles and biological sex

- traditional gender roles, which suggest that men are (or ought to be) sexually aggressive, whereas women are passive and often helpless, are reinforced by popular culture and much of science

- traditionally, both religious and secular views portray sexual desires as threatening civilization and reason; sexuality has been targeted for a whole array of regulations partly because it is often confused with reproduction and gender

- racial and national rivalries often involve the use of sexuality as a vehicle by which to label others as immoral, primitive, or deviant; men involved in warfare sometimes use sexual violence to assert their political dominance

- there is no one "natural" or normal sexuality; every society has a number of different sexualities that can be studied at the level of observable behaviour and at the level of personal sexual identity

- psychoanalysis, pioneered by Freud, is one of the most important theoretical approaches to sexuality; Freud argued that the human psyche is moved by two opposed drives, the erotic or pleasure drive and the death drive; his theory of gender development posited early stages common to both sexes, followed by an adult stage that is highly gender-differentiated, but his view of women has been questioned by feminist psychoanalysts such as Chodorow

- sexuality is not just a private matter; it has given rise to a variety of public discussions and policy debates — for example, on the regulation of pornography and on the legal status of same-sex relationships

MARIANA VALVERDE
University of Toronto

■ INTRODUCTION

In order to understand sex, sexuality, and gender sociologically, it is necessary first to analyze how relatively minor anatomical differences between the sexes have been used to justify socially constructed gender systems. I do this here by exploring the difference between "sex" and "gender" and by analyzing the process by which social distinctions and hierarchies are "naturalized" — that is, made to look as if they are either entirely natural or based on nature.

This analysis opens the door for a consideration of some of the major ways in which sexuality is defined and regulated. I emphasize how fears and anxieties about sexuality interact with fears about nationality, religion, and race. Reasons why different societies insist on recognizing as valid only one form of sexuality are also considered.

One of the most influential theoretical frameworks in the study of sexuality is psychoanalysis, which I explore in this chapter at some length. In the final section, I address some of the current political controversies about sexuality and its regulation, focussing in particular on recent Canadian obscenity law and on the legal recognition of same-sex relationships.

■ SEX: NATURAL OR SOCIAL?

There are some human practices and institutions that are universally regarded as social rather than natural — for instance, cosmetics, French cuisine, and federal elections. And yet, all these practices are often promoted as somehow replicating, imitating, or enhancing nature. Advertising for certain cosmetics stresses that they give a "natural look," and fancy restaurant menus assure diners that the fare consists not of processed, "unnatural" foods but of fresh ingredients cooked in a way that enhances their natural properties. Even federal elections (difficult to justify as natural, given the absence of political parties in the animal kingdom) are often regarded as a key element of the kind of government considered most natural to humans — namely, parliamentary democracy. Other political forms are dismissed by many on the grounds that they do not accord with "human nature." Thoroughly social institutions are thus naturalized — that is, justified as arising out of natural necessity rather than human inventiveness. This process is called **naturalization**.

Social institutions that have been naturalized seem transhistorical (that is, they seem to have existed as they are now throughout history) and therefore unchangeable. Of all spheres of social life, sexuality is probably the one most affected by the ideology of "the natural": People imagine that, as technology and other aspects of human society change throughout the centuries and from culture to culture, sex remains the same because it is natural rather than cultural.

Advanced industrial cultures have brought about the extinction of many natural species and have wrecked good parts of the "natural" world; our own society rarely allows "nature" to develop outside human control, and it relies on millions of human inventions, from blue jeans and rubber-soled shoes to computers and furnaces. Nevertheless, "nature" remains a very powerful myth, perhaps growing in emotional importance as our everyday lives are increasingly technologized. Advertising often appeals to a certain nostalgia for the very nature that large corporations are busily destroying. For example, Kraft processed cheese is sold through soft-focussed commercials portraying a small, preindustrial cheese-making operation rather than the factories in which Kraft actually makes its products. But many social practices and institutions have been so thoroughly naturalized that advertising strategies appealing to our nostalgia for nature are no longer necessary. Most North Americans, for instance, believe that the only natural response to a runny nose is to reach for a Kleenex. This gesture has become second nature, and nobody remembers that Europe prospered for centuries before handkerchiefs (never mind tissues) were invented. Norbert Elias's (1978) study of the invention of "manners" shows how the handkerchief, the fork, the four-legged chair, and the bathroom fairly quickly became second nature to well-to-do Europeans, so that other ways of meeting human physical needs became unthinkable.

The purpose of sociology is to debunk the myth of "nature" and to demonstrate that human beings, even when they believe they are acting out of natural instincts, are in fact regulated by complex and historically specific social structures and cultural norms. The main argument of this chapter is that there is no one natural human sexuality, but rather a wide range of sexual possibilities developed through the ongoing interaction of human agency and social structure. Each culture will regard only a few of these as natural, with all other options being labelled not just as statistically unusual but as downright *unnatural*. But this arbitrary labelling of some sexual possibilities as natural and others as unnatural is about as suspect as Kraft's attempt to claim that its cheeses are somehow more natural than those of other multinationals. There is, of course, a physiological basis for sex and sexuality, but the process by which we name, recognize, stimulate, suppress, act upon, and shape those feelings is thoroughly cultural.

If you feel reluctant to contemplate the possibility that your innermost sexual desires are socially and culturally constructed, think instead about other everyday practices that seem natural to you but are really cultural. You will perhaps agree that the disgust Westerners feel when presented with birds' nests at the table, for example, tells us more about Western culture than about the natural tastiness of the nests in question. Or think about the average Westerner's reaction to going to a Japanese restaurant and being asked to sit cross-legged on the floor. Feeling cramped and uncomfortable, the Westerner is likely to assert that only four-legged chairs truly fit the human body, not knowing that, even in Europe, chairs were unknown until a few centuries ago. The point is that our gut sense of what is edible or what feels comfortable is culturally specific.

Emotional and physical needs can be satisfied in a wide variety of ways, as anthropology (or even just attentive travelling) demonstrates, but the way things are done in our particular culture will seem natural and hence unremarkable to us. If this is true with respect to hunger and comfort needs, it is equally true in the area of sexuality. To many people, the only "natural" form of sex involves a man lying on top of his legally wedded wife, on a bed, in a bedroom, with the door firmly closed and the lights out. But neither doors, bedrooms, nor privatized heterosexuality are by any means universal or natural. Peasant families in many parts of the world have neither doors nor bedrooms, and many cultures and subcultures manage quite well with sexual arrangements other than monogamous heterosexuality. Polygamy is "natural" for many cultures, and some societies, such as ancient Greece, regard homosexual sex between older and younger men as the norm, not the exception.

To return to the food analogy: Fortunately for Canada's cosmopolitanism, eating out at "ethnic" restaurants is now very common, so most people are receptive to the idea of the cultural construction of tastiness. But the sexual imagination of many Canadians in the 1990s remains as limited as the food habits of the 1950s. One major reason for this is the inability to distinguish between *biological sex* and *social gender*.

▲ SEX VERSUS GENDER

In the 1970s, feminist sociologists argued that if we are going to understand the cultural formation of masculine and feminine human beings, it is necessary to make a distinction between the biological sex that can be discerned at birth and the social **gender** that is regarded as suitable to that sex. It is true, of course, that there are two sexes in the human species, male and female, and that one's sex usually remains the same for life. Even biological sex, however, is not as fixed as people believe. In the nineteenth century, there were people around with genitals of both sexes (hermaphrodites); today, medical science insists on surgically altering children born with unusual genitals, in the interests of perpetuating the illusory belief that all human beings are clearly sexed (Foucault, 1980). And, of course, a number of people change sex as adults, with help from hormones and other medical techniques. However, the previous sex of these transsexuals is usually not apparent; once again, the facts are managed in an attempt to sustain the false belief that everyone is either male or female once and for all.

Physiological sex, therefore, is not quite as immutable and easily determinable as most people think (Laqueur, 1990). But gender is much more obviously subject to the vagaries of culture. Babies are not born with any gender identity; if they were, pink and blue blankets would be unnecessary! Gender has to be instilled in them through the collective efforts of parents, relatives, nursery-school teachers, television, and the advertising industry. Children are subtly and not so subtly trained to "fit" the social gender role that is regarded as naturally flowing from their assigned biological sex, so that the social role becomes a kind of second nature. The process by which the two gender roles, masculinity and femininity, are instilled in children and constantly reinforced in adults has been studied by many scholars (for masculinity, see Kaufman, 1993 and Connell, 1987; for femininity, see Brownmiller, 1984 and Wolf, 1990). This is known as gender *socialization* — that is, the process by which particular social roles, in this case masculinity and femininity, are internalized by individuals, often so successfully as to appear natural.

Gender socialization, however, is not the focus of this chapter. I have briefly discussed the socialization process and the consequent naturalization of socially created gender roles in order to proceed to the heart of the chapter — the analysis of how nat-

There is no one "natural" or normal sexuality; every society has a number of different sexualities that can be studied at the level of observable behaviour and at the level of personal sexual identity. This gay parade float illustrates the point. Can you guess which person (if any) is the woman? SOURCE: Dick Hemingway.

uralized gender identities then make certain sexual practices appear "natural." In the following section, we will see how the naturalization of masculine sexuality works in popular views of male sexuality.

▲ MASCULINE POWER AND FEMININE HELPLESSNESS

Scene from a Harlequin paperback romance: An apparently self-sufficient young woman at first rejects her boss's sexual advances, but slowly (and inexplicably) comes to see his very aggressiveness, which had initially made her afraid, as enticing: "His lean, hard body held a menacing sexuality, an implicit threat of sexual violence that attracted women like iron filings to a magnet" (quoted in Valverde, 1985: 138).

Scene from Walt Disney's musical on ice, Snow White: The powerful evil queen controls magical technologies, including talking mirrors and poisoned apples, but she is eventually defeated by what the script calls "the power of love" — which turns out to be not a property of love in general but rather a

"natural" feature of a certain kind of heterosexual male. Neither the dwarves (working stiffs with hillbilly accents) nor the usually resourceful Snow White can undo the evil queen's spell. The erotic power of a strong, blond, "naturally" heterosexual prince is required to bring the erotically passive princess to life; but unlike the queen's power, the prince's charms are presented as natural, not technological or magical. In the final scenes, the "happily-ever-after" cliché combines with the gender conventions of ice dancing to quietly instil in the audience the belief that a certain type of masculinity is absolutely necessary for aesthetic enjoyment as well as for sexual pleasure, social respectability, and emotional security.

Aggressiveness, physical and/or emotional, is popularly portrayed as the essence of male sexuality both in the animal kingdom and among humans of all cultures. Like other stereotypical sexual characteristics, male aggressiveness is portrayed not only as something that men in fact do, but as a norm, as something that men, as proper men, *ought* to do. The process of making aggressiveness into a norm to which males must conform functions at three levels: physiological sex, gender identity, and general cultural values. Since the same cultural ideal permeates all three levels of everyday male experience, with the various levels reinforcing one another, it is extremely difficult to challenge.

At the level of physiological sex, male sexuality is generally identified with an obsession for competing with other males for the best-looking female, taking possession of her as one would a piece of property. This view is, of course, at the heart of both pornography and westerns, but it gets scientific reinforcement from such sources as Darwin's sexist view of animal behaviour, which regards even the passively preening male peacock as somehow the leader of the dating game (Darwin, 1871). Men who do not play the game are usually regarded as non-men rather than as men with a different sexuality; hence, the long-standing identification of male homosexuals with "sissies" — that is, nonmasculine beings. A failure to act according to the norm of masculinity in the sexual arena is often thought of

The level of aggressiveness and forms of affection generally regarded as appropriate to men and women in different settings are culturally defined. SOURCE: David Madison/ Tony Stone.

as connected to a general failure to exercise power in other arenas (think of the many meanings of the word *wimp*).

At the level of gender, there are countless social norms tying masculinity with aggressiveness, both physical and social. Sports, business, and war are three arenas in which masculine identity is formed, and all three are characterized by a premium on aggressiveness. The necessary result is that women who excel in any of these areas will be assumed to be non-women, since all forms of aggressiveness, social and political as well as sexual, are coded as masculine.

Finally, our society is based on economic competition among individuals, corporations, and nations. Aggressiveness is thus highly valued by being linked to economic and political success. "Tough" decisions are usually portrayed as the right ones; politicians who are "soft" (i.e., feminine) on issues such as crime, trade unions, or welfare are immediately suspect. Such views perpetuate the belief that men are generally better suited to positions of power than women, and that those women who do exercise power somehow lose their femininity in the process. Masculine aggressiveness thus travels from the level of innermost sexual feelings to that of male bonding and gender identity, to that of general cultural values (being, for instance, involved in the choosing of political leaders).

The identification of male sexuality with masculine aggressiveness is thus held together by different but complementary networks of institutions and norms, from media depictions of sexual attraction, to the culture of football, to the language of economic and political competitiveness. As Michael Kaufman (1993) has shown, this means that challenging prevailing sexual mores is extremely difficult, since it necessarily involves a challenge to gender identity — which is psychologically fundamental to us as individuals — and also a profound if implicit challenge to a great many apparently nonsexual social values and institutions. Building a less competitive and less sexist sexual culture would therefore involve challenging some of our society's most cherished institutions, from the stock exchange to the Blue Jays.

One of our culture's most cherished myths is that men and women are opposites, as suggested by the phrase *the opposite sex*. This rather arbitrary categorization — after all, men and women, as members of the same species, share a great deal, especially if they belong to the same culture — results in the rather odd situation of making it necessary for women to become everything that men do not want to become or are not supposed to become. Our cultural norms could be arranged in such a way that strength and courage, for instance, were norms for all humans, but this would undermine the myth of the two sexes as "opposites"; consequently, for every masculine quality, there is an opposite and complementary quality that women are supposed to have. Even in the relatively egalitarian world of *Star Trek: The Next Generation,* for instance, in which women understand difficult science and are part of the spaceship's technical crew, the two main female characters hold the stereotypically feminine positions of caregiver and emotional anchor — that is, doctor and psychologist. They are always portrayed as caring for others and, in the case of the psychologist, as using typically feminine intuition to supplement and complement the "hard" science of the other officers. Those officers include the android Commander Data, who, as an artificially created being with no sex, has no reason to be gendered, but who is portrayed as masculine because of the association between scientific knowledge and masculinity.

If popular culture — most of which is far more sexist than *Star Trek* — relies on the myth of "opposite" gender characteristics, the social sciences reinforce that myth. Psychologists engaged in what are known as "brain lateralization studies" have claimed that men and women have brains with different capacities. Although, overall, men show more aggressiveness and women more caring in psychological studies, the studies often neglect to mention that there is a great deal of overlap between the distribution of each of these qualities among men and women (see Figure 4.1). In other words, observed characteristics (which in any case say little about "nature," given the obvious bias created by child gender socialization) do not justify any claim of oppositeness, because many women are more aggressive than many men.

The fact that most men have more upper-body physical strength or a higher aggressiveness rating on a test than do most women does not justify any claim that women are the "opposite" sex. One might as well claim that, because most Europeans are taller than most Chinese, Chinese and Europeans are opposite races.

But the myth of opposites, the fundamental element of traditional heterosexual romance, was never based on evidence in the first place, and will not be abandoned even if most people become aware of the flaws of both popular and scientific portrayals of the sexes and gender as opposite rather than merely different. In order to understand the source

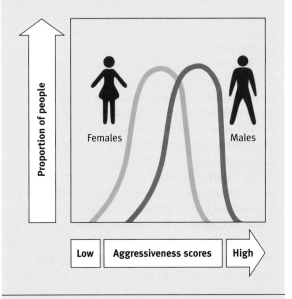

♦ **Figure 4.1** Overlapping Normal Curves of Aggressiveness

SOURCE: Marlene Mackie, "Gender Relations," in Robert Hagedorn, ed., *Sociology,* 5th ed. (Toronto: Harcourt Brace, 1994), p. 127.

and the power of this myth, we need to take a little detour to consider a few concepts that arise in the analysis of sex and sexuality.

▲ SEX VERSUS SEXUALITY

It should be clear to you by now that the sociology of sexuality does not necessarily involve studying what people do in bed. Sex in the sense of having genital sexual relations is a small part of the much wider social field of sexuality. The French philosopher Michel Foucault (1978), the most influential thinker in the sociology of sexuality since Freud, points out that the word *sexuality* did not exist until the nineteenth century. For him, this demonstrates that, although people have had sex since Adam and Eve, *sexuality* is a peculiarly modern term behind which several distinctly modern preoccupations lurk.

One way of making the distinction between sex and sexuality clear is to point out that "sex" in the narrow sense takes a very small amount of time, rarely more than a few hours per week, whereas sexuality does not disappear as people leave the bedroom to go to work or take care of their children. People talk about "*my* sexuality," as though it were

Box 4.1
Coming Out Isn't Everything: Young Gays Seek Acceptance

When Lisa scrawled "A dyke was here. Get used to it!" on the bathroom wall at Northern Collegiate, it wasn't to make a political statement or even for the thrill of defacing school property.

At 15, she did it to test whether it was safe to come out as the only openly gay student at her school.

The answers she received were mixed.

"Some people wrote stuff like 'Burn in hell,'" she said. "Others were like 'Right on.' I found out there were other lesbians."

Finding others is one of many hurdles faced by the first generation of openly homosexual students in high school, an environment where "fag" and "dyke" remain common epithets.

Teenagers like Lisa tell stories of isolation and fear of discovery so profound that many have tried to commit suicide.

But a growing number refuse to accept the "high-school-is-hell-and-then-you-go-to-university" status quo, said Jane, the first openly lesbian student at Branksome Hall, a private girls' school in downtown Toronto.

Many gay teenagers are starting their own support groups and helping each other come out to their schoolmates and parents. Four lesbian and gay youth groups have cropped up in Toronto in the past two years. There are 150 such organizations, in addition to those in schools and universities, across Canada and the United States.

Although open about their sexual orientation at home and school, Lisa and Jane use pseudonyms to protect their families and girlfriends.

Tony Gambini, a social worker with the Toronto Board of Education's human-sexuality program, offers counselling services to homosexual teenagers. He estimates that they are three times as likely to commit suicide as their heterosexual peers. But Mr. Gambini said there is a dramatic change in the number of students coming out and in young people's attitudes toward homosexuality.

"Kids these days have the feeling they have the right to be themselves," he said. "They are aware of what lesbians and gays are, so they can label themselves. In the past, there wasn't even enough information to do the labelling. I can see the difference on a yearly basis." . . .

Most are popular and successful, which they say makes it more difficult for their peers to reject them.

"I had a lot of friends, so people couldn't just ridicule me," said Lyn, an 18-year-old student at St. Joseph's College, a Catholic school. . . .

. . . Lyn announced she was a lesbian to her religion class during a presentation on homosexuality. Then she told her Filipino-Canadian family. "My mom's like, 'If you are, you are, but right now you're in an all-girls environment.' My brother's like, 'Why are you telling me this?'"

Sue Careless, founder of Citizens United for Responsible Education, a group made up primarily of conservative parents, said teenagers are too young to know whether they are really homosexual. She said students like Lyn are confused between an "adolescent phase of homosexuality," which includes "same-sex crushes that have a lot to do with admiration or role models," and adult homosexuality.

The too-young-to-know argument—usually coming from family and teachers—is what is most frustrating to gay teenagers. Many acknowledge that their orientation could change, but that is beside the point, Jane said. "It's so insulting. You're not signing any contracts. The important thing is now I'm a lesbian. Now you have to deal with it."

(continued)

Box 4.1
(continued)

The Toronto board's human-sexuality program is trying to improve the learning environment for gay teenagers. Primarily at students' requests, Mr. Gambini's group made 150 presentations on sexual orientation in high schools last year, an increase of more than 25 percent from the previous year. At many schools, he said, gay teenagers still face violence when they are found out.

. . . Mr. Gambini's greatest opposition comes from Ms. Careless's group, CURE, which is trying to keep him from speaking to classes or counselling students without written parental permission. Ms. Careless said the group also wants AIDS pamphlets that are targeted at gay teens banned from the schools.

Ms. Careless said the solution to high suicide rates and health problems among young homosexuals is to try to cure students of their homosexuality by inviting formerly gay people to speak to them about "leaving the gay lifestyle."

Meredith Cartwright, a Branksome Hall graduate who has worked extensively on gay issues and is currently studying religion at Harvard University, says important information about acquired immune deficiency syndrome and sexuality is being blocked by homophobic parents and teachers. "It hits on the real fears parents have about homosexual pedophilia and recruitment."

Jane said that although her sexual orientation is a "personal tragedy" for her parents, they still support her. She warns that parents who reject their gay children are causing great damage.

"Parents are going to lose their children if they can't get over their homophobia," she said. "Would they prefer queer or dead? Young queers are dying of AIDS and suicide." . . .

. . . When [Lisa] thought she might be a lesbian, she looked up "gay" in the telephone book to get some information. A gay organization referred her to Lesbian Youth Peer Support. When Lisa went to her first group meeting in February, there were 9 or 10 people; now 40 or 50 young women attend weekly meetings. She estimates that 300 to 400 people have passed through the two-year-old organization.

Lisa, who is switching from Northern Collegiate to an alternative school next year, explains that "artsy" teenagers are more accepting of homosexuality. "The more artsy the school, the less homophobia there is."

But students coming out in private schools, which depend on their reputations for financing, face a particular set of pressures.

"It challenges the idea of the perfect little private school where you can concentrate solely on school, but that's stupid," said Jane, whose date for last month's graduate formal was another girl. "Life invades anywhere you go. You can't create a sheltered environment, but you can create a safe environment." . . .

[Jane's] private girls' school principal said she is not sure whether the decision to come out in high school is the right one. "I don't know whether it's good or not for the individual."

Lyn says that when she came out at St. Joseph's College, on the edge of the downtown gay ghetto in Toronto, she was pressed by some students and teachers to keep things quiet. "A lot of people don't want to be labelled a lesbian school."

However, she was not deterred. "I think coming out on your own is pretty cool."

Raised in the aftermath of the sixties and seventies sexual revolution and in the wake of the eighties culture of individualism, openly homosexual teenagers are adding the nineties "get-used-to-it" mantra of gay liberation. The closet is the last place these outspoken and self-assured teenagers want to be.

(continued)

Box 4.1
(continued)

"I wasn't ready to compromise myself," said Lisa, now 16. "I wasn't ready to go around my life without talking about my life."

This new breed is shocking to even the most open-minded parents and teachers.

"I did hear things when I was a kid like, 'I'll love you no matter what,'" said Jane, a prefect at Branksome Hall who has been awarded a scholarship to go to university. "That's got to register somewhere, even though I know this wasn't what they were thinking of. Nonetheless, they created a strong person."

While there is definitely a new movement of in-your-face gay high-school students, for many students there's still a long way to go, said Frances Kunreuther, executive director of the Hetrick-Martin Institute for gay youth in New York City. "There are a lot of brave young people willing to be the only ones out. But there are still a lot who are hiding."

Lisa has had it with hiding. She walks the hallways of Northern Collegiate wearing a T-shirt with a pink triangle on it. When other kids ask her what it means, she tells them it's the symbol of gay pride. Sometimes people mutter "dyke" as she walks by, but as it says on the bathroom wall, "Get used to it."

SOURCE: Excerpted from Naomi Klein, "Coming Out Isn't Everything," *The Globe and Mail*, July 15, 1993, pp. A1, A4. Reprinted with permission of *The Globe and Mail*.

▲ FREUD AND THE SCIENTIFIC IDEAL

In the late 1870s, Sigmund Freud began to study medicine and neurology in Vienna, capital of the Austro-Hungarian Empire and a great centre of learning. Then he went to Paris, where world-famous studies of a feminine disease known as "hysteria" that were being conducted at a large women's asylum convinced him, along with many other European intellectuals, that many physical symptoms were caused not by brain lesions or other physiological faults but rather by purely psychic causes. Freud then began to move away from neurology and physiology in the direction of a purely psychological theory of mental disorder. After experimenting with hypnosis and other treatments, he and his friend Josef Breuer stumbled upon the method labelled by one of their patients as "the talking cure," technically known as psychoanalysis (Freud and Breuer, 1974 [1895]).

Psychiatry as we know it dates from the innovations developed in the 1890s by Freud and his colleagues, particularly the practice of letting patients talk about anything that came to mind with respect to their fears, dreams, and thoughts, in a technique called "free association." At that time, "alienists" (medical men in charge of asylums) never thought that asking patients to discuss their feelings had any therapeutic value, a context that highlights how radical Freud's method was at the time (see Box 4.2).

When faced with the fact that many patients sought to involve the analyst in their unfinished psychic dramas (for instance, by more or less obviously attempting to have the analyst fall in love with them), Freud, rather than ignoring such behaviour, reflected on it and found that the patient's *transference* was actually an important part of the cure. Transference, the process by which patients transfer onto the analyst feelings and fears (most typically, about their fathers) that have lain dormant for many years, was innovative in that it involved acknowledging that unconscious emotional dynamics, not just rational talk, had to play a part in recovery. An even more radical break with nineteenth-century science was Freud's discovery that the unconscious of the analyst also played an active part in the therapeutic process. The recognition that the doctor projected traumas and desires from his or her own life onto the patient, a phenomenon known as *countertransference*, undermined forever the ideal of a completely detached, emotionally neutral doctor.

Freud nonetheless found it difficult to let go of nineteenth-century science and its ideal of the all-seeing, detached observer. It is perhaps symptomatic of his own scientific egoism that, while noting that countertransference can and does take place, he seldom analyzed his own feelings toward the patients in his detailed case studies. He was comfortable only in positions of intellectual power, and made only token efforts to analyze the workings of his own unconscious. His writings, however, betray his unconscious investment in the myth of the Superman-superscientist, especially in his rather self-serving descriptions of his struggles for mastery with his patients. The most notable case of such a struggle, analyzed to Freud's disadvantage by many contemporary feminists, is the case of the young woman known as Dora (Freud, 1977b [1905, 1909]; Bernheimer and Kahane, 1985).

Freud's contradictions reveal intellectual limitations as well as personal foibles. Although many of his discoveries threatened not just particular medical theories but the whole quest for empirically verifiable, universally valid knowledge of human behaviour, Freud nevertheless retained his youthful reverence for medical science and for himself as a scientist. Freud's ambivalence toward medicine has given rise to endless debates. Some psychiatrists, notably in the United States, have developed the scientific side of Freud, often with very conservative implications. Meanwhile, cultural critics and social theorists have used psychoanalysis to undermine the ideal of scientific objectivity by highlighting the workings of the unconscious of the scientists themselves.

Putting aside the question of the controversial relationship between psychoanalysis and medical science, what are Freud's key ideas on sexuality? I will begin by discussing his theory of the basic human drives and then go on to his views on gender and sexual development.

▲ FREUD ON PLEASURE AND DEATH

While young, Freud developed the theory that the human psyche is always driven by a quest for pleasure, and that even self-denying activities such as

---

Box 4.2
Freud on Society's Resistance to Psychoanalysis

Society believes that no greater threat to its civilization could arise than if the sexual instincts were to be liberated and returned to their original aims. For this reason society does not wish to be reminded of this precarious portion of its foundations. It has no interest in the recognition of the strength of the sexual instincts or in the demonstration of the importance of sexual life to the individual. On the contrary, with an educational aim in view, it has set about diverting attention from that whole field of ideas. That is why it will not tolerate this outcome of psychoanalytic research and far prefers to stamp it as something aesthetically repulsive and morally reprehensible, or as something dangerous. . . . Now it is inherent in human nature to have an inclination to consider a thing untrue if one does not like it, and after that it is easy to find arguments against it. Thus society makes what is disagreeable into what is untrue. It disputes the truths of psychoanalysis with logical and factual arguments; but these arise from emotional sources and it maintains these objections as prejudices, against every attempt to counter them.

SOURCE: Excerpted from "Introductory Lectures on Psychoanalysis," in Sigmund Freud, *The Standard Edition of the Complete Psychological Works of Sigmund Freud,* vol. 1, ed. and trans. James Strachey (London: Hogarth Press, 1994), p. 48. Reprinted with the permission of Sigmund Freud Copyrights, The Institute of Psycho-Analysis, and The Hogarth Press.

studying hard are merely sublimated, socially acceptable routes to ego gratification. Using a biological analogy, he argued that organisms always seek to eliminate accumulated frustration and tension and restore a steady state; the tension–release dynamic was for him characteristic not only of genital sexual activity but of human behaviour generally. As he grew older, however, he became interested in the dynamics of masochism, since many of his patients, rather than using therapy in order to overcome their traumas and lead more pleasurable lives, seemed intent on constantly repeating their traumas, re-enacting with the therapist and with others the same feelings of loss or hurt that they had previously experienced in their early childhood.

In *Beyond the Pleasure Principle* (1955 [1920]; see also Boothby, 1990), Freud developed the theory of "repetition compulsion" — that is, the seemingly masochistic but very common tendency to repeat and re-enact traumas, sometimes overcoming and transcending them in the process but, more commonly, simply re-enacting them. He criticized his earlier view that **Eros,** or the *pleasure principle,* reigned supreme, and supplemented it with the new theory that human beings also have a **death drive,** or a wish for destruction. The death drive could be directed outward in aggression or inward in self-defeating behaviour.

How the new death-drive theory could be used to revise previous insights may be illustrated with an example from Freud's own life. Freud was a chain-smoker, and while smoking is at one level an attempt to recapture and repeat the oral eroticism of early childhood, the fact that he died of throat cancer — at a time when at least some scientists argued that smoking was dangerous — could suggest that smoking, for him, represented a simultaneous pursuit of pleasure and death.

This new interest in negative behaviour in individuals was paralleled by a growing interest in large-scale, socially destructive behaviour such as war and ethnic hatred. One of Freud's final works, *Civilization and Its Discontents* (1985 [1929]), lays out a bleak picture of a smug European civilization hurtling toward inevitable self-destruction. Freud argued that, as civilization advanced, people increasingly needed to suppress and repress their drives in the service of social harmony. And yet, the two main drives, toward pleasure and toward destruction, were fundamental to human identity and could never be truly mastered, either by individuals themselves or by social authorities. The drives would burst through the veneer of politeness sooner or later. The rise of fascism, Nazism, and anti-Semitism in Europe's most "civilized" nations gave this bleak view credence in the eyes of many people. Freud, in fact, was forced to flee the Nazis in 1938, when Hitler invaded Austria, and he died the following year in exile in London. Some people have argued that Freud's musings on culture and civilization are invalid attempts to treat whole societies with methods suitable only to individual patients. Nevertheless, some sociologists and political scientists do use Freudian concepts to explain cultural and political phenomena that are not easily explained by reference to economic interest or other rational and pragmatic factors.

▲ FREUD ON SEX AND GENDER

If the average educated person were asked to discuss Freud's views on sexuality, he or she would probably say, "Oh, Freud was the guy who thought everything had a sexual motive, like smoking a cigar was supposed to be a substitute for oral sex, or maybe for sucking on the mother's breast, I forget."

As in most popular views, there is a grain of truth in this comment, especially with respect to the early work, before the theory of the death drive. Freud did indeed believe that there was a fundamental continuity between sexual pleasure and other activities, from breast feeding or sucking a soother to smoking a pipe — or, for that matter, composing a piano sonata. However, again like most popular views, this fictional comment fundamentally distorts the psychoanalytic method.

The interpretation of dreams, for Freud a key route to unravelling the workings of the unconscious, is a case in point (Freud, 1976 [1900]). Most people believe that Freud provides some sort of a dictionary that can help us interpret certain dream images as symbols of this or that sexual desire. In fact, Freud heaps scorn on those who think that a certain dream image always has the same meaning. In Freud's view, in order to decipher the meaning of a dream or any other unconscious mental process, such as an inadvertent verbal slip (a "Freudian" slip), we need to know how the particular individual's psyche is constituted. The processes of the unconscious do not follow the rules of logic, which are universal and the same for everyone. In one person's dream, a waterfall might have a certain meaning because that person was many years ago molested by a camp counsellor when on a day trip to a waterfall; this meaning would not be universal but strictly individual. Or two people could be phobic about flying in airplanes, but the causes of their phobias, and hence their meanings, would be entirely different.

Hence the difficulty of psychoanalysis: Although there are some general methodological rules that can guide the analyst, the particular chain of association that leads back to the original trauma or repressed desire is always specific. Freud compared psychoanalysis to detective work, pointing out that clues acquire their proper meaning only when they are put in the right sequence of events. In murder mysteries, a cigarette stub in an ashtray will mean different things depending on the particular crime being investigated; the same holds true for clues in psychoanalysis.

The work of the analyst or psychic detective is made difficult by the fact that the patient is generally not concealing the evidence so much as repressing it. **Repression** is the process by which wishes or experiences unacceptable to the conscious mind are filed out of sight, out of the reach of consciousness (Freud, 1973 [1915–17]). Repressed wishes or experiences, such as incestuous fantasies or behaviours, go to form the **unconscious**. People often visualize the unconscious as a separate part of the brain, like a drive in a computer; however, the unconscious does not exist prior to repression and is therefore not a *place* at all. It is more accurate to speak of unconscious wishes than of a thing called "*the* unconscious."

Repression is never wholly successful, however. Unconscious wishes or traumas are constantly breaking out, though usually in distorted and unrecognizable form. Psychoanalysis takes these eruptions, which are usually not meaningful to the person having them, and painstakingly constructs the chain that leads back, past the barriers thrown up by repression, to the original desire or trauma. Repression of some desires that are often held to be universal, such as incest, is socially necessary, but Freud stresses that the individual can never really repress all infantile wishes and fantasies. Freud believes that these early and usually antisocial desires have a certain amount of psychic energy, which, if not released directly, will be displaced onto other people or will erupt in some indirect way that is likely to be surprising even to the individual concerned. An example is the common experience of taking a sudden and intense dislike to a person one barely knows: Freud would argue that one may be unconsciously using the new person to release an early hatred or jealousy connected with one's father or mother, or a sibling.

Repression is crucial to our sexual lives, since our feelings about who or what we find sexy are, Freud would argue, determined by early experiences that we cannot recall. Regardless of individual variation, however, Freud believes we all go through

the same three stages, more or less successfully. These are the oral, anal, and genital stages. The passage from one stage to another is not a smooth developmental process but rather a sharp break involving the repression of earlier desires. The first two, oral and anal, are common to both sexes; disregarding Victorian views about the inseparability of sex and gender (Russett, 1989), Freud believed that, for at least some time in our lives, we are sexual but not yet gendered.

The oral stage involves deriving pleasure from sucking, chewing, and otherwise trying to incorporate foreign objects. It is perhaps best exemplified by the notorious addiction of babies and toddlers to pacifiers. In the oral stage, pleasure is sought freely, without fear of parental or other prohibition. There is no repression here, and hence nothing is unconscious. Babies can, of course, be unhappy, but their displeasure is caused by external frustration such as the absence of milk or of a loved person, not because of any internal repression.

The anal stage is linked to the beginning of social authority. Toddlers are trained over many months to control their bodily functions and, more important, to prize this self-control. (Hence the popular if simplistic use of the term *anal retentive* to refer to people who are obsessed with order and control.) Toddlers thus learn to gain approval from others, and from themselves, by manipulating their own bodies as well as objects around them. This learned behaviour stands in contrast to the much more immediate and innocent pleasures of the oral stage. Small children going through the anal stage are very proud when they can finally produce feces as expected, and this for Freud is the basis for adults taking pleasure in a job well done.

Ironically, this new pleasure in social approval of deferred gratification is based on a new sense of bodily functions as dirty, as experiences to be conducted silently and in private, and certainly not to be enjoyed. Through toilet training, toddlers learn to repress the delight in satisfying simple bodily needs immediately — the hallmark of the oral stage. From now on, they will feel deep shame rather than delight if they fail to exercise control over excretion. A lifetime of repression and guilt has begun.

According to Freud, the simple pleasures of the oral stage, including masturbation and clitoral stimulation, never quite disappear, even in adulthood. But he believes that, in adults, these infantile erotic pleasures should be subordinated to the only *mature* erotic pleasure — that derived from genital sex. (This theory is similar to today's popular view that oral sex is acceptable as long as it is preliminary to "real" sex — namely, intercourse — and is not found sufficient in itself.) For Freud, as for many contemporary experts, the original infantile capacity to eroticize any person or thing has to give way to a narrowly defined normal, adult, heterosexual sexuality.

Freud's distinctly antimoralistic, sex-positive descriptions of children's pleasures contrast sharply with his highly moralistic injunctions in his discussions of genital sexuality, particularly with regard to the strict gender roles that he believes are necessary to heterosexuality. Boys, he believes, naturally develop an active, even aggressive, sexuality. Freud, like many other people then and now, believed that the penis is somehow aggressive by nature; he did not entertain the possibility that men might be encour-aged by their culture to become aggressive, using possession of a penis as a justification for doing so.

According to Freud, the penis is not just men's only erotic zone; it is virtually the only human erotic zone. Freud did not try to investigate women's sexual interests and capacities, but rather assumed that an adequate characterization of women consisted in noting how they differed from men. Thus, for Freud, the essence of womanhood and, consequently, of femininity is a negative feature — the lack of a penis. He wrote, in what has become a famous phrase, that "women are castrated." Women are thus condemned to a sense of inferiority to men, since nature dictates their fate as incomplete beings (see Box 4.3).

Box 4.3
Freud on Women's Penis Envy

Every analyst has come across certain women who cling with special intensity and tenac-ity to the attachment to their father and to the wish in which it culminates of having a child by him. We have good reason to suppose that the same wishful fantasy was also the motive force of their infantile masturbation. . . . But the first step [is not the girl's love for the father], but a momentous discovery which little girls are destined to make. They notice the penis of brother or playmate, strikingly visible and of large proportions, at once recog-nize it as the superior counterpart of their own small and inconspicuous organ, and from that time forward fall a victim to envy for the penis. . . .

She makes her judgement and her decision in a flash. She has seen it and knows that she is without it and wants to have it.

Here what has been named the masculinity complex of women branches off. It may put great difficulties in the way of their regular development toward femininity, if it cannot be got over soon enough. The hope of some day obtaining a penis despite everything and so of becoming like a man may persist to an incredibly late age and may become a motive for strange and otherwise unaccountable actions. . . .

After a woman has become aware of the wound to her narcissism, she develops, like a scar, a sense of inferiority. When she has passed beyond her first attempt at explaining her lack of penis as being a punishment personal to herself and has realized that sexual character is a universal one, she begins to share the contempt felt by men for a sex which is the lesser in so important a respect, and, at least in holding that opinion, insists on being like a man.

Even after penis envy has abandoned its true object, it continues to exist: by an easy dis-placement it persists in the character trait of jealousy. Of course, jealousy is not limited to one sex and has a wider foundation than this, but I am of the opinion that it plays a far larg-er role in the mental life of women than of men and that that is because it is enormously re-inforced from the direction of displayed penis envy.

SOURCE: Excerpted from "Some Psychical Consequences of the Anatomical Distinction be-tween the Sexes," from *On Sexuality,* in Sigmund Freud, *The Standard Edition of the Com-plete Psychological Works of Sigmund Freud,* vol. 7, ed. and trans. James Strachey (London: Hogarth Press, 1994), p. 335. Reprinted with the permission of Sigmund Freud Copyrights, The Institute of Psycho-Analysis, and The Hogarth Press.

Reading Freud, one wonders why women persist in heterosexual sex, since they have no active sexual desire of their own and being with a man is a constant reminder of their inevitable inferiority. Given his assumptions, it is very difficult for Freud to explain why women have sex at all, especially heterosexual sex. He is therefore led to the claim that women have intercourse not out of active desire but for two quite different reasons. One involves the old myth of woman-as-masochist. Freud claimed that normal women derive pleasure or, perhaps more accurately, some sense of fulfilment from passively submitting to male initiative. To women (including many of his patients) who suggested that they enjoyed clitoris-centred sexual activity more than vaginal intercourse, Freud responded that they were obviously trying to regress to the baby stage, before the development of gender, and that they needed to get over their "masculinity complex," grow up, and become real women.

The second reason is equally sexist but much more original. Freud believed that what women really want is not sex so much as the powerful penis itself, and since they can't actually have one, they settle for a symbolic substitute for the penis — a baby. (Childbirth, with which Freud was clearly not very familiar despite having fathered several children, is for him a kind of grand intercourse, with the baby as oversized penis.) If the resulting baby is a boy, and has an actual penis, the mother can now vicariously enjoy the power and pleasure of having a penis.

For Freud, women who do not enjoy intercourse or who refuse to become mothers or who pursue masculine occupations are examples of arrested development. These "masculine" women are immature insofar as they are refusing to go through all of the ordained stages of sexual development. For Freud, the development of gender is also the establishment of a sexual division of pleasure, with men getting all the direct pleasure and women getting only vicarious or derivative pleasures. Women are also condemned to being jealous of men. Freud thought that feminists who were trying to expand job opportunities for women were unconsciously acting out their envy of the male sexual organ.

In his practice, Freud extended much insight and sympathy to women with "masculine" desires, since he realized that his own theory had condemned women to such a mediocre social and sexual life that they could not be blamed for trying to escape it. But his sympathy would have been unnecessary if his theory had been less coloured by his own masculine perspective.

Today, Freud's highly questionable views on gender, best expressed in *Three Essays on the Theory of Sexuality* (in 1977a [1905]), are increasingly being rejected, even by practising psychoanalysts. Many people, including the feminist thinker discussed in the next section, believe that one can retain much of Freud's theory, particularly his fine understanding of the workings of repression, without accepting his views on gender.

▲ CHODOROW AND FEMINIST PSYCHOANALYSIS

A very influential feminist psychologist, Nancy Chodorow (1978), has reworked Freud's theory of sex and gender identity. Her theory is, not coincidentally, much less "naturalistic" than Freud's, and much less sexist. She also differs from Freud in acknowledging the active role of parents, particularly mothers, in children's development. In general, her model regards social identities as emerging in social interaction, not through a quasi-natural progress from one inevitable stage to the next.

Chodorow points out that most human societies involve a very unequal division of parenting, with mothers (or other women) providing the vast majority of the nurture and care that babies require. The early interaction of the mother with the baby, however, is likely to differ significantly with the child's sex. Mothers tend to treat boys, almost from birth, as more active and independent than girls, and they perceive girls as more psychically similar to, and more dependent on, their mothers. Apart from the mother's behaviour, all social institutions conspire to give boys a clear message — beginning as soon as they can speak — that they have to grow up to be independent men. Boys often go through a period (which can last many years) of rejecting and despising everything female, even their mothers. They refuse to play with girls, show great anxiety if taken for a girl, and use an idealized image of their fathers to create an ego ideal for themselves that values autonomy, especially from the mother. Encouraged to go out and play sports, to take risks, and to show independence, boys grow up into men who are often afraid of intimacy or lacking in emotional skills. Talking about one's feelings is dismissed as "girl talk," as if emotional literacy were not as useful for males as it is for females.

Girls, in contrast, do not have to break their early identification with their caregiver to become adults. This closer and longer bond with the mother establishes the groundwork for girls' later tendency to sympathize with others, to care for them, and to value emotional closeness more than boys do. Women's responsibility for the care of young children thus results in what Chodorow calls "the reproduction of mothering" across generations, including the reproduction of conventional gender roles.

Freud believed that men were the lucky ones in the sexual sphere, because they have the only sexual organ that matters. In contrast, Chodorow, who is interested in emotional dynamics and not in physiology, tells us that men often lead emotionally impoverished lives. Her work has thus been very influential not only among feminists but also among men who are attempting to transform the masculine role; it is in keeping with Chodorow's recommendations for transcending rigid gender roles that these nontraditional men are often very intent on playing a much more active role than their fathers did in the care of young children. Chodorow and many other psychologists believe that if babies bond with men as well as with women in early childhood, boys will not grow up feeling that they have to reject everything female and idealize masculinity in order to become adults. Their own sense of identity will no longer be based on a rejection of maternal and feminine values.

■ SEXUAL POLITICS IN CONTEMPORARY SOCIETIES

Sexuality has thus far been discussed in relation to personal identity and gender roles. There is also, however, a political dimension to sexuality, not in the narrow sense of party politics, but in the wider sense of the public agenda — the issues that are highlighted by the state as well as by various social movements, from abortion to sexual harassment in the workplace. Here I will focus on only two: obscenity legislation and the legal regulation of same-sex relationships. These are among the most heated debates on sexual politics in Canada today, and they are interesting in that they involve not only individual ethics but also decisions about the role the government ought to play in sexual regulation.

▲ SEXUAL REPRESENTATION AND THE STATE

Very few people believe that they are themselves susceptible to being corrupted by pornography. But obscenity laws exist because nearly everyone believes that others are easily influenced, and that the distribution of sexually explicit material ought therefore to be regulated. This rather contradictory, if not hypocritical, popular view is reflected in the criterion used by the courts to determine obscenity — namely, whether a particular image or text is believed by most Canadians to corrupt *others* who might see it. To save a sexually explicit movie from prosecution, for example, it would not be enough for a poll to determine that most Canadians are not particularly offended by the movie; the poll would have to show that most Canadians would be willing to let others see it as well.

The only thing the Criminal Code has to say about "obscenity" is that it is defined as "the undue exploitation of sex." This definition is not useful (what would constitute "due" exploitation?), and governments have therefore made some efforts to modernize and reword obscenity law. In the late 1980s, the Conservative government introduced a new bill, using the modern word *pornography* rather than the old moralistic term *obscenity,* but after much criticism from different quarters, the bill was withdrawn. The old law still stands.

In the absence of effective legislation, police and other public officials, especially in Canada Customs, have exercised a great deal of discretion in determining what Canadians can or cannot see. Those officials often apply censorship criteria from outside the Criminal Code, with little legal backing; the criteria are characterized by inconsistency and a lack of public accountability. Particularly notorious is the bureaucratic (rather than judicial) decision making that goes on within Canada Customs. In this branch of the civil service, nameless officials confiscate shipments of books and magazines before any judge or lawyer, or even the business that ordered the materials, can see them and challenge the ban.

This censorship without a trial was legally challenged by the Vancouver gay bookstore Little Sisters in a long and expensive constitutional challenge that nearly bankrupted the small business. The judge made a finding that sexual minorities have indeed suffered discriminatory treatment at the hands of Customs officials, and that the whole process of bureaucratic confiscation of materials that the bookstores have to pay for, whether or not they sell it, is fraught with inconsistencies. But, while calling for Customs management to improve its procedures and to cease targeting gay bookstores, the judge nevertheless stopped short of declaring the legislation under which this censorship occurs unconstitutional (Cossman and Ryder, 1996).

Part of the problem faced by lower-court judges such as the one in *Little Sisters Book and Art Emporium v. Canada (Minister of Justice)* ([1992] B.C.J. No. 2351 (S.C.)) is the fact that Parliament has not managed to clarify how the guarantee of freedom of expression in the Charter of Rights and Freedoms applies or fails to apply to pornography. Given this legislative vacuum, the Supreme Court of Canada has been reluctantly led to provide standards to guide the regulation of sexually explicit representation. The key element in the court's attempt to harmonize and rationalize censorship practices is the novel interpretation of obscenity law given in the *Butler* decision of 1992, a landmark ruling (see Box 4.4).

The *Butler* decision was perhaps most notable for trying to take feminist complaints about pornography into account. Judge Sopinka agreed with the feminist position (as put forward in a presentation by the Women's Legal Education and Action Fund, or LEAF) that the question of whether "harm," including social harm to women, was promoted by a text or image was more important than its level of sexual explicitness. Although moralism was by no means absent from the judge's decision (as evidenced by the previously cited phrase "dirt for dirt's sake"), the traditional focus on level of explicitness was in fact abandoned in favour of the feminist buzzword *harm*.

It is not clear whose harm was being discussed, however, since the decision uses gender-neutral language, and some of the material sold by Mr. Butler in his store involved only gay men. Feminists have argued, with some degree of success, that sexist heterosexual pornography contributes to a climate in which violence against women is trivialized and even glorified. But it would be rather a stretch to say that the feminist arguments about social harm provide any firm criteria for regulating gay male sexual imagery. Furthermore, it is not at all clear who would evaluate the harm: mostly male judges? women? and, if women, which ones?

Some women's groups, particularly LEAF itself, applauded the decision and saw it as the court's signal to move away from a moralistic interest in hiding sex and toward a more modern concern for the possible harmful effects, particularly on women, of the stereotypes of pornography. Other feminists, however, were sceptical, pointing out that it would be up to the police and the prosecution, not women's groups, to define what is or is not "harmful." The sceptical feminists felt that their suspicions were confirmed by the fact that the first charge laid by police after the *Butler* decision involved a small lesbian magazine sold in very small numbers in Toron-

to's gay bookstore (long a target of Canada Customs harassment). LEAF agreed that this was not a good application of *Butler;* the "harm" they had in mind was that caused by male heterosexual mainstream pornography. But they continue to have faith in the text of the *Butler* decision itself, which they believe ought to be applied in ways that target the real source of women's oppression (for the LEAF position, see Women's Legal Education and Action Fund, 1996; and Busby, 1993).

The debate within the women's movement on the legal regulation of pornography continues, and is unlikely to be resolved, since some feminists put more emphasis on the need for freedom of sexual expression, whereas others would rather err on the side of caution in their efforts to curtail the proliferation of sexist and racist pornography.

This debate is obviously not the exclusive province of feminists. Throughout the public sphere, from church groups that condemn "smut" to magazine publishers who argue that a little skin is a healthy thing, people have conflicting views about what role the state ought to play in the regulation of sexually explicit representations. These social and political debates, however, often take place in the absence of a more fundamental prior discussion of what we mean by "sex." Perhaps the different groups are not even talking about the same things, since, as we have seen in this chapter, people can mean a lot of different things when they use terms such as *sex* and *sexuality*.

▲ HETEROSEXISM AND THE STATE

Heterosexism refers to the institutional practices and attitudes that single out the heterosexual couple as the social norm, relegating all other sexual behaviours and identities to the realm of the deviant. Like racism, heterosexism is often present even when no individuals are showing obvious prejudiced attitudes; there are structures that promote heterosexism, just as there are structures that promote systemic racism. It is heterosexist, for example, for tickets to a school dance to be priced per couple, since this has the effect of making both single heterosexuals and gays (who are unlikely to count as couples even if they show up in pairs) into exceptions, regardless of the moral views of the organizers.

Individual gay people and many gay-rights organizations have, since the mid-1980s, launched a variety of legal challenges against discriminatory definitions of "couple" and "family." In 1987, Toronto librarian

Box 4.4
Obscenity Chill: Artists in a Post-*Butler* Era

Is it "dirt for dirt's sake," or is it art? This is the question which the Supreme Court of Canada in all its wisdom has directed law enforcers and interpreters to ask themselves when they are trying to determine whether or not a particular work is obscene. If it is art, then the exploitation of sex in the work, with the work considered in its entirety, must advance the plot or the theme, and have "a legitimate role when measured by the internal necessities of the work itself." I think that what the Court is asking is how much sex does the work itself cry out for, and how much sex is gratuitous. But what if the work is about sex? Do we trust Project Pornography officers to assess what the "internal necessities" are? Or will they decide that if it is about sex it must be obscene? Welcome to Canada in the post-*Butler* era.

Donald Victor Butler was the operator of a store that sold and rented sex videos in Winnipeg, Manitoba. He was convicted of violating obscenity sections of the Criminal Code, and was able to appeal his convictions all the way to the Supreme Court of Canada. That Court was asked to consider whether or not the definition of obscenity in the Code violated the guarantee of freedom of expression in the Charter of Rights and Freedoms, and if so, whether this infringement was justified under section 1 of the Charter. The Court unanimously answered both of these questions in the affirmative.

On February 27, 1992, all nine judges of the Supreme Court in *R. v. Butler* also agreed . . . on a "new" definition of obscenity. Two judges stated that they would have liked the definition to have gone a little further. The fact that all nine judges were assigned to hear this case gives an indication of the importance that the Court placed upon the decision. A unanimous verdict of the entire Supreme Court is extraordinary. *Butler* is immovable. It is a legal brick wall. As we cannot in the near future make any changes in its definition of obscenity, the question then becomes how the decision will be interpreted.

Under the heading "Offences Tending to Corrupt Morals," section 163(8) of the Criminal Code of Canada defines "obscene" as "any publication a dominant characteristic of which is the undue exploitation of sex, or of sex and any one or more of the following subjects, namely, crime, horror, cruelty, and violence." So the question has been and still is: What is the *undue* exploitation of sex?

In attempting to define "undue," courts developed the "community standard of tolerance" test. What the community would not tolerate would be held to be obscene. This begs the questions of who is the community, and how will courts determine what this community will allow? Often the community is in the judge's mind, and it is not required that the court hear evidence as to levels of tolerance. Must the same standard be applied in large urban and small rural areas? *Butler* upholds the line of cases which state that there must be one single national community standard. It states that the community standards test is concerned not with what Canadians would not tolerate being exposed to themselves, but what they would not tolerate other Canadians being exposed to. The Supreme Court lifted this statement from an earlier Supreme Court decision on obscenity, *R. v. Towne Cinema Theatres Ltd.* In that case, three out of seven judges had gone on to say that the audience to which the allegedly obscene material is targeted must be relevant, and that it was quite conceivable that the Canadian community would tolerate varying degrees of explicitness depending upon the audience and the circumstances. Unfortunately, these three

(continued)

Box 4.4
(continued)

judges were in the minority, and this did not become the law. In any event, *Butler* maintains the single national standard.

In the last ten years, the "degradation or dehumanization" test began to appear in court decisions as a means of defining community standards. This coincided with the growing body of anti-pornography work which developed within the feminist community, such as books by Catharine MacKinnon and Andrea Dworkin, and reflected the efforts of the anti-pornography feminists to get their viewpoint across to the courts. Their position, stated simplistically, is that pornography leads not only to physical harm to women by men, but also to inequality between the sexes. The Women's Legal Education and Action Fund (LEAF) was granted intervenor status before the Supreme Court in *Butler*, and presented a factum on which the Court relied in writing its decisions. LEAF argued that pornography constitutes sex discrimination against women. They stated that the "degradation or dehumanization" test which had evolved had begun to acknowledge the harms pornography causes to women and to recognize the sex equality interest in its regulation. LEAF quoted studies by such experts as Donnerstein, Malamuth, and Check to support their position that "it is uncontroversial that exposure to such materials increases aggression against women in laboratory settings, increases attitudes which are related to violence against women in the real world, and increases self-reported likelihood to rape. As a result of exposure, a significant percentage of men . . . come to believe that violence against women is acceptable." Perhaps LEAF's most succinct statement of its position was as follows: "Restriction of pornography on a harms-based equality rationale is not regulation because of content, although clearly it is tied to content. The purpose of regulation is not to restrict freedom of expression but rather to prevent harm."

The Supreme Court in *Butler* bought this completely. "Degrading or dehumanizing materials place women (and sometimes men) in positions of subordination, servile submission, or humiliation. They run against the principles of equality and dignity of all human beings. . . . This type of material would apparently fail the community standards test not because it offends against morals but because it is perceived by public opinion to be harmful to society, particularly to women. *While the accuracy of this position is not susceptible to exact proof* [author's emphasis], there is a substantial body of opinion that holds that the portrayal of persons being subjected to degrading or dehumanizing sexual treatment results in harm, particularly to women, and therefore to society as a whole."

What must be remarked upon and questioned is why only the voices of the pro-censorship feminists have been heard and adopted by the courts. Indeed, both in the judicial system and in society at large, the pro-censorship position is often assumed to be *the* feminist position. This is not accurate, so why is this assumption made? My theory is that it is precisely because of the agreement between pro-censorship feminists and conservative and right-wing groups that censorship should occur, that courts and other conservative groups in society have adopted the so-called feminist anti-porn position.

SOURCE: Excerpted from Clare Barclay (lawyer), "Obscenity Chill," *Fuse,* Winter 1992/1993, pp. 18–22. Reprinted with permission of the author.

Here is an example of the way "appropriate" sex roles are transmitted in popular culture. SOURCE: Preziosi Postcards.

Karen Andrews sought health-care coverage for her female partner and her two children. The case was lost, with the judge declaring that one of the purposes of the provincial health plan (OHIP) was to uphold the traditional family (*Andrews v. Ontario (Minister of Health)* (1988), 49 D.L.R. (4th) 584 (Ont. H.C.)).

In 1991 and 1993, two similar cases were successfully brought before the Ontario Human Rights Commission. The precedent-setting case was that of Michael Leshner, a provincial employee who sought to have certain benefits extended to his male partner of ten years. By 1991, many insurance companies and many employers, including the Ontario government, were already extending benefits to same-sex partners, but *Leshner v. Ontario* ((1992), 16 C.H.R.R.) resulted in a directive to make this practice universal. The decision was upheld in a similar 1993 case that involved a hospital nurse claiming benefits for her female partner (*Clinton v. Ontario Blue Cross* (1993), 18 C.H.R.R.).

Whereas provincial human rights commissions have often responded favourably to claims of discrimination on the basis of sexual orientation, the federal government has been much less flexible. In the *Leshner* case, for instance, lawyers for the federal government argued that the costs of a change in the Income Tax Act to provide survivor benefits for same-sex couples as well as heterosexual couples would be too great. Gay groups, however, have argued that gay workers ought not to be forced to contribute to plans from which they can never benefit. In any case, along with the financial argument, there is often a whiff of the old moral objection to recognizing the validity of same-sex relationships.

The 1995 decision of the Supreme Court of Canada in *Egan and Nesbit v. Canada* ([1995] 2 S.C.R. 513) was expected to clear up the legal status of same-sex couples once and for all, and to clarify to governments and to employers what their responsibilities were to such couples in the area of health benefits, pensions, and so forth. The court, however, split down the middle. Several judges, led by practising Catholic Gerald La Forest, repeated traditional views about marriage being the unit of society and about heterosexuality being intrinsic to marriage, and denied the claim made by an elderly gay male couple for pension benefits equal to those of heterosexual couples in similar circumstances. Another group of judges expressed diametrically opposed views, writing an eloquent defence of equal rights for all regardless of sexual orientation. Judge Sopinka provided the "swing vote," agreeing with the progressives that discrimination on the basis of sexual orientation is banned by the Charter, but voting with the conservatives to deny same-sex couples equal financial benefits. The net effect of the *Egan* decision is therefore a peculiar, and perhaps typically Canadian, mixed message: On the one hand, it is now the law of the land that discrimination against gay people is prohibited; but, on the other hand, the courts will not compel governments to change their laws even if gay people can be shown to be subsidizing plans from which they are excluded.

The mixed message of the *Egan* decision is perhaps not inappropriate, however, given the wide range of views on a variety of sexual and moral questions that are found across Canadian society today. Courts always reflect public opinion, and Canadian public opinion on issues of sexuality is changing rapidly but very unevenly. Some Canadians appear to have fallen under the influence of the U.S. "Moral Majority," at the same time that many other Canadians are far more tolerant of sexual pluralism now than they were even ten years ago (see

Figure 4.3). The evidence provided by popular culture also indicates that, at least among the younger generation, sexual pluralism is increasingly accepted. Ten or fifteen years ago, it would have been career suicide for Top 40 musicians to publicly "come out of the closet," but today nobody is too bothered by k.d. lang's "dyke" style, or by the fact that Melissa Etheridge's lesbian lover is pregnant by some unspecified means. It may be, then, that there is growing support for replacing heterosexism with a nonjudgemental pluralism in which people are judged by their actions rather than by their sexual identity or family status. ▪

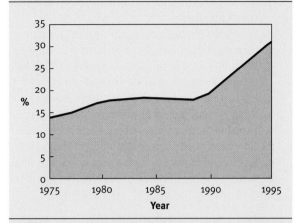

◆ **Figure 4.3** Percentage of Canadians Saying that Homosexuality Is "Not Wrong at All," 1975–1995

SOURCE: Adapted from Reginald W. Bibby, *The Bibby Report: Social Trends Canadian Style* (Toronto: Stoddart, 1995), p. 72. Used with permission of Stoddart Publishing Co. Limited, Canada.

● SUMMARY

1. Sexual behaviour may appear, even to the people involved in it, to be determined by nature and biology, but this is deceptive. Sex has been naturalized but is in fact thoroughly cultural.

2. One way to appreciate the cultural and social construction of sex is to understand that social gender roles are different from biological sex.

3. "Sex" refers to sexual activity, which takes place in every society. "Sexuality" as an inner quality that becomes an object of scientific knowledge is a modern preoccupation.

4. Traditional gender roles suggest that men are, or ought to be, sexually aggressive, whereas women are passive and often helpless. Both popular culture and science reinforce these myths.

5. Both Christian and secular traditional views portray sexual desires as threatening civilization and reason.

6. Sexuality has been targeted for a whole array of regulations partly because it is connected to, and often confused with, reproduction, as well as gender.

7. Racial and national rivalries often use sexuality as a vehicle by which to label others as immoral, primitive, or deviant. In turn, men involved in warfare sometimes use sexual violence to assert their political dominance.

8. There is no one "natural" or normal sexuality; in every society, a number of different sexualities are present. This variety can be studied at the level of observable behaviour and at the level of personal sexual identity.

9. Psychoanalysis is one of the most important theoretical approaches to sexuality. It was pioneered by Freud, a scientist sometimes at odds with the scientific method.

10. Freud theorized that the human psyche is moved by two opposite drives — the erotic, or pleasure, drive and the death drive. According to his theory of gender development, there are two early stages common to both sexes — the oral and the anal stage — followed by an adult genital stage that is highly differentiated by gender. His traditional view of women has been questioned by feminist psychoanalysts such as Chodorow.

11. Sexuality is not merely private, but gives rise to a variety of public discussions and policy debates, for example, on the regulation of pornography and the legal status of same-sex relationships.

QUESTIONS TO CONSIDER

1. Consider how traditional gender roles are naturalized by reference to "natural" sex in one or two popular television shows.
2. Why does Foucault claim that sexuality is a modern invention?
3. How do racist views about Africans interact with myths about sexuality?
4. What methods were used by Kinsey and his fellow researchers to study sexuality? How do these methods compare with those of other researchers?
5. Explain the two fundamental human drives, as conceived of by Freud.
6. What is Freud's view of women's sexual capacities?
7. Explain Freud's concept of repression. What are some of its consequences for individuals and societies?
8. How does Nancy Chodorow modify Freud's views on gender?
9. Why is the *Butler* Supreme Court decision a landmark case?
10. What is the significance of the legal recognition of same-sex spousal relationships?

GLOSSARY

death drive In Freud's thought, people's tendency to repeat early traumas and to seek out situations that are destructive to themselves or to others.

Eros Also known as the *pleasure principle:* according to Freud, a fundamental human drive (in his early writings, he saw it as the only instinctive drive).

gender Social role ascribed on the basis of biological sex: males are socialized to become masculine, whereas females are expected to become feminine. Gender roles differ among cultures, but are justified by reference to human biology and nature throughout the world.

heterosexism Institutions and values that promote the heterosexual couple as a superior sexual choice, one that is somehow more natural than any other.

naturalization The process by which a culturally determined phenomenon, such as sexuality, comes to be experienced as natural.

repression In Freud's thought, the process by which the conscious mind censors out unacceptable wishes and memories, which, rather than disappearing, become unconscious.

unconscious According to Freud, everything that is repressed and hence unavailable to the conscious mind. Unconscious wishes nevertheless continue to exercise influence over one's life, as evidenced, for example, in dreams and slips of the tongue.

SUGGESTED READING

Duggan, Lisa, and Nan Hunter (1995). *Sex Wars: Sexual Dissent and Political Culture.* New York: Routledge. This American collection critically examines recent judicial decisions infringing on sexual freedom, particularly in the areas of obscenity and gay rights.

Freud, Sigmund. (1973 [1915–17]). *Introductory Lectures on Psychoanalysis.* Trans. James Strachey; ed. James Strachey and Angela Richards. Vol. 1 of the Pelican Freud Library. Harmondsworth, UK: Penguin Books. There are many possible starting points for the study of psychoanalysis, but Freud's own writing is quite accessible, and the *Introductory Lectures* are perhaps the best place to start.

Gay, Peter, ed. (1989). *The Freud Reader.* New York: Norton. A useful collection of Freud's essays, providing a good introduction to psychoanalytic theory.

Snitow, Ann, Christine Stansell, and Sharon Thomson, eds. (1983). *Powers of Desire: The Politics of Sexuality.* New York: Monthly Review. An excellent anthology of articles by key scholars in the field of the sociology of sexuality.

Valverde, Mariana. (1985). *Sex, Power and Pleasure.* Toronto: Women's Press. An accessible Canadian overview of feminist views of sexuality.

Weeks, Jeffrey. (1986). *Sexuality.* London: Tavistock. An excellent short textbook on the sociology of sexuality.

CHAPTER FIVE
The Mass Media

IN THIS CHAPTER YOU WILL LEARN THAT

- the mass media may be examined in terms of their economic and political organization, the way they represent ideas, and their effects

- newspapers are local monopolies with high levels of ownership concentration; dependency on advertising has an enormous impact on news content because it limits the survival prospects of newspapers with a politically radical view of the news

- in the case of television, advertising dependency has discouraged the production of English-Canadian entertainment programming, particularly drama, because American shows are cheaper and more popular; while some analysts view this as a "sellout" of Canadian culture, others regard it as an effect of globalization and argue that it does not undermine the institutional structure of society

- some analysts claim that news coverage has a left-liberal political bias that is unrepresentative of the mainstream of society, while other analysts argue that news coverage is ideologically conservative in that it defines reality from the point of view of the most powerful groups in society (the wealthy, men, whites, and so forth) and views issues and events as problems demanding the control of subordinate groups (the less well-to-do, women, nonwhites, and so forth)

- the major effect of the news media is through agenda-setting: the media shape the way in which issues and events are perceived and evaluated as priorities

- many analysts believe that there is a causal link between television violence and violent behaviour, but studies that demonstrate this alleged connection have been criticized on the grounds of flawed methodology; and among those who believe that television violence causes aggressive behaviour, there is disagreement about how it does so, with some researchers arguing that television viewing counteracts socialization by weakening self-control and others arguing that television socializes children into how and when to use violence

- studies on the viewing habits of TV audiences indicate that women and men not only prefer different types of programs, but also watch TV in different ways: men tend to use TV in a more planned way than women, and watch more intently, whereas women are more likely to use TV as a focus for social interaction

GRAHAM KNIGHT
McMaster University

■ INTRODUCTION

By the early 1990s, the average Canadian spent almost 19 hours a week listening to radio and 23 hours a week watching TV, for a total of nearly 42 hours a week (Statistics Canada, 1990; 1994). Although radio listening had remained relatively stable, TV viewing had actually declined slightly from a peak of 24.3 hours a week in 1984 to 22.8 hours in 1993. Viewing varied, moreover, by age and sex. Women tended to watch more than men, and seniors more than the middle-aged, adolescents, or children. Women over 60 spent the most time watching TV, logging almost twice as many hours each week than adolescents or children (Statistics Canada, 1994: 21). This may come as something of a surprise, since we tend to associate too much TV viewing and its effects with young boys, not elderly women.

Add to this 42 hours a week spent listening to radio and watching TV the amount of time people also spend reading newspapers or magazines, and it becomes clear that most of us spend more time interacting with the mass media than doing anything else, including working. The term *mass media* itself is an abbreviation of "mass communications media," and it is increasingly being abbreviated even further, to "the media." All three words derive from Latin. **Mass** originally meant a large, shapeless piece of matter, like a lump of dough for making bread (R. Williams, 1976). Applied to people, the term *mass* has retained the sense of a large grouping that lacks any distinct characteristics or relationships, and whose members are anonymous and transient. The term **media** is the plural of "medium," or middle — hence, the idea of media as the means or the channels connecting two or more points. Finally, **communication** means to bring together or unify by establishing shared meanings and understandings among groups and individuals. This occurs through the transmission of information, knowledge, or beliefs by means of language, visual images, and other sign systems such as music.

Throughout this chapter, the terms *media* and *mass media* will be used to refer to television, radio, movies, newspapers, and magazines, which meet the two criteria for defining mass communications. The first is that communication goes from an identifiable point, such as a radio station, to an anonymous and rather nebulous body of people whose only relationship with one another is that they happen to be listening to the same station at the same time. The second criterion is that mass communication is largely one-way; there is little or no exchange of roles between sender and receiver. In both respects, mass communication differs from telecommunications, of which the telephone is an example, wherein communication occurs between one identifiable point and another and involves a two-way flow of messages.

The growing prominence of the mass media raises the issue of their role in modern society. The questions that first come to mind are: How do the media affect us? What impact and influence do they have, particularly in ways of which we are unaware? At the same time, we must also pose the opposite questions, in order to gain a balanced understanding of the media's role: How does society influence the media? What do the media tell us about the wider society? This chapter will address these two sets of questions by examining three aspects of media sociology: political economy, representation and ideology, and effects of the media. Each aspect represents a stage of mass communication: the organization of media production, the message as a cultural and ideological product, and the reception of the message by the audience. For each aspect, we will look at both the news media and television entertainment.

First, however, let us consider some of the theoretical foundations of media analysis. Theories of the social role of the media fall into two broad types, functionalist and critical. Both work primarily at the macrosociological level of analysis — that is, they focus on large-scale, institutional social processes — but they differ sharply in the nature of their analysis and in their interpretation of how the media function.

▲ THE FUNCTIONALIST PERSPECTIVE

The **functionalist perspective** analyzes social institutions in terms of their contribution to the integration and maintenance of society as a whole. Following Wright (1975), we can identify four major ways in which the media do this. First, the media help to *correlate* or co-ordinate the various parts of the social system by gathering and disseminating valuable information. In modernized societies, the growth of social differentiation poses crucial problems for integration as roles and institutions become more specialized, and the increasing scale of social life makes direct, face-to-face social interaction less and less viable as the central means of communication.

Second, the media act as powerful agents of *socialization* by transmitting society's cultural heritage and its basic system of norms and values. Notwithstanding general concerns about the effects of media violence, media messages are chiefly about reinforcing shared ideals such as justice, individualism, democracy, and respect for the law. On a more practical level, this socializing role, particularly that of TV, has become more extensive as the medium dispenses advice — "tele-advising" — on everything from talk shows to sitcoms about how to cope, adapt, and flourish in a complex world (White, 1992).

Closely related to the media's socializing effect is their third function, that of *social control*. By gathering information, the media engage in surveillance of the social environment. This is undertaken primarily within the frame of reference of society's central norms and values. The attention the media pay to crime, for example, reflects the way they uphold and reproduce moral order by exposing deviants, providing role models, and displaying the forces of law and order at work in maintaining social stability.

Finally, the media also provide pleasure and *entertainment*. As societies become more differentiated and complex, strains and conflicts arise. In this respect, the media function as part of society's "tension-management" process that enables the release of emotional tensions and stress in a manner that does not jeopardize social integration.

▲ THE TECHNOLOGICAL PERSPECTIVE

The technological perspective derives primarily from the work of two Canadian scholars, Harold Innis and Marshall McLuhan. From his survey of the history of human communication, Innis (1951) made the distinction between time-biased and space-biased media. **Time-biased media** are modes of communication that endure over time but that are not very mobile across space, such as writing on stone or clay tablets. **Space-biased media,** in contrast, can cover much greater areas of space but are much less durable over time — for example, writing on paper or sounds transmitted over the airwaves.

The two types of media foster different arrangements of institutions and cultural values. Time-biased media, for example, are conducive to a strong sense of tradition and custom, and these promote religious forms of power and belief. Space-biased media, in contrast, lead to territorial expansion, empire building, and more secular forms of power and

culture, as manifested in the dominance of military institutions and the growth of the state. These different forms of power, in turn, create different types of social division and conflict. The elite that controls the means of communication tries to use it to preserve its own privilege and interests. Those excluded from power struggle against elite control, and in the process stimulate the development of new, alternative forms of communication. Historically, such a struggle over the means of communication resulted in the shift from time- to space-biased media.

McLuhan (1964; 1969) was influenced by Innis's ideas about the effect of communication on institutions and culture and how this effect changes over time. He argued, however, that the relationship was mediated by the way that forms of communication change our sense perceptions and cognitive processes. The invention of printing, for example, undermined oral communication and its emphasis on hearing, and ushered in a more visually oriented culture. Because print consists of visually separated words strung together in a linear sequence, it encourages us to see the world around us as composed of separate objects, and to interpret that world in a linear, cause-and-effect way. Print removes — it literally abstracts — communication from face-to-face interaction, and so it makes information more abstract. This abstracting effect of print, in turn, fosters individualism and privacy, rationality and social differentiation. Historically, these further effects of print coincided with the rise of nationalism and the weakening of social ties. Print then served to standardize the national language and became a principal mechanism of social identity.

For McLuhan, the spread of electronic media, particularly TV, is spelling an end to the era of print dominance. The impact of TV is crucial for two reasons. First, unlike print, TV does not rely exclusively on one sense (ie., sight) — it integrates sight and sound and achieves a better *sensory balance*. In fact, for McLuhan, the effect of this balance is to make TV a kind of tactile medium in the sense that it "touches" its audience more easily than print. Second, TV allows communication to be *instantaneous* — there is no significant delay between transmission and reception of the message. These differences make TV more socially inclusive than print. This observation has led some of McLuhan's adherents to claim that TV is also more accessible and less hierarchical than print in its effects (Znaimer, 1996).

A similar implication can be found in the work of Meyrowitz (1985). Meyrowitz has applied McLuhan's views about the sensory and social effects of different media to Erving Goffman's (1959) ideas about the organization of social space, especially the ability of social groups to maintain a strict boundary between *front-stage* behaviour, which is publicly visible, and *back-stage* behaviour, which is private behaviour that is visible only to group members. Enforcing this distinction is crucial to a group's identity, solidarity, and power, but it depends, Meyrowitz argues, on the control of information — that is, on communication.

Electronic media such as TV can intrude more easily on the distinction between the two stages, blurring them to a greater extent than can single-sense media like print. This blurring allows outsiders to see back-stage behaviour — the private lives, personalities, and past histories of group members. On the one hand, this feature of electronic media can be exploited to intensify social control, as when surveillance cameras are used to police those who are considered deviant. On the other hand, social status and authority can be demystified when media allow us to glimpse the private side of those with power. Electronic media can thereby enable people to make interpretations of social reality that are not officially sanctioned or intended.

McLuhan's views, however, have proved to be controversial, not least because he tended to see media technologies as something of an autonomous force outside of social control and direction. He has been dismissed as a *technological determinist,* particularly by those who subscribe to the critical perspective.

▲ THE CRITICAL PERSPECTIVE

According to the **critical perspective,** institutions such as the media, and processes such as socialization and social control, cannot be understood from the viewpoint of society as a whole, but only from that of unequal and conflicting groups and classes. In fact, there are really two variants of the critical perspective: one that emphasizes the relationship between media and inequality, and one that emphasizes the relationship between media and social conflict.

The first variant of the critical perspective is derived from the orthodox interpretation of Marxism. In this perspective, the role of the media is defined in terms of how the media serve the economic interests and political power of the dominant class, those who own and control the means of material production. To maintain and consolidate its power and interests, the dominant class also exercises control over the means of cultural and moral production — that is, the production of the ideas, beliefs, values, and norms that constitute a society's **dom-inant ideology**. The media, by disseminating this dominant ideology, create acceptance and legitimization of the status quo. This view originates in the ideas of Max Horkheimer and Theodor Adorno (1982 [1947]), who saw the media as part of a broader "culture industry" that involves commodity production, profit making, and capital accumulation in its own right. (In fact, according to Smythe (1981), the audience itself, as potential consumers, is turned into a commodity that the media sell to advertisers.) But the culture industry also creates a kind of "mass deception" that distracts people and prevents them from recognizing the truly exploitive and oppressive character of capitalism. The masses are manipulated and pacified by standardized, uniform messages that do not admit alternative ways of thinking.

The second variant of the critical perspective also acknowledges that the capitalist class and other powerful groups use dominant ideology to reinforce their position and maintain the status quo. They do this through **hegemony** — the use of the media and other cultural institutions to represent the interests, values, and understandings of the capitalist class and other powerful groups as natural and universal. But dominant ideology is not the only ideology. Inequality also engenders resistance and struggle, which result in other, more critical perspectives from which social reality and the dominant ideology can be interpreted. A distinction should be made here between **alternative** and **oppositional viewpoints**. Oppositional viewpoints represent the experiences of subordinated groups against those of the powerful; alternative viewpoints occupy an intermediate position, reflecting compromise or "negotiated" understandings, which blend elements of the dominant and oppositional viewpoints (Hall, 1980). Although the media usually promote understandings that conform with dominant ideology, their messages are always at least partially open to the challenge of alternative and oppositional interpretations. To be successful, hegemony has to be flexible enough to accommodate and incorporate a range of different viewpoints.

■ POLITICAL ECONOMY OF THE MEDIA

For sociologists, the contribution of the discipline of political economy stems from its focus on the ownership and control of economic resources, and on the effect of technology and economic power on cultural values and social structure. Media are organizations that usually are owned and controlled by large corporations or the state, and that function like other bureaucracies. They have to sustain themselves economically through commercial revenue, government funding, subscriber fees, and donations, or some mixture of these. What, then, are the primary goals of media organizations — to inform and entertain, or to capture market share and make money? And in whose interests do they operate — those of owners, advertisers, or audiences? These questions are especially pertinent in democratic societies, where values such as freedom and diversity of opinion and the promotion of both minority and national cultural identities are strong.

Ownership and control of the media are generally becoming more concentrated into a smaller number of larger corporate hands. This trend is part of the wider process of economic globalization, and it is leading to the creation of large **multimedia chains**. These are corporations that own a diversified array of media operations and outlets in different fields, such as radio, TV, and publishing. The world's largest multimedia chain is Time Warner Inc., which has just added considerably to its size, scope, and power by taking over the Turner Broadcasting System. With this acquisition, Time Warner now has annual revenue of U.S.$18.7 billion from, among other things, magazine and book publishing, television production and distribution, cable systems, popular music, and sports teams (see Box 5.1) (Variety, 1995: 28).

To secure and enhance their market position, multimedia chains practise both horizontal consolidation and vertical integration. **Horizontal consolidation** is the sharing of facilities and resources between different plants and outlets; **vertical integration** is the controlling of resources and assets at the different stages of production, such as ownership of a major league sports team along with the stations and cable channels over which the games are televised.

Despite the trend toward growing concentration, there are variations among different media fields in both the extent and the social and cultural effects of media ownership and control. Some of these variations can be seen in a comparison of newspapers and television.

▲ NEWSPAPERS: CONCENTRATION, MONOPOLY, AND ADVERTISING

In Canada, the ownership and control of daily newspapers are now the most highly concentrated of all media fields. One corporation, Hollinger Inc., is now in a position of undisputed dominance, controlling 58 of the 104 dailies in the country, or 43 percent of total circulation. These include some major urban papers such as the Montreal *Gazette, The Ottawa Citizen,* and *The Edmonton Journal.* In addition to its Canadian papers, Hollinger also controls major papers in Britain, the United States, and Israel. As a result, Hollinger now claims to be the third-largest newspaper chain in the Western world (*Maclean's,* Nov. 11, 1996: 57).

By 1987, newspaper chains accounted for slightly more than 80 percent of all daily circulation in Canada. This situation stands in marked contrast to that which prevailed until the late nineteenth century, when chain ownership took root. Until then, newspapers were usually owned and operated on an independent, local basis. They were enterprises on a far smaller scale, with small circulations. Each paper catered primarily to a particular group or class of readers, rather than to a mass audience. Small circulations meant that the economic situation of many papers was precarious. Among newspapers, as among small businesses generally, rates of birth and death were high. And in many, if not most, cases, the point of running a newspaper was not to make money but to promote a particular ideology or cause (Rutherford, 1982).

Chain ownership altered this picture in a radical way, although even today some CEOs, such as Hollinger's Conrad Black, resemble the earlier newspaper proprietors in being outspoken and controversial public figures. Newspapers are now operated primarily as profit-driven business enterprises, a fact that relates to two other developments. First, newspapers have become increasingly dependent on advertising rather than subscription fees for their revenue. By 1980, 80 percent of the revenue of the average Canadian daily came from advertising. Second, both the scale and the cost of production have grown as owners try to expand circulation to attract more advertising. The increased cost of doing business has helped drive less-efficient newspapers out of business, resulting in the demise of competition and the emergence of local press monopolies. Even where more than one newspaper serves a local market, as in large metropolitan areas such as Toronto, papers have to specialize and serve particular market segments in order to survive.

The critical perspective views chain ownership, monopoly, and advertising dependency as being associated with the homogenization of news coverage and the decline of diversity in news topics and viewpoints. However, the evidence supporting that link is not conclusive. Studies of the 1980 closure of com-

Box 5.1
The Number One Global Media Corporation

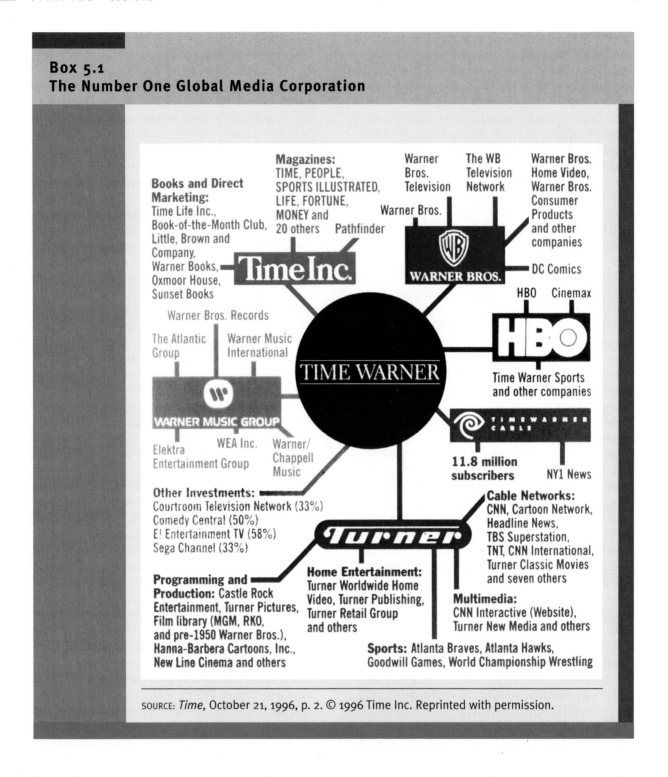

SOURCE: *Time*, October 21, 1996, p. 2. © 1996 Time Inc. Reprinted with permission.

peting papers in Winnipeg and Ottawa argue that, after monopolization, the amount of space devoted to the news declined, the number of national and international stories decreased, news stories became shorter, and local government coverage shifted in emphasis toward stories with higher-profile sources (Trim, Pizante, and Yaraskavitch, 1983; Candussi

and Winters, 1988). In contrast, McCoombs (1988: 136), in a comparison of Winnipeg and Montreal, claims that monopolization brought about no significant change. If anything, he argues, the quality of the news coverage actually improved somewhat after the closure of competing papers. Similarly, a U.S. study of the effects of chain ownership found that there was no significant change in the structure and quality of the editorial pages of papers that had previously been independently owned (Hale, 1988).

The adverse effects of advertising dependency in limiting the diversity of perspectives and voices in the news is easier to substantiate. Advertising dependency forces owners to maximize readership in order to attract advertisers. Particularly in the case of monopoly papers, this means appealing to as broad a cross-section of the market as possible. To do this, newspapers tend to orient their content to the "lowest common denominator" by avoiding topics and viewpoints thought to be either too radical or too offensive for the mainstream reader, or of interest only to minority tastes and perspectives.

The effects of advertising dependency are quite specific and direct. First and foremost, papers avoid ignoring or offending the interests of the advertisers themselves. In the 1970s, two attempts to establish newspapers in Quebec failed because advertisers found the papers' political orientations threatening. *Québec-Presse* (1969–74), a weekly paper established as a co-operative with representatives from the union movement and other activist groups, adopted an explicitly left-wing, Quebec-nationalist orientation. *Le Jour* (1974–76), a daily paper born out of the Parti Québécois's defeat in the 1973 Quebec election, also sought to bring a social-democratic and overtly sovereignist perspective to the news (Raboy, 1984). Although both papers succeeded in achieving reasonable circulation levels (about 30 000 copies) neither was able to overcome persistent financial difficulties caused by the lack of advertising from private businesses and government. *Le Jour*'s main rival, *Le Devoir*, at that time a pro-federalist paper, had about the same circulation as *Le Jour*, but three times the advertising revenue. This imbalance was attributable in part to the government's decision not to advertise in *Le Jour* because of its separatist affiliation (Raboy, 1984: 112).

▲ TELEVISION: ECONOMY, CULTURE, AND IDENTITY

Dating back to the Royal Commission on Radio Broadcasting (the Aird commission) of 1928–29, the development of broadcasting in Canada can be interpreted from the perspective of the role that first radio and then television have played vis-à-vis Canadian culture and national identity, and the threats to them. The main external threat to Canadian culture and identity has come from the prox-

imity and power of the U.S. media; the main internal threat has come from the persistent cultural, linguistic, and political differences between Quebec and the rest of Canada. The Aird commission saw broadcasting as having the potential to counter these threats, but only if it was developed as a "public service" devoted to the public interest rather than to private commercial gain (Raboy, 1990).

The Aird commission recommended that all broadcasting be controlled by a unified public monopoly that would be funded by Parliament but that would operate at arm's length from the government, in order to preserve its autonomy. Although this recommendation resulted in the eventual formation of the Canadian Broadcasting Corporation (CBC) and its French-language counterpart, Le Société Radio-Canada (SRC), private broadcasters remained in operation, and today they constitute the dominant sector by far of both the radio and television industries in Canada. In fact, CBC television itself has always been partly commercialized, because it has had to rely for part of its income (currently about 25 percent) on advertising.

For television, as for newspapers, commercialization and advertising dependency have had the greatest impact on the content and role of the medium. Private television is driven by the profit motive rather than by cultural goals such as the promotion of Canadian content and national identity. Income and profits come largely from advertising, which means that TV has to cater to large audiences. To attract audiences and advertisers, private Canadian broadcasters have often relied on imported, mainly U.S., programming. Even though the cost of licensing U.S. programming has been increasing, it is still less than the cost of producing comparable Canadian programming. The CTV network, for example, claims that, for every hour of Canadian-made entertainment programming it broadcasts, it loses $5 million from its profit margin (Canada, 1991: 39).

This issue of Canadian content pertains largely to entertainment programming, particularly English-language drama. Audiences have long shown a strong preference for U.S. dramatic programming and, as a result, the audience for domestic programs is not large enough in economic terms to make Canadian drama an attractive proposition, particularly for private broadcasters. Reaction to this situation is split. On the one side are nationalists, who argue that broadcasting should be an instrument of Canadian culture and identity, meaning that it should actively promote Canadian content (Collins, 1990; Hardin, 1985; Canada, 1986). The nationalists single out drama because of its popularity and because of its capacity to promote and reinforce the cultural myths and values that solidify a distinct national identity. Indeed, in this respect, the Canadian television drama that has been produced to date is considered to be significantly different from U.S. drama, in that it is more realistic and its narratives are more ironic and more morally ambivalent (Miller, 1987; Wolfe, 1985).

Support for the argument about the relationship between television drama and cultural identity can be found in the case of Quebec, where there is a stronger commitment to francophone drama and other entertainment programming on the part of both public and private television (Canada, 1991: 113–17). This commitment is matched by stronger audience interest and the strengthening of national and cultural identity on the part of francophone Quebeckers. In 1993–94, only 7.6 percent of programming available on the SRC was Canadian-made drama, but this accounted for 16.5 percent of total viewing time (Canada, 1996: 64, 66). Between 1985–86 and 1993–94, viewing time for Canadian programs on the CBC, the main source of Canadian programming, rose by about 4 percentage points, whereas on the SRC it rose by over 8 percentage points (see Table 5.1).

The dearth of English-Canadian drama and other entertainment programming has a long history. The federal government has made some attempts to redress the imbalance, establishing content requirements and offering inducements such as production subsidies to try to ensure more Canadian content. As we can see from Table 5.1, these efforts have had only a limited effect, at least for the CBC's English-language audience. The number of hours spent watching Canadian drama increased from 4.4 percent of the total in 1985–86 to 6.9 percent in 1993–94, staying roughly in proportion to the amount scheduled. Canadian drama remains one of the least watched and least scheduled forms of CBC programming. The decline in the proportion of foreign-program viewing, moreover, can be attributed to the huge increase in the amount of sports watched on the CBC. This increase also came at the expense of a drop in news and current-affairs viewing.

The dominance of the U.S. television industry is a global phenomenon, and Canada simply represents a more extreme example of subjection to what has been called **media imperialism,** a situation in which one society's media exert an overwhelming and unilateral influence over another's culture (Boyd-Barrett, 1977). Proponents of the theory of media imperialism argue that international traffic in cultural products such as television programs is very one-sided, with the influence coming from a handful of economically developed, Western societies that export cultural products but do not import them. This characterization is particularly true of the United States. In 1983, only 2 percent of the programming available in the United States was imported, a figure that had remained unchanged from a decade earlier (Varis, 1984). The United States is the world's biggest exporter of television programming, and its smallest importer.

The view that Canadian culture and identity are threatened or undermined by the consumption of U.S. television programs has not gone unchallenged. According to Collins (1990: xii), Canada is becom-

◆ **Table 5.1** Viewing By Program Type, 1985–1986 and 1993–1994 (CBC/SRC-Owned and -Operated Stations Only)

	CBC TV (English)		SRC TV (French)	
	1985–86	1993–94	1985–86	1993–94
Canadian programming	**66.0%**	**70.2%**	**75.5%**	**84.0%**
News	18.7	17.7	10.0	16.1
Public affairs	15.1	10.4	11.2	14.0
Sports	16.9	26.6	15.4	12.8
Drama	4.4	6.9	16.4	16.5
Variety	7.7	4.8	18.1	20.6
Other	3.2	3.8	4.4	4.0
Foreign programming	**34.0**	**29.8**	**24.5**	**16.0**

SOURCE: Compiled from Canada, *Making Our Voices Heard: Canadian Broadcasting and Film for the 21st Century* (Ottawa: Supply and Services Canada, 1996), p. 66, Graph 2. Used with the permission of the Minister of Public Works and Government Services Canada, 1997.

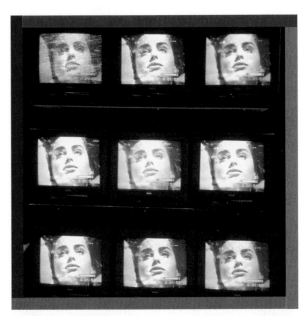

The dominance of the U.S. television industry is a global phenomenon, and Canada represents an extreme example of subjection to what has been called media imperialism. SOURCE: Dick Hemingway.

ing a "postnational" society. This is a condition that is becoming increasingly common among Western societies generally, as the association of the nation-state with particular economic, political, and cultural institutions breaks down under the effect of globalization. Canada is a pluralistic society linguistically, ethnically, and subculturally, so it may not have a strong symbolic culture in the sense of a single, unified system of symbols, representations, and identities. It does, nevertheless, have a strong culture in the anthropological sense of shared institutions and practices (Collins, 1990: 35). And this culture, Collins argues, is undiminished by the preference of English Canadians for U.S. cop shows and sitcoms.

Collins's argument reminds one of the current theory that developed, Western societies are becoming "postmodern." In this view, as the social structure becomes increasingly differentiated, social roles, identities, and experiences become increasingly fragmented and dissociated from one another. Postmodernists believe that **fragmentation** allows groups and individuals greater scope to play with and reconstruct their identities and understandings. It can foster new forms of consciousness, particularly in terms of the popular culture — music, fashion, lifestyle — that is associated with the mass media (Fiske, 1987).

Fragmentation is also occurring at the level of political economy, with the proliferation of new television services such as cable specialty channels, "superstations," pay-per-view channels, and home-

shopping channels, in addition to more conventional broadcast TV stations and networks (Ellis, 1992). As television becomes more differentiated, audiences become more fragmented, a process that is captured by the term *narrowcasting* (as opposed to broadcasting). With this development, the role of TV as an agent of common culture is being questioned.

Concomitant with audience fragmentation, a contrary process, **technological convergence,** is also at work. The term refers to the merging and integration of previously separate communications technologies, such as telephony, computers, television, and radio (Ellis, 1992). Hints of the imminence of this process were perhaps present in the very notion of "home entertainment," which is now being transformed to include a whole array of social activities such as shopping, banking, and even working ("telecommuting") at home. The implication is that everyday life will become privatized in the household as people find they have less and less need for face-to-face interaction with others. Some evidence to support such a trend can be found in a study of the consequences of the introduction of television reception to a community in British Columbia (T.M. Williams, 1986). The researchers found that the introduction of TV led to the **displacement** of other activities, such as participation in the community's social and recreational life, as people stayed at home more to watch television.

■ REPRESENTATION AND IDEOLOGY: THE MEANING OF THE MESSAGE

Analysis of the media from the perspective of political economy alone is ultimately limited, because it takes for granted the nature of the messages that the media communicate. The emphasis here is on the plural — *messages*. The media communicate on different levels — the pleasurable as well as the meaningful, the entertaining as well as the informative. Such communication entails the process of representation — that is, the use of language, visual images, and other symbolic tools to create messages that people can understand and find satisfying or enjoyable. Representation, however, is a selective process. It involves countless decisions — only some of which are conscious — about what is to be included and what is to be left out, what is to be emphasized and what is to be downplayed, and about the sequence in which the elements are to be connected into a coherent message. Any representation — a news report, an advertisement, a TV show — is ideological to the extent that it contains any particular inflection or bias. Every representation is only one of several ways of seeing and talking about something.

▲ NEWS AND IDEOLOGY

Outside our immediate experience, the news media are one of our principal sources of information about social reality. Conservative and critical writers have disagreed considerably about the nature of selectivity in the news, and its ideological effects. Conservatives argue that the news media have a "left-liberal" bias that runs counter to the views and interests of the mainstream of society. They believe that this bias operates in two ways: (1) the media give greater or more favourable attention to the views of more marginal and/or radical interest groups and constituencies — for example, unions, environmentalists, and, in the case of foreign news, left-wing regimes or political movements (Cooper, 1994); and (2) the media concentrate on negative events, issues, and news angles, ignoring the positive aspects of social life (see Box 5.2).

The conservative perspective is evident in the work of the National Media Archive (NMA). In its analysis of immigration coverage, for example, the NMA found that both CBC and CTV, "rather than reporting the successes . . . focussed on the negative experiences of refugees and immigrants in Canada" (National Media Archive, 1993: 3). CBC reporters, in particular, have been identified as guilty of unbalanced coverage: "CBC journalists were more than twice as likely to express negative as positive views on privatization, free trade, the management position in labour disputes, and private delivery of health-care services" (National Media Archive, 1989: 7). Although NMA research does not systematically examine the origins of these biases, its analyses imply that they stem primarily from the individual biases of reporters, editors, and other news staff.

In contrast to the conservative perspective, those who employ a critical perspective believe that the news media function chiefly to reproduce dominant ideology. This is not seen as a conscious conspiracy, but as the unconscious effect of the values and practices that journalists employ when they define and gather news. Let us consider the critical perspective in greater detail.

Defining the News

What is news? In the first place, it is a representation of reality, which, like all representations, is un-avoidably selective. We must therefore ask what criteria, or **news values,** that the media use to select what goes in the newspaper or on the newscast. There are three major criteria: immediacy, personalization, and extraordinariness.

IMMEDIACY By definition, news is about what is new or immediate. Although the media are often unable to capture events as they actually happen, the accent is on reporting them as quickly as possible after they occur. Immediacy has always been a major element in the competition among different media, and the history of media technology is dominated by the goal of making communication faster. Whenever possible, news is written in the present tense, to convey the sense that events are still ongoing.

The emphasis on immediacy, however, goes beyond the present to the future. To generate interest and curiosity on the part of the audience, news stories often create some sense of uncertainty about what will happen next. The effect of this approach is that news tends to be concerned with the consequences of events and issues at the expense of their causes and development (Knight, 1982b). Causes belong in the past, and news generally lacks a strong sense of historical perspective and context.

PERSONALIZATION When news does deal with causes and explanations, it often reduces them to the level of individual motives and psychology. This is an effect of personalization. To communicate with an anonymous audience, news has to enable the reader or viewer to identify with news events that are often remote from everyday experience by making them more concrete and familiar. This emphasis on personalities has been intensified by the growth of TV news, where the need to be visual makes it more difficult to deal in abstractions, such as unemployment, and easier to deal with people, such as the unemployed. Personalization is especially strong in political news coverage, as the media focus on party leaders and other prominent politicians and their respective popularity in the opinion polls. Critics often charge that this approach detracts from a fuller understanding of the political system and the more substantive aspects of political policy (Taras, 1990).

EXTRAORDINARINESS Above all else, news concerns events and issues that are *out of the ordinary*, and that entail *conflict, confrontation, deviance,* or *disorder* (Hall et al., 1978; Knight, 1982a). The implication of this, as conservative critics also point out, is that news is usually about the *negative*. For critical theorists, however, the negative emphasis of news does not un-

Box 5.2
The Conservative Critique: Is News too Negative?

Anybody scanning the news would be hard pressed to avoid concluding that the Canadian economy is dog-paddling into a sludge of slow growth and perpetual joblessness. *Maclean's* magazine set the national tone with a cover headline six centimetres high that said: "1,550,000 UNEMPLOYED: Will they find work in the '90s?"

The same headline, of course, could have been written ten years ago. In fact, if often was. In early 1983, the total number of unemployed in Canada reached 1,512,000, generating a stream of stories about how the unemployment rate will remain high for years to come. Where on earth, everybody asked them as they do now, will the jobs come from?

Other themes from a decade ago: The unemployment rate didn't really capture the true level of unemployment because it didn't include all the discouraged workers who simply gave up looking. Youth unemployment remained disturbingly high and job prospects looked impossible. Most jobs, moreover, were part-time rather than full-time.

That was 1983, when unemployment peaked at 12.8 percent and the headline was: Will they find work in the 1980s? In the following years, of course, the number of jobs created soared, contrary to the worst expectations. They *did* find work.

As the graph shows, the number of jobs—employed people—rose to more than 12.5 million from 10.5 million in 1983. Two million jobs created during the period drove the unemployment rate down to 7.5 percent.

Despite all the turmoil of the past two years, including the rise in the unemployment rate to a high of 11.6 percent, the number of people employed has remained well above 12 million. In recent months, it has been climbing, reaching 12,431,000 in June, about 200,000 more jobs than existed in June last year.

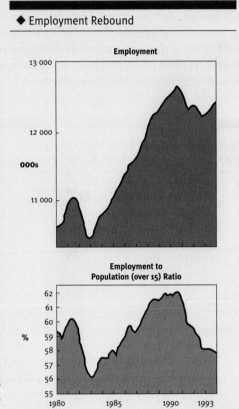

◆ Employment Rebound

Employment

SOURCE: Data from Statistics Canada.

SOURCE: Terence Corcoran, "12,431,000 Employed—And Climbing!" *The Globe and Mail*, July 30, 1993, p. B2. Reprinted with permission of *The Globe and Mail*.

dermine mainstream values and beliefs, but in fact reinforces dominant ideology in at least two ways.

First, by dwelling on the negative, news invokes and reproduces dominant definitions of what is socially normal and desirable. It identifies events and actors that deviate from these definitions, and represents them as a threat to what is socially desirable (Knight, 1982a). News media do not work in a vacuum, inventing the reality they represent out of thin air. Rather, they take up the dominant values, assumptions, and understandings of the society in which they are themselves embedded. The raw materials of news are already given in the preoccupations and concerns of the wider social context. These preoccupations and concerns, however, are themselves the result of an ongoing selection process that values the experiences and viewpoints of dominant groups over those of others. The events and issues that make it into the news are already defined in negative terms — as dangerous, sickening, bizarre, threatening, and so on — by the dominant culture (see Figure 5.1).

By assuming that the dominant culture generally reflects the interests, values, and understandings of society as a whole, the news media tend to reproduce a tacit consensus about what is right and wrong, normal and deviant, desirable and undesirable. One effect of this is to exclude or downplay oppositional and alternative perspectives by associating them with deviant or marginal behaviour. In his study of press coverage of the peace movement in Canada during the 1980s, for example, Hackett (1991) shows how the orientation to "bad" news helped stigmatize peace activists by focussing on the visibly more disruptive aspects of their actions, such as street demonstrations, at the expense of their arguments about the need for arms control and disarmament.

Second, news coverage of deviance and conflict tends to focus on the actions of the appropriate social-control authorities — the government, the police, the experts — to restore social order and limit disruptive effects. Newsworthy events and issues come to the attention of the media because the media rely on organized ways of knowing about the activities of official control agencies and organizations, including news releases, tip-offs from inside contracts, and routine monitoring of the radio communications of the police and other emergency services. Because they exercise official authority, these agencies are seen as the major source of credible and reliable information about what has happened, how it has happened, who is involved, and what the immediate consequences seem to be.

Crime news, for example, consists largely of information derived from the police about incidents of lawbreaking. This information deals primarily with police activities and procedures such as investigation, interrogation of witnesses and suspects, and the charging of the accused (Ericson, Baranek, and Chan, 1989). The ideological effect is that the media view crime from the perspective of the police and police procedures. Consequently, deviance and disorder are represented in the news as discrete, isolated events, rather than as broader social processes that are part of the structure and functioning of society. Deviance and disorder are, moreover, portrayed after the fact, in terms of the process of social control and restoration of order by the authorities. In this way, the threat of bad news is offset by reassurance that things are being put right: News of crime is news of police activities to solve crime and catch offenders.

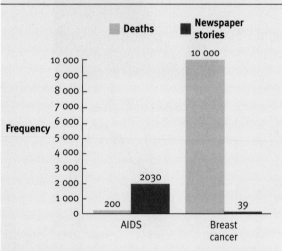

◆ **Figure 5.1** AIDS and Breast Cancer: Female Deaths and Press Coverage, Canada, 1990–1992

Note: The graph shows the number of stories about AIDS and breast cancer that appeared in the *Halifax Chronicle-Herald*, *Montreal Gazette*, *Toronto Star*, *Winnipeg Free Press*, *Edmonton Journal*, *Calgary Herald*, and *Vancouver Sun* from 1990 to 1992, as reported in the *Canadian News Index*; and the approximate number of female deaths from AIDS and breast cancer recorded in that period. AIDS is the single most popular medical story in the news, even though it accounts for far fewer deaths than other diseases. It is such a popular story because well-organized and relatively powerful groups have promoted it (the medical research establishment, gay groups) and because it is most prevalent among deviant (and therefore especially newsworthy) groups, such as prostitutes and gays.

SOURCE: Adapted from Chris McCormick, *Constructing Danger: The Mis/representation of Crime in the News* (Halifax: Fernwood, 1995), pp.104–105. Used with permission.

Gathering the News

News consists of information that has to be gathered from other sources, usually by means of interviewing. These sources include politicians, officials, spokespeople, experts, victims, and others involved in newsworthy issues and events. Ideological bias results from the media's reliance on certain sources of information and commentary over others. There is a hierarchy of access to and for the media, and this reflects the general distribution of power in society.

The media have easier access to certain sources, and certain sources have easier access to the media. For example, public representatives, such as elected politicians, have a much greater obligation to speak to the media than do private-sector officials, such as corporate executives, who can invoke the values of private property as a way to justify their own and their organizations' privacy. At the same time, because of their power and status, corporate officials can easily gain access to the news media when they choose to do so.

This hierarchy of access comprises two broad layers of news sources (Knight, 1988). The top layer consists of the most important sources, or **primary news sources**. These are usually official voices that provide what the media assume to be credible, authoritative information defining the basic contours of an event or issue. Primary sources usually represent the official viewpoint of dominant institutions, such as government, the police, the private sector of the economy, as well as major professions, such as law, medicine, and academe (Gans, 1979). At the same time, primary news sources are often presented as speaking on behalf of society in general.

When reporting on the economy, for example, the media often rely on the representatives of private business rather than organized labour as their source of information about what is really happening and why. Corporate spokespeople (including private-sector experts, such as professional economists) often speak on behalf of the economy as a whole, whereas labour spokespeople usually speak only on behalf of the interests of organized labour. The two sources are treated unequally: Even though both represent particular voices, the more powerful one is able to speak in general or universal terms. This means that the more powerful speak on behalf of the less powerful, as if there were no conflict of interest or of viewpoint involved. For example, in news coverage of Ontario's Bill 40, a 1993 law that outlawed the use of strikebreakers during legal strikes, the concerns of the strong and vocal business opposition to the legislation were represented in the news media largely in terms of lost jobs and harm to workers, rather than lost profits and harm to business (Knight and O'Connor, 1995; Knight, 1982b).

The bottom layer of sources consists of **secondary news sources,** mainly unofficial voices that provide reaction to news events and issues, usually in negative terms. This secondary reaction falls into two broad types. The first is reaction from ordinary people who are actual or potential victims, those directly afflicted, deprived, or harmed by an event or issue. The other type of secondary reaction comes from more organized sources, such as activist groups or social movements, that are usually opposed to government policies, but on general rather than particular grounds. Examples are the peace movement in the 1980s and the environmental movement in the 1990s. As Hackett (1991) shows, however, these groups often face the dilemma of attracting media attention in ways that associate their views with disruptive behaviour. An example of this is the coverage of the Toronto Days of Action Protest in 1996 against the policies of the Ontario government (see Table 5.2).

The news media usually represent both types of secondary sources as reacting to an event or an issue in emotional terms — anger, frustration, fear, or anxiety. Although these reactions tend to have negative implications, they are nonetheless structured within the definition of the situation established by the primary sources. In this respect, news imposes a division of labour on its two types of sources, a division that pits them against each other to some extent. Secondary sources are mainly heard to complain rather than analyze, to emphasize what is wrong rather than offer solutions, to express feelings rather than rational ideas, and to call on others, notably the government, to act rather than take the initiative themselves. The overall implication is that ordinary people are relatively powerless, passive, and socially dependent — but noisy nonetheless.

An example of this role of secondary sources can be seen in an article that appeared in *The Toronto Star* on November 1, 1996, about the reactions of nurses to government cutbacks in health care (see Box 5.3). The headline, which is the most important device that alerts the reader to the general tone or angle of a story (van Dijk, 1991), establishes the report's emotional, reactive focus through the use of the verbs "blast" and "hurts." This initial tone is reinforced throughout the first two-thirds of the story, which focusses on the Ontario Nurses' Association's claims about the harmful, victimizing effects of government policies. These claims are balanced by denials on the part of the minister of health, who is quoted as saying that the nurses' views about health-care reform are similar to the government's. Yet the report never explains what the nurses' views on this subject actually are, so the reader never has an opportunity to judge whether the nurses' view are, in fact, similar to the government's or whether they have merit. The nurses are simply assigned the role of complaining and grieving about the suffering that others are causing. As a source of reform proposals, they have been silenced.

◆ **Table 5.2 Toronto "Days of Action" Headlines: Disruption-Related Themes in *The Toronto Star*, 1996**

These headlines illustrate the way the media emphasize the disruptive or confrontational effects of news events rather than their causes or effects on social solidarity. They also highlight the way labour and other social movements are often portrayed as the source of social disruption and conflict.

Oct. 24: "Brace yourself for tough tomorrow," p. A1

Oct. 25: "Don't be intimidated by protesters: Harris," p. A1
"Ambulances, police go on high alert," p. A29 (continuation of previous report)
"No mail, trash but beer's on. TTC in doubt as protest affects many services," p. A1
"Days of Action hits many services," p. A29 (continuation of previous report)
"Parade, rallies expected to jam city tomorrow," p. A6

Oct. 26: "Day of Disruption," p. A1
"Day of frustration, frayed nerves," p. A18 (continuation of previous report)
"Shut out: Pickets block mayor from city hall," p. A26
"Protest a pain for many StarPhone callers," p. A26
"TTC workers didn't ask for help: Police. Chief says heavy police presence kept trouble to a minimum," p. A27
"Barely a blip. The labor protest pretty much failed to disrupt Bay Street. The TSE hummed along nicely," p. E1
"Protesters failed to tarnish Metro's image," p. E3
"Employers cope with disruptions," p. E1

SOURCE: *The Toronto Star*, October 24–26, 1996.

The news media do not take the perspectives of the powerful as representative of society as a whole in an absolute or monolithic way. Hegemony entails the need to appear objective, so the media sometimes allow dissenting voices to offer alternative or oppositional definitions of an event or issue that break with the dominant definition provided by primary sources. For example, media coverage of government deficits and debts has presented the issue overwhelmingly in terms of the need for governments to reduce their "spending," particularly on social programs. This perspective takes for granted that deficits are caused by an excess of government expenditure over government revenue. An alternative perspective, however, is that the problem lies not with government expenditure (which can be defined as a form of social investment), but with a tax system that brings in insufficient revenues because it unduly favours the wealthy, or with an interest and exchange rate policy that unnecessarily increases the cost of servicing government debt (McQuaig, 1995).

This alternative perspective has been absent from the media, with some exceptions (for example, Dobbin, 1993). From a critical perspective, these exceptions are an example of what Barthes calls **inoculation**. Inoculation refers to the small doses of alternative or radical points of view that

immunize the "collective imagination" and "protect it against the risk of a generalized subversion" (Barthes, 1973: 150). The composition and size of these doses are limited by the broader interests of dominant ideology (Fiske, 1987). When the media allow oppositional voices to speak, they often position them as secondary sources, and marginalize them as emotional and disruptive or incorporate them into the general consensus of dominant values and goals that the media reproduce: Who *does* want nuclear war, environmental disaster, or an unfair tax system?

Although critical theorists see the media as representative of dominant ideology, they also recognize that relations between journalists and their sources involve an ongoing struggle for control on both sides (Ericson, Baranek, and Chan, 1989). The outcome of the struggle depends chiefly on the status of the sources and the power they can exercise over the flow of information. In the case of crime news, the police enjoy an effective monopoly over the supply of information, because there is no alternative, competing source on which the media can rely. With politics, on the other hand, journalists have more leverage over sources by virtue of the adversarial structure of the political process, at least in democratic societies. This does not, however, alter the fact that the government exercises

Box 5.3
Secondary News Sources: The Negative Reaction

NURSES BLAST TORY POLICIES
"Dismantling" of Medicare Hurts Many, Group Says

More people will die in hospital and medical costs will leave others bankrupt if the provincial government follows current policies, Ontario's largest nurses' group predicts.

"We are witnessing the insidious dismantling of medicare leading to two-tiered medicine," said Jane Cornelius, president of the 50,000-member Ontario Nurses' Association.

Cornelius warned patients will face "more out-of-pocket costs," because of government policies so that "seniors (will have) to mortgage their homes for necessary medical services."

In a news conference yesterday afternoon, Cornelius blasted Health Minister Jim Wilson for offering doctors a $100 million raise in a recent deal at the same time that other areas of health care are being cut back.

In a toughly worded letter to Premier Mike Harris, Cornelius warned that the Canada Health Act, which guarantees comprehensive, universal health care, will soon be "rendered meaningless" in Ontario.

She also predicted that within two to three years:

- The rates of sickness and death in hospital will more than double because of staff cuts.
- The quality of health care will plummet to become "dangerous" to patients.
- Roughly 15,000 nurses will lose their jobs because of health-care cuts.
- Ontario will see a two-tiered health system where those with money can get better, faster medical services than others.
- The two-tiered system will hurt Canada's standing in the global marketplace by increasing health-care costs for businesses and individuals.

In her seven-page letter to Harris, Cornelius complains that she has been unable to meet with Wilson to discuss her concerns.

But Wilson yesterday said flatly that is "not true" and insisted his office has tried several times to arrange a meeting with representatives from the Ontario Nurses' Association.

"(The nurses') vision for reforming health care is almost identical to my own," he told reporters yesterday.

"I would like to discuss it with them."

Thousands of nurses have lost their jobs across Ontario as hospitals struggle to cut millions from their budget. Wilson has vowed to cut $1.3 billion from hospitals. Much of the money will come from hospital closings, but all hospitals took a cut in funding this year as well.

The nurses have developed a new plan for health care management that would feature more co-ordination between the various types of health care.

SOURCE: Kelly Toughill, "Nurses Blast Tory Policies," *The Toronto Star,* November 1, 1996, p. A4. Reprinted with permission—The Toronto Star Syndicate.

the greatest control over the flow of information because of its political authority and control over policy. What the government does or says is intrinsically newsworthy, and governments attempt to use this fact to manage the media and mobilize popular consent and support for their actions. Among the tactics governments employ to try to maximize favourable news coverage and minimize unfavourable coverage are the following (Taras, 1990):

- providing the media with prepackaged news releases and photo opportunities that create media dependency on government sources
- "freezing out" hostile media by denying or curtailing access to information
- giving hostile media "flak" — that is, complaining about negative coverage (Herman and Chomsky, 1988)
- staging events to attract media attention
- timing the release of information to maximize positive coverage and/or minimize the opportunity for coverage of oppositional viewpoints
- sending out "trial balloons" by means of informal leaks of information, or manufacturing a sense of crisis to create uncertainty or lower public expectations

▲ TELEVISION DRAMA AND IDEOLOGY: THE ISSUE OF GENDER

Unlike news, which concerns the facts and meanings of an external social reality, television drama deals in fictional creations, albeit ones that are understood to some extent in terms of their realism or plausibility by comparison with real life. Because it is an area in which meaning and values intersect and interact with entertainment and pleasure, television drama is important for the study of ideology. Its two main forms are the action drama and the soap opera.

Action dramas and soap operas differ in a number of ways. Action dramas usually cost more per episode to make and are initially aired in prime time. Soaps are produced more cheaply, using video rather than film, and are shot on studio sets rather than on location. Their daytime slots indicate that they are targeted primarily at an adult female audience. Soap-opera plots, more than action-drama

plots, feature women in central roles and are structured around women characters and their concerns. Gender, in fact, is one of the central axes around which television drama revolves, but, as we can see from Table 5.3, overall gender representation is uneven. There are simply more men than women in dramatic roles, particularly in English-Canadian drama and among characters aged 35–64.

Gender-role differences are also evident. Women outnumber men in activities "traditionally associated with women, such as presence in a family setting, child care, and home management" (CRTC, 1990: 23), whereas men are more likely to appear in situations in which they have paid employment or are the perpetrators or victims of physical violence (CRTC, 1990: 23). Television drama generally reproduces the structure of gender stratification in occupational roles. Men are more likely than women to be portrayed as managers, professionals, military personnel, or law-enforcement officers (though at rates far higher than those that apply in real life for *either* men or women), whereas women are significantly more likely to appear as office or sales workers.

These findings can be interpreted in two ways. On the one hand, television drama can be assessed as to how well it reflects reality; from that perspective, television drama generally does correspond to a social reality in which men are more likely to be managers and women are more likely to be clerical or sales workers. On the other hand, television drama can be assessed as to how well it serves to promote social change toward gender equality; from that perspective, the very realism of television drama suggests that it still has far to go in providing an egalitarian representation of gender. Whichever perspective is adopted, however, these imbalances in gender portrayals also point to the major difference between action dramas and

◆ **Table 5.3** Gender Representation in TV Drama

Point of origin	1984		1988	
	Male	Female	Male	Female
English-Canadian	74%	26%	70%	30%
French-Canadian	51	49	56	44
U.S.[a]	61	39	62	38

[a]The figures for U.S. drama include programs in both English and French (dubbed).

SOURCE: Compiled from Canadian Radio-television and Telecommunications Commission, *The Portrayal of Gender in Canadian Broadcasting: Summary Report* (Ottawa: CRTC, 1990), Tables 12 and 31.

soap operas: Action dramas are clearly male-oriented, and the characters, plot structures, and audiences of soap operas are female-oriented.

The dramatic world of the soap opera is distinct in a number of ways. Most soaps are set in small or mid-sized fictitious cities, rather than in the large, bleak urban landscapes characteristic of action shows. The choice of smaller cities is telling. The world of the soap is a familiar, intimate, interior world, dominated by interpersonal relationships, primarily those of family, friends, co-workers, and rivals or opponents. The family is a central motif in the soap opera. In this respect, the soap opera contrasts with the action drama, which often focusses on the lone individual struggling against a hostile or indifferent world. Although the family also plays a central role in the sitcom, it is in a different guise there — primarily child-centred as opposed to the adult-centred family of the soap, and focussed primarily on laughter and fun in contrast to the more serious world of the soap. At work, most soap-opera characters perform jobs in which they are continually dealing with others — listening, advising, helping. Themes often encountered in the news — harm, loss, victimization — run through soap-opera plots. Conflicts and other disruptions constantly arise, but they are defined primarily in terms of the middle-class values of small-town America, such as trust, loyalty, caring, and self-sacrifice, or of their negative counterparts, deceit, betrayal, malice, and revenge (Rosen, 1986).

Soap plots hinge on constant talk between characters; they are about interaction and reaction more than action. The sudden, dramatic events that move the plot forward, such as disasters, accidents, and crimes, often occur off-screen, entering the drama only after the fact, as subjects to talk about. The talk is concerned with the moral dilemmas of everyday life and the emotions and feelings that accompany them. Soap characters are constantly trying to determine and analyze one another's true feelings and motives, to unravel people's deep silences by getting them to open up and talk about the secret problems that plague them, to share their innermost selves with those around them. In this respect, women play a crucial role as agents of therapeutic talk, especially in relation to male characters, who are frequently emotionally blocked and in need of help to heal themselves through talk. But it is a role fraught with its own anxieties, as female characters agonize over whether they are sufficiently sensitive, compassionate, knowledgeable, and supportive (Modleski, 1983).

The ideology of daytime soaps is one of idealized averageness — close enough to the real world of viewers to seem realistic, different enough to stimulate the desire to watch and identify. The intimacy of the soap opera is conveyed in its content and in the way it addresses its audience. The camera work, for example, features frequent use of tight facial close-ups to convey emotional intensity and uncertainty, and to enhance the viewers' ability to identify with the characters and their predicaments. The typical soap narrative features multiple, intersecting plotlines that give the individual episode a fragmented structure in which the resolution of problems is repeatedly deferred. This deprives viewers of the satisfaction that comes with problem resolution, but simultaneously stimulates their desire to keep watching in order to achieve that elusive goal.

Soap-opera plots move slowly, developments are constantly interrupted, and there is frequent repetition. For some, this makes soap opera an essentially trivial, tedious form of drama, a form of low-brow escapism of no cultural value. However, for many of the women who watch soaps, these features parallel the real tempo, experiences, and contradictions of life (Modleski, 1983; Flitterman, 1983). What soaps lack, in contrast to action dramas and sitcoms, is a happy ending. Female characters in particular are thwarted in their quest for happiness as new problems, conflicts, and contradictions are thrown up in their path. This creates what Ang (1985: 121–30) calls a "tragic structure of feeling" as the dominant message. On the one hand, soaps reinforce images of the feminine ideal — caring mother, loving wife, supportive friend, successful professional; on the other hand, they confront their women characters with constant problems, conflicts, and anxieties not unlike those that women experience in their real lives.

Through the use of all these elements, soaps create a kind of identification with and for women viewers that has a particular resonance or appeal. In this respect, soap operas are part of a growing strategy on the part of TV programmers to appeal to audiences generally in terms of emotions and feelings. Andersen (1995) argues that emotional appeal has become increasingly important as the link between TV programs and the advertising that effectively subsidizes them. **Focus groups** of sample viewers are used by market researchers to assess the kinds of images, characters, and values that evoke positive and negative emotional responses. Advertisers and programmers are able to incorporate these findings into their respective representations in a complementary way. Advertising works by associating products with images of a desirable, idealized lifestyle, and this lifestyle, in turn, is replicated in the programs that surround the ads (Andersen, 1995).

lated to programs in terms of their realism vis-à-vis everyday life. This "search for realism" resulted in a more distanced and critical attitude toward TV, and this reduced their ability to identify strongly with the characters and personalities. Paradoxically, however, they claimed to value TV more highly than the middle-class women in the study for whom realism was less important, and who more easily identified with characters and situations. This paradox, Press argues, points to the way that the reality depicted on TV is essentially a middle-class one from which working-class women are in many ways separated.

The effect of age also was found to be, to some extent, paradoxical. The older women in the study, who were less likely to have worked full-time outside the home, were more likely to relate to TV in "feminist" terms (Press, 1991: 176). They respond-ed positively to the way TV had broadened their outlook, and particularly to the way it portrayed women characters in occupational roles. Among the younger women, however, talk of TV was focussed more on portrayals of the family than of work. Particularly among working-class women, TV's portrayal of life in the ideal nuclear family provoked mixed feelings of scepticism and criticism on the one hand, and sadness and nostalgia on the other (Press, 1991: 176). The pleasures that women get from TV, then, may foster not only feelings of guilt, but other contradictory emotions as well.

The findings of these studies help to validate the assumption that viewers do not assimilate what they see and hear in an uncritical, conformist, and uniform way. As they do with other media, viewers make selective use of TV. ■

SUMMARY

1. Newspapers have a high level of ownership concentration and function largely as local monopolies. The factor that has the greatest impact on news content, however, is dependency on advertising. In fact, the survival prospects of newspapers with alternative or politically radical perspectives on the news are limited because of it.

2. In the case of television, advertising dependency discourages the production of English-Canadian entertainment programming, particularly drama, because U.S. shows (which are cheaper to license than Canadian shows are to produce) are more popular, and therefore draw more advertising revenues. Nationalists view the situation as a "sellout" of Canadian culture, whereas postmodernists see it as part of the general effect of globalization and do not believe that it undermines the institutional structure of Canadian society.

3. Conservatives claim that news coverage has a left-liberal political bias that is unrepresentative of society's mainstream. Critical theorists argue that news coverage is ideologically conservative, in that it defines reality from the perspective of dominant ideology and views issues and events through the lens of social control.

4. Types of television are distinguished primarily in terms of gender. Soap operas in particular pertain to the dominant ideology of femininity by appealing to a largely female audience. Soaps generate lines of identification and pleasure for women, and simultaneously confront women with the endless contradictions between feminine ideals and female realities.

5. The major effect of the news media is its role in setting the public agenda. The media shape the public's perception and evaluation of the social priority of issues and events. The news media's agenda-setting influence varies over time and in accordance with the objective importance of the event or issue, its relevance for individuals on a subjective level, and the presence or absence of alternative sources of information and interpretation.

6. The majority of observers believe that there is a causal link between television and violent behaviour, but the studies that support this view have been criticized on the grounds of flawed methodology. Moreover, the majority view is split on the issue of how television causes aggression. Some argue that watching television counteracts the effects of socialization by weakening self-control; others believe that watching television in fact socializes children in the use of violence.

7. Studies of audiences indicate that TV viewing and the responses to it vary according to gender. Men and women tend to prefer different types of programming. Men are more likely to watch attentively and privately, whereas women watch in a more interactive, social way. Women also tend to be more open about their TV viewing, and use TV as a topic of casual social interaction and conversation.

QUESTIONS TO CONSIDER

1. Why is news primarily bad news? Is it because of a bias on the part of the news media toward issues and events that are negative, or is there an appetite for bad news in society generally?

2. Why, despite the lack of strong, consistent, and unequivocal evidence to confirm a direct connection between violence on television and violence in real life, are many people convinced that such a link exists? Television also conveys images and messages that are positive (in the normative or ethical sense). Why do we not assume that these have just as much effect as images of violence?

3. Compare the central male characters in a television action drama with the central female characters in a soap opera. What are the main similarities and differences? What does the comparison tell us about our ideologies of masculinity and femininity? How easy would it be to reverse the characters and roles, putting the men in the women's roles and vice versa?

4. Critics of media imperialism often point to Canada as an example of a country overwhelmed by U.S. popular culture — movies, magazines, music, and television. What is so appealing about U.S. popular culture, not only in Canada but in other countries as well? In what respects is U.S. popular culture specifically American, and in what respects is it now simply the leading culture in a world moving toward cultural globalization?

5. Do you think that, in the long term, the convergence of communications technologies such as television, telephones, and computers will result in a society in which people become increasingly isolated in their homes — working at home; shopping at home; being entertained, informed, and schooled at home — with little reason or desire to interact directly with the outside world? Do you see any factors or developments that might counteract the effects of technological convergence?

6. Why do females and males watch TV differently? Does this begin in childhood, or is it confined to adults? How would you make TV programming that is watched primarily by women, such as soap operas, more appealing to men without making it less appealing to women? Conversely, how would you make traditionally masculine programming, such as sports, more appealing to women without losing male viewers?

GLOSSARY

agenda setting The influence of the news media on the public agenda — that is, the public's perception, evaluation, and ranking of social issues and concerns in terms of their social importance.

alternative viewpoints Interpretations that differ from the meanings contained in society's dominant ideology, representing compromises between the latter and the meanings promoted by oppositional viewpoints. *See also* oppositional viewpoints.

bidirectional effect Self-reinforcing cycle in which television violence contributes to aggressive behaviour, and aggressive tendencies lead to a preference for violent television.

communication From the Latin, meaning "to bring together or unify"; now used to denote the transmission of knowledge, ideas, meanings, and understandings.

critical perspective The view that the media reinforce dominant ideology and the position of the dominant class and other powerful groups. The theory has two variants: one sees this process as more open to challenge and resistance than does the other.

desensitization The effect of prolonged exposure to television violence that makes people indifferent toward, or tolerant of, real violence by others.

disinhibition The effect of prolonged exposure to television violence that weakens the mechanisms of self-control acquired through socialization, and thereby contributes to aggressive behaviour.

displacement The consequence of devoting time to watching television that involves reducing the amount of time spent on other activities, such as reading or interacting socially.

dominant ideology The interests, perspectives, viewpoints, and understandings of the dominant class and other powerful groups.

focus groups Small groups of sample viewers tested and interviewed in-depth by market researchers to ascertain which media images, characters, and narrative themes evoke positive and negative emotional responses. These data are then used in the design of both advertising and TV programming.

fragmentation At the level of the individual, the differentiation of social identities and experiences; at the collective level, the increasing specialization and segmentation of audiences in terms of media tastes and interests.

functionalist perspective Analysis of the role of the media from the perspective of social integration. It identifies four distinct functions of the media: correlation or co-ordination, social control, socialization, and tension management.

hegemony The exercise by the dominant class of cultural leadership by using the media to naturalize and universalize dominant ideology and to absorb the challenge of alternative and oppositional points of view.

horizontal consolidation Co-ordination of different outlets in a media chain for purposes of sharing resources.

inoculation An immunizing effect that strengthens the resistance of dominant ideology to subversive views.

mass A large, anonymous social group that lacks distinctive characteristics and relationships.

media Plural of *medium;* from the Latin, meaning "middle"; refers to television, radio, newspapers, magazines, and movies as means of communication.

media imperialism A situation in which one country's media dominate another country's culture.

modality The degree to which a media image approximates real life; for example, an animated cartoon has a low modality, whereas news footage has a high modality.

multimedia chains Corporations that own and control a string of different media operations or outlets in different fields of mass communication, such as television, radio, and magazines.

need for orientation The extent to which individuals need to rely on the media for their basic information and understanding about an event or issue.

news values Criteria such as immediacy, personalization, deviance, and conflict, in terms of which news media define and represent events and issues.

obtrusiveness The extent to which an event or issue in the news impinges directly on people, lessening their need to rely on and be influenced by the news media.

oppositional viewpoints Ways of interpreting reality in terms that contradict the meanings of dominant ideology, representing the experiences of subordinated groups against those of the powerful.

primary news sources Official, authoritative voices that the media use to define the basic meaning of an event or issue — for example, politicians, police officers, and professional experts.

priming The process whereby the agenda of issues set by the media also influences the way in which members of the public evaluate politicians.

promotionalism The merging of advertising and its surrounding (e.g., written text or TV programs) in which each becomes an element in a chain of two-way promotion. For example, when a celebrity pitches a certain product in a TV ad, the product also promotes the celebrity and the fictional character that person plays.

salience The objective importance of an issue or event as a determinant of how effective the media's agenda setting will be.

scripts for violence The packaging of images of violence on television in a way that gives people, particularly children, a model of when, where, and how to use violence in real life.

secondary news sources News sources that provide reaction to news events and issues, often of a negative, emotional kind and typically from the point of view of victims. These voices are usually framed within the definition of the situation established by the primary sources.

space-biased media Media that enable communication over extended distances, such as print, radio, or television. The messages, however, are not long-lasting. Space-biased media promote territorial expansion together with secular beliefs and military-political forms of power.

sponsor effect The potential biasing effect of researchers in laboratory experiments on the effects of media violence. By showing violent images, researchers may give the impression to research subjects that they are condoning aggressive or other antisocial responses.

technological convergence The integration of different communications technologies, such as television and telephony, into a single system that obliterates the distinction between mass communications and telecommunications.

time-biased media Media that are durable (the messages last over time), but are relatively immobile, such as stone carvings or inscriptions on clay tablets. Time-biased media promote a sense of tradition as well as religious forms of belief and power.

vertical integration A media corporation's ownership and control of the means of production at all stages of the production process — for example, from producing newsprint to delivering newspapers.

SUGGESTED READING

Andersen, R. (1995). *Consumer Culture and TV Programming*. Boulder, CO: Westview Press. The principal argument of this book is that the content of TV programming is increasingly linked to the goals and techniques of advertising and the promotion of consumerism. The analysis follows a critical perspective, and shows how the relationship between advertising and programming limits what can and cannot be represented on TV.

Bacon-Smith, C. (1992). *Enterprising Women: Television Fandom and the Creation of Popular Myth*. Philadelphia: University of Pennsylvania Press. A social anthropological study of TV fan subculture and community, based on participant observation and in-depth interviewing methods. Bacon-Smith focusses primarily on female fans of such shows as *Star Trek* who produce their own stories, poems, artwork, etc., which they circulate via fanzines, conventions, and informal social contacts.

Collins, R. (1990). *Culture, Communication and National Identity: The Case of Canadian Television*. Toronto: University of Toronto Press. A study of the effects of the Americanization of Canadian television (especially in the area of drama) from the perspective of increasing globalization. It argues that these effects are not as harmful to national identity as nationalists assume.

Cooper, B. (1994). *Sins of Omission: Shaping the News at CBC TV*. Toronto: University of Toronto Press. This analysis of CBC TV news, with particular attention to foreign coverage, finds a bias in the reporting that favours left-wing political regimes and movements. The obverse face of this bias is that the violent or repressive actions of these regimes and movements are overlooked or underreported. Cooper is critical of the CBC for being more concerned to promote "progressive opinion" than with "the provision of reliable information about the world" (p. 221).

Winter, J. (1996). *Democracy's Oxygen: How Corporations Control the News*. Montreal: Black Rose. An analysis of the corporate control of Canada's news media from a critical perspective. The book addresses the relationship between the political economy of the press and the ideological nature of news coverage. The author is critical of "junk food news" and the depoliticization and resignation this fosters. A good contrast to Cooper (above).

CHAPTER SIX
Religion

IN THIS CHAPTER YOU WILL LEARN THAT

- religion is something that can be examined by social scientists, and has been studied from the beginnings of sociology
- religion has both individual and social components — people display a wide range of levels of commitment, but groups play a major role in instilling and sustaining personal religiosity
- since religious groups are organizations, they can best be understood in terms of organizational concepts and frameworks
- for the vast majority of people, religious commitment and involvement are rooted in social institutions, particularly in the family
- religion's influence on individuals tends to be noteworthy but not unique, while its broader influence in most societies supports social structure and culture
- despite the numerical problems of some groups, religion's future seems secure, grounded in ongoing spiritual interests and needs

REGINALD W. BIBBY
University of Lethbridge

■ INTRODUCTION

Religion has been present in virtually every society. Its influence has varied from culture to culture and from century to century. In different places and in different eras, religion has known both dark and golden ages.

The early social scientists were convinced that religion's days were numbered, that it would just be a short time before it was discarded in favour of science. Through the 1960s, the widespread consensus was that religion's influence was declining and that Canadians and people in other technologically advanced countries were leaving religion behind.

Those observers are proving to be wrong. On the verge of the twenty-first century, religion lives on, embraced by significant numbers of people in virtually all cultures. Moreover, there are claims and indications that, if anything, spirituality is on the upswing in many parts of the world, including North America, Russia, and China.

In this chapter, I will examine what some of the early social scientists had to say about religion and then show how sociologists study religion in both its individual and organized forms. I will clarify what sociologists mean by religion and then analyze "how much of it" we have in Canada, what kinds of factors contribute to people being religious, and the influence that religion has on both individuals and societies. I will also reflect on what religious developments can be expected in the foreseeable future.

Although I will take other societies, especially the United States, into account, I will pay particular attention to Canada. Why? Because, until recently we have known very little about religion in our society. And, to be frank, I have made religion in Canada my primary research interest and I can't wait to tell you what I've been finding.

■ SOCIOLOGY AND RELIGION

In using the scientific method of investigation to study social life, sociologists seek to understand social reality by relying on what can be perceived through the senses. Proponents of religion, in contrast, have traditionally asserted that the world we know through the senses is only part of a greater reality that, because of the limitations of perception, can be known only through faith.

Science and religion, then, approach the world, and how it is known, from different directions. In principle, these approaches are compatible. Science limits itself to what is perceivable, and religion maintains that reality includes the nonperceivable. Sociologists therefore cannot address claims concerning the existence of God or miraculous healing. But, as Émile Durkheim (1965 [1912]: 479) pointed out, religion "can affirm nothing that [science] denies, deny nothing that it affirms" (see Box 6.1). Conflict between science and religion arises only when they invade each other's territory, such as when scientists refute the plausibility of answered prayer, or "Biblical creationists" want equal time in the science classroom with proponents of evolution.

Although sociology cannot assess the accuracy of supernatural claims, it can explore issues relating to the social aspects of those claims: who believes what; the nature and extent of spiritual needs; involvement in religious groups; why some people tend to be more committed than others; and the consequences, for individuals and societies, of people being religious. "The essence of religion," said Max Weber, is not a concern of sociologists; "we make it our task to study the conditions and effects of a particular type of social behaviour" (1963: 1). For our purposes, whether religious beliefs are true is not as important as whether they are *believed* to be true, and therefore what potential consequences they have for individual and social life.

■ THEORETICAL TRADITIONS

The sociology of religion has been strongly influenced by three early theorists: Karl Marx, Émile Durkheim, and Max Weber.

▲ MARX AND CONFLICT

Karl Marx worked from the assumption that religion is a human creation. He maintained, however, that it plays an important role in compensating people who are economically deprived. Its very presence symbolizes the inclination of people to reinterpret rather than change their oppressive conditions. Using the language of the day, Marx (1970 [1843]: 131) wrote: "Man makes religion; religion does not make man." He argued that man has "found only his own reflection in the fantastic reality of heaven,

Box 6.1
Evolution Has Pope's Blessing

Vatican City (Reuter)—Pope John Paul has lent his support to the theory of evolution, proclaiming it compatible with Christian faith in a step welcomed by scientists but likely to raise howls from the religious right.

The Pope's recognition that evolution is "more than just a theory" came in a written message he sent to a meeting of the Pontifical Academy of Sciences, a body of experts that advises the Roman Catholic church on scientific issues.

It broke new ground by acknowledging the theory of the physical evolution of man and other species through natural selection and hereditary adaptation appears to be valid.

Though the Pope made clear he regards the human soul to be of immediate divine creation and so not subject to the process, his remarks brought banner headlines in the Italian press.

SOURCE: *The Calgary Sun*, October 25, 1996. Reprinted with permission of Reuters.

where he sought a supernatural being," and that being religious characterized "the self-consciousness and self-esteem of a man who has either not yet gained himself or has lost himself again."

Central to Marx's thought on religion was the belief that religion serves to hold in check the explosive tensions of a society. Aligned with the interests of the dominant few, religion soothes the exploited majority like an anesthetic — "the opium of the people" (Marx, 1970 [1843]: 131) — blinding them to the inequalities at hand and bottling up their creative energies. Consequently, those who hold power encourage religious belief among the masses as a subtle tool in the process of economic exploitation. So intertwined are society and religion, maintained Marx, that attacks on society are often attacks on religion. Historically, attacks on feudalism were, above all, attacks on the church, while revolutionary social and political doctrines were simultaneously regarded as theological heresies (Marx and Engels, 1964: 132).

Marx saw religion as an inadequate salve for a sick society. When the sickness is remedied, there will be no need for the salve. Accordingly, he viewed his criticism of religion as an attempt to expose the chain that was binding people, so that it could be removed. Freed from the panacea of religion, individuals would be able "to think, act, and fashion their reality with illusions lost and reason regained" (Marx, 1970 [1843]: 132).

▲ DURKHEIM AND COLLECTIVITY

Émile Durkheim was the son of a rabbi but he was raised in a Catholic educational tradition. He himself was an atheist and an anticleric, believing that a scientific understanding of society has the potential to raise the quality of social life to utopian heights.

In his classic work *The Elementary Forms of the Religious Life* (1965 [1912]), Durkheim argued that religion's origin is social. People who live in community come to share common sentiments, and as a result a **collective conscience** is formed. It is experienced by each member, yet is greater than the sum of the individual consciences. When individuals have the feeling of being in the presence of a higher power, the experience *is* real. But what they actually are experiencing is the collective conscience. So vivid is the experience that people feel the need to label it. In reality, Durkheim asserted, "God" is the group experiencing itself.

Once proponents of religion experience such an alleged supernatural reality, they proceed to designate some objects as **sacred** and others as **profane**. Christians, for example, have accorded special status to the cross, the Bible, and holy water, in contrast to most everything else. In Durkheim's view, religious beliefs articulate the nature of the sacred and its symbols, and religious rites provide guidelines as to how people should act in the presence of the sacred.

Religions assert that the world we know through the senses is merely part of a greater reality. However, the sociology of religion analyzes the observable social causes and consequences of religious thought and behaviour. SOURCE: Dick Hemingway.

Since all groups feel the need to uphold and reaffirm their collective sentiments, people come together as a church. According to Durkheim (1965 [1912]: 62–63), "the idea of religion is inseparable from that of the Church," since it is "an eminently collective thing." Even when religion seems to be entirely a matter of individual conscience, it still is nourished by social sources. Besides meeting needs at the individual level, he claimed, religion creates and reinforces social solidarity. Collective life is thus both the source and the product of religion. Accordingly, he defined religion as "a unified system of beliefs and practices relative to sacred things ... which unite into one single moral community called a Church, all those who adhere to them" (Durkheim, 1965 [1912]: 62).

Durkheim (1965 [1912]: 475) observed that "we are going through a stage of transition and moral mediocrity." He readily acknowledged the decline of traditional Christianity. However, he did not think that religion would disappear. Although the forms of expression might change, Durkheim predicted that the social sources that give rise to religion will remain and, with them, religion. He also contended that there will always be a place for religious explanations. Science is fragmentary and incomplete, Durkheim wrote, advancing too slowly for impatient people. Religion will therefore continue to have an important "gap-filling" role.

▲ WEBER AND IDEAS

Max Weber's interest in the origin and nature of modern capitalism led him into extensive debate with Marx's ideas, and stimulated much of his work in the sociology of religion. Unlike Marx and Durkheim, Weber was not interested in the question of whether religion is ultimately true or false. Rather, he maintained that religion, in addition to having a supernatural component, is largely oriented toward this world. As a result, religious ideas and behaviour should frequently be evident in everyday conduct. In *The Protestant Ethic and the Spirit of Capitalism* (1958 [1904–5]), for example, Weber examined the possibility that the moral tone that characterizes capitalism in the Western world — the **Protestant ethic** — can be traced back to the influence of the Protestant Reformation. He hoped that his work would contribute "to the understanding of the manner in which ideas become effective forces in history" (Weber, 1958 [1904–5]: 90).

Weber maintained that ideas, regardless of whether they are objectively true or false, represent one's definition of reality, and therefore have the potential to influence behaviour. Accordingly, Weber emphasized the need to interpret action by understanding the motives of the actor (a method he called *Verstehen,* or understanding). To achieve such an awareness, he said, one should place oneself in the roles of those being studied.

Weber understood the need to study diverse societies in order to examine culture's influence on religion. He therefore embarked on a comparative study of religion. In *Sociology of Religion* (1963), Weber noted that god-conceptions are strongly related to the economic, social, and political conditions in which people live. The gods of light and warmth and of rain and earth have been closely related to practical economic needs; heavenly gods that rule the celestial order have been related to the more abstract problems of death and fate. In political conquest, the gods of the conquered are fused with the gods of the conqueror, and reappear with revised characteristics. Furthermore, the growth of **monotheism** (belief in one god) is related to goals of political unification.

Beyond the social sources of the gods, Weber dealt with such major themes as religious organization and the relationship between religion and social class. He reflected on religious leadership and the important process whereby a personal following is transformed into a permanent congregation, which he referred to as "routinization." He noted that different groups in society vary in their inclination to be religious: peasants are religious when they are threatened; the nobility find religion beneath their honour; the middle class sees religion largely in ethical terms; the working class supplants religion with other ideologies.

THE NATURE OF RELIGION

The term "religion" is widely used, but not everyone has the same thing in mind when they use it. In attempting to study religion, therefore, it is important to clarify what we mean by the term. Charles Glock and Rodney Stark (1965) have offered some helpful insights. They point out that, in defining religion for social scientific purposes, we should begin by recognizing that humans develop systems of meaning to interpret the world. Some systems — commonly referred to as "religions," including Christianity, Judaism, and Islam — have a supernatural referent. Others, such as a science-based system (scientism) or political "isms" (communism, fascism), do not. These latter systems, they suggested, might be viewed as human-centred or **humanist perspectives,** in contrast to *religious perspectives,* which are succinctly referred to here as **religions**.

The two types of perspectives differ on one critical point: Religion is concerned with discovering life's meaning, and humanist perspectives are concerned with making life meaningful. Humanist Bertrand Russell stated the difference well: "I do not think that life in general has any purpose. It just happened. But individual human beings have purposes" (in Cogley, 1968: 171). Religious perspectives suggest that our existence has meaning, preceding that which we, as humans, decide to give it. In contrast, humanist perspectives assume that life has no "ultimate meaning" and therefore focus on giving it meaning.

▲ PERSONAL RELIGIOSITY

Individuals vary in their levels of religious commitment. Thus, a major issue in the scientific study of religion is how to define and measure **personal religiosity**.

Most of the early religion research used one of three basic indicators to determine the religiosity of a person. All three assumed group involvement: identification, membership, and attendance. People were asked questions such as, "What is your religious preference?" "Do you belong to a congregation?" and "How often do you attend worship services?" People who indicated that they had a religious preference, belonged to a local group, or attended services with regularity were regarded as religious.

Simply knowing that someone is a "Protestant," however, tells us very little about the person's actual commitment to the Christian faith. Similarly, mere identification with religious cultural groups such as Hindus and Hutterites hardly guarantees that a person takes religion seriously. Likewise, church and temple members may be active or inactive, committed or uncommitted. And service attendance, while measuring participation in a group, excludes people who could — by our definition — be very committed yet not be active in a religious organization.

Since the 1960s, social scientists have responded to the limitations of these three measures by viewing religious commitment as having a variety of dimensions. In one of the more helpful frameworks devised, Stark and Glock (1968) suggested that the religions of the world typically expect their most devoted followers to hold key beliefs, engage in certain practices, have supernatural experiences, and be aware of the central tenets of their faiths. Stark and Glock refer to the belief, practice, experience, and knowledge components of commitment as **dimensions of religiosity**. It is not enough to believe *or* practise *or* experience *or* know; all four traits are expected of the committed.

The ongoing Project Canada national surveys, which began in 1975, have been providing pioneering, comprehensive data on personal religiosity in this country. The surveys have found that Canadians exhibit relatively high levels of religious belief, practice, experience, and knowledge (see Table 6.1). Indeed, 8 in 10 say they believe in God, 7 in 10 maintain there is life after death, and 6 in 10 acknowledge that they pray privately at least once a month.

On the surface, late-twentieth-century Canadians seem to be a highly religious people. However, the surveys have also found that only about 40 percent claim to be committed to Christianity or some other religion (2 percent), and less than half of these demonstrate the belief, practice, experience, and knowledge characteristics that Stark and Glock deem to be central to commitment. Among the other 60 per-

cent of Canadians, 40 percent indicate that they are interested in but not committed to any religion, and the remaining 20 percent simply say that they are not religious (Bibby, 1987, 1993). According to the 1995 Project Canada survey, only 26 percent of Canadians say that religion is "very important" to them, and among those there are clear, regional variations. The levels range from a high of almost 40 percent in the three Prairie provinces, to 30 percent in the Atlantic region and 25 percent in Ontario, to a low of 20 percent in both Quebec and British Columbia.

In short, isolated religious beliefs and practices abound. But the majority of Canadians are not strongly committed to either traditional or nontraditional kinds of religion. As we will see, as we move into the twenty-first century, such a pattern is hardly unique to Canada.

◆ **Table 6.1** Religion Commitment along Four Dimensions, Canada, 1995

Dimension	Response	Percentage
Belief		
God	Yes, I definitely do	57%
	Yes, I think so	23
	No, I don't think so	11
	No, I definitely do not	9
Divinity of Jesus	Yes, I definitely do	48
	Yes, I think so	24
	No, I don't think so	15
	No, I definitely do not	13
Life after death	Yes, I definitely do	40
	Yes, I think so	30
	No, I don't think so	17
	No, I definitely do not	13
Practice		
Private prayer	Daily	30
	Several times a week	10
	About once a week	8
	About once a month	9
	Hardly ever/never	43
Experience		
God	Yes, I definitely have	21
	Yes, I think I have	21
	No, I don't think I have	32
	No, I definitely have not	26
Knowledge	The first book in the Old Testament? (Genesis)	51
	Who denied Jesus three times? (Peter)	47

SOURCE: Derived from Reginald W. Bibby, Project Can95 National Survey.

▲ COLLECTIVE RELIGIOSITY

It is frequently argued that one can be religious without having anything to do with religious organizations such as churches or synagogues. However, most social scientists, beginning with Durkheim, would maintain that personal religiosity is highly dependent on **collective religiosity,** or group support of some kind. Such dependence is not unique to religion. It stems, rather, from a basic fact of life: The ideas we hold tend to come from our interaction with other people. However creative we might like to think we are, the fact is that most of the ideas we have can be traced to the people with whom we have been in contact — family, friends, teachers, authors. Moreover, if we are to retain our ideas, they must continuously be endorsed by at least a few other people. In modern societies where religious ideas compete with a wide variety of other ideas, it is essential for the maintenance of religion that religious groups exist to transmit and sustain religious ideas.

The Church–Sect Typology

Those who have examined religious groups in predominantly Christian settings have recognized two major kinds of organizations. First, there are numerically dominant groupings — the Roman Catholic Church in medieval Europe, the Church of England, the so-called mainline denominations in Canada and the United States (Anglican, United, Presbyterian, Lutheran), and so on. Second, smaller groups have broken away from the dominant bodies. For example, in the sixteenth century, "protestant" groups including the Church of England broke away from the Roman Catholic Church; but Methodists in turn broke away from the Church of England, and the Salvation Army emerged as a breakaway group from the Methodists. Today, additional "emerging" groups include an array of Baptist and Pentecostal denominations and congregations that are found in virtually every North American city.

From this pattern of dominant groups and breakaway groups, sociologists who are trying to make sense of religious groups developed an analytical scheme known as the **church–sect typology**. This framework attempted to describe the central characteristics of these two types of organizations, as well as account for the origin and development of sects.

In perhaps its earliest formulation, Max Weber distinguished between church and sect primarily on the basis of theology (churches emphasize works, sects stress faith) and relationship to society (for churches, accommodation; for sects, separation). Weber noted the irony in the sect's development: initially a spinoff from an established church, the sect gradually evolves into a church itself (Gerth and Mills, 1958). The sect is at first characterized by spontaneity and enthusiasm. In time, however, these traits give way to routinization and institutionalization.

Although the church–sect typology has been used extensively, alternative ways of understanding religious groups are now becoming popular.

Organizational Approaches

In sociological terms, religious organizations are no different from other social organizations. Therefore, there has been a growing tendency to analyze religious groups by making use of the same frameworks we use in studying social organizations in general. For example, from an organizational point of view, religious groups in Canada are in effect corporations of different sizes: The Roman Catholic Church is "a multinational corporation," the United Church is a company that is "Canadian-owned and -operated," the Baptist Union of Western Canada is "a regional company" with links to other "regional companies" in central and eastern Canada, and an individual congregation in a given city or town is "a local outlet."

Apart from provocative marketing language and corporate analogies, a general organizational approach to religious groups might lead us to examine them in terms of some basic features, including (1) the nature and the sources of their members, (2) their formal and informal goals, (3) the norms and roles that are established to accomplish their purposes, (4) the sanctions that are used to ensure that norms are followed and roles are played, and (5) the success that groups experience in pursuing their goals.

MEMBERSHIP When one studies the membership of Protestant churches, one immediately notices that many members have parents who are involved as well. A 1994 national survey of the United Church of Canada, for example, found that about 70 percent of active members acknowledged that their mother or father had been United Church members (Bibby, 1994). Surveys of Anglicans, Roman Catholics, and members of evangelical churches — referred to as conservative Protestant groups by sociologists — have uncovered the same intergenerational pattern. As a result, new additions to almost any given congregation are primarily active members who are on the move geographically. By the same token, one of the major reasons for a decline in participation is the simple fact that people make a residential move and don't become involved with a congregation in their new setting (Bibby, 1997). Research into the growth patterns of twenty conservative Protestant groups in Calgary over 25 years has found that about 70 percent of the new members come from similar evangelical churches, while 20 percent are children of members. Only about 10 percent have roots outside of conservative groups. To the extent that such outsiders are recruited, it is friendship and marriage that draw them in, rather than such highly publicized activities as mass evangelism, religious television programming, and door-to-door visitation (Bibby and Brinkerhoff, 1973; 1983; 1994).

Because most new members come from existing pools of people who view themselves as Roman Catholics, Anglicans, Presbyterians, evangelicals, and so on, churches frequently compete with each other for members, especially in urban areas where choice abounds. One area of competition is leadership. Smaller, lower-status congregations are usually at a severe disadvantage to larger and more prestigious groups. Over the years, ministers within major Canadian and American denominations have been found to have standards comparable to those of secular managers and executives when it comes to interchurch movement (Mitchell, 1966). It is not only ministers, priests, and rabbis who equate "large" with "successful"; so do denominations and individual congregations. And, "attractive" congregations usually have the resources to search further for their ministers, and hold them longer, than congregations that are regarded as less attractive. It is widely known in religious circles that the dominant pattern of ministerial movement is from smaller to larger congregations. This view is so strong and pervasive that a failure to move is regarded as career failure (see, for example, Wimberley, 1971).

Competition among congregations does not stop with ministers and other workers. A congregation's physical resources and its range of services are also significant. The result is that groups tend to build structures as lavish as their resources will permit. In recent years, a number of "megachurches" have come into being in both Canada and the United States. They typically have seating for 1000–4000 people, are serviced by multiple full-time staffs, and have annual budgets in the millions of dollars. They are found in major cities such as Toronto, Montreal, Winnipeg, Edmonton, Calgary, and Vancouver. But they also are appearing in smaller communities such as Abbotsford, Red Deer, and St. Catharines. These megachurches make it difficult for other congregations to compete.

Churches, like secular businesses, also expand their services and personnel in keeping with their economic means. Some of the megachurches, for example, offer many of the typical worship and educational opportunities of more traditional, older groups. But they also develop extensive programs aimed at children, teenagers, young adults, and seniors. The programs offered range from small but sophisticated groups studying in homes ("cell groups"), to well-developed music and drama programs, to multimedia education, entertainment, and production. A foyer in one British Columbia megachurch is decorated to resemble a 1950s diner — complete with car front, jukeboxes, booths, and stools. As the church's head youth minister told me, "The young people love this room; but, I have to admit, the seniors love it too."

In their pursuit of members, congregations are sensitive to the tension between maintaining their integrity and compromising their "product" in order to attract "consumers." Indeed, competition among groups may be resolved in favour not of the most religious but of the least (Demerath and Hammond, 1969). Then again, there are others who argue that the congregations most likely to "win" are those who place greater, rather than less, demand on their members (Kelley, 1972; Finke and Stark, 1992).

GOALS The conscious and unconscious goals of Protestant churches vary by congregation and members. Like the goals of other social groupings, these conscious and unconscious goals commonly appear to be in conflict. Formal goals derived from religious doctrine, such as spiritual growth, frequently exist in tension with "survival goals," including numerical growth (Metz, 1967). Glock, Ringer, and Babbie (1967) have suggested that churches have difficulty in reconciling the pastoral or "comfort" function with the prophetical or "challenge" function. Even apart from the goal of offering comfort, efforts to be prophetic can sometimes have unsettling effects. For example, the national leadership of the United Church of Canada has viewed itself as prophetic in its call, since the mid-1980s, for the denomination to allow homosexuals to be eligible for ordination as ministers. In taking such a controversial position, however, the United Church lost a large number of dissenting members and, in some cases, entire congregations (see O'Toole et al., 1993). Prophecy has its organizational price.

Still other observers (Hadden, 1969; Crysdale, 1961; Luidens and Nemeth, 1989) have noted that North American Protestants experience tension in pursuing the goals of individual versus social redemption. Roman Catholics have had difficulty in combining social and individual ministry. Hewitt

(1992: 156) concludes that, despite its seemingly high-profile identification with justice, even a group like the Roman Catholic Church in Canada "has largely failed to marry rhetoric to concrete action."

Ironically, there may sometimes be more consensus about goals than religious groups themselves appreciate. In the wake of the divisive homosexual ordination issue in the United Church, many members accused the leadership of having different priorities from those of the laity. Yet the 1994 Unitrends national survey of the denomination disclosed that leaders agreed with average members that primary emphases of the church should be worship, spirituality, and ministry to youth. The leaders differed in maintaining that other emphases, notably social and justice issues, should also be given high priority. At the same time, leaders can misjudge the laity — for example, by underestimating their willingness to change. Conrad Kanagy and Leo Driedger (1996) recently found that among Mennonites — a group widely stereotyped as resistant to change — there have been noteworthy changes in attitudes toward women, political participation, and pacifism since the early 1970s.

NORMS, ROLES, AND SANCTIONS If groups are to achieve their official or formal goals, they must establish norms for thought and action, and roles for members to play. These norms and roles are in turn facilitated by communication, which co-ordinates the interaction, and by the use of social controls in the form of rewards and punishments.

Many Protestant groups, because they rely on volunteers, find it very difficult to execute goals in the norms/roles/communication/social control pattern of efficient organizations (Brannon, 1971; Bibby, 1993). Congregations compete for volunteer members and depend on them for attendance, financial support, and general participation. Although churches can establish norms concerning belief and behaviour, and assign organizational roles for members to perform, they have few and weak methods of social control in such a "buyer's market." In short, churches are extremely vulnerable organizations. The clergy receive no exemption from such organizational fragility. On the contrary, they are highly dependent on volunteer parishioners. This has important implications for what clergy can do and how they can do it.

SUCCESS In their studies of religion in Canada, researchers have tended to emphasize "the numerical bottom lines" of religious groups, and focussed on such indicators of success as attendance, membership, and finances.

Through the end of the 1990s, the research news has not been particularly good for organized religion. Overall, attendance and membership is down, with some groups feeling great hardship as a result of inadequate finances. The mainline Protestant groups — the United, Anglican, Presbyterian, and Lutheran churches — have been the most severely hit, along with Roman Catholics in Quebec. Despite some attendance and membership losses, the Roman Catholic Church outside of Quebec appears to be relatively healthy. And while their numbers are not as large as many people think, conservative Protestant groups have at least been able to hold their own and grow modestly — a significant accomplishment, given that they have represented only about 8 percent of the population since 1871, and could have readily been absorbed by larger competitors. To date, other faith groups such as Hindus, Muslims, and Buddhists have had a difficult time growing their membership, because so many of their offspring have married Catholics and Protestants.

What is particularly disconcerting for religious leaders in Canada, however, is that most groups are top-heavy with older people, and many groups do not seem able to replace them with comparable numbers of younger people. As a result, it is estimated that, by the year 2015, weekly attendance will drop dramatically for mainline Protestants (to 425 000) and Quebec Catholics (550 000), while remaining stable for conservative Protestants (900 000) and Roman Catholics elsewhere in Canada (1 200 000). The result? In just two decades, the dominant players on the Canadian religious scene may well be Roman Catholics and evangelical Protestants.

Given these numbers, there is obviously a need to evaluate organizational success using more than just participation indicators. The societal impact and individual influence of religious groups needs to be more clearly understood. To what extent, for example, does organized religion contribute to the instilling of interpersonal values that are essential to everyday civility? To what extent do religious groups respond to the spiritual needs expressed by many people? Is the decline of participation in organized religion associated with any noteworthy personal and social losses?

In addition to these questions, some of the important "latent" functions of religious involvement need to be better understood. Despite differences of opinion as to what groups should be doing, and confusion over what they are doing versus what they think they are doing, religious groups may often be playing significant roles in the lives of many of their members, and thereby living on. An extreme but informative example is the skid road mission (Bibby and Mauss, 1974). The mission operators, skid roaders, and suburban supporters all appear to have very different informal goals. The operators need employment, the skid roaders need food and lodging, and the suburbanites need an outlet for their talents. Nonetheless, the mission functions in such a way as to allow these varied goals to be attained. Thus, somewhat ironically, the skid road mission survives, even though it largely fails to accomplish its official goal — rehabilitate homeless derelicts. The same discrepancy between stated purpose and actual achievement is often evident in congregations. Many don't achieve what they say officially they are trying to achieve; but because the needs of those involved are at least partially met, the organizations themselves survive.

The Canadian Situation

Affiliation with religious groups has been widespread in Canada since the founding of this country. Close ties have always been apparent between Canadians of British descent and the Church of England, Methodism, and Presbyterianism; between the French and the Roman Catholic Church; and be-

tween other ethnic groups and the churches of their homelands. Such general affiliation continues to be very common in Canada. Indeed, according to the 1991 census (Statistics Canada, 1993), just 13 percent of Canadians indicated that they had no religious preference. Although group preferences differ in various parts of the country, on a national basis Roman Catholics comprise 46 percent of the population and Protestants 36 percent. The remaining 5 percent consist of those with other religious preferences (see Table 6.2). These data suggest that it is an exaggeration to think of Canada as a highly diversified religious mosaic.

These demographic findings are confirmed by a survey conducted for historian George Rawlyk shortly after the 1991 census (Nemeth, 1993). The poll found that about 75 percent of Canadians defined themselves as Christians, and about 75 percent of those claimed affiliation with a Christian denomination.

The Christian faith also continues to be pervasive in the United States, where surveys show that close to 9 in 10 Americans continue to identify with Christian groups. However, the numerically dominant groups in the United States are not the same as those in Canada. For example, whereas 1 in 2

Table 6.2 Religious Identification, Canada and the Provinces and Territories, 1991 (in percent)

	Canada	BC	AB	SK	MB	ON	QC	NB	NS	PEI	NF	YK	NWT
Catholic	46	19	27	33	30	36	86	54	37	47	37	20	38
Roman	45	19	26	31	27	36	86	54	37	47	37	20	38
Ukrainian	1	<1	1	2	3	<1	<1	<1	<1	<1	<1	<1	<1
Protestant	36	44	48	53	51	44	6	40	54	48	61	43	50
United	11	13	17	23	19	14	1	11	17	20	17	9	6
Anglican	8	10	7	7	9	10	2	9	14	5	26	15	32
Presbyterian	2	2	2	1	1	4	<1	1	4	9	<1	1	1
Lutheran	2	3	5	8	5	2	<1	<1	1	<1	<1	2	1
Baptist	3	3	2	2	2	3	<1	11	11	4	<1	4	1
Pentecostal	2	2	2	2	2	2	<1	3	1	1	7	2	4
Other	8	11	13	10	13	9	2	5	6	9	10	10	5
Other faiths	5	6	5	3	5	7	4	<1	1	1	<1	2	1
Eastern Orthodox	1	1	2	2	2	2	1	<1	<1	<1	<1	<1	<1
Jewish	1	<1	<1	<1	1	2	1	<1	<1	<1	<1	<1	<1
Islam	1	1	1	<1	<1	1	1	<1	<1	<1	<1	<1	<1
Hindu	1	1	<1	<1	<1	1	<1	<1	<1	<1	<1	<1	<1
Buddhist	1	1	1	<1	1	1	1	<1	<1	<1	<1	<1	<1
Sikh	<1	2	1	<1	<1	<1	<1	<1	<1	<1	<1	<1	<1
Other	<1	<1	<1	<1	<1	<1	<1	<1	<1	<1	<1	1	<1
No religion	13	31	20	11	14	13	4	6	8	4	2	35	11

SOURCE: Derived from Statistics Canada, *Religions in Canada,* 1991 Census of Canada, Cat. no. 93-319 (Ottawa: Industry, Science and Technology Canada). Used by authority of the Minister of Industry, 1997.

Canadians are Catholic, the same is true of only 1 in 4 Americans. Furthermore, only about 1 in 10 Canadians identify with conservative Protestant (evangelical) groups, in contrast to more than 3 in 10 Americans. Again, beyond cold demographics, there is good reason to believe that to be a Catholic, a mainliner, or a conservative in Canada is not necessarily the same as it is in the United States. A 1996 Angus Reid poll of Canadians and Americans found, for example, a higher proportion of commitment among U.S. Catholics and mainline Protestants than among their Canadian counterparts. Among evangelicals, the proportions exhibiting commitment were about the same (Fledderus, 1997).

When asked about actual *membership* in religious groups, as opposed to mere affiliation or identification, more Canadians — about 30 percent — claim to belong to churches than to any other single voluntary group. According to various polls, about 1 in 4 say they attend services weekly, and roughly the same proportion of people with school-age children expose their children to church schools.

At the same time, however, there has been a considerable decline in church attendance in recent years, as indicated by the Gallup poll findings summarized in Figure 6.1. Gallup asks Canadians if they have attended a service "in the last seven days" — the phrasing of the inquiry adds sporadic attenders

to those who claim they attend every week. Using such a measure, Gallup has found that, in the years since World War II, Protestant attendance dropped from around 60 percent to about 30 percent in the mid-1970s, rebounding to 40 percent by the mid-1990s — led by conservative Protestant groups. The decline in Roman Catholic attendance appears to have started around 1965, dropping from roughly 85 to 40 percent in the 1990s — led by low church-going in Quebec. No such dramatic decline in attendance has taken place in the United States.

The downward pattern of involvement in Canada may, of course, change. Indeed, some observers contend that it is changing, that there is a renewed interest in religion. Critical to discerning such trends are the individual and societal factors that influence the prevalence and depth of religious commitment.

■ THE SOURCES OF RELIGION

Much of the early work in the scientific study of religion focussed on primitive or simple cultures in which religion was pervasive. Everyone seemed religious. Consequently, it is not surprising that observers sought to understand the origin of religion itself, rather than the sources of individual variations in commitment.

However, individual differences in religion's importance in modern societies have called for explanations as to why some people are religious and others are not. These explanations focus either on individuals or on social structure.

▲ INDIVIDUAL–CENTRED EXPLANATIONS

At least three dominant "person-centred" explanations of religious commitment have emerged.

Reflection

The desire to comprehend reality is widespread among humans. Anthropologist Clifford Geertz (1968: 15) notes:

> it does appear to be a fact that at least some men — in all probability, most men — are unable . . . just to look at the stranger features of the world's landscape in dumb astonishment or bland apathy without trying to develop . . . some notions as to how such features might be reconciled with the more ordinary deliverances of experience.

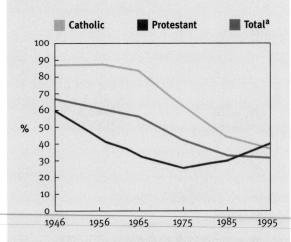

◆ **Figure 6.1** Attendance at Religious Services, Canada, 1946–1995

Percentage of people indicating that they attended church or synagogue in the last seven days.

■ **Catholic**   ■ **Protestant**   ■ **Total**[a]

[a] "Total" refers to all Canadians, regardless of faith.

SOURCE: Gallup Canada, Inc., surveys, 1946–1995.

In the course of reflecting on the meaning of existence, people have commonly concluded that life has a supernatural, "transempirical" dimension. As Weber (1963: 117) put it, religion is the product of an "inner compulsion to understand the world as a meaningful cosmos and take up a position toward it."

There is little doubt that Canadians reflect on life's so-called big questions. Some 80 percent say they think about such issues as the origin and purpose of life, the meaning of suffering, and what happens after we die. Yet such reflection is not strongly related to religious commitment. Fewer than 1 in 3 Canadians who often raise these questions give evidence of being religiously committed.

Socialization

A second person-centred explanation sees religious commitment as the product of learning. Freud (1962 [1928]) went so far as to say that religion is learned pretty much like the multiplication table. He may not have been exaggerating. In the terms of Durkheim's analysis, personal religiosity depends on collective religiosity, since ideas tend to be instilled through individuals and institutions. Therefore, one would expect that people who are religious have been exposed to social environments that are positive toward religion, whether those environments consist of an entire society, a community, an institution, an ethnic group, or — especially — family and friends.

Accommodation to social pressures, notably those of primary groups, seems to be another source of religious-group involvement. For example, one marital partner may become more active in response to the hopes and expectations of the other; friends in response to friends; and some "baby boomer" parents in response to having young children (see, for example, Roozen, McKinney, and Thompson, 1990; Brady, 1991). In communities where religion is pervasive, accommodation appears to act as an important source of religious involvement.

Research by Bruce Hunsberger (1980; Hunsberger and Brown, 1984) involving students at Wilfrid Laurier University and the University of Manitoba led him to conclude that emphasis on religion in childhood is positively associated with later religiosity. Similarly, the Project Canada surveys have documented a noteworthy relationship between the commitment of respondents and their parents (Bibby, 1993, 1996). Some 90 percent of Canadians with Protestant parents are Protestants themselves. The same level of identification is also found for children of Roman Catholic parents. Furthermore, about 80 percent of today's weekly attenders were also weekly churchgoers when they were growing up.

One of the strongest predictors of adult religiosity is childhood religious practice. When parents participate in religious observance with their children, the early socialization experience is often imprinted for life. SOURCE: Bushnell Soifer/Tony Stone.

It is important to keep in mind that socialization appears to be a *necessary* but not a *sufficient* cause of religiosity. That is, to the extent that Canadians are currently involved in religious groups, most had parents who also were involved. However, the fact that Canadians had parents who were involved does not ensure that they will follow suit. Although about 80 percent of today's weekly attenders had parents who attended weekly, only about 1 in 3 Canadians whose fathers or mothers attended services weekly are themselves weekly attenders.

As a result of declining service attendance over the past few decades, a decreasing number of parents are actively involved in religious groups and, therefore, passing the experience of organized religion on to their children (see Table 6.3). In view of the lack of such religious socialization, adult participation levels can only be expected to decline in the future.

Surveys have also found that the commitment level of one's spouse is strongly related to person-

	Age of respondents			
	18–34	35–54	55+	Total
Their mothers	49%	61%	69%	59%
Their fathers	43	49	57	49

◆ **Table 6.3** Parents' Attendance at Religious Services during Respondents' Childhood, Canada, 1995

SOURCE: Derived from Reginald W. Bibby, Project Can95 National Survey.

al involvement and the valuation of religion. In more than 7 in 10 cases, if one partner is a weekly attender, so is the other. In fewer than 2 in 10 cases does a person attend weekly if the spouse does not. The same pattern of spousal influence is evident among respondents who view religion as "very important."

Deprivation

A third person-centred explanation of religious commitment is that the religious are drawn primarily from society's deprived or disadvantaged. Religion provides "pie in the sky by and by," a means of compensating for deprivation. The roots of such thinking are found in the work of Karl Marx and Sigmund Freud.

The deprivation argument has been developed more fully by Glock and Stark (1965). They contend that five types of deprivation are predominant in the rise and development of religious and secular movements: economic, social, organismic (that is, physical or mental), psychic, and ethical. The first three types of deprivation are self-explanatory. Psychic deprivation refers to the lack of a meaningful system of values, and ethical deprivation refers to having values that are in conflict with those dominant in a society.

Research suggests that if deprivation is measured using so-called objective indicators such as income, health, and social relationships (which gauge economic, organismic, and social deprivation, respectively), deprivation is not strongly related to religious commitment in either the United States (Roof and Hoge, 1980) or Canada (Hobart, 1974). This is not to say that deprivation is never a significant factor for some individuals and religious groups. But the findings indicate that, as a whole, the religiously committed in North America are not, as a whole, any more or less disadvantaged than others.

▲ STRUCTURE-CENTRED EXPLANATIONS

Thus far, we have been examining what we might call "kinds of people" explanations of religious commitment. What these explanations have in common is their emphasis on individuals, who are said to turn to religion as a result of reflection, socialization, or deprivation. An adequate understanding of commitment, however, must also take into account the influence of the societal context in which people find themselves.

S.D. Clark (1948), for example, has argued that, historically, the emergence of sect-like groups in Canada was tied to the existence of unstable conditions, which were produced by factors such as immigration and economic depression. With industrialization and increased prosperity and stability, sects tended to evolve into denominations — a process referred to as **denominationalism**. A further example of the impact of societal factors on religion can be found in Quebec. Much of the drop-off in Roman Catholic attendance between 1965 and 1980 was related to the accelerated modernization of Quebec, including the church's relinquishing much of its important role in education and social services to the province (see, for example, Rouleau, 1977; Beyer, 1993, 1997).

The climate that contemporary societies provide for religion is a subject of considerable controversy. There are some observers who maintain that increasing industrialization and postindustrialization contribute to a decline in the pervasiveness and influence of religion. This **secularization thesis** can be found in Comte, Durkheim, Marx, and Freud. But there is also a **persistence thesis**. Proponents of this thesis claim that religion — traditional or otherwise — persists in industrial and postindustrial societies, continuing to address questions of meaning and purpose, and responding to widespread interest in spirituality.

In Canada, we can readily explore the relationship between religious commitment and some of the correlates of social and cultural change — such as urbanization, greater education, workforce participation, and exposure to mass media, along with the passage of time. If the secularization thesis is correct, we would expect commitment to be low, with minor differences by social characteristics such as community size and education. Over time, people in rural areas should come to resemble their urban counterparts in being less religious; the same should also be true of high-school drop-outs and college graduates, the elderly, and young adults. The culture should be so secularized that no sector of the population remains untouched.

What do the findings show? Differences continue to exist by age, reflecting at least in part the different eras in which Canadians were raised. But as education and workforce participation *increase,* commitment tends to *decrease* only moderately (see Table 6.4). These data suggest that Canada is already a highly secularized society. Significantly, there is a tendency for the modernization–secularization pattern to be reflected regionally: The somewhat less industrialized Atlantic provinces have a higher level of commitment than the other four regions of the country.

To the extent that people in Canada are religiously committed, the key sources of that commitment are neither institutions such as the media or education, nor the desire for compensation in the face of deprivation. Rather, those who place a high value on religion tend to be those who have been exposed to proreligious socialization by family, friends, and other significant people. This is not to say that reflection about meaning, felt needs, or a desire for spiritual satisfaction do not play roles. It is, however, to say that the key links to religious commitment and religious involvement are invariably people.

■ THE CONSEQUENCES OF RELIGION

Does religion have an impact on the way individuals live their lives, or is it largely irrelevant? If such an influence exists, does religion tend to contribute

◆ **Table 6.4** Attendance at Religious Services and Importance of Religion by Modernization Correlates, Canada, 1995

	Current weekly attenders	Those viewing religion as "very important"
Era (date of birth)		
1940 and earlier	40%	40%
1941–60	20	21
1961–77	15	20
Education		
High school or less	28	30
Some postsecondary	23	25
Degree or more	21	23
Workforce participation		
Not employed outside the home	29	30
Employed outside the Home	19	20
Region		
Atlantic	38	31
Quebec	19	19
Ontario	23	25
Prairies	28	38
British Columbia	19	20

SOURCE: Derived from Reginald W. Bibby, Project Can95 National Survey.

to individual and societal well-being, or does it more often produce anxiety and guilt, social indifference, and bigotry? And if religion does have an impact — adding, say, to civility — to what extent is its influence unique?

Those who value faith claim that religion has positive consequences for individuals and, in turn, for societies. Christians, for example, are likely to tell us that, ideally, mature followers are personally in-fluenced by their faith, experiencing emotions like joy, hope, and empowerment. They also aspire to show compassion in their dealings with others, exhibiting qualities such as concern, tolerance, forgiveness, and honesty. At the same time, because religious groups differ considerably on specific norms, such as sexual orientation, gambling, and abortion, the attitudes of the committed would be expected vary considerably.

Among other questions, the sociology of religion asks: Does religion influence the way individuals live? Does religion contribute to individual and societal well-being? SOURCE: Jean Paul Lemieux, *Lazare* (1941). Oil on masonite, 101 x 83.5 cm. Transparency provided by the Art Gallery of Ontario. Reproduced with permission of the Lemieux family.

Social scientists have explored the effects of Christianity on personal characteristics and interpersonal relations. Here is what they have been finding.

▲ PERSONAL CONSEQUENCES

Marx and Freud conceded, in essence, that religion contributed to positive personal characteristics such as happiness, contentment, and hope. Their criticism of religion rested in their belief that such qualities were based on illusion rather than reality.

Actual research on the consequences of individual commitment is surprisingly limited and suffers from serious methodological flaws. *Time-order* is often vague, so one does not know whether religion is the cause, the effect, or simply correlated with something like happiness; the *strength of relationships* is not always specified; and *controls* for other factors that might explain the relationships are commonly inadequate (Bouma, 1970; Wuthnow, 1973; Levin and Markides, 1986).

Apart from methodological shortcomings, the research findings on religion and what we might refer to generally as "mental health" are contradictory. Highly respected social psychologist Milton Rokeach (1965: 2), summing up a number of his studies, wrote: "We have found that people with formal religious affiliation are more anxious [than others]. Believers, compared with non-believers, complain more often of working under great tension, sleeping fitfully, and similar symptoms."

Yet researchers have consistently found a negative relationship between religious commitment and *anomie* (Lee and Clyde, 1974) — a characteristic of valuelessness and rootlessness that Srole (1956) sees as related to anxiety. Furthermore, involvement in groups such as sects and cults has been shown to provide improved self-images and hope in the face of economic and social deprivation (e.g., Whyte, 1966). Frankel and Hewitt (1994), among others, have found that religious group involvement and mental health are positively related. What seems apparent is that some forms of religiosity are connected with psychological and emotional well-being, while others are not (for overviews, see Bergin, 1983; Gorsuch, 1988).

Canadian analyses suggest that, overall, people who exhibit religious commitment are slightly more inclined than others to claim a high level of happiness, to find life exciting, to express a high level of satisfaction with family, friends, and leisure activities, and to view death with hope rather than with mystery or even fear (Bibby, 1987; 1993; 1995; and see Figure 6.2). However, when controls are introduced, and the impact of other variables such as age, education, community size, and region is taken into account, the apparent modest influence of commitment typically disappears, or at least has to be qualified. For example, Gee and Veevers (1990) found that religious involvement and life satisfaction were positively related nationally, but not in British Columbia.

In short, religious commitment by itself appears to have a very limited influence on valued personal characteristics. Moreover, it is often less important than such variables as age, education, or employment in predicting personal well-being.

This "no-difference" finding does not mean that faith is not adding something to the lives of people who value faith. Rather, in the light of the relatively high levels of happiness and contentment reported by Canadians generally, it suggests that large numbers of other people are finding alternative pathways to personal well-being. Religion is having an impact, but it is not a unique impact.

▲ INTERPERSONAL CONSEQUENCES

One of the first empirical attempts to examine the relationship between religious commitment and compassion was carried out by Clifford Kirkpatrick

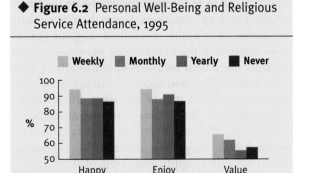

◆ **Figure 6.2** Personal Well-Being and Religious Service Attendance, 1995

SOURCE: Derived from Reginald W. Bibby, *The Bibby Report: Social Trends Canadian Style* (Toronto: Stoddart, 1995), p. 136. Used with permission of Stoddart Publishing Co. Limited, Canada.

Box 6.2
Bishops Blame Balanced Budget

Halifax (CP)—Canada's Catholic bishops say governments are shirking their responsibility for society's poor—especially women and children—in the name of balanced budgets.

"The church is willing to do its share," said Archbishop Marcel Gervais of Ottawa as the Canadian Conference of Catholic Bishops released a statement attacking the dismantling of the country's social safety net.

"But when governments are foisting on to agencies and churches the responsibility of people most in need, then I must protest," Gervais said Thursday, which the United Nations deemed an international day for the eradication of poverty.

"It is simply not acceptable."

Churches across Canada are seeing growing lineups at food banks, soup kitchens and shelters as federal, provincial and municipal governments cut social programs to eliminate deficits.

In a sharply worded pastoral letter, the Catholic bishops say Christians must speak out for the 4.8 million Canadians who live in poverty.

"To think that almost one Canadian child in five lives in poverty in one of the richest societies in world history is nothing less than a damning indictment," says the eight-page pastoral letter, prepared for the bishops' annual meeting in Halifax.

The letter quotes a recent report by an interchurch coalition: "In our society, if a parent denies a child food, clothing, and social security, it is considered child abuse. But when our government denies 1,362,000 children the same, it is simply balancing the budget.

SOURCE: Canadian Press, October 17, 1996. Reprinted with permission of Canadian Press.

Proponents of the secularization thesis, you will recall, maintain that religion is bound to be replaced by science and reason as society modernizes. Dobbelaere (1981) argues that this process has three aspects. *Institutionally,* secularization involves a reduction in the number of areas of life over which religion has authority and meaning. *Personally,* individuals increasingly use the observable world rather than religion as a frame of reference for interpreting and giving meaning to life. *Organizationally,* religious groups become increasingly conformist and routine rather than radical and spontaneous.

Opponents of the secularization thesis counter that humans have needs, such as the need to come to grips with death, that only religion can satisfy. Thus, even if secularization leads to the demise of some religious groups, new expressions of religiosity are bound to appear. New religious forms include sects, or groups that break away from established religions, and **cults,** or groups with origins outside of older religions. Given the emergence of

such new groups, secularization may actually stimulate the growth of religion (Stark and Bainbridge, 1985). Moreover, it has been predicted that such growth will be most evident in places where the "religious marketplace" is robust. In the United States, for example, when established religions fail to meet human needs, new religious "firms" move in to increase their "market share." From this point of view, shifts in the overall "religious economy" over time involve "the rising and falling fortunes of religious firms, not the rise and fall of religion per se" (Finke and Stark, 1992: 275).

Much anecdotal evidence can be mustered to support either side of this debate, but systematic and representative observations are preferable. Consider Campbell and Curtis's (1994) data on religious involvement, beliefs, and religious self-image in 21 countries in the period 1981–1983. Although they found that there was a decline in religious involvement overall, they noted that the United States and the United Kingdom were exceptions to this trend. Moreover, the 6 countries that exhibited the highest levels of involvement differed considerably in terms of their levels of industrialization and urbanization, along with their Catholic versus non-Catholic mix. Thus, there is no consistent pattern between industrialization or postindustrialization and religiosity (see Table 6.6). Campbell and Curtis also considered the merits of the argument that religiosity will be highest in countries characterized by pluralistic and competitive marketplaces. They concluded, on the basis of their research, that such interpretations were roughly consistent with the comparative data, but there were exceptions, notably Australia and Japan. In those countries, pluralism is high and regulation is low, but involvement levels are weak.

Viewed in an international context, Canada presents us with a paradox. Personal beliefs and practices are high, yet involvement in religious groups is well below that in such countries as Mexico and the United States, and shows signs of dropping to levels found in countries such as England, France, and Germany.

Research has failed to support the idea that large numbers of Canadians are actually deserting the churches in favour of other religions, old or new. Few Canadians are interested in such alternatives as New Age, Transcendental Meditation (TM), Hare Krishna, Eckankar, Scientology, Mormonism, or the Jehovah's Witnesses, and such interest as exists is often fleeting (Bibby and Weaver, 1985). Furthermore, few "drop-outs" from mainline Protestantism and Roman Catholicism are ending up in conservative Protestant groups such as Pentecostals and Baptists. At present, conservative Protestant groups comprise about 7 percent of the population, compared with 8 percent in 1871. Evangelical groups rely heavily on retention of their members and their members' children to maintain their numbers.

Nor is it the case that many Canadians are substituting TV's "electronic churches" for attendance at religious services. Fewer than 5 percent of Canadians say they regularly watch religious services on TV — a decline from 29 percent who were watching such programs on television or listening to them on radio in 1958. Eight out of 10 regular TV viewers also attend services weekly, suggesting that the TV programs are largely a supplement for those involved in religious groups, rather than a substitute for the uninvolved.

If Canadians are not flocking to new religions or to evangelical services and TV programs, then neither is their religion taking a less visible, more private form. At least 60 percent of Canadians do not claim to be religiously committed, privately or otherwise. Can we then conclude that the number of

◆ **Table 6.6** Practices, Beliefs, and Religious Self-Image for Selected Countries

	Practices				Beliefs				Self-image
	Attend weekly	Attend monthly+	Church role	Pray	God	Life after death	Hell	Rein-carnation	A religious person
Ireland	82%	88%	7%	80%	95%	75%	54%	27%	63%
Mexico	54	75	9	83	97	76	50	46	74
South Africa	43	61	21	85	95	70	40	26	69
United States	42	59	21	85	96	71	68	23	81
Spain	40	53	10	69	86	55	33	25	62
Italy	32	48	5	70	82	46	28	21	80
Canada	**31**	**45**	**15**	**73**	**91**	**61**	**38**	**29**	**74**
Germany	18	34	6	55	68	29	13	18	54
Australia	17	23	11	34	80	49	35	25	58
Britain	14	23	6	49	73	54	26	26	53
France	11	16	3	41	59	35	14	22	48
Hungary	11	16	—	45	44	13	9	7	42
Sweden	5	14	9	33	52	27	10	14	32
Japan	3	12	4	41	39	21	16	30	24
Iceland	2	10	5	42	77	55	12	27	67

SOURCE: Derived from the World Values Survey as reported in Robert A. Campbell and James E. Curtis, "Religious Involvement across Societies," *Journal for the Scientific Study of Religion, 33* (1994), pp. 215–29. Used with permission.

religious Canadians is declining and that the future of religion in Canada is that it has no future? It is true that the number of Canadians claiming in the census that they had no religion rose from 4 percent in 1971 to 12 percent in 1991. However, most of these people are single and young. As they marry and have children, many leave the "no-religion" category and affiliate with the Catholic or Protestant churches. And the group with which they identify is usually the same one as their parents. Most of them appear to re-affiliate, not out of spiritual urgency, but because of the desire for rites of passage pertaining to marriage, the birth of children, and death (see Table 6.7).

In short, the search for religious drop-outs in Canada yields an intriguing result: Few have actually left home. Almost 9 in 10 Canadians in the 1990s are continuing to identify with fairly established, predominantly Christian groups. A nucleus of only about 25 percent attend services weekly, but another 65 percent attend at least occasionally.

Most of the casual attenders expect to receive rites of passage from their identification groups when they are needed. Of particular importance, very few indicate that they have any inclination to turn elsewhere (Bibby, 1993; 1996).

It is clear that religious group identification is valued in this country. But it is equally clear that Canadians differ considerably in the role they want religion to play in their lives. Some embrace it wholeheartedly, seemingly as a meaning system that informs much of their lives. Others want some beliefs, some practices, some specialized services. Still others — a small minority — want nothing from religion or religious organizations.

It seems, therefore, that the significant religious development associated with industrialization and postindustrialization in Canada has not been the abandonment of religion but the tendency of Canadians to reject Christianity as an authoritative system of meaning. Instead, they draw on Judeo-Christian "fragments" — certain beliefs, practices, and

◆ **Table 6.7** Desire for Rites of Passage (Expected to Be Performed in the Future), by Age and Attendance at Religious Services, Canada, 1995

		Roman Catholics		
	Nationally	Outside Quebec	Quebec	**Protestants**
Birth-related	**25%**	**29%**	**35%**	**19%**
18–34	33	42	52	25
35–54	21	25	31	19
55+	17	17	21	15
Weekly	24	32	31	17
Less than weekly	25	28	37	21
Wedding ceremony	**31**	**35**	**36**	**25**
18–34	45	55	49	36
35–54	27	27	33	27
55+	18	17	25	16
Weekly	26	30	33	19
Less than weekly	33	39	38	28
Funeral	**57**	**63**	**57**	**58**
18–34	60	66	64	59
35–54	59	68	59	63
55+	53	57	47	56
Weekly	60	63	51	67
Less than weekly	57	65	60	57

SOURCE: Derived from Reginald W. Bibby, *Project Canada Consultation on Research and Ministry* (Lethbridge, AB: University of Lethbridge, 1996), p.23.

organizational offerings — in a highly specialized, consumer-like fashion. In a similar manner, Canadians select fragments of other non-naturalistic systems — astrology, ESP, New Age, and so on — without adopting them as substitutes for Christianity. As Stark and Bainbridge (1985) suggest, these other systems function as "consumer cults," providing "add-ons" to their Christian main courses.

Although religious groups might decry such selective consumption, over time they have adapted to this consumer mentality. In the face of consumer demand, Canada's main established groups — the Roman Catholics, United Church, Anglicans, and conservative Protestants — have been offering increasingly varied "religious menus." The diversification of functions by Canada's religious establishment has made it extremely difficult for new rivals to penetrate the country's religion market. Churches have also been patient with individuals who want minimal involvement, seldom withholding from them basic rites of passage, denying them admission to services, or removing them from membership rolls.

The stability of the religious scene in Canada, along with its prevalent "fragment" style, has been further documented by national surveys of teenagers between the ages of 15 and 19 (Bibby and Posterski, 1985, 1992). The surveys have found that the country's "emerging generation" differs negligibly from adults when it comes to religion. About 90 percent of teenagers claim the same group affiliation as their parents, and only about 2 percent indicate any strong interest in the new religions. Their belief, practice, experience, and knowledge levels are similar to those of adults. Their interest in other supernatural phenomena is also very high, as is the acknowledgement of spiritual needs (see Table 6.8).

Yet, when it comes to commitment, only about the same proportion of teens as adults — some 25 percent — say that religion is "very important" to them. Fewer than 1 in 5 attend religious services regularly, and only 15 percent of teens say that they receive a high level of enjoyment from church or synagogue life (this figure includes only half of the regular attenders). When they are 15 years of age, 19 percent are going to services frequently; by the time they are 19, that figure drops to about 13 percent, similar to the level of attendance of adults in the 18–29 age range.

Like their parents, however, young people are not particularly angry with religious groups. About 40 percent indicate that they have a high level of confidence in religious leaders, which places the clergy behind educational leaders (67 percent) but ahead of politicians (30 percent). Moreover, teenagers seldom make religion a target of humour. But the dominant tendency is to draw selectively from re-

◆ **Table 6.8** A Profile of Religion and Spirituality in Canada: Teenagers and Adults

		Adults	Teenagers
Beliefs	God	81%	81%
	Divinity of Jesus	72	80
	Life after death	71	64
	Spirit world contact	43	44
	Will personally be reincarnated	27	32
Practice (weekly)	Pray privately	48	30
	Read horoscope	28	42
	Read the Bible	20	17
	Attend religious services	25	18
Experience	Have experienced God	43	34
Knowledge	Know Peter denied Jesus	46	41
Salience	High religious commitment	26	24
Spirituality	Have spiritual needs	52	58

SOURCE: Reginald W. Bibby, The Project Canada Survey Series.

ligion, rather than allowing it to become an all-embracing system of meaning. Like their parents, young Canadians appear to be highly selective consumers who, rather than wanting much, want very little from the nation's religious groups.

It may well be that the structural and cultural changes associated with Canada's entry into the postindustrial "information age" have made meaning systems that encompass all of an individual's life incongruent with the varied roles people must play. In other words, fragments may be more functional than all-encompassing religions in a society that requires people to compartmentalize their experiences in order to play diverse roles. Religious systems may also seem frequently at odds with dominant cultural values such as rationalism, consumption, and enjoyment.

If that is the state of religion in postmodern society, then we do not choose belief, practice, and service fragments over systems because there are no system options. Rather, we choose fragments because they are more conducive to present-day life. As Bryan Wilson (1975: 80) has put it, modern societies offer "a supermarket of faiths; received, jazzed-up, homespun, restored, imported and exotic. But all of them co-exist because the wider society is so secular, because they are relatively unimportant consumer items."

In assessing the Canadian situation, Peter Beyer (1997: 25) speculates that, in at least the immediate future, "most religious consumers, with a relatively modest demand for purely religious product, will consume eclectically, with perhaps a fair degree of 'brand' loyalty, but more often than not without membership and the sort of commitment that produced regular participation." He is probably right. But what also bears watching is the extent to which religious groups can more adeptly respond to the apparent widespread and persistent interests and needs relating to meaning, the supernatural realm, and

spirituality. In 1995, no less than 63 percent of Canadians indicated that they would consider being more involved in religious groups if they found it to be worthwhile for themselves or their families. That figure included 64 percent of people who currently are attending on a yearly basis, and 42 percent who say that they never attend. Equally interesting is the finding (Bibby, 1996) that those who express openness to greater involvement included 72 percent of Canadians between the ages of 18 and 34 (see Figure 6.3).

Whether fragments will become meaning systems, and religion more significant personally and socially, will depend, it seems, not only on changing structural and cultural conditions, but also on the ability of religious groups to function far more effectively than they are at the present time. ■

◆ **Figure 6.3** Receptivity to Greater Involvement in the Church, Protestants and Catholics, by Age

Percentage of people indicating that they would consider being more involved in the church if they found involvement to be "worthwhile for myself or my family"

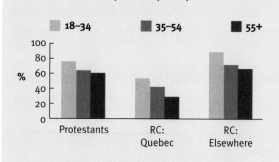

SOURCE: Derived from Reginald W. Bibby, *Project Canada Consultation on Research and Ministry* (Lethbridge, AB: University of Lethbridge, 1996), p. 34.

SUMMARY

1. Sociology uses the scientific method to study religion, in contrast to religion, which explores reality beyond what can be known empirically.

2. The sociology of religion has been strongly influenced by the theoretical contributions of Marx, who stressed the compensatory role of religion in the face of economic deprivation; Durkheim, who emphasized both the social origin of religion and its important social cohesive function; and Weber, who gave considerable attention to the relationship between ideas and behaviour.

3. Religion can be defined as a system of meaning with a supernatural referent used to interpret the world. Humanist perspectives make no such use of the supernatural realm, attempting instead to make life meaningful.

4. Personal religious commitment has come increasingly to be seen as having many facets or dimensions. Four such dimensions are commonly noted: belief, practice, experience, and knowledge. Personal commitment is created and sustained by collective religiosity. In Canada, organized religion has experienced a considerable decline in participation in recent years, a trend that has had critical implications for commitment at the individual level.

5. The variations in the levels of individual commitment that characterize complex societies have led to explanations that emphasize individual and structural factors. Reflection, socialization, and deprivation have been prominent among the individual explanations, while the dominant structural assertion has been the secularization thesis.

6. At the individual level, religion appears to be, at best, one of many paths leading to valued characteristics such as personal happiness and compassion. Although religion can be socially disruptive, it more commonly seems to contribute to social solidarity, frequently mirroring the characteristics of groups and societies.

7. Historically, observers of religion have been divided on its future, asserting both secularization and persistence theses. Internationally, there is growing qualitative and quantitative support for the persistence thesis.

8. The search for alleged religious drop-outs in Canada reveals that few have turned to new religions, conservative Protestant groups, privatized expressions, or the "no-religion" category. Most still identify with the established groups.

9. The apparent paradox of widespread beliefs and practices existing at the same time as relatively low commitment suggests that many people in Canada find it useful to draw selectively on religion, rather than embracing it as an all-encompassing system of meaning. Such a pattern seems to be common to highly advanced societies more generally.

10. Religion's future will depend not only on social and individual issues, but also on the extent to which religious groups are effective as organizations in responding to widespread interest and need.

QUESTIONS TO CONSIDER

1. Which of the three key theorists do you find to be the most helpful in understanding religion — Durkheim, Marx, or Freud?

2. What does it mean to be religious?

3. To what extent are people in Canada today interested in (a) spirituality and (b) organized religion? What do you mean by the term "spirituality"?

4. What kinds of people do you find are interested in (a) spirituality and (b) organized religion?

5. Does religion make any difference in the lives of the people you know? Would Canadian society be any different if organized religion disappeared next weekend?

6. Are Canadians interested in the supernatural? What is the evidence?

7. Do you think it is true that secularization stimulates religious innovation — that the decline of old groups provides the opportunity for new groups to surface and prosper?

8. Imagine that you are serving as a consultant to a major Canadian religious group. What might you suggest it consider doing in order to (a) keep the young people it has, and (b) gain the interest of Canadians who are not actively involved?

GLOSSARY

church–sect typology A framework, originating with Weber, in which religious organizations are studied in terms of ideal-type, church, and sect characteristics.

civil religion The tendency for nationalistic emphases to be nurtured by a society's religions, so that a culture takes on many religious-like characteristics; most often used with respect to the United States.

collective conscience Durkheim's term, referring to the awareness of the group being more than the sum of its individual members, and believing that what is being experienced is the supernatural.

collective religiosity Religious commitment as manifested in and through religious groups; key to the creation and sustenance of personal religiosity.

cults Religious groups that have their origins outside of older religions; sects, in contrast, are groups that have broken away from established religions.

denominationalism The tendency for a wide variety of Protestant religious groups to come into being, seemingly reflecting variations not only in theology but also — and perhaps primarily — in social characteristics.

dimensions of religiosity Various facets of religious commitment; Glock and Stark, for example, identify four: belief, experience, practice, and knowledge.

humanist perspectives Systems of meaning used to interpret the world that do not have a supernatural referent (e.g., communism, scientism).

monotheism Belief in one god.

persistence thesis The assertion that religion will continue to have a significant place in the modern world, because it never has actually declined, or because people continue to have interests and needs that only religion can satisfy.

personal religiosity The level of religious commitment characterizing an individual.

profane See *sacred and profane*.

Protestant ethic A term associated with Max Weber, referring to the Protestant reformation emphases of John Calvin, Martin Luther, and others on the importance of work performed well as an indication of living one's life "to the glory of God"; key characteristics include hard work, diligence, frugality, and good use of time.

religions Systems of meaning for interpreting the world that have a supernatural referent (e.g., Christianity, Hinduism).

sacred and profane Two categories by which Durkheim claimed all things are classified; the sacred represents those things that are deemed to warrant profound respect, and the profane encompasses essentially everything else.

secularization thesis The assertion that religion as it has been traditionally known is continuously declining, resulting in a loss of religious authority, societally and individually, as well as changes in religious organizations themselves.

● SUGGESTED READING

Bibby, Reginald W. (1993). *Unknown Gods: The Ongoing Story of Religion in Canada*. Toronto: Stoddart. This book draws on the work of the author and others in examining the widespread receptivity of Canadians to religion and spirituality, and assesses why religious groups are failing and what might be done to turn things around.

Clark, S.D. (1948). *Church and Sect in Canada*. Toronto: University of Toronto Press. A Canadian classic that examines the social factors contributing to the rise of different types of religious groups in this country.

Dawson, Lorne L., ed. (1996). *Cults in Context: Readings in the Study of New Religious Movements*. Toronto: Canadian Scholars' Press. A superb collection of readings of some of the best material available in the key areas of new religious movement research.

Greeley, Andrew M., ed. (1995). *Sociology and Religion: A Collection of Readings*. New York: Harper Collins. A diversified collection, ranging from classic Durkheim, Marx, Weber, and Freud, to prominent Americans today; the material is creatively organized to provide background and permit exchanges on a wide variety of key topics.

Hewitt, W.E., ed. (1993). *Sociology of Religion: A Canadian Focus*. Toronto: Harcourt Brace. Leading Canadian social scientists provide students with a good introduction both to the work being carried out in the country and to some of the scholars who are most active in this area of research.

Niebuhr, H. Richard. (1929). *The Social Sources of Denominationalism*. New York: Henry Holt and Company. A classic attempt to probe the role social factors (e.g., economics, nationality, race, and region) had in creating denominationalism in Europe and America. In the process, the author sensitizes students to the social sources of religion more generally.

Part Three INEQUALITY

MANY SCHOLARS REGARD THE STUDY OF SOCIAL
INEQUALITY — BETWEEN CLASSES, GENDER
GROUPS, ETHNIC AND RACIAL GROUPS, AND
NATIONS — AS THE CHIEF FOCUS OF SOCIOLOGY.
THIS PAINTING DEPICTS A WORLD WAR II
PARACHUTE ASSEMBLY LINE. IT CAPTURES A
MOMENT IN CANADIAN HISTORY WHEN WOMEN
MADE IMPORTANT INROADS INTO THE LABOUR
FORCE ON THEIR WAY TO ACHIEVING GREATER
GENDER EQUALITY. IT THUS REMINDS US OF
SOMETHING THAT THIS SECTION ILLUSTRATES
IN DETAIL: SOCIAL INEQUALITIES, ALTHOUGH
ALWAYS IN FLUX, CONTINUE TO BE TYPIFIED BY
SOCIAL AND ECONOMIC SEGREGATION.

CHAPTER SEVEN
Social Stratification

IN THIS CHAPTER YOU WILL LEARN THAT

- persistent patterns of social inequality are based on statuses assigned to individuals at birth and on how well individuals perform certain roles; societies vary in the degree to which mobility up and down the stratification system is possible

- explanations of the origins and impact of social stratification include: the theory of Karl Marx, which emphasizes the exploitation of the working class by owners of land and industry as the main source of inequality and change; the theory of Max Weber, which emphasizes the power that derives from property ownership, prestige, and politics; structural-functionalist theory, which holds that stratification is both inevitable and necessary; and several revisions of Marx's and Weber's ideas that render them more relevant to the late twentieth century

- although there has been considerable opportunity for upward occupational mobility in Canada, wealth and property are concentrated in relatively few hands, and one-sixth of Canadians live in poverty; because of labour-market changes, income inequality has been increasing; thus, the stratification structure we see in the future will probably not resemble the pattern that emerged in the affluent middle decades of this century

- one's position in society's stratification system has important consequences, both for lifestyle and the quality of life; those who are situated higher in the economic hierarchy tend to live better and live longer

HARVEY KRAHN
University of Alberta

■ INTRODUCTION

I pick up the weekend newspapers and flip through them quickly. Although the news writers don't use the term, I find myself reading about **social stratification** — that is, persistent patterns of social inequality within society. A top story on Friday describes how Edmonton inner-city social-service agencies are struggling with increased demand for their services from citizens with no income (*Edmonton Journal*, Dec. 20, 1996). The agencies put the blame on provincial government "welfare reform." After welfare benefits were reduced by 17 percent and many former welfare recipients were pushed into training programs, the number of people receiving official welfare assistance dropped dramatically. But, at the same time, food-bank use increased by 122 percent, and other "front-line" social-service agencies (e.g., shelters and drop-in centres) also experienced problems coping with increased demand. Judged by the number of people receiving welfare benefits, "welfare reform" has been successful. If finding decent jobs for all these people is the measure of success, we have to draw a different conclusion.

Near the front of Saturday's paper, I find an article describing how three of Canadian Airlines' unions have agreed to the wage rollback they were told to accept, even though their legally binding contracts had not yet ended. Fearful that they will lose their jobs if they do not agree to the company's demands, the workers have voted to accept the wage concession that the airline insists is necessary if it is to remain profitable (*Edmonton Journal*, Dec. 21, 1996). Immediately beneath this major story is a tiny article noting that the number of people who earned more than $250 000 but paid no taxes rose in 1994. A total of 290 Canadians made it into the tax-free, quarter-million club, up from 250 the year before. However, 1992 was a better year, with a total of 340 individuals in this exclusive group.

Further inside, Saturday's paper contains a story about a court case in Regina, where two young white men who admitted killing an aboriginal prostitute were found guilty of manslaughter, although they were originally charged with first-degree murder. Part of the defence was that the two men were too drunk to understand that, by viciously beating the victim, they could kill her. Aboriginal groups in Saskatchewan were outraged by the jury's decision, claiming that it revealed two justice systems in the province, "one for the Indian people and one for the white people" (*Edmonton Journal*, Dec. 21, 1996).

The common theme in these quite different stories is the existence of groups — welfare recipients, rank-and-file workers, nonwhites, women, and the unemployed — that are ranked lower than others in the social stratification system. A low position in this ranking typically means having little power, little wealth, and little prestige, whereas a higher position generally implies the opposite. In this chapter, we begin by discussing some of the ways in which sociologists study social stratification. We then examine a variety of theories of social stratification that attempt to explain its origins and impacts. The last section of the chapter focusses on occupational and class structures and material inequality in Canada, and concludes by asking whether inequality has been increasing in the recent past.

■ STRATIFICATION: A CORNERSTONE OF SOCIOLOGY

Standing back and looking at the whole discipline of sociology, we see four basic areas of inquiry. Sociologists study *social structure,* or the way in which society is organized, both formally and informally. We also ask questions about *social order.* What is it that holds together a society composed of individuals with different interests, and when and why does social order break down? Inquiries about *social change* form a third key area within the discipline. How and why do societies, the institutions and power structures within them, and the values and beliefs held by individual members change? Finally, sociologists spend a lot of time studying *social stratification,* the manner in which valued resources — that is, wealth, power, and prestige — are distributed, and the way in which advantages of wealth, power, and prestige are passed from generation to generation.

In fact, it could easily be argued that social stratification is the cornerstone of sociology. Descriptions of social structure that ignore the stratification system are clearly inadequate. For example, imagine describing Canadian society to someone from another country without referring to some features of stratification. Would the listener really have an adequate understanding of our society if she or he did not know that most businesses are run by men, that aboriginal Canadians are much more likely than most others to be living in poverty, and that disagreements about the relative power of the English-speaking majority and the French-speaking minority have dominated federal politics for decades?

Furthermore, inequalities in wealth can threaten social stability (the poor resenting the wealthy, for example, and demanding more equality), and inequalities in power can be used to maintain social order. For example, powerful companies might lobby provincial governments for changes in the labour laws that would make it more difficult for unions to organize company employees. In less democratic countries, direct control of the police and military by a powerful minority can lead to the quick and violent suppression of any unrest among the masses.

An understanding of social stratification is also essential for studying social change, since, frequently, it is the stratification system that is undergoing change. For example, changing gender roles and the slow movement of women into positions of power and authority in North America in the past few decades are really features of a changing stratification system. The massive social, economic, and political changes that began in the former Soviet Union in the late 1980s and that continue today are, among other things, changes in stratification systems, as the main source of power shifts from control of the political system to include control of the emerging free-market economy.

■ SOCIAL HIERARCHIES IN STRATIFIED SOCIETIES

Imagine a society in which stratification did not exist, in which all things of value were distributed equally. Even if you picture a very small group, perhaps a pre-industrial society with only a few hundred members, living on some isolated island where the necessities of life are easily obtained, it is still difficult to imagine a nonstratified society. A social hierarchy might emerge as a result of skill differences in fishing, in nursing the ill back to health, or in communicating with the spirits, for example. Inequalities in wealth might develop simply because some families were fortunate enough to have a larger number of children, providing more of the labour needed to accumulate valued possessions. And once accumulations of wealth began to be passed from generation to generation, a structured and relatively permanent pattern of inequality would emerge.

Perhaps you imagined some contemporary society composed of adults who, believing in the importance of equality, decided to live and work together, sharing all their possessions. Again, it is easy to imagine how some kind of social hierarchy could

emerge, as those with more useful skills found themselves playing a more central role in the society. No doubt, when important decisions needed to be made, these individuals would be more likely to influence the outcome.

We do not need to repeat this mental exercise too many times before we see that social stratification in one form or another exists in all societies. But our hypothetical examples are hardly typical. In most societies, stratification is much more pronounced, and basic skills are seldom the foundation of primary social hierarchies. Nevertheless, there are variations in the criteria by which individuals and groups are ranked, the degree to which they can move from one position to another within the hierarchy, and the extent of inequality in wealth and power that exists within the hierarchy.

▲ ASCRIBED AND ACHIEVED STATUS

Let's begin by defining the rank or position that one has within a social hierarchy as one's **status**. We can further distinguish between an **ascribed status** and an **achieved status**. The former is assigned to individuals, typically at birth. An ascribed status can be connected with race, gender, age, and other factors that are not chosen or earned, and that cannot be changed. (A few people do choose their gender status, but they are rare exceptions.) In contrast, an achieved status is precisely that — a position in a hierarchy that has been achieved by virtue of how well one performs in some role. The most obvious example is that of occupational statuses — for instance, individuals who have performed well in law school are entitled to become lawyers, and high-performance athletes strive to achieve the status of "professional athlete." By the same logic, one could achieve the status of "bum" by performing poorly in educational, employment, family, and other social roles.

Although we may accept that a completely nonstratified society is impossible, most of us would probably agree that a stratification system in which higher positions were achieved, not ascribed, would be preferable. In a **meritocracy,** such as this, everyone would have an equal opportunity to compete for higher-status positions and, presumably, those most capable would be awarded the highest rank. Such a society would exhibit a considerable degree of **social mobility,** as those who were more qualified moved up the social hierarchy to replace those who were less competent and who were consequently compelled to move down.

▲ OPEN AND CLOSED STRATIFICATION SYSTEMS

When we compare Canada with some other societies, or look back at our history, we find that this country has had what appears to be a fairly **open stratification system,** in which merit, rather than inheritance (or ascribed characteristics), determines social rank, and in which social change is therefore possible. For example, dramatic changes in the status of various groups have occurred in this country over time. Although the practice was not nearly as widespread in Canada as in the United States, slaves (most of them Native people) were bought and sold in Canada during the 1600s and 1700s (Pentland, 1981: 1). Chinese labourers, brought into the country to help build the railways, were kept out of most "white" jobs by law until well into the twentieth century (Li, 1982). Similarly, it was not until the 1960s that black Canadians were allowed to compete for anything but the lowest-level positions in the Canadian railway industry (Calliste, 1987). By the early 1800s, slavery had disappeared in Canada, and we now have laws against discrimination on the basis of race.

Comparing ourselves with other contemporary societies, we note that Canada does not have an aristocracy such as the one that exists in Britain, where children of wealthy and powerful families of long standing inherit positions and titles. The degree to which Canadians compete for higher-status occupations (in the education system and, later, within the workplace) stands in clear contrast to the situation in India, for example, where the caste into which an individual is born largely determines the type of work that he or she will be allowed to do. Although discrimination on the basis of caste membership has been illegal in India for several decades, the **caste system** continues to underpin an almost totally **closed stratification system**. Compared with India, then, Canada offers many more opportunities for upward social mobility, an indication of a more open stratification system.

It is all too easy, however, to overlook the extent to which ascribed statuses continue to limit opportunities for many Canadians as well. Discrimination against Native Canadians and against members of visible-minority groups continues to occur in Canada today (see Box 7.1). So too does discrimination against members of the gay community, against the disabled and the elderly, and against women. These people are in their lower-status positions not because they competed poorly for some higher ranking in the social hierarchy, but because they are old, disabled, gay, or female.

These are fairly obvious examples of the ways in which ascribed statuses continue to play a prominent role in Canada's social stratification system. But what about the child from a wealthy family who graduates from an excellent high school in an affluent neighbourhood, completes a degree or two in a prestigious and costly university, and then begins a career in a high-status, well-paying profession? Is this simply an example of someone achieving a deserved high-status position, or did the advantages of birth (ascribed status) play some part in this success story? Similarly, going back to the weekend newspaper, what about the 15 000 unemployed Alberta healthcare workers? Did their downward mobility reflect their failure to compete in an open, merit-based stratification system, or were they simply unfortunate enough to be employed in an industry that was being downsized?

As these examples illustrate, the social stratification system consists of a number of different hierarchies, some based on ascribed characteristics, others on achievement. If you flip through this textbook, you will see chapters devoted to dimensions of stratification and inequality such as gender, race, and ethnicity. Other chapters address activities (e.g., work) and institutions (e.g., education) in which stratification processes are extremely important, and still others focus on inequalities between regions and countries. Once you have read all these chapters, you will, no doubt, be convinced of the central importance of social stratification to the discipline of sociology.

▲ CLASS AND CLASS STRUCTURE

You will also notice that, even though studies of gender, race, ethnicity, and work take you in quite different directions, all frequently share an emphasis on inequalities in income and wealth or property, and on resulting inequalities in power. On average, women earn about two-thirds of what men earn. Older women are much more likely than older men to be living in poverty. Members of visible minorities and, particularly, aboriginal groups are more likely to be unemployed and, if they are employed, to be in low-paying jobs. Owners of large workplaces (employers, in other words) are wealthier than most other members of society, and employees in professional and managerial occupations typically earn a great deal more than lower-level employees. Owners, self-employed professionals, and managers typically have more job security than do nonmanagerial employees who are either paid by the hour or salaried. Recognizing, then, the extent to

Box 7.1
Aboriginal, Female, Poor, and Dealing with the Law

RCMP Commissioner Norman Inkster has formally apologized for the force's "inconsiderate and unprofessional" treatment of an Inuit rape victim who was dragged across the country in handcuffs to testify against her attacker.

In a recent letter to Kitty Nowdluk-Reynolds, Inkster said he was "absolutely appalled" at the behaviour of several Mounties, which brought discredit to the entire national police force. . . .

The 27-year-old woman's nightmare began in June 1990 when she was knocked down, choked, and raped in her home town of Iqaluit, N.W.T. A local man was arrested and, six days later, Nowdluk-Reynolds moved with her fiancé to Surrey, B.C., deciding to put the whole incident behind her.

She was arrested by the RCMP at her home a few months later when she didn't obey a subpoena ordering her to return to Iqaluit to appear as a witness.

It took almost eight days to return to Iqaluit—in part because her RCMP escort overslept and they missed their flight.

In all, Nowdluk-Reynolds spent time in five jail cells—at one point working three days in a prison laundry—and went for days without a shower.

She ended up riding to court in handcuffs in the same van as her rapist, separated only by a wire mesh.

Inusiq Shoo eventually pleaded guilty to aggravated assault and was sentenced to four years in prison. Nowdluk-Reynolds was not called to testify and was given a plane ticket back to Vancouver.

When she arrived at the airport late at night, the Mounties refused to drive her home and she was dropped off on a highway to catch a bus. . . .

SOURCE: Excerpted from Stephen Bindman, "Inkster Apologizes to Mistreated Rape Victim," *The Edmonton Journal,* February 15, 1993, p. A12. Reprinted with permission of Southam News.

which such material inequality (i.e., differences in income and wealth or property) parallels and overlaps other social hierarchies, the rest of this chapter will focus primarily on material inequality or, after we define the terms, on *class* and *class structure.*

Although the concept of **class** is seldom absent from discussions of social stratification, the definitions attached to it vary considerably. We will examine some of these definitions in the next section, which outlines several different theories of stratification. My own preference is to use the term in a fairly general sense, to indicate the position of an individual or a family within an economic hierarchy, along with others who have roughly the same amount of control over or access to economic or material resources (Grabb, 1990: 5). Thus, an individual can be said to be a member of a particular class,

whether this is a class of large landowners, a class of wage-labourers and salaried workers (i.e., the "working class"), or a "professional/managerial class." It is their similar economic situation and opportunities, a result of their shared position within a society's system of economic production, that makes these individuals members of the same class. In turn, we can use the term **class structure** to refer to the overall economic hierarchy composed of all such classes, choosing the word *structure* deliberately to indicate the relative stability and prominence of this social ranking.

Do you think of yourself as a member of a specific social class? Probably not. Like most North Americans, you probably have a reasonably good idea of how well off you are compared with others in your community. You probably have some sense of where your education, occupation, and income, or the education, occupation, and income of adult members of your household, fit in some general hierarchy of **socioeconomic status**. "Class," however, is unlikely to be part of your everyday vocabulary. Nor is it typically part of the media's vocabulary. The newspaper stories we examined earlier, for example, identified a number of different dimensions of stratification, including gender, race, and employment status, but class was not among them.

Does this make "class" a useless concept? I argue the opposite. As I have already suggested, and as you will see in this and other chapters, pronounced patterns of material inequality exist in our society, and overlap with most other dimensions of social stratification. The economic hierarchy is obviously not completely closed, but it is relatively stable and permanent, and is composed of some fairly distinct categories of individuals with similar amounts of control over material resources. Hence, it is useful to try to identify the "classes" that make up the stratification system (or class structure), to seek to understand their origin, and to examine the effects of membership in them on individuals and families. Rather than discarding the concept of "class" because few people think in these terms, we can ask why few people think about classes despite their prominence. In fact, we will see that some of the major theories of social stratification address this issue directly, inquiring about the conditions under which members of an economic class begin to recognize their shared interests, and perhaps begin to act accordingly as a group.

In the following section, we begin with a detailed look at the ideas of the nineteenth-century social and political philosopher Karl Marx, who put class at the very centre of his discussions of social structure and his theory of social change. In turn, some of the theories of social stratification developed in the twentieth century downplay the role of class or even ignore it completely, because the theorists appear to believe that material inequalities are decreasing. Summing up this line of reasoning, Terry Nichols Clark and Seymour Martin Lipset (1991: 397) write that

> class is an increasingly outmoded concept, although it is sometimes appropriate to earlier historical periods. . . . Class analysis has grown increasingly inadequate in recent decades as traditional hierarchies have declined and new social differences have emerged. The cumulative impact of these changes is fundamentally altering the nature of social stratification — placing past theories in need of substantial modification.

As you read about the various theories of social stratification in the next section, and as you examine the data on material inequalities in Canada in the section after that, keep in mind Clark and Lipset's question: "Are social classes dying?"

■ EXPLANATIONS OF SOCIAL STRATIFICATION

So far, we have considered some examples of social stratification and its effects, and have added to our vocabulary a number of useful concepts that allow us to discuss the phenomenon and to compare our society with others. But we have not really tried to explain social stratification, to account for its origins and its impacts. In this section, we will briefly examine the theories (or explanations) of social stratification elaborated by a number of important social theorists, some who were analyzing society decades ago and others who are writing about it today. As we will see, it is important to take into account the time and place in which a social theory was developed, since theorists construct their social explanations on the basis of what they see around them and expect to see in the future.

▲ KARL MARX: CAPITALISM, EXPLOITATION, AND CLASS CONFLICT

Karl Marx had an immense impact on how we think about social stratification. He was born in Germany in 1818 but lived in England from 1849 until he died in 1883. His writings about the social and economic forces that brought about economic change look back over history, but focus particularly on the rapidly changing European world that he observed during his lifetime. This was a time when industrial capitalism was transforming the economy and society. Large, mechanized, factory-based systems of production were emerging; cities were growing rapidly as rural peasants were being forced off the land or, perhaps, were attracted to the city by the possibility of jobs in factories; and material inequality was extreme, as factory owners and merchants made huge profits while labourers lived in poverty. Trade unions, labour laws, and other arrangements that came to offer some protection to workers did not yet exist. Thus, as Marx observed, the Industrial Revolution was a time when both the level of economic production and the degree of inequality in society increased tremendously.

Modes of Production and Social Classes

Marx called the overall system of economic activity in a society its **mode of production**. In turn, its major components were the **means of production** (technology, capital investments, and raw materials) and the **social relations of production** (the relationships between the main classes involved in production). Slavery had been the primary mode of production in some societies in earlier times, and feudalism, an economic system in which peasants worked for landowners, not for a wage but for some share of the produce, was the mode of production that gave way to industrial capitalism in Europe.

Within industrial capitalism, Marx identified two major classes — the capitalist class, or **bourgeoisie,** which owned the means of production, and the **proletariat,** or working class, which exchanged its labour for wages. He also described a middle class — the **petite bourgeoisie** — comprising independent owners/producers (farmers, for example) and small-business owners. Marx expected this middle class largely to disappear as capitalism matured and drew some of its members up into the bourgeoisie but most down into the proletariat. Of much greater importance in his theory of class inequality and social change was the relationship between workers and owners.

Marx reasoned that the value of a product sold was directly proportional to the average amount of labour needed to produce it. Thus, for example, an elegant piece of furniture was more valuable than its component pieces mainly because of the labour invested in it by the worker(s) who built it. Marx argued that the proceeds from the sale of goods produced by wage-labourers far exceeded the amount needed to pay their wages and the cost of raw materials, technology, and other components of the means of production. Marx referred to this excess as **surplus value**. According to Marx, when commodities were sold, their surplus value was turned into profits for the owner. Marx viewed this as an exploitive relationship, but one that differed from the exploitive relationships that characterized slavery or feudalism. After all, factory workers were paid a wage for their labour and were not legally forced to stay with the job. However, because most workers had few other options for making a living, and because owners controlled all aspects of the work, the legal freedom of wage-labourers to change jobs was, in practical terms, an illusion.

Class Conflict and Class Consciousness

The idea of **class conflict** between the major classes in a society was the driving force behind Marx's theory of social change. Marx noted that previous modes of production had collapsed and been replaced because of class conflict. Feudalism in Europe, for example, had given way to capitalism as a result of the growing power of the merchant class relative to the traditional alliance of landowners and the aristocracy, and the deteriorating relationship between landowners and peasants. Furthermore, Marx argued, capitalism would eventually be replaced by a socialist mode of production, in which private ownership of property would disappear, along with the exploitation and inequality it produced. The impetus for this massive change would again be widespread class conflict, this time between wage-labourers and the owners of the means of production, as inequality between these two classes became more pronounced.

Marx held that this revolution would take place only when members of the working class began to recognize that they were being exploited. In other words, Marx did not take it for granted that members of a class would see how their interests were similar. Whereas capitalists might be conscious of their group interests, wage-labourers needed to become aware of their common enemy. They needed to be transformed from a "class in itself" to a "class for itself." Thus, **class consciousness** was an important social-psychological component of Marx's theory of social inequality and social change. His vision of the future was that of a revolutionary upheaval in which the oppressed working class would recognize its enemy, destroy the institutions of capitalism, and replace them with a classless socialist society based on collective ownership of the means of production.

Responses to Marx's Theory

Over the years, many critics of Marx's ideas pointed to the communist countries, with their apparently socialist system of government and absence of private property, and noted that inequality had not disappeared there. Instead, a new hierarchy had emerged, in which control of the political and bureaucratic apparatus was the main basis of power. These observations were largely correct. (According to a Russian joke from the 1970s, under capitalism man exploits man, but under communism it is the other way around.) In fact, one wonders just how critical Marx himself would have been of the Soviet communist system, given the degree to which individual citizens were exploited and harshly treated by a powerful minority. However, it is slowly becoming apparent that the emergence of a capitalist economy in Eastern Europe is not eliminating material inequalities so much as changing their source. Today, individuals with control over some form of production or access to some marketing system are accumulating wealth while the majority of citizens appear to be no better off than before — indeed, many are worse off. In other words, while Marx's predictions about the inevitable emergence of a classless society have not been borne out, his type of class analysis may still have considerable relevance for understanding the changing stratification system in Eastern Europe.

Most theories of social stratification developed after Marx were essentially a "debate with Marx's ghost" (Zeitlin with Brym, 1991: 117). Some social philosophers and sociologists elaborated on Marx's ideas, while others attempted to refute them. Among the critics, some focussed on the absence of widespread class conflict, the growth of the middle class, and the relative decline in material inequality in Western Europe and North America in the twentieth century. We will examine some of these theories below, along with others that tried to develop more complex models of the contemporary class structure while basically following Marx's form of class-based analysis.

▲ MAX WEBER: CLASS AND OTHER DIMENSIONS OF INEQUALITY

Max Weber was born in Germany half a century later than Marx — in 1864. Like Marx, he built his analysis of social stratification on a careful reading of history as well as a thorough analysis of the economic and political events of his day. But because he was only beginning his university studies about the time Marx died, Weber had the advantage of seeing the direction in which a more mature industrial capitalism was taking European society. He continued to write about many aspects of social stratification and social change until his death in 1920.

Class, Status, and Party

Weber shared with Marx a belief that economic inequalities were central to the social stratification system, and that the ownership of property was a primary determinant of power, or the ability to impose one's wishes on others, to get them to do what one wants them to do. However, he argued that power could lie in controlling other types of resources as well (Weber, 1948 [1922]). Specifically,

he proposed that structures of social stratification could be better understood by looking at economic inequalities, hierarchies of prestige (or social honour), and political inequalities (control of power blocs such as political parties or other organizations) — or, in his words, at "class, status, and party." Although these different hierarchies often overlap, they need not do so. For example, suddenly wealthy individuals might not receive the prestige they desire, being rejected in "high society" by those with "old money." Similarly, a politician might have considerable power through control of government resources, but might not be very wealthy or, for that matter, have much prestige.

Since Weber lived to see the emergence of white-collar workers, the growth of large private- and public-sector bureaucracies, and the growing power of trade unions, he was able to write about these alternative sources of power in a stratified capitalist society. He provided an insightful analysis of how power resided in the control of top positions in large bureaucratic organizations, even if the office-holder was not an owner of the organization. He recognized that well-educated wage-labourers might not be as powerless as were the factory workers of an earlier era. He also saw that a new class of middle-level, educated workers might not necessarily align themselves with blue-collar workers, and was less inclined to conclude, as had Marx, that the middle class would disappear (Zeitlin with Brym, 1991: 118–19). In fact, he expected that the number of educated technical and professional workers in bureaucratic capitalist society would increase.

What Weber saw, then, compared with Marx, was considerably more complexity in the social stratification system because of the growing complexity of the occupational structure and of capitalist enterprises. And although Weber was sometimes pessimistic in his writings about the future of democracy in a bureaucratic capitalist society, he did not link inequality and class conflict to the ultimate demise of capitalism itself, as did Marx. Similarly, although Weber, like Marx, commented on how members of a class might or might not recognize their shared interests (Grabb, 1990: 55), he did not conclude that it was the inevitable destiny of the working class to become a "class for itself."

Social Class and Life-Chances

Despite the above-noted divergences in their thinking, Weber, like Marx, placed primary emphasis on the economic underpinnings of social stratification. However, he defined "class" more broadly. Rather than insisting that a limited number of class positions were based on an individual's relationship to the means of production, Weber saw a larger variety of class positions based both on ownership of property and on other labour-market statuses, such as occupation and education. Furthermore, he tended to emphasize the **life-chances** that class position offered. In other words, a higher position in the economic hierarchy, however obtained, provided more power and allowed an individual and his or her family to enjoy more of the good things in life.

It should be apparent, then, that the general approach to studying stratification that I outlined earlier, one that recognizes the central importance of class while acknowledging that gender, race, and other dimensions of social inequality can also be very important, is in the Weberian tradition. Similarly, my general definition of "class" as a relatively stable position within an economic hierarchy held by an individual or family, along with others with roughly the same amount of control over or access to material resources, follows Weber's use of the term.

▲ DAVIS AND MOORE: A FUNCTIONAL THEORY OF STRATIFICATION

Twentieth-Century Affluence and Structural-Functionalist Theory

Although a number of other social theorists in Europe and North America wrote about social stratification in the early decades of the twentieth century, we will skip ahead in our overview to 1945, when Kingsley Davis and Wilbert Moore published their short but much-debated statement on "some principles of social stratification." In other chapters in this text, you will read about the **structural-functionalist theory** in sociology, an approach that emphasizes consensus over conflict and that seeks to explain the function, for society as a whole, of social institutions and various aspects of social structure. Davis and Moore were part of this intellectual tradition, which arose in reaction to the conflict-oriented and socially radical theories of Marx (and, to a lesser extent, of Weber).

The emergence of structural-functionalism as an alternative theoretical approach can be better understood if we view it as reflecting the optimistic view in postwar North America that affluence was increasing, social conflict was decreasing, and a harmonious future for society was dawning. For example, Arthur Schlesinger Jr., an American historian writing in 1956, suggested that Americans should

start thinking about the "miseries of an age of abundance." Rather than worrying about economic growth, employment, and improving the standard of living, it was time to concentrate on "the bettering of our mass media and the elevation of our popular culture, in short, with the quality of civilization to which our nation aspires in an age of ever-increasing abundance and leisure" (as quoted in Longman, 1985: 75). Thus, during the several decades following World War II, many social scientists were attracted to theories that downplayed conflict and emphasized the benefits, to all, of an apparently ever-expanding economy.

The Functional Necessity of Stratification

Davis and Moore (1945) argued that, because inequality exists in all societies, it must be a necessary part of society. All societies, they noted, have a variety of occupational roles that need to be filled, some requiring much more training than others, some having more functional importance, and some being less pleasant and more difficult to perform. In order to get people to fill important roles and to perform these critical tasks well, and to spend time training for high-skill occupations, societies must ensure that the rewards for performance (money, prestige, and other intangibles) are greater. Thus, for example, doctors and schoolteachers need to be paid more than factory workers and truck drivers, and also must rank higher than the latter in terms of social honour and prestige.

In short, according to Davis and Moore, social inequality is both inevitable and functionally necessary for society. But theirs is not a class-based and conflict-prone stratification system. Rather, Davis and Moore describe a much more fluid socioeconomic hierarchy, with many different occupational statuses into which individuals are slotted on the basis of their effort and ability. The system is held together by consensus and shared values (not torn apart by conflict, as Marx theorized), because members of society generally agree that the hierarchy is fair and just. It also follows from this line of reasoning that efforts to reduce social inequality will be ineffective, and might even be harmful to society.

Criticisms of Davis and Moore

Various criticisms have been levelled against Davis and Moore's theory. For example, although some differences in pay might be justified to reimburse those who spend more years in school preparing for an occupation, are the huge income inequalities we see in our society really necessary? Why do women often earn less than men, even if they are doing the same type of work? Are movie stars, professional athletes, and chief executive officers with million-dollar-plus annual incomes really so much more important to society than nurses, day-care workers, prison guards, and most other low-paid workers? And how does a theory like this account for inherited wealth, for the fact that wealth leads to power and the ability to accumulate more wealth?

Given these criticisms, what accounts for the appeal of this theory? Perhaps it is the kernel of truth at its core that is so attractive — namely, the recognition that, *to some extent,* differences in income and prestige are based on different amounts of effort and ability. After all, we can easily think of examples of better-paying occupations that require long years of education and training. Nevertheless, this is far from the complete story about inequality in our society, which is much more pronounced than what such differences in effort and ability might lead us to expect. In fact, the theory's appeal probably lies more in its apparent justification of these large inequalities. You might test this hypothesis by explaining the theory, first to someone with a high income or inherited wealth, and then to someone who is unemployed or earning very little. The odds are that the functionalist explanation of stratification would sound much more plausible to the wealthier person.

▲ RALF DAHRENDORF: CONFLICT GROUPS IN ORGANIZATIONS

The structural-functionalist perspective on inequality, typified by Davis and Moore, replaced the notion of relatively distinct classes in society with an image of a much more open occupational hierarchy with many finely differentiated positions. In addition, this approach largely ignored power differences and conflict between groups at different locations in the economic hierarchy. But the theoretical pendulum soon swung back in the opposite direction, as several new theories placed conflict and power much more prominently in their explanations of social stratification (Grabb, 1990: 127–30).

The title of Ralf Dahrendorf's 1959 treatise — *Class and Class Conflict in Industrial Society* — was somewhat misleading, because Dahrendorf conceived of "class" very differently from Marx and Weber and because he argued that the Western world had been transformed into a "postcapitalist society." According to Dahrendorf, when Marx was analyzing early industrial capitalism, economic and political conflicts invariably overlapped, as the proletariat and the bourgeoisie fought it out in the workplace as well as in the political arena. But in "postcapitalist society," economic inequalities had been reduced, and industrial disputes were now largely separate from other conflicts.

Dahrendorf proposed that, in all organizations (or "associations," as he called them), one could identify two basic groups — those with power and those without — with the latter attempting to gain power at the expense of the former, who were making and enforcing the rules. In his model of the contemporary stratification system, these many **social conflict groups** replaced the limited number of economic classes described by Marx and Weber. Dahrendorf also claimed that the same individuals who held power in one organization might very well be those who lacked power in another group. For example, managers who hold power in a large corporation might be excluded from power in a community association that is controlled by members of a large ethnic group resident in the neighbourhood. Hence, according to Dahrendorf, conflict in modern society was diffused across many different sets of competing groups and was much less likely to lead to significant social unrest. Instead, conflict provided balance in society. Social stability was enhanced, moreover, because material inequalities had been reduced.

Compared with the structural-functionalists, who basically ignored power differences, Dahrendorf's emphasis on weak and powerful groups in conflict provided a more realistic picture of society. His recognition of conflict groups within organizations of all kinds was useful, since it encouraged sociologists to examine stratification within various organizations, such as religious, sports, or volunteer organizations, in addition to work organizations. However, there are a number of valid criticisms of Dahrendorf's theory (Zeitlin with Brym, 1991: 146–48; Grabb, 1990: 130–37). His argument that industrial disputes no longer go beyond the workplace stands in contrast to the fact that the powers of the state are frequently used to support employers in conflict with their workers (for example, through labour legislation and powers of arrest). Similarly, the notion that the powerless in one conflict group might be the powerful in another is difficult to support with real examples. As we look around us, we seldom see the poor and unemployed in power in some noneconomic organization. Instead, we frequently observe powerful lawyers at the top of political hierarchies, and wealthy business leaders sitting on the boards of voluntary

Ralf Dahrendorf proposed that, in all organizations, one can find two basic groups: those who hold power, and those who lack power but attempt to gain it. Dahrendorf also maintained that those who hold power in one group do not necessarily hold power in another group. SOURCE: Gary Silverberg, *11 Dancing Stars* (1993). Oil on canvas, 48 x 36 inches. Slide provided by the artist. Reproduced with permission of the artist.

organizations or educational institutions (e.g., universities). And, by ignoring class as traditionally defined and focussing instead on generic conflict groups, Dahrendorf drew attention away from large and long-lasting patterns of economic inequality within society, patterns that reflect the domination and exploitation of some groups by others (see Box 7.2).

▲ GERHARD LENSKI: TECHNOLOGY AND STRATIFICATION SYSTEMS

Writing in the 1960s, a time of economic expansion and growing prosperity in North America, Gerhard Lenski (1966) developed a theory of "power and privilege" that attempted to explain the extent of material inequality in both contemporary and past so-

cieties. Like Dahrendorf's theory, Lenski's explanation recognized power and conflict much more explicitly than had the Davis and Moore functionalist explanation of stratification. And, like Weber, he identified a number of different dimensions of social stratification, such as education and ethnicity, while emphasizing the centrality of economic inequalities. Although he used the term *class,* he did not define it precisely, choosing instead to talk about the ruling elites in society in general terms, and about how they managed to maintain their wealth and power at the expense of the masses.

Lenski reasoned that a society's technological base largely determines the degree of inequality within it. In simple hunting-and-gathering societies, he argued, the few resources of the society were distributed primarily on the basis of need. But as societies became more technologically complex, resources in excess of

Box 7.2
Salaries of the Top Brass Fuel Ethical and Political Debates

Is there any justification for executive pay soaring by 75 percent in North America over the past decade, while the average working stiff's hourly wages have declined by about 10 percent?

The question is embarrassing and disturbing—embarrassing for the limousined and comfortably perked corporate brass, disturbing for Canadians struggling to make ends meet in the lingering recession.

People like Toronto entrepreneur Peter Munk, who pocketed an unprecedented $32.3 million in salary, bonus, and stock-options last year as head of American Barrick Resources Corp., are not exactly winning popularity contests these days, as companies post record losses and continue laying off thousands of workers. . . .

A new front of outspoken investors, management consultants, and analysts argues that the performances of many firms—poor, adequate, or even excellent—often don't justify the multimillion-dollar paycheques and bonuses their senior executives automatically get.

Last year, for example, Coca-Cola Co. chief Roberto Goizueta collected a heart-stopping $85 million (US), mostly by cashing in stock options.

In a more "normal" year, like 1990, Goizueta hauled in a measly $3 million. Authors Donald Barlett and James Steele point out that in 1953, his predecessor made $134,600. If a lowly factory worker's pay had gone up at the same pace, they say, the worker would be making $81,000 today. In fact, the average American worker makes about $20,000. Corporate executives make about 100 times that, three times the pay gap fifteen years ago.

SOURCE: Excerpted from Southam News, "Salaries of the Top Brass Fuel Ethical and Political Debates," *The Edmonton Journal,* June 27, 1992, p. D1. Reprinted with permission of Southam News.

those required to fulfil basic needs were produced. Control of those surplus resources, or **privilege,** came to be based on power, allowing ruling elites to take a much larger share of these resources for themselves. Thus, the more complex agricultural societies, such as that of precolonial India, developed highly structured governing and tax-collecting systems, through which the privileged ruling elites accumulated immense amounts of wealth, while the masses lived in poverty.

As a result of industrialization and the complexity of modern technology, this "age-old evolutionary trend toward ever-increasing inequality" (Lenski, 1966: 308) was reversed. Owners of the means of production could no longer control the production process directly and had to rely instead on well-educated managerial and technical workers to keep the complex system operating. Education broadened the horizons of these middle-level employees, introducing them to ideas of democracy, encouraging

them to demand a larger share of the profits they were helping to produce, and making them more articulate in their demands for equality.

Thus, Lenski's theory proposed a causal link between complex industrial technology, the higher education of workers, and workers' insistence on sharing the growing wealth of an industrial society. But why would employers give in to such demands? Because, argued Lenski, the industrial elite needed educated workers — they could not produce without them. Equally important, the much greater productivity of industrial societies compared with preindustrial societies meant that the elite could "make economic concessions in relative terms without necessarily suffering any loss in absolute terms" (Lenski, 1966: 314). Because the economic "pie" was so much bigger, everyone could have a larger slice.

In one obvious sense, Lenski's theory resembled the functionalist theory of stratification — both noted that better-educated and more highly skilled workers are paid more. However, unlike the functionalist approach, Lenski's theory clearly took power differences into account, emphasizing how the extent of accumulation of wealth by elites, or the degree of material inequality, depends on the power and bargaining ability of middle-level workers. Compared with Dahrendorf, who treated all kinds of power differences relatively equally, Lenski placed material inequality at the centre of his theory of stratification. But in contrast to Marx's nineteenth-century predictions of growing inequality as industrial capitalism matured, Lenski, writing in the middle of the twentieth century, saw a movement toward a more equal distribution of society's wealth.

▲ ERIK OLIN WRIGHT: A NEO-MARXIST APPROACH

In reaction against functionalism, Dahrendorf and Lenski brought power and conflict back into their explanations of social inequality. Lenski placed material inequalities resulting from one group's domination of another at the centre of his model, thus coming closer to the approach taken by Marx and Weber. But neither of these writers attempted a Marxist analysis built around the relationships of different classes to the means of production. That is just what Erik Olin Wright did. He updated the original Marxist model so that it could be applied to the twentieth century.

Although Marx acknowledged the existence of a middle class composed of several distinct groups, including independent producers and small-business owners, he predicted that the class would disappear, and so spent much more time writing about the relationship between the two primary classes (capitalists and workers). Wright's contribution lies in recognizing that, as industrial capitalism matured, the middle class had grown and become more diverse, and in trying to understand the class dynamics of our more complex capitalist system of production. Of particular importance in Wright's theory is the emphasis on **contradictory class locations** — that is, on occupational groupings that have divided loyalties within a class structure. For example, although managers work for capitalists, supervising lower-level employees and trying to get them to produce as much as possible, managers are themselves employees, potentially exploited by owners. Considering the substantial numbers of people

While high technology has created many new jobs, it has eliminated even more. For the chronically unemployed, the closest they may get to high technology is a computer at the local unemployment office. SOURCE: Dick Hemingway.

in such contradictory locations, one can begin better to understand why the widespread class conflict envisioned by Marx has seldom emerged.

In his most recent reformulation of his ideas, Wright (1985) argued that exploitation of one class by another can occur through control of property or the means of production (as Marx had insisted), as well as through ownership of skill or credential assets and control of high positions within organizations. Thus, he identified three classes of owners (the bourgeoisie, small employers, and the petite bourgeoisie with no employees), and nine classes of wage-labourers (non-owners), differentiated on two dimensions, the possession of organizational assets and of skill/credential assets (Wright, 1985: 88). For example, "expert managers" (e.g., engineers or lawyers in senior management positions within large companies) fill a class location characterized by extensive organizational assets and high skill/credential assets, in contrast to basic "proletarians," who have no specific skill/credential assets and no management or supervisory responsibilities (see Figure 7.1).

Despite his intention of developing a neo-Marxist theoretical model updated to the late twentieth century, Wright's theory is similar to Weber's view of class structure in some ways (Grabb, 1990: 157). Specifically, the different class locations created by

the intersection of organizational and skill/credential assets remind us of the different classes Weber described as he commented on how similar educational and occupational statuses resulted in similar control over and access to material resources. Even so, Wright's theory of class structure and his observations about contradictory locations within it are useful because he deliberately attempts to incorporate the complexities of modern capitalist society into his explanation of social inequality.

▲ EXPLANATIONS OF SOCIAL STRATIFICATION: SUMMING UP

There are other theories of social inequality in addition to those reviewed above (Grabb, 1990). However, having been introduced to Marx and Weber, the functionalist theory of stratification, and a number of more recent approaches, you will now have some sense of the range of existing explanations. Davis and Moore's functionalist approach stressed that inequality was inevitable and useful, and downplayed social conflict resulting from inequality. In contrast to this *consensus* approach to stratification, a variety of *conflict* approaches highlighted differences in power result-

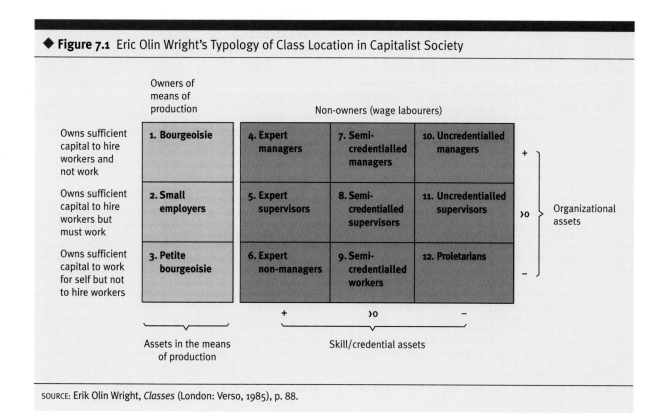

◆ **Figure 7.1** Eric Olin Wright's Typology of Class Location in Capitalist Society

SOURCE: Erik Olin Wright, *Classes* (London: Verso, 1985), p. 88.

ing from and contributing to material inequality, the exploitation of some groups by others, and the social conflict that could result. Marx was the most explicit in this regard, arguing that class conflict would eventually transform capitalist society itself.

The theories we have reviewed differ in the assumptions they make and the conclusions they draw about the future of material inequality. Marx clearly saw inequality and exploitation of the working class increasing, and predicted that class conflict would lead to the death of capitalism. Although Weber was not convinced that a socialist society would eventually emerge, neither did he embrace the theory that inequalities would gradually decrease (Grabb, 1990: 67–70). Although Wright's emphasis on the growing number of middle-class locations (Wright and Martin, 1987) does not suggest an increasing level of material inequality, neither does it imply the opposite. However, the functionalists, Dahrendorf, and Lenski, all writing in an era of economic growth and widespread optimism about the ability of capitalism to raise the overall standard of living, clearly felt that material inequalities were shrinking in Western industrial societies.

The various explanations also differ in the degree to which they emphasize class differences in access to and control of material resources. For Marx, class was the primary determining factor in this regard. Weber, using the term *class* somewhat more broadly, emphasized its central role but recognized other important dimensions of social stratification. Davis and Moore basically ignored the concept of class, while Dahrendorf substituted the concept of conflict groups. Although Lenski again focussed more directly on economic inequality, he did not really describe society in terms of distinct classes, as Wright, in his neo-Marxist approach, did. Thus, if we view these theories in chronological order, it appears that class, at least as defined in the Weberian sense, has made a comeback as an explanatory concept.

Furthermore, we see that those who felt that the level of material inequality was remaining high or increasing viewed society from a class-based perspective. In other words, they focussed on the distinctly different life-chances of individuals and families with similar amounts of access to and control over material resources. In contrast, theorists who thought economic inequalities were declining preferred a model of society composed of many different overlapping strata that reflected a variety of equally important dimensions of social stratification.

Clark and Lipset, whose question "Are social classes dying?" introduced this section, make the latter point explicitly when they state that "one simple,

powerful change has affected the economy: growth. And economic growth undermines hierarchical class stratification" (1991: 405). As you turn to the next section of the chapter — an overview of statistics on occupational and class structures and material inequality in Canada today — keep this argument in mind, because the statistics allow us to assess its validity.

■ OCCUPATIONS, SOCIAL CLASS, AND INEQUALITY IN CANADA

▲ OCCUPATIONAL SHIFTS OVER TIME

As noted above, explanations of social stratification differ in the extent to which they emphasize social class compared with other bases of social inequality. Some theories focus more on how occupational patterns have changed as industrial capitalism matured. But even theorists such as Erik Olin Wright, who place social class at the centre of their explanations, rely to a considerable extent on occupational data. So it would be useful to begin this section by examining occupational shifts in Canada over the past century.

Table 7.1 displays the types of occupations most common at the beginning (1911), in the middle (1951), and near the end of this century (1991), using data from the Canadian census. The most prominent occupational shift over the course of the century is the decline in agricultural occupations, from one-third of all labour-force participants in 1911 to only 3 percent in 1991. We also observe a decline in other natural-resource-based occupations (forestry, fishing, mining). Manufacturing and transportation occupations increased in relative terms between the beginning and middle of the century, but had declined by 1991.

Manufacturing, construction, transportation, and resource-based occupations are typically called *blue-collar occupations,* in contrast to *white-collar occupations* in the managerial, professional, clerical (office jobs), sales, and service categories. It is apparent from Table 7.1 that white-collar occupations have come to greatly outnumber blue-collar occupations as industrial capitalism has matured. In 1991, 12 percent of labour-force participants were identified as having managerial occupations, up from only 5 percent in 1911. Professional occupations had more than quadrupled in relative terms, from 4 to 18 percent, as had clerical occupations. Sales and service occupations also had become more common.

◆ **Table 7.1** Occupational Distribution of Labour-Force Participants,[a] Canada, 1911, 1951, 1991

Occupation type	1911	1951	1991
Managerial	5%	8%	12%
Professional	4	7	18
Clerical	4	11	18
Sales	5	7	9
Service	8	10	13
Manufacturing	14	17	11
Transportation	6	8	4
Construction	5	6	6
Agriculture	34	16	3
Forestry/fishing/mining	5	4	2
Other occupations	10	6	4
Total	100	100	100

[a] Labour-force participants include both the employed (paid employees and the self-employed) and the unemployed (those who want a paid job but who are unable to find one); based on the population aged 15 and older.

SOURCE: 1911 and 1951 data: adapted from 1911 and 1951 census results, presented by Jeff O'Neill, "Changing Occupational Structure," *Canadian Social Trends*, Winter 1991, p. 10; 1991 data: adapted from 1991 census results, Statistics Canada, *Occupation: The Nation*, Cat. no. 93-327, March 1993, Table 1.

What do these occupational changes tell us, with respect to our previous discussions of the bases of social stratification? First, as various theories have indicated, the proportion of occupations requiring higher education has increased, while the proportion of traditional blue-collar, "working-class" occupations has declined. With the expansion in white-collar occupations, average incomes rose, at least until the early 1980s. Thus, to the extent that occupational data can inform us about class structure in the Weberian sense, occupational shifts over the past 90 years suggest greater class diversity, rather than a polarization of classes, as a strict reading of Marx's theory would predict, and a rising standard of living for Canadian workers, rather than increasing poverty and exploitation.

And what do the numbers in Table 7.1 fail to tell us? First, they do not distinguish between the occupations typically held by women and those typically held by men. Since the middle of the century, a rising proportion of women have been entering the labour force. But, as we will see (Chapter 8), women have been more likely to find employment in the clerical, sales, and service occupations (what might be called a "pink-collar sector") than in blue-collar occupations or in higher-status and better-paying managerial and professional occupations, even though there has been some movement by women into higher-level white-collar occupations in the past decade (Hughes, 1995). Thus, gender-based labour market stratification continues to exist, intersecting with class-based stratification.

Second, even though we might draw some conclusions about social class from the occupational data in Table 7.1, the data do not directly describe workers' relationships to the means of production, in Marx's terms. However, research conducted in the early 1980s does provide us with one picture of the Canadian class structure. Based on a nation-wide survey and using an early version of Erik Olin Wright's class framework, Black and Myles (1986) demonstrated that only 1 percent of the labour force could be considered large employers (the bourgeoisie), 3 percent were small employers, and 12 percent fit into the petite bourgeoisie category. In contrast, 44 percent of the labour force fit into the traditional "worker" category (the proletariat), while the remainder were in contradictory class locations. Thus, we can see why Wright felt compelled to revise Marx's more simplistic three-class model.

Third, neither Table 7.1 (which displays occupational change over time) nor the Black and Myles (1986) study (which used "class" data from only one point in time) can give us a sense of how the Canadian class structure might be changing. But we can get one indication of this from other data on self-employment. Over the course of the century, particularly with the decline in the number of people employed in agriculture, the proportion of self-employed Canadians dropped dramatically. By 1971, only 11 percent of the Canadian labour force was self-employed. However, beginning in the 1980s, we began to see a slow reversal in the trend in Canada, the United States, and other Western industrialized countries. By 1994, about 9 percent of employed Canadians were own-account self-employed (without any employees) and 6 percent employed others (Krahn, 1995). Researchers still have not determined whether more Canadians are voluntarily choosing self-employment, or are being pushed into it as a result of higher levels of unemployment and growing corporate and public-sector "downsizing." Nevertheless, this reversal of the decline in self-employment — this increase in the size of the petit bourgeois class — is something that theorists are trying to explain as they attempt to further update Marx's ideas of class-based stratification (Myles and Turegun, 1994; Breen and Rottman, 1995: 87–88).

Finally, the data in Table 7.1 do not reflect some of the dramatic changes in employment opportunities and outcomes that have been occurring in the past two decades. I will return to this topic later, but for now I will simply note that unemployment rates have risen, part-time and temporary work has become much more common, and income growth appears to have stopped while income inequality has increased. Consequently, the higher standard of living that accompanied occupational changes observed earlier this century is no longer guaranteed for all those in middle-status occupations. Thus, it is essential that we look carefully at the distributional side of the occupation and class structures, at "who gets what" in return for their employment, as well as at the occupational and class positions that people hold (Westergaard, 1995). But before beginning our examination of changing patterns of material inequality in Canada, we will first discuss another important feature of stratification systems in modern societies — opportunities for occupational mobility.

▲ OCCUPATIONAL MOBILITY

Many people move up the occupational and income ladders over the course of their careers, frequently after investing in higher education of some kind. And some move down, often because of economic circumstances beyond their control. Sociologists have conducted a great deal of research on such **intra-generational occupational mobility** (mobility within an individual's lifetime), as well as on **intergenerational occupational mobility,** the process of reaching an occupational location higher or lower than the location one's parents held. Research of this type is interesting in itself, since we all like to compare how well we have done relative to others. However, such research is also theoretically important, since it tests hypotheses derived from theories of inequality (the functionalist perspective, for example) that propose that higher positions in society are generally filled by those most qualified, not by those who inherit them.

Canadian researchers Creese, Guppy, and Meissner (1991) have used data from Statistics Canada's 1986 general social survey, a large random sample of more than 16 000 adults, to examine the factors that influence occupational mobility opportunities or, in other words, the process of **occupational status attainment**. They demonstrated, not surprisingly, that the most important influence on the status of an individual's current job is the status of that person's first job. Individuals who enter the labour market as articling lawyers, for example, typically make their way higher up the occupational ladder than do those who began as unskilled labourers. In turn, the status of that first job is heavily influenced by the amount of education completed.

These findings obviously lend some support to theories that suggest that more qualified people, as indicated by higher education, end up in higher-status and better-paying occupations. However, the researchers also traced the education–job linkages back to the previous generation, showing that those who obtained more education and hence better jobs were more likely to come from families with well-educated fathers in high-status occupations. (Comparisons were not made with the occupations of sample members' mothers since relatively few women in the previous generation held paying jobs.) In other words, for a variety of reasons (e.g., more money for higher education, more well-educated role models), children from more advantaged backgrounds can build on their initial advantages. The same study also revealed that, on average, men experienced slightly more upward mobility than did women, even though women had completed more years of schooling. Similarly, Francophones were disadvantaged compared with Anglophones, and immigrants did not fare as well as native-born Canadians, even if they had equivalent educational credentials.

In brief, this recent study of occupational status attainment by Creese, Guppy, and Meissner demonstrates that the Canadian stratification system is relatively open. There are opportunities for upward mobility within the occupational hierarchy, and education plays a critical role in determining who gets ahead. In fact, comparisons with similar studies in other countries, such as Australia, France, Sweden, and the United Kingdom, suggest that Canada is a somewhat more open society in terms of mobility opportunities (Wanner, 1993: 174). Nevertheless, the 1986 general social survey also revealed considerable status inheritance, suggesting that the issue of who gets better jobs (with more status and higher income) is also class-based, and not just a matter of achievement based on merit. Furthermore, the research shows how other dimensions of social stratification, such as gender, ethnicity, and immigrant status, intersect with class-based inequalities.

Overall, the 1986 general social survey revealed more upward than downward mobility. Among women, 48 percent reported upward mobility relative to their father's occupation, 12 percent stayed at the same level, and 40 percent had moved down to some extent. The comparable statistics for men were 39 percent upwardly mobile, 25 percent stable, and 36 percent downwardly mobile (Creese, Guppy, and Meissner, 1991: 45–46). If the only intergenerational occupational mobility we were seeing was a result of better-qualified people moving up to replace those who were less qualified, we should also see an equivalent amount of downward mobility. Such a situation of "musical jobs" or, to use the technical term, **circulatory mobility** is not evident, however, because of the simultaneous presence of **structural mobility,** which results from a change in the shape of the overall occupational structure. As noted earlier, over the past half-century, industrial societies have experienced a great deal of growth in white-collar occupations (clerical, managerial, and professional positions) as traditional agricultural and blue-collar industrial jobs declined in relative importance. With an increase in the number of higher-status jobs, each generation had more chances than the preceding one to improve the status of their jobs.

In 1968, John Porter, a Canadian sociologist, observed this phenomenon and predicted that, in the future, the demand for people to fill highly skilled positions would exceed the supply of well-educated workers (Porter, 1968). Porter's fear seems ironic today, when almost one in four employed Canadians state that they are overqualified for their job (Krahn, 1992: 125). With many more well-educated labour-force participants in a labour market in which relatively low-skill part-time positions are increasing more quickly than high-skill full-time positions, underemployment has become a serious problem (Boothby, 1993). Expansion in the middle of the occupational structure appears to have slowed down, or perhaps even stopped, resulting in fewer opportunities for upward (structural) mobility. In fact, a recent U.S. study examined these trends and projected that, by the year 2000, immobility and downward mobility, especially for men, would be more common than upward mobility (Krymkowski and Krauze, 1992).

▲ THE DISTRIBUTION OF PROPERTY AND WEALTH

Evidence from various sources demonstrates that a limited number of people own or control a very large portion of the wealth in Canada. Antoniou and Rowley (1986), for example, showed that single owners held a majority of shares in more than one-third of the largest Canadian-owned corporations in 1979. Recognizing that control of a corporation can still be maintained with only a small minority of shares, so long as other shares are held in smaller blocks, Antoniou and Rowley also demonstrated that more than two-thirds of the largest Canadian-owned corporations were controlled by a single owner (holding 20 percent or more of the shares). At least half, if not more, of these owners were families, as opposed to financial corporations, government bodies, or other types of owners.

Richardson (1990) compared 1978 and 1985 data to make the same point about the pronounced and increasing concentration of corporate ownership in Canada. He showed that 76 percent of the assets of the 170 largest Canadian nonfinancial corporations were controlled in 1985 by only 17 large business enterprises (an enterprise consists of one or more corporations under common control), up from 64 percent seven years earlier. Two-thirds (11) of these 17 enterprises were controlled by a single owner. These two studies, and others like them, highlight the immense wealth held by families such as the Bronfmans, the Reichmanns, the Irvings, the Westons, and the Eatons, with business holdings spread around the globe as well as in Canada. Together with highly paid chief executive officers and corporate directors (see Box 7.2), these wealthy families clearly form a distinct upper class, the haute (or high) bourgeoisie in Marx's terms.

At the other end of this ownership scale are the roughly 9 in 10 Canadian families that report owning no publicly traded stocks (Osberg, 1981: 36). But although shares, particularly in large numbers, are owned by only a small minority of Canadian individuals and families, there are obviously other forms of wealth to consider, including property (homes and other real estate, and unincorporated businesses), other possessions (such as automobiles), cash savings and bonds, and money held in RRSPs and pension plans. This wealth is also distributed unequally. In 1984, more than half of all wealth (51 percent), including corporate stocks, was owned by the wealthiest 10 percent of Canadians (Oja, 1987: 25).

Over the long term, the economic growth experienced in Western industrialized countries, along with some income redistribution efforts by governments, has had an equalizing effect on the distribution of household wealth. Wolff (1991), for example, showed that inequality in household wealth decreased between 1920 and the 1970s in Sweden, Britain, and the United States. In the United States, the share of all household wealth owned by the top 1 percent of families fell from 38 percent in 1922 to 19 percent in 1976. Although comparable data are not available for Canada for the same period, it is likely that a similar decline occurred here as well (in 1970, the top 1 percent of Canadian families owned 20 percent of all household wealth). However, Wolff also noted that, in the mid-1970s, wealth inequality began to increase again in the United States and Sweden (it remained constant in Britain). Thus, in 1981, the top 1 percent of American families owned 24 percent of all household wealth. It is very likely that rising levels of unemployment over the past two decades, accented by the recessions at the beginning of the 1980s and the 1990s, have meant a continuation of this trend toward greater wealth inequality.

▲ INCOME DISTRIBUTION

High-Paying and Low-Paying Occupations

Although most of us have virtually no contact with the wealthiest 1 percent of families in Canada, we are much more aware of, or perhaps are even members of, a larger, not quite as wealthy, but still very affluent group of households containing one or more individuals in high-paying occupations. Table 7.2 lists the ten highest-paying and lowest-paying occupations in Canada in 1990. All of the ten highest-paying occupations are either professional occupations (e.g., lawyer, doctor, dentist, engineer, professor) or middle- or upper-level managerial oc-

cupations. Using the term *class* in the Weberian sense, we might be justified in viewing individuals in managerial and professional occupations (the top ten and others near the top of the earnings hierarchy) as members of an upper-middle class, given their high incomes and their access to and control of material resources through their employment positions. In contrast, the ten lowest-paying occupations, the majority of them in the service industries (e.g., food and beverage services, child care), include some of the insecure occupations that we might classify as constituting a lower working class.

For the ten highest-paying occupations, the average annual income (women and men averaged) was more than $73 000 in 1990, almost five times as high as the average for the ten lowest-paying occupations (about $15 000). But these figures are calculated only for the full-time, full-year employed, in order to provide a standardized comparison across occupations. Since part-time and part-year work is more common in the industries in which the lowest-paying types of occupations are typically found, the gap between the average annual income of all managers and professionals and the average for all those employed in low-paying service-type occupations is in fact considerably larger. Table 7.2 also shows that, across all occupations, women earned only two-thirds of what men earned in 1990, demonstrating the extent to which gender inequalities cut across occupational inequalities.

Income Inequality

The data in Table 7.2, based on the 1991 census, give us some indication of the current distribution of employment earnings, the largest component of total income. If we were to look back to the middle of the century, we would see that the distribution of total income (from employment, investments, government assistance, and all other sources) across households (families and individuals living alone) in Canada has changed relatively little. In 1951, the most advantaged 20 percent of households (the top quintile) received 43 percent of total Canadian income, whereas the bottom quintile (the 20 percent with the lowest incomes) received only 4 percent of all income (Statistics Canada, 1984: 6). In 1995, the distribution looked quite similar, with the top quintile receiving 44 percent of all income, and the bottom quintile taking home 5 percent (Statistics Canada, 1996: 159).

But while the proportion of total income received by each population quintile shows us how equally or unequally income is being distributed, it tells us

◆ **Table 7.2** Average Earnings of Full-Year, Full-Time[a] Working Men and Women in Ten Highest- and Ten Lowest-Paying Occupations, Canada, 1990

	Average earnings		
Occupation[b]	Total	Men	Women
Ten highest-paying occupations	**$ 73 313**	**$ 79 463**	**$ 48 609**
Judges and magistrates	102 646	109 313	79 204
Physicians and surgeons	102 370	111 261	73 071
Dentists	95 776	99 280	67 997
Lawyers and notaries	76 966	86 108	50 012
General managers and other senior officials	67 997	74 425	40 633
Other managers in mining and petroleum	64 893	73 281	39 151
Air pilots, navigators, and flight engineers	64 316	66 087	31 026
Osteopaths and chiropractors	64 299	68 404	45 368
Management occupations, natural science and engineering	63 566	66 668	41 800
University teachers	62 064	65 671	49 000
Ten lowest-paying occupations	**15 092**	**18 794**	**13 673**
Livestock farm workers	16 600	19 279	11 788
Sewing machine operators	16 540	22 991	15 933
Other farming occupations	16 227	19 537	12 174
Crop farm workers	16 191	19 814	12 421
Bartenders	16 067	18 558	13 952
Lodging cleaners	15 718	19 238	15 178
Service station attendants	15 586	16 135	13 359
Housekeepers and servants	14 479	19 210	14 053
Food/beverage serving occupations	14 100	17 822	13 037
Child-care occupations	13 518	20 987	13 252
All other occupations	**32 850**	**36 957**	**26 354**
Total	**33 714**	**38 648**	**26 033**

[a] Worked 49–52 weeks in 1990, mostly full-time.

[b] Although athletes were in the top-ten occupations, and trapping and hat-making were in the bottom-ten occupations, their very small numbers rendered their income statistics unreliable. Hence, the individuals in these three occupations were excluded from the high and low groups and included in all other occupations.

SOURCE: Statistics Canada, *The Daily,* Cat. no. 11-001E, April 13, 1993, p.11. Reproduced by authority of the Minister of Industry, 1997.

little about the standard of living of individuals and families within each quintile. For example, if total income doubled but the percentage received by each quintile stayed the same, the bottom 20 percent with their 5 percent of total income would now have twice as much income as before (of course, the same would apply to the top quintile, who would also have twice as much). In fact, when we look back over the past four decades, we find that average family income increased by more than 150 percent, after taking inflation into account. In other words, the Canadian standard of living increased substantially in the decades following World War II. But most of this increase took place in the 1950s and 1960s. By the 1980s, inflation was typically as high

as, or higher than, the income gains of Canadian families (Love and Poulin, 1991). In terms of purchasing power, then, incomes stopped rising.

Similarly, if we look at average annual wage increases (Figure 7.2), it is very apparent that it was during the middle decades of the century (the 1940s, '50s, and '60s) that Canadian wages were growing much faster than inflation. Adjusted for inflation, average wages increased by 350 percent between 1920 and 1990 (Rashid, 1993). (By the 1980s, this growth in wages and in the standard of living had basically stopped.) However, Figure 7.2 also shows that unemployment was steadily rising throughout this era. Thus, by the start of the 1990s, when real wages had stopped growing, a much larger propor-

Box 7.3
Measuring Absolute and Relative Poverty in Canada

The low-income cut-off lines estimated by Statistics Canada are indicators of *relative poverty*, linked to the average incomes of Canadians in families and communities of various sizes. Hence, if average incomes rise during periods of economic growth, but the distribution of income (the share of total income received by those at the top, in the middle, and at the bottom of the income hierarchy) does not change, the proportion of all Canadians who are poor will also remain the same, even if the standard of living increases for everyone. Christopher Sarlo criticizes the use of such relative poverty lines, arguing that "estimates of the extent of poverty in Canada are grossly exaggerated."[1] Using an *absolute poverty* line that estimates the costs of "basic needs" and nothing more, Sarlo concludes that "poverty, as it has been traditionally understood, has been virtually eliminated."[2]

Sarlo proposes that poverty means "a genuine deprivation of life's basic necessities" that could negatively affect "long-term physical well-being."[3] If a person's income is too low to allow a basic but nutritious diet, basic shelter and clothing costs, and basic health care, they should be considered "poor." Thus, among other basic-necessity calculations, Sarlo eliminates food items that lack nutritional value (e.g., coffee, ketchup, and jam) from his list of basic food costs, estimates basic housing costs at 10 percent below the average rental for an apartment of "adequate" size (e.g., one bedroom for a two-person household), assumes that utility costs are part of the typical rental agreement, excludes non-essentials such as radios and TVs, proposes $245 per person per year (in 1988) for all clothing and footwear costs, assumes that family members will cut each other's hair, and also assumes that dental societies will provide free dental service to low-income families and that Lions Clubs will provide free eyeglasses.

On the basis of his calculations, Sarlo concludes that slightly less than one million Canadians *might* be considered poor—about one-quarter the number estimated using Statistics Canada's low-income line. Arguing, however, that some of these people are senior citizens whose homes are paid for, students receiving loans and assistance from parents, individuals who are not declaring all their income, and so on, Sarlo suggests that the figure is even lower, and therefore concludes that Canada does not have a major poverty problem.[4] Sarlo's critics question many of his assumptions about the basic costs of living and, more important, his central arguement that only those who do not have access to basic necessities are poor. Poverty, they argue, is a relative concept. Measured against the average standard of living, a significant number of Canadians can be considered poor, even if they are basically surviving.

[1] Christopher A. Sarlo, *Poverty in Canada* (Vancouver: The Fraser Institute, 1992), p. 2.

[2] Sarlo, *Poverty in Canada*, p. 2.

[3] Sarlo, *Poverty in Canada*, p. 27.

[4] Sarlo, *Poverty in Canada*, p. 193.

ations within each group. Using 1982 data, the Economic Council of Canada (1992: 14) filled in some of the detail, suggesting that about 5 percent of working-age Canadians were "destitute" (no market income at all), about 6 percent were "margin-ally employed" (incomes up to 50 percent of the low-income line), about 8 percent were "working poor" (incomes between 50 percent and 100 percent of the low-income line), and about 11 percent were "hovering poor" (incomes up to 150 percent of the low-income line). The labour-market changes we have witnessed in the past decade suggest that the number of working poor and hovering poor has increased since then.

Social Assistance for the Poor

Recognizing, then, that not all of the poor are equally poor, where would people dependent on social assistance be located in this hierarchy of low income? There is a fairly common belief in our society that "welfare" and unemployment insurance are much too easy to obtain and that the amount of money received is enough to encourage people to avoid seeking work (Krahn et al., 1987). Is this true? Because welfare regulations vary across provinces, we will examine data from Ontario, the largest province and the province with the highest welfare income in 1994.

Figure 7.3 shows that a single "employable" adult (i.e., an adult who was not disabled, elderly, or considered unable to seek work because of family responsibilities) who was eligible for Ontario social assistance received about $8550 in 1994, an amount just over half (55 percent) of the poverty line and less than one-third of the average income for single adults in the province (National Council of Welfare, 1995). Disabled welfare recipients received a larger total annual transfer payment, putting them three-quarters of the way between no income and the low-income line, but at only 41 percent of the average income for single adults. Relative to other welfare recipients, single parents fared the best, with their total income set at 80 percent of the poverty line for one-adult households. Their incomes seem relatively high compared with the average income, but only because the average income for all single parents is very low. In contrast, the level of welfare assistance provided to a couple with two children was only 34 percent of the much higher average income of two-adult, two-child households in Ontario in 1994.

In short, in Ontario and the rest of the provinces, the amount of welfare assistance provided is very low. Since 1994, social-assistance rates have been significantly reduced in many provinces, but particularly in Ontario. Consequently, it is difficult to accept the argument that overly generous welfare systems discourage people from looking for work. Many of those who receive assistance cannot work outside the home, and the money that is provided seldom pushes the poor who receive it anywhere even close to the poverty line.

Moving In and Out of Poverty

Discussions of poverty such as this one can leave the impression that the poor and the nonpoor are basically separate groups, and that there is little mobility from one status to the other. In fact, according to the Economic Council of Canada (1992: 22), the annual turnover rate in and out of poverty (as defined by the low-income line) was about 27 percent between 1982 and 1986. In other words, about 1 in 4 Canadians (roughly 400 000 in total) who had been poor in a given year rose above the poverty line the next year, and were replaced among the ranks of the poor by about the same number of downwardly mobile individuals. However, many of those moving up would not have made it beyond the "hovering poor" category and, depending on the circumstances, might again find themselves categorized as "poor" in the subsequent year. The point remains that poverty is not a static status, as a sizable number of Canadians move in and out of poverty each year. In fact, about 1 in 3 Canadians can expect to be poor (below the low-income line) at some point during their adult working life (Economic

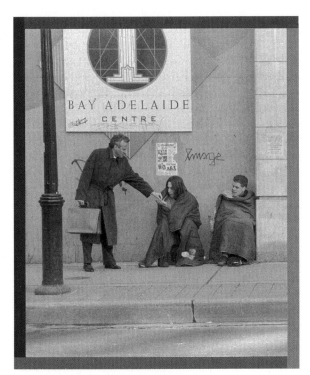

In 1992, the Economic Council of Canada suggested that about 5 percent of working-age Canadians were "destitute" and had no market income at all. Living on the streets is a dangerous alternative to a more socially acceptable struggle for survival. SOURCE: Dick Hemingway.

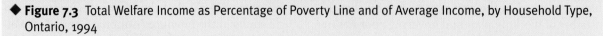

Figure 7.3 Total Welfare Income as Percentage of Poverty Line and of Average Income, by Household Type, Ontario, 1994

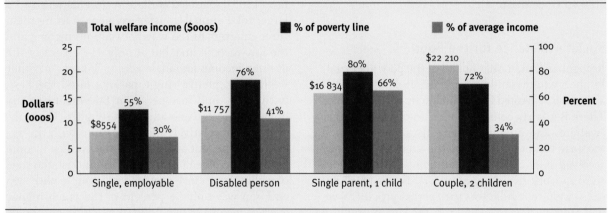

SOURCE: National Council of Welfare, *Welfare Incomes, 1994,* Cat. no. H68-27/1994E (Ottawa: Supply and Services Canada, 1995). Reproduced with the permission of the Minister of Public Works and Government Services Canada, 1997.

Council of Canada, 1992: 27). As we noted above, losing a job, becoming a single parent, or being widowed can have devastating effects on one's income.

▲ MATERIAL INEQUALITY IN CANADA: SUMMING UP

Is Inequality Increasing in Canada?

Compared with some other countries, and compared with the situation in Canada a century ago, the level of material inequality in this country today is relatively low. Even so, we have seen evidence of a great deal of inequality in wealth and income (see also Box 7.4). Furthermore, there are indications that, for at least a decade and perhaps two, the level of inequality has been slowly rising. Corporate concentration has been increasing as a small number of huge business enterprises, many of them family-owned or -controlled, have gained control over a larger share of the assets of Canada's largest corporations. Wealth inequality in general appears to be increasing, income inequality has risen, and the number of poor in Canada, particularly the working poor, has increased.

Looking more closely at the labour market, we see that unemployment rates have been rising steadily for several decades. Although these rates have gone up and down a number of times, the long-term trend since mid-century has been upward. Hence, in 1995,

the average annual unemployment rate was 9.5 percent, representing 1.4 million unemployed Canadians, a number roughly equal to the total adult population of the provinces of Nova Scotia, New Brunswick, and Prince Edward Island. Similarly, the part-time employment rate has been rising. Forty years ago, fewer than 4 percent of employed Canadians worked part-time. Today, almost 1 in 5 are in part-time jobs (18.6 percent in 1995); of these workers, one-third (32 percent) would prefer full-time jobs but cannot find them. Since the 1980s, we have also seen a significant increase in temporary jobs, as employers have begun to cut long-term wage costs by offering more limited-term contract positions (Krahn, 1995). Real wages are no longer increasing, inequality in earnings has risen as a result of polarization in hours worked (Morissette, Myles, and Picot, 1994), and opportunities for upward mobility have declined.

A More Polarized Society?

It is difficult to avoid the conclusion that, in Canada, the gap between the advantaged (those with full-time, permanent jobs) and the disadvantaged (those with part-time, temporary, or no jobs) is slowly increasing (Krahn and Lowe, 1993: 98; Myles, 1996). A similar pattern has been observed in Britain (Westergaard, 1995) and in the United States (Bellin and Miller, 1990; Ryscavage, 1995). This is not to suggest that a new era of massive inequalities is dawning. However, the evidence is clear enough

Box 7.4
The Information Highway—Will It Bypass Poorer Households?

More and more Canadians are travelling the information highway. In the last nine years, the proportion of households with a home computer has almost tripled to 28.8% in 1995 from 10.3% in 1986. In 1995, almost 42% of these home computers had a modem, permitting the user to connect to the services of the Internet.

However, income is the passport to this electronic network. In 1995, households in the highest quintile (the 20% of households with the highest income) were more than four times more likely to have a computer than those in the lowest quintile (52.6% compared with 11.9%). For single-parent households the comparison between the highest-to-lowest income group was considerably better at three to one (53.7% vs 17.1%).

The future shape of interactive services continues to unfold. Telephone and cable lines as well as satellite links are all poised to become the providers of new communication networks. The ability to access the growing online services will be dependent not only on having the necessary hardware (cable lines, computer, modem, etc.) but also being able to afford any user fees charged by the providers. It remains to be seen whether or not access to the information highway will be universally affordable.

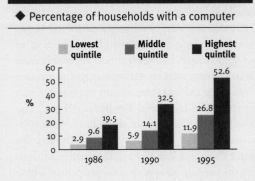

◆ Percentage of households with a computer

SOURCE: Statistics Canada, *Household Facilities by Income and Other Characteristics, 1995,* Cat. no. 13-218, pp. 10–11. Reproduced by authority of the Minister of Industry, 1997.

that material inequalities are rising, not declining, and that society is becoming more polarized in terms of access to and control over economic resources. Using Weber's definition of the term *class,* we could conclude that class differences in Canada and the United States (and in other countries like Britain) are becoming more pronounced.

There are obviously many interrelated factors contributing to this growth in material inequality, this increased polarization of North American society (Krahn and Lowe, 1993: 44–54). Although some new high-skill and well-paying jobs have emerged with the introduction of automated production technologies, the overall outcome still appears to have been a reduction in employment opportunities. Globalization, the process whereby goods and services are produced by business enterprises operating in many different countries, has led to a much more competitive economic environment. Business enterprises have responded by shifting some of their activities to countries in which lower wages and less rigorous environmental and labour laws allow higher profits to be made. In North America, layoffs have been a frequent response, along with the replacement of full-time permanent jobs with part-time and temporary positions. Labour unions, which traditionally resisted attempts to cut wages and jobs, have lost some of their power. At the political level, a belief system or ideology emphasizing that "the market knows best" and that we need less rather than more government intervention in the economy and labour market has led to fewer government efforts to reduce material inequalities (Myles, 1996).

Less Economic Growth and Greater Inequality?

We will leave it to other chapters in this text to examine the relevant economic, labour-market, political, and ideological trends in more detail, and will conclude instead with a speculative comment about a much broader phenomenon that may also be influencing trends toward greater inequality. In brief, evidence is mounting, as demands for raw materials by a rapidly growing global population come to outstrip supply, that the half-century of economic growth and mass consumption that started after World War II may be coming to an end. Summarizing some of this information, Lester R. Brown (1993: 19) writes:

> When the history of the late 20th century is written, the 1990s will be seen as a decade of discontinuity — a time when familiar trends that had seemed likely to go on forever, like smooth straight roads, came to abrupt bends or junctures and began descending abruptly. The world's production of steel, for example, had risen almost as reliably each year as the sun rises in the morning. The amount of coal extracted had risen almost uninterruptedly ever since the Industrial Revolution began. The harvest of grain had grown much faster than population since the middle of this century and the oceanic fish catch had more than quadrupled, doubling the consumption of seafood per person. These rising curves were seen as basic measures of human progress; we expected them to rise. But now, within just a few years, these trends have reversed, with consequences we have yet to grasp.

Brown goes on to note that these are only some of the indications that, on a global basis, the rate of economic growth has dropped off. On average, world economic growth increased 5.2 percent per year during the 1960s. The comparable figure in the 1970s was 3.4 percent, and dropped to 2.9 percent in the 1980s. Between 1990 and 1992, average world economic growth was only 0.6 percent per year. From this three-decade perspective, it appears that the recession that introduced the 1990s to North America may be the end of a long-term trend rather than merely a temporary setback. In Brown's opinion, the underlying problem is that world population growth is increasing rapidly (e.g., by 91 million people in 1992), while the supply of raw materials needed to sustain this growing population is being exhausted. Thus, despite changes in the way production takes places, and even with further scientific advances in agriculture and industry, it is clear that the economic growth we have come to expect is unlikely to continue.

This is certainly a sobering thought, particularly alongside the warnings from environmental groups about the destructive manner in which we have been consuming our natural resources. Its implications are no less serious in the light of our discussion of increasing material inequalities. Recall Gerhard Lenski's optimistic predictions of declining inequality as technological change and economic growth produced a larger "pie" for distribution, and the other twentieth-century social theorists' belief that class-based inequality and conflict would decline with increasing prosperity. Forty years ago, Arthur Schlesinger Jr. advised us to start thinking about the "miseries of an age of abundance" (quoted in Longman, 1985: 75). And even as late as 1991, Clark and Lipset were arguing that "economic growth undermines hierarchical class stratification" (1991: 405).

To the extent that these social scientists were correct about the impact of economic growth on inequality in North America, their theories would also suggest an *increase* in material inequality today as a consequence of declining economic growth. These theorists were writing in (or thinking back to) a time when the economy was expanding rapidly, when unemployment rates were low, and when the standard of living was clearly increasing. For example, automobile ownership in the United States increased from 10 million in 1949 to 24 million in 1957 (Reich, 1991: 45). As "a car in every driveway" became the American way of life, social inequality appeared to be on the decline. But that expansionary, optimistic era seems to be over. Economic growth has slowed down, if not stalled, and a higher level of material inequality may now characterize North American society. In response to their question "Are social classes dying?" Clark and Lipset (1991) answered yes, but they may have misread the evidence.

▲ CONSEQUENCES OF MATERIAL INEQUALITY

Other chapters in this textbook will go into more detail about some of the many consequences of material inequality for individuals and families. You will see that position in the class structure has an effect on belief systems, behaviours, and lifestyles, that the poor, the middle classes, and the very wealthy frequently hold different opinions on various subjects, may vote differently, and certainly enjoy different lifestyles. But, much more important, people in different positions in society's economic hierarchy experience different life-chances, to use the term introduced by Max Weber.

Consequences for Individuals and Families

Children from poorer families typically do not do as well as more affluent children in school, are more likely to drop out before completing high school (Tanner, Krahn, and Hartnagel, 1995), and are less likely to go on to higher education (Krahn and Lowe, 1993: 120–22). As we noted above in our discussion of occupational mobility, such effects of poverty are largely responsible for the perpetuation of class inequalities from one generation to the next.

For a variety of reasons, including better nutrition, access to better health care, and less hazardous working conditions, those who are situated higher in the economic hierarchy are typically healthier than the poor (Roberge, Berthelot, and Wolfson, 1995). On average, the poor do not live as long as those who are better off (Wilkinson, 1992). Similarly, when dealing with the criminal-justice system, those with greater access to and control over economic resources tend to fare better. The poor are consequently overrepresented in jails (Reiman, 1979; Box, 1987). I could go on, but these examples are probably sufficient to make the point that life-chances are a function of position in the class structure, and that those higher up in the economic hierarchy enjoy a better quality of life.

Consequences for Society

In addition to the above-described consequences of material inequality for individuals and families, can material inequality have other social outcomes? Specifically, given the relatively high and apparently increasing level of inequality in Canada, can we expect to see more social unrest? Will conflict between the "haves" and the "have-nots" increase? Those committed to a classical Marxist theory of social change might welcome such conflict; for them, it would indicate that capitalism was beginning to give way to a socialist society. Others might view such conflict much more negatively. Whatever our response to such a possibility, it is clear that our values and beliefs directly influence the way we respond to evidence of inequality and its consequences.

But returning to our question, can we expect to see an increase in social unrest and conflict as a result of higher levels of inequality? During the early 1980s, for example, the Solidarity Movement in British Columbia brought together members of trade unions, social-welfare organizations, and various community-based groups in opposition to the Social Credit government's cutbacks in government programs and attempts to change labour legislation. Bryan Palmer (1986) described the protests and rallies that took place as evidence of growing class conflict. However, these events were exceptional. Much more often, the poor and the near-poor put up with their less-advantaged position because they have few of the resources (e.g., money, education, organizations) that make it possible to fight for social change (Brym, 1979) In fact, in the past few years, we have seen more opposition from a better-organized middle class, in response to government cutbacks in health and education, than from the poor in response to welfare cutbacks. Thus, it is by no means clear that a higher level of inequality and fewer opportunities for upward mobility will translate into greater social unrest. Nevertheless, greater inequality means greater hardship and more limited life-chances for more people. As Paul Krugman, the influential American economist, wrote: "The ultimate effects of growing economic disparities on our social and political health may be hard to predict, but they are unlikely to be pleasant" (Krugman, 1994: F9).

■ RESPONDING TO INEQUALITY

Some of us believe that more equal distribution of society's resources would be preferable to the current level of inequality. We believe that the existing differences in life-chances are unjust, and look for ways in which social institutions, laws, and tax systems might be changed in order to reduce material inequality. Others, equally offended by inequality and its consequences, reject this reformist approach in favour of a more radical position, advocating the replacement of capitalist society by some kind of socialist alternative. Still others respond to evidence of extensive inequality with little ambition to change it, believing, simply, that this is "the way things are." Although perhaps bothered by its consequences, members of this group might still conclude that the existing level of inequality is inevitable, and that well-intentioned efforts to reduce it will, in the long run, have little effect. They might even conclude that inequality is functional, as Davis and Moore argued half a century ago, and that efforts to reduce it will be counterproductive. In short, our reactions to the fact of inequality, and our recommendations about what, if anything, should be done about it, directly reflect our values and our political orientation.

Assuming that a lower level of inequality *is* a goal worth striving for, it is clear that the government has a role to play in trying to reach that goal. The Canadian state has an impact on the distribution of wealth and income through tax systems that redistribute wealth from the rich to the poor, through minimum-wage and other types of legislation, and through transfer payments such as pensions for the elderly and the disabled, social assistance for low-income individuals and families, and unemployment insurance (now renamed employment insurance). Even so, compared with a number of other industrialized countries, Canada spends considerably less on attempts to reduce poverty (Economic Council of Canada, 1992: 9–10).

Canada's "liberal" welfare policies place much more faith in the power of a "free market," unregulated by government legislation and policies, to produce wealth and jobs that should, it is expected, trickle down to the poor (Esping-Andersen, 1990). Unfortunately, as our review of labour-market trends indicates, there is little evidence that the "free market" has performed successfully in this regard (Myles, 1996). Instead,

unemployment rates have risen and inequality has increased. Furthermore, during the past decade or so, the political mood has changed, and concerns about reducing the deficit, streamlining government, and making Canada more competitive in the global marketplace appear to have been influencing government policy much more than concerns about reducing inequality. In fact, some deficit-reducing initiatives (e.g., reductions in social-assistance payments) are leading to increases in material inequality in Canada. But there are other approaches to deficit reduction that do not involve this trade-off. For example, job-creation strategies may be as useful in the long run as some deficit-cutting efforts, and tax alternatives that would raise corporate income taxes or eliminate some of the tax write-offs enjoyed by the upper and middle classes (such as tax deductions for pension plans and RRSPs) might also be appropriate.

A large part of the problem lies, of course, in the fact that any serious effort to redistribute the wealth and income from the well-off to the poor would probably be opposed by the former, by many of us. If we really want to do something about material inequality in Canada, if we want a different kind of society, many of us have to be willing to accept less so that others can have more. ▓

SUMMARY

1. Persistent patterns of social inequality within a society are referred to as a structure of social stratification. Some social hierarchies within a society are based on ascribed statuses such as gender, race, or age, which are typically assigned to an individual at birth. Other social hierarchies are based on achieved statuses, which index how well an individual has performed within some role. A society in which considerable social mobility between statuses is possible is said to have an open stratification system.

2. Social theorists have proposed a variety of different explanations of the origins and effects of social-stratification systems. In his class-based theory of social stratification, Karl Marx emphasized the exploitation of the working class by the owners of the means of production and the capacity of class conflict to generate social change. Max Weber also put considerable emphasis on the power that resides in ownership of property, but argued that other hierarchies, those of prestige and political power, are influential as well.

3. The structural-functionalist theory of social stratification suggests that inequality is both inevitable and functionally necessary for a society, ensuring that the most qualified individuals are selected to fill the most important (and most rewarding) roles. Power differences are downplayed in this theory, as is conflict between different social classes. A number of more recent theories of social stratification, including those put forward by Ralf Dahrendorf, Gerhard Lenski, and Erik Olin Wright, have placed much more emphasis on power and conflict. Wright, in particular, has tried to develop a class-based theory of stratification that adapts many of Marx's ideas to the circumstances of the late twentieth century.

4. Examination of occupational shifts in Canada over the course of this century reveals some of the changing features of Canada's stratification system. However, we can get only partial glimpses of the class structure of our society. Studies of occupational mobility reveal that Canada is a relatively open society. Even so, there is considerable evidence that class-based advantages are passed from one generation to the next.

5. A detailed analysis of material inequality in Canada reveals that ownership of wealth and property is highly concentrated, and that income inequality is relatively high. Using a relative measure of poverty, we observe that 1 in 6 Canadians are living below the "poverty line." There is considerable evidence that the poor and others near the bottom of the social hierarchies in our society enjoy fewer life-chances than do the well-off. For example, they are less likely to do well in school and to continue on to higher education, they are less healthy and have a shorter life expectancy, and they do not fare as well when dealing with the criminal-justice system. But because of their more limited access to social and material resources, the poor have seldom become an active force for social change.

6. Some theories of social stratification developed in the middle of the twentieth century suggested that material inequality was declining as the North American economy expanded. However, the period of rapid economic growth and relative affluence that characterized the middle decades of the century appears to have ended. And, as unemployment rates rise, as part-time and temporary work becomes more common, and as governments cut back on social-assistance programs, evidence accumulates that material inequality is also slowly increasing in Canada.

QUESTIONS TO CONSIDER

1. Does social class play a more or less significant role than do ascribed statuses (such as race and gender) in determining patterns of inequality within Canadian society?

2. How are social and material advantages passed from one generation to the next, resulting in persistent patterns of social inequality?

3. What role, if any, should governments play in addressing persistent patterns of social inequality? How successful have such attempts been in the past?

4. What does "poverty" really mean, and how should we measure it? Does Christopher Sarlo's "absolute poverty" approach (see Box 7.3) make more sense to you than the "relative poverty" approach underlying Statistics Canada's "low-income cut-off lines"? Why or why not?

5. Some people believe that computers and the "information highway" will open doors for disadvantaged Canadians, and will help reduce social inequalities. Others disagree, arguing that those who are already better off will be able to benefit the most from new information technologies. What do you think?

GLOSSARY

absolute poverty The state of existence of those who have so little income that they can barely stay alive.

achieved status A changeable status that is achieved on the basis of how well an individual performs in a particular role.

ascribed status A status such as age, gender, or race that is assigned to an individual, typically at birth, not chosen by the individual.

bourgeoisie According to Marx, one of the two main classes within a capitalist mode of production, comprising the owners of the means of production.

caste system A closed stratification system, most common in India, with strict rules regarding the type of work that members of different castes (the strata of society into which people are born) can do.

circulatory mobility The occupational mobility that occurs within a society when better-qualified individuals move upward to replace those who are less qualified and who must consequently move downward.

class The position of an individual or a family within an economic hierarchy, along with others who have similar amounts of access to or control over material resources.

class conflict According to Marx, conflict between major classes within a mode of production, which eventually leads to the evolution of a new mode of production.

class consciousness According to Marx, the phenomenon whereby members of a class recognize their shared interests in opposition to members of another class.

class structure The relatively permanent economic hierarchy composed of different social classes.

closed stratification system A stratification system in which little or no social mobility occurs, because most or all statuses are ascribed.

contradictory class locations According to Erik Olin Wright, the locations within a class structure populated by occupational groupings with divided loyalties (for example, managers who both supervise others and report to owners).

intergenerational occupational mobility An individual's occupational mobility, either upward or downward, in relation to her or his parents' (typical) occupational status.

intragenerational occupational mobility An individual's occupational mobility, either upward or downward, within his or her own lifetime.

life-chances According to Weber, the opportunities (or lack thereof) for a higher standard of living and a better quality of life that are available to members of a given class.

low-income cut-off line Also known as the "poverty line"; an estimate of the income level below which one might be considered to be living in (relative) poverty; defined by Statistics Canada as the level of income at which more than 55 percent of income is spent on basic necessities.

means of production According to Marx, one of the main components of a mode of production, consisting of the technology, capital investments, and raw materials used in production.

meritocracy A society in which most or all statuses are achieved on the basis of merit (how well one performs in a given role).

mode of production According to Marx, the overall system of economic activity within a society, comprising the means of production and the social relations of production.

occupational status attainment The process whereby an individual obtains a particular occupational status, and the factors that influence this process.

open stratification system A stratification system in which merit, rather than inheritance (or ascribed characteristics), determine social rank.

petite bourgeoisie According to Marx, a secondary class within the capitalist mode of production, including independent owners/producers (for example, farmers) and small-business owners.

privilege Control of a society's surplus resources.

proletariat According to Marx, one of the two main classes within a capitalist mode of production, comprising workers who exchange their labour for a wage.

relative poverty The state of existence in which individuals have significantly less income than most others in their society, causing their lifestyle to be much more restricted and their life-chances substantially curtailed.

social conflict groups According to Dahrendorf, the groups that hold power and those that lack it (with the latter trying to obtain power and the former attempting to maintain it) in the variety of organizations that constitute contemporary society.

social mobility The process whereby individuals, families, or other groups move up or down a status hierarchy.

social relations of production According to Marx, one of the main components of a given mode of production; specifically, the relationships between the main classes involved in production.

social stratification Persistent patterns of social inequality within a society, perpetuated by the manner in which wealth, power, and prestige are distributed and passed on from one generation to the next.

socioeconomic status One's general status within an economic hierarchy, based on income, education, and occupation.

status One's rank or position within a social hierarchy.

structural-functionalist theory A theoretical approach that seeks to explain the function for society as a whole of specific social institutions and other societal characteristics; emphasizes consensus over conflict as an agent of social change.

structural mobility Occupational mobility within a society resulting from changes in the occupational structure (for example, the upward mobility of many individuals resulting from the creation of more middle- and upper-level jobs in the economy).

surplus value According to Marx, the value added to a product through a worker's labour; the profit taken by the owners.

working poor Individuals who work, but whose income leaves them below a designated low-income, or "poverty," line.

SUGGESTED READING

Curtis, James E., Edward Grabb, and Neil Guppy, eds. (1993). *Social Inequality in Canada: Patterns, Problems, Policies,* 2nd ed. Scarborough, ON: Prentice Hall. An interesting and useful collection of readings on the various dimensions of stratification in Canada.

Grabb, Edward G. (1990). *Theories of Social Inequality: Classical and Contemporary Perspectives,* 2nd ed. Toronto: Holt, Rinehart and Winston. This advanced but very readable book discusses various theories of social inequality, some of which were summarized in this chapter.

Gunderson, Morley, L. Muszynski, and J. Keck. (1990). *Women and Labour Market Poverty.* Ottawa: Canadian Advisory Council on the Status of Women. A very useful analysis of poverty among employed Canadians, particularly women, that carefully examines labour-market processes that allow poverty to exist among the employed, and government interventions in the labour market that are meant to reduce the number of working poor.

Menzies, Heather. (1996). *Whose Brave New World? The Information Highway and the New Economy.* Toronto: Between the Lines. The author asks important and provocative questions about who is really benefiting the most from new information technologies and changing employment practices, and suggests ways in which the benefits might be more equally shared.

Ross, David P., and Richard Shillington. (1994). *The Canadian Fact Book on Poverty, 1994.* Ottawa: Canadian Council on Social Development. This short book discusses the measurement of poverty and provides detailed statistics on the extent of poverty in Canada today, as well as comparisons over time and with other countries.

CHAPTER EIGHT

Gender Inequality: Economic and Political Aspects

IN THIS CHAPTER YOU WILL LEARN THAT

■ a main source of inequality between women and men is the greater exclusion of women from public economic and political activity; the persistent tendency of many women to be relegated to domestic affairs leads to less income, prestige, and power for women

■ although women have entered politics and the paid labour force in increasing numbers in the course of this century, they still tend to be chiefly responsible for meal preparation, cleaning, laundry, and child care

■ in the paid labour force, women and men still tend to be segregated in different kinds of jobs; "women's jobs" typically pay less, carry less prestige, offer less security, and bestow less authority

■ although women make up over half the Canadian population, fewer than 20 percent of members of Parliament are women

■ in recent years, employment equity policies and policies requiring equal pay for work of equal value have been implemented to help lessen gender inequalities, but much research and political action is still required before gender equality is achieved

MONICA BOYD
Florida State University

■ INTRODUCTION

As we look back on the twentieth century, one fact is inescapable — enormous change has occurred in the attitudes, expectations, and behaviours of women and men in Canada. One way to see this change vividly is to compare the likely lifestyle of a man and a woman born in 1925 with that of another man and woman, born in 1950, and of a third man and woman, born in 1975. The pair born in 1925 would have been 25 years old in 1950, and 35 in 1960. During that ten-year period in the 1950s, they would almost certainly have married and had children. In the 1950s, women were expected to work exclusively in the home and take complete responsibility for domestic tasks and behaviours. Sociologists use the term **social roles** to refer to the behaviours that are expected of people occupying particular social positions. In the 1950s, the attitudes and activities expected of women — that is, their social roles — were those of wives and mothers. In contrast, men were expected to have paying jobs, and their responsibilities were to meet their family's needs for food, clothing, and shelter. Their social roles were those captured by the terms *provider* and *head of household.*

For a woman and a man born in 1950, this idealized "script" would be less rigid than it had been for the couple from the previous generation. Both pairs would have been raised at a time when mothers were expected to stay in the home and fathers were expected to be away for most of the day earning a living. But by the time the pair born in 1950 turned age 25 in 1975, the belief that women should marry and work exclusively in the home was rapidly eroding. The average age at marriage had increased, indicating that many women and men were postponing legal marriage. After the divorce laws were revised in 1969, divorce rates also rose, giving a clear signal that fewer women and men would have a spouse for the duration of their adult lives. Other changes were blurring the line between work in the home and work in the labour force. Men were starting to become more involved in household maintenance and child rearing, and more and more women were joining the paid labour force.

The scenario for the pair born in 1975 and turning 25 in the year 2000 is not yet complete. In fact, many of you were born during the mid-1970s, so you can draw the picture both as it currently exists and as you think it will look by the turn of the century. Most of you, both men and women, probably continue to see yourselves as eventually having spouses or partners and raising children. Unlike the generation born in the 1920s, you probably also see yourselves as sharing domestic responsibilities with your spouse or partner and as both holding paid jobs in either the private or the public sector.

However, a changed world does not necessarily mean an equal world. Although the term *revolution* is often used in reference to the changes in the direction of gender equality that have been made to date, those changes can hardly be said to constitute a finished revolution. In the "Cathy" cartoon on the next page, we see Cathy marvelling at the many options that Shawna now has — only to be reminded of the low wages often paid to women, the need for affordable child care, and the importance of paid work for economic security. As I will show in this chapter, gender inequality still exists in Canada, and is likely to persist into the twenty-first century. This means that, throughout your lifetime, you have probably seen and are likely yet to see at least some of the gender inequalities discussed here. At the same time, you are also likely to witness a variety of interventions aimed at reducing these inequalities.

The chapter begins with a definition of gender inequality, then explores the major dimensions of the phenomenon and the three main arenas in Canadian society in which it is evident: the home, the labour force, and politics. The chapter ends with a review of the actions, policies, and legislation that could reduce gender inequality in the future.

■ UNDERSTANDING GENDER INEQUALITY

▲ GENDER INEQUALITY DEFINED

We frequently use the term *inequality* in reference to differences between groups of people that can be described by phrases such as "less than" or "greater than," or "more/less important." Social scientists usually refer to inequalities between men and women as "gender inequalities" rather than as "sex inequalities." The term *gender* is favoured because it refers to the *social* meanings associated with being a man or a woman, whereas the term *sex* refers to the *biological* characteristics of men and women. For sociologists, social meanings are constructed from social relations. For example, heterosexual marriage is a relationship in which one person becomes the husband and the other person becomes the wife. Although the terms *husband* and *wife* are inherently neutral, we quickly realize that, in our society, they carry expectations about people's obligations to each other, about their behaviour, and about the sex of the partner labelled "husband" and the partner labelled "wife." If you were to write down all the thoughts that occur to you when you think of the terms *husband* and *wife,* you would probably include such phrases as "provider" or "decision-maker" versus "homemaker" or "caregiver."

Gender Stereotypes

Phrases such as "provider" and "caregiver" do more than describe the expected behaviour associated with being a partner in a marriage. They also cause us to evaluate types of behaviour as "masculine" or "feminine." Once in place, these images of masculinity and femininity influence how people see themselves and how they experience the world. For example, the observation "it's a boy" often causes North American parents to decorate the child's room in bold colours, or at least in pale blue as opposed to pink. A male child is likely to receive stuffed animals, trucks, and play tool-kits rather than the dolls, play dishes, and play make-up that are likely to be given a girl. Through parental behaviour, television, movies, and print media (including schoolbooks), children learn to define certain social behaviours as inherent in being chromosomally male or female, even when such traits are probably learned rather than an inevitable consequence of an XY or XX chromosomal structure. By the time children have grown into adults, they have adopted and identified with many of these "masculine" or "feminine" personality traits and related behaviours. In turn, they

are likely to treat others around them through the lenses of their own identities and understandings of masculinity and femininity. In many instances, these conceptualizations are **gender stereotypes** — that is, oversimplified beliefs that men and women, by virtue of their physical sex, possess different personality traits and, as a result, may behave differently and experience the world in different ways.

Images of masculinity and femininity often emphasize opposites. The fixation on polarizing characteristics of men and women is evident in phrases such as "opposite sex" or "vive la différence." The polarized approach is also evident in psychological studies of gender stereotypes. In one famous study, several U.S. psychologists asked respondents to indicate which traits, from a checklist of 122 adjectives, characterized average men and women. They found that men were described as very aggressive, very independent, very active, very competitive, very logical, able to make decisions easily, and almost always acting as leaders. Women were described as not at all aggressive, not at all independent, very emotional, very passive, not at all competitive, very illogical, able to make decisions only with difficulty, and almost never acting as leaders (Broverman et al., 1972).

These results were obtained from respondents in the late 1960s; a study today would almost certainly have some different results. However, a Canadian sociologist, Marlene Mackie (1980), still found evidence of polarized gender stereotypes in research conducted about a decade later. The persistence of stereotypical thinking of feminine and masculine characteristics as polar opposites should sensitize us

SOURCE: *Cathy* © 1994 Cathy Guisewite. Reprinted with permission of Universal Press Syndicate.

to two things. First, the idea of difference is apparently a powerful one, and hard to dispel even when it is contradicted by research: Psychological studies of personality traits show that the personality traits of men and women actually overlap quite a bit (Basow, 1986). Second, in these polar depictions, feminine traits are viewed as less desirable than masculine ones. You need only reread the lists in the preceding paragraph to see that this is true.

Dimensions of Inequality

Gender stereotypes shape our attitudes about girls and boys, men and women, and they are often important factors in determining the ideologies that perpetuate gender inequalities. Sociologists usually define **gender inequalities** as hierarchical asymmetries between men and women with respect to the distribution of power, material well-being, and prestige (as recognized through deference or honour). This definition does not imply that men as individuals always have greater prestige, wealth, and power than do individual women. It does imply that, in general, compared with women, men have more wealth and greater power, and positions that are accorded higher prestige.

Power refers to the capacity to impose one's will on others, regardless of any resistance they might offer. It thus refers to the capacity to influence, manipulate, and control others. Power is exercised not only in the overt imposition of the will of one individual on others, but also in the control or support by groups or organizations of agendas that either uphold or challenge existing conditions (Duffy, 1986).

Material well-being refers to the ability to obtain the economic resources necessary to pay for adequate food, clothing, housing, and possessions. Two important sources of material well-being are work-related earnings and wealth.

Prestige refers to the social evaluation or ranking, by general consensus, of occupational activities and positions in a hierarchical order that reflects the degree of respect, honour, or deference the person engaged in the activity or occupying the position is to be accorded. Not everyone has to agree with the evaluation. For example, university professors are usually highly respected by the Canadian public, yet you may have no use for a particular professor. (One clear signal of the high general regard for professors is the regulation that Canadian passport applications can be witnessed by them.) Commonly, two or more differently evaluated positions are described as having higher or lower prestige, or "status."

The three dimensions of inequality just defined — power, material well-being, and prestige — are found in discussions of **social stratification,** which is the unequal ranking of groups in a society and the unequal and asymmetrical distribution of prestige, material possessions, and power among those groups. Stratification is the result, achieved over time, of routine and frequently recurring practices and often unstated rules. From this broader perspective, gender inequality can be seen as a particular type of social inequality.

Throughout this chapter, you will find examples of gender inequalities in prestige, material well-being, and power. However, we can also witness gender inequality in the distribution of power in relationships *between* men and women, and in the separation of women and men in private and public spheres. Let us now examine these issues in turn.

▲ EXERCISING POWER

For many analysts of gender inequality, the asymmetry of power whereby men influence and control women is a very important aspect of the phenomenon. Since the ability to control and influence — to use power — indicates the twin processes of domination and subordination, most sociologists describe the power relations between men and women as those of male domination and female subordination.

Male influence and control over women is not narrowly defined. It does not, for example, refer just to the predominance of men rather than women in political positions or in the military. Instead, the concern with power is broadly based, including all social relations, routine behaviours, and commonly accepted practices. For example, denying women the right to vote clearly denied them a voice in choosing who would govern them and, equally important, denied them direct input into the formulation of laws that affect them, bestowing that right on men instead. Similarly, a workplace regulation that had women fired upon marriage, such as the one that existed in the federal public service through the 1950s, made it impossible for married women to earn income and forced them to be dependent on their husbands for money. Power is also evident in day-to-day situations, such as when a young woman becomes the object of sexual innuendo or leering by her male classmates, co-workers, or even strangers. In our society, such behaviour on the part of males is often considered "normal"; it draws on concep-

Table 8.2 Occupational Distributions of the Canadian Labour Force, Females and Males Age 15 and Over, 1991

Title	Male	Female	Percentage of total labour force that is female[a]
All occupations, percent[b]	100.0	100.0	44.9
Managerial, administrative, and related occupations	13.9	10.0	37.5
Natural sciences, engineering, and mathematical	5.9	1.8	19.9
Social sciences and related fields, religion	1.9	3.1	57.4
Teaching and related occupations	2.9	6.3	64.1
Medicine and health	1.9	9.0	79.2
Artistic, literary, recreational	1.8	1.7	44.3
Clerical and related occupations	7.1	31.6	78.4
Sales occupations	9.0	9.4	46.0
Service occupations	10.1	16.0	56.3
Farming, fishing, forestry, logging, mining, and quarrying	6.8	2.3	21.9
Processing, machining, and fabrication	15.9	5.7	20.6
Construction	10.5	0.4	2.7
Transport equipment	5.9	0.7	9.2
All other	6.7	2.3	21.7

[a] Percentages are specific for each row. For example, for persons in the total labour force who reported occupations (row 1), 44.9 percent are female. Of persons reporting occupations in natural sciences, engineering, and mathematics (row 3), 19.9 percent are female.

[b] Percentages will not add up to exactly 100 percent, because of rounding procedures employed by Statistics Canada.

SOURCE: Statistics Canada, *Occupation: The Nation*, 1991 Census of Canada, Cat. no. 93-327 (Ottawa: Industry, Science and Technology Canada, 1993), Table 1. Reproduced by authority of the Minister of Industry, 1997.

added paid work to the unpaid work they were already doing, and now work a "double day" or even a "triple day" as they combine hours in a paid job with housework and child care. The fact that women do more unpaid work than men cannot be attributed solely to the higher percentages of women relative to men who hold **part-time** jobs, and thus have fewer hours of paid work each week. Even when they work at full-time jobs, women continue to spend more time than men on unpaid housework, including child care, cooking, cleaning up after meals, house cleaning, laundry, shopping, maintenance and repairs, and volunteer activities (Devereaux, 1993). The hours spent on unpaid work is highest for women age 25–44 who have children. Figure 8.1 shows that such full-time employed women, whether married and living with their husbands or single parents, spend over 4 hours a day on unpaid work, amounting to over 30 hours a week. In contrast, full-time employed married men with children spend a little over 3 hours a day on unpaid work, or under 22 hours a week. The gender gap per week amounts to more than what we would consider a normal

"working" day of 8 hours. Judith Frederick, who analyzed the 1992 general social survey at Statistics Canada, also found that the full- or part-time employment of wives did not generate more hours of unpaid work by husbands. However, she did find that husbands with full-time employed wives were more likely than others to reallocate their time to the "deadline" everyday chores of meal preparation and washing up (Frederick, 1995). We should remember that single parents usually do not have another adult present to help with unpaid work.

Not surprisingly, women report spending less time than men watching television, pursuing hobbies, and playing sports and games (Devereaux, 1993). Also, women are more likely than men to report feeling stressed due to lack of time; this is especially true for women who are working full-time and who have young children. Among dual-earner couples in which both partners were working full-time and the youngest child was under the age of 10 in 1992, 16 percent of the men and 34 percent of the women reported being severely stressed due to lack of time (Frederick, 1993: 9).

◆ **Figure 8.1** Average Daily Hours Spent on Unpaid Work Activities, by Marital Status, Children, and Gender, for the Full-Time Employed, Age 25–44, Canada, 1992

SOURCE: Judith A. Frederick, *As Time Goes By . . . Time Use of Canadians*, Cat. no. 89-544E (Ottawa: Statistics Canada, 1995), Tables 2.4 and 2.5. Reproduced by authority of the Minister of Industry, 1997.

■ LABOUR-FORCE INEQUALITIES

▲ OCCUPATIONAL SEGREGATION AND SEX TYPING

Although more and more Canadian women are now paid workers, they are frequently in jobs that involve caregiving, nurturing, and the sort of management functions typically found in the home. Women tend to be secretaries (the "office wife"), nurses, social workers, teachers, seamstresses, and waitresses. In contrast, men tend to be managers, doctors, professors, and factory and construction workers. This concentration of men in some occupations and women in others is often called the **sex segregation of occupations,** and the notion that a given occupation is appropriate for one sex versus the other is referred to as **sex typing (or sex labelling) of occupations**.

Occupational Segregation

Men and women can be compared across occupations in a designated place (a firm, a city, or a country). If men and women are concentrated in different occupations, the occupational structure is considered sex-segregated. Table 8.2 shows that, according to the 1991 census, sex segregation does exist in Canada. When we collapse 500 occupa-

tional titles into fourteen major groups, we see that nearly one-third of Canadian women are employed in clerical and related occupations and another 16 percent are employed in service occupations. Men are not hired for jobs in these two occupational categories to the same extent as women (17 percent versus 48 percent). Instead, the largest percentages of men are in processing, machining, and fabricating occupations (16 percent) and in managerial, administrative, and related occupations (14 percent).

The degree of occupational sex segregation has declined somewhat since the 1960s. This decline is attributable mainly to the movement of women into previously male-dominated occupations rather than that of men into female-dominated occupations. However, the persistently large percentages of women employed in clerical occupations, creating a so-called female ghetto, are an important source of continued high levels of occupational segregation between women and men. We also learn from the last column in Table 8.2 that women represent 45 percent of workers in all occupations. However, nearly 80 percent of the workers in clerical occupations and in medicine and health are women. Fewer than 3 percent of workers in construction occupations are women; 97 percent are men. This overrepresentation and underrepresentation of women (using the 45 percent figure as a standard) indicates the stereotypical labelling of certain occupations and jobs as suitable for women and others as suitable for men. We can say that clerical and medicine and health occupations are female-labelled occupations and those in construction are sex-typed as male. In actuality, the degree of sex labelling, or sex typing, is often greater than is suggested by Table 8.2, since the occupational categories given here are very broad. For example, if we look at Statistics Canada 1991 census data for specific occupational titles, we find that within the health-related occupations, 16 percent of osteopaths and chiropractors and 95 percent of registered nurses, graduate nurses, and nurses-in-training are women (Statistics Canada, 1993c: 10).

Why Care?

Why should you be concerned about sex typing and sex segregation? Because the occupations in which women are concentrated are often lower than those held predominantly by men in terms of authority, responsibility, skill requirements, mobility opportunities, and earnings. We will discuss many of these inequalities later. The important point for now is that these inequalities indicate male advantages in the labour force. Furthermore, the nature of the sex typ-

Sex typing or sex labelling is the designation of an occupation as "female" or "male" depending on the sex for whom it is considered appropriate. Secretarial work and data entry are traditional female jobs. SOURCE: David Oliver/Tony Stone.

ing in our society implies that the work traditionally performed by women in the home has created sex stereotypes about the work that women should do in the paid labour force.

▲ POWER AT WORK

Male power over women is evident in the labour market and in public arenas such as law, politics, the military, and the media. We have seen that substantial occupational segregation exists, and that it hints at greater male power, in that men are more likely than women to be managers. But in order to document gender asymmetry in the ability to influence and control others, we must find out whether men are indeed able to make more decisions and exercise authority over women.

In analyzing the 1994 Statistics Canada general social survey, my colleagues and I found that men were more likely than women to describe their jobs as managerial and/or as supervising others. For example, 25.3 percent of women, but 40.4 percent of men, described themselves as supervisors. We also found that male supervisors had more employees to supervise than did female supervisors. As well, male managers were more likely than female managers to hold positions in the top rungs and to plan the activities of all parts of the business. Women were in the lower managerial rungs. They were less likely to be involved in planning business activities and more likely to be only partly involved (Boyd, Hughes, and Miller, 1997). This pattern illustrates the **glass-ceiling** effect: Women face invisible barriers in penetrating the highest levels of organizations where power is concentrated and exercised. Box 8.1 shows that the glass ceiling is prevalent in many of the 300 largest Canadian companies listed on the Toronto Stock Exchange.

Our current and earlier research (Boyd, Mulvihill, and Myles, 1991) indicates that men are more likely to hold jobs characterized by the ability to control people and influence outcomes. However, demonstrating gender inequalities in the distribution of power is not quite the same as showing that men have power over women. Studies of specific firms do indicate that men, as managers, foremen, or union organizers, often have control and influence over women workers. Our analysis of a 1982 Canadian survey found that it is common for women to be supervised by men; when women supervise, they usually exercise authority over other women. Only rarely do men have a female superior (Boyd, Mulvihill, and Myles, 1991: 424). In the labour force, men have power over both men and women, whereas women have power primarily over other women.

▲ GENDER AND SKILL

The jobs that women often hold are characterized not only by being less powerful, but also by having lower skill requirements than jobs held by men (Boyd, 1990; Myles and Fawcett, 1990). Since higher-skilled jobs usually differ from lower-skilled jobs in pay and security, employment in lower-skilled jobs implies economic and quality-of-work inequalities between men and women.

Why are women less likely than men to be employed in high-skilled jobs? One possible answer

Box 8.1
The Glass Ceiling

Among the top TSE [Toronto Stock Exchange] 300 [Canadian] companies, based on 1994 data, 91 companies had no women either in senior management or on the board of directors.

We rated the companies as having a strength in diversity if they have a board that is even 15 percent female or a senior management that is at least 25 percent female. According to the 1994 figures, only 35 TSE-300 companies registered a strength in one of these two areas. Only one TSE-300 company received a strength rating in both areas. But even these numbers can be deceiving. Many women included in these statistics hold positions in areas such as human resources and public affairs, jobs which normally do not involve them in strategic corporate operating decisions.

The jury may still be out, but the fact that about one-third of the largest companies in Canada do not have any women board directors or senior managers last year suggests that the pace of change in these companies leaves much to be desired.

SOURCE: Excerpted from the "Letter to the Editor" column, *The Globe and Mail,* August 28, 1995, p. A16. Letter written by Michael C. Jantzi, President, Michael Jantzi Research Associates, Inc. Reprinted with permission from *The Globe and Mail* and Michael C. Jantzi.

is that there is gender bias in the definition of **skill**. Sex typing and a general devaluation of work done by women influence common-sense evaluations of what is or is not "skilled" work. For example, nursing occupations may require a high level of interpersonal skill — for example, in dealing with relatives of dying patients — but because this ability to handle a diversity of distraught and upset people is considered "natural" in a woman, it is not recognized as a professional "skill" in a nursing occupation. In contrast, plumbing jobs (usually performed by men) require knowledge of toilets and sinks, soldering, and pipe fitting — so-called technical skills. Bias in the evaluation of skills occurs when such technical knowledge is considered more valuable than knowledge about personal interactions and caregiving.

This example indicates that our definitions of skill are socially constructed. That is, what we define as "skill" reflects other social evaluations and hierarchies — in this case, hierarchies based on gender (Gaskell, 1986; Steinberg, 1990). If we think of women as being worth less than men, we are likely to let this attitude influence how we define the skill requirements of jobs held primarily by

women or primarily by men. Jane Gaskell (1986) suggests that women are disadvantaged in the skill definitions assigned to jobs sex-typed as female because, historically, women have not been represented by strong unions that have lobbied in their interest. Furthermore, women are less likely to be trained on the shop floor as apprentices. Instead, the training required for "female" jobs is often incorporated into high-school curricula, with the result that the skill-training component is less visible than it is in occupations in which training is provided on the job.

Skill undervaluation of female sex-typed occupations is a concern for two reasons. First, wage levels are associated with skill requirements. Thus, if the skill requirements of jobs in which women predominate are undervalued, the pay rates in those jobs are likely to be lower. Second, current pay-equity policies often ask whether men and women are receiving equal pay for performing jobs of comparable worth. The "worth" of a job, however, includes its skill requirements. If the skill requirements of jobs employing predominantly women are already devalued, then fair comparisons between appropriate sets of jobs may not be made (Gaskell, 1991; Steinberg, 1990).

While women have made inroads into many traditionally male-dominated professions, their progress is often exaggerated. What proportion of the people in this photo of the trading floor of the Toronto Stock Exchange are women? Do their jobs appear to differ from those performed by the men? SOURCE: Dick Hemingway.

▲ NONSTANDARD WORK

As another example of gender inequality, let us now examine gender differences in **standard** and **nonstandard work**. What do these terms mean? If asked to describe a typical job in the labour market, most of you would probably mention full-time, full-year employment with job-related benefits. This is usually what we mean by standard work. In contrast, nonstandard work includes part-time work, part-year employment, limited-term contract employment, employment through temporary-help agencies, self-employment, and multiple job holding (Economic Council of Canada, 1991: 71; Krahn, 1995).

Women and Part-Time Work

Compared with men at every age, women in the labour force are much more likely to be part-time workers. In 1991, for example, 1 in 4 employed women (26 percent) worked part-time compared with only 1 in 11 employed men (9 percent); the gaps were most pronounced among women and men age 25 and older (Ghalam, 1993: 13). Gender differences remain when the definition of part-time is extended beyond hours worked per week to include weeks worked per year. According to the most recent Canadian census, 65 percent of all women working in 1990 were *not* working full-time–full-year, whereas only 41 percent of men fell into this category (Statistics Canada, 1993a: 5).

As a share of all employment, part-time work has been increasing. The restructuring of the economy is a primary explanation for this increase. Many workers now take part-time employment because they cannot find full-time employment. By 1993, 35 percent of women in part-time work and 38 percent of men indicated they were working part-time because they could not find full-time employment, up from 11 percent for both women and men in 1975 (Best, 1995).

Women and Nonstandard Work

During the past two decades, women have consistently made up around 70 percent of the part-time labour force. Part-time work can thus be seen as an employment ghetto for women. Women are also overrepresented in nonstandard work defined more broadly. Using a definition of nonstandard employment that includes self-employment, temporary work, part-time work, part-year work, and multiple job holding, a 1994 Canadian study found that 40 percent of all currently employed women, compared with 27 percent of men, were working in nonstandard employment. Percentages were extremely high for young men and women like yourselves. Among those age 15–24, 62 percent of young women and 52 percent of young men had nonstandard employment (Krahn, 1995: Table 3).

Concerns about Nonstandard Work

Employment in nonstandard work is of concern for two reasons. First, it is becoming more and more common, especially among young people. Second, compared with full-year, full-time jobs, nonstandard jobs generally provide less job security, lower pay, and fewer fringe benefits. Part-time workers, for example, are often excluded from employer fringe benefits, including pension plans (Duffy and Pupo, 1992). Thus, nonstandard employment, in general, and part-time work, in particular, imply a marginal work force — marginal in terms of earnings, benefits, and job security. Statistics indicate that more women than men are employed in this marginal work world.

▲ EARNINGS

In addition to gender inequalities in terms of occupations, power, skill, and type of work, women in Canada, on average, earn less than men. In 1991, the average annual income of women was $18 050, compared with $29 328 for men; in other words, the average income of women was 62 percent of the average income of men (Ghalam, 1993). Shocking as it may be, this ratio represents an improvement over the situation in earlier times. In the late 1960s and early 1970s, the average earnings of women were roughly 46 percent of the average earnings of men (Ghalam, 1993: Table 3.1).

Explanations of Women's Lower Pay

Observers have offered four sets of explanations for the pay gap between women and men: (1) gender differences in the characteristics that influence pay rates; (2) gender differences in the type of work performed; (3) discrimination; and (4) societal devaluation of women's work. All four explanations have strong advocates, and all have critics (England, 1993; Phillips and Phillips, 1983).

Explanations of the first type usually assume that earnings reflect the productivity of workers and that productivity is increased by factors such as higher education, longer labour-force experience, and length of time on the job. Advocates of this explanation argue that the lower wages of women are caused by lower productivity levels resulting from women's lower or different educational achievements and from labour-force interruptions attributable to women's family responsibilities.

The second type of explanation argues that the gender gap in pay reflects the concentration of women in certain occupations and industries characterized by lower wages, and their concentration in nonstandard work, particularly part-time work.

The third type of explanation focusses on discrimination, identified here as differential pay being assigned to women on the basis of their gender. Such discrimination can be personal and deliberate, but it is often impersonal, produced by the standard, unquestioned practices of assigning women to certain jobs and men to others, and of paying men and women different wages even when they hold the same jobs. Much of this impersonal discrimination is called **statistical discrimination,** the process whereby employers make decisions about whether to hire and how much to pay any given woman on the basis of the employers' perceptions of the average characteristics of *all* women. For example, if an employer believes that women typically leave the labour force for long periods to raise children, or will not travel extensively or work overtime because of family responsibilities, the employer may impose those generalized beliefs on particular women. Thus, a single woman with no children might find herself being paid less than a man because of the employer's belief that women, in general, are less productive than men. Alternatively, she might find herself denied opportunities for job training or advancement because of her employer's belief that women, in general, will leave their jobs to have families or will not perform certain tasks, such as long-distance travelling, because of family obligations.

The fourth explanation holds that the lower earnings of women reflect a general devaluation of "women's work" — that is, of tasks initially performed in the home — and the incorporation of that devaluation into pay practices. As we have seen, the work women perform in the home can be invisible and often is not viewed as "work." People who do domestic work for money receive low wages. The devaluation of women's labour is also rooted in the historical image of every woman having a male breadwinner to provide for her and not "needing" to be paid the same wage as a man who, after all, has a family to support! Once in place, pay practices persist and fuel a faulty logic that not only sustains pay differences between men and women in the same jobs but also provides a rationale for the lower wage rates paid in sex-typed occupations and jobs. Research by Paula England, a U.S. sociologist, has shown that the wages paid in occupations decline as the percentage of workers in those occupations who are female rises (England, 1993: Chap. 3).

Assessing the Explanations

Most sociologists emphasize discrimination and the devaluation of work performed by women as the main explanations for gender inequalities in earnings. Sociologists point to the absence of proof that women are less productive than men or that they expend less effort (England, 1993: 27). They also observe that earnings gaps persist even when women and men have comparable levels of education; are in full-time, full-year jobs; and/or are in the same occupations (Best, 1995). For example, according to Canada's 1991 census, the average 1990 earnings of women employed full-time, full-year as secretaries and stenographers, cashiers and tellers, and hotel clerks were 70 percent, 79 percent, and 82 percent, respectively, of the average earnings of men in those occupations. Although women constituted 97 percent of all full-time, full-year child-care workers, their average earnings in 1990 were only 63 percent of the average earnings of male child-care workers. These are but a few examples in a much longer list of gender gaps in pay by occupation (Statistics Canada, 1993b: Table 1).

▲ BIRTHPLACE AND COLOUR MATTER

So far, my discussion of gender inequality in work has proceeded as if all women were alike and all men were alike. In fact, as other chapters in this book show, this is not the case. Some women and men are young, some are old; some are married or living with a partner, others are not. Some women are born in Canada, others are born elsewhere. In addition, women differ in their colour and ancestral origins, as do men.

The intersection of gender inequality with inequalities stemming from birthplace and colour is of interest to many Canadians. That interest is fuelled by the changing ethnic and colour composition of Canada's population, initiated by changes in Canada's immigration policies starting in 1962. It has become evident since that time that foreign-born women and women of colour experience not only gender inequality but also the inequalities that arise in a society that allocates privileges to certain groups and not to others on the basis of their colour, ethnicity, birthplace, and class.

Table 8.3 gives us an idea of labour-force inequalities by gender, birthplace, and colour for 1991. In this table, persons of race or colour are referred to as members of "visible-minority" groups. In popular usage and government parlance, the term **visible minority** is used to identify those Canadian residents who are not recognized as part of the white mainstream population (of European or U.S. origin) and who thus may experience discrimination. However, the term is an umbrella label for diverse groups. In government statistics, Canada's aboriginal peoples are not included in the "visible-minority" category, but rather appear as a separate group. It should also be noted that the table refers only to persons living in Montreal, Toronto, or Vancouver, where many of Canada's foreign-born and visible-minority groups reside (see Boyd, 1992, for further discussion on these points). This restriction distorts the overall situation of the aboriginal population, most of whom live either on reserves or in other Canadian cities.

The information in Table 8.3 prompts at least four conclusions. First, gender differences remain pronounced. For all groups defined by birthplace or membership in a visible-minority or aboriginal group, women are less likely than men to be in the labour force; they experience higher rates of part-time work and they are usually more likely than men to work in low-skill occupations. Other studies show that, within the Canadian-born, foreign-born, visible-minority and non-visible-minority groups, women earn less than men (Boyd, 1992; Pendakur and Pendakur, 1995).

Second, birthplace, visible-minority status, and aboriginal status do matter. For both men and women, the foreign-born population is more likely than the Canadian-born population to be employed in low-skill occupations. The same findings apply to the occupations of the total visible-minority population compared with those of the non-visible-minority population.

Third, foreign-born women and women of colour are the most likely to be employed in occupations characterized as low-skill occupations. Many of these women in fact hold production-fabrication jobs and

◆ **Table 8.3** Socioeconomic Characteristics of Canadian-Born, Foreign-Born, Select Visible-Minority Groups, and Aboriginal Groups for Females (and Males in Parentheses), Age 25–55, Living in Montreal, Toronto, or Vancouver Census Metropolitan Areas, 1991[a]

	Percentage in labour force[b]		Percentage of labour force			
			That is part-time		That holds low-skill[c] occupations	
Females (Males)	77	(90)	11	(5)	9	(9)
Birthplace						
Canadian-born	78	(91)	20	(5)	6	(8)
Foreign-born	75	(89)	17	(5)	13	(11)
Member of a visible-minority group[d]						
No	78	(91)	20	(5)	8	(9)
Yes	74	(86)	14	(5)	14	(11)
Minority group[e]						
Aboriginal	71	(85)	21	(7)	7	(9)
Arab	58	(80)	19	(6)	9	(8)
Black[f]	78	(86)	15	(7)	15	(12)
Chinese	76	(88)	13	(5)	10	(7)
Filipino	89	(92)	11	(4)	11	(13)
Latin American[g]	65	(78)	20	(7)	18	(19)
South Asian	73	(90)	11	(4)	18	(11)
Vietnamese	67	(83)	10	(4)	16	(14)
West Asian[h]	60	(76)	25	(9)	9	(8)

[a] Excludes persons who are not permanent residents of Canada.

[b] Refers to the labour-market activity of the noninstitutionalized population during the week prior to enumeration (June 4, 1991).

[c] "Low-skill" refers to the lowest of four categories of skill used by Statistics Canada to classify occupational information on the basis of the following occupational characteristics: education, training or skill level required to enter the job, and the kind of work performed as determined by the tasks, duties, and responsibilities of the occupation.

[d] All persons categorized as "visible-minority" members according to Statistics Canada are included in this category even if they indicated other nonvisible ethnic origins.

[e] Includes persons who indicate membership in a single minority group; persons who indicate multiple memberships in one or more minority groups; and those who indicate membership in two or groups or in one or more minority groups and one or more nonminority groups.

[f] Includes persons who reported Caribbean ethnic origins such as Ghanaian, Barbadian, Cuban, Guyanese, Haitian, Jamaican, or Trinidadian and Tobagonian.

[g] Includes persons who reported Latin Amercian origins or Central and South American ethnic origins.

[h] Includes persons who reported Afghan, Armenian, Iranian, Israeli, Kurdish, Turk, and other West Asian ethnic origins.

SOURCE: Special tabulations produced especially for this chapter from Statistics Canada, 1991 Census of Population (Ottawa: Industry, Science and Technology Canada), Public Use Sample Tape of Individuals, Full Count. Used by authority of the Minister of Industry, 1997.

are employed as seamstresses in the garment industry (Boyd, 1996). We know from other studies that have examined earnings inequalities in Canada's large cities that foreign-born and visible-minority women have the lowest earnings of all labour-force participants, in comparison both to their male counterparts and to women who are Canadian-born or not members of visible-minority groups (Boyd, 1992; Pendakur and Pendakur, 1995). These wage and occupational characteristics imply that foreign-born and/or visible-minority women experience a double or triple disadvantage in the labour force. For feminists of colour, these disadvantages are indicative of power relations based on race, colour, and birthplace, which diversify female subordination and create relations of domination and subordination between white women and visible-minority women, and between Canadian-born women and foreign-born women.

Fourth, considerable diversity exists among women and among men. The figures confirm that one should not think of women (or men) as a homogeneous group. To give a few examples, labour-force participation rates are highest for Filipino, black, and Chinese women and lowest for Arab and West Asian women. Aboriginal, Latin American, and West Asian women are the most likely to be employed part-time, and South Asian, Filipino, and Vietnamese women are the least likely. Occupational characteristics also vary by membership in specific groups. These findings reaffirm the criticisms voiced by minority and foreign-born women — namely, that, for them, inequality issues are not restricted to gender, but also include race and immigrant status, and that each group is unique in the kinds of disadvantages and subordinations it experiences.

■ GENDER IN POLITICS

The voice of government, as the Royal Commission on the Status of Women observed [almost 30] years ago, is still a man's voice. Women remain governed rather than governors, legislated rather than legislators. (Brodie, 1991: 9)

So far, I have discussed the increasing movement of women out of the home and into the labour force. The economy, however, is only one of several arenas in the public sphere from which women have historically been excluded, and in which their participation remains very limited. Politics is another important arena, one that initially excluded women, but that women have now begun to penetrate.

Politics is an important area of gender inequality for three reasons: It is here that the exercise of power is most obvious, that laws determining rights and entitlements are formulated, and that public policies are set. As political scientist Janine Brodie observes (1991: 9), politics and political representation are the mechanisms whereby the interests of groups are translated into political demands and actions. If groups are politically disenfranchised or face barriers to the representation of their interests, two consequences follow: The needs of the groups may not be met through policies and legislation; and the premise that democratic governments represent all the people is false.

For the first 50 years after Confederation, the notion that the private sphere was the appropriate place for women went hand in hand with the exclusion of women from politics. In the course of the twentieth century, however, women did move into the political arena. The effects of their entry are threefold: (1) they obtained and exercise the right to vote; (2) they participate in political parties and can be elected to political office; and (3) they have created and use associations to represent the special interests of women. Such interests include, but are not limited to, access to abortion, child care, equality in the labour force, family violence (including spousal violence and child abuse), prostitution, rape, pensions, and participation in politics.

▲ VOTING RIGHTS

Throughout the early part of the twentieth century, Canadian women did not have the right to vote; without that right, they could not elect candidates to represent their interests in government. Between 1916 and 1925, however, all provinces except Quebec enfranchised women. Quebec granted women the vote in 1940. The federal government granted voting rights in 1917 to women who were British subjects and who had served with the military or had a close relative in the military; it extended those rights to women unconnected with the military in 1918. But voting rights were not given to women or men of Chinese, East Indian, or Japanese ancestry until the late 1940s, or to male or female Inuit until 1950, or to registered Indians living on reserves until 1960 (Maille, 1990: 1).

The suffrage movement in English Canada was a factor in obtaining the vote for women (Bashevkin, 1993: Chap. 1). However, Sandra Burt (1993: 216) observes that the vote was granted on the premise that women would use it only to improve the quality of home life, and that enfranchisement would not divert women from their "natural and sacred" duties in the domestic sphere.

Such sex stereotyping of women also led to the expectation that women would not be interested in the realm of politics. Male legislators in the early 1900s believed that women would not vote at the same rate as men. Men also believed that women would vote in a politically naïve and parochial way as a result of being isolated at home. But these stereotypes proved to be false. In Canada today, voting rates — that is, the percentages of eligible voters who cast a ballot — are similar for women and men. The political agendas of men and women do differ, but not because women's views are parochial. Research in the late 1980s showed that women were more likely than men to oppose free trade, foreign investment, cruise missile testing, and military spending and to be more concerned with social-welfare policies (Bashevkin, 1993: Chap. 2). In dispatching the notion that women vote in a conservative or parochial way, Thelma McCormack suggests that female–male differences in voting interests result because women and men operate in different political cultures (which have been moulded by gender differences in political socialization) and have different opportunities to participate in politics. Again and again, women hear that "politics is a man's world." Excluded from political life, women are more likely to be concerned with moral and community-based political issues than with issues pertaining to the acquisition or exercise of power (McCormack, 1975: 25–26). However, there is no evidence that women act as a cohesive voting bloc on all issues (Brodie, 1991).

▲ PARTICIPATING IN THE WORLD OF POLITICS

McCormack's description of women as excluded from political life was written when fewer than 4 percent of Canada's members of Parliament (MPs) were women. The situation has changed since then. In the 1993 election, nearly 1 in 5 elected federal MPs (18 percent) were women. However, enthusiasm over such progress should be tempered by the recognition that women represent half of Canada's electorate. Thus, assuming that present trends continue, it will take seven more elections before gender equality is achieved in the House of Commons. And if future elections are held five years apart, that means that gender equality will not be realized for another 35 years, taking us to the year 2027! (These calculations assume that the increment of fifteen additional women that occurred between 1988 and 1993 will be repeated with each future election, and that the number of seats in the House of Commons will remain at 295.)

Women are also seldom found in the upper ranks of political parties. To be sure, Margaret Thatcher was elected prime minister of Great Britain, and Kim Campbell served briefly as prime minister of Canada until the 1993 election. In striking his cabinet shortly after that election, Jean Chrétien appointed Sheila Copps as deputy prime minister. However, the presence of these women in the upper echelons of power is rare enough to be newsworthy. If gender made no difference, why would the cover of *Maclean's* run a photo of Kim Campbell over the caption "When the Boss Is a Woman" (Oct. 4, 1993) and picture Sheila Copps under the title "Rebel with a Cause," accompanied by a text portraying Copps as "the latest national lightning rod for the prevailing ambivalence about women in power" (Apr. 4, 1994)?

Figure 8.2 illustrates the truth of the saying "the higher, the fewer" with respect to the participation of women in Canadian political parties. Sylvia Bashevkin (1993: Chap. 3) found that women are more likely to be local riding secretaries (as opposed to presidents) and they do the necessary clerical work, paralleling the "pink ghetto" of female-typed clerical work found in the labour force. In the almost 80 years since most women gained the vote federally, only three women have been elected as party leaders, all within the last decade. Audrey McLaughlin served as leader of the NDP between 1989 and 1995; Kim Campbell as leader of the Progressive Conservatives between June and December 1993; and Alexa McDonough was elected leader of the NDP in October 1995 (Young, 1997: 82). Campbell was prime minister briefly, but the PC failed to retain a majority in the subsequent 1993 election.

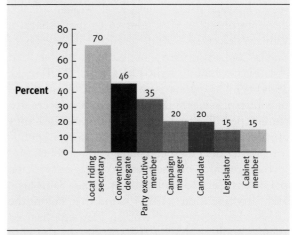

◆ **Figure 8.2** The Higher, the Fewer: Women's Participation in Major Canadian Party Organizations, 1992[a]

[a] Levels of participation are approximate.

SOURCE: Sylvia B. Bashevkin, *Toeing the Lines: Women and Party Politics in English Canada,* 2nd ed. (Toronto: Oxford University Press, 1993), Figure 3.1. Copyright © Sylvia B. Bashevkin 1993. Used by permission of Oxford University Press Canada.

Explaining the Political Participation of Women

Four major explanations exist for the underrepresentation of women in Canadian politics. The first relies on sex-role stereotypes. It argues that certain characteristics of women keep them from participating in politics. According to this argument, women are less assertive than men, more oriented to family than to politics, and conditioned, through childhood socialization, to view politics as an inappropriate activity (Brodie, 1991). For two reasons, this explanation is currently far less popular than it was in the past. First, it stereotypes all women and fails to acknowledge that the traits of men and women often overlap and that women themselves are very diverse, just as men are. Second, it invokes the behaviour of men as the standard, implying that women are "deficient," and that the problem is to be found in women rather than in the characteristics of political life.

The second explanation reverses the emphasis by arguing that the culture of politics is both "male" and hostile to the participation of women. Descriptions of political life as "gladiatorial" create the image of a highly combative blood sport in which the stakes are the acquisition and display of power (Bashevkin, 1991). This is a highly masculine image that reinforces the notion of politics as "a man's world." It creates a chilly climate for female participants, who may have interests beyond those of domination and who may prefer to resolve conflicts in nonconfrontational ways.

Few observers of Canadian political life doubt that politics is still very much a male domain. As we have seen, at the federal level, women are underrepresented as MPs relative to their share of Canada's electorate. And, recently, the success of Sheila Copps was partly attributed to the fact that she "knows how to fight like a man" (McDonald, 1994: 19). The emphasis on male traits in the world of politics also means that women in politics are sex-stereotyped. They are given attention because they are "deviant" or "different" from the "normal" politician, rather than for their competency as politicians. In their research on the media coverage of women politicians, Gertrude Robinson, Armande Saint-Jean, and Christine Rioux (1991) found that, before the 1970s, the portrayal of women MPs emphasized themes such as that of the spinster or the club woman, or focussed on the politician's relationship to significant family members, including her husband. According to these researchers, all the labels that were used emphasized a woman's gender and looks or affiliation rather than her competence. Between the 1970s and 1990s, new labels and stereotypes came to be used, but they still failed to evaluate women's political competence. Robinson, Saint-Jean, and Rioux (1991: 142–46) describe these new labels and stereotypes as follows:

- *Superwoman:* A young, intelligent, active, and ambitious woman who succeeds on all levels and has it all.
- *Champion:* Similar to "superwoman," but tends to be used in reference to older women politicians who have led a more traditional life.
- *One of the boys:* A female politician who "adopts a masculine stance, which means either that she does not resort to what are called feminine wiles to achieve her goals (charm, coquetry, wheedling) or that she accepts and operates by the conventional rules of the game."
- *Wife of . . . :* Invoked whenever the interests and activities of the female politician are linked by the media to those of her spouse.

Robinson and her co-authors conclude that the media continue to emphasize the personal characteristics (e.g., looks, hair, and dress) of female politicians. This emphasis is evident in the captions accompanying the photographs, reproduced in Box 8.2, of Hillary Rodham Clinton, Flora MacDonald, and Margaret Thatcher, which appeared in *Maclean's* magazine on October 4, 1993. Robinson, Saint-Jean, and Rioux note three additional characteristics of media descriptions of female politicians: (1) they fail to recognize the prior political activities of female politicians, with the result that the women's histories of acquiring competency remain unknown; (2) they suggest that female politicians are responsible for women's issues, when, in fact, gender interests may or may not be on the agenda of any politician, male or female; and (3) they use the term *feminism* or *feminist* to denote negative personal characteristics.

The third reason for women's underrepresentation as politicians is gatekeeping. By controlling the nomination of candidates for elected office, political parties influence the gender composition of their electoral slate and the ridings that the nominees represent. In the past, women candidates were often "sacrificial lambs," allowed to run primarily in ridings in which the chances of winning were small. Janine Brodie (1991: 6) observes that, in today's climate of striving for gender equality, few parties can afford to provide a slate of candidates with few or no women. But parties can and still do assign women to ridings in which their chances of winning are poor. According to Brodie, many of the representational gains that women have made are attributable to a volatile electorate

Box 8.2
Gender Stereotypes in Politics

"She is so smart and I like her so much that I feel like squeezing her."

—Congressman John LaFalce (D–N.Y.), on Hillary Rodham Clinton's plans to reform health care

"Tell me, Madame Minister, how was it that a woman was able to keep a secret like that for three months?"

—A male interviewer, after then-External Affairs Minister Flora MacDonald helped to engineer the 1980 escape from Iran of six Americans

"She would throw little temper fits, she would be sweet and coquettish. Of course, men find that slightly uncomfortable."

—Sir Tim Bell, Margaret Thatcher's former public relations adviser, on how Thatcher used her femininity to get her own way

SOURCE: *Maclean's*, October 4, 1993, pp. 18, 19. Photo credits: Hillary Rodham Clinton: Westenberger/Gamma/Ponopresse; Flora MacDonald: Chuck Mitchell/Canapress Photo Service; Margaret Thatcher: Frank Gunn/Canapress Photo Service.

and last-minute voter shifts that carry ridings in which female candidates were not expected to win.

Insufficient resources are the fourth reason for the lack of gender parity in Canadian politics. Money is a very important resource for winning nominations and mounting publicity campaigns. In the late 1980s, for example, the cost of contesting a nomination in a winnable urban riding was in excess of $50 000 (Brodie, 1991: 40). Women may be at a fiscal disadvantage to the extent that they earn less than male candidates and consequently have less to put into a campaign. Bashevkin (1991) notes that, whereas men who enter politics tend to come from law and business, women candidates tend to come from social work, journalism, and education, where earnings are lower. Social networks are also important among the resources needed for contesting nominations and elections. Networks are useful for obtaining financial contributions and generating the volunteers who lobby voters. Yet, to the extent that politics is "an old boys' club," women may not have access to insider or "old boy" networks.

Finally, although this is not a major reason for the lower representation of women in politics, the clash between political life and family life is a factor influencing the participation of some women. The culture that emphasizes politics as a man's world or as a man's sport fails to recognize that politicians also have personal lives and family responsibilities. Indeed, the lifestyle that is part of this culture is almost antifamily. (This has been cited as one reason for the recent efforts of the Reform Party to establish a "code of conduct" for its MPs.) Ignoring the family needs and responsibilities of politicians affects both men and women. However, because women more than men are designated as the primary childcare providers, their participation in politics can require greater personal and child-care costs.

Representation by Women; Representation for Women

Until recently, most research on women in politics focussed on the question of how many women held party positions or were elected legislators. However, representation by women is not always the same as representation for women. Although both men and women may use their legislative roles to place women's issues on the political agenda and to support party policies and legislation that reflect women's situations and concerns, they may not.

Jane Arscott and Linda Trimble (1997) summarize the views of a number of social scientists and women's groups when they call for "representation by women as if women mattered" — that is, the election of women who will act in the interests of women. However, it also raises another issue: How are differences of class and race among women to be represented? Specifically, can women legislators and party officers understand and speak for women who are different from them and who may have different experiences and concerns? As Arscott and Trimble (1997: 4–5) note, the vast majority of Canadian female legislators are white, middle-class, publicly heterosexual, and well educated. Do they understand, stand for, and speak for other women,

including aboriginal women, women of colour, immigrant women, elderly women, poor women, homeless women, lesbians, and women who are victims of spousal abuse (cf. Vickers, 1997: 28)? Furthermore, if mainstream women cannot speak for all women, then should targets or quotas be set for women of colour, poor women, lesbians, etc.? Currently, the answers to these questions are under debate. However, in the late 1990s, Canadian governments at all levels appear less willing to exercise the political will, spend the money, and change the electoral laws and party practices that would accommodate difference.

▲ WOMEN'S GROUPS: ORGANIZING FOR CHANGE

Besides seeking election to public office, women participate in politics by taking action for change not only as individuals but in groups. The term *women's movement* is the most general term used to describe the extremely varied actions that have been and are being taken by women's groups on behalf of women. A **social movement** consists of collective action aimed at change. The **women's movement** is a social movement that takes action to improve the situation of women. Feminism is an important part of the women's movement in Canada. **Feminism** refers to the body of thought on the causes and nature of women's disadvantaged and subordinate position in society, and to efforts to minimize or eliminate that subordination. The familiar phrase "I'm not a feminist, but . . . " belies the fact that anyone who is concerned about the subordinate position of women and seeks change is a feminist. However, many different forms of feminism exist, reflecting different understandings of the causes of gender inequality and subordination and of the action required to improve the situation.

Organizing for change has many different forms and objectives. For example, when students meet informally to discuss and resolve gender-related problems facing women in universities or to develop plans for a drop-in women's centre, they are involved in a collective attempt at change. Groups marching to protest the lack of safety for women at night or lobbying governments for improved pension benefits for elderly women are similarly participating in collective action. Although small, community-based groups are the backbone of the women's movement, larger groups are often more visible to the public and their activities are more likely to be reported in the media.

Many of these larger associations, which usually have a formal organizational structure, with an executive board and, in some cases, a permanent office staff, evolved from smaller associations. The history of the establishment of the Royal Commission on the Status of Women, in 1967, and the formation of the National Action Committee on the Status of Women (NAC), in 1972, reflects such a pattern. Through her position as president of the Canadian Federation of University Women, Laura Sabia assembled representatives of more than 30 organizations to create a new organization focussed on the status of Canadian women. Struck in June 1966, the Committee for the Equality of Women (CEW) in Canada represented, through its members, a broad-based coalition of women's groups. The Royal Commission on the Status of Women, formally established by Prime Minister Pearson on February 3, 1967, was the result of the lobbying efforts of CEW. The report of the royal commission was completed in 1970. It included 167 recommendations, and quickly became both a sourcebook documenting gender inequality and a benchmark for change. In 1971, in response to their concern that pressure had to be sustained if the royal commission's recommendations were to be implemented, many of the former members of CEW formed the National Ad Hoc Committee on the Status of Women. In turn, the National Action Committee on the Status of Women (NAC) emerged from the subsequent Strategies for Change conference, in 1972, which involved more than 500 women representing a diversity of groups (Bashevkin, 1993: Chap. 2; Vickers, Rankin, and Appelle, 1993). An umbrella organization, NAC today represents more than 500 member organizations. It shapes public discussion and policy debate by lobbying the federal government and serving as a source of information and expertise for the media (Vickers, Rankin, and Appelle, 1993).

Many other associations also advance the interests of women. Sylvia Bashevkin (1993: Table 8.2) lists seventeen of the major women's organizations created since 1960, which either represent a large number of members or have proved to be effective agents of change. Recently, associations that represent the interests of women of colour, immigrant women, and lesbians have been important additions to the landscape of women's associations in Canada. The attention they have directed to issues of racism, sexual identity, and class has forced mainstream groups representing primarily white, heterosexual, and often middle-class women to become more inclusive in their membership base and their agendas. Women of colour have argued that these groups fail to ac-

knowledge concerns other than those of white middle-class women. The mainstream argument that gender subordination reflects the restriction of women to the private sphere fails to recognize that many women of colour have always engaged in paid work and that issues of racism in employment are of equal importance for them. Furthermore, to the extent that women of colour work as domestics, it is white women who have power over them as their employers, and the important issues are both gender oppression and racial oppression. Immigrant women also have their own concerns, which include language training, job-skill training, culturally sensitive child care, and culturally sensitive assistance in situations of domestic violence. For lesbian women, areas of interest are gay rights and related issues, such as the inclusion of sexual orientation in human rights codes, the prohibition of employment discrimination on the basis of sexual orientation, and the extension of married-equivalent benefits to same-sex couples.

The creation of associations that address the specific concerns of groups such as immigrant women, women of colour, lesbians, prostitutes, battered women, and women with disabilities is not entirely new. For example, many groups that represent the interests of immigrant women have existed in Toronto and other large cities since the 1970s. In November 1986, the National Organization of Immigrant and Visible Minority Women was formed, having been preceded by the Visible Minority Women's Coalition (1983) and the Canadian Congress of Black Women (1980).

Women's groups are important participants in the Canadian political arena, where they lobby for change and apply pressure on federal, provincial, and municipal governments to undertake reform in areas of interest to women. However, despite major successes — such as ensuring that women's rights were enshrined in the 1982 Canadian Charter of Rights and Freedoms and securing legislative changes that ensure fairer division of assets in divorce cases — the efforts of women's groups have been limited by at least three factors, according to Sandra Burt (1993). First, because many women's groups rely on governments for funding, their role as critics of government policy can be easily compromised — they may change their agenda or adopt a conciliatory style of confrontation in order not to bite the hand that feeds them. The consensus-building approach adopted within many women's organizations constitutes a second constraint on their effectiveness. This decision-making style can be very time-consuming, and it can place groups at a disadvantage, given that political interventions often require quick reaction. The heterogeneity of women's groups is a third factor limiting their impact. There are many different women's groups, and not all of them agree on what should be done for women. For example, diverse opinions exist among women's associations on child-care issues and on access to abortion, and it is often impossible to create a coalition among groups to lobby for one clear policy.

In addition to co-optation risks, decision-making styles, and the challenge of creating unity out of diversity, women's groups can also be underfunded. Lack of funds can severely constrain a group's capacity to assist individual women, to inform individual and government organizations about the concerns and issues facing women, and to exert pressure for solutions. Invoking fiscal restraint and changes in federal–provincial financial transfers and responsibilities, governments in the late 1990s are reducing funding to organizations, including women's groups. In addition to budget cutbacks, in 1995 the federal government disbanded the Canadian Advisory Council on the Status of Women, which was an arm's-length body mandated to inform the public and the Canadian federal government on issues of concern to women.

■ ELIMINATING GENDER INEQUALITY

Although the magnitude of the change in women's participation in Canada's economic and political life during the twentieth century has been great, gender inequality still exists. In this section, I consider the mechanisms that can be used to lessen the degree of gender inequality in the future, starting with a review of the general approaches, then looking at specific interventions designed to reduce inequalities in the labour force and in political representation.

▲ MODELS OF CHANGE

One's choice of mechanism for bringing about change will depend very much on how one explains gender inequality. If we see gender inequality as arising out of personality differences between men and women, we are likely to prefer a mechanism that influences personality traits — for example, we may seek ways of altering the messages that boys and girls and men and women receive about masculinity and femininity. And if we see in-

equalities as resulting from organizational rules and practices governing recruitment and promotion, we are likely to emphasize changing those rules and practices.

Starting in the 1970s, North American research on inequality began to shift away from perspectives that attributed unequal outcomes to individual differences in talent, educational achievement, and opportunity. That viewpoint, still prevalent in Canada in the early 1970s, resulted in social programs and public policies oriented to individuals, such as efforts to increase access to education and training for members of less privileged groups (Agocs and Boyd, 1993).

By the 1980s, people were becoming more aware of power relations and the influence of workplace cultures and practices as sources of gender inequality. This awareness was partly fuelled by feminism, with its twin emphases on the undervaluation of women and on the presence of men's influence over women in diverse areas — from family law to hiring practices in the labour force, to the nomination of candidates in political ridings. Accompanying such changing intellectual perspectives was a growing impatience with waiting for organizations to change their practices voluntarily. Increased pressure was also put on governments to develop public policies that lessened or eliminated gender inequalities.

Public policy refers to the statements made and the actions taken — or not taken — by governments with respect to a given problem or set of problems (Pal, 1989: 4). State intervention influences the magnitude of gender inequality, and sustains or minimizes male relations of power over women, in three areas: reproduction, family, and the labour force. In the category of reproduction are government actions pertaining to medical care, new reproductive technologies (such as *in vitro* fertilization), contraception, and abortion. In the category of the family are government policies regarding family law (including regulations governing divorce and property division) and child care. Government intervention in the labour force affects gender inequality through unemployment insurance policies, maternity- and parental-leave policies, job-training programs, employment policies, and pay policies. So far, there is no government policy targeted explicitly at gender inequality in politics.

▲ PUBLIC POLICY AND GENDER INEQUALITY IN THE LABOUR FORCE

Two areas of policy development that bear specifically on gender inequality in the labour force are **em-**

ployment equity, including **affirmative action,** and pay equity, as expressed in the principle of **equal pay for work of equal value** (or "work of comparable worth"). Policies in both areas seek to correct inequalities in the realm of paid work by removing barriers that handicap certain groups, including women. However, these policies differ in the populations they cover, the mechanisms they employ to determine and eliminate inequalities, and the aspects of labour-force inequality that they address (i.e., terms, conditions, and systems of employment versus pay). These differences are outlined in Box 8.3.

Assessing the Impact

Numerous publications have outlined the specifics of the various Canadian employment-equity and equal-pay policies (Agocs, Burr, and Somerset, 1992;

Box 8.3
Differences between Employment Equity and Pay Equity

EMPLOYMENT EQUITY

- covers all employment systems, such as recruitment, selection, training, development, and promotion, and all terms and conditions of employment, including compensation, layoff, and disciplinary action
- addresses discrimination and disadvantages in employment affecting women, aboriginal peoples, racial minorities, and people with disabilities
- applies to all jobs

- involves a current and continuing process
- is based on an analysis of unequal treatment, adverse impact, lack of accommodation, and underutilization
- includes the following typical activities:
  — workforce and availability analysis of representation and distribution
  — employment systems review covering formal and informal policies, practices, and decision making, and organizational culture
  — goals and action plans
  — training and communication
  — policy statements
  — monitoring

PAY EQUITY

- covers compensation only

- addresses discrimination in earnings affecting women

- applies to jobs in which women predominate, and in which there are male "comparator" jobs within the employer's establishment
- generally involves a one-time analysis and remedy
- is based on an analysis of unequal treatment

- includes the following typical activities:
  — determination of proportion of male and female employees or jobs or job groups
  — evaluation of jobs using a gender-neutral job evaluation plan
  — comparison of pay lines or comparison groups
  — pay adjustments

SOURCE: Adapted from Carol Agocs, Catherine Burr, and Felicity Somerset, *Employment Equity: Cooperative Strategies for Organizational Change* (Scarborough, ON: Prentice Hall, 1992), pp. 6–7. Used with permission.

Weiner and Gunderson, 1990). Do such policies work? Have related programs succeeded in moving women into jobs from which they were previously excluded? Is the real monetary worth of women's work in female job ghettos being acknowledged?

In answer to these questions, there is some "good news" and some "bad news." The good news is that cases do exist in which inequalities have elicited legally mandated action. In the mid-1980s, for example, litigation forced CN Rail to hire women in the St. Lawrence region. At the time of the complaint, women held fewer than 1 percent of the blue-collar jobs in the company, and a pattern of discriminatory hiring practices was revealed (Agocs, Burr, and Somerset, 1992: 104). The company was ordered to discontinue a number of these practices (including that of testing women's but not men's capacity to lift heavy objects) and to adopt new recruiting and hiring practices. Similarly, equal-pay-for-work-of-equal-value legislation has resulted in pay adjustments in a number of cases. For example, the salaries of federally employed librarians have been raised to match those of historians, and nurses' pay has been raised to match that of orderlies.

Nevertheless, a few isolated victories do not amount to winning the war. Critics of employment-equity policies note three types of "bad news." First, the legislation is limited in its jurisdiction, and does not apply to a large part of the population. For example, the federal Employment Equity Act of 1995, which replaced the Employment Equity Act of 1986, covers the public service, federally regulated employers, and portions of the public sector specified by orders-in-council, such as contractors doing business with the government who have 100 or more employees. In 1994, the total population covered by federal employment-equity legislation represented less than 5 percent of the Canadian labour force (calculated from Human Resources Development Canada, 1995: 3, 11). Second, failure to comply with the legislation is penalized only lightly. Although the federal Employment Equity Act of 1995 imposes fines on employers who do not report the required data or who knowingly provide false or misleading information, the amount cannot exceed $10 000 for a single violation and $50 000 for repeated or continued violations (Canada, 1995: Section 36(2)).

Numerous criticisms have been voiced about equal-pay-for-work-of-equal-value policies. First, many of the policies exclude small firms. Second,

they compare men and women within the same firms, with the result that they do not apply to women employed in firms in which the labour force is all female. Third, the method of establishing the comparable worth of two jobs is based on existing job descriptions. Jobs that are considered similar by virtue of pay or classification are evaluated on the basis of knowledge and skills, effort, responsibility, and working conditions (England, 1993; Steinberg, 1990). But such evaluation does not correct for the a priori undervaluation of certain skills (see the discussion of gender and skill earlier in this chapter).

For many feminists, these and other criticisms suggest that limited change can be expected from employment-equity and pay-equity policies in their current forms. Supporters are likely to press for stronger policies and broader coverage in the decades to come. However, government and business support for such changes is not assured. As Box 8.4 shows, business owners may argue that equity is unaffordable in times of economic downturn. In Quebec, protests by business leaders caused amendments to the provincial bill on pay equity in the private sector, effective January 1, 1997. As a result of these changes, pay-equity legislation will not be fully implemented until the year 2006 (Séguin, 1996).

▲ CORRECTING THE BALANCE: WOMEN IN POLITICS

As noted above, there is no federal policy aimed at reducing gender inequality among elected politicians. Political parties are sensitive to the issue of increasing the number of women representing them. However, there are at least six other types of actions that, if undertaken, could increase the numbers and percentages of women in Canadian politics in the years to come. All have to do with reducing barriers erected as a result of social roles and with changing organizational aspects of political recruitment and elections.

The first, and probably the least effective, action can be described as "displaying good intentions." It is commonly manifested in the form of party statements indicating commitment to the principle of gender parity. Compared with other mechanisms, however, party commitments tend to be limited and to have a limited impact. In the 1980s, for example, the only guaranteed commitments written into the constitutions of the Liberal and Conservative parties

Box 8.4
Recession Used as Excuse to Delay Employment Equity

Many Canadian companies are using the recession as an excuse not to promote more women or minority groups, claiming they've got bigger problems to worry about, according to a Bank of Montreal vice-president.

"Among the top 100 companies in Canada, the tough economy has meant that many of them don't have to start a workplace equality program or they can chop the ones they have," said Johanne Totta, vice-president of workplace equality with the bank.

But these companies could be gambling with their futures through such lack of vision, Ms. Totta said in an interview.

When a company offers flexible work arrangements for women with families or provides more training opportunities which lead to management, that makes your employees happier and more productive.

"And this attitude ends up on the bottom line, because you have less staff turnover and more pleased customers."

The bank, which has 28,000 employees, 75 percent of whom are women, began its equitable workplace program in January 1992.

"The number of women at executive levels in the bank has risen from 9 percent to 13 percent in two years," [Ms. Totta] said.

At the very top of the bank, four out of 10 senior vice-presidents are women. However, only four out of 28 members of the board of directors are female.

SOURCE: Excerpted from John Davidson, "Equality Slowdown Denounced," *The Globe and Mail,* December 9, 1993, p. B9. Reprinted by permission of Canadian Press.

---

were to ensure fair representation of women at national party conventions, and fair representation of the national parties' women's groups on governing bodies such as the parties' national executives (Brodie, 1991: 30).

A second way to increase women's participation in politics is to reduce the economic constraints they face in connection with winning nominations and running for office. Reducing the financial burden facing women and some men can be achieved by introducing legislation that would allow candidates the right to take unpaid leave from employment to contest party nominations and elections; setting spending limits for nomination contests and party leadership campaigns; making contributions for nomination contests tax-deductible; reimbursing money spent on nomination contests if the candidate gets a minimum level of support (say, 15 percent of the vote); using centralized party funds for nomination battles; and treating child-care and

housekeeping costs as part of the overall campaign costs, thereby making them subject to reimbursement (Brodie, 1991: 49–50; Erickson, 1991).

Although the recommendation to recognize childcare and housekeeping costs is a financial one, it may also be considered part of the third set of actions, which are designed to recognize family needs and responsibilities and the social roles of women. Lynda Erickson (1991) suggests that a fixed term for governments would increase the predictability of politicians' lives rather than leaving them at the mercy of a vote of nonconfidence or a leader's prerogative to call an election. Changing the rules of elections might indirectly help politicians to better anticipate their futures, taking into account the needs of their families.

Eliminating or weakening the gatekeeping tradition is the fourth potentially useful action. It could be accomplished by basing the amount of the government subsidy paid to political parties for their campaign expenses on an upward sliding scale according to the proportion of their elected candidates who are women (Brodie, 1991: 50). Under this system, the amount of the subsidy would vary with the number of women elected.

To the extent that it rewards parties for having women elected and may increase the number of women in politics, such an action can also be seen as a form of affirmative action. Other affirmative action measures include setting quotas to ensure that women are on riding nomination lists and establishing guarantees that a certain percentage of women are nominated for and are present in the party organization.

Research suggests that affirmative action measures can be difficult to implement in a single-member electoral system. Under the single-member system in Canada, a person running for office in a riding wins by getting the most votes. This approach is conducive to the control of nominations by local party organizations. However, attempts to increase the numbers of women holding office are most effective in electoral systems that place decision making about nominations and party representation at levels higher than the local ridings. A more centralized decision-making structure gives party elites more control over the representation of women and other minority groups. Modifying Canada's single-party system is thus the sixth area in which action could be taken to increase the percentage of women politicians (Erickson, 1991).

Which, if any, of these possible changes will be adopted remains to be seen. Many of the recommendations were made as part of research conducted for the Royal Commission on Electoral Reform, and most would require changes in existing legislation governing how political expenses are handled and how elections are run. In the course of the next decade, you will be able to monitor whether any of the above-described changes are implemented. ■

● SUMMARY

1. Many sociologists view the segregation of women and men into the private and public spheres as a very important source of gender inequality. Exclusion from the economic and political arenas of Canadian life can mean disadvantages in access to income, economic well-being, prestige, and power. Restricted in the past to the domestic sphere, women have been economically disadvantaged and have had little or no opportunity to influence legislation directly. In addition, their unpaid work in the home has been considered low in prestige, or at least lower in value than their spouses' paid work.

2. During the twentieth century, women have entered the labour force and the political arena in ever-increasing numbers. Today, more than half of all women are in the labour force. Politically enfranchised, women have also entered the political arena, either as politicians or in connection with groups associated with the women's movement. Many of these changes have occurred — or, at least, have accelerated — since the time most of you were born. Between the 1970s and the early 1990s, the labour-force participation rate of women more than doubled, and the number of elected women MPs quadrupled.

3. If the glass is half full, it also is half empty. Although they do paid work, many women are still responsible for most of the meal preparation, cleaning, and laundry needs of their families. Women still tend to be considered the primary caregivers of children. In short, women are more likely than men to work a double or triple "shift" every day.

4. In the labour force, women and men are occupationally segregated, with women concentrated in jobs stereotyped as "women's jobs." Women are more likely than men to be employed in jobs that are part-time or otherwise nonstandard. They earn less than men, on average, and their skills tend not to be fully recognized or fairly evaluated. To be sure, these issues affect women to varying degrees, depending on their birthplace, race, and ethnicity. Nevertheless, the overall picture is one of gender inequality in the labour force, with women disadvantaged relative to men.

5. There is still evidence of a gender gap in politics as well. Women represent slightly more than half of Canada's adult population, but only about 18 percent of federally elected legislators. This imbalance notwithstanding, substantial gains *have* been made in recent elections. And, as agents pressing for improvements in their own status, Canadian women have left a considerable legacy of influence and change.

6. Many of the challenges that remain are documented in this chapter. Future generations will have to combat not only gender-role stereotypes, but ideologies and structures that privilege men and handicap women as well. In recent years, employment-equity and equal-pay-for-work-of-equal-value policies have been developed to remedy some of the inequalities in the labour force. Analysts have also documented the various ways in which women's participation and influence in the political arena can be enhanced. As you finish your schooling, live with a spouse or partner, hold a paying job, and become politically involved, you will experience or witness some of the gender inequalities discussed in this chapter. However, you may also witness and work toward remedying the gender inequalities that currently exist.

QUESTIONS TO CONSIDER

1. If you grew up in a two-parent household, describe the types of activities that each parent did around the house. Were they different? Did the amount of time each spent on activities in the home vary? Why?

2. Think back to jobs you have held in the past three years that involved working with other people. Reflecting on the type of work you did compared with the work of others, would you say that sex segregation or sex typing existed? Why or why not?

3. In some of the occupational skill assessments that have been conducted in recent years, the job of dogcatcher was deemed more skilled than the job of child-care worker. Why do you think such an evaluation was made? Do you agree with the ranking? Why or why not?

4. Your readings discussed the principles of political "representation by women," "representation for women," and "representation of difference." Should women legislators be elected only if they champion women's causes? Should electoral rules be changed to allow for the proportionate or even disproportionate election of women of colour and other disadvantaged women in order to represent their interests and experiences?

GLOSSARY

affirmative action Policies and programs designed to create opportunities for and to further the achievements of historically disadvantaged groups in the labour force. One form of action to correct past inequalities involves setting targets and quotas for the hiring and promotion of members of groups that have faced barriers and discrimination in the past. The term is often used interchangeably with *employment equity;* strictly speaking, it is one aspect of employment equity.

employment equity The principle of equal treatment of all groups in the labour force. Employment-equity policies and programs seek to dismantle barriers and alter workplace cultures in order to create opportunities for and to further the advancement of historically disadvantaged groups.

equal pay for work of equal value Also known as "equal pay for work of comparable worth," this principle is supported by policies and programs that seek to equalize the wage rates offered for different jobs that are of comparable worth or value in terms of factors such as knowledge, complexity, responsibility, and skill.

feminism Both the body of knowledge about the causes and nature of women's subordination to men in society, and the various agendas, often involving political action, for removing that subordination.

gender inequalities Inequalities between men and women in the distribution of prestige, material well-being, and/or power; also, relational inequalities, as manifested in men's power over women, or in relations of male domination and female subordination.

gender stereotypes A set of prejudicial generalizations about men and women based on the oversimplified belief that physical sex determines distinct personality traits and, as a result, causes men and women to experience the world and behave in different ways.

glass ceiling The level in an organization above which women and minorities are seldom found.

labour-force participation rate The percentage of the population, age 15 and older, that is in the labour force.

material well-being The ability to obtain the economic resources necessary to pay for adequate food, clothing, housing, and possessions.

nonstandard work One or a combination of the following types of employment: part-week employment (reduced hours per week), part-year employment, limited-term contract employment, employment through temporary-help agencies, self-employment, and multiple job holding.

part-time work Jobs with reduced hours of work.

power The capacity to influence and control others, regardless of any resistance they might offer.

prestige The social evaluation or ranking, by general consensus, of occupational activities and positions in a hierarchical order that reflects the degree of respect, honour, or deference the person engaged in the activity or occupying the position is to be accorded.

public policy The government's stance on issues and problems, as expressed through its statements and actions, or its inaction.

sex segregation of occupations The concentration of women and men in different occupations.

sex typing (or sex labelling) of occupations The designation of an occupation as "female" or "male," depending on the sex for whom it is considered appropriate.

skill An ability or expertise in performing a given technique or task. Researchers describe tasks as requiring more or less skill on the basis of their complexity and the degree of autonomy required to perform them. Existing rankings, incomes, and levels of education associated with various occupations are often accepted by researchers as proxy measures of skill.

social movement Collective action aimed at change.

social roles The expectations and behaviours associated with particular positions in society.

social stratification The unequal ranking of groups in a society, and the unequal and asymmetrical distribution of prestige, material possessions, and power among those groups; stratification is the result, achieved over time, of routinized and frequently recurring practices and often unstated rules.

standard work Full-time, full-year employment, usually accompanied by job-related benefits, such as vacation leave, sick leave, and parental leave, as well as health and pension benefits.

statistical discrimination The discrimination that occurs when negative decisions concerning the hiring or promotion of a given individual are made on the basis of the average characteristics of the group to which the individual belongs. Thus, an employer may not hire a particular woman because of a belief that women, in general, are likely to take time off work to have children, even though the woman in question may intend not to have children.

visible minority A group of people (other than Native people) who are nonwhite and who, because of their race, may face discrimination in hiring and promotion.

women's movement A social movement that takes action to improve the conditions of women.

⬤ SUGGESTED READING

Arscott, Jane, and Linda Trimble, eds. (1997). *In the Presence of Women: Representation in Canadian Governments*. Toronto: Harcourt Brace. In addition to chapters focussing on issues of representation, many chapters provide in-depth analyses of women's experiences in provincial politics.

Burt, Sandra. (1993). "The Changing Patterns of Public Policy." In Sandra Burt, Lorraine Code, and Lindsay Dorney, eds., *Changing Patterns: Women in Canada*, 2nd ed. (pp. 212–37). Toronto: McClelland and Stewart. This short but information-packed chapter traces the development of Canadian public policies that affect women from the mid-1800s to the present.

Duffy, Ann, and Norene Pupo. (1992). *Part-Time Paradox: Connecting Gender, Work and Family*. Toronto: McClelland and Stewart. An excellent source of data on the growth of part-time work, the concentration of women in part-time jobs, and how women rely on part-time work to handle family and employment responsibilities.

Gaskell, Jane. (1991). "What Counts as Skill? Reflections on Pay Equity." In Judy Fudge and Patricia McDermott, eds., *Just Wages: A Feminist Assessment of Pay Equity* (pp. 141–59). Toronto: University of Toronto Press. An overview that explains how our notions of "skill" are socially constructed and how socially determined definitions of skill can influence equal-pay-for-work-of-equal-value settlements.

CHAPTER NINE
Race and Ethnic Relations

IN THIS CHAPTER YOU WILL LEARN THAT

- the study of race and ethnic relations involves the analysis of the unequal distribution of power and resources, and involves a number of sociological approaches; frustration-aggression, sociobiology, socialization, and power-conflict approaches are among the most important

- *ethnicity* and *race* are terms used to categorize groups on the basis of cultural and physical criteria; although the concept of race has no basis in biology, and although ethnic identities and boundaries are situational, variable, and flexible, race and ethnicity are important parts of social reality

- aboriginal people in Canada are made up of Indians, Métis, and Inuit; there are two main sociological interpretations of aboriginal people's socioeconomic status in Canada — the culture of poverty thesis and the internal colonial model

- the nationalist movement in Quebec has deep historical roots; the contemporary nationalist movement is united around the goal of maintaining the French character of Quebec; one of the main problems facing the nationalist movement in Quebec is exactly how to define the boundaries of the nation

- immigration played a central role in both the early and later phases of Canadian capitalist development; Canada accepts refugees, family class, and independent immigrants, each of which are subject to different selection criteria

- John Porter's description of Canada as a vertical mosaic is no longer an accurate way of describing the structure of Canadian society

- there are historical, conceptual, and empirical grounds for believing that "Canadian" is an emerging ethnic category

VIC SATZEWICH
McMaster University

■ INTRODUCTION

Leo LaChance did not know that the Northern Gun and Pawn Shop he walked into the night of January 28, 1991 was owned by a white supremacist. LaChance, a Cree trapper from northern Saskatchewan, needed a few dollars and thought he would sell his hunting rifle in Prince Albert. Carney Nerland, the shop's owner, did not want to buy the gun. As LaChance left the shop, a bullet from an M-56 assault rifle hit him in the back, puncturing his spleen, pancreas, gall bladder, and liver. Six hours later, LaChance was dead (Cannon, 1995).

Twenty-nine-year-old Carney Nerland was well known in Prince Albert. He liked to strut around town with a brush cut and polished jackboots. As a teenager, he had painted swastikas anywhere he could. He had a picture of Adolf Hitler pinned to a wall in his shop. He had fired shots at Natives in the city before. At the time of the shooting, Nerland was under investigation for distributing anti-Jewish and anti-Native literature. He was a member of the Aryan Nations, a violent white supremacist group, and liked to call himself the future "Führer of Saskatchewan." He once told a group of journalists that his hunting rifle was his form of "Native birth control." When he turned himself in after shooting Leo LaChance, he told the arresting officer, "If I'm convicted of killing that Indian, I should get a medal and you should pin it on me" (Cannon, 1995).

At his trial in December 1991, Nerland said he didn't know that there was a bullet in the chamber of the M-56 when he pointed it at LaChance; "it was just a joke," he said, "an accident." In his ruling, the judge recognized that Nerland was a racist, but he did not believe that racism played a role in LaChance's death. The judge accepted Nerland's version of events and sentenced him to four years in prison for manslaughter. As turned out, Nerland was an ideal prisoner. He was paroled after serving just over a year of his sentence (Cannon, 1995).

Few Canadians hold the same racist ideas as Carney Nerland. Even fewer are prepared to translate their hatred of certain ethnic and racial groups into acts of physical violence. But other kinds of ethnic and racial problems exist. Aboriginal people are prepared to put their lives on the line to resolve decades of injustice. Black parents in Toronto argue that they need to establish black-focussed schools that cater to the specific educational needs of their children. Others holler that this is racism in reverse. A group of former RCMP officers in Lethbridge, Alberta, claim that they have several thousand signatures on a petition demanding that the force change its policy allowing Sikh officers to wear turbans. Two years ago, the country was on the verge of collapse after nearly half the voters in the province of Quebec voted in favour of separation. Writer Neil Bissoondath (1994) recently set off a firestorm of controversy when he argued that the government's policy of multiculturalism is undermining the unity of our country.

These examples all touch in some way on the issue of what different ethnic and racial groups are allowed, and able, to do in our society. In other words, they all say something about the distribution of power and resources in Canada. The sociology of ethnic and racial relations concerns primarily the study of how power and resources are unequally distributed among ethnic and racial groups. Sociologists who are interested in race and ethnic relations ask a number of interrelated questions: What are the conditions under which ethnic and racial groups come into contact? Which ethnic and racial groups hold power in a society? How do they exercise power? Are there social and economic advantages associated with having a particular ethnic or racial background? What are the social consequences of the unequal distribution of power and resources? How have ethnic and racial groups challenged inequality and power imbalances? How have governments tried to manage and contain ethnic and racial conflict?

My aim in this chapter is to provide some sociological answers to these questions. I begin by examining what sociologists mean by the terms *ethnicity, race,* and *racism,* and then discuss various theoretical approaches to the study of ethnic and racial relations. Next, I examine the three main forms of ethnic and racial relations in Canada: aboriginal–nonaboriginal relations; French–English relations; and immigrant–nonimmigrant relations. In each of these cases, you will see how power and resource imbalances play important roles in structuring relationships among groups. I conclude by suggesting that, despite our ethnic and racial differences, there are good reasons to think that "Canadians," as a whole, are becoming an ethnic group.

■ ETHNICITY AND RACE: THE SOCIAL CONSTRUCTION OF DIFFERENCE

We use the terms *race, racial, ethnic,* and *ethnicity* in a variety of ways in our everyday lives. Some students in my classes talk about how they are under pressure from their parents to marry someone of the same "race" or "ethnicity." Others are concerned that "race relations" in Canada seem to be getting worse. Yet others describe the joys of living in a "multiethnic" country, of eating meals in a variety of "ethnic" restaurants, and of observing and participating in the rituals and festivals of "ethnic" groups from around the world.

The assumption underlying our common-sense understandings of these terms is that race and ethnicity are *ascribed* characteristics. That is, we assume that we are born with a certain race or ethnicity and that that fact cannot be changed. Sociologists, on the other hand, recognize that, while we cannot change our birth parents, and generally cannot change our skin colour, we do not necessarily have fixed and unalterable ethnic and racial characteristics or identities. Instead, sociologists believe it is more useful to see race and ethnicity as certain kinds of *achieved* statuses — statuses that are acquired by virtue of social definition. Box 9.1 shows how Statistics Canada measured ethnicity and race in the 1991 census.

▲ ETHNICITY AND RACE

Ethnicity

Sociologists do not agree on how to define and measure ethnicity. *Objective definitions of ethnicity* assume that ethnic groups exist because of people's social attachments (Isajiw, 1977). From this point of view, ethnicity is something that people possess because of differences in language, culture, customs, national origin, and ancestry. *Subjective approaches to ethnicity* focus on the process of ethnic identification. Sociologists who emphasize the socially constructed nature of perceived reality insist that ethnicity is a "transactional" process. Ethnic groups are made up of people who identify themselves, or who are identified by others, as belonging to the same ancestral or cultural

Box 9.1
The Ethnicity Question in the 1991 Census

Ethnic Origin

15. To which ethnic or cultural group(s) did this person's ancestors belong?

Mark or specify as many as applicable.

Note:

While most people of Canada view themselves as Canadian, information about their ancestral origins has been collected since the 1901 Census to reflect the changing composition of the Canadian population and is needed to ensure that everyone, regardless of his/her ethnic or cultural background, has **equal opportunity** *to share fully in the economic, social, cultural and political life of Canada. Therefore, this question refers to the origins of this person's* **ancestors**.

See Guide.

Examples of other ethnic or cultural groups are: Portuguese, Greek, Indian from India, Pakistani, Filipino, Vietnamese, Japanese, Lebanese, Haitian, etc. ▶

08 ○ French
09 ○ English
10 ○ German
11 ○ Scottish
12 ○ Italian
13 ○ Irish
14 ○ Ukrainian
15 ○ Chinese
16 ○ Dutch (Netherlands)
17 ○ Jewish
18 ○ Polish
19 ○ Black
20 ○ North American Indian
21 ○ Métis
22 ○ Inuit/Eskimo

Other ethnic or cultural group(s) — *Specify*

23 [ ]
24 [ ]

SOURCE: Statistics Canada, *1991 Census Handbook,* 1991 Census of Canada, Cat. no. 92-305 (Ottawa: Supply and Services Canada, 1992), p. 50. Reproduced by authority of the Minister of Industry, 1997.

group. Whether they actually display any of the cultural characteristics of the group with which they identify, or whether they are merely born into that group, is largely irrelevant. When subjective definitions are used, then, "ethnicity" is self-defined and reflects "a shared 'we-feeling' within a collectivity (groupness) whose symbolic components can vary from time and place" (Fleras and Elliot, 1996). From this perspective, ethnic identities and boundaries are situational, variable, and flexible.

Race

For much of the twentieth century, there was little difference between common-sense understandings of **race** and the way that race was analyzed in the social and natural sciences. Most scientists believed that races were real and objective subdivisions of *Homo sapiens.* These divisions were supposedly based on a combination of unalterable physical and genetic characteristics. Characteristics such as skin colour, hair texture, body and facial shape, genetic diseases, metabolic rates, and distribution of blood groups were used to construct various racial typologies. The most common typology was the division of humanity into "caucasoid," "mongoloid," and "negroid" races (Montagu, 1972).

During the 1930s, scientists began to raise serious doubts about the scientific validity of the concept of race (Barkan, 1992). Since the 1950s, the scientific consensus is that racial classifications of humanity are arbitrary, that genetic differences between groups are small, and that genetic differences are behaviourally insignificant (Montagu, 1972). Racial classifications based on a characteristic, such as skin colour, are as illogical as racial classifications based on the length of index fingers (Miles, 1982). Moreover, only 0.24 percent of all human genes are necessarily shared by members of the same race, genetically defined. Thus, from a strictly genetic point of view, Jean Chrétien may have much more in common with Oscar Peterson than with Lucien Bouchard.

In sum, differences between races are arbitrary, extremely small, and without behavioural consequences. Ethnic boundaries and identities are flexible, negotiated, and historically variable. We should not conclude, however, that race and ethnicity are unimportant aspects of modern society. According to W.I. Thomas's famous sociological dictum, if people define situations as real, they are real in their consequences (Thomas and Znaniecki, 1918: 79). Even though race is a hollow biological concept, and even though ethnic identities and boundaries are neither fixed nor unchanging, many people believe in the existence of ethnicity and race, and or-ganize their relationships with others on the basis of those beliefs. Therefore, race and ethnicity are important parts of our social reality.

Racism

If race is a biological myth, what is racism? Is a school racist if it puts on hot dog days but not chow mein days? Are black people in Toronto subject to racist policing? Is Don Cherry a racist because he denigrates European hockey players who compete in the National Hockey League? Is Professor Phillipe Rushton of the University of Western Ontario a racist because he believes that black people have smaller brains than whites and Asians? Is a black woman racist if she wants to marry only a black man? Is a white man racist if he wants to marry only a white woman?

Before we can begin to answer these questions, we need to define racism. Sociologists define racism as both a certain kind of idea and a certain kind of institutional practice. I will consider each of these definitions in turn.

RACIST IDEAS Traditionally, sociologists defined racism as "the belief that humans are subdivided into distinct hereditary groups that are innately different in their social behaviour and mental capacities and that can therefore be ranked as superior or inferior" (Marger, 1997: 27). By this definition, only a small minority of Canadians could be called racist. A survey conducted in 1990 by Decima Research Ltd. (cited in Reitz and Breton, 1994: 68) showed that 90 percent of Canadians agreed with the statement, "All races are created equal." It might be argued, then, that the 10 percent who either disagreed or did not know are racist. How can we reconcile the fact, on the one hand, that so few Canadians believe in the inherent superiority of some races over others with the fact, on the other hand, that people and institutions are so often called racist?

One answer is that, because ideas about the inherent superiority and inferiority of groups have been so thoroughly discredited, racism has taken new forms (Omi and Winant, 1986). Biological versions of racism may very well be "dead," but researchers have developed the concept of **new racism** as a way of analyzing its changing manifestations.

The concept of new racism was developed by Martin Barker (1981) to analyze the way that racist ideas were being expressed in the 1970s by British members of Parliament (MPs) when they were speaking out against British immigration policy. That policy permitted people from former British colonies in Asia, Africa, and the Caribbean unrestricted entry to the country. In their speeches, the MPs did not make references to British *biological* superiority or to Indian, African, or Caribbean *biological* inferiority. Instead, they regarded immigrants from these areas as *culturally* different from British people, and alleged that the ability of British people to advance the moral level of humanity was being undermined by immigration policy. The MPs' statements could not be considered "racist" by the traditional definition of racism. However, the statements had the real consequence of helping to stop almost all nonwhite immigration from those countries.

These events suggested that the definition of racism had to be broadened. Accordingly, Barker (1981: 21) argued that the new racism "is a theory of human nature. [It is the belief that] human nature is such that it is natural to form a bounded community, a nation, aware of its differences from other nations. They are not better or worse. But feelings of antagonism will be aroused if outsiders are admitted." Thus, the new racism involves the beliefs that, although races of people cannot be ranked biologically, with some being inferior and some superior, they are naturally different from each other, and that social problems are created when different groups try to live together. These beliefs should be considered racist because of their underlying intent: to socially exclude, marginalize, and denigrate certain groups of people, but to do so without reference to unalterable biology.

One indication of how widespread these kinds of ideas are in Canada is given in Table 9.1. It presents selected results from a 1991 national survey conducted by the Angus Reid Group about Canadians' limits to tolerance.

◆ **Table 9.1** Canadians and the Limits to Tolerance, Angus Reid Poll, 1991

	General agreement	General disagreement	Neither agree nor disagree
1. It is best for Canada if all people forget their different ethnic and cultural backgrounds as soon as possible	46%	30%	24%
2. The unity of this country is weakened by Canadians of different ethnic and cultural backgrounds sticking to their old ways	33	39	28
3. It is a bad idea for people of different races to marry	65	25	10
4. If employers only want to hire certain groups of people, that's their business	47	32	21
5. Nonwhites living here should not push themselves where they are not wanted	57	31	12
6. It makes me angry when I see recent immigrants on television demanding the same rights as Canadians	41	36	23
7. Recent immigrants should have as much say about the future of Canada as people who were born here	23	38	39
8. People who come to Canada should change their behaviour to be more like us	24	48	28
9. Ethnic groups are mainly made up of persons who are born outside Canada	35	45	20
10. Whites in Canada discriminate against nonwhites	12	51	37
11. Nonwhites in Canada tend to discriminate against whites	14	57	29

SOURCE: Angus Reid Group, *Multiculturalism and Canadians: National Attitude Study 1991* (Ottawa: Multiculturalism and Citizenship Canada, 1991), pp. 9–12.

INSTITUTIONAL RACISM The concept of **institutional racism** refers to "discriminatory racial practices built into such prominent structures as the political, economic and education systems" (Doob, 1996: 6). Institutional racism can take three forms. First, there are circumstances where institutional practices are based on explicitly racist ideas. There are plenty of examples of this form of institutional racism in Canadian history (Bolaria and Li, 1988). Chinese people were excluded from certain jobs and were denied the right to vote in federal elections until 1947. Japanese-Canadians were denied their basic civil rights, were forcibly expelled from the west coast of British Columbia, and had their property confiscated during World War II (Bolaria and Li, 1988). Status Indians were denied the right to vote in federal elections until 1960. Residential segregation was widespread for black people living in Canada. Restrictive covenants in wills, deeds, and leases were used to ensure that property was not sold or leased to blacks or to Jews. Blacks were frequently refused service in restaurants, theatres, and recreational facilities (Henry et al., 1995: 66). Canada had the worst record of all Allied countries in allowing Jewish immigration during World War II, when millions of Jews were being gassed in Europe (Abella and Troper, 1982). In each case, ideas about the alleged inferiority of these groups underpinned institutional practices.

Second, there are circumstances where institutional practices arose from but are no longer sustained by racist ideas (Miles, 1989). For example, in 1966, the federal government admitted a handful of black workers from the Caribbean to work on Canadian farms. Now, over 10 000 migrant workers from the Caribbean enter Canada each year to harvest fruits, vegetables, and tobacco in southern Ontario during the summer months. Canadian government officials originally justified this practice, in part, by arguing that black workers were racially suited to backbreaking labour under the hot sun, but racially unsuited to the cold Canadian winters (Satzewich, 1991). The present migrant-labour policy had its origins in racist thinking, but racist ideas are no longer used to justify this migration stream.

Third, there are circumstances where institutions unintentionally restrict the life-chances of certain groups through a variety of seemingly neutral rules, regulations, and procedures. This is sometimes referred to as *systemic discrimination*. For example, height and weight requirements for jobs with police forces and fire departments did not necessarily originate in racist ideas, but these requirements meant that, for many years, certain Asian groups could not get jobs as police officers or firefighters.

Systemic discrimination involves institutions unintentionally restricting the life-chances of certain groups, such as blacks, through a variety of seemingly neutral rules.
SOURCE: Bruce Ayres/Tony Stone.

Word-of-mouth recruiting in organizations and inflated educational requirements for nontechnical jobs are also forms of systemic discrimination, because they unintentionally put minority groups at a disadvantage in the distribution of scarce resources like jobs (Special Committee on the Participation of Visible Minorities in Canadian Society, 1984).

▲ THEORIES OF RACE AND ETHNIC RELATIONS

There are a number of sociological approaches to the interpretation of race and ethnic relations (Rex and Mason, 1986). In this section, I will discuss four approaches that seek to explain various forms of ethnic and racial hostility. Such hostility is multifaceted and, depending on the circumstances, is described as racism, prejudice, ethnocentrism, and/or xenophobia.

Social Psychology

Social-psychological approaches to the interpretation of race and ethnic relations focus on how **prejudice** — an unfavourable, generalized and rigid *belief* applied to all members of a group — and racism satisfy the psychic needs of certain people. *Frustration-aggression* is a popular variant of social-psychological theory. It explains prejudice and racism as forms of hostility that arise from frustration. The theory suggests that people who are frustrated in their efforts to achieve a desired goal — a better-paying job, for example, or entry to a university — respond with aggression (Marger, 1997). Since the real source of frustration is usually too powerful to confront directly, or may not in fact be known, people take out their frustrations on the less powerful. From this perspective, minority ethnic and racial groups are convenient and safe targets of displaced aggression. This displacement is also referred to as scapegoating. The concept of scapegoating is sometimes used to explain *anti-Semitism* — negative attitudes and everyday discrimination directed against Jews (Brym and Lenton, 1993).

There is a seductive, almost common-sense, appeal to this kind of explanation. We all have bad days at work or at school, and when we get home we sometimes lash out at the people close to us. However, the theory has limitations. First, people respond to frustrating circumstances in a variety of ways. Displaced aggression does not always follow frustration. We sometimes internalize our frustrations and end up giving ourselves an ulcer, or we may direct our frustrations at the real source of our problems. The theory does not say why we respond to frustrating circumstances in different ways. Second, the theory does not explain why some groups, and not others, are chosen as scapegoats.

Primordialism

The **primordialist thesis** suggests that ethnic and racial attachments reflect an innate tendency for people to seek out, and associate with, others who are similar in terms of language, culture, beliefs, ancestry, and appearance (Scott, 1990). From this point of view, ethnic prejudice and racism are ways of maintaining social boundaries. *Sociobiologists* offer a popular form of primordial theory. They suggest that prejudice and **discrimination** — practices that deny members of particular groups equal access to societal rewards — stem from our supposedly biologically grounded tendency to be nepotistic. Sociobiologists argue that the process of natural selection does not operate at the level of individuals, but rather at the level of kin-related groups. Clusters of genes are assumed to be passed on through kin selection (Wilson, 1978). Ethnic and racial groups are seen to be nothing more than very large extended families. Since there is a "natural" tendency for people to want to pass on their genes, they favour their own "families." Thus, people are inherently altruistic (prepared to sacrifice their own individual interests for the sake of the group) and **ethnocentric** because they want to pass on their genes to their own group. Humans, therefore, naturally favour members of their own ethnic or racial group — their "relatives" — and have a natural distrust and dislike of "nonfamily" members (van den Berghe, 1986: 255).

Are racism, prejudice, and discrimination programmed by our genes? It seems unlikely. The first problem with sociobiology is that shared ethnicity or race does not prevent conflict from erupting. In the history of the United States, white workers have struck against white-owned factories, and Americans have killed members of their own ethnic or racial group without concern for common ethnicity or race (Bonacich, 1980). Second, sociobiology is not able to explain how and why we frequently break out of our supposed genetically programmed nepotism. For example, Canadians of diverse ethnic and racial origins participate together in various kinds of antiracist social movements (Henry et al., 1995). Ethnic and racial relations, therefore, are not necessarily zero-sum games in which one group wins at the expense of another.

Normative Theories

Normative theories of ethnic and racial prejudices concentrate on the way in which prejudices are transmitted through socialization and the social circumstances that compel discriminatory behaviour (Marger, 1997). For example, the *socialization approach* focusses on how we are taught ethnic and racial stereotypes, prejudices, and attitudes by our families, peer groups, and the mass media. For instance, as a teenager in Saskatchewan in the 1970s, I remember watching the TV show *All in the Family*. People in Saskatchewan at the time held many prejudicial attitudes, particularly toward aboriginal people. However, *All in the Family* exposed my generation to a repertoire of ethnic and racial slang and stereotypes that we had not heard before. Archie Bunker, the show's central character, was supposed to be a caricature of an American "bigot." He taught us terms like "wop," "dago," "spic," and "nigger," and the corresponding stereotypes.

As Box 9.2 shows, there are subtle ways in which the English language places different values on the colours black and white. Our language, in turn, shapes how we perceive and socially evaluate different racial groups.

Socialization approaches are superior to the first two approaches because they emphasize the way in which ethnic and racial prejudices and attitudes are learned through social interaction. The limitation of socialization theories is that they are unable to explain how prejudicial ideas, attitudes, and practices arise in the first place. This is where power-conflict theories come into play.

Power-Conflict Theories

Karl Marx (1967 [1867]: 751) said that "the turning of Africa into a warren for the commercial hunting of black-skins signaled the rosy dawn of the era of capitalist production." Marx did not take his analysis of slavery and racism much further than this. Later generations of Marxist scholars, however, have sought to link racism to the overall structure of capitalist societies.

Orthodox Marxists argue that racism is an *ideology* — a set of statements shaped by one's economic interests about the way the social world "really works." Racism is ideological insofar as it is

Box 9.2
Language, Colour of Race

Language is an integral part of our culture. Language not only expresses ideas but shapes our thought. Our childhood socialization involves, in part, the ability to use language. In the following "Short Play on 'Black' and 'White' Words," Robert Moore shows how aspects of our language help unwittingly to reproduce both negative and positive racial imagery.

Some may blackly (angrily) accuse me of trying to blacken (defame) the English language, to give it a black eye (a mark of shame) by writing such black words (hostile). They may denigrate (to cast aspersions; to darken) me by accusing me of being blackhearted (malevolent), of having a black outlook (pessimistic, dismal) on life, of being a blackguard (scoundrel)—which would certainly be a black mark (detrimental fact) against me. Some may black-brow (scowl at) me and hope that a black cat crosses in front of me because of this black deed. I may become a black sheep (one who causes shame or embarrassment because of deviation from the accepted standards), who will be blackballed (ostracized) by being placed on a blacklist (list of undesirables) in an attempt to blackmail (to force or coerce into a particular action) me to retract my words. But attempts to blackjack (to compel by threat) me will have a Chinaman's chance of success, for I am not a yellow-bellied Indian-giver of words, who will whitewash (cover up or gloss over vices or crimes) a black lie (harmful, inexcusable). I challenge the purity and innocence (white) of the English language. I don't see things in black and white (entirely bad or entirely good) terms, for I am a white man (marked by upright firmness) if there ever was one. However, it would be a black day when I would not "call a spade a spade," even though some will suggest a white man calling the English language racist is like the pot calling the kettle black. While many may be niggardly (grudging, scanty) in their support, others will be honest and decent—and to them I say, that's very white of you (honest, decent).

The preceding is of course a white lie (not intended to cause harm), meant only to illustrate some examples of racist terminology in the English language.

SOURCE: Robert Moore, "Racism in the English Language," in Paula Rothernberg, ed., *Race, Class and Gender in the United States: An Integrated Study* (New York: St. Martin's Press, 1995), p. 377.

used by capitalists to mystify social reality and justify the exploitation and the unequal treatment of groups of people.

This justification can take many forms. For example, in the seventeenth century, American and Caribbean plantation owners justified the use of Africans as slaves by denying the humanity of Africans (Williams, 1964). In Marxist terms, the existence of racist ideas did not "cause" slavery; rather, slavery was a particular system of labour control that was justified by racist ideology.

In the case of advanced capitalism, racism is viewed by Marxists as an ideology that justifies the especially intense exploitation of racial minority and immigrant workers (Castles and Kosack, 1984; Bolaria and Li, 1988). From this point of view, racist ideas are used by employers as a means of creating artificial divisions in the working class so as to prevent the formation of a class consciousness that would threaten the social and economic order (Bolaria and Li, 1988; Castles and Kosack, 1984; Nikolinakos, 1973). Also, racist ideas help to justify the allocation of certain groups to low-wage, socially marginal jobs.

RACE AND THE SPLIT LABOUR MARKET **Split labour-market theory** was developed by Edna Bonacich (1972, 1979) because of the limitations of orthodox Marxism in analyzing racism. She argues that orthodox Marxism tends to assume that the capitalist class is all-powerful, and that other classes play no role in the development of racist thinking. This is inaccurate; racism may be found in all classes to varying degrees. Second, orthodox Marxism portrays racism in overly conspiratorial terms. There is little evidence to demonstrate that capitalists sit around plotting new and devious ways of using racism to stop workers from developing a class consciousness. Third, orthodox Marxism has trouble explaining why racialized conflict so often results in *exclusionary practices* — practices that deny employers access to cheaper, more exploitable labour. In 1885, for example, the Canadian government instituted a "head tax" on new immigrants from China. Chinese immigrants had to pay $50 to the federal government. In 1900, the tax was raised to $100, and in 1903 to $500 (Li, 1988: 30). The Chinese Immigration Act of 1923 completely barred Chinese immigration until 1947 (Li, 1988: 30). If racism is developed by capitalists to justify exploitation, then why does it so often result in efforts to *block* the entry of new immigrants, and limit the job opportunities of those already in the country? Bonacich feels that more attention has to

be paid to the way in which the competititon for jobs and other scarce resources among the working class creates and sustains racism.

Split labour-market theory suggests that racial and ethnic conflict is rooted in differences in the price of labour. For historical reasons — mainly involving military conquest — nonwhite workers have often received low wages and white workers high wages. Employers try to replace high-paid white workers with low-paid nonwhite workers. Meanwhile, high-paid workers, faced with displacement or the threat of displacement, try to protect their own interests by limiting capitalists' access to cheaper nonwhite workers. Thus, cheaper nonwhite workers are the victims of a complicated process of class struggle between expensive labour, cheap labour, and capitalists.

The theory applies well to Canada. During the late nineteenth and early twentieth centuries, the presence of Chinese workers and merchants in British Columbia provoked a negative response on the part of various segments of the white working class. As split labour-market theory would predict, the hostility of whites was rooted in differences in the price of labour. According to evidence presented at the Royal Commission on Chinese and Japanese Immigration in 1903, Chinese workers earned about one-half of the wages that white workers earned in the same jobs (Li, 1988: 44). A number of racist organizations emerged, including the Anti-Chinese Association, the Asiatic Exclusion League, and the Anti-Mongolian Association. They successfully limited the places where Chinese people could work and helped stop Chinese immigration (Roy, 1989).

Split labour-market theory makes three other points that are relevant to the analysis of ethnic and race relations in general. First, it argues that individual racism, ethnic prejudice, and institutional racism emerge from intergroup conflict. Second, the theory maintains that prejudicial ideas and discriminatory behaviour are ways of socially marginalizing minority groups whom the dominant group sees as threats to their position of power and privilege. Third, the theory suggests that, in order to understand ethnic and racial relations, we need to look beyond individual personalities and sociobiological processes and analyze processes of economic, social, and political competition between groups (Marger, 1997: 98).

Keeping these three observations in mind will help you understand the three main patterns of ethnic and racial relations in Canada: aboriginal–nonaboriginal relations, French–English relations, and immigrant–nonimmigrant relations. These are the topics that we turn to next.

■ ABORIGINAL PEOPLES

Have you ever fumbled trying to find the right way to refer to someone who is ethnically or racially different from yourself? Are we supposed to say that a person is a "Native," an "Indian," an "aboriginal," or a member of the "First Nations"? Are you sensitive about how you want others to refer to your own ethnic or racial origins? In contrast, you may think that this sensitivity is yet another indication that political correctness has run amok. If so, you should not dismiss the issue of labels and names so easily.

Ethnic and racial labels are about power. Take the term *Indian*. A hopelessly lost Christopher Columbus thought he found a sea route to India when he was discovered in 1492 by people indigenous to this part of the world. He mislabelled the people he met "Indians." Britain's military, political, and economic domination of North America in the 1700s meant that it had the power to ignore the linguistic and cultural differences between indigenous groups and define them in any way they saw fit. They chose the term *Indian*.

As indigenous people have acquired more power, they have begun to challenge externally imposed labels. In the 1980s, for example, the National Indian Brotherhood renamed itself the Assembly of First Nations, and people in Alberta who were defined by Europeans as Sarcee Indians for most of this century renamed themselves the Siksika nation. Groups have rejected externally imposed labels as part of a search for forms of consciousness, identity, and culture that are untainted by the colonizing power's definition of the situation (Jenson, 1993).

One, albeit imperfect, way to make our way through the complex issue of naming is to use the definition of "aboriginal peoples" that is contained in the 1982 Canadian Charter of Rights and Freedoms. In the Charter, the "aboriginal peoples" of Canada include Indians, Inuit, and Métis. According to the 1991 census, there were 783 980 Indians, 212 650 Métis, and 49 260 Inuit people in Canada, who made up 3.7 percent of the total population (Statistics Canada, 1995).

At its simplest level, the term *Indian* (or *status* or *registered Indian*) refers to people who are recognized as "Indians" by virtue of the federal government's Indian Act. But deciding who is an Indian under the Indian Act is a much more complicated question. Until 1985, Indian women who married non-Indian men, along with their children, lost their federally recognized Indian status; they be-came *non-status Indians*. In 1985, Bill C-31 was passed. It allowed these women and their dependent children to regain their Indian status.

There are two different definitions of *Métis*. Métis organizations in Western Canada tend to focus on a person's objective "roots" as the condition for being considered Métis. Thus, the Métis National Council defines "the Métis" as "descendants of the historic Métis who evolved in what is now Western Canada as a people with a common political will" (Métis National Council, 1983). Métis organizations in Eastern Canada, such as the Native Council of Canada, argue that the Métis should include descendants of the historic Métis in Western Canada *and* anyone of mixed European–Indian ancestry who defines himself or herself as Métis, and is accepted by other Métis people as such.

Finally, *Inuit* people are part of a diverse group of people who have lived for many centuries north of the tree line. In Canada, the name Inuit has replaced the earlier name Eskimo. The language of the Inuit is Inuktitut (McMillan, 1988: 240).

▲ EXPLANATIONS OF ABORIGINAL CONDITIONS

The socioeconomic conditions of Canada's aboriginal people amount to a national tragedy (Royal Commission on Aboriginal Peoples, 1996). Canada has made admirable efforts to condemn social inequality and the denial of human rights in other countries, such as South Africa when apartheid — its policy of legalized ethnic separation and inequality — was still in force. Ironically, though, the commitment to social justice for aboriginal peoples in our own country has not been as strong. In the 1980s, the South African government routinely defended itself against our criticisms of apartheid by saying that we should first clean up our own backyard (Bourgeault, 1988; York, 1989).

Statistical evidence shows that aboriginal peoples are the most socially and economically disadvantaged groups in the country. About three-quarters of all existing housing for status Indians who live on reserves fails to meet the basic standards for safe and healthy living, such as running water, central heating, sewer connections or septic tanks, and electricity (Frideres, 1993: 195–96). On average, aboriginal people have much lower family incomes, lower rates of labour-force participation, and higher rates of unemployment than nonaboriginal Canadians (Frideres, 1993: 165–67). The age-standardized death rate for aboriginal people in Canada was 9.2 per 1000 in 1991, compared with a rate of 6 per 1000 for Canada as a whole. In 1991, the life expectancy of status Indian men was 68 years, 6 years lower than the Canadian average. Life expectancy for status Indian women was higher than that for Indian men, but was still below life expectancy for other Canadian women: 73.1 compared with 80 years. In 1988, the infant mortality rate (the number of deaths of children under 1 year old per 1000 people) for status Indians was 12.7, much higher than the national rate of 7.2. Tuberculosis, which is widely regarded as a disease of poverty, is on the rise in Indian communities, yet it has been virtually eliminated from non-Indian communities in Canada.

For many years, Canadian politicians, bureaucrats, and social scientists have puzzled over where these differences and inequalities come from, how and why they persist, and what can be done about them. Indeed, when the federal government announced in 1991 the establishment of the Royal Commission on Aboriginal Peoples, Ovide Mercredi, the chief of the Assembly of First Nations, caustically commented that "Indians have been studied to death." I want first to consider the federal government's historical explanation of these conditions and then examine two sociological accounts of them: the culture of poverty thesis and the conflict theory.

The Government's View

Throughout the first half of the twentieth century, government Indian policy was premised on the belief that aboriginal culture was both different from and inferior to European culture. Armed with this ethnocentric attitude, the federal government sought to assimilate aboriginal people into mainstream Canadian society (Gibbins and Ponting, 1986). In 1920, this approach was summed up in the following terms by Duncan Campbell Scott, the deputy minister of the federal government's Department of Indian Affairs: "[O]ur object is to continue until there is not a single Indian ... that has not been absorbed into the body politic and there is no [longer an] Indian question." (quoted in Titley, 1986).

The government, therefore, forcibly tried to Europeanize aboriginal people and culture. Traditional cultural practices like the potlatch, a winter exchange of gifts and property on the British Columbia coast, and the sun dance, a summer solstice religious ceremony on the Prairies, were outlawed. Such practices were regarded as pagan, anticapitalist rituals that inhibited the development of both Christianity and a capitalistic work ethic (Cole and Chaikin, 1990; Pettipas, 1995). The federal government also tried to assimilate and Christianize aboriginal children by establishing a series of residential schools. These boarding schools were located far from the children's families and home communities. While in school, the children were forbidden to speak in their mother tongue, were forbidden to speak with siblings of the opposite sex, and had their hair shorn. Boys were given extensive training in manual labour and girls were taught domestic labour skills. The goal of this schooling was to resocialize aboriginal children and to instil in them a new European identity (Titley, 1986). The government's legislative, regulatory, and educational approach to aboriginal people reflected the view that inequality, poverty, and poor social conditions were rooted in aboriginal cultural and racial inferiority.

The Culture of Poverty Thesis

In the 1960s and 1970s, many sociologists also saw aboriginal culture as the source of the "Indian problem." To account for the origins and persistence of the problem, some sociologists proposed a variant of the **culture of poverty thesis**. The concept of a culture of poverty was first developed by Oscar Lewis (1961), an American anthropologist interested in explaining the slow pace at which Mexican-Americans and Puerto Ricans were being assimilated into U.S. society. He suggested that some ethnic groups do not readily assimilate, and hence are poor, because their culture does not value economic success, hard work, and achievement.

Nagler (1972) applied Lewis's framework to the conditions of aboriginal people in Canada. In his view, Indian culture displayed the following characteristics: a present rather than a future time-orientation; a high value on mutual aid without the expectation of return; a lack of emphasis on the possession of material goods; a lack of appreciation for the monetary value of time; and the absence of a capitalist work ethic. These cultural characteristics meant that "a large segment of the Indian population refuse or find themselves unable to partake in full time economic pursuits" (Nagler, 1972: 131).

Sociologists like Steven Steinberg (1981) criticize culture of poverty explanations by arguing that groups generally do not get ahead or lag behind because of their cultural values. Instead, they are born into certain stations in life and adopt the values and attitudes that are consistent with their life-chances. If aboriginal people do not value hard work or if they have low aspirations, it is likely due to a realistic assessment of their dismal job prospects and a resignation born out of bitter personal experience. For Steinberg, the *culture* of poverty is the consequence, not the cause, of poverty.

Conflict Theory

Since the 1970s, sociologists have focussed on blocked opportunities rather than culture as the explanation for inequalities between aboriginal and nonaboriginal people. The *internal colonial model* is the most popular variant of the conflict approach (Frideres, 1993). The internal colonial model analyzes the problem of inequality in terms of power imbalances and the exploitation of aboriginal people and lands by white society.

Theorists of internal colonialism argue that the Indian Act, which outlines the federal government's policies and procedures for dealing with Indian issues, is a paternalistic document that disempowers Indian people (Frideres, 1993). It places real limits on the actions of both individual Indians and their band councils. When Indians from Brantford, Ontario, wanted to sue the federal government over unfulfilled treaty promises in the 1920s, the government passed a law making it illegal for them to use band funds to hire lawyers to pursue their claims (Titley, 1986). Indians did not get much help from federal or provincial politicians either. Since Indians could not vote in either federal or provincial elections until 1960s, politicians had no need to stand up for the interests of Indians who lived in their constituency. Chiefs who failed to co-operate with the government's designs were routinely removed from their positions (Satzewich and Mahood, 1994). Band councils are still required to have their decisions approved by the federal minister of Indian affairs. Thus, rather than helping to create the social conditions that would afford Indian people greater autonomy over their lives, government policy has fostered social marginality and dependence.

Furthermore, most of the present-day conflicts between aboriginal people and various levels of government originated in the past misuse of power by government officials. Present-day land claims disputes sometimes go back 100 years, when government officials could arbitrarily lop off chunks of Indian reserve land and sell it to white interests (Frideres, 1993). The Canadian government and private business have derived tremendous economic benefits from the exploitation of land appropriated from aboriginal communities. According to internal colonial theorists, the time has come for Canadians to pay the rent. The Métis in Alberta, for example, estimate that they are owed over $60 million in unpaid royalties on 200 oil and gas wells that are on their land (Frideres, 1993: 8).

▲ CLASS AND GENDER DIVERSITY

Criticisms of the internal colonial model have focussed on its tendency to overgeneralize about the conditions of aboriginal people in Canada. As significant as the inequalities between aboriginal and nonaboriginal people are, conflict and feminist sociologists argue that it is worth remembering that there is also socioeconomic diversity within aboriginal communities. These sociologists analyze class and gender differentiation within aboriginal communities and the implications of such differences for both individual life-chances and wider community life (Satzewich and Wotherspoon, 1993).

Feminist sociologists have been interested in the role of gender in recent debates about the inclusion of the right to self-government in the Canadian constitution. During the debate about the Charlottetown accord in 1992, many aboriginal women were concerned that the proposal for self-government, which was advanced by the predominantly male leadership of aboriginal organizations, did not contain any guarantees of sexual equality between aboriginal women and men (Krosenbrink-Gelissen, 1994: 357–60; Fiske, 1996). The Native Women's Association of Canada, therefore, fought against the accord in the months leading up to the referendum.

Other conflict theorists are interested in the political and economic implications of socioeconomic differentiation within aboriginal communities. Researchers challenge the stereotype that all aboriginal people are either poor, unemployed, living on welfare, or working in low-skill, dead-end jobs. In fact, a small but nevertheless significant proportion of aboriginal men and women work in highly skilled professional and technical occupations, and others are owners and managers of both small and large businesses (Gerber, 1990). Menno Boldt (1993: 124) argues that most Indian reserves are characterized by a two-class social order. The first class consists of "a small, virtually closed élite class comprising influential landowners, politicians, bureaucrats, and a few entrepreneurs," while the second consists of "a large lower class comprising destitute, dependent, powerless [and wage-earning] people" (Boldt, 1993: 124). Boldt argues (1993: 125) that this two-class structure has important consequences for community life and community politics:

With the élite class controlling the political agenda, lower-class interests get neglected. Elite class interests tend to be primarily "power" not "problem" oriented; that is, such interests are related to expanding their jurisdiction and control over band/tribal political and administrative structures. . . . [These] are given preference over the problems that afflict the Indian lower class: high unemployment; excessive rates of family disintegration; alcohol and substance abuse; extraordinary levels of violence, suicide, incarceration, and so on.

Researchers are also studying the formation of a capitalist class within aboriginal communities. Land-claim settlements, although ostensibly earmarked for the benefit of all community members, are frequently controlled by small ruling elites. In the case of the Inuit, Marybelle Mitchell (1996: 449) argues:

The state's acknowledgment in 1973 of its responsibility to negotiate land settlements with Native people led to the formation of an Inuit ruling class. Created by the state to facilitate access by the multinationals to the Arctic's natural resources, these leaders, a wholly new kind of talking chief, are signing away the land and aboriginal rights of their fellow Inuit in return for limited entitlement to land, some managerial powers and varying amounts of cash channeled through development corporations.

This new capitalist class is different from other Canadian capitalists, in that they do not personally own all the wealth and capital that is at their disposal. They do, however, control the compensation that communities receive from land-claims settlements. They establish development corporations, hire and fire employees, make capital-planning and investment decisions, and decide what and how much to produce. The unanswered sociological question is whether this capitalist class will make decisions about the future that are in their own material interests or in the interests of the community as a whole.

■ QUEBEC: NATIONALISM AND IDENTITY

On the evening of October 30, 1995, most adult Canadians were tuned to TV or radio coverage of the Quebec referendum on separation. I followed the results that night with mixed emotions. On the one hand, as a second-generation Canadian with no ethnic roots in the old British Empire, I could empathize with people in Quebec. On the other hand, as a child of the Trudeau years, I was socialized to believe

in a vision of Canadian unity. Many on the "No" side believed that a lot of Quebeckers were just bluffing in the prereferendum rhetoric; when it came to the crunch, they would vote in favour of staying in Canada. Then the results came in. In some parts of Quebec, 90 percent of voters were in favour of separation. As the results from around Montreal were tabulated, the "No" side gained ground. When the final count was tallied, 49.6 percent of Quebeckers voted for, and 50.4 percent voted against, separation. Across Canada, people were both exhilarated and downcast because Canada had "won."

Is the issue of separation going to go away? The answer is clearly no. As with other areas of ethnic relations in Canada, an understanding of the contemporary scene must begin with an appreciation of history and of power relations. In this section, I examine three main sociological questions: (1) What is the historical basis for the emergence of Québécois nationalism? (2) Who is a Québécois? (3) What does the close vote mean for ethnic relations in the province and the country?

▲ THE SOCIAL BASIS OF QUÉBÉCOIS NATIONALISM

Even though the 1867 British North America Act asserted that there were two founding peoples of Canada, the English and the French, and that they had equal places in Canadian Confederation, *les Québécois* are one of the oldest colonized peoples in the world (Milner and Milner, 1973). The French government controlled the colony of New France from the early 1600s to 1763. The inhabitants of New France were expected to serve the interests of France. The colony was established in part to pursue the fur trade and to transfer economic resources to the mother country. Much of the French commercial and political elite left the colony following the British victory over France in 1763. When New France was transferred to British control — what the Québécois refer to as "The Conquest" — a new colonizing power came to dominate the society.

An anglophone — a unilingual, English-speaking — elite gradually took over the economic and political affairs of the province. Most French-Canadian peasants (*habitants*) remained subsistence farmers. During the nineteenth century, some of them emigrated to the northeastern United States to work in the expanding cotton and linen mills; others moved to other provinces in Canada; and still others became part of the urban industrial working class in the province (Ramirez, 1991). By the late nineteenth century, Quebec was a province where "capital speaks English and labour speaks French" (Whitaker, 1993: 22) — a telling description of the way in which linguistic and class structures overlapped. The French Canadians in Quebec, who formed a numerical majority, were worse off than the anglophone minority in virtually every material way (Whitaker, 1993: 22).

The Catholic Church occupied a unique position as a social, political, and religious intermediary between the two groups. In addition to attending to the religious needs of its French-speaking parishioners, the Catholic Church acted as an agent of social control over French-Canadian workers and farmers. The church promoted social ideologies that were conservative and antimodern. It devalued the importance of formal education for the masses, discouraged workers from forming and joining secular trade unions, encouraged married couples to have large families, and vigorously discouraged French Canadians from taking up professions or establishing businesses of their own. These ideas were not in the best material interests of French-Canadian workers and farmers, but they helped ensure the survival of French-Canadian culture (Latouche, 1993).

This social structure began to change significantly during the rapid industrialization stimulated by World War I, as the industrial working class became a significant player on the political scene. One of the biggest changes in the 1940s and 1950s was the rise of a new francophone middle class of technical workers and professionals. The upper echelons of the corporate world, still under the control of anglophones, remained hostile to the advancement of francophones, even if they were bilingual. The new francophone middle class, therefore, faced a situation of blocked social mobility, which was partly responsible for the Quiet Revolution in Quebec.

The term **Quiet Revolution** describes the social, political, and cultural changes that occurred in Quebec in the 1960s, in part because of the initiatives of this new middle class. These changes included the secularization of the educational system, the reform of the civil service, growth in the provincially controlled public sector, greater involvement of the Quebec provincial government in the economic affairs of the province, and a questioning of the Catholic Church's authority in all areas of life. Facing blocked mobility in the corporate world, francophones created their own economic opportunities by expanding the power of the provincial government.

Social scientists and political pundits have poured over referendum and federal and provincial election results over the last 30 years in an effort to determine which social forces are responsible for sustaining the push for sovereignty. Some see the present-day sovereignty movement as an expression of *middle-class nationalism* that is a continuation of the Quiet Revolution. From this perspective, separation is being promoted by middle-class professionals as a way of continuing to further their own material interests. Emboldened by the success at expanding the activities of the provincial government during the Quiet Revolution, they desire even more control over their affairs (Whitaker, 1993).

However, likening the sovereignty movement to a massive job-creation project is too simplistic. First, francophone professionals are no longer shut out of the corporate sector in Quebec. Over the past 30 years, middle-class francophones have achieved upward mobility in both the private and the public sectors. Second, there is a diversity of class interests within the sovereignty movement. Many francophone professionals support sovereignty, but there is also social democratic tradition within the movement that is trying to mobilize working people against foreign (anglophone and U.S.) capitalist domination. Their vision of a sovereign Quebec involves a reorganization of power relations between francophones and nonfrancophones, and between workers and capitalists. Some francophone capitalists also support the sovereignty movement (Whitaker, 1993).

Clearly, the contemporary sovereignty movement is not based on the support of only one social class. According to Fleras and Elliot (1996), the nationalist movement is sustained by a broadly based desire among most francophone Quebeckers to achieve a common goal — to create the political and economic conditions that will allow them to preserve their French language and culture. Fleras and Elliot argue that, rather than defining support for the sovereignty movement in class terms, it is more useful to conceptualize the movement as made up of groups who have differing views about how best to maintain their language and culture. Thus, the present-day sovereignty movement consists in part of moderates who want to strengthen Quebec's position within the federal system. This involves a new constitutional division of powers that has yet to be settled. Radical supporters, on the other hand, argue that the best way for the French language and culture to survive is for the people of Quebec to have their own state. They argue that they will always be a minority if they stay in Canada and that they will always be subject to the tyranny of the majority. As Louise Beaudoin of the Parti Québécois put it, "I want to be a majority in my own country" (Fleras and Elliot, 1996: 270).

▲ WHO IS QUÉBÉCOIS?

The population of Quebec is ethnically heterogeneous — 19.4 percent of the population of Quebec is made up of people whose mother tongue is not French: Jews, anglophones, allophones (people whose mother tongue is neither French nor English), visible-minority immigrants, and aboriginal people (Fournier, Rosenberg, and White, 1997: 282). One of the central issues facing the nationalist movement in Quebec is the definition of a Québécois. This question cuts to the heart of ethnic relations in the province.

Benedict Anderson (1983) regards nations as "imagined communities." They are imagined in the sense that, even though members of the smallest nation can never know everyone in the community, there is still a common feeling of fellowship with others in the nation. People in Shawinigan do not personally know all other Quebeckers; nevertheless, they have a comradeship that extends beyond personal relationships. Nations also possess physical and symbolic boundaries that define who is a member and who is not. Sociologists interested in nationalism want to identify the symbolic boundaries of the nation. In the case of the nationalist movement in Quebec, this issue is translated into the question of who is "in" and who is "outside" the imagined community. And if some groups are "out," will they ever be accepted as Québécois?

A majority of nationalists, on the one hand, define the imagined community as all those people who now live in the province of Quebec. For them, the social and symbolic boundaries of the nation correspond with the present-day provincial boundaries. Sociologists call this a form of **civic nationalism** (Balthazar, 1993). A minority of nationalists, on the other hand, reject civic nationalism in favour of cultural and linguistic criteria for membership in the nation. *Ethnic nationalists* define the Québécois as people who possess a particular history, culture, ancestry, and/or language. This is where the concept of *pure laine* ("pure wool") Québécois becomes important. Some nationalists regard the true Quebeckers as only those who are the direct descendants of the French people who settled in the colony of New France before the conquest of 1763. Other groups in the province are defined as "cultural communities" (GRES, 1997: 107). According to the province's policy of interculturalism, these cultural communities must learn to accommodate themselves to the dominant francophone culture and language.

The debate about how to define a nation is not academic hairsplitting. Premier Jacques Parizeau commented on referendum night that the prosovereignty forces were defeated by "money and the ethnic vote." After his resignation, Parizeau commented further that it was the first time in Canadian history that the majority (60 percent) of francophone Quebeckers voted in favour of sovereignty. These statements implied that ethnic minorities were not really part of the nation and that *pure laine* votes should be worth more than the votes of others. Parizeau's remarks also confirmed the worst fears of ethnic minorities — namely, that sovereigntists are not civic nationalists but rather ethnic nationalists at heart, and that ethnic minorities will never be considered full and equal citizens in a sovereign Quebec (Ha, 1995). Many people within the sovereignty movement distanced themselves from Parizeau's comments, and the movement is still trying to repair the damage that they caused to ethnic relations. Clearly, the challenge for sovereigntists is to find a place for nonfrancophones in the imagined community (GRES, 1997: 109).

■ IMMIGRATION: STATE FORMATION AND ECONOMIC DEVELOPMENT

The third aspect of ethnic and racial relations in Canada that I consider is immigrant–nonimmigrant relations. In 1991, there were 4.3 million immigrants living in Canada, representing 16.1 percent of our population. In large cities, the impact of immigration is even greater. In 1991, immigrants made up 17 percent of the population of Montreal, 30 percent of the population of Vancouver, and 38 percent of the population of Toronto (Badets, 1993). Canada accepts more immigrants and refugees in proportion to our population than virtually any other country in the world (Citizenship and Immigration Canada, 1996).

Migration has been a feature of our history for well over 300 years. However, the nature, sources, determinants, and consequences of immigration have varied through history. In the nineteenth century, immigrants contributed to the processes of capitalist state formation — the process of creating a capitalist system of production and governance. They did this in a number of ways. The early working class in Canada was made up largely of immigrants (Pentland, 1981; Avery, 1995). Immigrant workers helped build the canals, railways, and roads that became part of our economic infrastructure. Many nineteenth-century immigrants were also farmers. Their crops were used to feed Canadian workers and, as productivity increased, were exported to feed people in other countries. Those same farmers, in turn, helped stimulate capitalist industry through their role as consumers of goods. A significant proportion of the corporate elite in nineteenth-century Canada was made up of immigrants (Macmillan, 1985; Clement, 1975), as was a large segment of the early political elite. Canada's first prime minister, Sir John A. Macdonald, was an immigrant from Glasgow, Scotland.

Immigrants continue to make important contributions to the social reproduction of Canadian society. Demographers predict that, in the absence of new immigrants, the population of Canada would begin to decline by 2015. Without new immigrants to replenish our population, the next generation of taxpayers would have to pay far more in taxes and Canada Pension Plan contributions. Employers would face serious shortages of workers, and manufacturers would face a much smaller consumer market in which to sell their goods (Economic Council of Canada, 1991).

▲ FACTORS THAT SHAPE CANADIAN IMMIGRATION

There is no single variable that can explain the complex pattern of immigration to Canada. Over the past 100 years, five main variables have determined which groups of people have been let into the country as immigrants.

The first variable is social class. Most immigrants are admitted to Canada because they fill jobs in the Canadian economy or because they create jobs for other Canadians. As such, the flow of immigrants to Canada has been very closely linked to the overall structure of the Canadian economy. Between 1947 and the early 1960s, for example, immigrants were regarded by the Canadian government as what Australian economist Jock Collins (1988) calls "factory fodder." Immigrants were recruited in order to fill unskilled and semiskilled manual jobs in agriculture, construction, mining, logging, the garment industry, and heavy manufacturing. During this time, it was common for individual employers to demand that the government recruit as many as 300 immigrant workers at a time in order to fill job openings (Avery, 1995).

In the early 1960s, immigration policy began to place more emphasis on the recruitment of highly skilled professional and technical workers, and on immigrants with large amounts of investment capital. As a result, by 1991, immigrants made up 16.1 percent of the population but 19.5 percent of the total Canadian labour force, 20.5 percent of people in managerial occupations, and 20.3 percent of people in professional and technical occupations (Li, 1996).

The second determinant of immigration is ethnic and racial **stereotypes** — exaggerated, oversimplified images of the characteristics of social groups. Before 1962, there was a racialized hierarchy of desirability in Canadian immigration policy. Immigration policy was based on the assumption that European immigrants were racially and culturally superior to all other potential immigrants. Non-Europeans were stereotyped as racially and culturally inferior and, therefore, were not welcome. In the 1950s, for example, immigration officials could bar groups from entering Canada on the grounds that the groups were "unsuited to climatic and economic conditions" or that they were "unable to assimilate" (Bolaria and Li, 1988). These phrases were thinly veiled masks for racial preferences in the selection of immigrants.

Since 1962, ethnic and racial stereotyping in selecting new immigrants has become less important. Canadian immigration policy is now more open in terms of the ethnic and racial origins of immigrants. Before 1961, Europeans made up over 90 percent of total immigrants to Canada. In the period 1981–91, Europeans declined to 25 percent of total immigrants and people from Asia and the Middle East made up 48 percent of the total immigration flow to Canada (see Figure 9.1).

The third variable that shapes immigrant selection consists of a variety of geopolitical considerations stemming from Canada's relationships with other countries. Racist selection criteria were taken out of immigration regulations in the 1960s, in part because they interfered with Canadian international diplomacy. In the early 1960s, Canada began to assert itself as a middle power in world politics that could mediate social conflicts in and between other countries. Outside of Europe, though, our diplomats did not have much credibility because our immigration policy implied that certain groups were inferior and therefore not suited to life in Canada (Hawkins, 1989).

In the 1980s, the Cold War also played a role in shaping who was let in. According to Whitaker (1987) there was a double standard at work in the

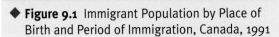

◆ Figure 9.1 Immigrant Population by Place of Birth and Period of Immigration, Canada, 1991

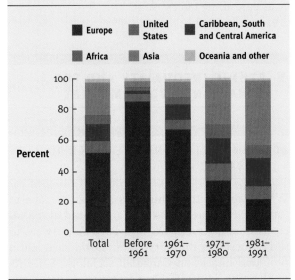

SOURCE: Statistics Canada, *The Daily*, Cat. no. 11-001E, December 8, 1992, p. 6. Reproduced by authority of the Minister of Industry, 1997.

gration but who were concerned that immigration had certain negative effects on Canadian institutions; 21 percent were "indifferent" in their attitudes toward immigration and ambivalent about the contributions that immigrants make; 19 percent were "reactionaries" who felt that the government has lost control over immigration and that immigration was largely negative for Canada. The remaining 15 percent had no opinion on immigration (Holton and Lanphier, 1994).

Holton and Lanphier (1994) suggest that these findings point to a hardening of Canadian attitudes toward immigration. Zong (1994) argues that the federal government has responded to this hardening of attitudes by cutting target levels of immigration, placing more emphasis on the skills that immigrants can bring to the labour market, recruiting European immigrants, and narrowing the definition of who can be sponsored under the family class (see next page). More research, though, is needed to substantiate the link between public opinion and immigration policy.

▲ THE CONTEMPORARY IMMIGRATION CATEGORIES

There are three main categories of immigrants in Canada: refugees, family class, and independent immigrants. Altogether, there were just over 250 000 immigrants to Canada in 1993 (Richmond, 1994: 257).

Refugees

About 30 000 refugees were admitted to Canada in 1993 (Richmond, 1994: 257). There are two categories of refugees that Canada accepts through its immigration program. *Convention refugees* are people who are defined as refugees by the 1951 Geneva Convention Relating to the Status of Refugees and its 1967 protocol. They are people who, by reason of their race, religion, nationality, membership in a particular social group, or political opinion live outside of their country of nationality or their country of habitual residence, and who are unable or unwilling, because of fear of persecution, to return to their country of origin (Citizenship and Immigration Canada, 1996: 28).

Canada also accepts *designated classes of refugees*. These include political prisoners and oppressed peoples who still live in their home countries but who are in refugee-like situations, and self-exiled persons.

admittance of refugees. People who managed to escape from the Soviet Union or other Eastern Bloc countries were routinely granted refugee status in Canada. In 1985, for example, it took a day for the brother of a Czech hockey star who played for the Toronto Maple Leafs to be granted refugee status in Canada. Canadian immigration bureaucrats were much more cautious, however, about admitting "socialist" refugees who were fleeing right-wing dictatorships in various Central American countries.

The fourth variable affecting immigrant selection is humanitarianism. Canada accepts immigrants and refugees partly on humanitarian and compassionate grounds. In 1986, Canada was the first country ever to be awarded the Nansen Medal by the United Nations for its generosity and commitment to international refugee programs (Fleras and Elliot, 1996).

The influence of the fifth variable, public opinion, is more difficult to determine, in part because Canadians do not speak with one voice regarding immigration. A 1991 poll found five distinct segments of opinion regarding immigration. Twenty-three percent were "protagonists" who supported increased levels of immigration and believed that immigrants made important contributions to the betterment of Canadian society; 22 percent were "concerned supporters" who approved of current levels of immi-

Canada also, from time to time, admits individuals and groups as refugees because of special hardships due to such events as civil war and political upheaval. For example, special measures have been introduced over the years to accept people from Iran, Sri Lanka, Vietnam, and Lebanon.

Family Class Immigrants

About 111 000 *family class immigrants* arrived in Canada in 1993 (Richmond, 1994: 257). Family class immigrants have close family members already living in Canada who are willing and able to support them. A sponsor must be a Canadian citizen or a permanent resident who is over 19 years of age and who is living in Canada. Depending on the specific circumstances, a sponsor must be able to provide for the lodging, care, maintenance, and normal settlement needs of the family member(s) for between one and ten years (Citizenship and Immigration Canada, 1996).

Independent Immigrants

Independent immigrants numbered about 103 000 in 1993 (Richmond, 1994: 257). The federal government is trying to increase the size of this category in total immigration flows, because it believes that they are of greater economic benefit to Canada than other categories of immigrants. There are five subcategories of independent immigrants. *Skilled workers* are selected by the federal government on the basis of merit as measured by the **points system**. As Table 9.2 shows, applicants are awarded points for various attributes that the Canadian government deems important in determining an immigrant's economic and settlement prospects. An applicant has to earn a minimum of 70 out of 107 points to gain admission to Canada as a skilled worker.

Immigrant entrepreneurs are people who establish or invest in a business in Canada that they will personally run, and that will result in the creation of at least one new job. *Immigrant investors* are capitalists who have a personal net worth of at least $500 000 and who plan to invest in a business in Canada. If immigrant investors plan to settle in British Columbia, Ontario, or Quebec, they have to invest a minimum of $350 000. In the other provinces and territories, they must invest a minimum of $250 000 (Wong and Netting, 1992). *Self-employed immigrants* have to establish or buy a business in Canada. The business must create a job for the applicant and make a significant contribution to the economic, cultural,

or artistic life of Canada. Finally, *assisted relatives* are sons, daughters, brothers, sisters, nieces, nephews, grandchildren, aunts, and uncles who do not qualify as part of the family class.

■ ETHNIC INEQUALITY AND THE CANADIAN LABOUR MARKET

▲ JOHN PORTER AND THE VERTICAL MOSAIC

What happens to immigrants after they come to Canada? How are they sorted and placed in the socioeconomic structure? John Porter's answers to these questions in *The Vertical Mosaic* have had a profound impact on Canadian sociology. Since its publication in 1965, Canadian sociologists have been interested in whether ethnicity and race affect the operation of the labour market, social mobility, and the composition of elites.

Porter argued that Canada is a **vertical mosaic,** a society in which ethnic groups tend to occupy different and unequal positions in the stratification system. He suggested that the first ethnic group to take control of a previously unoccupied or newly conquered territory is the *charter group* of that society. One of the prerogatives that go to a charter group is the ability to decide "what other groups are to be let in and what they will be permitted to do" (Porter, 1965: 62). Canada has two charter groups, the English and the French. Although their power was, and is, unequal, Porter argued that the two charter groups have been able to set the terms by which other immigrants are admitted to Canada. These charter groups also reserved for themselves the top positions in the occupational hierarchy. They also made up the upper ranks of the labour, political, bureaucratic, religious, and media elites.

Immigrants who arrived after these charter groups were assigned to less-preferred positions. Non-English and non-French immigrants were assigned an *entrance status* that was linked in part to the social evaluation of their cultural and racial capacities. Groups from northern and western Europe were considered more racially and culturally like the English and French, and were accorded a higher entrance status than southern and eastern European immigrants. The latter were regarded as culturally, if not racially, inferior to the charter groups and were therefore placed in lower levels of the occupa-

◆ **Table 9.2** The Points System for the Selection of Independent Immigrants, Canada, 1996

Criteria	Units of assessment (maximum)
Education	16 points
Experience	8 points
Specific vocational preparation	18 points
Age	10 points
Knowledge of French and/or English	15 points
Personal suitability	10 points
Bonus for self-employed immigrants	30 points
Demographic factor	10 points
Arranged employment or designated occupation	10 points
Occupation found on the General or Designated Occupations List[a]	10 points
Minimum selection points required per category	
Investor	25 points
Entrepreneur	25 points
Self-employed	70 points
Skilled worker	70 points
Assisted relative	65 points

[a] The General Occupation List is based on ongoing analysis of the labour market and of applications received abroad. It identifies occupations that are in demand and that can, on a national basis, absorb newcomers into Canada. The Designated Occupation List relates to labour-market needs currently identified by six provinces: Newfoundland, Ontario, Manitoba, Saskatchewan, Alberta, and British Columbia.

SOURCE: Citizenship and Immigration Canada, *You Asked About . . . Immigration and Citizenship* (Ottawa: Supply and Services Canada, 1996), pp. 22–23. Reproduced with the permission of the Minister of Public Works and Government Services Canada, 1997.

tional hierarchy and excluded from elite positions. Non-Europeans were defined as unassimilable and were virtually barred from entry (Woodsworth, 1972).

Porter argued that once the vertical mosaic was established, it took on a life of its own. Immigrants and their descendants who were initially allocated a subordinate entrance status faced limited prospects for upward social mobility. He thought two factors accounted for the rigidity of the vertical mosaic. One was blatant prejudice and discrimination by charter groups. The other was the retention by ethnic groups of cultural practices that were incompatible with economic success in modern, industrialized societies. In other words, certain immigrants and their descendants were caught in an *ethnic mobility trap* because of their continued identification with a subordinated and marginalized ethnic group (Wiley, 1967).

Taken in the context of its time, Porter's analysis was both powerful and insightful. As we have seen, before 1962, the selection of new immigrants was based on ethnic and racial stereotypes. These stereotypes also shaped charter group perceptions of what kinds of jobs other immigrants were fit to do. In the 1950s, for example, Italian immigrant men were regarded by immigration bureaucrats and members of the economic elite as culturally willing and able to "tolerate irregular employment, low wages and physically demanding work." They were recruited specifically for work in agriculture, mining, domestic service, the metal trades, and logging (Iacovetta, 1992: 28). Black women from the Caribbean, on the other hand, were recruited specifically as housekeepers and nannies for middle-class families in the 1950s and 1960s, in part because they were believed to be nurturing and passive (Daenzer, 1993).

▲ THE DECLINING SIGNIFICANCE OF THE VERTICAL MOSAIC?

Does the vertical mosaic still exist? Is the distribution of economic rewards still based on ethnicity? Over the past two decades, debates have raged among Canadian sociologists about whether race and ethnicity continue to shape our stratification system (Brym with Fox, 1989). Gordon Darroch (1979) and Edward Herberg (1990) argue that the vertical mosaic is no longer a useful way of describing our society. Later in his life, John Porter also had doubts about its existence (Pineo and Porter, 1985). Others argue that, while we may be moving in the direction of greater equality, the vertical mosaic is still a useful metaphor to describe our society. They suggest that the vertical mosaic has been recast along racial lines (Fleras and Elliot, 1996).

There are three main empirical findings that are relevant to the debate about the vertical mosaic in present-day Canada. First, Canadian society is much more open than it once was in terms of the social evaluation of European immigrants and their descendants. The European groups that Porter identified in the mid-1960s as occupying subordinate entrance statuses — particularly Ukrainians, Italians, Poles, Greeks, and Italians — have been able to move up the socioeconomic hierarchy (Hou and Balakrishnan, 1996). This mobility has occurred both within and between generations — that is, it has been both intra- and intergenerational. Long-settled European immigrants and their descendants have attained income and occupation levels that are comparable to the charter groups. They have also begun to occupy positions in various elites. For example, it is now common for members of these communities to be elected to federal and provincial legislatures (Iacovetta, 1992).

Second, the earnings and occupational distributions of visible-minority men and women who are born in Canada are comparable to those of the charter groups and of other Europeans. Boyd (1992) and Reitz and Breton (1994) demonstrate this by statistically controlling for variations in earnings due to factors such as occupation, age, region of residence, education, and number of weeks worked per year (see also Geschwender, 1994). Using these methods, they show that, on average, Canadian-born visible-minority men and women earn about the same incomes as other men and women in Canada earn. Thus, there does not seem to be a pattern of racially based disadvantage for individuals born, raised, and educated in Canada.

Third, however, evidence suggests that the vertical mosaic exists in modified form for non-European immigrants. Although immigrants from Europe have been able to make their way up the

The storefront of a downtown Toronto drugstore reflects the ethnic diversity of most large Canadian cities. SOURCE: Dick Hemingway.

occupational and income hierarchies, more recent visible-minority immigrants have been less successful. Despite having education levels that are, on average, higher than the Canadian population as a whole (Lian and Matthews, 1995), visible-minority immigrants earn less than both European immigrants and those who were born in Canada (Boyd, 1992). According to Table 9.3, when differences in earnings due to a number of other background variables are controlled for, foreign-born visible minorities earned $3068 less than the average for all Canadians, foreign-born white Canadians earned $1027 more than the average for all Canadians, and native-born white and visible-minority Canadians earned, respectively, slightly above and slightly below the average for all Canadians in 1991.

These findings suggest that there is not a single, clear-cut pattern of ethnic or racial economic disadvantage in Canada. Studies suggest that, in certain circumstances, ethnic attachments may be a resource that groups of people use to get ahead. Professionals in law, business, and medicine may achieve levels of upward mobility and economic security by offering services in their mother tongue and in ways that are sensitive to the culture of their ethnic group (Brym with Fox, 1989).

But ethnicity is not an advantage for all. There are two interrelated explanations for the lower earnings of visible-minority immigrants. First, the education credentials of visible-minority immigrants are devalued in the labour market and by certification authorities. In one celebrated case, an evalua-tion officer of the Ontario Ministry of Education wrote to a Jamaican immigrant that his honours degree from Harvard University and his Ph.D. from Stanford were equivalent to "at least Grade Thirteen in the Ontario school system" (Special Committee on the Participation of Visible Minorities in Canadian Society, 1984). Although this may have been a bureaucratic error, there is evidence showing that many immigrant teachers, doctors, nurses, and engineers find that their non-Western university degrees and diplomas are of little value in Canada (Henry et al., 1995).

Second, research on employers' hiring practices has documented the influence of racial discrimination in employment. Henry and Ginsberg (1985) organized a study in Toronto where they sent two actors with virtually identical résumés to apply for various jobs. The only difference between the two was the colour of their skin and/or their accent: One group consisted of actors who were white and who had Anglo-Canadian accents, and the other group of actors were members of visible minorities, some of whom had other accents. The study found that, in both face-to-face interviews and approaches over the telephone, whites received three job offers for every job offered to visible-minority applicants. Visible-minority applicants were five times more likely to be told that the job had been filled when a subsequent white applicant was invited for an interview (Henry and Ginsberg, 1985).

A follow-up study conducted in 1989 showed there was no racial discrimination in job offers fol-

◆ **Table 9.3** Average Employment Earnings of Groups by Racial Origin and Nativity, Canada, 1991

Racial groups	Number	Employment earnings as deviations above or below national average[a]	
		Gross	Net
Native-born white Canadians	341 670	−$57	$204
Foreign-born white Canadians	51 921	4 171	1 027
Native-born visible minorities	5 755	−4 894	−654
Foreign-born visible minorities	34 269	−2 710	−3 068
Aboriginal peoples	12 698	−5 992	−1 122

[a] The average employment earnings for all groups was $23 740. Gross earnings are actual differences from the mean when variations in other variables have not been statistically accounted for. Net earnings in deviations are residual differences after variations in years of education, age, nativity, full-time/part-time employment, gender, industry of work, occupation, and number of weeks worked have been statistically controlled for.

SOURCE: Peter Li, "The Market Value and Social Value of Race," in Vic Satzewich, ed., *Racism and Social Inequality in Canada: Concepts and Controversies* (Toronto: Thompson Educational, 1998). Reprinted with permission of the publisher.

lowing face-to-face contacts between applicants and employers. Blacks and whites received equal numbers of job offers. When it came to approaches over the telephone, however, callers with foreign accents were less likely to be invited for an interview, and more likely to be told that the job was filled when in fact it was not, than callers with North American accents (Henry, 1989).

■ "CANADIAN": MORE THAN A BRAND OF BEER?

In most of this chapter I have talked about the various ways that ethnicity and race are bases on which power and resources are unevenly distributed. Even though Canada is ethnically diverse, and even though racism, discrimination, and inequality are features of our society, compared with many other countries we live together in reasonable harmony. Certainly, most Canadians find the civil wars and ethnic cleansing in places like the former Yugoslavia, Rwanda, and Burundi incomprehensible. Despite our diversity and differences, we may have more in common than we sometimes think.

If any of you have travelled outside of North America, you probably came across someone who initially thought you were American. With the politeness characteristic of Canadians, I am sure that you gently informed the unknowing offender, "I'm not American, I'm Canadian!" Whether or not you were offended at being mistaken as American, being "not American" also means that we think of ourselves as being *culturally* different from Americans in terms of how we think, feel, believe, act, and relate to others. We are also saying something *positive* about our identity as Canadians.

The search for a Canadian identity and Canadian culture is elusive. It is not, though, a lost cause. There are sociological reasons why it is useful to start thinking about the term "Canadian" as more than the sum of our differences, or as just a brand of beer. It is entirely possible that "Canadians" are becoming an ethnic group.

The Caribana parade, a large annual celebration of Caribbean culture in Toronto. SOURCE: Dick Hemingway.

▲ IS "CANADIAN" AN ETHNICITY?

As we have seen, ethnic and racial categories and identities are socially constructed and negotiated. There is not a fixed number of ethnic groups in the world that have existed from time immemorial, and that cannot be added to or subtracted from. Assimilation and genocide occur. Some ethnic groups lose their distinctiveness and are amalgamated into other groups, and some, as in the former Yugoslavia, have been targets of ethnic cleansing. At the same time, new ethnic groups are created out of processes of assimilation, conquest, and migration.

Most of the ethnic categories that we now take for granted are actually recent historical creations. The ethnic category "English" would have been un-thinkable to the person who lived in the British Isles 800 years ago. People defined themselves, and were defined by others, as Celts, Saxons, Normans, and so on. Only some of those people came to be known as "the English" (Lieberson, 1991). Similarly, the people whom we now think of as "Germans" did not exist 150 years ago. As these examples suggest, the way in which people define themselves, and are defined by others, is in constant flux (Lieberson, 1991: 444). If we take a long view, it is common for ethnic categories and identities to be recast and created anew.

This is what seems to be happening in Canada now. There has crystallized a feeling of commonality that is the basis for a common ethnic identification.

In preparing for the 1991 census, Statistics Canada held meetings, organized focus groups, and tested different ways of posing questions that tried to measure the ethnicity of our population. One of the things that Statistics Canada found was that there "was a strong tendency [for respondents] to report Canadian as their ethnic origin and as their ethnic identity" (White, 1992: 166). In one trial, "Canadian" was listed as one of the sixteen possible responses (alongside ethnic groups such as "French," "English," "German," "Scottish," "Italian," "Ukrainian") to the question, "What are the ethnic or cultural origins of your parents and grandparents?" Thirty-six percent of respondents identified their "ethnic or cultural origins" as Canadian. When Statistics Canada tested questions about the ethnic group that people "identified" with (a subjective measure of ethnicity), 50 percent responded "Canadian" (White, 1992: 167; see also Pineo and Porter, 1985: 359).

Even though a significant portion of people who participated in the census pretests identified their "roots" and "identity" as "Canadian," Statistics Canada chose not to list "Canadian" as one of the possible response categories in the 1991 census. People could still write "Canadian" in response to questions about their ethnic identity, but when "Canadian" was not listed as a possible ethnicity, the number of people who identified themselves as such decreased dramatically, from between 36 and 50 percent in the test scenarios to 2.8 percent in the actual census. Largely because of political pressure, "Canadian" was included as a response category in the ethnicity question for the 1996 census.

Why do some of us define our ethnic roots or ethnic identity as "Canadian"? Some of us may simply be unaware or uninterested in our so-called roots and, hence, by default define ourselves as Canadian. For others, defining ourselves as Canadian is a political act used to express our dissatisfaction with the government's policy of multiculturalism (White, 1992: 168–69). At the same time, though, there are many of us who insist that we are Canadian because that is simply the group with whom we identify, and with whom we share a sense of belonging (Howard, 1996; Angus Reid Group, 1991). More than 130 years after the the creation of the Canadian state, it is clear that a Canadian ethnicity has been forged. ■

● SUMMARY

1. Racism refers to certain kinds of ideas and to certain kinds of institutional practices. Institutional racism refers to circumstances where social institutions operate, or once operated, on the basis of racist ideas. There are three forms of institutional racism.
2. Racism, prejudice, and discrimination have been analyzed from different sociological perspectives. Social-psychological theories, primordialism, normative theories, and power-conflict theories each offer different interpretations of ethnic and racial hostility.
3. The term "aboriginal people" includes people who are defined in the Constitution as "Indian," "Métis," and "Inuit." The terms used to describe aboriginal people are socially negotiated and change because of shifts in power relations among groups.

4. The culture of poverty thesis was used in the 1970s as a way of explaining the poor socioeconomic conditions of aboriginal people. Problems with the culture of poverty thesis led to the development of the internal colonial model, a variant of conflict theory. Conflict and feminist sociologists are beginning to be more interested in class and gender diversity within the aboriginal population.

5. French–English relations in Canada are about power relations. Material inequalities between French and English in Quebec provided the historical basis for the emergence of nationalism in Quebec. The contemporary nationalist movement has a diverse class base.

6. There are debates in the nationalist movement about who is Québécois. Tensions exist between ethnic and civic nationalists. Minorities in Quebec fear that they will not be included in the definition of a sovereign Quebec nation.

7. Immigration has played different roles in Canadian history. During the nineteenth century, immigrants contributed to capitalist state formation. Now, immigrants contribute to the social and economic reproduction of Canadian society.

8. There are five main variables that have shaped immigrant selection in Canada: social class, ethnic and racial stereotypes, geopolitical considerations, humanitarianism, and public opinion. Immigrants are categorized as refugees, family class, or independents. Independent immigrants are selected on the basis of the points system.

9. John Porter argued that Canada was a vertical mosaic, a social structure where ethnic groups occupy different, and unequal, positions within the stratification system. Evidence suggests that the vertical mosaic is declining in importance, at least for European immigrants and people born in Canada. Discrimination against visible-minority immigrants is still a problem.

10. Canadians may be an ethnic group. Ethnic categories and identities are not fixed and unchanging; they evolve socially and historically. Canadians display a strong desire to define their ethnicity as Canadian.

QUESTIONS TO CONSIDER

1. What are the strengths and weaknesses of different sociological approaches to the study of the social significance of race and ethnicity?
2. Does racism have any impact on the operation of social institutions in Canada?
3. How do you think the nationalist movement in Quebec will resolve the question of who is part of the imagined community of the nation?
4. Do you think that the importance of class and gender diversity within aboriginal communities will increase or decrease in the future?
5. Are Canadians an ethnic group? Why or why not?

GLOSSARY

civic nationalism A form of nationalism where the social boundaries of the nation are defined in territorial and geographic terms.

culture of poverty thesis The theory that some ethnic groups do not readily assimilate, and hence are poor, because their culture does not value economic success, hard work, and achievement.

discrimination Practices that deny members of particular groups equal access to societal rewards.

ethnocentrism A tendency to judge other groups by the standards and values of one's own group.

institutional racism Discriminatory racial practices built into such prominent structures as the political, economic, and education systems.

new racism A theory of human nature that suggests that it is natural for groups to form bounded communities. One group is neither better nor worse than another, but feelings of antagonism will be aroused if outsiders are admitted.

points system A system used by the Canadian government to select independent immigrants. Applicants are awarded "points" for various attributes that the Canadian government deems important in determining an immigrant's economic contribution to Canada.

prejudice An unfavourable, generalized, and rigid belief applied to all members of a group.

primordialist thesis The theory that ethnic attachments reflect a basic tendency of people to seek out, and associate with, their "own kind."

Quiet Revolution The social, political, and cultural changes that occurred in Quebec in the 1960s, due in part to the emergence of a francophone middle class.

race A socially constructed label that has been used to describe certain kinds of physical and genetic differences between people.

split labour-market theory The theory that racial and ethnic conflict are rooted in differences in the price of labour.

stereotypes Exaggerated, oversimplified images of the characteristics of social categories.

vertical mosaic A social structure where ethnic groups occupy different, and unequal, positions within the stratification system.

SUGGESTED READING

Boldt, Menno. (1993). *Surviving as Indians: The Challenge of Self-Government.* Toronto: University of Toronto Press. A controversial analysis of the challenges facing aboriginal communities in their pursuit of self-government. Boldt argues that there is a two-class social order in reserve communities and that this class structure has important implications for how self-government is defined and pursued.

Fleras, Augie, and Jean Elliot. (1996). *Unequal Relations: An Introduction to Race, Ethnic and Aboriginal Dynamics in Canada.* Scarborough, ON: Prentice Hall. An in-depth discussion that integrates a variety of theoretical approaches and empirical findings to explain why race and ethnicity matter in Canada.

Henry, Frances, Carol Tator, Winston Mattis, and Tim Rees. (1995). *The Colour of Democracy: Racism in Canadian Society.* Toronto: Harcourt Brace. A comprehensive discussion of the meaning and significance of racism in Canadian society, focussing on both institutional and individual-level racism.

Miles, Robert. (1989). *Racism.* London: Routledge. One of the best discussions of the meaning of race and racism in modern Western societies. Miles argues strongly for a social constructionist approach to race and racism.

Reitz, Jeffrey, and Raymond Breton. (1994). *The Illusion of Difference: Realities of Ethnicity in Canada and the United States.* Toronto: C.D. Howe Institute. A good discussion of how Canada compares with the United States in terms of how cultural minorities fit into the two societies. Reitz and Breton show that there are fewer differences between the two countries than Canadians often think.

CHAPTER TEN

Inequality among Nations: Perspectives on Development

IN THIS CHAPTER YOU WILL LEARN THAT

- transnational corporations are prepared to shift the site of work in order to maximize profits; this has massive implications for the employment and well-being of ordinary citizens
- 250 years ago there were only small gaps in living standards and levels of productivity between countries; now the gaps are huge
- the poor countries today are mainly those that were colonized by the West
- liberal development theory argues that if markets are allowed to function without state interference, prosperity follows; but although liberal theory has been adopted by the International Monetary Fund, transnational corporations, and the U.S. government, it has not led to policies that improve the well-being of most Third World citizens
- dependency theory suggests that underdevelopment is the result of foreign economic and political control; the spectacular development breakthroughs of Japan, South Korea, and Sweden illustrate that domestic control of corporations and activist governments can be the keys to economic success
- more democratic and egalitarian development policies, such as those of the Indian state of Kerala, will benefit all countries

GORDON LAXER
University of Alberta

INTRODUCTION

Human history is long; individual lives are short. World War II (1939–45) truly ended only when the Berlin Wall fell in 1989 and the Soviet Union collapsed two years later. The period up to the final end of the war and of the partition of Europe was a short time in human history, but it was the majority of the lifetime of those who lived through it.

When we think of **development,** we must think in terms of the time span of human history rather than that of individual lives. Not that much has changed in the economic-development rankings of nations since I was born in 1944. The countries that were more "developed" in the 1940s are by and large the ones that are more "developed" now. Only a few countries have made spectacular moves up or down. Hong Kong[1] and Singapore, two small city-states, are the only ones to have broken through to development levels comparable to those of the advanced Western countries. South Korea and Taiwan have shifted from low to middle levels. A few, such as Argentina and most of the former communist countries of Eastern Europe, have deteriorated badly, moving down from middle to somewhat lower levels. In the 1940s, Japan was already the sixth-largest industrial economy, a strength reflected in its sustained military challenge to the United States during World War II.

Economic development is usually portrayed as involving anonymous processes and inevitable movement in one direction. "Urbanization," "industrialization," "technological progress," "rising standards of living" — all imply unstoppable processes. Are there human decision-makers behind these changes, or are we captives of nonhuman forces?

I will argue in this chapter that the anonymous phrases connected with development hide the major actors of the past two centuries: business in its pursuit of profits, and the most powerful states. Since World War II, **supranational** agencies and associations closely connected to business, such as the **International Monetary Fund (IMF),** the **International Bank for Reconstruction and Development (IBRD;** also known as the **World Bank),** the **G-7,** and the **European Union (EU),** emerged as a third set of actors shaping world development. As communications technologies evolved, corporations could move around more, as if location did not matter. States were less mobile, tied as they were to political territories and to gaining political legitimacy from immobile labour — that is, the citizens of a country. But the most powerful states could extend their influence over weaker states by two ways. Formal colonization was the old means. The new ways involved dominant states exercising influence over supranational agencies such as the IMF and by championing the interests of "their" **transnational corporations.** Other means used to coerce weaker states involved using diplomacy or applying trade and investment sanctions, or by virtue of the fact of their superior military strength. The world's sole remaining superpower, the United States, has exercised considerable influence over other countries, largely by the newer means.

Much of the motivation for changing the world's economy derives from periodic crises of profitability for the major businesses and corporations. These crises have affected the location of economic development. In the early phases of **industrialization** (1760–1960), modern industry and infrastructure developed in a few countries that were to become the advanced **capitalist** economies. Increasingly, profits were made by continuously expanding production and consumption in the economically advanced countries. The leading businesses and the states in which they were located saw the rest of the world as a source of cheap raw materials and as a captive market for their products. Colonization of much of the world ensured that businesses in the economically advanced countries held monopoly positions over the resources and markets of the colonies. For the most part, little interest was shown in locating manufacturing or services in the colonies.

From the late 1960s, capitalist strategy changed. In the few developed countries, wage-earners had gained more economic and political power. Democratic electorates demanded that generous social services be provided and that businesses be regulated to serve the interests of the wider community. These gains for the majority of citizens led to one of capitalism's periodic profitability crises. In response, the new corporate strategy was to escape the "pay explosion" in the rich countries and restore profit rates by shifting production to some of the poor countries (Arrighi, 1993).

Early capitalists reaped high profits through the superexploitation of workers. Later, leading transnationals, such as Reebok, General Electric, and McDonald's, copied their predecessors. Some hired

I benefited greatly from the outstanding critique Josee Johnston provided of an earlier version of this chapter. Peter Puplampu did extensive research in preparation of the earlier version.

Part Four INSTITUTIONS

INSTITUTIONS PERFORM THE BASIC FUNCTIONS OF SOCIETY. FOR EXAMPLE, THE FAMILY USUALLY SERVES AS THE BASIS FOR PROCREATION AND EARLY SOCIALIZATION OF CHILDREN. EDUCATIONAL INSTITUTIONS THEN PROVIDE SECONDARY SOCIALIZATION AND TRAINING. APPROPRIATELY SOCIALIZED AND TRAINED PEOPLE ARE THEN SLOTTED INTO WORK ORGANIZATIONS THAT PROVIDE THE MATERIAL BASIS FOR SOCIAL LIFE. THIS PAINTING EVOKES THE RECRUITMENT OF PEOPLE INTO VARIOUS INSTITUTIONAL ROLES, THUS INTRODUCING US TO THE SUBJECT MATTER OF THIS PART.

CHAPTER ELEVEN
Families

IN THIS CHAPTER YOU WILL LEARN THAT

■ while common sense suggests that current dilemmas in family life are private problems, sociology helps uncover their public sources and solutions

■ the family does not take a universal form and its structure is therefore not a product of some biological imperative: families vary widely in the way they are organized across different cultures and through history, and family organization is loosely related to the way material production is organized

■ our society is organized around a sexual division of labour and the heterosexual nuclear family; this is the main reason why families that assume a different form — especially lone-parent families — have a particularly hard time meeting the needs of their members

■ as women have increasingly assumed part of the financial support of their families, men have not substantially increased the work they do in the home, nor has society changed in ways that accommodate this changed reality for families

■ the sexual division of labour that makes it possible for nuclear families to care for young children involves sizable liabilities for women and children: the social isolation of full-time mothers and the stress attached to their high-demand, low-control situation reduce the quality of child care

■ the chief negative effect of divorce, for women and children, is the loss of income that follows; the most effective solution to this problem — government support of all children — has not been adopted by the Canadian government, although most advanced industrial societies do have such a policy objective

BONNIE J. FOX
University of Toronto

■ INTRODUCTION

Contemporary life presents difficult choices for those of us who live in or plan to live in families. The constraints on these choices affect our lives profoundly. I begin this chapter by reviewing dilemmas in family life in the light of popular myths. Because family life is so familiar to us, we all too easily accept common-sense understandings that portray family problems as personal, private, and attributable to "human nature." Common-sense solutions prescribe individual change and ignore the social context. In contrast, sociology uncovers the social origins of family patterns and the problems they entail.

As a way of challenging the common-sense perspective, the second section of this chapter examines two patterns of family life that are different from our own. In these cases, it is clear that the family patterns people have created are a response to the problems posed by the needs of daily survival. Next, I review the history that produced our own family arrangements.

In the chapter's fourth section, I explore some of the main features of family life today: heterosexuality, marriage, parenthood, and the **sexual division of labour** (i.e., the difference in the work men and women do). My aim is to analyze how these activities are organized in order to give you an idea of the sources of problems that often plague modern families. I then discuss divorce and its aftermath, lone-parent and reconstituted families. I finish with a brief discussion of possible government policies to support families.

■ EXPLORING THE FAMILIAR: THE FAMILY IN WESTERN SOCIETY TODAY

▲ DILEMMAS OF CONTEMPORARY FAMILY LIFE

When you imagine yourself at age 39, you probably think of yourself as married, with a child or two. You probably also assume — or at least hope — that your children will enjoy full-time mothering for their early years. You are not unusual if you envision your adulthood in family terms. Moreover, when you think of family, you probably think of the conventional nuclear family, in which the man is the main breadwinner and the woman has primary responsibility for the children.

At the same time, you probably have nagging concerns about your future. Full-time mothering seems a luxury few women can afford these days. Most married women — even those with young children — now have to assume some of the responsibility of breadwinning. Indeed, women attending university anticipate building a career, which involves far more commitment and time than does simply holding a job. Building a career virtually precludes taking time out for children, because the necessary commitment is at odds with the demands of motherhood. These realities beg obvious questions: Women wonder when there will be time to have children and how they will care for them once they arrive.

Whereas women's concerns about family tend to focus on the difficulties of combining employment and child care, men's concerns probably centre on the growing elusiveness of the breadwinner role in this uncertain economy. At the same time, men are increasingly pressured by the women they live with to change in ways for which they are unprepared. Manhood was once equated with occupational success, but such success is now both harder to achieve and insufficient for a happy marriage. Today, many women expect men to be emotionally open in ways that women tend to find easy, in addition to aggressively pursuing occupational success *and* sharing the housework.

Although the conventional nuclear family is in jeopardy, our society still seems to be organized around it and the gender roles it involves. For instance, whether or not the nuclear family is the best unit for raising children, our society offers almost no support for any alternative. Aside from the flurry of gift giving and visiting that occurs when a baby is born, few friends help a new mother with her child-care responsibilities. Whatever support grandparents are inclined to offer is inhibited by the fact that they live in another house, if not another city, as well as by the demands of their employment. In the end, new parents (usually mothers) typically face the dirty diapers and dishes on their own. Moreover, we equate loving, supportive relationships with family. Consequently, when we find ourselves in personal crisis or in need of money, few of us can turn to people outside our immediate families for help.

Conventional gender roles also seem central to the organization of our society. It is difficult to keep a family going with no one home to buy groceries, plan and make meals, organize doctors' appointments, and meet repair persons. The dearth of good, affordable day care means that having children is difficult unless the mother becomes a full-time homemaker. And men have depended on the emotional support and caring work provided by their wives to keep them sane and productive.

Generally, the conventional division of labour by sex has solved the problems created by an economy in which employers bear no direct responsibility for the welfare of their employees' families. Men's ability to return to their paid work every day has depended on women's homemaking to restore and sustain their energy (Luxton, 1980). Thus, women's work of caring for others has been essential to the economy as well as to people's welfare.

Clearly, the future poses various dilemmas. How will we earn enough money to support a family and raise our children at the same time? How will we sustain loving relationships with our partners while coping with the problems outlined above? Indeed, are our ideals about family sustainable? And if the conventional nuclear family is an unlikely prospect for most of us, how will we live in a society that still assumes it to be an essential part of life?

▲ MYTHS ABOUT FAMILY

Thinking through these dilemmas is especially difficult because myths about family pervade our culture. Measured against the idealized image of family life that emerged during the 1950s and was beamed into homes across the country by television, the problems in family life today assume crisis proportions. "The family" seems to be disintegrating. Actually, real families in the 1950s bore little resemblance to those depicted in *Leave It to Beaver* and *Father Knows Best*. Nevertheless, the 1950s was an unusually "familistic" decade: People married earlier, had more children, and were less likely to divorce than the generations that preceded and followed them (E. May, 1988). The 1950s are thus an odd benchmark.

Also mythical is the popular view that the traditional European family consisted of three generations living harmoniously under one roof, caring for all its members. In fact, **extended-family households** — consisting of three generations — were rare in preindustrial Europe. Moreover, children spent as much of their childhood in the care of people other than their parents as they did at home; and the elderly did not expect to be cared for lovingly by their children. Where large extended families

Idealized images of the "traditional" family and the perfect marriage were beamed into homes by television in the 1950s. SOURCE: Dick Hemingway.

were common — for instance, among the wealthy in ancient China — the lives of all but the male patriarch were wholly circumscribed by his authority over life and limb.

▲ "FAMILY VALUES"

Some politicians have taken advantage of the popular belief that the family is in crisis. The call for a return to "family values" has been especially pronounced in the U.S. political arena. Although it is not clear exactly what "family values" are, the phrase evokes an undefined past, free of today's social problems, a time when the values we associate with family — community, decency, morality — were dominant. The family in political rhetoric is the symbol of all that is good and decent, and the bedrock on which society rests. Of course, the family in question is the heterosexual breadwinner–homemaker family, and deviations from this ideal are held responsible for myriad social problems.

In practice, family-values advocates call for policies that punish deviations from the nuclear-family ideal. They want to outlaw abortion, prohibit gay and lesbian marriages and parenthood, and encourage women to stay home with their children rather than provide funding for day-care facilities. It seems obvious that what family-values politicians seek to promote is the continued assumption of responsibility for people's welfare by families, with services provided largely by women — at little or no cost to the state. Adopting an ideology of "less government," these politicians seldom promote policies that actually support families of any kind.

Aside from the political implications of family-values arguments, there are a number of problems with the assumptions and logic of the arguments themselves. Highlighting these problems will raise some of the issues addressed in this chapter. First, the idea that the family is in crisis is problematic because it assumes that there is only one kind of family — the heterosexual, nuclear, breadwinner–homemaker family. Closely related is the assumption that children are always best raised at home by full-time mothers. The third flawed assumption — one that is more subtle, and of special concern to sociologists — is that "society" is simply the sum of individuals who live in it. This assumption is convenient for the family-values proponents because it suggests that the "good old days" could be restored if only large numbers of individuals adopted "family values."

The idea that society is simply the sum of the people who live in it is worth examining. This idea ignores social structure, and, by doing so, misses what is arguably the most important insight of sociology — namely, that the organization of various aspects of society puts constraints on, and creates opportunities for, individuals. In other words, social structure generates powerful social forces that cannot be reduced to individual motivation. Market forces, for example, rather than the greed of individual capitalists, explain much of what occurs in the marketplace.

Consider the following example: A footnote in *Das Kapital,* Karl Marx's pathbreaking analysis and critique of capitalism, tells the story of the efforts of nineteenth-century potter and factory owner Josiah Wedgewood (whose products are still available) to fight the brutal practice of child labour, which was common during early industrial capitalism. Although he was disturbed by the practice, Wedgewood was forced to use children in his own factory in order to keep up with his competition. He therefore wrote to the government to request legislation prohibiting the practice. He explained that market forces made it impossible for him not to use cheap child labour, and he wanted the state to intervene, to

curb those forces. He was not alone. Eventually, after campaigns by organized labour along with a general public outcry, the government passed child-labour laws.

Market forces are perhaps the most obvious and easily understood example of influences that arise from the way society is organized. They are not reducible to individual behaviour. In the Wedgewood example, although it is true that individual capitalists themselves had made the decision to hire children as young as 7 to work in their factories, they had been pressured to do so by the dynamics of a capitalist economy, which generates competition around the prices of products and thus forces participants to minimize costs. Consequently, once one producer opted to use child labour, all the others had to follow suit — or find some other way to drastically reduce labour costs. At that point, the situation was out of the hands of individuals.

Systems of class, gender, and racial inequality are also structural. Although sexism, racism, and other such phenomena are partly a matter of individual attitudes, they are also built into the structure of our society — most fundamentally, as divisions of labour. Indeed, a variety of social forces influence family patterns. Although individuals make choices about whether to marry, have children, and so on, the social forces guiding them toward those decisions are so powerful that most individuals end up making the same choices. The regularities or patterns that result attest to the power of social structure, and are what allow the development of "social science." They also are what make the family an institution — that is, a relatively stable set of roles and practices. Family-values advocates ignore the social forces that shape family patterns; instead, they define family problems and solutions as individual and private.

In sum, the family-values argument represents a popular ideology that confuses attempts to think clearly about family. Sociology offers a more fruitful approach to a subject that is important for us to understand, because we count on family relations to meet our most fundamental needs for love and support. This chapter develops a sociological analysis of family, after debunking what has become a very popular myth.

▲ THE MYTH OF THE NATURAL FAMILY

There is a strong ideology in this culture holding that families should be heterosexual and nuclear — that is, composed of a man, who is the primary breadwinner; a woman, who functions primarily as mother and homemaker; and their children. Because only about 15 percent of Canadian families in 1991 consisted of a married couple in which the man was the exclusive breadwinner, the woman was a full-time mother, and there were unmarried children living at home (Statistics Canada, 1992a, 1993b), concern about the status of families has escalated.

One reason for the popular fixation on the nuclear, breadwinner family is that it seems to derive from the biology of reproduction. Common sense suggests that biology produces the family. Heralded by the news media, arguments based on **biological determinism** are immensely popular these days. One common variant of this approach, known as **sociobiology,** attempts to apply the laws of biological evolution to social behaviour. Sociobiologists hold that, as with physical traits, social behaviour is inherited biologically — in other words, that behaviour can be linked to specific genetic configurations. Typically, sociobiologists construct a story about the history of human evolution that assumes genetic encoding of behaviour — a problematic assumption since there is no evidence to support it (Lewontin, Rose, and Kamin, 1984).

The sociobiological argument about family is that, over the course of human history, certain behaviours were adaptive because they contributed to "reproductive success." Specifically, males who were more aggressive and females who were more nurturant had more offspring. Thus, these behaviours were "naturally selected," and turned up in more and more individuals over the generations. According to this perspective, today's behaviour is the product of human evolution — and thus inevitable.

The family, consisting of the biological mother and father and their offspring, is also a product of evolution, according to sociobiologists. Because children represent people's genetic investment, they argue, evolutionary forces have selected a pattern that is most likely to ensure the survival of offspring — namely, the union of two biological parents in a lasting relationship.

Although sociobiology accords with common sense, its claims do not accord with observable evidence. Evidence on family patterns across various cultures indicates that, although the nuclear family is common in many cultures, it is not always the unit that provides care for children. In many cultures, the nuclear family exists primarily to provide sex and companionship for adults. It is often embedded in larger households or communities, which are the units that govern production, consumption, and child care.

Although parenthood may seem attributable to biology, the cross-cultural evidence makes it clear that fatherhood, at least, is strictly a socially derived identity. Not all societies recognize the role of the father in conception; in some, the mother alone is assumed to provide the matter that becomes a baby. More to the point, fathers are not always expected to assume responsibility to provide for their biological children; often the larger household or community does so.

More basically, **gender** — that is, the behaviour patterns and personality traits typically associated with being female or male — is not a product of biology. Cross-cultural variations in gender make this clear, but so too does current psychological research. For instance, although researchers usually find that boys and men tend to be more physically aggressive than girls and women, there is no evidence from studies of humans that male hormones cause aggressiveness (Fausto-Sterling, 1985). Nurturing behaviour in women is so much assumed that it is seldom studied, but the studies that have been conducted offer no clear evidence of a biologically based tendency.

In short, neither conventional gender roles and the sexual division of labour nor the nuclear-family structure they support are given in our genes. Indeed, many of the things we often assume to be natural and universal are neither. There is a diversity of family patterns across history and cultures: The ways in which people organize to ensure their survival, and that of their children, vary.

▲ CONCEPTUALIZING AND DEFINING FAMILY

Structural Functionalism

It is widely believed that the best unit in which to raise children is the nuclear family. This common-sense notion was promoted by Talcott Parsons (Parsons and Bales, 1955), whose writings on family constituted the dominant perspective in post–World War II sociology. In arguing that an institution (in this case, the family) exists because of the useful functions it performs for the larger society, Parsons was making an argument within the school of thought called **structural functionalism.**

Although structural functionalism dominated the study of families until recently, there are obvious problems with this perspective. First, just because an institution performs a social function, there is no reason to assume that some other institution might not perform that function equally well. Whether exclusive care by the biological mother and father is best for children is an empirical question.

The other key problem with the functionalist perspective is its focus on how institutions create social *order*, and its consequent failure to analyze the tensions in family life that can generate social *change*. Moreover, the functions that are emphasized allegedly meet the needs of society, not necessarily of the individuals in it. So, for instance, while Parsons recognized the problems faced by full-time housewives, it was not until feminists analyzed family life that the power dynamics and conflicts common to families were highlighted.

Definitions

When social scientists define *family,* some of them still assume the nuclear unit. This tendency has often resulted in a focus on the frequency with which nuclear-family patterns appear across history and cultures. Conceptualizing family in a way that focusses on common properties does not serve the interests of good empirical inquiry, however. Focussing on diversity in social patterns can, in contrast, help us acquire a better understanding of the nature of family. By studying diversity, and by noting the social circumstances that vary with family patterns, we can derive some idea of the social forces and factors that influence those patterns.

How one defines family has practical, as well as methodological, consequences. Rights and responsibilities follow from one's definition. For instance, state-regulated institutions such as schools and hospitals often use legal definitions of marriage and family to determine which people will be informed and consulted about the status of someone in the institution. Accordingly, critically ill patients may find that family members with whom they have had little recent contact are admitted to their rooms and entitled to make important medical decisions on their behalf, whereas the friends who have been constant companions and who know them best are excluded. Government entitlements such as widows' pensions and tax deductions for the support of dependants apply only to family relations as defined by the government. A wife of a few years may be entitled to a widow's pension, whereas a same-sex lover of twenty years is not. A woman supporting an elderly and disabled friend cannot take the same tax deduction as a father supporting a child. In short, the matter of definition is of great practical importance.

For the purposes of my analysis, I define *family* as the sets of relationships people create to share resources daily in order to ensure their own and their children's welfare. What this definition offers is a focus on what is of critical importance across many cultures to both individual survival and generational reproduction. At the same time, it does not exclude groupings of people who are in essence functioning as family, though they may lack formal recognition as such (e.g., lesbian or gay partners with children, or female relatives who live separately but co-operate daily to care for their children).

This definition holds family to be the unit of **social reproduction.** As opposed to biological reproduction, social reproduction refers to a wide range of activities that "maintain existing life and ... reproduce the next generation" (Laslett and Brenner, 1989: 381–403). In other words, social reproduction refers to feeding, clothing, and otherwise looking after people's subsistence needs, as well as nurturing and socializing children and emotionally supporting adults. In short, "family" refers to the sets of relationships that work to reproduce life on a daily and a generational basis.

■ A LOOK AT OTHER FAMILY PATTERNS

In order to gain some perspective on family life, it is useful to examine family patterns that are significantly different from our own. When we do, one of the things we notice is that family patterns vary with the way people organize themselves to acquire their subsistence. To illustrate this point, I describe two interesting configurations: the communal households characteristic of many foraging (or hunting-and-gathering) societies, and the household economies typical of agricultural societies in preindustrial Europe.

▲ FORAGING SOCIETIES: THE COMMUNAL HOUSEHOLD

In **foraging societies,** people acquire subsistence by gathering edibles and hunting live game. Foragers live in fairly small camps, or bands, comprising people who are compatible, and not necessarily related by marriage or blood (as sociobiologists would predict). Because they live off the resources available to them in the local area, foragers are nomadic. Their ability to move when necessary is critical to survival, so they cannot accumulate possessions and they must keep the ratio of dependants (children and the aged) to active foragers low (Lee, 1979).

The uncertainty of subsistence based on available resources means that survival depends on co-oper-ation and sharing. Successful hunters distribute game to all members of the camp. In the context of foraging, it is wise — indeed, economically ration-al — for the individual to be very generous, since giving establishes obligations to reciprocate. Be-cause hunting is an especially uncertain occupa-tion, sharing the product is a sort of personal in-surance. For the group, sharing ensures that a valuable source of protein is distributed widely.

In addition to sharing, a division of labour by sex and age organizes the acquisition of subsistence in foraging societies. Women typically gather and men typically hunt, although men also gather after an unsuccessful day of hunting and women hunt in some societies. Among the !Kung San of the Kala-hari Desert in Botswana, as among many foragers, the food that women gather provides the bulk of sub-sistence — about 80 percent (Lee, 1979). In forag-ing societies, children and older adults typically do not forage for food.

The co-operation that is the basis of foragers' sur-vival strategy influences the organization of their so-cieties. Probably because it is necessary for every able individual to participate willingly in the work of the camp, decisions affecting everyone are made democratically (Leacock, 1981). Also related to the need for co-operation is the communal nature of these societies. What this means for family life is that it is **collectivized** rather than **privatized,** with the community (rather than the family) assuming re-sponsibility. Marriage establishes the mother–fa-ther–child (i.e., nuclear) unit, but the group of co-operating adults that is crucial for survival — the unit of social reproduction — is the camp.

Just as subsistence is shared, so too is responsi-bility for children (Turnbull, 1961; Leacock, 1981). Thus, although women do most of the child care — which is considerable, when children are carried constantly, as they are among the !Kung — they do not bear the burden alone. Women care for one an-other's children; they even breastfeed one another's babies. Men also often tend babies and children.

Living in a communal society seems to produce an absence of possessiveness toward children and spouses. This attitude is clear in the comment of a seventeenth-century Montagnais-Naskapi (Innu) man in response to a Jesuit missionary's attempt to impose European norms on him: "Thou hast no sense. You French people love only your own chil-dren; but we all love all the children of our tribe" (Leacock, 1981: 50). With respect to spouses, an-thropologist Colin Turnbull (1961: 125) writes of the Pygmies of Congo:

> They think of responsibility as communal. If you ask a father, or a husband, why he allows his son to flirt with a married girl, or his wife to flirt with other men, he will answer, "It is not my affair," and he is right. It is their affair and the affair of the other men and women, and of their brothers and sisters. He will try to settle it himself . . . but if this fails he brings everyone else into the dispute.

In addition to a minimized sense of personal life as private, another consequence of communal liv-ing is that quarrelling and especially violence be-tween spouses are seen, and treated, as communi-ty problems rather than private problems. Whatever disrupts the peace of the community is likely to be stopped — whether it is a beating or an extramar-ital relationship that takes an adult away from his or her responsibilities.

At the same time, the members of these com-munal societies have considerable autonomy. On consideration, the reasons are clear: Every adult has access to what is necessary for subsistence, so no per-son is in a position of dependency on some other, more powerful, person, and because individual co-operation is essential for the survival of the collec-tive, every person's happiness matters. For these and other reasons, relations between women and men are egalitarian — men have no more power or privileges than women (Leacock, 1981).

Individual autonomy is evident in many aspects of family life. Although a girl's first marriage is typ-ically arranged by her parents, a divorce is fairly easy to obtain (Lee, 1979). Similarly, although women typically have babies only about every four years (be-cause they breastfeed each infant for several years and because they have low body fat), they can also decide not to keep every child. Women can choose infanticide if a child is born before other children are able to fend for themselves (thereby overbur-dening the mother), or if a child is born who requires too much special care (thereby jeopardizing the lives of others). Sexuality is also quite unconstrained. Al-though monogamy is usually expected in marriage, women and men are typically able to enter into ex-tramarital sexual relations as long as they do not in-terfere with the performance of their duties.

As this brief sketch demonstrates, the unit of so-cial reproduction among foragers is larger than the nuclear family. Because foragers' survival depends on co-operation and sharing, the larger community assumes responsibilities that belong to nuclear families in our society. In turn, the communal basis of life and the absence of private households in foraging societies have far-reaching implications, including collective responsibility for people's welfare, individual autonomy, and gender egalitarianism.

▲ PREINDUSTRIAL AGRICULTURAL SOCIETIES: HOUSEHOLD ECONOMIES

Our family patterns developed out of the patterns that were typical of precapitalist agricultural societies. In those societies, the household itself was the productive unit; producing subsistence was its main objective. This was true of craftsmen's households as well as those of the peasants and nobility who lived directly off the land. Thus, the social relations of family life in precapitalist households — that is, relations between spouses, between parents and children, and among residents of the same household — were also the relations of production. The chief relationship was that between husband and wife. Wives did necessary work that was complementary to their husbands', so an able-bodied wife was quite indispensable to the survival of the household (Tilly and Scott, 1978).

Land, which was the key means of production, was privately owned in preindustrial Europe. That meant that marriage — and thus adulthood — was predicated on acquiring land, or some other means of livelihood. Consequently, people often married late (Mitterauer and Sieder, 1982). Typically, one son waited to inherit the land, his brothers were apprenticed to learn a skilled trade, and his sisters were given dowries. In the interim, children's dependence on their father to set them up for adulthood gave him considerable authority over them (Greven, 1973).

Land scarcity, and the fact that landlords extracted a substantial portion of the year's produce from the peasantry, meant that the struggle to survive was the chief household dynamic in these societies. It was constantly necessary to balance the number of productive adults against the number of dependants and the available economic resources (Tilly and Scott, 1978). Accordingly, household composition varied with economic requirements, especially labour requirements. In fact, much of the nature of household and family life was governed by economic considerations. So, in contrast with foragers, the interests of individuals in precapitalist agricultural societies

were subordinated to those of the larger kin group and of the land from which they derived subsistence.

Labour requirements dictated household membership. Various types of labourers were taken into households as they were needed. Wives who died were quickly replaced. In peasant households, children were kept home only if their labour was needed. Otherwise, they were sent to wealthier households to be raised. For this reason, and because of extra adult workers, wealthy households were often huge, consisting of 15 to 30 people (Flandrin, 1979).

It was not only poor children who were sent away, however; few children from any economic background were raised at home by their mothers. Indeed, raising a child usually involved several households. Babies were often sent to wet nurses, peasant women who were paid to care for them. About 1 in 2 children survived and returned home after several years, to be looked after, in most cases, by an older sibling. In their early teens, children were then sent off to be trained for adulthood in yet another household. They were either apprenticed to learn a skilled trade or simply sent to another household to learn basic domestic skills (Mitterauer and Sieder, 1982). Women's critical economic role precluded their spending much time on child care or being distracted by the needs of loved ones.

Although parents no doubt loved their children and missed those who were living in other households, in many marriages sentiment and emotional connection probably took a distant back seat to practical imperatives (Mitterauer and Sieder, 1982). Similarly, the household privacy that we take for granted was absent in preindustrial households. Because the household was a place of work, business and family life were not distinguished. Moreover, rooms were not reserved for special purposes like sleeping. In peasant hovels, entire families often slept in the same bed (Flandrin, 1979). In wealthier households, servants often slept with members of the family. Even sexuality was not entirely a private matter. This is clear from evidence of the community's intervention to regulate behaviour — whether to humiliate newlyweds it deemed inappropriate matches, to punish women suspected of adultery, or to force men to stop beating their wives. The interests of the collective — whether the household or the peasant community — always took precedence over individual autonomy.

Moreover, these were truly patriarchal households: Married women owed their husbands absolute obedience and, according to British common law, could not hold property, enter into contractual arrangements, or, in the rare event of divorce, get custody of the children. Many historians conclude that most married women were entirely subordinate to their husbands.

Nevertheless, women's work was vital to the on-going survival of the household. Whereas men did the heavy farm work (or supervised those who did), women were typically in charge of the dairy, the poultry, and the garden, as well as household management — mostly supervising the full range of household chores (Tilly and Scott, 1978). Evidence from men's wills testifies to the trust, respect, and love that developed between some spouses (Hanawalt, 1986). Accordingly, some historians argue that a rough equality often developed between husbands and wives.

Instances of near equality notwithstanding, women's and children's interests were generally subordinated to the needs of the household far more than were men's. For example, women had little control over their sexual and reproductive lives; at a time when childbirth was life-threatening, they were subject to frequent pregnancies.

Finally, it is a myth that preindustrial agricultural households involved extended families, with three generations living under the same roof (Laslett and Wall, 1972). Short life spans tended to preclude the co-residence of three generations. Equally, however, the establishment of the next generation's family was often delayed because male property owners avoided turning the land over to their sons — on whom they would then become dependent — for as long as possible (Mitterauer and Sieder, 1982). In fact, elderly men typically retired only after carefully specifying (in writing) how they were to be provided for by their heirs; feelings between the generations were ambivalent enough that the elderly had to protect themselves against possible neglect by their children.

In sum, the nuclear unit was scarcely distinguishable from the larger household in preindustrial Europe. Nor was the nuclear unit sustained by sentimental or romantic feelings. Family and household relations were primarily relations of work, and individual needs were subordinated to those of the household, to ensure its survival. Whereas the absence of privatized family life empowered individuals in foraging societies, private ownership of the means of production and a considerable struggle to survive meant that, in agricultural societies, all individuals were subordinated to the household enterprise, women were subordinated to men, and children were subordinated to parents.

■ THE ORIGINS OF CONTEMPORARY FAMILY PATTERNS IN WESTERN SOCIETIES

Given how different family life today is from what I have just described, how did contemporary family patterns develop? Actually, it is only in recent history that family life took on its distinguishing characteristics — namely, the sexual division of labour in which women assume domestic responsibilities and men are the breadwinners, motherhood as women's primary role, the privatized nature of the home, and the sentimentality attached to family relations.

Before the nineteenth century, "family" generally referred to all the people who lived under the same roof, many of whom (as we saw) were not related by blood or marriage (Flandrin, 1979). Only when household economies eroded and an economy developed outside the household did our concept of family take root. As we shall see, the concept of family and many of its defining features are products of the separation of public and private spheres that accompanied industrialization: As people grappled with the problems of survival in a new social order, patterns of family life changed.

▲ THE MIDDLE CLASS

The concept of family was a notion constructed by the middle class as it emerged in the nineteenth century. This was a class struggling to assert its social identity and establish its right to political power by claiming a moral superiority over the aristocracy and the labouring masses (Davidoff and Hall, 1987).

Religion provided a moral code essential to that struggle, but family life became the expression of middle-class morality (Davidoff and Hall, 1987). A "cult of domesticity" developed in reaction to and as a critique of an unfolding capitalist economy that people experienced as cruel, immoral, and beyond human control (Cott, 1977). It was an economy in which impersonal forces of supply and demand were replacing face-to-face negotiations and customs such as those reflected in the phrases "an honest price" and "a fair day's wage." It was an economy in which one could be rich one day and penniless the next. The domestic sphere was defined, in contrast, as a moral abode characterized by peace, virtuous behaviour, and the selfless care of loved ones — a "haven in a heartless world" (Lasch, 1977). Dissociating themselves from a world devoid of morality, the middle class wore the cult of domesticity as a social badge — a symbol of their moral distance from the business world they inhabited.

Meanwhile, the reality behind the ideology was that men's work was increasingly moving out of the household. Home and business were separating as the scale of business increased. The middle-class home became a peaceful retreat, where the concerns and evils of the world of business were banished. Domesticity was a way of coping with rapid social change.

Mirroring the separation of men's and women's work, a new conception of gender difference emerged in the nineteenth century. Probably in an attempt to make sense of the new social order, people came to believe that men and women had fundamentally different natures. Women were assumed to belong naturally in the domestic sphere, as its guardian, and to be naturally nurturing. Men were believed to be suited to battle in the amoral world of business, although their objective there was to provide for their families. Thus, an ideology of gender difference made sense of the unfolding social order, and an evolving sexual division of labour complemented the physical separation of public and private spheres.

Women themselves seem to have had a hand in fashioning the role of mother, which was equated with womanhood in the nineteenth century. Moreover, mothers' socialization of their children, coupled with more formal education, solved an emergent problem — that fathers could no longer ensure their children's futures by passing on property and skills. Nevertheless, motherhood entailed women's economic dependence on their spouses: The ideals of domesticity entailed gender inequality.

Finally, the turn toward domesticity brought about a change in the emotional texture of family relations. When the need to produce subsistence was no longer the driving dynamic in daily household life, time and space became available for exploring and meeting emotional needs. By the end of the nineteenth century, children were the sentimental focus of family life (Davidoff and Hall, 1987).

Ironically, although there was more space for intimacy in the nineteenth century, the separation of men's and women's daily work undermined emotional closeness between them. In the increasingly sexually segregated world, women's emotional en-

By the late nineteenth century, mothers and children were idealized. This image depicts a well-to-do mother and her children, 1894. SOURCE: Dummer Collection, Schlesinger Library, Radcliffe College.

ergy seems, in many cases, to have been directed largely toward other women, friends, and kin (in addition to children) rather than toward their husbands (Smith-Rosenberg, 1975). Indeed, same-sex, live-in relationships were more tolerated in the nineteenth century than in the twentieth.

▲ THE WORKING CLASS

While family life was becoming a sentimental focus for the middle class, it was nearly endangered for the working class. Men's wages were so low in the nineteenth century that their children were often forced to work for pay — at long shifts, in horrible factory conditions, for cruel bosses, and risking illness and early death. Although working-class wives attempted to keep up their households in the tradition of peasant wives, they lacked vital means of production, especially land, because of their working-class status. In turn, women's dependent status resulted in strained relations between men and women, marital tensions that focussed on money, and probably frequent violence against women (Stansell, 1987). When unemployment, illness, or death undermined their fragile ability to cope, many working-class families were periodically forced to place children in orphanages (Bradbury, 1982).

At the same time, however, it was often family relations that ensured the survival of working-class people trying to cope with the ravages of developing capitalism. As they had in preindustrial times, families developed collective survival strategies. Accordingly, individual needs were often sacrificed to the imperatives of family survival. Teenagers in the labour force brought home most of their earnings, and young adults postponed marriage until their parents could withstand the withdrawal of their earnings (Hareven, 1982); married women did whatever they could, over and above child care and homemaking, to contribute to household provisions — from keeping farm animals and cultivating gardens (even in cities) to taking in boarders (Stansell, 1987). Moreover, families doubled up to save on rent; there were more extended-family households during the Industrial Revolution than before or after it (Anderson, 1971). In the end, working-class people survived because of the collective efforts of families and kin.

Meanwhile, the trade-union movement responded to the straits of working-class life with a campaign for a **family wage** — that is, a wage paid to a man sufficient to support a wife and children (M. May, 1985). Social historians continue to debate the reasons why the goal of the campaign was a family wage rather than simply decent wages for all. Whatever the reasons, defining the struggle in these terms undoubtedly had the effect of reinforcing a working-class conception of family that was not unlike the middle-class ideal — with women defined as dependants and men as breadwinners.

To conclude, the breadwinner–homemaker division of labour that has characterized many families in this century arose out of people's struggles to survive or succeed materially, to care for their children, and to hold onto a sense of identity during times of massive social change. In turn, the patterns that have emerged during the course of the twentieth century are clearly connected to the problems and possibilities men and women face in an industrial capitalist society.

■ SOCIAL RELATIONS IN FAMILIES TODAY

▲ MAIN FEATURES

We have seen how the development of an economy characterized by competition among people led to a mistrust of the public sphere and a turn toward domesticity. The family became the exclusive location of caring relationships. At the same time, relations between many husbands and wives were hardly romantic. Only in this century do we expect romantic love, sex, and marriage to be intimately bound together (Rapp and Ross, 1986).

An emotionally intense relationship between a man and a woman and even more intense mother–child relationships are two key characteristics of twentieth-century family life. But raising children has not always been a privatized parental responsibility. Although capitalist employers bear no responsibility for the next generation of employees, feudal master craftsmen housed and fed their young apprentices as they trained them and used their labour. In precapitalist times, several households usually contributed to the rearing of every child. Community responsibility for children extended to more recent centuries as well. In the British colonies in North America, community leaders had the power to order households to take in orphans and raise them to adulthood.

Forty years after the idealized mother and children photo, we have this harrowing photo of a migrant mother and children. This striking juxtaposition illustrates the difference between ideal and reality. SOURCE: Dorothea Lange, *Migrant Mother, Nipomo, California* (1936). The Museum of Modern Art, New York.

During the twentieth century, the state has avoided the assumption of responsibility for the welfare of children, except for their schooling, and instead has enforced men's responsibility for the financial support of their children. Accordingly, when "mothers' allowances" were started early in the century in Canada, they were paid only to widows, even though other types of lone mothers were equally in need of assistance (Baker, 1995). Newer forms of social assistance have involved "man-in-the-house" rules, which disqualify women who appear to have a man in their life. Moreover, one of the key government responses to growing concerns about child poverty is to strengthen attempts to force fathers who are separated from their wives to meet their child-support obligations. This strategy turns attention away from governmental and community responsibility for children's welfare.

In the 1950s, 1960s, and 1970s, many men's earnings approached the family-wage level, so a majority of married women stayed home. A sexual division of responsibility and labour was the key strategy by which families met the daily needs of adults and children. Because wages and salaries have eroded since the late 1970s and most women (even those with preschool children) work outside the home, the issue of who cares for the children is now a social problem: Privatized child care no longer works.

Meanwhile, many women, living in a society that has failed to change, are faced with the need to juggle the fundamentally incompatible demands of employment and family every day. The stress of their "double day" of work generates considerable tension between women and their male partners, as men typically have failed to assume their share of the housework and child care (Hochschild, 1989). Many heterosexual nuclear families are, then, under stress.

At the same time, many Canadians are living in different types of families — subject to the same pressures, and others. Women and men who are cohabiting, and not married, represent the fastest growing type of family in Canada. They have more than doubled in number between 1981 and 1991; 1 in 10 Canadian families in 1991 consisted of a "common-law" couple (Statistics Canada, 1993a: 15). These relations are more unstable than those involving marriage (Marcil-Gratton, 1993), yet many produce children.

Lone-parent families are not new in Canada, but their numbers have increased in recent decades. In 1991, 13 percent of families consisted of one parent — usually a mother — and her dependent child(ren) (Statistics, Canada, 1993a: 15). Early in the century, such families usually involved a widow and her children; now more than half of them in-

volve separated or divorced women, and about 20 percent involve never-married women (Statistics Canada, 1992b: 5). As of 1991, 17 percent of Canadian children lived with only one parent (Statistics Canada, 1992b: 5), and over half of these families are poor (National Council of Welfare, 1996).

There are, no doubt, racial, ethnic, and class differences in family patterns in Canada, although our knowledge of these is limited. Almost 18 percent of black women and 15 percent of aboriginal women in Canada are lone parents, compared with only 7 percent of all nonaboriginal women (Statistics Canada, 1992b: 14, 19). We do not know whether a pattern common to black Americans (at least in the early 1970s) holds for these Canadians. That pattern involves black women coping with unstable male–female relations by creating personal-support networks of kin and friends who share scarce resources and co-operate in child rearing (Stack, 1974). Nor do we know whether there are distinct family patterns for different ethnic groups in Canada, for immigrant populations, or even for the working class. The evidence of systematic differences is sketchy. It appears, for instance, that Italian immigrants to Toronto in the period following World War II typically helped relatives adjust to their new surroundings by sharing housing (Iacovetta, 1992).

We know more about families reconstituted after divorce and about gay and lesbian families, both of which are increasing in number. We know much about gender differences and divisions in families, and I pay special attention to them as I discuss sexuality, housework, and parenting in the sections that follow.

▲ SEXUALITY AND FAMILIES

We think of our sexuality as a private, personal matter. Nevertheless, the modern state has historically attempted to exert control over its citizens' sexuality. The most obvious reason sexuality has been the object of state control is that the family is the unit of social reproduction: Society depends on families to produce and care for the next generation. Accordingly, with the aim of tying sexuality to reproduction, most Western governments in the nineteenth century passed laws banning the use of all forms of contraception. In Canada, section 179c of the 1892 Criminal Code made the selling or advertising of any contraceptive or abortifacient an indictable offence. This legislation was not only a form of **pronatalism** (a policy aimed at increasing the population), it was also the product of *eugenist* *fears* that white middle-class Canadians of northern European descent were not reproducing in large enough numbers, while immigrants of darker skin were doing just that. Not until 1969 was the Criminal Code amended to make contraceptives legal. Abortion remained a criminal offence until 1988, after Dr. Henry Morgentaler's repeated challenges of the law.

The state continues to attempt to control sexual behaviour in its refusal to grant gay and lesbian couples the same privileges as heterosexual couples. Because gays and lesbians living in long-term same-sex relationships cannot be legally married, they pay higher taxes, are denied various spousal benefits (e.g., survivors' pensions), and have no legal rights to any nonbiological children they raise. The most punitive of these practices is the denial of child custody to lesbian mothers, solely on the grounds that their homosexuality proves them to be immoral and unsuited for motherhood. The practice is on the decline, but still is not uncommon (O'Brien and Weir, 1995).

The gay and lesbian community has persistently pressed the government to end discriminatory practices. Some positive changes have occurred, but on the issue of allowing same-sex couples to marry there has been little movement. Nevertheless, some large employers now extend spousal benefits to their gay and lesbian employees.

Conservatives have lobbied against the extension of family status to gay and lesbian couples and have presented themselves as defenders of "the family." Popular discussion has thus frequently posed an opposition between family and same-sex relationships (O'Brien and Weir, 1995). In fact, the gay and lesbian communities have not been united on this matter. Some see family as an inherently inegalitarian institution that they avoid replicating, while others — especially those raising children — identify themselves as families.

Many gays and lesbians live with a memory of family that is disturbing. If they "came out" while still living at home, they stood the risk of rejection by their parents. That many parents reject children who declare themselves to be gay or lesbian is clear in the unusually high rates of suicide among homosexual youth (O'Brien and Weir, 1995) and in the absence of any relationship between many adults who are openly gay or lesbian and their parents (Weston, 1991).

Yet gays and lesbians often form lasting relationships. Contrary to stereotypes, these relationships are no more likely to break up than those of heterosexual married or co-habiting couples (O'Brien and Weir, 1995). Moreover, lesbian and gay couples are more likely to be egalitarian in how they arrange housework and child care (Blumenstein and Schwartz, 1983).

Given the obstacles facing same-sex couples, some researchers have stressed the extent to which their families are the product of choice (Weston, 1991). Thus, while convention may move some heterosexual couples to marry, same-sex couples defy the society they live in when they live as families. Similarly, although married women often allow "fate" to decide whether or not they have children, lesbians choose to get pregnant. That the state refuses to acknowledge same-sex families attests to how central heterosexuality is to our notion of family.

▲ GENDER AND FAMILIES

We go to great lengths to ensure that children develop into heterosexual beings. We also spend much time and effort — often unconsciously — making sure that girls and boys turn out differently. The differences that are promoted are directly related to the sexual division of labour that organizes nuclear families. Accordingly, surveys of Canadian high-school students consistently find that marriage and family tend to take strong precedence over other aspirations for girls but not for boys.

There is plenty of evidence that girls and boys are socialized differently as they are growing up, probably in part because of a pervasive conviction that boys and girls are naturally different. For example, it appears that, in subtle and not-so-subtle ways, parents encourage their sons' independence and discourage their daughters', and that girls learn interpersonal skills while boys work on acquiring more mechanical and analytical skills (Weitzman, 1984). Moreover, research indicates that teachers tend to treat boys differently from girls, in ways that build boys' confidence and undermine that of girls (Russell, 1987).

Relying on the concept of socialization to explain gender differences is not totally satisfying, however. Theories of socialization often assume that individuals are passive objects in the process. They overlook how active people are — even infants, toddlers, and children — in fashioning their life course. A better explanation of girls' tendency to focus on domesticity emphasizes that they make decisions in the light of the opportunities and constraints they face. American sociologist Arlie Hochschild (1989) has argued that young adults develop a **gender strategy** that involves a prioritization of either career/job or family/relationships. That prioritization then guides their life decisions. People's gender strategies result from a combination of ideas about gender in the culture, emotionally charged reactions to childhood (especially parents' gender roles), and the opportunities and constraints that they face as they become adults.

A good illustration of gender strategy can be found in Jane Gaskell's study of the expectations of young people graduating from three high schools in working-class areas of Vancouver. Most of the girls judged paid work to be more satisfying than the domestic roles of mother, wife, and housewife: Their socialization had not produced a desire for domestic roles. At the same time, they overwhelmingly agreed that they would eventually assume primary responsibility for housework and child care. They saw their futures as bound up with domesticity for a number of reasons. First, they assumed that they would have a male partner and that he would be unwilling and unable to share the household work. Second, they predicted that their future earnings, relative to their spouse's, would be low, and that it would therefore make economic sense for them to assume household responsibility rather than paid employment. Third, they felt that babies were better off at home with their mothers. The boys in the study concurred with the girls about who should take on housework and child care (Gaskell, 1983). Gaskell's findings indicate that girls become domestic largely because of the lack of opportunities facing them, from good jobs to good day care to egalitarian men.

Similarly, a U.S. study of the decisions that women make about whether to prioritize family or paid work found that the degree of the women's success in the labour market was a more important factor than the effects of their socialization. Women who ended up prioritizing family and the care of loved ones often did so because of a negative experience of paid work (Gerson, 1985). Thus, gender inequality in the labour force promotes the sexual division of labour in the home. It also pushes women toward marriage. Women's relatively poor market position and the growing need for two incomes when there are dependants to support means that if women want children and a decent standard of living, marriage is a wise "choice."

At the same time, labour-market inequality forces impossible choices. Employers still define jobs, especially professional jobs, in terms of employees who are unencumbered by family responsibilities and are able to work after 5 P.M., at night, on weekends, and so on. Job sharing, part-time work with good benefits, workplace day-care facilities, and paid leave for tending sick children are still not common in Canada. As a result, many women find that they must somehow choose between jobs and family. Thus,

many successful career women are single. And the ages of marriage and childbearing are rising as women postpone the balancing act that combining family and paid work entails.

▲ MARRIAGE

Today, because relatively few men earn enough to support a family, and women also need to do paid work, the conventional sexual division of work and responsibility is no longer viable. Old patterns die hard, however. And the contradictory nature of old family patterns existing in new circumstances has generated an increase in divorce, pressures on men to assume new family roles, and a need for new social policies.

Family law has changed to reflect the new circumstances. Before the late 1970s, the marriage contract stipulated a simple but unequal exchange between a woman and a man: He was responsible for his and her maintenance, she owed him domestic and sexual services. Meg Luxton (1980) explored the personal consequences of the conventional sexual division of labour in her study of working-class, breadwinner–homemaker families living in Flin Flon, Manitoba, in the late 1970s. Her clearest finding was that breadwinning translated into privilege. Because men's families depended on them, their needs assumed priority — whether that meant meals prepared according to their taste, children kept quiet for the sake of their need for peace, or any other accommodation. Conversely, housewives' economic dependence typically meant an inability to get their own needs met in the relationship.

That these inequalities were typical in a conventional marriage is suggested by statistics on physical and mental health. Comparisons of men's and women's physical and mental health in the 1960s and 1970s show that men benefited from the care they received in marriage, while the work of personal care took a toll on women. Married men were significantly better off physically and mentally than single men, whereas the opposite was true for women (Bernard, 1972).

Divorce has gradually become more common over the course of this century, and more rapidly since 1968, when federal law was changed to include more grounds for divorce. Recently, the divorce rate has levelled off. According to popular opinion (and some sociologists), the rise in the divorce rate testifies to increased selfishness, unwillingness to make the compromises required by a relationship, and laziness when it comes to "working out" interpersonal problems. This explanation denies the rights of individuals to happiness and emphasizes instead the importance of maintaining the institution of marriage. It ignores the fact that there have tended to be two experiences of marriage — "his" and "hers" — and that women are typically the ones called on to overcome selfishness, make compromises, and work to create happy homes. In the worst marriages, women are the ones subject to severe violence (Crawford and Gartner, 1992). Not surprisingly, women have been more likely than men to initiate separation and divorce (Furstenberg and Cherlin, 1991).

A more reasonable explanation of the rise in the divorce rate might begin with inequalities in the household division of labour. In view of the fact that women have entered the labour market in increasing numbers — and thus gained the possibility of self-support — and have been exposed to the climate of change brought about by the women's liberation movement, it is not surprising that divorce rates have risen. It is estimated that about 30 percent of marriages in Canada will end in divorce, which is considerably below rates in the United States and Sweden, but high when the consequences for children are considered. (The aftermath of divorce is considered below.) Although the majority

of adults who divorce later remarry, marriage is now no longer the only basis of family formation. By the late 1980s, 1 in 5 Canadian babies were born out of wedlock; in 1990, 38 percent of Quebec newborns' parents were not married, though most were co-habiting (Marcil-Gratton, 1993).

Meanwhile, marriage as an institution has changed. In the late 1970s, with the explicit aim of recognizing the work that women do in the home, provinces across Canada reformed their family laws to omit any mention of gender-specific obligations and exchanges. The old model of a "community" of interdependent men and women was replaced by a new one that emphasizes individuals. The spousal relationship is now seen as a partnership of equals, both of whom contribute to the marriage and are responsible for themselves. Under the old laws, a woman had no right to "family assets," including property that resulted from her own work over the years (because she owed her husband her labour). Now, "family assets," which include the fruits of advanced educational degrees and pensions, are to be divided equally upon divorce (Morton, 1988). The new laws encourage people leaving a marriage to become independent as quickly as possible; women are not entitled to continued support, as they were under the old laws.

The Canadian divorce rate was about five times higher in 1994 than it was in 1968, although it declined somewhat after the late 1980s. SOURCE: Andrew Benyei, *Pink Couch* (1993). Fiberglass, 24 x 15 x 19 inches. Photo by Ron Giddings. Reproduced with permission of the artist.

Ironically, because the new laws treat women and men equally, the results are inequitable. The assumption that women can support themselves as men do is simply incorrect, given the gender inequality that is characteristic of the labour market. For many working-class women, there is the additional problem that sharing "family assets" simply means sharing the poverty. Not surprisingly, the chief result of divorce is a significantly lowered standard of living for women and the children who usually live with them (Finnie, 1993).

▲ HOUSEWORK AND MOTHERWORK

Although the new family laws stipulate equality, a sexual division of labour still predominates in households. Women may have assumed part of the responsibility of breadwinning — in 1991 they contributed an average of 26 percent of family income (Statistics Canada, 1993a) — but they remain largely responsible for the housework (Hochschild, 1989; Marshall, 1994). Men do more when their partners are employed, and more than they used to, but women continue to bear most of the responsibility and do most of the necessary daily chores. Consequently, employed women generally work longer hours than their partners every week, and have less time for sleep, leisure, friends, and children than do full-time homemakers and men.

Why is this so? Some men translate higher earnings into privilege at home. Marriage involves negotiations — if not daily, then at least periodically, and especially early in the relationship. Women's bargaining power in those negotiations is undermined by the following factors: women's disadvantage in the labour market; women's perceived disadvantage on the remarriage market (which weakens their courage to push for change in the relationship); and both men's and women's perceptions of other couples' division of labour (Hochschild, 1989).

The causes of unequal workloads are not solely material. A U.S. study based on in-depth interviews found that, even when women make more money and are more committed to their careers than their partners, some men refuse to do more at home (Hochschild, 1989). Sometimes, the simple need to be dominant in the relationship explains men's refusal. At issue, according to Arlie Hochschild, is a cultural and personal equation of manhood with a balance of power that gives men the edge in their intimate relations with women. Moreover, feelings about gender express deep psychic needs. For some men, their wives' caring for them is central to the relationship.

Meanwhile, surveys show that couples who share housework are significantly happier than others. Among couples who do not share housework, the resulting tension in the relationship affects the men and the children as well as the women (Hochschild, 1989). Research also shows that equality in the labour market and at home go hand in hand: Couples who do similar work, especially dual-career couples, seem to be more likely to share household work (Hertz, 1986). Given that gender inequality is still present in the labour market, the unequal division of housework is likely to persist for some time.

Having children also contributes to the division of labour between women and men. Although becoming a parent typically means that a woman is wholly absorbed in the responsibility of caring for the baby, at least for the first six months, fathers usually become much more devoted to making money, often increasing their hours at work (Fox, 1997).

There is a growing conviction that full-time mothering is bad for women and, consequently, for their children, and that men's physical absence from the home also can be detrimental to the social development of children, if men's absence leads to emotional distance from children. For women, the privatized nature of parenting causes problems. Because full-time mothers are home alone much of the day, many suffer from social isolation. A British study of full-time mothers with young children found that, although motherhood enhanced the meaning of their lives, most women (especially middle-class women) were quite unhappy with the daily experiences connected with it (Boulton, 1983). Alone with the responsibility, most women find the full-time care of young children stressful because it combines high demands and reduced control over time (Rosenberg, 1987). A Canadian study likened the work of full-time mothers with young children to that of "front-line" workers servicing people with pressing needs, among whom "burnout" is a common problem. At work and on call 24 hours a day, they have no "down time" and often only minimal sleep (Rosenberg, 1987). For single mothers, of course, all these problems are intensified.

These problems are the result of the social organization of child care in this society. The responsibility for child care is privatized, which means that it rests with the parents alone. Neither the health-care system nor the educational system provides many services for the early years of children's lives. Drop-in facilities, frequent home visiting, and good-quality day care have yet to be considered a basic part of our social infrastructure.

At the same time, most of us are certain it is best for babies and toddlers to be at home with their mothers. On dispassionate and careful consideration, however, the more logical conclusion is that toddlers and even infants fare better when they are cared for by several adults and when they spend at least part of the time outside the home. A single, isolated care-giver inevitably loses some inspiration, enthusiasm, and even warmth over the course of 24 hours a day, seven days a week. Moreover, the home is not de-signed for toddlers; it is both more dangerous and less stimulating than it should ideally be. Indeed, adult needs for order compete with infant and tod-dler needs to explore and manipulate their envi-ronment: Housework and child care conflict. More-over, there is considerable evidence that children who are in good-quality day care from early ages bene-fit more in terms of social development than do those who stay at home (Rutter, 1981).

The majority of mothers of young children today are working outside the home, unable to afford full-time motherhood even if they prefer it. The prob-lem they confront is having to handle a stressful bal-ancing act every weekday. Although attention to this problem, and that of housework, has typically focussed on increasing men's contribution, perhaps there is just not enough time in the day to do the work that many couples face. Solutions require a col-lective response; however, the Canadian govern-ment's main response to the problem has been to recruit foreign workers, obliging them to provide do-mestic service for several years before they can ob-tain permanent-resident status. Using nannies to solve the problem involves the continued privati-zation of domestic labour, which, in effect, allows the community to avoid solving the problem of child care. It allows wealthy professionals, who might otherwise combine forces to put political pressure on the government for a solution that would help everyone, to solve the problem privately. This solu-tion also means having child care and housework done by workers who are highly vulnerable to ex-ploitation, given their long hours of work, their low pay, their social isolation, their lack of citizenship rights, and the private nature of their relationship with the employer (Arat-Koc, 1993). Moreover, gen-erally, this arrangement puts Third World women in the position of subsidizing the dual careers and comfortable lifestyles of middle-class Canadians.

▲ PARENTHOOD

Childbirth

Parenthood is about more than work; it involves a unique and wonderful relationship and also a pro-found responsibility. In all human societies, women are assisted in the process of giving birth. The ways in which they are assisted vary greatly, however. In many societies, it was customary for women giving birth to be assisted by other women, who contin-ued to care for them in the weeks following the birth so that they could concentrate on caring for the baby. They also taught new mothers how to care for the baby. In our society, the aid that is extend-ed to women as they become mothers involves med-ical management of the birth, with the sole aim of protecting the physical health of the mother and es-pecially the child.

Apparently, medicalized birth does not meet the interests of many women. Research shows that after a highly medicalized birth involving machine mon-itors, drugs, and so on, women typically experience a range of negative emotions, from upset and anger to shock and even grief (Oakley, 1980; Rosenberg, 1987). A majority of new mothers get "baby blues" (transitory emotional volatility) in the days and weeks following the birth. Because baby blues are absent in some societies, the usual explanation in-volving hormones is clearly problematic (Oakley, 1980). Some researchers have found that baby blues are related to the degree of medical intervention in the labour (Oakley, 1980). The use of drugs and medical technology can leave many women feeling that the medical staff, and not they, delivered the baby. Other researchers, however, find that the amount of medical intervention is less important, with respect to women's feelings, than how they are treated — how responsive and caring the people around them are (Brown et al., 1994).

Although the medical model of birth defines it as a potentially hazardous physiological process, the midwifery movement presents an alternative model of childbirth. Concerned with the emotional and psychological state of the woman as well as with her physical well-being, midwives assist women through much of the pregnancy and for months after the baby is born. Now that midwives are being licensed in some Canadian provinces, the medical profession may find it necessary to be more responsive to women's needs. Meanwhile, it is profoundly disturbing that, in this society, the process of giving life can leave women feeling disempowered.

Becoming a Family

The first year of parenthood is very stressful for almost all couples. Their lives change dramatically. Even their relationships with other people often change. To obtain help with their huge responsibility, new mothers are much more likely to turn to their own relatives than to friends. Moreover, mothers and fathers of young children spend much less time with friends than they did previously. Their rare socializing is likely to be with kin, who become more important to the couple than they were for years (Fox, 1997). It seems that as people create families, their social world constricts, bounded mostly by kinship.

▲ THE AFTERMATH OF DIVORCE

As we have seen, families are units based on exchange between two adults. Men still provide the bulk of financial support, while women are responsible for child care and most of the housework. When families come apart, the disruption of that exchange brings predictable consequences: emotional turmoil for all members (for what researchers refer to as a two-year "crisis" period), women assuming custody of and responsibility for the children, men abandoning their responsibility for financial support of the children, and a decline in the standard of living for women and children. Many men do not voluntarily make the child-support payments they are responsible for, and most, over time, withdraw from regular contact with their children (Furstenberg and Cherlin, 1991).

That women usually get custody of the children is in part a consequence of the fact that women generally care for children. When divorce settlements are being negotiated, mothers' first priority is usually to keep the children. Fathers' abandonment of their responsibility for, and relationship with, the children is probably the result of several factors: a desire to avoid contact with the former spouse, the demands on a man's time and resources of a new relationship that may involve children, and the difficulty of being a father without a mother on the scene (Furstenberg and Cherlin, 1991).

Probably the most important consequence of divorce for women and the children who live with them is a significant decline in family income. This decline is often so great that many fall out of the middle class, lose their family home, move, and thus change schools (Finnie, 1993). A majority of single-parent mothers with dependent children — 57 percent in 1994 — are living in poverty (National Council of Welfare, 1996: 1). Low income is especially significant because it reduces mothers' ability to provide what researchers find to be most important for children's adjustment after divorce — additional emotional support and a predictable daily schedule (Furstenberg and Cherlin, 1991).

The conflict between spouses that precedes and accompanies divorce (and persists for some couples who do not divorce) is certainly damaging for children. Yet, in the vast majority of cases, children return to normal development about two years after divorce. Nevertheless, some research indicates that women whose parents divorced are more likely to marry and have children early, to give birth before marriage, and to have their own marriages break up (McLanahan and Bumpass, 1988: 147). The reasons are not clear, but it is possible that the children of divorce carry emotional baggage from their childhood. As for the adults who divorce, most remarry. In the short term, the vast majority feel after a while that their divorce improved their lives. Even women struggling with poverty can feel relieved at least to be in control of the money (Graham, 1987).

Lone Parents

In the last two decades, in addition to an increase in the divorce rate, there has been an increase in the proportion of mothers who are unmarried. By 1991, 13 percent of all Canadian families (and 20 percent of Canadian families with children) were lone-parent families. Seventeen percent of children lived in one-parent families (Statistics Canada, 1992b). There are also racial and ethnic differences in the likelihood that children will be raised by one parent: In 1986, 23 percent of aboriginal families living off reserves were headed by one parent, nearly twice the rate for all Canadians (McKie, 1993: 59).

The chief problem facing lone-parent families is poverty. Most are headed by women, and the majority are poor. The reasons for the poverty are clear. A woman — someone disadvantaged in the labour market — is expected both to earn money and to care for children, since support from the former spouse (if there is one) and the state is meagre. Thus, the tension between employment and family is acute in these families. The evidence is that children who grow up in female-headed families are less likely to complete high school than those living in two-parent families. The same evidence indicates that such children are less likely to complete high school because of the financial stress that lone parents face, and not because of the absence of a father figure (McLanahan, 1985).

Reconstituted Families

Adults who divorce usually remarry, so they and their children establish new families. Although these reconstituted families find themselves in a much better financial situation than lone-parent families, they face their own problems. Stepparents are in a difficult position with respect to their spouses' children; stepmothers especially face considerable challenges. According to the research, the outcomes of these new situations are uncertain. In many reconstituted families, both stepparents and stepchildren establish very close relationships; in a sizable number of such families, though, the tensions continue (Furstenberg and Cherlin, 1991). Many reconstituted families do not survive the early years of adjustment — divorce rates are higher for second marriages, especially if children are present. As well, children in reconstituted families have developmental and social problems with the same frequency as children in lone-parent families. The risk of problems may be relatively small, but, nevertheless, it is greater than that for children living in two-parent families that have not experienced divorce.

▲ POLICIES TO SUPPORT FAMILIES

The chief problem for families today seems to be the difficulty of caring for children while earning money sufficient for family support. The problem assumes crisis proportions for lone-parent families, but is also of major importance in two-parent families. The policies that most industrial countries have developed to address this problem include direct family subsidies, significant paid parental leave following birth, and good-quality, subsidized child-care facilities — especially preschool for children over $2\frac{1}{2}$ years of age (Eyer, 1996). Such policies are pred-

SOURCE: *Cathy* © 1996 Cathy Guisewite. Reprinted with permission of Universal Press Syndicate.

icated both on the assumption of the community's responsibility for all its children and on state actions to support women as mothers *and* wage earners. In Canada, in contrast, children are assumed to be a private responsibility, as is the problem women face in juggling family and employment.

We can look to Sweden for a model of state policies that support families. There, it is assumed that children are a collective responsibility, and it is an official policy objective to promote gender equality in the home and the labour force. Behind this orientation lies a role of the Swedish state that is very different from that of the Canadian state: The state in Sweden directly acts to contain and condition the effects of market forces in order to pursue the goals of social equity and meeting human needs.

The Swedish government actively redistributes income from families with high incomes and without children to those with lower incomes and children. Its universal family allowances were $4\frac{1}{2}$ times the amount paid in Canada in 1991. Lone parents receive supplemental child support. Consequently, fewer than 5 percent of lone-parent families in Sweden are poor (Baker, 1995: 72, 126–27).

In Sweden, all new parents can take eighteen months of parental leave (i.e., for either a mother or father) — twelve months at 80 percent of their previous wage or salary, the next three months at a low flat rate, and the last three months without pay (Eyer, 1996). Most families take twelve months of maternity leave. Because of fathers' general failure to stay home with their babies, a 1995 law requires that fathers take at least one of the first twelve months of paid parental leave. In addition to parental leave, new parents can reduce their working hours to 30 per week and retain their job until their child is 8 years of age. And all employees can get up to 120 days per year of leave to care for a sick child (at 90 percent of their wages or salary) (Eyer, 1996).

Although Swedish babies are cared for at home by their parents, from age 6 months to 7 years (when they enter school) all Swedish children are eligible for day-care services. Since 1988, over 70 percent of children under 6 years of age have been enrolled in day care, usually in a day-care centre, but also in family day care (where a woman takes up to four children in her home and is supervised regularly) (Baker, 1995). Most 5- and 6-year-olds go to kindergarten. Before-school and after-school care is also available for children to the age of 12. Because of such support, about 90 percent of Swedish women are employed.

Contrast Canada. Here, meagre universal family allowances were discontinued in 1993 and replaced with a child tax benefit for low-income families. Maternity leave (for those who have been employed for some time) consists of fifteen weeks paid at about 55 percent of the mother's previous wage or salary (up to a maximum). Couples have the right to parental leave as well, for ten weeks, paid at about 55 percent of the previous wage or salary. Although most Canadian infants and toddlers are cared for by at least one person other than their parents, only a small minority are in day-care programs. Care for infants that is not provided entirely by parents is supplemented mostly by relatives or by unlicensed "family day care" (i.e., by nonrelatives in their own home). About 3 percent of infants are in licensed day-care facilities (Goelman et al., 1992). Although about 33 percent of 3- to 5-year-olds are in kindergarten, there is increasing talk about eliminating kindergarten altogether. In short, Canada's support for children looks good only in comparison with the support that is available in the United States, where new parents have no right to paid parental leave and the state does not fund day-care facilities.

CONCLUSION

Cross-cultural and historical evidence shows the diverse ways in which people have organized their lives to meet their own and their children's needs. People of all classes and races have called upon relatives and friends to help them care for their children and to meet the entire range of adult family responsibilities — from finding jobs and paying for housing to coping with emergencies. Governments that prioritize deficit reduction over social programs are counting on such efforts to sustain people.

Research shows, however, that there is no consensus about what obligations people have toward their kin: Help from relatives is never automatic (Finch, 1989). Moreover, people's time is more scarce as the hours of paid work increase and women remain committed to paid work. At a time of both growing economic uncertainty and state cutbacks to social services, nuclear families can neither continue to shoulder so much of the responsibility for people's welfare nor rely on relatives and friends to help them out. The situation calls for an expansion of community responsibility. ■

SUMMARY

1. Common-sense arguments hold that current dilemmas in family life, such as how women can balance the responsibilities of family and paid work and how men can succeed at breadwinning and also do their share of the housework, are private, individual problems. Similarly, family-values advocates argue that change by individuals is the solution to family problems. In the absence of a sociological analysis, the public sources of these problems — and of their potential solutions — remain unclear and unrecognized.

2. Biology does not produce the family, which varies in its organization considerably across different cultures and through history. Although the nuclear family unit is common, it is not always responsible for child care; often, the family is embedded in a larger household or community that collectively assumes responsibility for all the children of the group.

3. Family organization can be seen as loosely related to the organization of production, especially if *family* is defined as the sets of relationships that people create to meet the daily needs of adults and children.

4. In foraging societies, the nuclear family is embedded in a larger group that co-operates with respect to subsistence, consumption, and child care. Paradoxically, the communal nature of these societies grants considerable autonomy to the individuals living in them.

5. In the agricultural societies of preindustrial Europe, households were primarily units of production in which the need to survive took precedence over all else. Household composition, even the texture of emotional life, reflected economic pressures.

6. Contemporary family patterns are the product of a particular history. Our history is marked by the development of an economy outside the household, in which the relations of paid employment are separated from the relations that provide for daily personal needs and the needs of children. A sexual division of labour corresponds to this separation.

7. As women have increasingly come to share the burden of family financial support, men have not proportionally increased the work they do in the home. That jobs are usually geared to people who lack family responsibilities is partly what prevents men from taking on more housework — their time is too limited. However, ideas about gender also make men reluctant to do "women's work."

8. The sexual division of labour that makes it possible for nuclear families to care for young children involves significant liabilities for women, and even for children. The social isolation that full-time mothers experience, combined with the stress attached to their high-demand, low-control situation, reduces the quality of child care they are able to provide. Now that so many mothers are working outside the home, however, the problems associated with privatized responsibility for child care may prove too burdensome, and government supports are likely to provide the only viable solution.

9. Because of fairly high rates of divorce, and an increasing incidence of births to unmarried women, many Canadian children will spend some part of their lives in lone-parent families. Most problematic about this type of family is its typically low income and the attendant stress on the parent.

10. The policies of the Canadian state pertaining to families are premised on the assumption that the welfare of family members — even children — is not the responsibility of the government or of the community. Accordingly, family law in Canada now views marriage as the union of two individuals who are responsible for their own support, even in the case of a divorcing woman who was a full-time homemaker.

QUESTIONS TO CONSIDER

1. Common sense holds that, if everyone embraced family values, problems in family life today would disappear. Explain why this perspective is naïve, and describe some of the barriers in the way of solving problems such as child care, the difficult balance between the responsibilities of family and paid employment, and the unequal allocation of housework.

2. Explain how family patterns are related to the ways that people acquire their subsistence in foraging societies. Do the same for our society.

3. It has been argued that the concept of family takes its meaning from the separation of private and public spheres in some societies (Collier, Rosaldo, and Yanagisako, 1982). In fact, the term itself was not in popular use in Europe until the eighteenth century, when an economy was beginning to develop outside the household. Explain why the idea of family would make little sense in foraging societies and in preindustrial agricultural Europe, and why it does have meaning in our society.

4. Explain how the development of capitalism influenced family ideals in the nineteenth century. Then sketch how the marketplace today influences family life — even aspects of it as basic as conceiving and having children.

5. Describe some of the "crises" typical of family life today, and speculate on possible solutions.

GLOSSARY

biological determinism The argument that individual behaviour or social organization is directly caused by biology or biological processes.

collectivization The opposite of privatization. *See* privatization.

extended-family households Residential units of people who are blood relatives but consist of more than the members of a nuclear family (e.g., an extended family may consist of children, their parents, and a set of grandparents living together).

family wage An ideal of the trade-union movement in the nineteenth century; it refers to a wage that is paid to a man and is sufficient to support him, his wife, and his children.

foraging societies Also known as hunting-and-gathering societies; societies in which people acquire their subsistence from the resources around them, without cultivating the earth.

gender A concept popularized by feminist scholars to distinguish what is socially created from what is clearly biological. Gender encompasses individual behaviour, personality traits, relational orientations, and so on, which are socially produced and associated with being a woman or a man. "Gender relations" refers to regular patterns of social interaction between women and men in institutions, such as families, and in large-scale organizations, such as labour markets.

gender strategy An individual's "plan of action" or, more generally, orientation to life based on (1) cultural notions of gender, (2) emotional reactions to gender roles as played out by parents and other important people, and (3) choices made about one's life, given the opportunities one faces and an assessment of one's abilities. Hochschild (1989) argues that there are three basic gender strategies today: traditional, transitional, and egalitarian.

privatization The assumption of responsibility by the individual, the household, or the family; the opposite of collectivization.

pronatalism Usually, inducements by government to encourage women to have children.

sexual division of labour The division of work by sex; the separation of the tasks men and women regularly do.

social reproduction As opposed to biological reproduction, social reproduction refers to all that is necessary to meet the needs of adults and children, from feeding them and clothing them to meeting their emotional needs and socializing them. It is "the activities and attitudes, behaviors and emotions, responsibilities and relations directly involved in the maintenance of life on a daily basis, and intergenerationally" (Laslett and Brenner, 1989: 382).

sociobiology A type of biological determinism that involves arguments in which human behaviour or social organization is held to be the product of human evolution.

structural functionalism A school of thought that argues that social organization is analogous to a biological organism, or system, in which the parts (or organs) exist because of the functions they perform in maintaining the whole. Thus, institutions such as the family exist because of vital functions they perform in maintaining societal equilibrium.

● SUGGESTED READING

Coontz, Stephanie. (1992). *The Way We Never Were: American Families and the Nostalgia Trap.* New York: Basic Books. Fascinating to read, provocative, and very well researched, this book thoroughly reviews and criticizes "family-values" arguments by analyzing family life, past and present.

Gottlieb, Beatrice. (1993). *The Family in the Western World: From the Black Death to the Industrial Age.* New York: Oxford University Press. A fascinating social history of preindustrial family life. The description is so rich and the writing is so good that it reads like a novel.

Hochschild, Arlie. (1989). *The Second Shift: Working Parents and the Revolution at Home.* New York: Viking. This unsettling study addresses the question of why men are so slow to take on household responsibilities as their wives take over some of the responsibilities of breadwinning. On the basis of in-depth interviews, Hochschild offers some important insights about relations between women and men.

Luxton, Meg. (1980). *More than a Labour of Love: Three Generations of Women's Work in the Home.* Toronto: Women's Press. Now a Canadian classic, this is a study of three generations of housewives in Flin Flon, Manitoba. It shows the changes that have occurred in women's household work over time and also how the capitalist economy shapes women's work and gender relations.

Stack, Carol. (1974). *All Our Kin: Strategies for Survival in a Black Community.* New York: Harper and Row. An American classic, this anthropological study of a poor black community makes sense of a family pattern that is very different from the pattern common among middle-class North Americans, whether black or white.

CHAPTER TWELVE
Work and Occupations

IN THIS CHAPTER YOU WILL LEARN THAT

- work in Canada is dominated by the service economy: jobs are becoming polarized into good and bad jobs, and nonstandard or part-time jobs are becoming more prevalent

- the labour market is segmented into areas of good and bad jobs: job ghettos in the labour market trap certain groups of workers, such as women and visible minorities; labour-market shelters help some workers protect their access to better jobs in the economy

- the degree to which technology enhances or degrades jobs is contingent on the goals of management, what type of technology is used, and how workers react to the technology

- management uses a variety of strategies to organize work: from scientific management to Japanese management, these strategies attempt to help management reduce costs and increase the productivity of workers

- working in organizations presents specific challenges to women and minorities: women managers may be perceived as less effective than their male counterparts

- job satisfaction measures how workers feel about their jobs, and the characteristics of organizations and jobs are the primary determinants of satisfaction: if employers provide workers with challenging jobs, opportunities for advancement, and adequate pay, workers are more likely to be satisfied

- alienation is a structural condition reflecting workers' lack of power over their work and lives: several types of workplace behaviour, such as sabotage, playing games, and strikes, are typical reactions to alienating conditions

SANDY WELSH
University of Toronto

■ INTRODUCTION

▲ WORKING FOR McDONALD'S

In April 1991, 14-year-old Sarah Inglis started working at McDonald's in Orangeville, Ontario. Like lots of other teens, she was trained on how to work the counter, arrange food on trays, and keep the customers smiling. And like lots of other McDonald's employees, she discovered that working there was not all fun and games. As Sarah herself said, "There's a lot more to a counterperson's job than what you see. They don't let you rest. As soon as you're done with your customer you can help somebody else out with another order, or you can stock up, or you can clean, but *just don't stop*. It's like you're a robot" (Inglis, 1994: 20).

Unlike a lot of teenagers, Sarah didn't quit her job when a new manager made working conditions even harder. Instead, she decided it was time for a more daring approach to her working conditions. By the time she was 16, Sarah joined forces with her co-workers and looked into forming a union with the help of the Service Employees International Union. Yet, as Sarah discovered, organizing a union is not simply about presenting your side to management and convincing your co-workers to sign a card and vote for the union.

McDonald's used its skills at selling hamburgers to sell anti-union sentiment. The manager of the McDonald's franchise where Sarah worked organized parties and meetings to encourage workers to vote down the union. He used comic books, music, and slide shows to encourage workers to "Just Say No." Previously hard-to-get hours and shift times were now available. And behind these management strategies lay threats that McDonald's would close the franchise if the union was voted in. Ultimately, the management strategies worked, and the union was voted down by employees.

Whatever your opinion of unions may be, I think you'll agree that Sarah's response to her working conditions went beyond the ordinary. Most of us who find ourselves in jobs that we don't like or that force us to work like a robot would probably quit or quietly cope. Or we might throw ourselves into our life outside of work, knowing that at least we were getting a paycheque from our job. What Sarah did, though, was engage in a century-old practice used by workers to change their workplace conditions.

And McDonald's responded in the way that management has for the past century, by fighting back to keep the balance of control firmly in management's hands.

Sarah's work experience mirrors a lot of the issues facing all of us who are current and potential employees. She is part of the rising legion of service workers. Her concerns are ours: How can we have a job that pays a decent wage, treats us with respect, and offers some satisfaction? This chapter will take you through many of the key issues facing workers today. We'll discuss what the service economy means for our working lives, how employees and employers battle to gain the upper hand in determining what jobs will be like, what factors lead to "good jobs" or "bad jobs," and if these jobs will be satisfying to workers. Whether we look at a 16-year-old McDonald's worker asking for respect, or doctors in Ontario fighting the provincial government for the right to choose where they practise, the study of work and occupations is a study of both the constraints and struggles that happen every day in Canadian workplaces.

■ INDUSTRIAL REVOLUTIONS: A LOOK BACK AT WORK IN CANADA

▲ THE FIRST AND SECOND INDUSTRIAL REVOLUTIONS

Sarah Inglis working at McDonald's represents the most recent phase in our economic development. To understand how we reached this phase, we need to look back to the various shifts in the Canadian economy.

Most researchers speak about changes in the economy and the world of work as revolutions. First in importance is the Industrial Revolution. Starting in England in the late eighteenth century, the economic and social structure began to shift from feudalism to capitalism. Under feudalism, most people worked as peasant farmers, and a few skilled artisans created the necessary tools and goods. As a result of a combination of factors, including the growth of the textile industry and nonlocal markets for wool, landowners started to use their land for sheep grazing and other cash crops. Displaced by this shift in land use and in need of work, peasant farmers migrated to urban areas, looking for jobs in the emerging factories and artisan shops.

The organization of work dramatically shifted during the Industrial Revolution. Under feudalism, most farmers produced enough to meet their own needs. Work and leisure were not clearly separated. And agricultural labour also had its own work rhythm, connected to the seasons. The transition to capitalism, however, transformed peasant farmers into wage-earning factory workers. Now individuals worked for others and no longer controlled their own work schedules. It was during this time that the division of labour expanded. Work that had been done by skilled craftsmen was broken down into smaller components, so that semiskilled workers, who were paid less than the skilled craftsmen, could perform the jobs in factories. This whole process — a "great transformation" in social and labour organization — led to the rise of an urban capitalist class and working class (Polanyi, 1957).

Canada also went through its own industrial revolution, though it occurred later here than in Europe or the United States (Laxer, 1989). As late as the early twentieth century, 40 percent of the Canadian population worked in agricultural pursuits (Campbell, 1996). When industrialization did begin, activity centred on Canada's vast natural resources, such as lumber and minerals.

In the early twentieth century, the second industrial revolution started. This revolution included the rise of consolidated companies, where large companies bought up smaller companies engaged in similar types of production, in such industries as steel and railroads. Henry Ford's assembly line and other mass-production technologies contributed to this expansion, as company owners increased their ability to dominate the market and control the activities of workers. Simultaneously, an "administrative revolution" transformed office work (Lowe, 1987). Because of the vast amounts of information produced by companies, such as personnel and transaction records, management needed efficient systems to organize their offices. This led to the creation of a white-collar job sector and the growth of bureaucratic organizations, and with all these changes came an increasing division of labour. Now, there was management to manage, clerical workers to handle paperwork, and production workers to do smaller and smaller parts of the production process.

What this brief background tells us is that work as we know it in Canada and other capitalist economies is a relatively new phenomenon. A hundred and fifty years ago, most of us would not have been living in cities and going to work for an employer in a large bureaucratic organization. Although we still see vestiges of the first and second industrial revolutions in our working lives, many things have changed. Most prominent is the movement away from a manufacturing-based economy toward a service economy.

The second industrial revolution started in the early twentieth century. Henry Ford's assembly line and other mass-production technologies date from this era. SOURCE: Diego M. Rivera, *Detroit Industry — North Wall* (1932–33). Fresco (detail). Photograph © 1997 The Detroit Institute of Arts.

■ WORK IN THE SERVICE ECONOMY

Many researchers argue that, in the years since World War II, Canadians have been witnessing — and living through — a third industrial revolution (Toffler, 1980). Our economy has shifted from its early industrial base of primary production (mining and logging) and secondary production (manufacturing) to tertiary production (service industries). As Table 12.1 shows, from 1980 to 1995, the number of Canadians employed in service industries grew from 67 percent to 73 percent. Increased global competitiveness contributed to the lowering of labour costs as companies tried to maintain their market position. Global markets also facilitated the movement of some goods production to low-wage areas. These factors have helped pushed many manufacturing jobs out of Canada. Free-trade agreements with the United States and Mexico and the drive to reduce labour costs have also played a role in the decline of the goods sector (Canadian Labour Congress, 1993). Fewer jobs in the goods sector means that most new jobs will be in the service sector.

Much debate has ensued about the rise of the service, or "postindustrial," economy. Writing in the early 1970s when this trend began, Daniel Bell (1973) presented an optimistic picture of the rise of the "postindustrial" economy. In his view, work would be transformed from repetitive, low-skilled production work to highly skilled, knowledge-based work. Today, however, more pessimistic analyses of the postindustrial economy are prevalent. We are witnessing an increase in low-skilled, low-paying service jobs and a steady rise in the level of unemployment. It may be too early to tell whether the optimistic or pessimistic scenario will eventually prevail. As stated by sociologist John Myles (1991: 128), "the issue for the future is not whether we will have a service economy but what kind of service economy" we will have.

▲ GOOD JOBS OR BAD JOBS?

One way to discover what kind of service economy we will have in Canada is to look at the mix of good and bad jobs available for workers. At minimum, good jobs are those that provide **extrinsic rewards,** such as good wages, benefits, employment security, and opportunities for advancement. Good jobs should also provide **intrinsic rewards,** such as decision-making opportunities, challenging nonrepetitive work, and autonomy that allows for self-direction and responsibility over work tasks.

A misconception about the service economy is that the service sector creates only bad jobs and that the goods sector is the source of good jobs. This scenario assumes that all service jobs are alike and ignores important divisions within the service sector. Instead, we should think of the service sector as having a lower tier made up of traditional services,

◆ **Table 12.1** Canadian Labour-Force Characteristics, 1980 and 1995

Labour-force characteristics	1980	1995
Total number employed (thousands)	10 708	13 506
Percent in goods sector	33	27
Percent in service sector	67	73
Percent part-time	13	17
Women's labour-force participation rate (percent)	51	57
Unionization rate (out of all paid workers) (percent)	32	33[a]

[a] Based on 1993 data.

SOURCE: Compiled from Statistics Canada, "Social Indicators," *Canadian Social Trends,* Winter 1988, p. 31; and Statistics Canada, "Social Indicators," *Canadian Social Trends,* Autumn 1995, p. 31. Used by authority of the Minister of Industry, 1997.

such as retail trade, food, and personal services, and an upper tier consisting of other services, such as finance and business, utilities, health, education, and public administration. Whether you find yourself in a lower- or upper-tier service job has implications for your wages, job security, and the skill content required in your work (Krahn, 1992; Economic Council of Canada, 1991).

Debates also revolve around changes in the skill level of jobs in the service economy. Conventional wisdom suggests that skill requirements are increasing as a result of technology (Spenner, 1983). As Daniel Bell and other postindustrialists propose, we should experience an upgrading of jobs in the economy as skill requirements increase within specific occupations. This group also predicts that job growth will occur in the higher-skilled occupations. In contrast, Harry Braverman (1974) and other postindustrial critics believe that skill levels are being downgraded. In this view, although some highly skilled professional and technical jobs will be created, the majority of jobs will be lower-skilled industrial and service jobs.

So which is it? Are we moving to the postindustrial world of Bell or the downgraded world of Braverman? When we examine the shifts in the Canadian occupational structure, a more complex picture than the ones sketched by Bell and Braverman emerges: Blue-collar jobs in the middle are declining and job growth is occurring at the top and the bottom of the occupational structure (Myles, 1988; Economic Council of Canada, 1991). Thus, we see an increasing polarization of jobs in the service sector — higher-skilled knowledge jobs on the one hand and lower-skilled "hamburger" jobs on the other (Myles, 1988).

As this trend continues, we should be concerned about those who minimize the significance of the goods or manufacturing sector for our economic well-being. Such a view is shortsighted: It is increasingly clear that the goods and services sectors are interdependent and that manufacturing is important for the creation of good jobs (Economic Council of Canada, 1991). For example, the production of telecommunications technology drives the development of telecommunications services in Canada (Myles, 1991). We need both sectors to fuel our economic growth. This is why trade agreements that threaten Canadian manufacturing may be detrimental to our overall economy. The movement of goods-producing industries to other countries could ultimately hurt the ability of the service economy to generate good jobs.

▲ NONSTANDARD JOBS

One crucial outcome of the shift to a service-based global economy is the rise of **nonstandard jobs.** These are jobs that provide temporary, part-time, or part-year employment. For employers, nonstandard jobs can reduce labour costs since part-time and temporary workers receive less in pay and benefits (Economic Council of Canada, 1991; Krahn, 1992). As Table 12.1 shows, 17 percent of Canadians worked in part-time jobs in 1995. Figure 12.1 also shows that the lower-tier service industry is leading the way in the creation of nonstandard jobs.

In order to respond to changes in demand for their products and services, some employers now rely on temporary workers, ranging from clerical help to computer programmers, hired through temporary-employment agencies. Like part-time workers, temporaries tend to be young and/or women (Economic Council of Canada, 1991). They are usually hired for short-term contracts to fill in for absent full-time workers, or as part of a "just-in-time" labour force called in to fill production or service demands. Al-

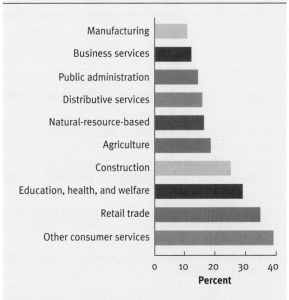

◆ Figure 12.1 Nonstandard Employment by Industry, 1989

SOURCE: General Social Survey, reported in Harvey Krahn, "Nonstandard Work Arrangements," *Perspectives on Labour and Income*, Cat. no. 75-001, Winter 1991, p. 39. Used by authority of the Minister of Industry, 1997.

though some workers are drawn to temporary work for its perceived flexibility in scheduling, the reality for most workers is that such jobs are often inflexible. As a result of work shortages, many temporary workers find themselves taking whatever work is available, even if it means putting up with inappropriate work, such as cleaning offices while on a clerical assignment (Henson, 1996).

Some employees, particularly women and young workers between the ages of 15 and 24, prefer the flexibility of nonstandard work. They voluntarily choose part-time work because it allows time for school attendance and family responsibilities or because they do not want to work full-time. Most disturbing, though, is the growing number of involuntary part-time workers — part-time workers who would prefer full-time work (Noreau, 1994). In most industrial countries, including Canada, one-quarter to one-third of all jobs are now nonstandard (Economic Council of Canada, 1991).

▲ WHAT IS HAPPENING TO THE STANDARD WORK WEEK?

In 1995, only 54 percent of Canadians worked a "normal" 35–40 hour work week (Gibb-Clark, 1996). Along with the rise in nonstandard jobs, we are experiencing a polarization in the hours we work per week. Members of certain occupations, like managers and factory workers, are working well over 40 hours per week, while lower-tier service workers are seeing their work hours drop to under 30 hours per week (Gibb-Clark, 1996).

There are various explanations for the increasing polarization of work hours. The rise of the service industry and employers' demands for a more flexible workforce have increased the number of part-time jobs. In companies that are downsizing, remaining core employees may face greater demands and pressure to overwork. A poll of U.S. chief executive officers (CEOs) found that a majority of CEOs expected their high-level and middle managers to work 50–59 hours per week (Solo 1990). When asked how many hours they work, 70 percent of the CEOs reported that they work at least 60 hours per week. Pay-for-performance schemes, where employees are paid for outcomes, have contributed to the rise in hours for managers (Morissette and Sunter, 1993). Globalization and technological innovations, such as fax machines and computers, have also increased the likelihood of overwork. As one senior partner of a U.S. law firm put it, "We used to type up drafts of contracts on seven-page car-

bons, and by 9:30 at night you had to give them to the typing pool. Then you went home. [Now] we can print out a contract, fax it to London, and wait around until 3 a.m. when they've finished reviewing it, and we can start working on it again" (O'Reilly, 1990: 41). More and more, we face a situation in which there is too much work for some people and not enough work for others.

The polarization of work hours has sparked interest in shortening the work week. The hope is that shorter hours will create jobs for the unemployed and underemployed. In the early 1990s, workers at Volkswagen in Germany agreed to reduce their work week from 37 hours over five days to 29 hours over four days, as well as to take a 10 percent pay cut, in order to save 30 000 jobs (B. Wallace, 1994). Ontario's controversial "Rae Days," a government-imposed work arrangement in which civil servants earning over $30 000 per year were required to take twelve days off without pay, kept 40 000 people from being laid off. Recently, the CAW agreed to reduce overtime at the Chrysler plant in Windsor in order to add a third shift of 800 workers. For these schemes to work, we must ensure the underemployed and unemployed have the skills needed for these additional jobs created by decreasing working hours of those already employed.

■ LABOUR-MARKET SEGMENTATION

All of us hope to have an equal chance of getting a good job. But do we really have an equal chance? As you know from your study of stratification and inequality (see Chapter 7), some groups of workers, such as individuals from upper-class families or more educated workers, are more likely than less-advantaged workers to end up in good jobs. Another factor that affects your chances is the structure of the labour market. Although some economists, especially human-capital theorists, conceive of the labour market as a single and open competition in which people are rewarded in proportion to their education and skills (Becker, 1975), **labour-market segmentation** theory offers a different perspective. Instead of assuming that we all have an equal chance of getting good jobs, labour-market segmentation theory shows that where you enter the labour market may limit your chances of getting a different, better job.

Labour-market segmentation theory emphasizes that jobs are divided according to their location in the "core" or "periphery" of the economy. A core industry is a group of companies in a relatively noncompetitive market, such as the automobile industry. Core industries tend to be capital-intensive, large, and unionized, and they tend to exert control over their environment (e.g., by influencing governments to limit foreign competition). For a variety of reasons, such as the need to maintain skilled workers that can operate expensive capital equipment, and in response to the presence of unions, jobs in core industries tend to be stable and to offer good wages and access to benefits (Morissette, 1991).

The periphery, in contrast, is characterized by lower-tier service jobs and jobs in highly competitive markets. Firms in this sector tend to be smaller, labour-intensive, and nonunionized, and the employment they offer lacks security and pays low wages. Work is also characterized by high turnover rates, owing to product-demand fluctuations and seasonal work cycles, such as in the fisheries on the east and west coasts of Canada.

Your chances of finding a good job are determined not only by the sector of the economy you enter, but also by the existence of **primary labour markets,** both external and internal to firms. Internal labour markets provide opportunities for advancement by providing the chance to climb up the job ladder as you gain skills and knowledge (Althauser, 1989). Secondary labour-market jobs do not offer much of a job ladder. These jobs are sometimes referred to as "dead-end jobs" because of their lack of upward mobility. Workers at McDonald's may be able to move from being on the crew to assistant manager, but unless they buy their own franchise (which is rare), that is the extent of their mobility.

Employers often create primary labour markets for some employees but not for others. In a single firm, managers can have access to mobility through an internal labour market while their clerical, production, and maintenance staff may have little room to move up. Employers' increasing use of temporary and part-time workers is another way in which secondary labour markets are created within companies. Increasingly, these types of secondary markets are found outside the lower-tier service industries. At the university where I work, and in all other Canadian universities, departments have full-time professors to do research and teach. In addition, "sessional" instructors are hired to teach one or two classes each. Substantial differences exist between these two groups in terms of pay, job security, and mobility opportunities. As a full-time professor, I have a multiyear contract and may be promoted if I fulfil my job duties. My colleague, who is a part-time instructor, has no access to promotions or job security. Instead, she receives year-to-year contracts only if the department needs her

to teach a specific course. Although having secondary labour-market positions gives organizations the "flexibility" to unload employees when they are not needed, it increases the insecurity of these employees and decreases their chances of getting ahead, both in their jobs and in life.

Geography also plays a role in our chances of ending up in the primary or secondary labour market. Even if you are a highly skilled and motivated worker, you will have trouble finding a good job in Newfoundland, where the cod fisheries have fallen on hard times (Krahn and Lowe, 1993: 135). Those of us who live in the major urban and industrial areas of Canada are more likely to end up in a better job simply because there are more of these jobs in our regional labour markets.

We may conclude that whether you end up in a good job or a bad job is due to more than your individual characteristics or the occupation you choose. Your chances of landing a rewarding job depend on what sector of the economy your job is in and whether your job has an internal labour market as-

Jobs in the secondary labour market are sometimes referred to as "dead-end jobs" because they offer little or no opportunity for upward mobility. SOURCE: Chris Jones/ First Light.

sociated with it. In the next section, I develop this idea by showing how some groups of workers find themselves stuck in job ghettos.

▲ JOB GHETTOS AND DISADVANTAGED GROUPS

Job ghettos are parts of the labour market that trap certain groups of workers. Structural barriers based on stereotypes work to keep some individuals from entering the primary labour market and the best jobs. The labelling of occupations as "female" or "male" jobs is one such example. In the health-care industry, women are still more likely to become nurses than doctors, and, as doctors, women are more likely to be found in pediatric and family medicine than the higher-paying specialities of neurology and cardiology. Chapter 8 discusses how female job ghettos are formed through occupational sex segregation, sex typing, and other forms of discrimination.

Although most Canadian women in the paid labour force are segregated in jobs traditionally dominated by women, they are making advances in traditionally male-dominated jobs. SOURCE: Dick Hemingway.

People with disabilities face barriers to good jobs because of the inaccessibility of education and workplaces. Lack of financial resources to attend school, inflexible workplace schedules, and lack of employers' commitment to hiring disabled workers are some of the reasons people with disabilities have trouble getting good jobs. Jamie Hunter, a 29-year-old with minimal control over his limbs as a result of a diving accident, experiences these barriers firsthand. Speaking about looking for work, he states (quoted in McKay, 1993: 170):

> I recall one fellow, from the personnel department of a major corporation, who was so uncomfortable he couldn't even bring himself to take me to his office. So we sat in the lobby and he read me back my resume. "You're Jamie Hunter? You graduated from York University? You worked for a summer at Ontario Hydro?" Then he said thanks and left. That was it. The interview was over and I never heard from him again.

Hiring disabled workers is not as costly as some employers believe. Recent studies show that only 20 percent of people with disabilities require changes to the physical accommodations of workplaces in order to work (Shain, 1995). Until more employers make the effort to hire people with disabilities, disabled workers will continue to face barriers to good jobs.

Ethnic job ghettos are a pervasive component of past and current labour markets throughout the world. In Canada, between 1860 and 1960, black railroad workers were restricted to sleeping-car porter jobs and were not allowed to compete for the higher-paid jobs of sleeping-car conductor and dining-car steward (Calliste, 1993). Today, employer prejudice can keep qualified minorities from being hired. Since most visible minorities are also recent immigrants, their ability to move into better jobs is constrained by this dual status, unless they are entrepreneurs. Often, employers will request "Canadian work experience" before hiring white-collar workers. And some professional occupations, like doctor and veterinarian, require additional training for professionals emigrating from certain countries. Highly educated visible minorities in these situations may find themselves forced to take low-level service jobs, such as taxi driver or restaurant worker.

Aboriginal people face formidable barriers in their search for employment. Living in remote areas limits both their job opportunities and their access to education and work training. Even when aboriginals move to areas where jobs are more readily available, they often lack crucial work experience. Aboriginal workers are especially vulnerable to the "bad-work syndrome" (Krahn and Lowe, 1993). Having access only to low-skill and part-time work gives individuals a spotty work history. They are then caught in a cycle where one low-skill job leads to another. For many, the "bad-work syndrome" makes it impossible to get better jobs.

Finally, *young and old workers* may find themselves trapped in job ghettos that are based on age. Some employers view younger workers as less serious and less interested in full-time jobs. In many ways, trying to improve the jobs in the teenage-student job ghetto was the motivation behind Sarah Inglis's union drive at the McDonald's in Orangeville. Older workers, who are defined as those over 45, also face employment limitations. As a result of downsizing and early-retirement incentives, older workers may find themselves out of a job before they are ready to stop working. Access to better jobs is also limited by the prejudices of employers, who tend to view older workers as less productive and more resistant to new work methods.

Labour-market segmentation creates areas of better and worse jobs in the labour market. Although we would like to think that we all have an equal chance of getting the better jobs, the research on job ghettos shows that some groups of workers may get trapped in the worse jobs. And, as I show in the next sections, some workers are able to protect their good jobs through the labour-market shelters of professional occupations and unions.

▲ PROFESSIONS

The occupations of doctor, lawyer, and other professions are some of the most desirable jobs in the labour market. High pay, autonomy, and respect from the outside community are some of the advantages bestowed on members of professional occupations. Many of us consider these occupations to be different from other occupations. This special status has caught the attention of sociologists.

Early studies of professions attempted to delineate their general characteristics or hallmarks. First, all professional occupations control a special body of abstract knowledge, held only by members of that profession. Second, professional occupations are autonomous. Third, professionals generally have authority over their clients and subordinates because of the special knowledge they possess. Finally, professional occupations are supposed to be altruistic due to their focus on helping clients.

But are these four characteristics all there are to professions? Many sociologists believe that the hallmark model is really an "idealized model that im-

perfectly describes reality" (Hodson and Sullivan, 1990: 266), and that it provides only a checklist for determining which occupations are more or less a profession. Overlooked by this approach is how these occupations became "professions" in the first place. To address this issue, we need to consider power and the contested nature of professions. Doing this will uncover how professions act as **labour-market shelters,** protecting their members' access to good jobs.

In many ways, relationships between professional occupations can be considered "battles" for control over professional knowledge (e.g., Friedson, 1970). For example, until recently, only doctors had the authority to deliver babies. Doctors maintained their authority because of their monopoly over the relevant knowledge and used their national associations to lobby provincial and federal governments to deny others the right to practise. As a result of current public demands for access to midwives and the development of professional midwifery schools, doctors have lost some control over the birthing process and have lost their monopoly over this body of professional knowledge.

Some occupations are continually striving for professional status. Semiprofessions are occupations that have some professional characteristics, but to a lesser degree than full-fledged professions (Hodson and Sullivan, 1990). Examples of semiprofessions are nurses, engineers, accountants, pharmacists, and teachers. Although we may call these occupations "professions" in our everyday use of the term, the sociological definition of professions requires us to view these occupations as "not quite" or "semi" professions. Often semiprofessions do not have full control over their body of knowledge, or their autonomy may be constrained by a more powerful profession, as is the case with nurses. Furthermore, female-dominated semiprofessions, such as teachers or librarians, face additional barriers to professionalization because of occupational sex segregation.

Third parties, such as the government, can threaten professional power by intervening in the decisions of professional organizations. We become most aware of this when the government pays for part or all of the services received by a client, as is the case for the Canadian health-care system. During the summer and fall of 1996, doctors in Ontario fought the provincial government over who has the right to decide where doctors work. Doctors wanted to maintain their professional autonomy to work and live where they choose, while the Ministry of Health believed it had the right to force doctors to work in underserviced areas. Some doctors did not accept new patients to protest what they saw as government in-

New technologies require job retraining, even for middle-aged and elderly workers.
SOURCE: David Pollack/First Light.

According to Shoshana Zuboff (1988), management can design computer-based jobs to either increase or decrease the need for workers to use knowledge and judgement on the job. She provides examples of jobs being enhanced, on the one hand, when workers were given the opportunity to use computers in complex ways. On the other hand, she also found that, if management is interested only in productivity and efficiency, technology can have detrimental effects on the quality of work. For example, one office used computers to automate and speed up the work of clerks. Any decisions that clerks formerly made about their work were now programmed into the computer. Box 12.1 describes some of the experiences of these workers. The stick-figure drawings represent the drastic change in workers' views of their jobs. What makes these pictures compelling is knowing that a consultant recommended further automation of the clerks' jobs. But management held back. As one manager acknowledged, the company realized it couldn't remove all variety from tasks because "there's a limit to how boring you can make a job if you want even reasonably capable people" (Zuboff, 1988: 134). This example shows us, then, that management can choose to implement technology in a way that either enhances work or downgrades it.

From video cameras to computer programs, workers are finding themselves increasingly monitored by technology. In one high-tech firm, management used scanners to detect motion in rooms that were not supposed to be used (M. Wallace, 1989). Air Canada uses electronic surveillance to make the job of telephone airline reservation agents more visible and easily controlled (Robertson and Wareham, 1990). Detailed information can be collected about how many phone calls an agent handles, the duration of each phone call, and how long each agent is "out of the system" or unavailable for calls. This information is then used to determine who is working up to speed. Reservation agents complain that these computer measures do not adequately capture all components of their job, such as providing friendly and useful service to customers. As the use of computers and high-technology systems becomes more common, more of us may find ourselves monitored electronically. How far monitoring will go in the name of increasing employee productivity will hinge on the ability of workers and unions to participate in decisions about the implementation of technology.

Technological Unemployment and Job Creation

Technology has the potential to change not only jobs, but also who will be working. When high-tech systems and robots were brought into a General Motors plant in Linden, New Jersey, production jobs were phased out while new skilled mainte-

Box 12.1
How Technology Can Change the Workplace

What can computer technology do to the quality of worklife? In her study of technological change, Shoshana Zuboff asked office workers to draw pictures that "represented their 'felt sense' about their job experience before and after the conversion to the new computer system" that automated and standardized work. Below are two workers' views of how their work experience changed. Note the shifts in facial expressions and the loss of mobility. Even the flower on the benefits analyst's desk has wilted. As one office manager said about work after the conversion: "The system controls the transfer assistants in some ways because it ties them to the desk. It forces them to do the input and to really be tied to the machine. That forces control in terms of physically having to just be there."

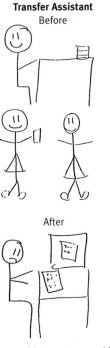

Transfer Assistant
Before

After

"Before I was able to get up and hand things to people without having someone say, what are you doing? Now, I feel like I am with my head down, doing my work."

Benefit Analyst
Before

After

"My supervisor is frowning because we shouldn't be talking. I have on the stripes of a convict. It's all true. It feels like a prison in here."

SOURCE: Adapted from Shoshana Zuboff, *In the Age of the Smart Machine: The Future of Work and Power* (New York: Basic Books, 1988), pp. 138–41. Copyright © 1988 by Basic Books, a division of HarperCollins Publishers, Inc. Used by permission of Basic Books.

nance and repair jobs were created (Milkman and Pullman, 1991). Overall, more jobs were lost than created. At Dofasco in Hamilton, computer technology is partly responsible for reducing the work-force from 12 500 to 7000 over the past ten years (Campbell, 1996). Automated banking machines have already reduced the number of teller positions in banks (McLaughlin, 1983) while creating a small number of jobs for those who repair and maintain these machines. These examples show technology's initial effect on employment. Although some skilled jobs directly connected to the technology are created, a greater number of lower-skilled jobs are lost. And, more often now, workers facing technological unemployment can find only lower-tier service jobs to replace their previous jobs (M. Wallace, 1989).

■ BUREAUCRACIES AND WORK ORGANIZATION

We live and work in a bureaucratic society. According to Max Weber, bureaucracies are the most efficient and rational organizational form for reaching the goals of capitalism. In bureaucracies, written rules provide guidelines for handling routine situations. A complex division of labour ensures that workers know what is required of them and helps to identify who is responsible when something goes wrong. Although a clear hierarchy of authority clarifies who makes decisions, bureaucracies are not without their problems. They can be rigid, full of "red tape," and lead to communication problems between managers and workers (Jones, 1996).

▲ MANAGERIAL STRATEGIES FOR ORGANIZING WORK

In the past 100 years, several approaches to organizing work in bureaucracies have come and gone. Some, like Taylorism and human relations, have endured the test of time (Braverman, 1974). While Taylorism was geared toward removing the need for workers to think on the job, more recent strategies have paid more attention to the ability and desire of workers to participate in workplace decisions. Whether these strategies offer real participation is a question to keep in mind as you read the following sections.

Taylorism

Frederick Taylor, an American industrial engineer, was the founder of scientific management or **Taylorism**. Originating in the 1890s, scientific management was an attempt by management to regain direct control of the labour process. Based on his own experience in factories, Taylor discovered that workers knew more than their managers about the work processes. As long as this was the case, workers could control how fast they worked and how much they produced. To shift control back to management, Taylor recommended a detailed division of labour that broke complex tasks into several subtasks. To do this, management needed to learn how workers did their jobs and then convert this knowledge into formal procedures. Using time and motion studies, managers documented the exact movements of workers and the length of time required to complete the task. Taylor also believed that conceptual work should be separated from the execution of tasks. It was management's job to design work procedures, and the workers' job to follow those procedures. By breaking jobs into their smallest components and removing the need for workers to think, Taylorism opened the door for management to reduce their reliance on skilled labour. Cheaper, unskilled workers could now be hired to perform simplified tasks. Managers and intellectuals worldwide, including the Russian communist leader Lenin, hailed Taylor as a pioneer in the rationalization of work.

Taylorism is not limited to factory work. Lowe (1987) shows how Taylorist principles rationalized office work in early twentieth-century Canada. And Taylorism is still around in many jobs. Making hamburgers in a fast-food restaurant is broken down into minute tasks, and telephone reservation agents for airlines are given scripts to follow when dealing with clients. But today, as in the past, workers complain about the limited opportunities for creativity and self-fulfilment when working under scientific management.

Human Relations

One shortcoming of Taylorism is its assumption that workers are wage-pursuing machines, motivated only by desire for their paycheque (Jones, 1996; Bendix, 1974). In reaction to this simplistic view, the **human relations school of management** pushed management to rethink the Taylorist image of workers by showing the importance of the social aspects of work. Based on a series of experiments at the Western Electric Company's Hawthorne plant in Chicago, Elton Mayo and others found that friendly supervision and attention to the social environment increased workers' co-operation and productivity. These "Hawthorne studies" started the movement to consider how employers can fulfil employees' social needs, increase their satisfaction, and make them feel better about their jobs.

Although the validity of the Hawthorne studies has been called into question (Carey, 1967), most researchers agree that management strategies today still incorporate and build on elements of the human relations school. From suggestion boxes to workplace participation programs, organizations are trying to find the right "human touch" to decrease worker resistance and increase productivity.

Recent "Humanization" of Work and Worker Participation

During the 1970s, management efforts to "humanize" workplaces gave rise to quality-control circles, quality-of-work-life programs, and other forms of workplace participation. At minimum, management introduced some of these newer strategies in order to diminish worker resistance and boost profits (Rinehart, 1996). Unlike worker co-operatives and worker ownership, though, participation schemes implemented by management are not true examples of workplace democracy.

As their name implies, quality-control (QC) circles emphasize the need to improve production quality. QC circles involve a small number of employees working with a team leader or supervisor. Together, these labour–management teams brainstorm about how to solve production problems. Quality-of-work-life (QWL) programs are broader in scope than QC circles. Management promotes QWL programs as democratizing the workplace, by giving workers more responsibility and control over their work through self-regulating work teams and by providing more complex jobs for workers. Although both QC circles and QWL programs make reference to worker participation, the decision-making authority of workers is usually limited to improving individual work tasks or improving the atmosphere at work. Workers are left out of decisions about "what is to be produced, investments, distribution of profits, technology, size of the work force or plant closings" (Rinehart, 1996: 169).

The Shell chemical plant in Sarnia, Ontario, is considered to have the "flagship" QWL program in North America (Krahn and Lowe, 1993). Starting with the development of the plant in 1975, the union and management worked together to design work processes. The variety of tasks performed by autonomous teams of workers was expanded, initially at least, through job rotation and job enlargement. However, in his analysis of QWL programs, Rinehart (1986) questioned Shell's commitment to humanizing the workplace. Instead of being enlarged by the QWL program, work intensified as management added housekeeping and equipment maintenance to operators' duties.

Recently, concepts such as total quality management (TQM), Japanese management, lean production, and "just-in-time" production have been promoted as the panacea for productivity and quality "problems" of management. These programs emphasize quality control through communication and teamwork between management and workers. And the rhetoric surrounding these programs continues to promote the potential for democratizing workplaces and increasing the participation of workers. Because of the attention it has received in North America, I now consider the trend toward Japanese management and lean production in North American plants.

Japanese Management: Lean Production or Mean Production?

Many of you have probably seen the television commercial about the Saturn automobile employee and "the day he stopped the line." While doing his job, this worker noticed a problem with the cars going past him, so he reached up, pulled the cord that stopped the line, and received the help he needed to solve the problem. As part of their marketing campaign, Saturn uses this commercial to show how the commitment to quality production runs throughout the plant. When I first saw this commercial, I remember thinking that this looked like a change from the old forms of production, where workers were told to leave their brains at the door, to a new form of production, where workers were encouraged to use their mental skills. And, to confirm my initial impression, I found out at the end of the commercial that Saturn is a "different kind of company" producing " a different kind of car."

What is Saturn promoting with this commercial? What does this commercial signify about potential changes to the way that work is organized? Saturn, like CAMI in Ingersoll, Ontario, and Subaru-Isuzu in Lafeyette, Indiana, is part of the movement to **Japanese production techniques (JPT)**. Initial reactions to these Japanese transplants and joint operations were positive. "Just-in-time" production cut costs as companies reduced their parts inventories and the need for warehouses. And the use of participatory work teams led some academics and industry experts to consider JPT a "post-Fordist" way of organizing work (Womack, Jones, and Roos, 1990). Their version of post-Fordism emphasizes how Japanese production is an alternative to Taylorism and Fordism. JPT is seen as enhancing workers' skills and their participation at work and, in general, promoting the use of workers' mental capacities in conjunction with their physical labour. In addition, many believe these companies represent a new era in labour–management relations.

But does the Saturn dream of a different kind of company really hold true? A growing body of research from both the United States and Canada suggests that JPT is really a direct extension of Fordism and Taylorism (Dassbach, 1996; Robertson et al., 1993). Even though work is subdivided into teams, scientific management is apparent insofar as jobs are still broken down into small tasks. For example, instructions for the first few tasks of a welding shop job at the CAMI plant read as follows: "A) Press the cycle stop button to release the locking pin from the tray; B) Remove empty parts tray and roll over to parts bin; C) Load parts from bin into tray, using 2 hands, lifting approximately 10 parts at a time" (Robertson et al., 1993). This is followed by six or seven more detailed instructions. When the list is completed, another car has moved in front of the worker and the cycle starts all over again. Although JPT does involve some job rotation, it is usually between two similar jobs or it is instituted simply to reduce repetitive strain injuries. Also, as in plants run on Fordist principles, managers and the computerized assembly-line technology, not the workers, set the speed of the line and the pace of work.

Although early studies of Japanese management hailed the potential for increased worker participation, recent studies have redefined this as a form of social control where workers commit solely to the goals of the company. For example, to gain employment in one of these plants, workers must undergo several days of problem solving, teamwork, and psychological testing. Workers are told this testing is to build enthusiasm for and commitment to the company. It appears, however, that one of the goals of this pre-employment screening is to weed out employees with pro-union attitudes (Graham, 1995). The team concept also tries to develop a culture of egalitarianism. Employees are called "associates" and team members, and direct supervisors are called "team leaders." But under Japanese management, teams become sites of peer pressure and social control. For instance, if a team member takes a sick day, he or she may not be replaced. Since this leaves the rest of the team to take on the sick member's work, workers pressure each other to remain at work, even when family needs or illness demand that they take time off (Kamata, 1982; Graham, 1995).

Crucial to the success of JPT is the process of *kaizening,* or continuous improvement. *Kaizen* requires workers to provide suggestions for improving the production process. The philosophy behind *kaizen* is to use workers' knowledge of their jobs to reduce production time and to balance the line so that all workers are exerting the same effort (Dassbach, 1996). On the basis of a multiyear study at CAMI in Ingersoll, Ontario, researchers showed how *kaizening* encourages workers to play a role in speeding up their jobs while reducing costs for the company. The combinination of *kaizen* and the continual line speed-ups common under JPT led the researchers to dub Japanese management "management by stress" (Robertson et al., 1993).

Workers are beginning to question whether lean production represents a new type of worker participation. In 1990, 56 percent of workers at CAMI said they viewed the company as democratic. A little over a year later, only 26 percent viewed CAMI in the same light (Robertson et al., 1993). And when asked whether workers needed a union at CAMI, those who strongly agreed a union was needed increased from 57 percent to 81 percent between 1990 and 1991. A statement by a local union official at the Ingersoll, Ontario, CAMI plant sums things up nicely (quoted in Rinehart et al., 1994: 166):

> This empowerment, when it's cost saving or quality problem, okay, but when it's human problems, a comfort issue, whatever, there's no empowerment. It's one-sided. That's the bottom line.

Japanese management, QWL programs, and other work-humanization programs still have the potential to increase worker democracy. But as long as these programs continue to be linked solely to management's desire for productivity increases and "the bottom line," the participatory potential of these programs will be limited. Alternatives, such as worker-owned companies like Algoma Steel in Sault Ste. Marie, Ontario, may bring us closer to real worker participation (Livingstone, 1993).

■ MANAGING DIVERSITY

Organizations now talk about **managing diversity** within their boundaries. This is the catchphrase for programs designed to reduce barriers for women, visible minorities, aboriginal people, and people with disabilities. Managing diversity can include providing sexual harassment awareness seminars, actively hiring and promoting visible minorities, or establishing mentorship relationships. Most of these diversity programs aim to make the formal structures of organizations discrimination-free and tolerable for all members.

A complicating factor in the potential of these programs is the informal structure or *organizational culture* of organizations. Members have shared meanings about what life is like in their organizations. Organizational culture comprises, among other things, implicit understandings of how to complete work and shared assumptions about how to interact and how to treat co-workers. When the majority of workers are white and heterosexual, the organizational culture may implicitly discount the experiences of minority employees. One lesbian employee was distressed by her own self-betrayal as she attempted to fit into her organizational culture: "I'd just come back from a gay rights march . . . and yet in that situation with those people I worked with, I couldn't say anything . . . it was extremely upsetting" (quoted in Hall, 1993: 133). E.M. Bell (1990) describes the "bicultural life experiences" of black women professionals in the United States as they move between their home life in the black community and their work life in predominantly white organizations. As one manager stated, "The white world is where I feel the most at risk. I show my white side here, which means I must be more strategic, not spontaneous" (quoted in E. Bell, 1990: 473). This woman, like other minorities, is forced to hide the black side of her identity when she goes to work. What this thumbnail sketch of organizational culture tells us is that, to "manage diversity," we must do more than change the formal structures of organizations. We must also look at how the informal culture of organizations constrains members of minority groups.

▲ WOMEN IN MANAGEMENT

Much of the research concerning women working in organizations has focussed on the movement of women into management. In Canada between 1971 and 1991, the number of women managers increased from 6 percent to 38 percent of all managers (Andrew, Coderre, and Denis, 1994). However, since only 21 percent of senior managers in Canada are women (Andrew, Coderre, and Denis, 1994), the "glass ceiling" for women has by no means disappeared. Research suggests that it is not easy for women to move into the male-dominated world of management.

Do Women and Men Manage Differently?

One barrier that women have to overcome in moving up the managerial ladder is the perception that they are ineffective managers. On the one hand, one stereotype is that of the bossy and overly controlling female manager. On the other hand, as Box 12.2 points out, current research points to an image of women as more effective and participatory managers than men. So what are we to conclude? Are women managers authoritarian or consensus-oriented? Are they different from men managers?

In her classic study of a large, white-collar organization she called "Indsco," Rosabeth Moss Kanter (1977) demonstrates that whether women managers are participatory or authoritarian often depends on their position in the organization. Kanter found that women managers at Indsco tend to be in powerless positions in the lower managerial ranks. These positions offer little room for risk taking and limited authority over organizational decisions. These powerless positions also breed rule-mindedness and territoriality on the part of managers. Knowing the rules and being able to force subordinates to follow the rules represents one of the few areas of power for "powerless" managers. Kanter concludes that, regardless of gender, if managers find themselves in a powerless position, they will likely be narrow-minded and overly controlling. So we now have a partial answer to our question. To understand why some managers — male or female — are authoritarian, we need to know whether they are in relatively powerful or powerless positions.

Judy Rosener (1990) offers a different perspective by arguing that some female managers are more interactive and people-oriented than male managers. The women interviewed by Rosener see themselves as encouraging participation, sharing power and information, enhancing the self-worth of others, and energizing co-workers and subordinates. Indicative of this style is the decision-making approach of one female CEO, who stated: "When I face a tough decision, I always ask my employees, 'What would you do if you were me?' This approach generates good ideas and introduces my employees to the complexity of management decisions" (quoted in Rosener, 1990: 122).

At first glance, Rosener seems to be supporting the view that women and men make essentially different managers. This would lead us to believe that there is something about women — biology, socialization, or life experiences — that turns them into interactive, participatory managers. Yet Rosener also acknowledges that management style is determined by organizational context, such as the location of managers in the organization hierarchy, the degree of bureau-

Box 12.2
Do Women and Men Manage Differently? Women Better Managers, Study Says

WASHINGTON — Women do a better job than men in 28 of 31 key management categories including keeping productivity high and generating ideas, but they do poorly at handling frustration, a new study reported yesterday.

This was a departure from traditional presumptions, which credit women with being nurturing team players at work but not with skills associated with top management, Janet Irwin, one of the study's authors, told Reuters.

The study, distributed by the non-profit Foundation for Future Leadership, found that women have better intuitive skills than men, but also outperform men in logic-based skills such as meeting deadlines and problem solving. The study reviewed 6,403 questionnaires dealing with 915 corporate workers; the workers themselves filled out the questionnaires, as did their supervisors, subordinates and peers. — *Reuters*

SOURCE: *The Globe and Mail,* September 19, 1996, p. A16. Reprinted by permission of Reuters.

cratization and rigidity in the organization structure, and the presence — or absence — of a culture that allows for innovation. In addition, the way in which a woman's managerial style is perceived may lead to the development of different styles. In her study of Canadian managers, Sheppard (1993) found that, while both men and women managers made "gut-level" decisions, men's quick decision making was viewed as more credible than women's. Sheppard argues that the way in which male and female decision-makers are perceived may lead women to develop a slower, more participatory style of management.

The answer to the question about gender differences in managerial style, then, is not entirely clear. In some instances, we see differences, but just as often we do not. The consensus that seems to be growing among researchers, however, is that no real differences exist between male and female managerial behaviour and effectiveness (Powell, 1990). This body of research suggests that, rather than defining certain managerial styles as male and female, we should develop a contextualized understanding of managerial styles.

■ **"WILL I LIKE MY JOB?" JOB SATISFACTION AND ALIENATION**

Nine out of ten Canadians reported they were satisfied with their jobs in 1996 (Chamberlain, 1996).

Getting respect from their bosses and feeling in control of their job mattered most to Canadian workers. Less important was the amount of money they made. This reflects much of what we know about job satisfaction. To be satisfied at work, intrinsic rewards, such as autonomy and challenging work, are as important as extrinsic or material rewards.

▲ JOB SATISFACTION

Job satisfaction refers to the subjective feelings we have toward our work. Job satisfaction usually is determined by asking workers a question such as, "How satisfied are you with your job as a whole?" Managers care about job satisfaction because it is assumed that satisfied workers are the most productive workers. Even though some research does not support this assumption (Hodson and Sullivan, 1990), job satisfaction is still important. We all deserve to have jobs that bring meaning to our lives.

What Determines Job Satisfaction?

A multitude of factors affect how we feel about our jobs, ranging from our individual characteristics to the size of the firm we work in. To give you an idea of this range, I'll discuss some of the major predictors of job satisfaction.

INDIVIDUAL CHARACTERISTICS Based on what we know about job ghettos, it might be a safe assumption to predict that women, older workers, and younger workers will be some of the least satisfied groups of workers. Although it is true that younger workers are some of the most dissatisfied workers (see Table 12.2), older workers — at least those who have stable jobs — are actually a relatively happy group (Krahn, 1992). The higher job satisfaction reported by older employed workers may be the result of reduced expectations about work, more meaningful lives outside of work, or past advancement in their jobs (Krahn and Lowe, 1993).

When you consider occupational sex segregation and the differences in jobs held by women and men, you might expect women to be less satisfied than men. In a majority of studies, though, women and men report similar levels of job satisfaction (see Table 12.2 and, e.g., Krahn, 1992). However, when evaluating their feelings about their work, women tend to compare themselves with other women (Hodson and Sullivan, 1990). If women compared themselves with men, their reported level of satisfaction might be lower.

JOB AND ORGANIZATIONAL CHARACTERISTICS Opportunities for autonomous and complex work are important predictors of job satisfaction: Satisfaction increases with autonomy and decreases with repetitive or automated work. For example, fast-food workers who repeat the same phrases every day and autoworkers who must do the same task repeatedly are less likely to be satisfied than other workers. Opportunities for participation can increase satisfaction. Workers at the CAMI plant in Ingersoll, Ontario, initially were excited about Japanese management. But when the promise of participation faded, workers' negative feelings increased (Robertson et al., 1993).

Organizational structure, such as technology and firm size, affect how happy we are at work. Blauner's (1964) classic study, *Alienation and Freedom,* shows how workers' alienation increased as technology shifted from craft work to machine tending and assembly-line work. In contrast, technology that requires the use of conceptual skills increases job satisfaction. Employees in small companies experience higher levels of satisfaction. In 1996, 48 percent of Canadians who worked in very small companies were very satisfied, compared with 41 percent who worked in large companies (see Table 12.2). As company size increases, so do workers' feelings of isolation and powerlessness. Thus, workers in small, locally owned companies are more likely to be satisfied than those working in regional and national corporations (Hodson and Sullivan, 1985).

When I consider all the individual, job, and organizational factors that influence job satisfaction, I am struck by the realization that much of our satisfaction at work is determined by things over which we have little or no control. Our employers determine how much we are paid and how challenging and autonomous our jobs will be. And the chance to work in a small, locally owned company has much to do with the employment opportunities where we live.

◆ **Table 12.2** Job Satisfaction of Canadians, 1996

Employee characteristics	Percent who are "very satisfied" with their job
All Canadians	45
Level in company	
Senior manager	57
Middle level	44
Junior level	34
Size of company	
Very small	48
Small	43
Medium	46
Large	41
Age	
18–29	37
30–39	48
40+	46
Gender	
Women	45
Men	44
Employment status	
Full-time	44
Part-time	38
Self-employed	55
Union status	
Union member	41
Nonunion member	43

SOURCE: Compiled from an Angus Reid survey reported in "The Happy Gang," *The Toronto Sun,* October 8, 1996, p. B1.

▲ ALIENATION

For Karl Marx, organizational structure does more than make us "feel" dissatisfied or powerless. Rather, the way work is set up under capitalism creates a *structural* situation of **alienation,** or "objective powerlessness" for workers. Because workers do not control the means of production or what they are producing, workers lack power over their work and lives (Rinehart, 1996). As long as management controls the conditions of work, workers have little opportunity to alleviate alienating conditions. It follows that the only way to diminish alienation is to move toward more co-operative ways of organizing work.

▲ FIGHTING ALIENATION: INDIVIDUAL AND COLLECTIVE RESPONSES TO WORK

How we "behave" on the job tells us much about the structural conditions of alienation in our workplaces. Approached in this way, the "misbehaviour" of workers appears in a different light. For example, if a worker engages in sabotage or repeatedly skips work, we might be tempted to conclude that this worker is either destructive or lazy. In contrast, some researchers argue that the alienating conditions of work lead some workers to "fight back" or react to these conditions (Edwards and Scullion, 1982; Rinehart, 1996). You may have had similar reactions to work, such as slacking off if you believed your supervisor required you to work too hard, or turning your work into a game to make the time go faster. Engaging in these behaviours does not mean you are lazy or incompetent. Rather, they are typical reactions to alienating work.

To cope with poor working conditions, some workers quit their jobs. Those who cannot quit may respond passively by socializing with co-workers, playing games, or reducing their productivity (see, e.g., Burawoy, 1979). Some managers try to prevent these types of behaviours. Taylorism was motivated in part by management's desire to reduce opportunities for workers to restrict their output.

For management, one particularly bothersome behaviour is the theft and destruction of company property. But these criminal acts may be motivated by poor working conditions. A few years ago, an undergraduate student in my class confessed that, while working in a small T-shirt design factory, she purposely poked holes in some shirts. Because management had a policy of giving damaged T-shirts to employees, one might think she did this only to take advantage of her situation. As it turns out, though, employees were paid very low wages and worked under conditions of extreme heat. This student saw her behaviour as a protest against the inadequate pay and difficult working conditions. Other workers engage in sabotage to gain concessions from management or to gain control over the work process. Factory workers may damage the assembly line to slow down the pace of work, or clerical workers may hide files to reduce their workload (Hodson and Sullivan, 1990; Rinehart, 1996).

Collective responses, such as forming unions and striking, can be effective ways to diminish alienating workplace conditions. If Sarah Inglis's co-workers had voted to form a union, they could have bargained collectively for improved pay, job security, and working conditions. Wildcat strikes, where workers spontaneously walk off the job, are effective ways to protest poor working conditions and arbitrary treatment (Rinehart, 1996). In 1996, General Motors, Canadian Airlines, and Ontario provincial government employees went on strike to protest a range of issues, from job cuts and inadequate severance packages to the subcontracting of work. Chapter 19 provides more details about the role of strikes in the Canadian labour movement's struggle for economic and social rights. Although playing games and stealing may momentarily increase workers' feelings of control over their jobs, most researchers agree that, for lasting change to occur, collective responses are needed.

■ THE FUTURE OF WORK

Good and bad jobs, nonstandard jobs, alienating work — what will the future of work hold? Although sociologists don't usually try to predict the future, we can look at some of the current trends to see where we are going.

In the immediate future, we can expect employers to continue looking for ways to reduce operating costs. As in the past, the focus will be on reducing the cost of labour. Employers continue to move factories to countries with the lowest labour costs. This, along with labour-reducing uses of technology, may further the trend of downsizing and company restructuring. As a result, fewer employees will spend their lifetime with the same employer. As the head of production for the PowerPC microchip said in 1994, "I'm here for the duration, five years or so" (quoted in Osterman, 1995: 72).

Some researchers and futurists debate what jobs will look like. As in the debates over the service

The future of work is hard to determine. Optimists emphasize the "end of the job" as we know it and the rise of self-employed, autonomous entrepreneurs. SOURCE: Chris Windsor/Tony Stone.

economy, the debate divides along pessimistic and optimistic lines. Optimists emphasize the "end of the job" as we know it (Bridges, 1994) and the rise of self-employed, autonomous entrepreneurs. Pessimists like Jeremy Rifkin (1995) predict the "end of work." In Rifkin's view, unemployment levels will continue to rise and more of us will scramble for the few remaining jobs. Both optimists and pessimists agree, however, that the days of work in large corporations may be coming to an end. But it's too early to tell which scenario, if either, will emerge.

As you've learned in this chapter, employers and employees do have some control over whether technology creates good jobs or bad jobs or reduces alienating conditions. An important issue for the future of work is whether employers or employees will set the terms by which such changes will be judged. It is clear that the century-old battle between workers and management will probably continue. And it is workers like Sarah Inglis who will attempt to organize their co-workers, so that employees improve their chances of having a say in what work will look like in the future. ■

● SUMMARY

1. In the first industrial revolution, large segments of the population moved from being peasant farmers to wage-earning factory workers living in urban areas. During the second revolution, companies increased in size and developed administrative offices with a complex division of labour.

2. The rise of the service economy is changing the types of jobs available in the labour market. The types of jobs available in the service economy and being polarized into good jobs in upper-tier industries and bad jobs in lower-tier industries.

3. The proportion of Canadians employed in nonstandard jobs is growing. Much of this job growth is fuelled by the expansion of the lower-tier service sector. Fewer Canadians are working a standard 40-hour work week. As a consequence of the growth of the service economy, downsizing, and technological advances, work hours are polarizing, resulting in a situation of overwork for some employees and underwork for others.

4. Labour-market segmentation shows that different segments exist in the labour market. Good jobs are located in core industries and firms with primary labour markets, while bad jobs may be found in peripheral industries and firms with secondary labour markets. Job ghettos are areas of the labour market that trap disadvantaged groups of workers. Labour-market shelters, such as professional associations and unions, help their members maintain access to good jobs.

5. From Taylorism to Japanese management, various management strategies are used to control workers and increase their productivity. Most strategies fall short on their claims to be participatory.

6. Research does not show a difference in men's and women's management styles. Differences are due to the position of managers or their organizational context.

7. Job satisfaction measures how workers feel about their jobs. Work and organizational characteristics are the primary predictors of how satisfied workers are.

8. Alienation is a structural condition of powerlessness that arises from the organization of work in the capitalist economy. Workers respond to alienating conditions in various ways, such as engaging in sabotage or quitting their jobs. Strikes and other collective forms of resistance may have some success in changing the conditions of work.

QUESTIONS TO CONSIDER

1. Thinking about your own work experience, do you see evidence of the service economy creating good jobs or bad jobs?

2. Do Japanese production techniques (JPTs) represent a different way of organizing work from Taylorism? If yes, how are JPTs different? Do JPTs offer new forms of participation for workers?

3. Do men and women have different managerial styles? Design a study to answer this question. Whom would you study? Would it be better to interview managers or to observe them at work? How would you be certain that your results were conclusive?

4. What is the difference between the concepts of job satisfaction and alienation? Is Marx's concept of alienation relevant for understanding work today? Why or why not? Have you ever engaged in workplace behaviour that could be interpreted as a reaction to alienating conditions? Did these behaviours change the alienating conditions? Why or why not?

GLOSSARY

alienation In Marxist theory, a structural condition of "objective powerlessness." Workers do not have power or control over their work situation and are separated from the means of production. This situation is indicative of work in a capitalist economy.

extrinsic rewards The material benefits of working. Adequate pay, benefits, and opportunities for advancement are examples.

human relations school of management A theory of management that emphasizes the importance of the social aspects of work. Proponents argue that more satisfied workers are more productive workers.

intrinsic rewards The social-psychological benefits of working. They are derived from challenging work, nonrepetitive work, autonomy, and decision-making opportunities.

Japanese production techniques (JPT) A management strategy that combines teamwork and the philosophy of *kaizen* (continuous improvement) with assembly-line work to improve efficiency and productivity of workers.

job ghettos Parts of the labour market that trap certain groups of workers.

job satisfaction A measure of how workers feel about their jobs. It is determined by asking workers in a survey, "How satisfied are you with your job as a whole?"

labour-market segmentation The separation of the labour market into sectors of good and bad jobs.

labour-market shelters Organizations that protect the jobs of certain groups of workers. Professional associations and unions are examples.

managing diversity A management strategy to help women and minorities succeed in the workplace. This strategy consists of antiracism and sexual harassment policies and awareness classes, mentorship programs, and other nondiscriminatory procedures.

nonstandard jobs Part-time, temporary, or part-year employment.

primary labour markets Characteristics of good jobs. They have an internal labour market that provides a job ladder and the opportunity for upward mobility.

structural forms of control Work arrangements that embed control of workers in the structure of the organization. Using technology to set the pace of work is an example.

Taylorism Also known as scientific management; named after its developer, Frederick Taylor; a style of management that breaks job tasks into their smallest components. Work is also separated into conceptual and manual tasks, removing the need for workers to make decisions about their work.

● SUGGESTED READING

Betcherman, Gordon, Kathryn McMullen, Norm Leckie, and Christina Caron. (1994). *The Canadian Workplace in Transition.* Kingston, ON: Industrial Relations Centre Press. Using current survey information, this text provides an empirical overview of changes occurring in Canadian organizations.

Graham, Laurie. (1995). *On the Line at Subaru-Isuzu: The Japanese Model and the American Worker.* Ithaca, NY: ILR Press and Cornell University Press. This book supplies an informative ethnography of life as a worker in a Japanese transplant factory.

Krahn, Harvey J., and Graham S. Lowe. (1993). *Work, Industry and Canadian Society,* 2nd ed. Scarborough, ON: Nelson. This text provides an overview of major topics and research in the study of work and occupations in Canada.

Myles, John. (1988). "The Expanding Middle: Some Canadian Evidence on the Deskilling Debate." *Canadian Review of Sociology and Anthropology, 25* (3), 335–64. A key assessment of the polarization of the Canadian labour market into good and bad jobs.

Rinehart, James W. (1996). *The Tyranny of Work: Alienation and the Labour Process,* 3rd ed. Toronto: Harcourt Brace. A compelling look at the history and sociology of alienation and work.

CHAPTER THIRTEEN
Education

IN THIS CHAPTER YOU WILL LEARN THAT

- there are three different sociological perspectives on education: structural functionalism, conflict theory, and interpretive approaches
- Canadian education has been shaped by the history and social forces of the country, as well as by international pressures
- inequality in educational attainment has persisted despite educational reforms of many types because it is tied to inequality in the social and economic resources of families
- the curriculum that is taught in schools reflects the changing social context
- education is closely tied to economic objectives for individuals and for society as a whole

JANE GASKELL
University of British Columbia

■ INTRODUCTION

Sociologists have asked many questions about the educational system, but most of them can be related to questions of equality and inequality (who succeeds in school and why), questions of curriculum (what knowledge is transmitted in school and why), and questions of the relation between education and work (how are changes in education related to changes in the economy, and why). One could, of course, ask many other questions about parents and teachers, ethnicity and gender, and citizenship and school organization, but most of these other questions can be related back to a concern about equality, knowledge, or the economic uses of schooling.

After outlining three theoretical approaches to education, this chapter will explore issues concerning the organization of schooling in Canada, in the context of social forces that are international as well as national. The analysis is meant to provoke you to think concretely about equality, curriculum, and linkages to work in Canadian education today. What is it about the current system that makes sense and should be preserved? What should be changed? Why? These are the chief policy issues that will concern us.

■ THEORETICAL APPROACHES

Education is something every university student knows well. It is within the framework of an educational institution that you will study this chapter, and your work as a student can be the object of reflection as you work your way through the ideas presented here. How are you studying this text? Why are you studying it? What is included and what is left out? What do you expect to achieve as a result of the study? Who is studying with you? Each of you knows education a little differently from everyone else. In this chapter, you will draw on your own experience with schools to supply the particulars that are not presented here. You will have some opinions about what schools are like, why they are like that, and what (if anything) needs to be done about them. But sociology should challenge you to see education through a variety of lenses, to understand it in new ways that challenge your taken-for-granted knowledge.

Consider a classroom. You have experienced it, as a student, in any number of ways: as a site of competition for marks, as a boring performance by a teacher, as an exciting introduction to new ways of thinking, as a place where you felt confident, or as a place where you did not know the language or felt discriminated against, or as a place where you made friends or engaged in romantic adventures. Your teacher also knows something about classrooms, from a point of view different from your own. Perhaps she experienced it as a struggle for control, as a place to prove her competence and earn some money, as an intellectual challenge to present ideas clearly, as a drain on her time with her family. Parents, politicians, social workers, employers, taxpayers, and superintendents also have experiences of schooling that frame their questions about it and their understanding of it.

In this section, you will encounter three different ways of thinking about education, three different theories for understanding how it works and why. You will prefer some approaches to others. But try to understand who would be likely to see education each way, why it might make sense, and how you could pursue the analysis of education in the terms of each approach. Sociology of education is the study of how education takes the social forms it does, how it is linked to other institutions in the society, and how it affects the people who work in it. There is no single way of understanding education that is better than all others; rather, there is an exciting dialogue among different theorists, different models, and different bodies of evidence. The multiple perspectives offered by sociology are mirrored by the multiple experiences that people have of education, and by the multiple ways they come in contact with it. Keep your own perspective in mind as you read.

▲ STRUCTURAL-FUNCTIONALIST APPROACHES: SCHOOLS REFLECT SOCIETY

In a 1959 essay on education, Talcott Parsons encapsulated the structural-functional view of schooling. He argued that schools do two things. One is **socialization**; schools socialize students, developing in them attitudes, knowledge, and skills that are necessary in adult society. Schools also do **allocation,** matching students to positions in the adult social order, grading and sorting them for the labour market. In both ways, schools are integral to the functioning of the larger society. They reflect society; they allow a new generation to carry it forward in time.

Socialization does not take place only in the school. Families, churches, peers, baseball teams, gangs, and many other places teach children many things. But schools are sanctioned by the state to socialize children, to teach them what they need to know. And what they need to know consists of many things. Cognitive learning is important. Reading, writing, and arithmetic, as well as Canadian history, algebra, and Shakespeare, which are all subjects on the **formal curriculum,** are part of what students in Canadian schools are taught. But Parsons also drew attention to the values, attitudes, and predispositions that children learn in school — that is, the moral dimensions or **informal curriculum** of schooling, including work habits, initiative, and obedience. A good pupil is one who learns well both the cognitive and the moral dimensions of schooling.

The differentiation of students along axes of achievement is a necessary part of schooling for Parsons. Schools assign tasks and judge students on their performance. Grades signal relative achievement, and the adult society will then allocate students to adult roles based on their success. Because school reflects what is necessary in the adult society, those who do better in school will do better in adult society. Marks are the exchange system. Getting an A in class, on the one hand, suggests that someone deserves to be a leader, to take a position of responsibility when they leave school. On the other hand, those who receive poor marks, or who drop out of school altogether, deserve less responsible, less demanding, and less financially rewarding jobs.

Parsons's argument rests on the assumptions of functionalist theory. He assumes that schools are part of an organic social system where each part works in harmony with the others, much as heart and lungs and pancreas are interrelated and mutually supportive in the human body. Although institutions are not always in equilibrium, for the most part schools serve the rest of society by socializing children for their adult roles, and by allocating them to those adult roles where they can make their best contribution. Schools are necessary for a stable, fair, and orderly society.

Drawing on Parsons's argument, Robert Dreeben (1968) described, in much greater detail, what aspects of the curriculum students need to learn to function in adult society, and how the structure of schools serves these functions. His argument is a good illustration of the structural-functional analysis of what is learned in school. He calls attention to four norms involved in schooling and necessary for adult society — achievement, independence, universalism, and specificity — and he relates each to the organization of schools. He shows that the structure of schools is "functional" in helping children to move from their families to the larger social structure. In

their families, children are accepted for who they are. In schools, however, children are taught by an adult who knows little about their home life, and they typically have a different teacher every year, so that children learn that their value is dependent on what they achieve, not on who they are. So schools teach the norm of achievement. Although children can work with others at home, in schools they must learn to do their own work. Interestingly, working together is called "cheating" in most circumstances. So schools teach the norm of independence. In their families, children are treated differently from their siblings, depending on their own needs and personality, but in classrooms they learn about being treated alike, as members of an age-graded class where the same work is expected of all. So schools teach the norm of universalism. And although when children are at home all aspects of their personality and relationships can be taken into account, when they are in school, they learn to be treated specifically as students. Other aspects of their life become irrelevant as soon as they walk through the door of the classroom. So schools teach the norm of the specificity of roles.

For Dreeben, teaching the ability to accept, understand, and function under norms of achievement, independence, universalism, and specificity is one of schooling's major contributions. You might pick other norms that schools teach to illustrate the ways in which schools reflect the larger society and socialize students into it. For example, students learn to be bored politely, a habit that serves us well at work and at home. Students learn to deal with social exclusion, competition, and criticism. More positively, students learn that hard work pays off, and they learn rules of fair play and discipline. In these ways and many more, schools teach students to function in the adult social world.

Meritocracy

In functionalist theory, schools are important because they constitute a **meritocracy,** a system that allocates people to adult positions on the basis of their achievement. Functionalist theory deals with differences among students and differences among adults as benign if they are based on achievement in school and if they contribute to the more efficient allocation of resources in society as a whole. Differences based on ascription — that is, characteristics you are born with — are differences that get in the way of efficient and fair allocation of people in the social order, so they need to be reduced. An equal society, in this view, would be one where adult position is based more fully on school achievement, and more children were helped to achieve in school.

However, there is a great deal of research that shows that social class and ethnic background continue to predict how well students do in school and at work, even while measures of ability or IQ also show a relationship to school achievement. Parsons recognized that both ascription and achievement determined occupational status, but he believed that achievement was becoming increasingly important. In functionalist theory, the problem becomes how to put students from different social class, ethnic, or racial backgrounds on an equal footing to compete. Some students have families that are less supportive than other families, less educated, or less able to speak the language and help their children with schoolwork. This inequality among students readmits elements of ascription into the system, for these students are held back, not by their abilities, but by the position into which they are born. The problem, then, is to provide the kind of remedial help that will put them on a fair footing and allow them to learn and compete equally.

Many special programs for disadvantaged youngsters have been based on this kind of analysis. They are designed to compensate for the deficiencies of the home environment and help children adapt to the norms of the school. Since the school reflects the dominant norms and knowledge of the society, it is important that students learn them quickly, before they fall behind and are streamed into a program that confirms their disadvantage for another generation. Remediation is provided to "fix" inequalities of social class, ethnicity, language, and race that influence progress in the school. It is not inequality per se that is the problem, but inequality that prevents children learning and competing equally in the school environment.

The question of women's education was a problem for Parsons in the 1950s. He recognized that girls and women competed equally in school, but then did not do the same things as men when they became adults. Women worked primarily in the family, men in the paid labour force. Why should women and men get the same schooling for quite different functions in the society? Parsons concluded that schooling was useful for women because it taught them how to deal with their children and how to encourage them at school. Parsons took gender differentiation for granted. But he also thought that educating women for a man's world is appropriate.

The differentiation Parsons accepted as functional for the society, especially for the family and work, sounds very old-fashioned and discriminatory today. If women study the same social and intellectual curriculum as men, it is because we assume they want and deserve access to the same choices as adults. We treat gender as an ascriptive criterion that should not interfere with judging children and adults on the basis of their achievement. And statistics show that girls hold their own and then some in schools. They tend to get higher grades than boys and to drop out less often, and they are more likely than boys to go on to higher education today, although this has only happened in the past decade. The problem for women is not educational disadvantage, at least as measured in the traditional ways on marks and achievement tests, but disadvantage in turning education into achievement in the larger society.

Status Attainment and Human-Capital Theory

Much research in sociology of education looks at the relationship between achievement in school and

Statistics show that girls tend to get higher grades than boys and to drop out of school less often. SOURCE: Peter Beck/Masterfile.

achievement in the labour market, and concludes that schooling is the best predictor of success at work. In sociology, this research has produced what are known as **status-attainment models**. The biggest studies, by American and British researchers, have found a strong relation between success at school and success at work (Blau and Duncan, 1967; Jencks, 1972; Kerckhoff, 1990). All the Canadian evidence also shows similar relationships (Porter, 1965; Ornstein, 1983). Within the status-attainment tradition, this link between educational and occupational success is interpreted as meaning that those with more achievement in school are quite properly allocated to the best occupational positions (Knotterus, 1987).

The belief that school teaches what people need to know, and that those who learn most and best at school will contribute most to the society, is expressed in economic terms in **human-capital theory**. As the name implies, this theory suggests that the economy works on the basis of human, as well as physical, capital. Schools provide the human resources necessary for economic productivity. Those with the most human capital will be the most attractive to employers, and will be paid the highest wages, indicating the greater contribution they make to the economy. There is a good deal of evidence that more-educated people are more likely to be employed and to earn more than less-educated people.

There is evidence that countries with more educated people are wealthier than countries with fewer educated people. This is interpreted within human-capital theory as showing that education does pay off economically, and that education is increasingly important in a modern, global, technologically sophisticated, and knowledge-driven economy.

Human-capital theory has been very important in arguments for increasing our investment as a society in education. If more-educated people are more productive, spending money on education is an excellent investment, not a drain on our resources. In 1964, the Economic Council of Canada estimated that investments in education were much more likely to pay off than investments in new buildings, equipment, or small business. As a result, spending on universities and community colleges was increased across the country, and enrollments in higher education rose dramatically. In the 1990s, emphasis on the importance of human capital continues, and many policy-makers are again arguing that education is more important than ever before in a knowledge-based economy. In a report released in 1992, the Economic Council of Canada urged the adoption of a variety of education-system reforms in order to increase the ability of Canada to compete successfully in a global economy. It is through concepts like human capital and meritocracy that theories of the function and contribution of education have come to have important policy implications.

▲ CONFLICT APPROACHES: A CHALLENGE TO CONSENSUS

The functionalist view of how education reflects society is a happy one; it views education as benefiting both the individual and the collective. It is a view that fits with many people's experience of schooling, especially those who have done well in school and at work, and it fits with a basically liberal view of the world (Marchak, 1975). It is particularly popular with those who are successful in school, because it suggests that what they learn is important, and that their success justifies their continuing privilege as adults. However, this kind of sociological theory has been challenged in many different ways. Conflict theory does not see society as a whole as some cohesive unit that functions for the welfare of all. Instead, society is viewed as a site of struggle between groups with different kinds and amounts of power and resources. Groups with more power are likely to control schooling and to impose their culture on it. Control of the educational agenda will always be a focus of struggle, as many social groups and movements try to affect it.

In 1976, Sam Bowles and Herb Gintis presented a Marxist version of conflict theory to challenge the dominant functionalist view of schooling. Bowles and Gintis (1976: 11) agreed that schools reflect what is required to be successful in society, but they argued that this is the case only because the dominant classes control both the schools and the larger society and use them both to perpetuate their own power:

> Education plays a dual role in the social process whereby surplus value, i.e. profit, is created and expropriated. On the one hand, by imparting technical and social skills and appropriate motivations, education increases the productive capacity of workers. On the other hand, education helps defuse and depoliticize the potentially explosive class relations of the production process, and thus serves to perpetuate the social, political and economic conditions through which a portion of the product of labor is expropriated in the form of profits.

Notice the way in which Bowles and Gintis agree with Parsons. Schools teach values and knowledge; schools sort people out. However, they do it, not for the common good, but for the greater profitability of capital, for the greater good of the already privileged. Education does not serve everyone equally; it serves the privileged few best.

Bowles and Gintis show that, because the rich possess disproportionate economic power, they also control the educational system. Through it, they impose their knowledge, their culture, and their desired ways of behaving on everyone else. The less privileged are predictably less successful, because they are less familiar with the culture of the school, and are less willing and able to conform to its demands. They are soon sorted out into high-school streams where they are taught a curriculum that prepares them to accept their subordinate position and where they rehearse their docility, obedience, and respect for authority. Just as important, everyone is taught that this system of sorting is fair, because success at school is equated with achievement and merit, and this belief legitimizes the existing social order, preventing anyone from seeing the bias of the system.

Bowles and Gintis's analysis of schooling reflects a less benign experience of classrooms, but one that most people can empathize with. They show that schools do not teach what everyone needs to know to be fully functioning adults; rather, schools teach things from the culture of the dominant classes; they teach things that will encourage people to fit into the workplace. The norms of school are not what everyone needs to know as a citizen. Instead of teaching true democracy, co-operation, creativity, and autonomy, schools emphasize norms that will turn students into good employees. In school, say Bowles and Gintis, students learn about alienated labour, hierarchy, and the fragmentation of knowledge and tasks. Schools do not develop students' intellectual and social competencies; they fit students for a work process that exploits them and that emphasizes obedience and conformity rather than serious thought and initiative. School "corresponds" to work; neither school nor work is good for most people.

Bowles and Gintis (1976: 132) also emphasize that schools reproduce the class structure. Schools stream students, and those who are streamed into the lower tracks experience more alienation, more fragmentation of work, and more hierarchy: "Even within a single school, the social relationships of different tracks tend to conform to different behavioral norms. Thus in high school, vocational and gener-al tracks emphasize rule-following and close supervision, while the college track tends toward a more open atmosphere emphasizing the internalization of norms." And all students learn about the "IQ ideology," which says that those who do well in school deserve better jobs, higher wages, and more power. By teaching this belief, schools legitimate and perpetuate the inequalities they create. They prevent people from viewing equality as an ideal; they encourage youth to blame themselves if they end up in low-paying jobs. They provide the ideological underpinnings for an unjust social order.

Bowles and Gintis thus turn Parsons's analysis on its head. They agree that schools serve the larger social order, but they argue that the social order benefits mainly the most powerful people who exercise control over the economy.

Maintaining Dominance through Schooling

To understand why some groups benefit more from education than others, conflict analysis draws our attention to the question of whose knowledge is reflected in schools, and which groups are served by the norms that schools foster. Instead of calling for remedial programs for the disadvantaged, as Parsons would, conflict theorists argue that we should change the structure and organization of schooling so that it more fairly reflects the knowledge and norms of less-powerful groups.

Many scholars aside from Bowles and Gintis have made this kind of argument. The work of Pierre Bourdieu on "cultural capital" has been particularly influential in shaping the discussion of how education reproduces social inequalities. Bourdieu and Passeron (1977: 71) write that the sociology of education "endeavours to determine the contribution made by the educational system to the reproduction of the structure of relationships between classes, by contributing to the reproduction of the structure of the distinction of cultural capital among these classes." In other words, education teaches and sorts on the basis of culture. Those who have the kind of background or "habitus" that allows them to participate easily in the dominant culture that characterizes educational institutions will reproduce their privilege through education.

A Canadian study of music classrooms by Shepherd and Vulliamy (1983) explores how the reproduction of cultural capital works in Ontario schools. Teachers typically take up the study of music from within a classical European paradigm, emphasizing formal structure and musical notation. This manages to make students' understanding of "their" ethnic and emotionally charged in Ontario and Quebec, because the issue raises the question of whose heritage constitutes Canada's cultural legacy. The notion of two founding nations and languages, English and French, is challenged by the notion that other languages should also be taught in public schools.

A look at the content of history courses in the Quebec schools and in English-Canadian schools provides a second illustration of the way social and historical context shapes curriculum. Hodgett's study of Canadian civic education in 1964 found that textbooks in English Canada offered a bland, consensus interpretation of Canadian society, based on "nice, neat little acts of parliament." Quebec textbooks discussed quite a different history (Tomkins, 1986). In 1977, the Royal Commission on Biculturalism and Bilingualism worried that there were two mutually exclusive historical traditions representing the two different linguistic communities. In the constitutional debates of 1992, it was apparent that this situation had not changed. There is increased demand for a social history of Canada that includes Native people, rural communities, women's work in the home, and the organization of labour unions, but in many cases history texts continue to represent Canada's history as a political one dominated by powerful men of Anglo-Saxon or French background.

▲ RELATION TO WORK

With the economic challenges of a global economy and the economic restructuring that globalization is forcing on Canada, concern has been surfacing about the economic imperatives of having a well-educated labour force. Recent school-reform efforts have been driven by the rhetoric of economic competition, often with Japan, South Korea, and Taiwan, whose education systems are much more examination-oriented and where students do a great deal of school work at home (see Figures 13.2 and 13.3).

In 1992, the Economic Council of Canada wrote another report on schooling that included international comparisons of educational achievement which suggested Canada did not do very well. The council argued (Economic Council of Canada, 1992: 1):

> Educational attainment has a strong influence on earnings and employment, and since most Canadian adults participate in the labour market, this link is of vital importance to the economy. Indeed, education is a good investment: after taking account of the direct costs of schooling and of forgone earnings, the additional income from completing secondary school yields a rate of return of some 30 per-

◆ **Figure 13.2** Top 18 Countries in Science and Math Test Average Scores (Out of 41 Tested), 13-Year-Old Students, 1994–1995[a]

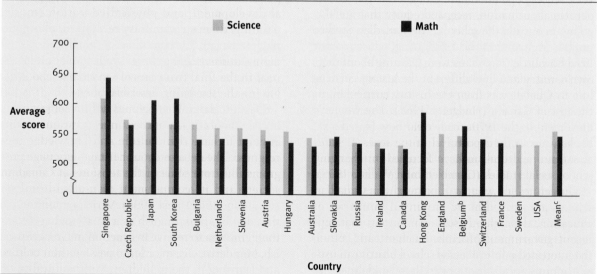

[a] Where only one bar appears for a given country, it means that the country was not in the top 18 on the test for which no bar appears.

[b] Flanders only (Wallonia recorded separately).

[c] Mean for all 41 countries tested.

SOURCE: Data from Third International Maths and Science Study (TIMSS), as reported in "Who's Top?" *The Economist*, March 29, 1997.

Notice the way in which Bowles and Gintis agree with Parsons. Schools teach values and knowledge; schools sort people out. However, they do it, not for the common good, but for the greater profitability of capital, for the greater good of the already privileged. Education does not serve everyone equally; it serves the privileged few best.

Bowles and Gintis show that, because the rich possess disproportionate economic power, they also control the educational system. Through it, they impose their knowledge, their culture, and their desired ways of behaving on everyone else. The less privileged are predictably less successful, because they are less familiar with the culture of the school, and are less willing and able to conform to its demands. They are soon sorted out into high-school streams where they are taught a curriculum that prepares them to accept their subordinate position and where they rehearse their docility, obedience, and respect for authority. Just as important, everyone is taught that this system of sorting is fair, because success at school is equated with achievement and merit, and this belief legitimizes the existing social order, preventing anyone from seeing the bias of the system.

Bowles and Gintis's analysis of schooling reflects a less benign experience of classrooms, but one that most people can empathize with. They show that schools do not teach what everyone needs to know to be fully functioning adults; rather, schools teach things from the culture of the dominant classes; they teach things that will encourage people to fit into the workplace. The norms of school are not what everyone needs to know as a citizen. Instead of teaching true democracy, co-operation, creativity, and autonomy, schools emphasize norms that will turn students into good employees. In school, say Bowles and Gintis, students learn about alienated labour, hierarchy, and the fragmentation of knowledge and tasks. Schools do not develop students' intellectual and social competencies; they fit students for a work process that exploits them and that emphasizes obedience and conformity rather than serious thought and initiative. School "corresponds" to work; neither school nor work is good for most people.

Bowles and Gintis (1976: 132) also emphasize that schools reproduce the class structure. Schools stream students, and those who are streamed into the lower tracks experience more alienation, more fragmentation of work, and more hierarchy: "Even within a single school, the social relationships of different tracks tend to conform to different behavioral norms. Thus in high school, vocational and gener-al tracks emphasize rule-following and close supervision, while the college track tends toward a more open atmosphere emphasizing the internalization of norms." And all students learn about the "IQ ideology," which says that those who do well in school deserve better jobs, higher wages, and more power. By teaching this belief, schools legitimate and perpetuate the inequalities they create. They prevent people from viewing equality as an ideal; they encourage youth to blame themselves if they end up in low-paying jobs. They provide the ideological underpinnings for an unjust social order.

Bowles and Gintis thus turn Parsons's analysis on its head. They agree that schools serve the larger social order, but they argue that the social order benefits mainly the most powerful people who exercise control over the economy.

Maintaining Dominance through Schooling

To understand why some groups benefit more from education than others, conflict analysis draws our attention to the question of whose knowledge is reflected in schools, and which groups are served by the norms that schools foster. Instead of calling for remedial programs for the disadvantaged, as Parsons would, conflict theorists argue that we should change the structure and organization of schooling so that it more fairly reflects the knowledge and norms of less-powerful groups.

Many scholars aside from Bowles and Gintis have made this kind of argument. The work of Pierre Bourdieu on "cultural capital" has been particularly influential in shaping the discussion of how education reproduces social inequalities. Bourdieu and Passeron (1977: 71) write that the sociology of education "endeavours to determine the contribution made by the educational system to the reproduction of the structure of relationships between classes, by contributing to the reproduction of the structure of the distinction of cultural capital among these classes." In other words, education teaches and sorts on the basis of culture. Those who have the kind of background or "habitus" that allows them to participate easily in the dominant culture that characterizes educational institutions will reproduce their privilege through education.

A Canadian study of music classrooms by Shepherd and Vulliamy (1983) explores how the reproduction of cultural capital works in Ontario schools. Teachers typically take up the study of music from within a classical European paradigm, emphasizing formal structure and musical notation. This manages to make students' understanding of "their" ethnic or regional music irrelevant for the purposes of instruction and imposes a dominant musical ideology. Instead of encouraging personal, individual statements through music, music classes encourage the impersonal and abstract manipulation of a simple harmonic-rhythmic framework. Shepherd and Vulliamy conclude, however, that the distinction between "school music" and "student music is less pronounced in Ontario classrooms than in British classrooms. That is because, in Ontario, music is a marginal subject in the curriculum and a wider scope of music is allowed into the classroom.

First Nations people have similarly argued that the structure and organization of schooling excludes their knowledge, their spirituality, and their understanding of the world. Many Native people have struggled to get more control over the schools their children attend, and to change the content and organization of what is taught. A case study of one secondary school in Vancouver (Kelly, 1995) illustrates the problems. The school developed a program called *Tumanos* ("guardian spirit" in the Coast Salish language) for First Nations students across the city. Aboriginal spiritual practices like smudging ceremonies were eventually introduced, but not without conflict. Kelly describes the initial reaction to the program as "We can't have any fire or any flame in any school building. You can't smoke on school grounds. And that concludes that." After a particularly difficult incident involving the loss of a teacher, the principal allowed the ceremony as a form of healing for the program. But still teachers asked, "What about the School Act? Isn't this religion? How come you're doing this in a public school?" The incident illustrates the fundamental ways in which the public school system reflects the values, culture, and practices of dominant groups, even though these can be challenged.

This kind of analysis of the ideology of schooling, of what knowledge is included, and how it is studied can be pursued in all subject areas. Studies of textbooks have pointed out that school versions of history are the versions held by employers rather than by workers, and Anglo-Canadians rather than aboriginal Canadians (Osborne, 1980; Apple, 1988). The language demanded in school is "standard English," the language of the dominant group, while dialects and intelligible but nonstandard speech are not allowed (Bernstein, 1977). School art and literature have been drawn overwhelmingly from the classic European tradition, including Canadian examples that share in the assumptions of this tradition. Whose knowledge and culture are reflected in schools? Your experience, along with sociological studies, will tell you that it is most often the knowledge and culture of men with a European heritage and a reasonable standard of living. This is the dominant culture, and the knowledge of the powerful.

The norms of schooling similarly reflect and justify the status quo. Students are taught that their grades reflect their ability and effort. They learn to accept inequality as a legitimate outcome of individual differences, rather than as a structure that perpetuates injustice. Schooling reinforces inequalities in contemporary society in that it works hard to convince students that inequalities are the result of individual effort and talent: "After all, if he didn't do his math homework, and failed the test, what do you expect?"

The conflict tradition, then, tends to see the inequalities involved in schooling as a function of social inequalities reflected in the structure of the school curriculum. It points to ways in which schools could adjust better to students and their families, rather than looking for better ways to fit students and their families into the school system. But because schools, like the society, are controlled by the relatively powerful, educational change depends on change in relations of power outside the school system.

Credentialing

Bowles and Gintis argue that schools reflect the needs of employers for a docile labour force. They reanalyze status-attainment data to argue that it is schooling, not ability, that accounts for success at work. Randall Collins (1979) takes the argument about school credentials further. He shows that **credentials** act as a signal to employers about the kind of culture that students have, and thus act as a barrier to equality in the labour market. Collins argues that credentials do not signal the knowledge or skills that are necessary to perform a job; instead, they signal the fact that someone has been able to get through school and therefore can display the ways of acting and thinking — the class and ethnic culture — that are demanded in the workplace. Many individuals could quite adequately perform the tasks involved in jobs that they are disqualified from because they do not have the right credentials. Educational credentials, then, are a kind of "cultural currency," and a barrier to equality in the labour market.

Collins's argument is based in a critique of the technocratic, industrial model of society espoused by functionalist theory. Instead of an increasingly complex society that demands more sophisticated skills in the workplace, Collins sees a society where jobs are deskilled by technology and access to good jobs is controlled by credentials that bear little relation to skill. He assumes most people can do most jobs and learn them in a short time at work. He shows how professional groups, like doctors and lawyers, manage to exclude anyone without the "proper" education in order to minimize competition and keep their incomes high. He also shows how the competition for credentials has produced "credential inflation," a highly irrational system that demands far more schooling from people than is necessary for the workplace or good for anyone.

Human-capital theory and status-attainment models assume that everyone competes with everyone else in the labour market, and that employers will hire the person with the best qualifications. But the fact is that people search for work in *specialized* labour markets, set apart by credentials and by personal characteristics. The analysis of "segmented labour markets" has been important in providing an alternative account of why the relation between education and work posited by functionalist theory is inadequate.

The argument can be seen most clearly with regard to women: Women earn less for each year of education they bring to the labour market than men do. Thus, as Figure 13.1 shows, for Canadians employed full-time and in their 40s, men earn more than women at all levels of educational attainment. In general, women have not been able to turn their educational advantage into labour-market success in the way that human-capital theory or status-attainment models would predict.

Why should this be so? Because women have been segregated into jobs where men do not work. Clerical and secretarial jobs, certain kinds of service occupations, and certain kinds of factory jobs are held almost exclusively by women, and these occupations tend to pay less for education than do male occupations. These jobs also tend to offer less on-the-job education to workers. So, even if women do get a great deal of education, unless they move outside these labour markets or change the nature of their jobs, they will not increase their wages. In order to turn their education into more income, women need to change the value placed on their credentials in the labour markets in which they compete. The problem is not lack of education; the problem is that education per se is not valued across the board by employers and used to allocate people to work in the simple way suggested by the status-attainment model. Firms, labour markets, and hiring practices need to be understood as complex institutional processes in themselves, ones that sometimes do and sometimes do not reward education and educational credentials (see Chapter 8).

▲ INTERPRETIVE APPROACHES: MEANING AND CULTURE

Both structural-functionalist and conflict perspectives paint a view of education in broad strokes. They provide a general interpretation of how schools

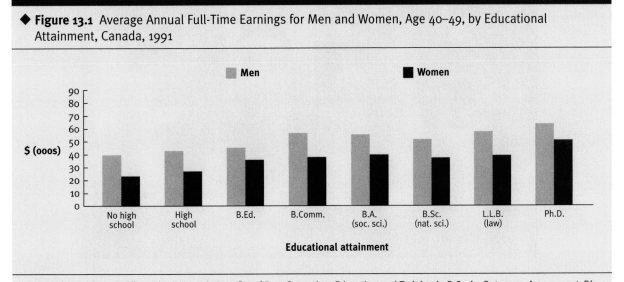

◆ **Figure 13.1** Average Annual Full-Time Earnings for Men and Women, Age 40–49, by Educational Attainment, Canada, 1991

SOURCE: Adapted from R. Allen, *The Economic Benefits of Post Secondary Education and Training in B.C.: An Outcomes Assessment*, Discussion paper DP-34 (Vancouver: Centre for Research on Economic and Social Policy, 1996).

either "correspond to" or serve the larger social structures of the society. Both try to understand the ways schools "really" are and why. In contrast, interpretive approaches to sociology are more interested in elucidating how people understand and therefore respond to schooling. Some would argue there is not, and cannot be, a single explanation of schooling. We each develop our own interpretations that reflect our own position in the world. Trying to communicate among the various interpretations, much less test which ones are correct, is difficult, and probably impossible. But making the effort to understand how others see things makes us better educators, better citizens, and better analysts of society.

Studies in the interpretive tradition of the sociology of education take a close look at the everyday interactions and understandings that constitute schooling. They examine how students, teachers, and parents make meaning out of their experience of school and act on it. This kind of scholarship is also concerned with reflecting on the standpoint of sociologists, who, after all, become participants in the process of producing meaning when writing up observations, interviews, and statistics.

In this section, you will find a description of some studies of school processes that try to explain what school feels like to the people in it, and then work from that explanation to an understanding of how school as an institution should be understood in its social context. These studies address many of the same questions addressed above: How do schools produce inequality? How is school related to work? How is the curriculum arrived at? But the interpretive approach to studying these issues focusses on people as makers of meaning, as interpreters of an ambiguous social world.

The Production of Inequality

One of the most important studies of the production and reproduction of understandings about schooling is Paul Willis's *Learning to Labour.* Willis, who takes a Marxist view of class reproduction in schools, starts his book with this observation (1977: 1):

> The difficult thing to explain about how middle class kids get middle class jobs is why others let them. The difficult thing to explain about how working class kids get working class jobs is why they let themselves.... There is no obvious physical coercion and a degree of self direction. This is despite the inferior rewards for, undesirable social definition of, and increasing intrinsic meaninglessness of manual work: in a word, its location at the bottom of a class society.

Studies in the postmodernist tradition of the sociology of education take a close look at the everyday interactions and understandings that constitute schooling. SOURCE: Tom and DeeAnn McCarthy/First Light.

Willis questions how the "IQ ideology" could possibly convince young people to take working-class jobs, and he wants to know how young people understand schools and work so that they "choose" working-class jobs. Why do they understand work as an attractive option, when most sociologists have seen it as a terrible option?

Willis hung around with a few working-class male adolescents known as "the lads." He interviewed them and followed them to their homes and leisure-time activities. He tried to understand their culture, their understandings of school and work, and the connections between them. He reported that the lads do not buy into the "IQ ideology" of the school; they do not believe the well-meant liberal platitudes that school is good for you and will open up opportunities in the class structure. Instead, they rebel against the school, its teachers, and its promise of upward mobility, vaunting their physical activity in the face of its bookishness, their masculinity in the face of its femininity, their outrageousness in the face of the demand for conformity, their rudeness to counter the demand for politeness, their self-assertion in the face of the demand for docility. He explores how their understanding of the school and of class structure is taken up within the culture of working-class masculinity and the shop floor to produce an understanding of the world that allows them to rebel, but at the same time confirms their position at the bottom of class society, in the working-class jobs of their fathers.

Willis examines class and school structure in relation to the production of meaning and culture. He sees the reproduction of class society, not as a structural necessity, but as a cultural achievement that must be accomplished over and over again in the school. The reproduction of class society is not determined by capitalism or any other structure of power, but is acted out within particular structural conditions, cultures, and ideologies by particular people. And every time it is done, it is done slightly differently, for each person reworks the culture, recreates it, and gives it new meanings. This is an active creation by inquiring human beings, not a passive reception of the already given.

A more recent study by Annette Lareau (1991) explores the interaction of parents with the school. Lareau wanted to know how social-class differences are given social meaning in the day-to-day interactions between parents and their children and between parents and teachers. She knew that children from working-class homes are less likely to do well in school, but she wanted to know how this is actually worked out in everyday interactions and un-

derstandings. Lareau therefore chose two different schools, one working-class and one middle-class. She interviewed teachers, parents, and children. She observed the classroom and attended parent–teacher interviews. She tried to understand what people actually do and why, from their own point of view.

Lareau shows how upper-middle-class parents have the competence to help their children in school, because of their understanding of the language and the social patterns that are practised there. Their social status itself is a resource they can use to get the attention of the teacher and have her take their opinions seriously. Their self-confidence and status convince them that they have the right and even the responsibility to intervene. They have the income and material resources, the social networks, and the expectation that work and home should be connected, not kept apart. Thus, a variety of beliefs, resources, and practices amount to effective intervention by middle-class parents that is denied to working-class parents.

Both Willis and Lareau examine a question raised by functionalist and conflict theories: How does sorting get accomplished and justified in schools? But both examine it by looking in great detail at the activities and understandings of the people who are involved. Both give a sense that "the system" is not a static monolith, because people and their action constitute that system, and people can change and rebel and change their minds. They do so within a structure that shapes what is possible and within a set of dominant beliefs that shape the meanings they are able to make.

Classroom Knowledge

The things that are taught in school can be seen as tightly determined by the social structure, either reflecting what everyone needs to know or reflecting the culture of the dominant group. But curriculum can also be seen as a struggle over meaning, as a daily negotiation between people with different conceptions of what is true and important, and what it all signifies. The curriculum is constructed in the daily interactions of students with teachers; it is influenced by teachers, school boards, students, parents, and employers, and it changes over time.

What is learned in school? Linda McNeil (1986) shows that what is taught in schools is no mere reflection of a larger social order; it is the product of teachers' decisions as they try to satisfy the requirements of their jobs within their own understandings of what is possible and desirable. In schools, teachers' primary concern must be to manage, to control students, and to turn out the grades for which they are accountable. Teachers take broad curriculum guidelines and turn them into little bits of knowledge, assignments, and tests that can be marked and used to grade and sort students. McNeil looks closely at how and why teachers fragment knowledge and insist on control, and how and why students in turn respond with disengagement from the knowledge and hierarchy with which they are confronted. Unlike Bowles and Gintis, she attributes the curriculum and the resultant reproduction of cultural knowledge and norms less to capitalist interests and more to the understandings and requirements of life inside schools. She explores how teachers think about their work and finds their concerns to be concrete and rooted in their working conditions, just as the concerns of students are.

The three different sociological approaches to schooling — functionalist, conflict, and interpretive — are not mutually exclusive. There is overlap between the way Parsons sees schools as being functionally related to the larger society and the way Bowles and Gintis see schools as a focus of the struggle between groups in society. Both suggest a fairly strong structural relation between the school and other social institutions. In contrast, most interpretive studies see the relation between schools and society as depending on the generation of meaning and culture. But the interpretive studies need some macrosociological understandings about where schools fit in the social order to make sense of their observations about how teachers understand their students, why students drop out of school, or what the curriculum represents in the way of compromise between students, teachers, and the state. Although the three approaches are related, they highlight different dimensions of schooling and reflect the different concerns and experiences of the sociologists who do the research and write the books. Within each kind of analysis, there is great variation in the themes sociologists have chosen to develop. There is much scope for interesting research and interpretation of schools, and the development of our understanding of Canadian education.

■ SCHOOLING IN CANADA

This section analyzes three important sociological aspects of the Canadian educational system: how ef-

fectively it promotes equality, how curriculum is shaped by social context, and how education is related to the world of work. It begins by considering the controversial question of equality.

▲ EQUALITY

John Porter, in his classic *The Vertical Mosaic* (1965: 198), emphasized the problems Canadian schools face in educating all students equally: "No society in the modern period can afford to ignore the ability which lies in the lower social strata. Whatever may be said about average intelligence and social class, the fact remains that in absolute numbers there is more of the highly intelligent in lower classes than in the higher." Porter showed, however, that those who stayed in school were disproportionately from families with higher socioeconomic status, as were those who went to university. He called for much greater effort to ensure the accessibility of higher education to students from lower-income backgrounds (1965: 198): "Without such policies intergenerational continuity of class will remain, mobility deprivation will continue, and external recruitment will still be required to meet the needs of a complex occupational structure."

It is clear that students from wealthier backgrounds perform better in Canadian schools and stay there longer. Students who leave before completing high school are more likely to come from poorer backgrounds. Canadian studies continue to show the correlation of social class with school achievement and university enrollment (Gilbert, 1993; Guppy and Pendakur, 1989). Aboriginal people have much lower rates of educational attainment than nonaboriginals. The 1991 census shows that 2.7 percent of aboriginal peoples have university degrees, compared with 20.8 percent of all Canadians. One-third of the on-reserve population in Canada had less than Grade 9 formal education, and Grade 9 has been defined as a minimal functional literacy level.

Staying in school beyond the compulsory leaving age and into university has always been closely related to social-class background. Axelrod (1990) notes that, from 1920 to 1950, nearly one-half of the student population at Memorial University of Newfoundland came from middle- and upper-class backgrounds, while only 10 percent of Newfoundland society was composed of these groups. Axelrod argues that Canadian universities in the interwar years "made the middle class" — that is, universities instilled in students the understandings and habits of middle-class Canada. Many of these habits and understandings excluded those who were not white males with an Anglo-Saxon heritage (Axelrod, 1990: 32): "Overwhelmingly white, Anglo-Celtic Protestant, and to a lesser degree Catholic, English Canadian universities were determined to preserve their cultural mix. Like those administering immigration policy, university officials did this not by banning minority groups, but by rigidly controlling their numbers." The "nonpreferred" students at the University of Manitoba, to take just one example, consisted of women, Jews, Ukranians, Poles, Dutch, Norwegians, Germans, Italians, and Mennonites. Students in these categories had to have much higher marks than "preferred" students to be admitted.

The expansion of universities since World War II has done little to change the class bias of the student body. Robert Pike (1981: 5), in his review of a variety of sociological studies, concludes that "there was no indication that the university expansion had been accompanied by more than a small increase in the participation rates of students of lower class origins relative to the participation of students from the more privileged classes." Neil Guppy (1984: 89) comes to the same conclusion: "The effects of higher educational expansion in Canada, as this relates to equality of opportunity, would seem to have operated to preserve the place of privilege at the university level." In 1985, the Report of the Royal Commission on the Economic Union and Development Prospects of Canada (the McDonald commission) reported that children whose parents hold bachelor degrees are three times more likely to attend university than children of parents without degrees. Parents of students at community colleges tend to have lower levels of education than parents of university students.

Until recently, women have been less likely to attend university than men, even though they have been more likely to graduate from secondary school since the turn of the century. Between 1920 and 1960, women constituted between 20 percent and 25 percent of university enrollments. This proportion has increased dramatically in the last 30 years. By 1970, women made up almost 37 percent of university enrollments, and, in 1988, women's enrollment surpassed men's. As Bellamy and Guppy (1992: 169) put it: "One way of illustrating the trend in enrollment patterns is to note that in the last 35 years, the number of male students has increased by 294 percent, while female enrollments have increased by an astounding 1420 percent." Gender difference remains clear in patterns of enrollment at universi-

ties, however. Women constitute about 11 percent of engineering students, 42 percent of medical students, and 45 percent of commerce students, but 59 percent of arts students, 70 percent of education students, and 96 percent of nursing students (Bellamy and Guppy, 1992).

The reasons for the differential success and enrollment patterns of different kinds of students can be traced to students' social characteristics and also to the character of the school system within which these differences are translated into differences in academic achievement. For example, school financing varies across the country. The Atlantic provinces spent $4800 per pupil for elementary and secondary schools in 1989–90, while Quebec and Ontario spent $6000. A recent study by the Economic Council of Canada (1992) concludes that, although this regional spending pattern plays a significant role in explaining the poorer educational achievement of students in the Atlantic provinces, it is far from a complete explanation, because levels of funding do not correlate closely with school achievement. Many studies have shown little relationship between measures of school resources and student-achievement scores.

Because children in Canada usually attend school in their own neighbourhood, they attend school with children who share their own social characteristics. Several studies, like the one by Lareau (1991), have shown the dramatic effect that neighbourhood composition has on the curriculum and social relations of even very early schooling. In recent years, the introduction of French-immersion programs, to which many English-speaking professional middle-class families send their children, has exacerbated the segregation of relatively privileged students in the public schools (Olsen and Burns, 1983).

The practice of grouping students within classrooms has also been seen as a factor in the differential success of students. Early in the elementary schools, different reading groups — the "robins" and the "swallows" — are separated out and subjected to different expectations and different methods of teaching. Stephen Richer (1979) has also looked at the organization of a kindergarten class with attention to gender divisions. He shows how a kindergarten classroom continues a process of gender identity formation through voluntary seating patterns that separate girls and boys, higher use of physical aggression by boys, and play patterns that reproduce stereotypical "mummy" and "daddy" roles. A more recent study of Grade 8 classrooms by Linda Eyre (1992) shows continuing informal separation of girls and boys in class, verbal harassment of girls and ethnic minorities, and gender-specific expectations about who performs technical and domestic tasks.

In secondary schools, a more formal streaming process tends to further separate students, ostensibly by academic ability and interest, but actually also by class, gender, and ethnicity. Until the late 1960s, students in secondary schools were clearly streamed into vocational or academic programs, each with its own course requirements, examinations, and diploma. Students from working-class homes were more likely to be in the vocational stream; girls were more likely to be in the typing classes; children from most ethnic minorities were more likely to be in the lower academic streams.

In the early 1970s, overt streaming mandated by the school was replaced by a system where students streamed themselves through their selection of courses. Today, streaming is more disguised in some provinces than in others by the organization of the secondary-school curriculum. Ontario has a clearly streamed system that is defended by the teachers' federation, but it is increasingly being questioned by the government. Ontario schools offer courses at different levels — labelled gifted, academic, general, basic, etc., and numbered hierarchically from 1 to 6. For example, a Grade 11 student could choose to take a level 6 history course, or a level 5 or a level 4. Only level 5 or 6 courses provide an "academic" credit that is counted at the university level. Students tend to see themselves as in one stream or another, although they do not have to take all their courses at the same level.

In British Columbia, the process is more subtle. Few courses are officially streamed. Only a few are labelled "modified," signalling a lower level of difficulty. Differences in students' programs arise through the type of course they select and whether these courses count toward university admission, rather than through the level of difficulty that is officially attributed to the course. The more academic students who are planning to continue their education take more mathematics, science, language, and history courses. Those who are not planning to continue take more vocational electives — for example, business math, home economics, media studies, and human biology (Gaskell, 1992).

Some of the studies of the changes in streaming practices in the 1970s stressed how pleased students were to take responsibility for their course choices, instead of having them imposed by the school. Students felt much more in control of their own school careers and, if they did badly or could not get into university, they would tend to blame themselves for selecting the wrong courses instead of blaming

teachers or the school for inadequate instruction (Fleming, 1974). In fact, though, streaming has merely become more difficult to describe and assess. Under the new system, statistics are hard to collect and rarely reported. The streaming is not hidden from the view of students themselves, who are fairly clear about their relative position, nor from postsecondary institutions, who deny entry to students who have not taken appropriate courses.

▲ KNOWLEDGE

School curriculum has been shaped by an ongoing series of debates about the nature of knowledge, the needs of children, and the needs of the society. These debates have been international, as well as national. Prestigious centres of scholarship like Oxford, Cambridge, the Sorbonne, and Harvard have had a huge influence on what is taught around the world, especially from the level of secondary education up. Students in Africa, Australia, and Thailand have studied many of the same texts in secondary schools. Today, arguments about a global economy have increased pressure to teach a curriculum that is global in its scope, while nationalist sentiments have increased pressure to teach local history, geography, and literature. Although the currency of high scholarship remains, educators have expanded the curriculum to attract a wider variety of students, and employers have often pressed to make the curriculum more practical.

The curriculum through most of the nineteenth century was dominated by Greek, Latin, and mathematics, with a smattering of history, English, and geography. After 1880, schools began to add science, modern languages, and technology. At the turn of the century, Canadian secondary schools offered an eclectic mixture of useful subjects for the local bourgeoisie (accounting, penmanship, surveying, navigation) alongside Latin and the more traditional subjects (Gidney and Millar, 1990). Most students would pick up a smattering of different kinds of courses.

In the early twentieth century, the introduction of subjects of use to the working class occasioned much debate. A 1918 report by the Royal Commission on Vocational Education recommended the inclusion of industrial and technical education, domestic science, and typing. Subject matter in the curriculum became an instrument through which students would learn to function in society, rather than the repository of general knowledge for all. Typing, manual arts, some technical subjects, and home economics were clearly labelled vocational and separated from academic courses. As enrollments increased, vocational offerings expanded, but they remained firmly segregated and were considered "second-class." Through the 1930s and 1940s, many schools resisted the incursions of the reformers, and the traditional academic curriculum held its place of prominence. But the belief that students destined for different positions in the economy needed different kinds of knowledge and skills became standard in Canadian schools.

Debates about the content of curriculum can be linked closely to the social context in which they arose. After the Russians launched Sputnik at the height of the Cold War, curriculum reform in Western countries centred on science and mathematics teaching. The "new math" came out of a major reform effort launched by university researchers and mathematicians, based in beliefs about children "learning by discovery." The curriculum was aimed at college-bound students, originally in the secondary grades. It revolutionized textbooks in the early 1960s, as concepts such as sets, nondecimal bases, prime numbers, and factors were introduced for the first time. The reform foundered on the noncomprehension, not just of teachers, but of parents, as it spread through the curriculum to all children, and all families. A concept developed by top-flight mathematicians was unable to change the culture of schools (Lazerson et al., 1985).

More recently, attempts to change the social-studies curriculum to include the experience of a more diverse school population have brought into the schools debates about nation, race, and equity that are also going on outside the schools. The Canadian Studies project originated in the 1960s when educators noticed how little Canadians were learning about their own country, and how different the history curriculum in Quebec was from the history curriculum in the rest of Canada (Hodgetts, 1964). The women's movement in the 1970s made clear how biased textbooks were in their portrayal of the sexes. Debates about multiculturalism have focussed on changing school social studies (Cornbleth and Walker, 1995).

Guidelines for what will be taught in Canadian schools are arrived at by provincial ministries of education, through advisory committees that represent government officials, teachers, and, often, the interested public. Elected school boards can usually approve local variations in these guidelines and develop their own courses. Curriculum is translated into practice by teachers in their own classrooms, with some supervision from principals, curriculum specialists at the provincial and local level, and other

teachers. The process is a political one, where the public has a clear role. The process is also fairly loose, especially when, as is almost always the case, testing and reporting to parents are controlled by teachers themselves. Province-wide examinations, which were the norm in Canada through the 1960s, were phased out in the 1970s, and then were gradually and selectively reintroduced in the 1980s.

The elementary curriculum is based largely in language arts and mathematics, with social studies, science, music, art, and physical education also having their place. Students tend to be taught several subjects by the same teacher, a structure that allows the integration of content from different areas, and encourages a "child-centred" pedagogy. There is virtually no explicitly vocational content in the elementary curriculum, although "relevance" to children's lives is an integral part of what most teachers espouse.

The secondary-school curriculum in Canada today has been described as a "smorgasbord" or "cafeteria." A wide range of courses is available for credit toward a high-school diploma, especially in large urban schools. Students are required to take some core subjects, usually English, mathematics, social studies, and science. Canadian history, social studies, and literature are introduced at some point in the curriculum, reflecting an emphasis on citizenship and nationalism. Some courses are vocational in their orientation (e.g., carpentry, cafeteria, electronics, marketing, accounting, home economics, typing, work experience); others are considered more academic (history, geography, calculus, French, physics, computer science); and others are in fine arts, personal development, and physical education (music, painting, drama, community recreation, photography, guidance). The requirements for all students are more extensive in the earlier grades, and quite minimal in the final two years of secondary school, allowing the streaming described above.

Debates about what belongs within subject areas in the school curriculum continue as various groups attempt to have their culture and knowledge represented. The debates about heritage-language programs illustrate some of the tensions of Canadian society and its commitment to multiculturalism (Cummins and Danesi, 1990). Various communities that do not speak English as a first language want their children to receive instruction in Greek, Spanish, Mandarin, etc., in order to pass on their culture and learning to their children. Multiculturalism is official policy in Canada, and some school boards have tried to accommodate these demands, allowing after-hours instruction or even integrating it into the school day. But debate has been particularly divisive and emotionally charged in Ontario and Quebec, because the issue raises the question of whose heritage constitutes Canada's cultural legacy. The notion of two founding nations and languages, English and French, is challenged by the notion that other languages should also be taught in public schools.

A look at the content of history courses in the Quebec schools and in English-Canadian schools provides a second illustration of the way social and historical context shapes curriculum. Hodgett's study of Canadian civic education in 1964 found that textbooks in English Canada offered a bland, consensus interpretation of Canadian society, based on "nice, neat little acts of parliament." Quebec textbooks discussed quite a different history (Tomkins, 1986). In 1977, the Royal Commission on Biculturalism and Bilingualism worried that there were two mutually exclusive historical traditions representing the two different linguistic communities. In the constitutional debates of 1992, it was apparent that this situation had not changed. There is increased demand for a social history of Canada that includes Native people, rural communities, women's work in the home, and the organization of labour unions, but in many cases history texts continue to represent Canada's history as a political one dominated by powerful men of Anglo-Saxon or French background.

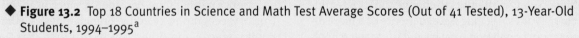

▲ RELATION TO WORK

With the economic challenges of a global economy and the economic restructuring that globalization is forcing on Canada, concern has been surfacing about the economic imperatives of having a well-educated labour force. Recent school-reform efforts have been driven by the rhetoric of economic competition, often with Japan, South Korea, and Taiwan, whose education systems are much more examination-oriented and where students do a great deal of school work at home (see Figures 13.2 and 13.3).

In 1992, the Economic Council of Canada wrote another report on schooling that included international comparisons of educational achievement which suggested Canada did not do very well. The council argued (Economic Council of Canada, 1992: 1):

> Educational attainment has a strong influence on earnings and employment, and since most Canadian adults participate in the labour market, this link is of vital importance to the economy. Indeed, education is a good investment: after taking account of the direct costs of schooling and of forgone earnings, the additional income from completing secondary school yields a rate of return of some 30 per-

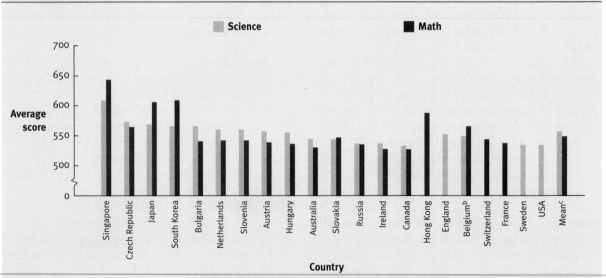

◆ **Figure 13.2** Top 18 Countries in Science and Math Test Average Scores (Out of 41 Tested), 13-Year-Old Students, 1994–1995[a]

[a] Where only one bar appears for a given country, it means that the country was not in the top 18 on the test for which no bar appears.

[b] Flanders only (Wallonia recorded separately).

[c] Mean for all 41 countries tested.

SOURCE: Data from Third International Maths and Science Study (TIMSS), as reported in "Who's Top?" *The Economist*, March 29, 1997.

Part Five CHANGE AND CONFLICT

POPULATIONS GROW, URBANIZE, GLOBALIZE,
AND TAX THE ABILITY OF THE NATURAL
ENVIRONMENT TO SUSTAIN THEM. PEOPLE
OFTEN COPE BY DEVELOPING NEW WAYS OF
LIVING THAT OFTEN CONFLICT WITH THE OLD.
WHETHER EXPRESSED AS DEVIANT
BEHAVIOUR, POLITICAL PROTEST, OR IN SOME
OTHER FORM, SOCIAL CONFLICT IS THUS
ENDEMIC IN ALL SOCIETIES. THIS PAINTING
COMMEMORATES A 1937 STRIKE IN CHICAGO
THAT LED TO THE SLAYING OF FIVE STEEL
WORKERS BY POLICE. BY PORTRAYING SOCIAL
CONFLICT IN ONE OF ITS RAWEST FORMS, THIS
PAINTING VIVIDLY EVOKES THE CENTRAL
THEME OF THIS SECTION.

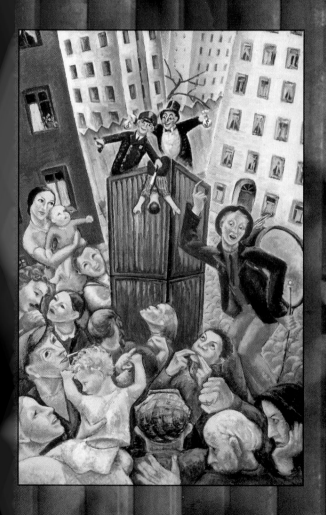

CHAPTER FOURTEEN
Urbanization

IN THIS CHAPTER YOU WILL LEARN THAT

- the choice of opportunities, experiences, and lifestyles available to urban residents is shaped and constrained by two sets of factors: those related to the physical environment and those dictated by the changing structure of the wider economy

- contrary to the theory that the core of Canadian cities is hollowing out like the hole in a doughnut, recent evidence suggests that city centres are remaining relatively stable economically and demographically; in contrast, the ring of older suburbs around the city core is stagnating, losing jobs and population to a constellation of edge cities in the surrounding region

- the fastest-growing middle-class neighbourhoods today are private communities, where control over local government, public services, and security rests in the hands of nonelected, professional managers; one popular form of such neighbourhoods is the gated community, where nonresidents are considered intruders and are monitored and kept out by guards, alarm systems, and surveillance cameras

- downtown areas of Canadian and U.S. cities are being transformed into urban theme parks whose planning and design reflect the requirements of a rapidly growing symbolic economy rooted in popular culture and entertainment

JOHN HANNIGAN
University of Toronto

INTRODUCTION

Recently, *The Globe and Mail* published an opinion piece by Elinor Florence, a British Columbia woman who, with her husband and three teenage children, had moved from Richmond, a rapidly developing suburb on the southern boundary of Vancouver, to Invermere, an alpine town of 3000 near the Alberta border. Leaving behind a mushrooming population, the stresses of urban driving, and "a junk culture that undeniably rears its head everywhere but snarls louder in cities" (Florence, 1997), the Florence family appears to have found happiness in the shadow of the Rockies. Among the benefits that she cites are a slower pace of life, more leisure time, a greater sense of personal security, no fast-food restaurants, and the ability to walk everywhere.

Elinor Florence's profile of small-town life highlights a theme that has resounded through the discipline of sociology since its founding in the late nineteenth century. Urban life, it is said, is qualitatively different from a rural or small-town existence: meaner, more stressful, more alienating. Obsessed as they are with efficiency and making money, urbanites are said to have no time for relating to others in a more holistic and humane way. Increasing population size and density, such as that which is beginning to plague Richmond, bring with them a host of urban problems, from traffic gridlock and pollution to family breakdown and crime.

The tale of the Florences illustrates one of the most influential ways of looking at residential settings. Termed **environmental-opportunity theory** (Michelson, 1973), it posits that people actively choose where they want to live depending on the extent to which a particular place either meshes with or constrains their preferred lifestyle. Not everyone, of course, gets to choose their community freely, but people will always strive to match their choices with their needs.

There is another approach that asserts that the urban experience is constrained not just by the nature of the physical environment, but also by the changing configuration of international, national, and local economic arrangements. In recent years, the emergence of a globalized economy has had profound implications for North American cities, changing both their physical form and their social-class patterns. In particular, it has resulted in an increasing polarization between rich and poor, affecting the homeless person sleeping in the park, the highly paid professional eating in the chic urban restaurant, and the suburban homeowner shopping in a "big-box" megastore on the fringes of the city (Kleniewski, 1997: 135).

In this chapter, we will look at this this dual influence of environment and structure on city life over the course of the twentieth century. In the course of our discussion, you will encounter three main types of cities: the industrial city, the corporate city, and the postmodern city. The industrial city originated in the nineteenth century and reached its zenith in the 1920s and 1930s; the corporate city arose after World War II and dominated during the 1950s and 1960s; and the postmodern city dates from the 1970s up to the present.

EARLY CITIES

Cities are defined as "relatively large, dense, permanent settlements in which the majority of the

Most Canadians live in urban areas, some of which are booming. Between 1986 and 1991, Vancouver (shown here) experienced the second-fastest urban growth rate in Canada. SOURCE: Stefan Schulhof/Tony Stone.

residents do not produce their own food" (McGahan, 1995: 1). By most accounts, the city as a distinct form dates back five or six thousand years to 3000–4000 B.C., when it first appeared in Mesopotamia (now southern Iraq) and Egypt. Initially, these ancient cities were established largely as centres of religious worship and were not much larger than most single-industry towns in Canada today. For example, Memphis, at the head of the Nile River delta, had an estimated population of 40 000 in 3000 B.C. Cities later swelled: Babylon had a population of 200 000 during the reign of Nebuchadnezzar in the seventh century B.C.; Alexandria, Egypt, surpassed 300 000 three centuries later; and Rome reached 800 000 at its peak in the second century A.D. (Chandler and Fox, 1974).

Three elements of prime importance characterized these preindustrial cities: the existence of a food surplus in fertile valleys, which permitted the specialization of labour in zones of dense settlement; the achievement of literacy among scribes, priests, and other elite members of society, which allowed for the keeping of financial and other records; and technological innovations, notably metallurgy, agricultural irrigation, and the harnessing of wind and water power for sailing and grain milling.

After the fall of Rome to Germanic tribes in the fifth century A.D., cities stagnated and declined over large parts of Europe. They continued to flourish, though, in the rising Islamic empire, which, at its zenith, stretched from Spain to India. More decentralized than the Roman world, the Islamic empire contained a number of cities that reached impressive levels of size and sophistication. For example, more than 500 000 people lived in Cairo in the fourteenth century, when Egypt held a trade monopoly on the east–west spice route (Abu-Lughod, 1991: 38).

From the eleventh century on, a number of city-states along the Mediterranean — Florence, Genoa, Venice, Pisa — succeeded in re-establishing trade routes to Asia and the Middle East by means of the Crusades. The commercial revival that followed was felt even in the merchant towns of the North Sea and the Baltic, which themselves had begun to develop a brisk trade in wool and cloth. From this renaissance there developed a distinct class of professional merchants who established their own municipal laws and institutions distinct from those in the surrounding feudal society, and there also emerged a market for housing and a variety of other goods and services, which generated further urban growth (Golden, 1981: 120–22).

Although preindustrial cities were important as centres of commerce, knowledge, and art, they never contained much more than a small fraction of the overall population. Even at their height, ancient and medieval cities were incapable of supporting urban populations of more than 5 or 10 percent of society, primarily because they could not generate a sufficiently large agricultural surplus to feed a huge urban populace. When the cities did begin to swell, periodic outbreaks of the bubonic plague (the notorious "Black Death"), spread by fleas from infected rats, killed as many as half the people in Europe's cities. Thus, by 1800, of the roughly 900 million people in the world, only about 3 percent lived in urban places of 5000 or more inhabitants (Hauser, 1965: 7). And, despite significant changes in architectural styles and building materials, the physical layout of the communities in which they lived had not changed all that much from antiquity to the eighteenth century — they were still built up within protective walls and organized around a central market square and places of worship, such as cathedrals, temples, or mosques (Abu-Lughod, 1991: 49–50).

■ THE INDUSTRIAL CITY

By the end of the eighteenth century, a brand new type of city had begun to emerge, first in England and later in continental Europe and America. This industrial city was larger, more complex, and more dynamic than any urban settlement that had preceded it. At century's end, more than 50 percent of the population of England and Wales was found to be residing in places with 20 000 or more people, compared with only 17 percent a century earlier (Weber, 1963 [1899]: 47). Global urbanization trends from 1800 to 2000 are shown in Figure 14.1.

What contributed to the growth of industrial cities? One popular theory emphasizes advances in transportation and agricultural technology, inasmuch as these factors contributed to the production and movement of agricultural surpluses from farm to city. Among the innovations were better methods of land drainage, the use of fertilizers, methods of seed selection, techniques of animal breeding, toll-road building, and the application of steam power to farm machinery and rail transport. Other scholars emphasize a boom in trade and commerce, which provided a powerful inducement to greater investment, technological improvements, and, ultimately, increased agricultural productivity.

Another key factor appears to have been a shift in the sources of capital accumulation — that is, how factory owners raised the investment money need-

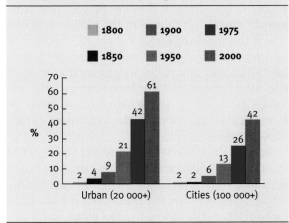

◆ Figure 14.1 Percent of World Population Living in Urban Areas and in Large Cities, 1800–2000

■ 1800 ■ 1900 ■ 1975
■ 1850 ■ 1950 ■ 2000

SOURCE: Adapted from Kingsley Davis, "The Origin and Growth of Urbanization in the World," *American Journal of Sociology, 60* (1955), p. 430. Used with permission.

ed to build and improve their manufacturing facilities. In England after 1850, capital investment was facilitated by the creation of the joint stock company, a business structure that pooled the capital of many investors and that had limited liability (i.e., the shareholders could not be held personally responsible for enterprises that failed).

Finally, urban growth has been linked to the invention of the factory. Previously, under the "putting-out" system, piecework was done in village or rural cottages and collected at regular intervals by the agents of merchant entrepreneurs. With the advent of the factory system, workers were required to work in a central location. Initially, factories had to be located next to rivers, in order to run directly on water power. Then, as steam-powered machines became the standard, factories concentrated in cities because steam power could not be distributed economically over a wide grid, as electrical systems can today.

▲ THE DEVELOPMENT OF AN URBAN-INDUSTRIAL ECONOMY IN CANADA

At the time of Confederation in 1867, Canada lagged significantly behind both Britain and the United States in the development of an urban-industrial economy. The British North American colonies, both inside and outside the new political union, traded very little with each other, looking instead to the United States or Great Britain. According to the first manufacturing census in 1870, such localized activities as sawmilling, flour milling, shoemaking, and clothing manufacture accounted for almost half the value of the manufactured goods produced in Canada (Nader, 1975: 207). At the same time, only a tiny minority of Canadians lived in urban areas: In 1871, fewer than 1 in 5 (18 percent) lived in a town or a city (Stone, 1967: 29).

By century's end, industrial cities had finally begun to emerge. While Toronto and Montreal were the largest industrial centres, factory towns also grew up elsewhere in Ontario, chief among them Windsor, because of its proximity to industry and markets in Detroit, and Hamilton, because of its port and strategic location on the Great Lakes. In addition to strategic location, the availability of investment capital played a significant role in directing where industry was established. The Canada Bank Act of 1871 was instrumental in concentrating economic power in a few national metropolitan centres, notably Toronto and Montreal. The act adopted the British model of a branch-banking system wherein a handful of major banks each established a network of branches. In contrast, under the U.S. unit-banking system, many more banks are independent. Investment capital was thus concentrated in a handful of urban centres rather than being widely dispersed across the country (Nader, 1975: 215).

Through various interventions by the federal government — the building of the transcontinental railroad, the imposition of a protective tariff system to encourage domestic manufacturing, a vigorous immigration policy that encouraged agriculture on the Prairies — a system of national economic markets was eventually established. In particular, at the turn of the century, these interventions found form in the expansion of wheat production for export. With cash from wheat sales jingling in their pockets, Prairie grain farmers were able to purchase manufactured goods from the factories of Ontario and Quebec, thus stimulating a marked upsurge in Canadian urbanization in the two decades from 1891 to 1911 (Stone, 1967: 20–21). By 1911, four cities had populations exceeding 100 000: Montreal (470 480), Toronto (376 538), Winnipeg (136 035) and Vancouver (100 401). However, the formation of a national market led to the deindustrialization of the Maritime provinces (see Brym, 1986).

As the twentieth century progressed, the proportion of the Canadian population that was classified as "urban" increased dramatically, crossing the 50 percent mark before 1931 and reaching 70 percent in 1951. By 1991, 77 percent of the Canadian population was living in towns and cities (see

Table 14.1). Toronto, Montreal, and Vancouver continued to hold the largest number of Canadians, but, as can be seen in Figure 14.2, the sharpest growth rates after 1951 were in the western cities of Calgary and Edmonton.

▲ RESEARCHING THE INDUSTRIAL CITY: THE CHICAGO SCHOOL

By the final quarter of the nineteenth century, U.S. cities were seeing jumps in population that rivalled and even surpassed those in Britain. Nowhere was this more dramatic than in Chicago, which mushroomed from 122 000 people in 1860 to 1.7 million in 1900 and 3.4 million in 1930. Such rapid growth left in its wake social dislocation and human misery. Among those who sought to address these problems was the chairman of the Sociology Department of the University of Chicago, Robert E. Park.

Park and his colleagues believed that they could improve conditions for the disadvantaged by discovering what made the city "tick" and then using this knowledge to help solve its "social pathologies" — crime, juvenile delinquency, family breakdown, and mental illness. To carry out this task, they employed an assortment of methods and models. On the one hand, Park argued that researchers should consider themselves urban anthropologists who would venture out into the field and study the natives, their customs, beliefs, and practices. This inspired a rich ethnographic tradition of urban research in which Park's colleagues and students rendered richly detailed, first-hand accounts of such things as homeless men, gangs, and "taxi-dance" halls. At the same time, Park also urged his

students to consider the city of Chicago as a kind of social laboratory in which various natural processes took place. One way of documenting these processes was through the development of urban-growth models (discussed in the next section) by which the changing social and spatial structure of the city could be depicted visually. Another was to use "ecological spot maps" in which differences in the rate of various deviant behaviours, such as juvenile delinquency and schizophrenia, could be plotted geographically in order to discover underlying patterns.

Some of the most memorable work to come out of the Chicago School tradition drew upon personal documents and other biographical materials. For example, Harvey Zorbaugh (1929) made use of a huge cache of letters, life histories, school essays, social-service agency records, and a school census. To contrast the experience of Polish peasants in the old country with that of urban migrants to America, William I. Thomas and Florian Znaniecki (1918–20) employed court and agency records, an in-depth autobiography, and thousands of letters exchanged between newcomers to Chicago and their relatives in Poland.

To put this mountain of data into some kind of theoretical order, Park and his colleagues used sev-

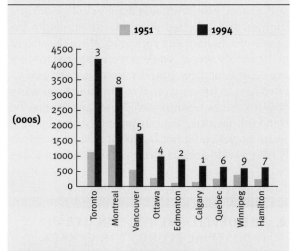

◆ **Figure 14.2** Population of Canada's Nine Biggest Metro Areas, 1951–1994

□ 1951   ■ 1994

Note: Numbers at the top of bars are growth-rate ranks.

SOURCE: Adapted from "Population of Major Metropolitan Areas," http://www.StatCan.CA/Documents/English/Faq/Glance/Tables/demo2.htm; Brian Biggs and Ray Bollman, "Urbanization in Canada," *Canadian Social Trends,* Vol. 2 (1994), p. 69. Used by authority of the Minister of Industry, 1997.

◆ **Table 14.1** Urban–Rural Population, Canada, 1931–1991

	1931	**1951**	**1991**
Rural farm	31%	11%	3%
Rural nonfarm	16	19	20
Urban	53	70	77
Total	100	100	100

SOURCE: Adapted from Statistics Canada, "Urban vs Rural Population," http://www.StatCan.CA/Documents/English/Faq/Glance/Tbles/demo11.htm (September 20, 1996). Used by authority of the Minister of Industry, 1997.

eral approaches. First, they tapped into a long tradition of exploring the contrast between rural and urban life. In the latter part of the nineteenth century, the German social philosopher Ferdinand Tönnies (1957 [1887]) had attempted to depict the difference between traditional and modern societies by introducing a distinction between a *Gemeinschaft* — the "community of feeling" that exists in villages, tribes, and small communities — and the *Gesellschaft* — the characteristic feature of social relations in the city. Tönnies favoured *Gemeinschaft* and saw its decline as a loss of all that is natural and satisfying about small-town life. In contrast, he wrote, *Gesellschaft* denotes a lifestyle based on money, commercial contracts, individual interest, and class antagonism. Although he was more positive about the possibilities for individual freedom in modern urban life, the German sociologist Georg Simmel (1950) used the same rural–urban contrast as a central method of dealing with the meaning of the shift to an urban society.

This rural–urban dichotomy runs through much of Chicago School theorizing. Thomas and Znaniecki, for example, depict the city as being responsible for destroying the traditional institutions of Polish peasant life — family, neighbourhood, church — and substituting nothing but an empty well of social disorganization. Freed from the ties that formerly bound the community together, marriages dissolve, teenagers run wild, and even murder is not uncommon. In his modification of Simmel's social-psychological profile of urban life, Louis Wirth (1938) proposed that the city is characterized by the concurrent trends of increasing size, density, and heterogeneity. In his view, the city creates a distinct way of life — "urbanism" — that economically efficient but socially destructive. Wirth's shortlist of urban characteristics includes the decline of the family, the disappearance of the neighbourhood, and the undermining of traditional bases of social solidarity. Urbanites are said to be superficial, unable to step outside their narrow occupational roles to relate to people in a holistic and meaningful way, and guided by an all-consuming drive for success and money.

▲ ECOLOGY OF THE INDUSTRIAL CITY

Industrial cities were also unique in their ecology — that is, their spatial layout, physical structure, and distribution of population. In order to depict the spatial or ecological patterns of the city, a group of sociologists and geographers from the University of Chicago devised a set of urban-growth models in the 1920s and 1930s.

Burgess's **concentric-zone model** conceptualized the expansion of cities as a succession of concentric rings, each of which contained a distinct resident population and type of land use (Burgess, 1961). This concentric model of urban growth identified five zones (see Figure 14.3).

Zone 1, the central business district (CBD), is the commercial pulse of the city. It is the site of the major department stores, live theatres, hotels, banks, and office space. The land here is the most valuable in the city, which means that residential and low-rent commercial uses are inevitably displaced in favour of big-money commercial enterprises.

Zone 2 is called the zone in transition. In the 1920s, large parcels of land in Chicago's transitional zone were being held by speculators who fully expected that the CBD would push outward, making them millionaires. In the meantime, zone 2 stood as an area of cheap housing that became the initial

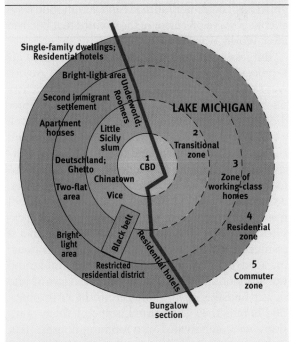

◆ **Figure 14.3** Burgess's Concentric Zone Model Applied to Chicago

SOURCE: Redrawn from Ernest W. Burgess, "The Growth of the City: An Introduction to a Research Project," in George A. Theodorson, ed., *Studies in Human Ecology* (Evanston, IL: Row, Peterson, 1961), p. 41.

resting point for each new wave of immigrants who took jobs in the nearby factories. Also located here were a variety of marginal businesses — pawn shops, tattoo parlours, second-hand stores — that could not afford the high rents of the city centre. The transitional zone also attracted a raft of illegal commercial activities — gambling, prostitution, drug dealing — that needed to be accessible to clientele in the CBD but that were considered socially unacceptable in the high-profile heart of the downtown area.

Zone 3, the zone of working-class homes, denotes the area settled by second-generation immigrants and rural migrants. In Burgess's time, zone 3 was a neighbourhood of semidetached, two-family homes where fathers still worked in inner-city factories but from which the upwardly mobile children aspired to escape, into the middle-class suburban zones.

Zone 4, the zone of better residences, was where the bulk of the middle-class could be found: small-business people, professionals, sales personnel, and office employees. Initially, it was an area of single-family detached houses, but, by the mid-1920s, it was increasingly characterized by apartment buildings and residential hotels.

Finally, zone 5, the commuter zone, was an area beyond the political boundaries of the city composed of satellite towns and suburbs. With the growth of commuter railroads and automobile travel, zone 5 was a precursor of the suburbs that boomed after World War II.

Burgess's concentric-zone model made three interrelated assumptions. First, all commercial growth was said to emanate from the dominant city-centre nucleus and proceed outward in an orderly and predictable manner. Second, residential growth took place at the periphery, where it was easier and cheaper to obtain open land for development purchases. New housing was added here but it was intended primarily for the middle and upper classes, who were increasingly able to take advantage of newly constructed commuter rail lines and, later, expressways. Third, the model was dynamic in that it assumed a sort of filtering-down process. As housing aged, it deteriorated, became less desirable, and was abandoned by better-off citizens, who moved into newer housing further away from the city centre. The homes they left behind, some of them mansions, were subdivided into rooming houses, flats, and dormitories for artists and students. In recent years, many of these have been restored to a measure of their former glory, either by residential "gentrifiers" or by commercial users such as restaurateurs or hair stylists. Furthermore, Burgess assumed that,

as immigrant newcomers to the industrial city found their balance and began to prosper, they would want to upgrade their housing. For example, the second generation of "white ethnics" — the acculturated sons and daughters of those who had come as part of the Polish, Italian, German, and other European immigration around the turn of the century — could be expected to settle in the zone of working-class homes, which possessed superior housing to that occupied by their parents in the transitional zone.

Burgess's urban-growth model appears to have fit Chicago in the 1920s reasonably well, but, as a scheme for understanding all cities in different places and times, it does not do as well. First, the notion of a single growth nucleus has not held up very firmly. Cities such as Calgary and Edmonton, which developed later in the century and which were shaped largely by the automobile, are more likely to possess more than one nucleus or growth centre. Similarly, Los Angeles is widely known as "the city without a downtown." This was first recognized in the 1940s by geographers Chauncey Harris and Edward Ullman (1945), who proposed a **multiple-nuclei model** of urban growth in which were located a series of growth centres — retail, wholesale, residential — each representing the concentration of a specific function or activity within the urban economy.

Second, Burgess seems to have underestimated the importance of transportation corridors as magnets for urban growth. Geographer Homer Hoyt (1939) developed a **sector model** of urban growth after studying 142 U.S. cities during the Depression years. He argued that cities grew not in concentric circles but in sectors or wedges along major transportation arteries extending like the tentacles of an octopus from the CBD. Within each sector, the social character of the residential housing would remain constant. For example, upper-income groups would follow a northward progression, and working-class groups a southward path, thereby producing a distinct sectoral pattern to the developing city. Montreal and Vancouver seem to fit this sector model, because their populations tended to spread out along the natural shorelines of the bodies of water on which they are located (Driedger, 1991: 90).

Third, Burgess failed to appreciate that some resident groups would develop strong residential attachments to their neighbourhoods and refuse to move on, even in the face of an aging housing stock. This was first pointed out by Walter Firey (1947) in his study of Boston. Firey gives several examples that span the socioeconomic spectrum, from Beacon Hill, an elite area near the city centre, to the North End, a blue-collar Italian area where the residents chose to remain in their old neighbourhoods because the places were cherished as symbols of the residents' family connections, traditions, and culture.

■ THE CORPORATE CITY

Although the industrial city continued to exist in North America into the 1970s, it began to lose ground after 1945 to a new urban form. Simply defined, the **corporate city** denotes the perception and organization of the city as a vehicle for capital accumulation — that is, as a money-making machine.

The corporate city is composed of five major elements (Lorimer, 1978; Reid, 1991). First are *corporate suburbs,* which are designed on the assumption that every family owns one or more cars. They incorporate a housing design that emphasizes large lots, single-family use, multicar parking, and huge fenced back yards. They also entail a new land development process by which a single developer assembles a large tract of land plus services such as sewers, lights, roads, etc., finances the new subdivision, and sells the lots and houses to home-owners at a price that includes the cost of servicing.

Second are *high-rise apartment buildings,* which are built at high densities in both older downtown neighbourhoods and on the fringe of the new suburbs. They offer minimum-standard housing at affordable rents on sites isolated from the surrounding urban fabric.

Third are *suburban industrial parks,* large tracts of land owned by a single developer and planned to accommodate one-storey factories and warehouses. Sprawling over acres of land, these areas have changed the geography of postwar cities by shifting industries out of the central city to the suburban fringe.

Concentrated in the central business district are *downtown office towers,* the fourth element of the corporate city. These are large-scale buildings rising to 60 storeys or more. The developers are the owners; businesses are the tenants. Office towers also combine office space with other profitable uses, notably ground-level or subterranean retail-shopping space.

Finally, *shopping centres* or *malls* are usually found in suburban or exurban areas. They are served primarily by cars and major roads, and typically remain inaccessible to public transit. They are located off the street, and the stores open internally into a central pedestrian passageway and courtyard. Most malls depend on large retail chains, especially department stores and supermarket "anchors," and often exclude small, independent retailers. The developers of malls control competition among retail tenants.

Each of these five elements of the corporate city has evolved over the years. Some of their central features have recently changed. Facing the spectre of shopper boredom and increased competition from both revitalized downtown retail districts and ex-urban "big-box" stores (e.g., Home Depot, Price Club/Costco, Walmart), shopping centres have been undergoing a redesign that includes a more diverse mix of retail tenants. In the face of changing demographics, suburban developments have also been forced to include a greater variety of housing types, including more townhouses and row houses and such innovations as "granny flats" (separate quarters for aged parents). After years of being half-empty, some downtown office buildings have begun to convert to condominiums. Nevertheless, the process by which the corporate city has been assembled and maintained remains much the same, and stands in marked contrast to that which undergirds the building of the industrial city. Nowhere has this been more evident than in the case of the corporate suburb.

▲ THE CORPORATE SUBURB

Before World War II, North American cities such as Toronto were configured in a grid system, with residential avenues crossing long commercial streets at right angles. Since most urban residents lived within a few blocks of neighbourhood stores and services, there was constant pedestrian traffic up and down the streets. This spawned a lively "front-yard culture" in which passers-by regularly interacted with porch sitters, since front yards and families faced the street rather than the house itself (Fowler, 1992: 205).

When cities expanded, they did so incrementally, often a dozen houses at a time. The cost of extending sewers, water lines, and other city services was assumed by the municipality and paid for over 20 or 30 years through tax increases or special bonds. Lots were narrow and houses two or three storeys high. Parking space was mostly on the street and, as auto ownership spread rapidly, increasingly scarce.

In the early 1950s, all this changed with the building of Don Mills, Canada's first mass suburb, on the northern fringe of Toronto. Don Mills emphasized a system of short curving roads in the form of circles and crescents. Initially, this layout was probably meant to convey a sense of privileged exclusivity, although over time it also came to reflect a desire to shield children from the perceived danger of through-traffic. In any case, it made public transit difficult, consigning buses to main arterial roads on the perimeter of the housing subdivision. Don Mills houses were placed on wider lots with larger setbacks from the streets. With no sidewalks, small front porches, and minimal pedestrian traffic (most residents drove to the nearby Don Mills Plaza to shop), the social action shifted to the fenced-in back yards, which were, in any case, favoured by parents, who appreciated being able to keep an eye on their toddlers from the kitchen window. Don Mills was one of the first residential areas in Canada to be planned completely from scratch and built all at once. In contrast to the development pattern in the central city, almost all the servicing costs, including that of a sewage treatment plant along the Don River, were assumed by the developer, E.P. Taylor. By doing so, Taylor changed the rules of urban development, relegating the municipality to a more passive role and introducing corporate success as a major planning consideration (Sewell, 1993: 95).

With the triumph of Don Mills, the corporate suburb spread rapidly across Canada and the United States. (The United States had already introduced its own early prototype of a planned, mass-produced suburb in Levittown, Long Island, 20 miles from New York City.) Although there were local differences, these first-generation postwar suburbs shared five main characteristics: a peripheral location, relatively low population densities, architectural similarity, a relatively low purchase price for houses, and a fairly high degree of economic and racial homogeneity (Jackson, 1985: 238–43).

▲ "SUBURBANISM AS A WAY OF LIFE"

In the 1950s, the suburbs were routinely disparaged as being sterile social and cultural wastelands where conformity ruled and individual taste and thought was stifled. This notion was given wide exposure in the 1956 best-seller *The Organization Man*, a study of Park Forest, Illinois, 30 miles south of Chicago, by *Fortune* magazine writer William H. Whyte. Suburban dwellers were invariably depicted as living in mass-produced housing that was uniform in design and decoration. This image is bitingly evoked in folk singer Malvina Reynolds's 1950s ditty "Little Boxes" (Reynolds, 1964: 28):

Little Boxes on the hillside
Little Boxes made of ticky tacky,
Little Boxes on the hillside,
Little Boxes all the same.

Not only was the physical appearance of suburban areas said to be homogeneous, but life there was said to revolve around a "dry-martini culture." During the work week, fathers commuted in car pools or by rail to jobs at IBM, General Motors, and other corporate giants, while mothers ferried the children around in the family station wagon and socialized at coffee parties. On the weekend, the husbands washed the cars and tended to well-manicured lawns, while the wives shopped for groceries at nearby plazas. At night, couples socialized in one another's homes, around the pool or the barbecue pit.

For sociological researchers, suburbanism represented an important trend. In a much-quoted 1956 article, "Suburbanism as a Way of Life," Sylvia Fava did a take on Louis Wirth's classic 1938 essay. Fava claimed that suburbanites were far more likely than their counterparts in the central city to be both sociable and socially active. Similarly, in a much-cited before–after study of middle-class couples in Toronto who chose to relocate during the early 1970s, Michelson (1973) found that suburban movers increased their involvement with neighbours, while city relocators increased interactions with friends and relatives.

Another key feature of the suburban lifestyle was its emphasis on children and the family. Perhaps the most influential study with regard to the importance of children in suburban communities was that by Seeley, Sim, and Loosley (1956) in *Crestwood Heights,* a profile of the affluent community of Forest Hill Village in 1950s Toronto. Although Crestwood Heights was more a neighbourhood on the northern edge of the city, its organization around the needs of its children (schools, camps, counselling) was said to be typical of the developing suburbs of the time.

Suburbanism was further depicted as a lifestyle choice rather than strictly an economic decision. City dwellers who packed up and left the central city were said to be embracing a new, family-oriented way of life, seduced by advertisements in the real-estate section of the Saturday newpaper promising "bourgeois utopias" (Fishman, 1987). Not all residents, however, embraced this lifestyle with equal enthusiasm. Women in the suburbs frequently felt cut off from the the social and cultural stimulation of the central city with its theatres, art galleries, restaurants, and shopping streets. Sociability in the corporate suburb was restricted to private gatherings in the home or the back yard with one's neighbours. Not sur-

About three-quarters of Canadians now live in urban areas, although in recent years most urban growth has taken place in the suburbs. SOURCE: Dick Hemingway.

prisingly, a number of researchers found that women were less satisfied than their husbands with their choice of residence, often having a sense of stagnation and isolation despite relatively frequent visiting and entertaining (Michelson, 1973).

Significantly, this lifestyle did not appear to be replicated in working-class suburbs, where people's values and social behaviours remained firmly anchored in blue-collar culture. Berger (1960) refers to the **myth of suburbia,** by which he means a standardized and stereotyped view of the suburbs as uniformly middle-class, homogeneous, conformist, child-centred, female-dominated, and hotbeds of sociability.

It is possible to discern three alternative interpretations of the relationship between suburban residence and lifestyle patterns (McGahan, 1995: 232–36). According to the *structural* interpretation, the environmental and demographic characteristics of the suburb encourage a distinct style of life. For example, by excluding stores and services such as restaurants, bars, and movie theatres from residential neighbourhoods and by discouraging public transit, the Don Mills model promoted a greater reliance on private sociability, as evidenced by the weekday morning coffee klatches and weekend pool parties that came to be identified with suburban life in the 1950s and 1960s.

In contrast, the *selective migration* interpretation denies that the suburban environment exercises any independent effect on behaviour patterns. Rather, it is suggested that those who chose to move to the corporate suburbs after World War II were already primed to embrace **familism** — a lifestyle that places a high value on family living, marriage at a young age, a brief period of childlessness after marriage, and child-centredness of the type that Seeley and his colleagues observed in Crestwood Heights (Bell, 1968: 147).

Finally, the *class and life-cycle* interpretation proposes that what Berger had branded the "suburban myth" was nothing more than a snapshot of middle-class life at mid-century. Today, many of the same characteristics — child-centredness, commuting, back-yard culture — can be observed in the second wave of gentrification in the central city. As the corporate suburb matured, it changed appreciably, with a new set of social activities replacing those which had prevailed at an earlier stage in the life cycle of both the suburb and the families who settled there.

▲ INNER-CITY URBAN RENEWAL

Starting in the 1950s, governments in the United States and Canada began to participate more actively in building the corporate city, by using their powers of appropriation and subsidization to make large-scale private investment attractive in areas where the potential payoff was too low to attract investors otherwise (Logan and Molotch, 1987: 114). The main tool for this was the urban-renewal program.

In the United States, renewal efforts were launched by the Urban Renewal Act of 1949. Initially, it was designed to aid in slum clearance and the provision of public housing, but it was broadened in the 1950s to include housing rehabilitation and community redevelopment. Sadly, what started out with good intentions was soon derailed. Money originally intended for housing improvements was captured and diverted by public officials who wanted to build downtown megaprojects, such as high-rise office complexes. Having quickly discovered that private developers were unwilling to build in the heart of the slums, city-renewal directors sought out "the blight that's right" — places with some substandard housing but basically in sound condition. By 1961, at least a fifth of the housing demolished for urban-renewal projects in fact had had nothing wrong with it. Especially targeted were low-income and minority families: Of all the American families displaced by urban renewal from 1949 to 1963, 63 percent whose race was known were nonwhite (Frieden and Sagalyn, 1989).

Large-scale urban renewal came a decade later in Canada, intensifying after 1964 when nonresidential as well as residential areas were targeted. Although some of these projects — the Jeanne Mance project in Montreal, Uniacke Square in Halifax — were converted to public housing for low-income families, other sites were targeted for office buildings and downtown shopping centres. What opened the door to this sort of development was the vague meaning of "blight," which came to be understood as just about anything the municipality wanted (McGahan, 1995: 263).

As was the case in the United States, urban-renewal programs required a massive dislocation of existing land uses and residents. In Montreal, for example, 15 000 inner-city dwellings were demolished by the city from the mid-1950s to the mid-1960s, and in Vancouver, one renewal program alone displaced 3300 residents, many of them of Chinese ethnic background (Ley, 1991b: 335). One of the best-known and most tragic victims of urban renewal was Africville, a black residential community on the northern outskirts of Halifax. The community lived for fifteen years under the label of a blighted area destined for industrial redevelopment before it was bulldozed in the mid-1960s (Clairmont and Magill, 1974). Little thought was given to the social and personal dislocation involved in these renewal schemes. One U.S. study of 350 small businesses displaced by renewal or highway-building projects in Providence, Rhode Island, between 1954 and 1959 found that one-third of these firms went out of business, and that 90 percent of the owners earned lower incomes afterward (Zimmer, 1964). In similar fashion, relocated families faced a slew of social and economic crises. A 1963 report from the Social Planning Council of Hamilton and District pointed out that urban renewal in that city's north end would disrupt local social networks without providing any meaningful replacement. In addition, the elderly and disadvantaged would be forced to depend more completely on welfare assistance and social agencies if their only viable source of rental accommodations was removed. Similarly, a York University study of six sections of the city designated as blighted by the Metro Toronto Planning Board in 1966 found that forced relocation represented a disruptive force to the extent that the residents, who were satisfied with and who identified with their present neighbourhood, felt unable to recreate current living patterns in another place (Jenzen, Mozoff, and Richmond, 1970).

Urban renewal was finally halted in the early 1970s when residents of inner-city neighbourhoods who faced being uprooted finally mobilized and fought back, aided by the legal and organizational skills of a cadre of middle-class reformers who took up their cause. One of the best known of these struggles was the campaign to stop the demolition of existing houses and shops in Trefann Court, just to the east of downtown Toronto. After this, the federal government shifted gears and moved to programs that stressed the rehabilitation rather than the razing of existing housing and that favoured a considerably lower profile for public-sector participants in the urban-renewal process.

Whether it was the Don Mills–style suburb or downtown urban renewal, the corporate city did not just happen: It was the deliberate product of an alliance between government and business interests. Logan and Molotch (1987) have termed this alliance an **urban-growth machine,** a loosely structured coalition of local economic and political interest groups with a commitment to sustained growth and development. Urban-growth machines can include an extensive cast of players: businesses, property owners, investors and developers, politicians and planners, the media, utilities, cultural institutions (museums, theatres), professional sports teams, labour unions, and even universities. Growth machines pursue a narrow band of interests, sacrificing the sentimental and symbolic value of places — which is associated with jobs, neighbourhood, home town, and community — in favour of a strict emphasis on land use as an investment and commodity to be bought and sold (Palen, 1995: 20). Although government and business may honestly believe that local communities thrive only if they continue to expand economically, it could also be said that the structure that growth machines impose on urban living gives people a minimum of freedom to live their lives in the corporate city as they would choose (Lorimer, 1978: 220).

THE POSTMODERN CITY

In recent years, a new kind of urban form has appeared on the landscape: the postmodern city. Although there is some debate over what exactly is meant by this term, several aspects do seem clear.

First, the postmodern city is powerfully shaped by the globalization of consumption. In contrast to the industrial city, the areas of which reflected the local content of the neighbourhoods in which they were situated, today's urban landscapes are more likely to embody global tastes, especially those influenced by the entertainment industry. For example, the typical restaurant in the industrial city was small, ethnic, and neighbourhood-based, but the typical restaurant in the postmodern city has an entertainment theme that is recognizable worldwide. Archetypal is Planet Hollywood, where patrons line up in hopes of seeing Hollywood celebrity-investors, such as Demi Moore, Bruce Willis, and Arnold Schwarzenegger.

Second, the postmodern city is characteristically fragmented, even chaotic. Elizabeth Wilson (1991: 136) describes it as resembling "a split screen flickering with competing beliefs, cultures and 'stories.'" Geographically and socially split, the postmodern city does not have a single "way of life" of the sort identified by Wirth for the industrial city and Fava for the corporate suburb.

Finally, the postmodern city is characterized by the privatization of public space. Privatization occurs across a wide spectrum of settings, from downtown malls and festival marketplaces to private, "gated" communities on the fringes of the city. Although suburban dwellers have always put a premium on private space, from the enclosed back yard to the drive-in theatre, this value is now washing over the city as a whole, and, in the process, drastically reducing the number of public places where people can come together to shop or socialize (Goldberger, 1996: 139).

In this section, we will examine three overlapping components of the postmodern city: the edge city, the dual city, and the theme-park city. Although each component has a real-life spatial component, none exists in pure form. Instead, they are constructions, formulated by academic researchers or journalists, that help us visualize an important dimension of the globalized, privatized, and fragmented postmodern city.

▲ THE EDGE CITY

Although they differed significantly in their patterns of housing, transportation, and shopping, the industrial city and the corporate city displayed more or less the same spatial configuration: an urban core containing the bulk of the office space, cultural institutions, and factories, and a ring of suburbs where much of the more affluent middle-class resided. Even with the growth of shopping centres and industrial parks in the 1950s and 1960s, the lion's share of jobs and services remained within the city itself and suburbanites were, by definition, daily commuters.

During the past quarter-century, however, this traditional pattern has been turned inside out with the rapid growth of **edge cities** (Garrau, 1991). Situated in exurbia — the rural residential area around the suburbs within commuting range of the city — these edge cities have no dominant single core or definable set of boundaries; they are typically "clusters of malls, office developments and entertainment complexes that rise where major highways cross or converge" (Fishman, 1990: 18). Some edge cities are expansions of existing satellite cities, but others sprout up in unincorporated townships, lacking clearly definable borders and legal status as places (Palen, 1995: 187).

What has led to the growth of edge cities? Leinberger and Lockwood (1986) offer five reasons for their recent emergence. First, there has been a major shift in North American economies from manufacturing to a service and knowledge base. One result of this shift is that middle-class employees are now more willing to live near where they work than they used to be when jobs were located in factories that were dirty, noisy, and unattractive. An example of the older pattern can be found in Ontario's steel industry, where the managers and executives at Stelco and

Dofasco traditionally settled on the other side of the Skyway Bridge in Burlington, while the mill workers remained in Hamilton. In contrast, Kanata, the outer suburban location of Ottawa's booming microchip computer industry, is solidly middle-class.

Second, there have been significant changes in transportation patterns that favour trucks and cars over fixed line carriers: subways, streetcars, and trains. As a result, urban facilities have scattered over the exurban landscape, unfettered by the requirement of locating along established transportation corridors.

Third, recent advances in telecommunications technology have reduced the necessity for offices to locate downtown in close physical proximity. Some types of businesses — stock brokerages, banks — still prefer to be close to one another and to central city services. But the tremendous growth of technology, such as fax machines, cellular phones, and e-mail, has geographically freed up many employees whose linkages to the workplace are now activated on the road or from home offices.

Fourth, as it has become increasingly expensive to operate in the city, offices, industries, and professional practicioners (lawyers, accountants, etc.) have pulled up their roots and moved to cheaper locations in exurbia. Among other things, parking is more plentiful and less expensive out of the city.

Fifth, the coming of age of dual-income, "baby-boom" families with one or two children has meant that people's lives are increasingly governed by considerations of time, convenience, and efficiency. The clustering of offices, shopping centres, and recreational facilities at the juncture of exurban highways meets the needs of this subpopulation, the members of which have little time left in their lives to commute downtown to shop, eat, or be entertained.

Edge cities have been of particular interest to urban sociologists because they are neither suburbs nor centralized cities but a hybrid that incorporates elements of each. Unlike the typical suburb, which is primarily residential, edge cities contain many of the functions of the traditional city — shopping, office space, housing, entertainment facilities. Also, in contrast to suburbanites, who commute to work in the central city by rail or car, edge-city residents are inclined to live and work in the same geographic area. Commuting now means driving to an adjoining suburb or exurb, rather than heading downtown. This can be seen in the "905 belt" surrounding Metro Toronto, where a number of areas now function as "magnets." That is, more people travel to jobs there each day than journey out of the community to jobs elsewhere in the greater Toronto area (see Box 14.1). Finally, in contrast to the typ-

ical suburb, which lacks a well-developed infrastructure of sports, entertainment, and cultural facilities, the edge city is increasingly the site of a burgeoning number of performing arts centres, sports palaces, and entertainment complexes.

Nevertheless, it would be wrong to think that there are no real differences between edge cities and the older cities. Unlike the industrial city, the edge city lacks a single centre. In the former, it was always possible to start downtown and eventually reach the outer boundaries of the city. In contrast, the spatial logic of the edge city dictates that centres and boundaries are not needed. Instead, the edge city is made up of three overlapping types of socioeconomic networks: household networks, networks of consumption, and networks of production. Each of these runs on the guiding principle of convenience. Two-income families with children, who make up the largest demographic segment of the edge-city population, are increasingly pressed for time and, as a result, frequently create their own "personal cities" out of the destinations they can reach within a manageable time (Fishman, 1990).

▲ THE DUAL CITY

With the edge city increasingly becoming the occupational, residential, and commercial centre for the middle classes, what has become of urban downtowns? The central city, some analysts suggest, has become balkanized between two starkly different realities that are spatially discrete and that have only the name of the city and some public places in common. Situated just blocks or streets away from one another, the "city of despair and squalor" and the "city of hope and splendour" are light years apart. This split reality has been called the "dual city."

The term *dual city* has come to refer to the urban expression of two increasingly divergent streams in the global economy. On the one hand, there is an information-based, formal economy rooted in financial services, telecommunications, and the microchip. Typically, those who are part of this upper-tier informational city live in a world of computer software, fax machines, mobile telephones, and Internet surfing. Residentially, they can be found in "gentrified" niches of the inner city (gentrification is discussed below) or in exclusive suburbs, where they isolate themselves both socially and geographically from the rest of the city. In Castells's (1989) description, these spaces constitute a microsociety with their own separate circuit of leisure, lifestyle, and services.

Box 14.1
"905 Belt"

Nowhere in Canada are the changing social demographics of the city more evident than in the four regions surrounding Metropolitan Toronto — Durham, Halton, Peel, and York. Nicknamed the "905 belt" after a new area code that was added in order to head off the crisis of a rapidly dwindling supply of new telephone numbers in the existing "416" area, the outer limits of Toronto have now become its major growth area. According to one estimate, Metro's population is expected to stay at around 2.3 million while Peel and York regions are projected to grow by more than 100 000 people every five years.

Furthermore, the communities in the 905 belt have shifted from being almost completely residential to being increasingly strong magnets for industry and jobs. As a result, many of these towns and cities now have a surplus of jobs over residents. For example, in York region, which runs along the northern perimeter of Metro, Markham has 82 200 workers but provides 90 200 jobs, and Vaughan is home to 58 500 workers but provides 67 300 jobs. Community patterns are changing as a result, with an increasing number of employees travelling each day among the 905 communities, or between the Toronto suburbs and these rapidly developing edge cities, rather than into the central downtown core.

Contrary to the theory that the core of Toronto is hollowing out like the hole in a doughnut, these figures suggest that the central core is still holding its own, while the 905 belt is the growth area of the future for new residents and jobs. Only the ring of older suburbs around the city core appears to be stagnating, as indicated by the outward flow of workers each day to the regions in the Greater Toronto Area (GTA).

SOURCE: Adapted from Alan Ferguson, "Urban Forecasting a Tricky Art but It's Safe to Predict Most Growth Will Be in the GTA Suburbs," *The Toronto Star,* April 30, 1995, p. A7; John Spears, "How the Burbs Woke Up to Become New Boardrooms," *The Toronto Star,* October 24, 1995, p. A26. Used with permission—The Toronto Star Syndicate.

On the other hand, juxtaposed to the informational city, there is an "informal economy" that has been excluded from the main loop. Residents here rely, not on high-technology communications, but on face-to-face social networks, usually established on the basis of shared race and ethnicity. People are engaged in a wide range of activities, from labouring in immigrant sweatshops in the clothing trade to offering such services as furniture making, home renovation, and auto repairs (Gordon and Sassen, 1992). Although this informal economy cannot be equated with urban poverty per se, its participants stand relatively little chance of ever penetrating the upper-tier informational economy.

Gentrification

In the 1970s and 1980s, considerable attention was paid by urban researchers to the phenomenon of **gentrification** in the dual city. By gentrification, we mean the transformation of working-class housing into fashionable downtown neighbourhoods by middle- and upper-income newcomers. Gentrification is neither anticipated nor accounted for by the ecological growth models discussed above. Similarly, it runs counter to predictions about the mass flight to the suburbs that dominated urban sociology in the 1950s and 1960s. A comparison of the suburban lifestyle and the postmodern urban lifestyle as typified by gentrification is set out in Table 14.2.

Four primary explanations for gentrification have been advanced (Ley, 1991a: 182–85). First, demographic changes led to gentrification in the 1970s and 1980s. At this time, the baby boomers who were born and raised in the suburbs began to look for housing of their own. Facing high demand levels and a shortage of supply, they turned to inner-city housing, which was cheap but in dire need of rehabilitation. They opposed demolition, favoured by urban-renewal advocates. Unlike suburban settlers in the previous period, these urban migrants were childless and career-oriented. This meant that schools, playgrounds, and parks were not their major concerns and they were happy with smaller housing units without the big back yards and basement recreation rooms that were characteristic of Don Mills–type housing. Since many of these young professionals worked downtown, they were willing to trade off space for proximity to their places of employment and to downtown cultural and entertainment facilities.

Second, gentrification may be accounted for by economic changes related to the flow of capital in and out of the housing market. In this view, gentrification functions as a "back to the city movement by capital not people" (Smith, 1979). As we have seen, in the 1950s and 1960s, financial capital flowed into the building of the suburbs under the guidance of governments that viewed the construction of large-scale projects by development companies as the fastest, most efficient way of coping with the pressures created by the baby boom. Developers were encouraged by an array of incentives: tax breaks, government-backed mortgages, guarantees, and insurance with low down payments. By the 1970s, the profit levels in suburban building had begun to shrink, and capital flow switched back to the urban centre to take advantage of the **rent gap** — that is, the difference between the current value of land in its "depressed" state and the value that could be charged given a higher or better land use (Smith and LeFaivre, 1984).

Third, middle-class newcomers to the central city arrived in search of a lifestyle that was more distinctive and cosmopolitan than that available within the constraints of suburban conformity. In the central city, they could express a distinctive aesthetic and style of consumption, characterized by a dislike of mass-produced goods and a penchant for objects and buildings from a bygone era, notably the Victorian age (Filion, 1991: 554). This new lifestyle also extended to the surrounding neighbourhood, which filled up with wine bars, California-style restaurants, franchise coffee outlets, and trendy boutiques.

A fourth explanation of gentrification looks to the kind of changes in the urban economy that were described at the beginning of the section on the dual city. With the tremendous boom in jobs in advanced service industries, such as those connected to the "globalized information economy," there has been a dramatic increase in the number of well-paying occupations located downtown. This growth has, in turn, produced a pool of middle-class workers interested in trying the experience of inner-city living.

It should be emphasized, however, that the image of gentrifiers as returning from the suburbs is false; gentrification is, in fact, a "stay in the city" rather than a "back to the city" movement (Wittberg, 1992: 27). Ley (1991a: 186) cites data from Canadian cities that indicate that only 2–3 percent of a sample of households moving into Toronto's Don Vale neighbourhood between 1966 and 1976 originated in the suburbs. Similarly, a high percentage of those in Ottawa's Centretown (55 percent), Vancouver's False Creek (78 percent) and Montreal's Milton-Parc, Plateau Mont-Royal, and Papineau (79 percent) neighbourhoods had previous addresses in the central city. This research suggests that gentrifiers are devoted to an inner-city lifestyle, even when they have reached a stage in the life cycle where one might have predicted that they would move to the suburbs.

◆ **Table 14.2** Comparison of Suburban and Postmodern Urban Lifestyles

	Suburban	Postmodern urban (as per gentrification)
Neighbourhood social involvement	Deliberate and sustained	Incidental
Lifestyle focus	Family	Consumerism
Typical activities	Home activities (gardening, entertaining)	Dining out, shopping
Typical occupation of resident	Middle manager	Architect, designer
Housing type	Split-level, detached	Victorian, semidetached
Social composition	Class-exclusive	Socially and culturally diverse
Ideology	Anti-urban	Pro-urban

SOURCE: John A. Hannigan, "The Postmodern City: A New Urbanization?" *Current Sociology, 43* (1) (1995), p. 180. Reprinted with permission.

Among those most likely to settle in gentrified areas of the inner city are women. Summarizing the empirical evidence available from these studies, Warde (1991: 228) lists the following as typical of gentrified enclaves:

> a female population increasing faster than the male population; an unusually high proportion of young and single women; very high proportions of women in professional and technical occupations; high levels of academic credentials; a high proportion of dual-earner households, but few families; presence of young professional women; and the postponement of marriage and childbearing.

Why do gentrified neighbourhoods appeal to these groups of women cited by Warde? One explanation is that inner-city communities help relieve some of the pressures of women's dual roles as both members of the workforce and as mothers of young children. The advantages include relatively cheap housing, public transit, and readily available child-care and social-support systems. Travel time is an especially important consideration. Female gentrifiers tend to have jobs in downtown office buildings, so inner-city housing allows them to lead their lives on a tight schedule, with services such as shopping, schools, day care, and medical clinics located nearby. In contrast, suburban residence requires long daily commutes, especially when the weather is bad, as well as the devotion of a good share of one's leisure time travelling to widely scattered stores and services. Gentrification thus represents an environmental solution to a potential set of social problems (Rose, 1984: 66).

Private Communities

In recent years, another phenomenon — the rise of private communities — has embraced an even greater number of middle-class home-owners than has gentrification. Located in the newer suburbs and in edge cities, private communities compete with central cities for residents, offering as incentives a homogeneous middle-class population, physical security, stable housing values, local control, and freedom from exposure to the social problems of the inner city (see Box 14.2; McKenzie, 1989: 257).

In the United States, nearly 4 million residents are estimated to live in closed-off, gated communities, and another 28 million in areas governed by private community associations. This makes private communities the fastest-growing residential communities in the nation (Egan, 1995). Of all the new housing developments in California, as much as one-third are thought to be gated communities (Kleniewski, 1997: 207). Growth has been less rapid in Canada, but private communities have begun to multiply in some areas, notably around Metro Toronto and in the Okanagan Valley in British Columbia. Typical of these are Casitas at Northtown, a gated condominium community built on the site of a failed indoor shopping centre, and Swan Lake Village, an "adult-lifestyle village" in Markham. The latter, a retirement community, employs a round-the-clock security guard at the controlled-entry front gate and a second guard who roams throughout the settlement looking for intruders. Northtown is no less security-oriented, with a gate house complete with smoked windows, surveillance cameras, and a personally encoded suite-intrusion alarm system to register any incursion by "outside elements" (Lorinc, 1996).

The Fortress City

At the same time as middle-class home-owners are barricading themselves in private gated communities, the public–private partnerships that increasingly dictate what happens to postmodern cities are said to be systematically privatizing and militarizing public space in order to secure it against the homeless and the poor. Emerging from such alliances is the "fortress city" in which the urban disadvantaged are isolated socially and spatially from office workers, tourists, and suburban day trippers.

The fortress city has been described in *City of Quartz,* Mike Davis's (1990) sweeping examination of present-day Los Angeles. LA, Davis notes, is a city obsessed with urban security. What passes for a downtown, a series of billion-dollar, block-square megastructures around Bunker Hill, has been insulated by removing almost all pedestrian linkages to the poor immigrant neighbourhoods that surround it on every side. To make public facilities and spaces as unlivable as possible for the homeless and the poor, the city is engaged in a virtual war against them. Tactics and defences include the establishment of barrel-shaped, "bum-proof" bus benches that make sleep impossible, the random deployment of outdoor overhead sprinklers in Skid Row Park to discourage overnight camping, and the removal of public toilets and washrooms in areas patronized by vagrants. To secure its garbage, one popular seafood restaurant has spent $12 000 to build a "bag-lady-proof trash cage" out of three-quarter-inch steel rods with alloy locks and vicious curved spikes. To cope with a burgeoning inmate population, law-enforcement agencies are venturing into **carceral development,** building downtown jails and prisons designed by celebrity architects to look like hotel-convention centres or office buildings, thus camouflaging their real purpose.

Nor is the fortress city restricted to Los Angeles. In the late 1970s, Henry Ford II persuaded the heads of 50 large corporations in Detroit to put equity cap- ital into the Renaissance Center, a $357 million megaproject along the Detroit River opposite Wind- sor, Ontario. Poorly planned, the hotel-office venture resembled a castle with virtually invisible pedestri- an entrances. It was cut off from downtown Detroit by a wide road and railroad tracks. It stands, Frieden and Sagalyn observe, as a "symbol of isolation: an ex-

Box 14.2
Walling Out the World

Gated communities are suburbs with big walls around them. Only residents and approved visitors get in. There are no surprise calls on Aunt Sally. Private security guards check identification at the entrances — the gates — and patrol the perimeter.

Those outside cannot see in. Equally important, those inside cannot see out. As one planner has explained, "Any significant changes that may befall an adjacent parcel of land due to uncertainty in the marketplace, a lack of adequate land use control and so on can be screened out. Thus, any adverse real-estate implications can be effectively minimized."

The richest of the gated communities behind their walls have private lakes and beaches and golf courses. They appear to be an American invention, specifically a Californian inven- tion. Not surprisingly, they have been copied in South Africa, the world's most violent coun- try not at war. They are also being copied in peaceful Canada — for example, in British Co- lumbia's Okanagan Valley and the affluent suburbs north of Toronto. Why in Canada? Perhaps because of the free trade in media images: the misperception of their country Canadians ac- quire from watching too much U.S. television and becoming convinced that U.S. urban may- hem has advanced north of the border.

I hope it is not for any perverse reason, but I have my doubts.

People proclaim that they live in gated communities as protection against crime. And, in principle, gated communities are no different from apartment buildings with locked doors, buzzers, and security guards sitting in the lobby. No surprise visits to Aunt Sally there either.

However, apartment security measures are necessary because apartment building corri- dors, unlike neighbourhood residential streets, do not have watchers. They are empty, ster- ile. The great urbanist Jane Jacobs discovered long ago that watchers — the neighbours who sit on porches and spend a lot of time peering out through their windows — are the most effective deterrent against crime.

I was struck by something a woman in a Kelowna gated community told a CBC inter- viewer. She said approvingly something to the effect of "You never see a stranger here." Let's think about this.

What this woman is talking about is what the planner quoted above is talking about — disengagement from society. You don't know whether there are children living on the streets if there are walls and security guards present to make sure they don't live on your streets. You don't know whether the number of street beggars is increasing if they are not allowed to beg on your streets.

You don't know what the human face of your country looks like if you live in a communi- ty where you never see a stranger. You're never surprised. You don't have to learn to con- front and become accustomed to new things.

(continued)

Box 14.2 (continued)

The husband of the woman who made the comment about strangers boasted that people driving by the community can't see in. If they could, they would be envious, he said. I'm more worried by what the planner said about people not being able to see out.

If one is cosseted behind great big concrete walls, it does not matter if some polluting horror occurs, if some criminally wasteful land-use practice takes place, if some stomach-churningly ugly development is built on the adjacent property. You don't see it.

This is the modern doctrine of what's mine is mine, what's yours is yours, a doctrine, says the Canadian Jewish scholar Rabbi Reuven Bulka, that can "create a syndrome of insensitivity, of noncommunication, of nonconcern, which eventually leads to hardness, callousness, and total disregard of the other individual, even producing the inability to help and, eventually, the desire to harm."

SOURCE: Adapted from Michael Valpy, "Walling Out the World," *The Globe and Mail,* May 23, 1996, p. A21. Used with permission from *The Globe and Mail.*

---

treme case of a self-contained, inward-facing complex, surrounded by fortress-like two-story walls covering the heating and ventilating equipment" (1989: 222).

▲ THE THEME-PARK CITY

The third and final component of the postmodern city is often called the "theme-park city." Its planning, design, and identity all reflect the influence of the exurban theme park, most notably Disney World in Orlando, Florida. Theme-park cities are both a product of and a part of the rapidly developing **symbolic economy** — that is, an economy that is based not on manufacturing and selling tangible goods, such as cars and refrigerators, but on the marketing of images and representations that derive from popular culture and entertainment.

Symbolic economies and their keenest promoters — large retail and entertainment giants, such as Disney, Universal Studios, Warner Bros., Sony, and Nike — have become so important to the future of contemporary cities because they are regarded as the best and, in some cases, the only chance for reversing the economic decline associated with deindustrialization. That is, cities are having to cope with the consequences of declining automotive, steel, textile, and other manufacturing industries, as a result of shrinking markets, increased foreign competition, or relocation of existing factories to regions of the world in which wages are low, unions are weak, and environmental regulations are lax. Local growth machines that once engaged in "smokestack chasing" — offering tax holidays and other incentives in order to attract industry — today seek out "mega-events" (Olympic Games, Expos, the Superbowl), tourist attractions, and professional sports teams. By doing so, they hope to lure out-of-town visitors, especially those attending conventions and trade shows.

West Edmonton Mall, at 4 million square feet, is the largest shopping mall in the world. The contractor, Triple Five Corporation, claims that the mall is also "the first real attempt to integrate leisure, retail, and hospitality under one roof." SOURCE: West Edmonton Mall.

Another important part of the planning process of theme-park cities is the creation of "place images" by which cities become known worldwide. Although some cities have distinctive images of considerable vintage (e.g., New Orleans, Paris), many of today's urban centres have found it necessary to invent a new set of attributes and then market them aggressively. Among the best known of these are Manchester, England, and Glasgow, Scotland, both of which have attempted with some degree of success to discard images as dirty, industrial cities and substitute a new identity as centres of European culture.

"Comeback cities" in Canada and the United States have been especially attracted by the possibilities of sports and themed entertainment as identity enhancers. Two leading examples are Baltimore and Cleveland, both of which have built highly acclaimed neotraditional baseball stadiums on the edge of inner-city neighbourhoods, as well as an ever-expanding infrastructure of other attractions, such as Harborplace, a waterfront festival market (Baltimore), and the Rock and Roll Hall of Fame (Cleveland). Other cities have looked to casino gambling, hoping to reinvent themselves as miniversions of Las Vegas, which still has one of the fastest-growing economies in the United States.

As they did the corporate suburbs of the 1950s, many urban commentators, critics, and researchers regard the theme-park city with some alarm. Sorkin (1992: xiii), for example, cites three characteristics that give the theme-park city a "sinister" twist.

First, the theme-park city is characterized by despatialization — that is, the severing of all natural ties between the city and local and physical geography. Whereas a community used to be unique because of its indigenous landscape, urban place images today are both generic and modular, capable of being inserted anywhere and everywhere. For example, the *Wall Street Journal* recently profiled the Irish Pub Co., a design and construction business that has exported 1000 "genuine" new Irish pubs to 35 countries. Each completely finished pub is delivered with everything from beer taps to old whisky bottles for decoration, and comes in a choice of five models: Victorian Dublin, Gaelic, Irish Brewery Pub, Irish Pub Shop, and Irish Country Cottage (Goldsmith, 1996). As such products spread globally, local space is departicularized — that is, stripped of its

The first large-scale amusement park developed in this country was Canada's Wonderland (now called Paramount Canada's Wonderland). A 150-foot artificial mountain is surrounded by several attraction areas, each with a different fantasy theme. SOURCE: Image reproduced by permission of Paramount Canada's Wonderland.

unique qualities that make it both distinctive and human (Hannigan, 1995: 160).

A second sinister aspect of the theme-park city is pervasive surveillance and security. **Festival marketplaces,** for example, may appear to be open to all, but in fact are meant only for affluent tourists and suburban visitors. To insulate them from surrounding neighbourhoods that are considered unsafe, developers have put in place a sophisticated security system, modelled in part on that used in Disney World.

And, finally, the theme-park city is a city of simulations. That is, urban cityscapes are deliberately constructed so as to replicate reality, but without any of the warts to be found in the original. A good illustration of this is City Walk, an urban entertainment centre at the Universal City complex in California. A "pseudo-city" street of shops and entertainment, City Walk thoroughly fuses — or confuses — the urban "real" and the entertainment "ideal." One is left asking, as Goldberger (1996: 141) does: Is it a city street masquerading as a theme park, or a theme park masquerading as a city street?

The various features that distinguish the industrial city, the corporate city, and the postmodern city are compared in Table 14.3. ■

◆ **Table 14.3** Industrial City, Corporate City, and Postmodern City Compared

	Industrial city	**Corporate city**	**Postmodern city**
Urban economy depends on	Manufacturing	Financial and retail	Information; leisure services; entertainment
Key retailing institution	Department store	Shopping centre	Urban entertainment centre
Class distance maintained by	Cost of real estate	Physical separation of suburb and central city	Privatization of urban space
Where the middle class live	Central city (outer edge)	Suburbs	Edge cities
Urban critics concerned with	Overcrowding; social disorganization	Mass conformity (suburbs); decline of downtowns	"Disneyfication" of the metropolis

SUMMARY

1. Cities are defined as relatively large, dense, permanent settlements in which the majority of the residents do not produce their own food.

2. Until the Industrial Revolution, cities were incapable of supporting more than about 5 percent of the total societal population, largely because of the absence of agricultural surpluses large enough to feed a huge urban population.

3. The best-known urban-growth model in the social sciences is Ernest Burgess's concentric-zone scheme in which the expansion of cities is conceptualized as a successive series or rings and circles, each of which segregates a distinct resident population and type of land use. Other, more recent explanations favour patterns of urban growth resembling pie-shaped wedges that develop along transportation routes or multiple nodes of economic activity each with its own nucleus.

4. The corporate city of the 1950s and 1960s was the product of an urban-growth machine in which a coalition of politicians, planners, real-estate developers, business people, and other interest groups joined forces in order to engineer economic development and progress. The main products of this alliance were: (a) the corporate suburbs, (b) shopping centres, (c) suburban industrial parks, (d) downtown office towers, and (e) high-rise apartment buildings.

5. Three alternative theories — structural, selective migration, and class and life-cycle stage — have been proposed to explain the relationship between suburban residence and lifestyle patterns. Although all these theories have merit, the suburban way of life observed by many researchers in the 1950s and 1960s appears to have been a unique product of a particular time and place.

6. In recent decades, the contemporary city has mirrored and incorporated a bifurcated global economy. On the one hand, there is an upper-tier informational city whose members work in jobs related to financial services, telecommunications, and high technology and live either in gentrified downtown neighbourhoods or in private communities on the edge of the city. On the other hand, there is an informal economy whose members are excluded from the informational city and who live in ethnic or racial ghettos that are often, but not necessarily, located in the inner city. Together, the informational city and the informal economy constitute the dual city whose residents have little in common with each other.

7. One of the defining characteristics of the postmodern city is the increasing privatization of public spaces. This is manifested in three ways: (a) the growth of private enclosed places, such as malls, festival marketplaces, and themed entertainment complexes, that offer pale imitations of urbanity; (b) the booming growth of gated communities and other private residential enclaves where outsiders are not welcome; and (c) in the construction of fortress cities where tourists and other affluent consumers are kept in while the homeless and the urban poor are kept out.

● QUESTIONS TO CONSIDER

1. Are edge cities real cities? Support your answer by including examples from both Canadian and U.S. urban areas.

2. Map out your own "personal city" by keeping a record for a full week of all the trips you take to work, school, shopping, medical and dental appointments, friends' houses, restaurants and night clubs, and so on. What proportion of these trips occur within your neighbourhood? Within the community in which you live? Across the wider metropolitan area?

3. To what extent does the big city in which you live or which you live closest to constitute a dual city?

4. How has suburban life been depicted in the mass media? Think, for example, of popular television series, such as *Clueless* and *The Simpsons*. To what extent do these depictions support the "myth of suburbia"?

5. Locate the Statistics Canada Web site (http://www.statcan.ca) on the Internet. What kinds of questions about cities could you answer from this data source?

● GLOSSARY

carceral development Building downtown jails and prisons to resemble hotels, convention centres, or office buildings in order to camouflage their real purpose.

city A relatively large, dense, permanent settlement in which the majority of the residents do not produce their own food.

concentric-zone model The classic urban-growth model proposed by Ernest Burgess in which the expansion of cities is visualized as a successive series of concentric rings or circles, each of which contains a distinct resident population and type of land use. As social groups become more established and prosperous, they move farther away from the city centre.

corporate city The perception and organization of the city as a vehicle for capital accumulation. The corporate city contains five major elements: the corporate suburb, high-rise apartments, suburban industrial parks, downtown office towers, and shopping malls.

edge cities Self-contained entertainment, shopping, and office areas that have emerged in formerly suburban areas or just beyond the fringe of suburbia.

environmental-opportunity theory The idea that people actively choose where they want to live depending on the extent to which a particular place either meshes with or constrains their preferred lifestyle.

familism A lifestyle that places a high value on family living, marriage at a young age, a brief period of childlessness after marriage, and child-centredness.

festival marketplace A themed specialty retail centre that is typically located on the historic urban waterfront.

gentrification The transformation of working-class housing to fashionable downtown neighbourhoods by middle- and upper-income migrants.

multiple-nuclei model A model of urban growth characterized by a series of growth centres — retail, wholesale, residential — each representing the concentration of a specific function or activity within the urban economy.

myth of suburbia A standardized and stereotyped view of the suburbs as uniformly middle-class, homogeneous, child-centred and female-dominated, conformist, and a hotbed of sociability and local participation.

rent gap The difference between the current value of land in its "depressed" state and the value that could be charged given a higher or better land use.

sector model A model of urban growth that proposes that the city expands outward from the centre in a series of sectors or wedges along major transportation arteries, such as highways and railroad lines.

symbolic economy An economy based on images and representations derived from popular culture and entertainment.

urban-growth machine A loosely structured coalition of local economic and political interest groups that hold in common a commitment to sustained growth and development.

SUGGESTED READING

Hannigan, John. (1995). "The Postmodern City: A New Urbanization?" *Current Sociology, 43* (1), 152–217. A critical guide to the postmodern city, including discussions of postmodern architecture and planning, gentrification, tourism, and theme parks.

McGahan, Peter. (1995). *Urban Sociology in Canada,* 3rd ed. Toronto: Harcourt Brace. Still the best urban-sociology text on the Canadian market. Note especially the discussions of urban migration, immigration, and ethnic residential segregation.

Palen, John J. (1995). *The Suburbs.* New York: McGraw Hill. A concise, information-packed, and up-to-date overview of the suburban experience, by the author of *The Urban World*. It includes a useful discussion of edge cities and private communities.

Sewell, John. (1993). *The Shape of the City: Toronto Struggles with Modern Planning.* Toronto: University of Toronto Press. A generously illustrated history of urban growth and planning in Canada's largest city, by a well-known activist, author, and former mayor of Toronto.

Sorkin, Michael, ed. (1992). *Variations on a Theme Park: The New American City and the End of Public Space.* New York: The Noonday Press. A fascinating collection of articles on the "ageographical" city. Of particular note are essays by Margaret Crawford on the West Edmonton Mall, Mike Davis on the "militarization" of Los Angeles, and Christine Boyer on "South Street Seaport," a festival marketplace in New York.

CHAPTER FIFTEEN
Sociology and the Environment

IN THIS CHAPTER YOU WILL LEARN THAT

- a major focus of the sociology of the environment is the conflict between environmentalists and their opponents in industry and science
- support for environmentalism has remained constant for nearly two decades, with a majority of people generally supportive of environmental values and a young, well-educated, urban, liberal group leading the movement for environmental change
- in order to mobilize the reluctant majority, organizers of the environmental movement develop and spread interpretations of events that play up the possibility of environmental crises
- the goals of conserving resources, reducing pollution, and restricting population increase are especially difficult to achieve in the Third World
- at the community level, willingness to act on environmental problems rises as trust in authority figures declines
- environmental problems are often contested on the basis of acceptable risk; and the definition of what is acceptable risk is strongly influenced by the distribution of power in society, with more powerful individuals and groups better able to determine what is and what is not risky

JOHN HANNIGAN
University of Toronto

■ INTRODUCTION

During the winter of 1994, hundreds of millions of television viewers worldwide watched the Winter Olympic Games in Lillehammer, Norway. The Lillehammer Olympics will be remembered not only for the media blitz that accompanied the figure-skating rivalry between Nancy Kerrigan and Tonya Harding, but also because they were the first "Green Games," at which the issue of environmental protection was placed front and centre. Among other measures, private cars were banned from routes into the Olympic area, the cutlery and plates at Olympic sites were made from biodegradable potato starch, and a special fuel was developed for the Olympic flame to reduce the amount of pollution from the symbolic fire (*The Globe and Mail,* Feb. 11, 1994: A1).

In this chapter, I examine how sociology has dealt with the rising global crescendo of environmental awareness, concern, and action that was symbolized by Norway's Green Olympics. After briefly discussing the traditional lack of concern with the environment in sociological theory and research, I outline the basic value conflict in contemporary societies between those who favour unlimited economic expansion and technological solutions to human problems and those

who embrace a new "ecological" view of the world, in which nature is accorded a central place. Next, I review theory and research in the four principal areas of sociological inquiry relating to the environment (Buttel, 1987): (1) environmental attitudes, concern, and behaviour; (2) the environmental movement; (3) the political economy of the environment; and (4) environmental risk and risk assessment. I conclude by arguing that it is important to deal with the environment from a "social-constructionist" perspective in order to bring more sociology into the sociological study of the environment.

■ TOWARD ENVIRONMENTAL SOCIOLOGY

In contrast to some other social sciences, notably anthropology and geography, sociology's interest in the environment is of relatively recent vintage, stretching back only about a quarter of a century. There are several reasons for this neglect (Dunlap and Catton, 1983).

First, for the early-twentieth-century pioneers of sociology, the term *environment* came to mean something quite different from our physical sur-

One focus of environmental sociology is the value conflict between environmentalists and "mainstream" citizens. According to the mainstream view, people have the unalienable right to dominate nature, even if that involves polluting the environment, as this McDonnell Douglas plant illustrates. SOURCE: Dick Hemingway.

roundings. In order to carve out a distinctive place for sociology as a new academic discipline, Émile Durkheim and the other founders of the field downplayed the role of biological and physical factors in influencing human affairs while at the same time elevating the importance of "social facts," such as norms, groups, and institutions. In accounting for the emergence of a wide range of behaviours, from juvenile delinquency to racism, sociologists opted for explanations that framed these behaviours in terms of "nurture" rather than "nature."

A second explanation for sociology's reluctance to embrace the study of the environment concerns sociologists' own view of technology, natural resources, and human progress. In the past, most sociologists shared the assumption of the general public that the world would see steady gains in material progress, fuelled by an apparently unlimited availability of natural resources such as coal, lumber, and water. From this perspective, technology functioned as the linchpin of economic development, allowing humans to overcome the challenges presented by hostile habitats such as jungles, swamps, and deserts. This **human-exceptionalism paradigm** featured the ideals of steadily evolving social progress, increasing prosperity and material comfort, and class mobility for all segments of society. There was little room in this world view for sociological attention to the environmental "costs" of growth — pollution, health hazards in the workplace, and the loss of diversity in plant and animal species. Nor was there much consideration given to the constraints that might be imposed on further economic expansion by declining resources, the exhaustion of nutrients in the soil, and the destruction of natural ecosystems.

Sociology's one major venture into environmental theorizing before the 1970s was the "human ecology" approach to the growth of cities, which dominated urban sociology from the 1920s to the 1960s. The language and principles of human ecology were borrowed from biological ecology, the science of the interdependence of plants and animals living together in a natural area. Robert Park, a founder of the Chicago School of urban sociology, with which the human ecology approach is most closely associated, drew an analogy between processes of invasion, succession, and competition in nature and patterns of location, movement, and relocation in cities. Park argued that the competitive struggle for existence among urban residents, including ethnic and racial groups, was especially evident in the "zone of transition," an area adjacent to the central core of the city where residential en-

vironments gave way to illegal commercial activities (drug dealing, prostitution, gambling), slum housing, and low-rent businesses.

Despite its inspiration in the biological sciences, human ecology failed to give much consideration to our relationships with the natural environment. Emphasis was placed on the contest among humans for land and space rather than on the impact of that struggle on natural ecological systems. Starting in the 1950s, some "neo-orthodox" human ecologists, notably O.D. Duncan and Amos Hawley, undertook to address the environmental dimension more directly. Duncan (1959) proposed that human settlements take the form of a weblike "ecological complex" in which four central variables — population, organization, environment, and technology — are closely interrelated. However, sociological human ecologists devoted most of their efforts to showing how social organization and technology enable human populations to adapt to their environment rather than looking at the limits imposed by the environment on human actions or at how human actions affect the natural environment (Dunlap and Catton, 1983).

By the early 1970s, stimulated by increased societal attention to urban decay, pollution, overpopulation, resource shortages, and so on, a number of sociologists began at last to study environmental issues. In 1973, the Society for the Study of Social Problems established an Environmental Problems Division. This was followed three years later by the founding of a Section on Environmental Sociology in the American Sociological Association. In 1983, *Sociological Inquiry* became the first English-language sociological journal to publish a complete special issue (vol. 53, no. 2/3) on "environmental sociology." Although natural-resource issues have long been central to sociology in Canada, it has only been in the last five years that environmental theory and research have come to the fore in this country. The *Canadian Review of Sociology and Anthropology* recently recognized this interest with a special issue entitled "Social Studies of the Environment" (vol. 31, no. 3, August 1994).

Nineteen years ago, in the first comprehensive review of the emergence of environmental sociology as a distinct area of inquiry, Dunlap and Catton (1979) distinguished between a "sociology of environmental issues" and "environmental sociology." The former, they observed, was concerned primarily with environmentally related phenomena, such as resource-management problems in wildland recreation areas or the origins, membership, and beliefs of the environmental movement. The latter focussed

"Say, we must be nearer civilization than we thought. This is oil!"

SOURCE: Drawing by Carl Rose; © 1970 The New Yorker Magazine, Inc.

on "the physical environment as a factor that may influence (or be influenced by) social behavior" (Dunlap and Catton, 1979: 255). This suggests that the environment can function as a contextual, an independent, or a dependent variable — that is, as background, cause, or effect.

Today, "environmental sociology" has become a catchall for the study of all social aspects of the environment. This has both advantages and disadvantages. On the plus side, it has propelled sociological inquiry into a number of important new areas — for example, studying public opposition to, and mobilization against, toxic wastes. At the same time, the very breadth of the field today has made it difficult to assemble a cohesive body of work built on strong theoretical foundations. Rather than emerging from a central core, the sociological study of the environment has developed from multiple nuclei, each reflecting a different philosophical position and a corresponding research agenda. This tendency has been exacerbated by the decision of some authors, journals, and organizations to consider both the natural and the human-built environments under the same umbrella. Furthermore, some terms — notably, *social ecology* — have come to acquire several very different meanings, depending on the branch of environmental sociology to which the researcher claims allegiance. One unifying element, however, is the widely shared recognition of the existence of a key value conflict in contemporary society between those who hold an "environmentalist" view of the world and those who do not.

ENVIRONMENTAL VALUE CONFLICT

Values, the most abstract level of culture, are guideposts that help us to sort out the choices we make in life. Although the vast majority of the Canadian population may be in agreement on some values (freedom, humanitarianism), other values are more controversial.

A central focus for many sociologists interested in the environment is the value cleavage between environmentalists and their opponents. At the core of this disagreement is the long-accepted notion that the environment is something to be actively used and exploited. Many of the key values that have governed North American life — activism, achievement, progress, pursuit of the good life, materialism

— permit this orientation toward the environment (Turner, 1981: 87). Environmentalists, in contrast, support a different value orientation, one that advocates a more passive, less manipulative approach to nature.

How environmentalists differ from the mainstream population has been most explicitly set out by British sociologist Stephen Cotgrove (1982). Cotgrove lays out two conflicting paradigms (a *paradigm* is a type of social lens through which we view the world) — the **dominant paradigm** and the **alternative environmental paradigm** (See Table 15.1).

The dominant paradigm is anchored by two core values: the moral imperative of material-wealth creation and the moral conviction that humans have the inalienable right to dominate nature and harness the environment to that end. All of our major institutions reflect the widespread acceptance of this paradigm. Governments at all levels operate ministries, consulates, and trade offices that have a mandate to promote commerce and attract foreign investment. University business schools run pro-

grams in "entrepreneurship." The media act as cheerleaders, linking political competence and achievement with an expanding economy and job creation. Economic growth carries with it a number of supplementary values: the view that society is best organized on a large-scale, centralized basis; respect for authority; the ascendancy of law and order; and confidence in science and technology.

Allied with this moral imperative of material wealth is the conviction that humans have a right and even a responsibility to dominate nature. Progress is interpreted as the increasing encroachment of civilization on jungles, deserts, frozen tundra, and other "wild" geographic environments. History, as it has been taught in our schools, is an account of how the explorers, missionaries, traders, and industrialists rolled back the frontier, "tamed" nature, and brought prosperity to "virgin" lands. Typically, one popular Hollywood epic of the 1960s was titled *How the West Was Won*. The great achievements of the last two centuries, including the opening of the Panama Canal, the completion of the

---

◆ **Table 15.1** Counter-Paradigms of the Environment

	Dominant paradigm	Alternative environmental paradigm
Core values	Material (economic growth)	Nonmaterial (self-actualization)
	Natural environment valued as resource	Natural environment intrinsically valued
	Domination over nature	Harmony with nature
Economy	Market forces	Public interest
	Risk and reward	Safety
	Rewards for achievement	Incomes related to need
	Differentials	Egalitarian
	Individual self-help	Collective/social provision
Polity	Authoritative structures (experts influential)	Participative structures (citizen/worker involvement)
	Hierarchical	Nonhierarchical
	Law and order	Liberation
Society	Centralized	Decentralized
	Large-scale	Small-scale
	Associational	Communal
	Ordered	Flexible
Nature	Ample reserves	Earth's resources limited
	Nature hostile/neutral	Nature benign
	Environment controllable	Nature delicately balanced
Knowledge	Confidence in science and technology	Limits to science
	Rationality of means	Rationality of ends
	Separation of fact/value, thought/feeling	Integration of fact/value, thought/feeling

SOURCE: S.F. Cotgrove, *Catastrophe or Cornucopia: The Environment, Politics, and the Future* (Chichester, UK: John Wiley & Sons, 1982). Copyright John Wiley & Sons Limited. Reproduced with permission.

Canadian transcontinental railway, and the landing of astronauts on the moon, all represent a triumph by science and industry over natural hazards and barriers.

The alternative environmental paradigm categorically rejects both of the pillars of enterprise culture (Cotgrove, 1982: 28–29):

> Not only do [environmentalists] challenge the importance attached to material and economic goals, they by contrast give much higher priority to the realization of non-material values — to social relationships and community, to the exercise of human skills and capacities and to increased participation in decisions that affect our daily lives. . . . They have little confidence in science and technology to come up with a technological fix to solve the problems of material and energy shortages. And this is in part rooted in a different view of nature, which stresses the delicate balance of ecological systems and possible irreversible damage which may result from the interventions of high technology.

Adherents of the alternative environmental paradigm value the natural environment for its own sake, thus questioning the human right to domination. The earth's resources, they claim, are limited and must therefore be conserved. Drawing on the insights of the economist E.F. Schumacher (1973), they believe that "small is beautiful." In this view, society should adopt small-scale, decentralized economic and political structures that are in harmony with nature.

The value conflict just described arches over a wide spectrum of issues and problems related to sociology and the environment. It is, for example, at the core of the dispute over commercial logging of the old-growth forests of Vancouver Island and the Lake Temagami region of Northern Ontario. It infuses the continuing debate over world population growth as a primary factor contributing to environmental degradation. It helps account for the rise of the "Greens" in Western Europe and of other political ecology parties whose vision closely parallels the alternative environmental paradigm.

A major attempt to bridge the differences between the dominant and alternative environmental outlooks can be found in the idea of **sustainable development**. This concept achieved global currency in 1987 as a result of its use in the report of the United Nations World Commission on Environment and Development, more commonly known as the Brundtland report (after the chair of the commission, Norwegian prime minister Gro Harlem Brundtland). The Brundtland report defined *sustainable development* as "development that meets the needs of the present without compromising the ability of future generations to meet their own needs" (World Commission on Environment and Development, 1987: 43). It foresaw a new form of economic growth, especially for Third World nations, that would be both environmentally aware and egalitarian, integrating objectives for social development with the demands of science. In short, the Brundtland report suggested that it is possible to have the best of both worlds: continued economic growth, but not at the expense of the environment.

However, many environmentalists have been critical of the concept of sustainable development. They argue that, in real life, it is not very easy to balance economic growth and natural-resource use with environmental protection. For example, they would argue that situating a jetport in the middle of an environmentally sensitive natural area would be ecologically destructive no matter what measures were taken to reduce noise pollution or catch the run-off of aviation fuel. In fact, environmentalists such as David Suzuki insist that the environmental dangers we face today are so extensive that we can survive as a species only by totally dismantling the "buzz saw of progress" in the industrial nations of the North, and by halting its advance in the less-developed countries of the Third World (see Box 15.1).

Furthermore, critics of the Brundtland report point out that sustainable development requires an extraordinary degree of mutual co-operation and a deep commitment to reform. This is difficult to achieve, especially in the nations of the Southern Hemisphere, where rural economies are still controlled by wealthy landowners, and the poor are forced to engage in ecologically damaging practices, such as stripping the rapidly dwindling forests for cooking fuel, in order to survive.

■ ENVIRONMENTAL ATTITUDES, CONCERNS, AND BEHAVIOURS

The existence of a distinct set of environmental attitudes and concerns in our society has been documented by a large number of polls conducted over the last quarter-century. One of the first and most important efforts to develop a research tool with which to measure an environmental view of the world was Dunlap and Van Liere's (1978) new environmental paradigm (NEP) scale. Using survey data from two samples of Washington state resi-

Box 15.1
The Buzz Saw of "Progress" Hits Sarawak

The Haida [Nation of British Columbia] bring to mind a remarkable speech delivered late last year before the United Nations by Anderson Mutang Urud, a Kelabit from Sarawak in Malaysia.

Sarawak is less than 2 percent the size of Brazil, yet it produces almost half the world's tropical timber. Even if the rate of logging were cut in half immediately, Mutang says all primary forest in Sarawak would be gone by the year 2000.

And as the forest is cleared there is a domino effect. "Fish, wild animals, sago palms, rattan, and medicinal plants disappear. The trees which bear the fruit which feeds the wild pigs are cut down for timber. The pigs disappear and with them vanishes the main supply of meat for our peoples.... Trees and vines with poisonous barks are felled and find their way into the streams, killing all the fish. Mud from the eroded lands pollutes the rivers, bringing us diseases and destroying our source of drinking water."

There is a fundamental clash between value systems. "The government says that it is bringing us progress and development.... For us, their so-called progress means only starvation, dependence, helplessness, the destruction of our culture, and demoralization of our people."

... Mutang says: "A high government official once told me that in order to have development, someone must make a sacrifice." I replied, "Why should it be us who must make this sacrifice? We have already become poor and marginalized. Now there is nothing left for us to sacrifice except our lives."

In our race to modernize, we must respect the ancient cultures and traditions of our indigenous people. We must not blindly follow that model of progress invented by European civilization. We may envy the industrialized world for its wealth; but we must not forget that this wealth was bought at a very high price. The rich world suffers from so much stress, pollution, violence, poverty, and spiritual emptiness. The wealth of indigenous communities lies not in money or commodities, but in community, tradition, and a sense of belonging to a special place.

SOURCE: Excerpted from David Suzuki, "The Buzz Saw of 'Progress' Hits Sarawak," *The Toronto Star,* March 17, 1994, p. B6.

dents and from the membership of a statewide environmental organization, Dunlap and Van Liere developed a twelve-item scale that measures the extent of agreement with such statements as "the balance of nature is very delicate and easily upset" and "humans need not adapt to the natural environment, because they can remake it to suit their own needs" (see Table 15.2). The researchers found that the general public moderately accepted the content of the emerging environmental paradigm, whereas environmentalists strongly endorsed it.

In addition to this "measured agreement" method favoured by Dunlap and his co-researchers, two other techniques have been used to measure environmental concern. One simple and straightforward approach is to ask people how worried or upset they are about a series of environmental problems. A second strategy, which strives for greater concreteness, is to ask respondents to weigh trade-offs between, for example, environmental protection and jobs (Freudenburg, 1991).

Has public concern with environmental quality changed since the first survey results were carried out in the early 1970s? Two complementary hypotheses address this question (Jones and Dunlap, 1992). Grossman and Potter (1977) formulated the **broadening-base hypothesis,** which predicts that environmental concern will eventually diffuse

Table 15.2 Average Scores on the New Environmental Paradigm (NEP) Scale by the General Public Sample (GPS) and the Environmental Organization Sample (EOS)[a]

	GPS	EOS
1. We are approaching the limit of the number of people the earth can support.	3.00	3.63
2. The balance of nature is very delicate and easily upset.	3.18	3.68
3. Humans have the right to modify the natural environment to suit their needs.	2.76	3.30
4. Humankind was created to rule over the rest of nature.	2.63	3.67
5. When humans interfere with nature, it often produces disastrous consequences.	3.03	3.49
6. Plants and animals exist primarily to be used by humans.	2.81	3.61
7. To maintain a healthy economy, we will have to develop a "steady-state" economy in which industrial growth is controlled.	2.85	3.48
8. Humans must live in harmony with nature in order to survive.	3.52	3.86
9. The earth is like a spaceship with only limited room and resources.	3.21	3.85
10. Humans need not adapt to the natural environment, because they can remake it to suit their own needs.	3.25	3.74
11. There are limits to growth beyond which our industrialized society cannot expand.	2.94	3.64
12. Humankind is severely abusing the environment.	3.11	3.81

[a] High scores indicate strong agreement with the pro-NEP position. Range = 1.0–4.0. Eight of the items are worded such that agreement reflects acceptance of the NEP, while for the other four (3, 4, 6, 10) disagreement reflects acceptance of the NEP. Respondents were assigned scores of 4 for "strongly agree," 3 for "mildly agree," 2 for "mildly disagree," and 1 for "strongly disagree" for the eight pro-NEP items; scoring for the four anti-NEP items was reversed.

SOURCE: Adapted from Riley E. Dunlap and Kenneth D. Van Liere, "The New Environmental Paradigm: A Proposed Measuring Instrument and Preliminary Results," *Journal of Environmental Education, 9* (1978), pp. 10–19.

throughout all groups in the nation. Buttel (1975) promoted the **economic-contingency hypothesis,** which suggests that the broadening of the social bases of environmental concern depends on prevailing economic conditions. Buttel argued that when economic conditions worsen or are perceived to be getting worse, those who are least well off will be the first to shift their focus from the environment to the economy. However, other researchers, using U.S. data for the years 1973–90, found little support for either hypothesis (Jones and Dunlap, 1992); they found instead that the level and social location of support for environmental protection have remained remarkably stable for nearly twenty years.

In Canada, support for the environment did not grow rapidly until the mid-1980s, when it suddenly spiked upward (see Figure 15.1). Nevertheless, ac-

cording to both Gallup polls and national election surveys, the environmental issue was easily outranked by concern with other issues, notably the economy, inflation, and unemployment (Bakvis and Nevitte, 1992: 146–47).

What are the social bases of environmental concern? It was originally thought that support for environmentalism was limited to the affluent. However, most surveys in the 1970s and 1980s found that income and occupational prestige were only weakly related to environmental concern (Buttel, 1987; Van Liere and Dunlap, 1980). Instead, higher levels of education, youth, political liberalism, and urban residence were found to be the best predictors of concern with environmental quality (Dunlap and Catton, 1979). The social bases of environmental concern have remained more or less the

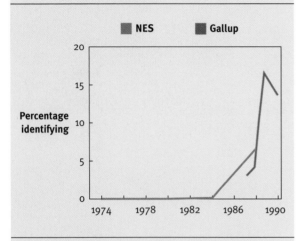

◆ **Figure 15.1** The Identification of Environment/Pollution as the Most Important Issue in National Election Surveys (NES) and Gallup Polls,[a] 1974–1990

[a] The questions posed were as follows: *NES* — What is/was the most important issue in this campaign to you? *Gallup* — What is/was the most important problem facing Canada today?

SOURCE: Herman Bakvis and Neil Nevitte, "The Greening of the Canadian Electorate: Enviromentalism, Ideology and Partisanship," in R. Boardman, ed., *Canadian Environmental Policy: Ecosystems, Politics and Process* (Toronto: Oxford University Press, 1992), pp. 144–63. Reprinted by permission of the authors.

studies of the relationship between environmental attitudes and behaviour and concluded that individuals who expressed a positive attitude toward the environment were more likely to report engaging in responsible environmental actions than were those who held a negative view. This relationship was strongest among those who supported recycling, energy conservation, and other individual behaviours, but it also applied to those who expressed a positive view toward ecology and the environment in general (Hines, Hungerford, and Tomera, 1986–87).

Most other studies, however, have failed to confirm these linkages. As Maloney and Ward (1973: 585) have noted, "most people say they are willing to do a great deal to help curb pollution problems and are fairly emotional about it, but in fact they actually do very little and know even less." For the most part, those who score positively in environmental-concern polls do not show any particular willingness to go beyond low-cost, personal actions (recycling, buying "green" products) to make deep-cutting sacrifices for the environment. Uusitalo (1990), for example, found that support for measures to help the environment declined when they required any change of personal habits.

From this evidence, it appears that most people are willing to pay lip-service to protecting the environment and will behave responsibly as long as it is not appreciably more expensive or inconvenient to do so. After studying recycling behaviour across the province of Alberta, Derksen and Gartrell (1993) concluded that the key factor accounting for participation in recycling programs was the easy availability of curbside pickups rather than positive attitudes toward the environment. In fact, those who were environmentally concerned were no more likely to recycle than those who were unconcerned.

same from 1973 to 1990, as have levels of support (Jones and Dunlap, 1992). Greenbaum (1995) has characterized the social bases of environmental concern as "complex and subtle." That is because environmental concern spans a wide variety of subject matters, from species extinction and the thinning of the ozone layer to the contamination of local drinking waters by toxic chemicals. Although it may be possible to isolate general clusters of environmental concern, as have Dunlap and Van Liere in their NEP scale (see Table 15.2), people may not be very consistent across various issues. Part of the reason for inconsistency is that individual environmental problems may affect us in very different ways. How concerned we will be about a particular environmental problem, or whether we even perceive it as a "problem," will depend on how the activity in question affects our "interests" — that is, how we will be affected by its benefits, costs, and risks (Greenbaum, 1995: 127).

Do these pro-environmental attitudes convert directly into environmentally friendly behaviour? The evidence is mixed. One set of authors reviewed 51

■ THE ENVIRONMENTAL MOVEMENT

Although environmental concern exists across a wide cross-section of the population, it has been most intensely concentrated in the environmental movement. Movement activists have waged environmental battles with loggers, utility companies, whalers, agri-corporations, developers, and other defenders of the dominant paradigm. Although the environmental movement has not always represented a "vanguard for a new society" (Milbrath, 1984), it does directly incorporate many of the elements of the alternative environmental paradigm in its philosophies and actions.

▲ SOCIAL BASE AND COMPOSITION

In its early manifestations in the nineteenth century, the environmental movement was largely the creation of an elite. For example, the leadership and much of the membership of American wildlife-preservation organizations such as the Sierra Club, the Save the Redwoods League, and the Boone and Crockett Club were drawn almost exclusively from a tightly knit network of lawyers, educators, and wealthy businessmen. Similarly, in England, preservationist causes were pursued primarily by members of the clergy and the aristocracy. Occasionally, these elite organizations would enlist the support of the general public in specific campaigns. In the fight to save Niagara Falls (1906–10), for example, a national publicity campaign waged in the pages of American popular magazines such as *Ladies' Home Journal* resulted in more than 6500 letters written in support of the preservation of the falls (Cylke, 1993: 22).

In Canada, the conservation movement developed in a different fashion. Environmental initiatives, such as the establishment of national parks and the protection of wildlife, were more likely to be developed by small groups of dedicated civil servants who were

The environmental movement has grown tremendously since the 1960s. Some members of the middle class in particular are now more personally involved in the environmental movement and raise environmentally conscious children. SOURCE: Dick Hemingway.

able to convince the federal government to take action (Foster, 1978). Two of the most significant events in early Canadian conservation history, the establishment of the first national park in Banff in 1887 and the signing of the Canada–U.S. Migratory Bird Convention in 1917, followed this pattern.

When the modern environmental movement emerged in the late 1960s and early 1970s, it was largely a creature of the upper middle classes. The dominant social groups in environmental organizations were well-educated professionals from urban and suburban backgrounds and college students from white-collar backgrounds (Gale, 1983). More recently, environmentalists have been identified as members of a "new middle class" drawn primarily from social and cultural specialists — teachers, social workers, journalists, artists, and professors — who work in creative and/or public-service-oriented jobs. This new middle class is on the firing line in the day-to-day conflicts between the engineers and technocrats who tend to ignore the human costs of progress and the ordinary citizens who are victimized by them.

There are two kinds of explanations for why members of the new middle class tend to be more radical as a group than the population as a whole. On the one hand, they are more likely to seek out jobs in the public sector, away from the pressures of a business environment that is hostile to their values. At the same time, they tend to become personally involved in the problems faced by their clients, even to the point of becoming advocates for their interests (Kriesi, 1989: 1084). For example, a doctor working in a community health centre whose patients suffer an unusually high incidence of asthma might recognize that the source of the illness is a local incinerator and may campaign to have the polluting facility closed.

Evidence for this new class theory of social movements comes from a number of different nations. Cotgrove and Duff (1981) found that nearly half (43.4 percent) of their sample of environmentalists in England (compared with only about 12 percent of the general public) were employed in service, welfare, and creative occupations. Kriesi (1989) found that 23 percent of those who reported having participated in the Dutch ecology movement (compared with 12 percent of the population as a whole) were social and cultural specialists. And Tindall (1994) showed that people who had higher levels of income and education and/or were employed in the public sector were more likely to join the Vancouver Island wilderness-preservation movement, although these factors did not affect their level of participation after joining.

▲ ENVIRONMENTAL MOBILIZATION

In addition to researching the social composition of the environmental movement, sociologists have also been interested in learning how environmentalists mobilize people to their cause.

Much of the research on this topic has focussed on community-based, grass-roots environmental organizations. Formed in opposition to the pollution problems caused by local industries and utilities, these citizens' groups differ somewhat from the rest of the environmental movement insofar as they draw their members from blue-collar as well as white-collar neighbourhoods. The prototype of the grass-roots, locally based environmental group is the Love Canal Homeowners Association, formed in the 1970s by some Niagara Falls, New York, home-owners whose properties had been contaminated by toxic waste buried 30 years earlier by a local chemical company (see Box 15.2).

It is by no means a simple matter to mobilize one's neighbours in the face of an environmental threat. In fact, most people want to avoid trouble and must be actively convinced that their present situation is both unjust and intolerable before they will consider taking action. Capek (1993: 11) describes the initial reluctance of home-owners in Carver Terrace, a contaminated residential subdivision in the U.S. South, to recognize the dangers facing them:

> Residents knew at some level about bad-smelling air, mysterious illness or deaths among people with no prior history of medical problems, plants that would not grow or grew strangely, animals becoming ill or [being] born deformed, and a variety of other experiences that lacked explanation. The amorphous and invisible nature of chemical exposure, however, and the difficulty of diagnosing its consequences either at a popular or professional level worked against the integration of this knowledge.

Caught up in the demands of everyday life, respectful of the voices of authority who downplay the problem, and blinded by the pride of home ownership, people tend to accept the status quo and must be persuaded to redefine their situation in such a way that they can see it as a violation of their basic rights. This is easier to do when citizens are ideologically primed to question the image of progress as continuous economic development (Ladd and Laska, 1991), but even those who lack this attitudinal underpinning can be brought around.

There are four stages through which local communities pass in the process of challenging polluters (Cable and Benson, 1993). In the first phase, residents come to see themselves as "victims" of corporate environmental crime. In phase two, they make individual appeals to government regulatory agencies to take action to force an end to the toxic dumping or other problem situation. In the third phase, the complainants become disillusioned with the slow pace or absence of official action and begin to seek environmental justice. In the final phase, increased democratic pressure has either convinced government regulators to enforce environmental standards or proven insufficient, in which case the problem continues unchecked.

Like other social movements, the environmental movement aims to convince as wide a segment of the public as possible that its interpretation of the world is correct and should, therefore, be acted upon. To that end, members of the movement develop "frames" — that is, interpretations of events and their meanings. Successful framing has three elements: diagnostic, prognostic, and motivational. Diagnostic framing involves identifying a problem and fixing the blame for it. Prognostic framing offers a proposed solution to the diagnosed problem. Motivational framing is a call to arms to potential recruits to take specific corrective action. The better these three frames are integrated, the greater their capacity for mobilizing people (Gerhards and Rucht, 1992: 583).

Contemporary environmental frames are frequently constructed around the image of an impending global collapse. In the early 1970s, this approach was typified by the bestselling book *The Limits to Growth* (Meadows et al., 1972), in which the authors forecast that earth's **carrying capacity** — that is, the optimum population size that the planet can support under present environmental conditions — would eventually be exceeded. With the aid of a computer model, they estimated how five interrelated factors — population growth, industrial output, food production, pollution, and nonrenewable natural resources — would interact over time. They predicted that, within a century, we would face a major crisis brought on by uncontrolled population growth and rising levels of pollution.

In the 1980s, the threat shifted to that of "biosphere crisis," generated by global climatic changes resulting from increased emissions of "greenhouse" gases, such as carbon dioxide, chlorofluorocarbons, methane, and nitrous oxide, into the atmosphere. Such changes in global weather patterns have the potential to trigger major environmental changes, including rising sea levels, hotter summers, more frequent and more severe droughts, dust storms, forest fires, and the rapid extinction of thousands of species of plants and animals.

Box 15.2
Love Canal

After World War II, the Hooker Chemical company, a subsidiary of the giant Occidental Petroleum Company, began to dump large drums full of waste chemicals into Love Canal, an uncompleted and abandoned nineteenth-century waterway near Niagara Falls, New York. In 1953, after thousands of drums had been deposited in the canal, it was filled in, and the land was sold to the local board of education for the token price of a dollar, as the site of a new primary school and playground. Significantly, the company insisted on a legal release from any future liability.

By 1976, after several years of unusually heavy rain and snow, the rotting drums had begun to break apart and more than 80 different chemical compounds were seeping into the basements of the several hundred homes that had been constructed along the canal.

Alarmed by the deteriorating health of her children, Lois Gibbs canvassed her neighbours and went on to found the Love Canal Homeowners Association. With the assistance of Dr. Beverly Paigen, a biologist who worked at a prestigious cancer research centre in nearby Buffalo, the association carried out a community health survey that revealed higher-than-average rates of miscarriage among pregnant women, kidney and bladder ailments, and disorders of the central nervous sytem. Further actions taken by home-owners included protest marches, public demonstrations, press conferences, political lobbying, legal injunctions, and, in one instance, a hostage-taking action. Finally, in 1980, U.S. president Jimmy Carter declared a state emergency at Love Canal, and 700 families living close to the canal were relocated at government expense.

The solution, environmentalists claim, is to embrace wholeheartedly the alternative environmental paradigm. In *Beyond the Limits* (1992), the sequel to *The Limits to Growth,* Meadows, Meadows, and Randers caution that we must draw back and ease down: conserve resources, reduce pollution, and adopt deliberate social constraints on population and industrial growth. In the less-developed nations, this means both controlling family size and finding new, more sustainable avenues of economic expansion. In the industrialized world, a new value system is said to be necessary so that people will stop trying to use material growth to satisfy what are in fact nonmaterial needs — for acceptance, self-importance, and community identity (Fields, 1993: 40).

More research is needed on the relationship between grass-roots mobilizations protesting toxic dumps, incinerators, nuclear power plants, and other pollution sources and these wider ecological world views. Although we might assume that environmentalists, in accordance with the popular slogan "think globally, act locally," first become imbued with the alternative environmental paradigm and then put it to practical use in their own neigh-bourhoods and communities, another possibility is that ecological values arise directly out of first-hand experience. In the latter view, it is the process of dealing with recalcitrant polluters, bureaucratic cover-ups, and overly cautious scientists that eventually causes the penny to drop for local environmentalists who previously had not given much thought to broad environmental philosophies. Members of community-based, grass-roots environmental organizations thus engage in a form of social learning as they go about researching their case against polluters. This social learning is further facilitated by the assembly of a widening net of environmental contacts. Irene Paparo-Stein, a Winnipeg woman who formed a citizens' lobby group to fight chemical spraying in her city, describes the environmental networking process this way (Stein, 1988: 52):

One thing I had discovered, there was quite a network in the U.S. And the Americans, once I explained the situation and the need for information, were ready with their help. They understood the enormity of the problem, of the lay persons up against the governments, bureaucracy, and industry, and knew what to do. They were generous with their aid. We had soon compiled a list of contacts from all over the U.S.

Inevitably, someone in the network introduces the community activist to an "ecological" perspective.

▲ IDEOLOGICAL DIVISIONS

Although we often speak of the environmental movement as a single entity, there has in fact long been a basic philosophical split between "value-oriented environmentalists," whose main concern is to change the way we view the world, and "success-oriented environmentalists," whose chief goal is to stop pollution and other activities that damage the physical environment (Eyerman and Jamison, 1989). These two factions differ significantly in their perceptions of the root causes of environmental problems, their preferences among strategies for coping, and their visions of an ecologically sound society (Cylke, 1993: 69).

This division became evident at the beginning of the twentieth century in the differing approaches to the environment taken by the two main wings of the U.S. conservation movement — the "resource conservationists" and the "preservationists." The former wished to "manage" natural resources by applying modern engineering and administrative techniques, whereas the latter, guided by aesthetic and even spiritual ideals, believed it was necessary for the government to intervene in order to preserve areas of natural beauty and scientific importance. For example, in a difference of opinion that has carried over to the present day, resource conservationists wanted to "harvest" public forests in a "scientific" manner, whereas preservationists advocated setting these lands aside as natural parks, in which logging would be prohibited.

Today, value differences over the true meaning of environmentalism have become the basis for the emergence of various alternative ecophilosophies, the best known of which are "deep ecology" and "ecofeminism." Whereas success-oriented environmentalists are primarily concerned with the direct effects of industrial pollution on individuals and communities, value-oriented environmentalists stress the survival of all living and nonliving things as components of healthy ecosystems. In doing so, they come closest to any segment of the environmental movement to popularizing the alternative environmental paradigm.

Deep Ecology

The **deep-ecology** argument was set out in the early 1970s by Norwegian philosopher Arne Naess (1973),

and was elaborated by U.S. ecological thinkers Bill Devall and George Sessions (1985). In contrast to the **anthropocentrism** that characterizes much of the environmental movement, deep ecologists believe in a "biocentric" approach, which emphasizes that humans are one species among many on earth and have no special rights or privileges. This **biocentric egalitariansism** states that all things on the earth have an equal right to live and blossom and reach their own forms of self-realization.

Although the intellectual roots of this principle are varied, it owes much to the thinking of John Muir, the leading preservationist in the early American conservation movement. A second touchstone for deep ecology is the "land ethic" of Aldo Leopold, an American naturalist. Formulated in 1949, Leopold's land ethic affirms the right of soils, waters, plants, and animals to co-exist in their natural state with humans, whose role is viewed not as conqueror of the land but as member and citizen of it.

Deep ecologists believe that the relation of the individual to nature cannot be fully grasped intellectually but must ultimately be experienced directly. This quite clearly sets deep ecology in oppo-

Tree-planting on Earth Day — an example of conservationism. SOURCE: Dick Hemingway.

sition to mainstream environmentalism, which is primarily concerned with gathering "facts" about nature and our despoiling of it. Indeed, deep ecologists regard science and scientists with a fair degree of suspicion, depicting them as being a part of the problem as much as a part of its solution. An exception to this is the "Gaia hypothesis," formulated in the 1980s by British scientist James Lovelock (1987), which holds that the earth is a living superorganism with its own internal system of regulation. From this perspective, it is possible to see ourselves as having a moral obligation not just to plants, animals, and other human beings but to the planet itself (Yearley, 1991: 145).

Ecofeminism

A second alternative ecophilosophy is **ecofeminism**. The term was first coined in 1974 by the French writer Françoise d'Eaubonne, who believes that the oppression and exploitation of women and the domination of the natural environment are part of the same phenomenon. Ecofeminists identify a distinctly "feminine" way of thinking and being that is more nurturing, more co-operative, and more communal than the mainstream, paternalistic culture. *Mother Nature,* a long-accepted term in the English language, is given a new meaning and significance by the ecofeminists, who celebrate the ancient pagan tradition of Goddess worship and nature cults; the Goddess is seen as the symbol of ecological wisdom.

Both deep ecologists and ecofeminists express the need for developing a new human consciousness and vision. However, there is also a certain degree of tension between these two ecophilosophies, centred on differing conceptions of the central cause of the current environmental crisis: Deep ecologists point to a gender-neutral anthropocentrism, whereas ecofeminists claim that "androcentrism" (male-centredness) is the real culprit. Furthermore, deep ecologists have trouble accepting the ecofeminist claims that women are more innately and more sensitively attuned to nature than men and therefore have the unique capacity to construct a new, more enlightened approach to the environment (Warren, 1990).

■ POLITICAL ECONOMY OF THE ENVIRONMENT

A third major area of inquiry within environmental sociology is the study of the political economy of the environment.

A starting point for many studies undertaken from a political-economy perspective is Alan Schnaiberg's *The Environment: From Surplus to Scarcity* (1980). Schnaiberg distinguishes between production and consumption activities in society and points the finger of blame for the environmental crisis at production activities. Rather than looking to irresponsible consumers who insist on embracing an extravagant, wasteful lifestyle despite its harmful environmental effects, Schnaiberg identifies the real villain as the relentless process of economic development that is controlled by industrial capitalists and buttressed by the state.

According to Schnaiberg, the political economy of environmental problems and policies is shaped by modern industrial society's **treadmill of production**. This term refers to the inherent need of our economic system to continually yield profits by creating consumer demand for new products, even where this means expanding the ecosystem to its furthest limits. Corporate producers create this demand primarily through the medium of advertising. For example, in a recent issue of a leading Canadian urban-living magazine, readers are advised that a Porsche will stir the "power of passion" in its owner, a Jenn-Air cooktop system is "the sign of a great cook," and a Kohler spray-and-brush attachment will "turn your shower into a personal luxury spa." Consumers are thus persuaded from earliest childhood to become part of a dominant materialistic culture in which personal identity depends on material possessions.

The state is said to buttress this treadmill of production by providing a variety of economic incentives to new industries, from tax breaks to worker-training programs. Traditionally, the state has also encouraged untrammelled economic growth by ensuring a continuous flow of natural resources to industrial producers. For example, in the latter years of the last century, the "gospel of efficiency" (Hays, 1959) in U.S. politics dictated that the growing power of the federal government be used to regulate competition and ensure a steady supply of lumber and other resources to industry. The idea was that only government measures could ensure that resources be set aside and, then, be exploited in a controlled fashion, rather than squandered in the cutthroat competition of the unregulated marketplace (Koppes, 1988: 234). In Canada, the prevailing view has been that nature can be privately requisitioned virtually without limit (Williams, 1992), as evidenced by our exportation of oil, natural gas, minerals, lumber, and, more recently, water, to industrial centres in the United States, often despite negative environmental consequences.

"So that's where it goes! Well, I'd like to thank you fellows for bringing this to my attention."

SOURCE: Drawing by Stevenson; © 1970 The New Yorker Magazine, Inc.

One recent and far-reaching example of this approach to natural resources is the Great Whale hydro-electric project, initiated by former Quebec premier Robert Bourassa and Hydro Quebec. Great Whale is the second phase of the massive James Bay hydro-electric project, which calls for the diversion or alteration of 20 northern rivers through the construction of 36 dams and more than 1000 dikes. When and if it is completed, after the year 2000, the development will have "flooded 23 000 square kilometres of land the size of Newfoundland island and Labrador combined and shattered two cultures that have flourished there — surviving both natural disaster and foreign intrusion — for 5000 years" (Dwyer, 1992: 30).

Of course, the despoiling of the environment is not limited to countries that have functioned under a capitalist system: Soviet-style societies devastated the environment to an even greater degree. Two of the most memorable photographic images to come out of Eastern Europe in the early 1990s were

of the Romanian town of Copsa Mica totally blackened by carbon dust from the local carbosin plant and of schoolchildren from the Czechoslovakian town of Most who had to wear face masks on "sulphur dioxide alert" days to filter the pollution-laden air. There are also indications that recent economic expansion in China has produced its own environmental nightmares. In 1988, for example, Benxi, a city covering 43 km^2, vanished from satellite photographs beneath a cloud of smog (Silvertown, 1989: 550). Thus, the accusing finger should be pointed not at the capitalist system, but at unbridled industrialism, with its accompanying lack of environmental responsibility.

Schnaiberg has described a pervasive conflict in advanced industrial societies between the treadmill of production and the rising public demand for protecting the environment. That is, governments are increasingly torn between a commitment to promote economic development and job creation and the goal of environmental preservation. The bitter conflict over the future of old-growth forests on Vancouver Island is a dramatic illustration of the conflict. Environmentalists argue that the temperate rain forests of Clayoquot Sound and other parts of the province have nearly disappeared and must be declared out of bounds to further logging, particularly if it employs "clear-cutting" methods. The forestry industry replies that this solution would cripple one of British Columbia's major industries, throwing tens of thousands of loggers out of work.

In such situations, governments search for a viable compromise. That search is typically complicated by the fact that the civil service is rarely of one mind, with various departments and diverse personnel defending conflicting positions. One approach to resolving these contradictions involves the adoption of "environmental-management" techniques. **Environmental management** refers to moderate government interventions that afford some limited protection to the environment without seriously curtailing economic development.

The continuing conflict between economic development and environmental preservation is illustrated in Novek and Kampen's (1992) comparative case study of two proposed pulp-and-paper megaprojects: the Japanese-owned Alberta-Pacific mill to be built on the Athabasca River in northern Alberta, and the proposed expansion of the Repap mill in The Pas in northern Manitoba. They found that the provincial governments attempted to resolve their contradictory commitments to economic development and environmental protection primarily by implementing the *environmental-assessment process*. This is a formal legal mechanism whereby the environmental impacts of proposed developments, such as these pulp-and-paper mills, are subjected to scientific and technical scrutiny. Novek and Kampen also found that this public review process failed to quell opposition from northern aboriginal groups and other opponents of the two projects, because it excluded consideration of broader social and environmental concerns, including, in particular, the terms under which the forestry companies were granted access to the land.

The treadmill of production exerts a major influence on the developing nations as well, where many people want access to the consumer culture that we enjoy. The unsustainable development that some industrializing countries have consequently espoused has led to considerable friction with environmentalists from Northern countries, who fear that it will lead to serious worldwide environmental problems (for example, increased destruction of tropical rain forests can lead to accelerated global warming). Third World leaders reply that, having enjoyed the benefits of a century of industrial growth, environmental activists from Europe and America cannot in fairness now deny developing countries the fruits of economic expansion on ecological grounds. (For an attempt to reconcile development with environmental integrity in the Third World, see Adams, 1990.) At the same time, Third World planners and politicians have not always learned from the mistakes of their counterparts in the North. For example, urban planners in São Paulo, Brazil's largest and most heavily polluted city, evidently modelled their transportation system on that of Los Angeles without taking into account the gridlocked traffic and persistent smog that characterize that city.

A second source of environmental degradation in the lower-income countries is that associated with "unsustainable impoverishment"; in other words, the poor engage in ecologically damaging practices just to survive from day to day (Gallopin, Gutman, and Maletta, 1989). For example, rural dwellers are often forced to strip the rapidly dwindling forests in order to obtain fuel for cooking. As the Brundtland commission recognized, it is futile to attempt to deal with environmental problems in the Third World without addressing broader issues of poverty and inequality. These problems in turn are rooted in a variety of social arrangements, from the continuing dominance of wealthy elites within the developing nations to economic dependencies on the industrialized countries, associated with massive debts.

■ RISK AND RISK ASSESSMENT

Risk refers to the probability that a particular hazard will actually occur. Everyday life is full of risks, from slipping on the ice on our front steps to being hit by a bolt of lightning on the golf course. Normally, we base our decision on whether to take a particular course of action that carries with it a degree of risk on a series of individual factors: past experience, confidence in our own abilities, our assessment of apparent safety of a situation. In the world of the 1990s, however, it is increasingly difficult to make such judgements, especially with regard to new technologies and environmental conditions. For example, a summer afternoon spent sunning on the beach may seem innocent, but it may in fact contribute to the onset of skin cancer unless a sunblock lotion is applied to counteract the ultraviolet rays coming through the thinned-out ozone layer. Many of today's environmental hazards (chemicals, radiation, electromagnetic currents) are, in fact, invisible to the naked eye.

In order to cope with such risks, we have increasingly come to rely on the judgement of medical and scientific experts, who appear to be best qualified to decide what is safe. We avoid high-fat foods, buckle our seat belts, and buy bottled spring water because risk professionals tells us that it may be risky not to do so.

Each week seems to bring some newly discovered risk to our attention. Increasingly, such risks are environmentally related — from dioxins and heavy metals in our drinking water to radiation leaks from nuclear power plants, to urban smog that can cause respiratory problems. Toxic hazards are particularly devastating because they render many of the seemingly innocuous or even beneficial things that we depend on — the air we breathe, the water we drink, the sea and soil that nourish the food we eat — quite dangerous (Clarke and Short, 1993).

Sociologists have taken a particular interest in three aspects of risk and risk assessment: the organizational basis of risk, the community perception of risk, and the social distribution of risk.

▲ ORGANIZATIONAL BASIS OF RISK

One consequence of the increasing size and complexity of modern industrial systems is that the source of risk has shifted to large-scale organizations that are all but beyond individual control. When environmentally threatening accidents happen, they are attributable to more than human error; they reflect a set of structural arrangements that make breakdowns inevitable. For example, the gigantic 1989 oil spill that occurred after the supertanker *Exxon Valdez* ran aground in Prince Edward Sound, Alaska, was attributable to cutbacks in maritime safety standards as much as to personal lapses by the captain (Smith, 1992).

Indeed, **normal accidents** — the inevitable failures in nuclear power facilities, petrochemical plants, air-traffic control nets, and other high-risk technologies — are common. Sometimes these flaws are identified during the construction process, but, on other occasions, design flaws manifest themselves only years later, in the form of disasters, such as the Three Mile Island nuclear accident. Rather than being anomalies, such technological accidents are the normal consequences of profit-driven, high-risk systems (Perrow, 1984).

Organizations are not only the source of accidents, but are responsible for responding to them as well. The ways in which they do so often amplify the risk (Clarke and Short, 1993: 392). For example, in the wake of the 1984 gas leak at a Union Carbide pesticide plant in Bhopal, India, in which 8000 people were killed and an estimated 300 000 injured, neither the company, which lacked the necessary support structure and contingency plans for dealing with major accidents, nor the immense government bureaucracy, which took a long time to mobilize, was able to move quickly enough to cope with the catastrophe (Shrivastava, 1987).

▲ COMMUNITY PERCEPTION OF RISK

Contrary to expectations, it is not possible to predict the public perception of risk accurately on the basis of the standard set of demographic and sociological variables (age, gender, political affiliation, etc.). Instead, the best predictor of whether people are likely to perceive risk is the degree to which they trust the ability of expert institutions, including local industries themselves (see Box 15.3), to manage danger (Freudenburg, 1993; Wynne, 1992). For example, during the Windscale inquiry into the establishment of a nuclear reprocessing facility on the east coast of England, the nuclear experts and the judge who chaired the inquiry approached the issue from a completely different

vantage point from local citizens. Whereas the former restricted the scope of the inquiry to technical risk considerations, the latter wished to deal with larger questions, such as how adequate the past performance of the nuclear plant had been and what should be the future of nuclear power. As a result, public trust in both the project and the inquiry was undermined and the perception of risk magnified (Wynne, 1992).

Trust in institutions varies among the members of a community. Those who trust institutions least are most likely to define environmental conditions as risky and therefore actionable. In the Love Canal case, the residents of the neighbourhood that was affected by toxic seepage could be divided into two types: "minimalists," who denied that there was a problem at all or acknowledged a problem of only minor significance, and "maximalists," who believed that the risks were substantial and that the chemical contamination might be more widespread than officially acknowledged. Minimalists were generally found to be social isolates in their neighbourhoods, without children at home, with occupational links to the chemical industry, and with strong attachments to their homes, which they viewed as their principal economic resource in old age. In contrast, the maximalists were typically young parents who shared common interests, placed greater emphasis on health than on property issues, and were active in seeking out risk information, especially from nonofficial sources (Fowlkes and Miller, 1987). In other cases, too, researchers have confirmed that a major motivation for families to become involved in neighbourhood action against toxic wastes is concern about the quality of the community for raising children (Hallman and Wandersman, 1992). Environmental-risk perception, then, is not only a product of how much trust citizens put in the explanations and assurances offered by those in authority positions, but is also linked to people's participation in family life, neighbourhood social networks, and community affairs.

▲ SOCIAL DISTRIBUTION OF RISK

Finally, recent research in the sociology of environmental risk has documented how marginal groups in society bear a disproportionate burden of the risk associated with oil refineries, chemical plants, toxic dumps, garbage and sewage incinerators, and other sources of hazardous exposure. Racial and ethnic minorities, women, low-income urban dwellers, and residents of poor, isolated rural regions are particularly affected. Disadvantaged communities are over-represented as risk sites because corporate polluters view them as constituting the path of least resistance, since their inhabitants are generally both economically poor and politically powerless. In many cases,

existing patterns of discrimination are closely linked with inequalities in the distribution of environmental hazards.

Disadvantaged people are the primary victims of pollution (most of it generated by or on behalf of the middle and upper classes) because they live clos-

Box 15.3
The "First Weed-Free Town in Canada"

A community's perception of the risk posed by a local industrial polluter cannot be separated from the role which that company plays in the life of the town or city. This message runs throughout the social history of Uniroyal Chemical's operation in Elmira, Ontario, a small, quiet town of 7000 residents located about 125 km northwest of Toronto.

Uniroyal (formerly Naugatuck Chemicals) first came to Elmira as part of a wartime economic-revitalization program. Situated in a former shoe factory, Uniroyal produced a variety of products over the years, some useful and relatively benign, and others that would surely claim their place on everyone's top-ten list of controversial chemicals: DDT, 2,4-D, Agent Orange, and Alar. When Dominion Rubber, Naugatuck's U.S. parent company, first announced plans to re-open the old shoe factory, the people of Elmira celebrated; the town had been mired in an economic funk for over a decade. The honeymoon lasted for nearly 30 years. It was cemented by political and economic ties between Uniroyal and the Elmira town council. In 1946, town officials agreed to a publicity campaign whereby the company provided the herbicide 2,4-D to the city at cost and residents were encouraged to participate at minimal expense in a lawn-spraying program. Most (85 percent) did and the community proudly assumed the label of the "First Weed-Free Town in Canada," for which it received national media attention.

In addition to its economic and political relationship, Uniroyal was a central element in the social life of the community. The company sponsored a local softball team, held annual summer picnics, conducted open houses and tours of the plant, and sponsored the Elmira Maple Syrup Festival. Bruce Marr, general manager of the plant from 1949 to 1951, became the local economic and social leader, serving at one point as the elected president of the Elmira Board of Trade.

From its first opening in 1942, noxious smells and dust drifted over the town. In April 1957, "fly ash" spewed out from the factory stack, blanketing surrounding homes. Tomatoes would not grow in back-yard gardens. In 1965, some cattle died after drinking water containing effluent from the plant. Most Elmirians seemed to accept company explanations that the smells and dust were harmless, and, given the trusted position of Uniroyal in the community, few were inclined to question this.

In the 1960s and 1970s, a number of factors combined to tarnish this trust. The company halted plant tours, began to hire from outside the town, cancelled advertising with the *Elmira Signet*, the local newspaper, and imposed an air of secrecy and security around the plant and its activities. Furthermore, Uniroyal began to secretly manufacture a range of more dangerous chemicals, including Agent Orange, a defoliant used to spray the jungle during the Vietnam War, and DMNA, a carcinogenic chemical that eventually got into the town's water supply.

(continued)

Box 15.3
(continued)

As the company's ties with the town weakened and a new cohort of younger, less conservative, and more outspoken people moved to the town, the opposition to Uniroyal grew. Whereas the *Signet* had long been respectful of the company, a competitor, the *Elmira Independent*, founded in 1974, was openly critical. When DMNA was discovered to be contaminating the drinking-water supply, local residents formed APT Environment (Assuring Protection for Tomorrow's Environment) and pressed the Ministry of the Environment to act. Eventually the ministry did act, ordering Uniroyal to discontinue discharging waste water and clean up its properties. Although some residents disapproved of such protest activities, the bloom was clearly off the rose and there were to be no more Elmira–Uniroyal joint ventures like the mid-1940s campaign to declare the town the "First Weed-Free Town in Canada."

SOURCE: Adapted from David Cameron, "The Making of a Polluter: A Social History of Uniroyal Chemical in Elmira," in Michael D. Mehta and Eric Ouellet, eds., *Environmental Sociology: Theory and Practice* (North York, ON: Captus Press, 1995), pp. 297–320. Used with permission.

est to the sources of pollution — power plants, industrial installations, and, in central cities, heavy vehicle traffic. Usually, they have no choice as to where they live. Discrimination created the situation, and those with wealth and influence have the political power needed to keep polluting facilities away from their homes. Living in a poor area is bad enough; high levels of pollution make it worse (Bullard, 1990).

Although the scale of environmental-risk inequality is smaller in Canada than in the United States, there are some striking parallels. For example, in July 1993, a Micmac band in Pictou Landing, Nova Scotia, was reported to have accepted a federal government package worth an estimated $35 million as compensation for the pollution of Boat Harbour, the body of water adjoining the band's reserve. At one time, Boat Harbour had clear beaches and was a source of fish and lobster for the Micmac, but in the mid-1960s, almost half the harbour was purchased for $60 000 to treat waste water from a kraft mill operated by Scott Maritimes, Ltd., a subsidiary of Scott Paper Company. The harbour subsequently became one of the most polluted spots in the province, with 87 million litres of a coffee-coloured effluent being processed each day by the provincial treatment lagoon (*The Globe and Mail*, July 6, 1993: A7).

A similar case occurred two decades earlier in northern Ontario, when the Reed pulp-and-paper plant at Dryden was found to be responsible for dumping nine tonnes of mercury into the English Wabigoon river system between 1962 and 1970 (Macdonald, 1991: 106). The Ojibwa who lived in the area suffered serious health and economic problems. Not only were they penalized by a commercial fishing ban, but they were found to be suffering from "Minimata disease" — mercury poisoning from fish — a toxic syndrome named after a fishing village in Japan, where victims took court action against Chisso Corporation, a large chemical firm.

Environmentally risky activities are also more likely to be located in peripheral communities, areas that are out of the mainstream by virtue of their relative geographic remoteness, their economic marginality, their political powerlessness, or their social isolation. For example, Sellafield, a town in northwest England on the Irish Sea, became a major repository for nuclear waste reprocessing. Sellafield was the archetype of a peripheral community, accessible only by twisting road and branch railway, situated in a area of high unemployment, and economically dependent on the local nuclear power plant (Blowers, Lowry, and Solomon, 1991). Cases such as this are often found in regions that Gidengil (1990) has termed the "vulnerable periphery" and the "depressed periphery," regions with chronic economic problems and dependencies and a high susceptibility to boom-and-bust industries.

Research on the social distribution of risk not only is important for humanitarian reasons, but also influences how we think about power, decision making, and institutional analyses of environmental risk (Clarke and Short, 1993: 394). Among other things, it suggests that risk decisions are not based entirely on "objective" technical and scientific criteria, but are also influenced by sociological factors related to inequality and power. This represents an important addition to public-policy debates on the dynamics of risk, which have tended to treat risk allocation as something that takes place outside of the normal workings of society.

■ SOCIAL CONSTRUCTION OF ENVIRONMENTAL PROBLEMS

Among the most promising new areas of research in environmental sociology is the "social-constructionist" approach. According to this perspective, environmental issues rarely arise spontaneously; rather, they must be discovered, presented, promoted, and kept alive. Furthermore, environmental problems, like social problems in general, are not free-floating but are owned and managed by policy entrepreneurs in science, environmental-movement organizations, and the media. These "environmental claims-makers" invest considerable time and resources in attempting to elevate problems such as acid rain, global warming, and ozone depletion onto national and international agendas for action.

Consider, for example, the issue of indoor air pollution from radon gas. In the United States, policy entrepreneurs in Congress aggressively pressed the Environmental Protection Agency to take action to publicize the problem. Citizen groups were influential in making the public aware of the dangers of radon, especially when these were first discovered in the state of Pennsylvania. In contrast, a lack of comparable environmental claims-makers in Canada meant that the problem never really "caught on" here beyond a few investigative stories in *The Globe and Mail* (Harrison and Hoberg, 1991).

Hannigan (1995) notes that there are three central tasks in the construction of environmental claims — assembling, presenting, and contesting — each of which involves its own activities, opportunities, and pitfalls. To secure public attention and support, prospective problems must surmount a series of hurdles. They have to be considered newsworthy; they must acquire a measure of scientific credibility; and they have to be skilfully navigated across the shoals of political interest and policy relevance. Finding a way around these roadblocks is more likely if several conditions are met. First, it helps to have onside one or more scientific "popularizers" like David Suzuki who can bridge the gap between environmentalism and science, packaging claims so that they appeal to editors, journalists, political leaders, and other opinion-makers. Second, success is more likely if there are positive incentives for taking action. Moral appeals can effectively direct attention toward an environmental problem, but, unless there are stakeholders in undertaking a concerted program of action, the issue may fizzle out. Protecting endangered species and conserving biodiversity in the tropical rain forest, for example, are made more attractive by the possibility that failure to do so would mean losing a wealth of as-yet-undiscovered pharmaceuticals that may be hidden there. Finally, it is crucial to recruit the support of institutional sponsors, such as the Rockefeller Foundation and the United Nations, to ensure both continuity and legitimacy as well as financial support.

Social constructionists depict environmental problems as passing through a series of stages, from initial discovery to the waning of public interest. Earlier work in political science characterized environmental concern as inevitably proceeding through the five stages of a fixed **issue-attention cycle** (Downs, 1972). In the preproblem stage, some highly undesirable social or environmental condition exists but has not yet captured much public attention, even though experts or interest groups may have identified it. In the second stage — "alarmed discovery and euphoric enthusiasm" — the public becomes aware of, and frightened by, the problem and is convinced that it can be solved if action is taken immediately. By the third stage, the public begins to realize the cost of significant progress and to perceive that solving the problem will not be as easy as it seemed; solutions require money, sacrifice, and loss of benefits for some. In the fourth stage, intense public interest gradually declines as the growing realization of how difficult any solutions will be sinks in. In the final, postproblem stage, the issue moves off the public-policy agenda, although it may recapture public interest at some point in the future.

More recent research has suggested that environmental issues rise and fall in the public eye in response to a number of different factors, including the clarity and viability of scientific evidence, the ability of environmental claims-makers to sustain a sense of dramatic crisis, and the rise of competing new environmental problems (Ungar, 1992).

A basic assumption of the social-constructionist perspective is that neither the appearance of collective values, such as those described by the alternative environmental paradigm, nor the documented existence of an actual environmental threat is sufficient, by itself, to create an environmental problem that ranks on the public agenda. For example, although tropical rain forest destruction in Malaysia is every bit as serious as its counterpart in Brazil (see Box 15.1), the latter has received extensive worldwide publicity whereas the former is rarely discussed. Rather, what is significant is the process through which environmental claims-makers pressure those who hold the reins of power to recognize definitions of environmental problems, to implement them, and to accept responsibility for solving them.

It is important to note that the social construction of environmental problems does not occur in isolation. Rather, just as socioeconomic structures influence the social distribution of risk, so the powerful in society have the ability to determine what is and what is not relevant with respect to the environment. It is this synergy between social definition and power inequality that makes social constructionism a distinctively sociological route to studying environmentalism and the environment. ■

● SUMMARY

1. Sociological interest in the natural environment is quite recent, having first developed in the early 1970s. Sociology's reluctance to embrace the study of the environment reflects its heritage, wherein biology and nature were banished from the discipline in favour of socially based theories of behaviour.

2. A central focus for much of the sociological examination of the environment has been the deep-seated value cleavage between environmentalists and their opponents in industry and science. The latter support a dominant social paradigm that stresses materialism, economic growth, and the human right to dominate nature. In contrast, environmentalists propose an alternative environmental paradigm that emphasizes the need to adopt small-scale, decentralized economic and political structures that are in harmony with nature. This value-oriented environmentalism has found its fullest expression in a number of "ecophilosophies" — deep ecology and ecofeminism — that have recently flourished on the margins of the environmental movement.

3. Support for environmentalism has remained remarkably constant for nearly twenty years. Although the majority of the population is generally supportive of environmental values, a young, well-educated, urban, liberal core has taken the lead in working for environmental change. Most other Canadians will recycle, purchase "green" products, and act positively toward the environment, but only to the extent that such action does not require any real sacrifice in terms of time and money.

4. In order to mobilize the reluctant majority, environmental-movement organizers develop frames (interpretations of events) that play up the possibility of an impending global collapse as a result of uncontrolled population growth and continued industrial growth. Global warming, expanding holes in the ozone layer, and the worldwide loss of biodiversity are the most recently identified symptoms of the impending crisis. The only solution, it is claimed, is to draw back and ease down, conserving resources, reducing pollution, and restricting population increase. However, these goals are especially difficult to achieve in the expanding economies of the Third World, where the environment is threatened by both unsustainable development and unsustainable impoverishment.

5. At the level of the local community, willingness to act on environmental problems rises as trust in expert institutions declines. This loss of trust is characteristic of neighbourhood-based environmental conflicts, in which citizens typically find the explanations and assurances offered by scientists and other authority figures to be faulty. Environmental-risk perception and action are also linked to people's participation in local social networks and community affairs.

6. The role of environmental entrepreneurs or claims-makers is vital in moving environmental issues from free-floating concerns to problems that are recognized and acted upon by those in power. These promoters, situated in science, environmental organizations, and the media, define problems such as acid rain, global warming, and ozone depletion; package them; and elevate them to action agendas.

7. The social construction of environmental problems does not occur in a vacuum but is shaped by political and economic factors, to the extent that the powerful in society have the ability to act as gatekeepers, determining what is and what is not relevant with respect to the environment. Environmental problems, then, are actively contested, often on the basis of acceptable or unacceptable risk. Social constructionism in the context of power inequality represents a promising sociological route to understanding the environment–society relationship.

QUESTIONS TO CONSIDER

1. What types of environmental hazards do you and members of your community routinely face? Who do you think determines what is an acceptable level of risk in these situations? Scientists? The government? The media?
2. Analyze the environmental content of your local newspapers and/or television news programs over the course of several weeks. Is environmental coverage balanced or does it favour a specific point of view? What types of media frames (interpretations of events) are used to organize information relating to environmental issues?
3. Keep a diary of all your consumer activities (shopping, transportation, leisure) for a week. Which of the products you buy and services you use are most likely to contribute to the deterioration of the environment? Which show signs of a "green" attitude among manufacturers, merchants, and service providers?
4. In the 1970s, Downs (1972) estimated that concern over the environment was about midway through the issue-attention cycle. Where in the cycle do you think it is now? What factors do you think have influenced its progression over the last quarter-century?
5. What is meant by the term *environmental management?* Think of some specific examples from Canadian political life in which governments have sought to use this strategy in order to distance themselves from environmental controversies.

GLOSSARY

alternative environmental paradigm A set of beliefs that challenge the centrality of economic growth, technological progress, and the human domination of nature as pillars of our society. The alternative environmental paradigm stresses the need to adopt small-scale, decentralized economic and political structures that are in harmony with nature.

anthropocentrism Human-centredness; an ideology that assumes that humans are separate from and superior to all other natural things, and judges human actions in the natural environment accordingly.

biocentric egalitarianism The principle, held by deep ecologists, that all things on earth have an equal right to exist. In this view, humans have no special rights or privileges that allow them to subdue and destroy their natural surroundings.

broadening-base hypothesis The hypothesis that environmental concern will eventually spread beyond its present social base — that is, of young, well-educated, urban, politically liberal citizens — to all of society.

carrying capacity The optimum population size that the planet can support under present environmental conditions.

deep ecology An environmental ethic emphasizing that all species in nature are of equal value. Our experience of nature, deep ecologists claim, should be the foundation for an energetic environmentalism that opposes the present domination by rational science.

dominant paradigm A widely accepted view of the world that emphasizes the moral imperative of material-wealth creation and the moral conviction that humans have the inalienable right to dominate nature and harness the environment to that end.

ecofeminism An environmental ethic that sees androcentrism (male-centredness) as the root of ecological destruction. Ecofeminists identify a distinctly feminine way of thinking and acting that is nurturing, co-operative, communal, and sensitive to nature.

economic-contingency hypothesis The hypothesis that the broadening of the social base of environmental concern is contingent on prevailing economic conditions. When economic conditions worsen or are perceived as worsening, those who are least well off will be the first to shift their focus away from the environment to the economy.

environmental management Moderate government intervention in environmental conflicts that accords some limited protection to the environment without seriously curtailing economic development.

human-exceptionalism paradigm A world view that features the ideals of steadily evolving social progress, increasing prosperity and material comfort, and class mobility for all segments of society, while ignoring the environmental costs of economic growth.

issue-attention cycle A five-stage sequence through which the "career" of most social problems is said to pass.

normal accidents Inevitable failures in nuclear power stations, petrochemical plants, air-traffic control nets, and other high-risk technological systems. Such accidents are regarded by corporate organizations as an inevitable consequence of operating a hazardous facility.

risk The relative probability that a particular hazard will actually occur.

sustainable development Economic development that meets the needs of the present without compromising the ability of future generations to meet their own needs.

treadmill of production The inherent need of our economic system to continually yield profits by creating consumer demand for new products, even where this means expanding the ecosystem to its furthest limits.

● SUGGESTED READING

Bullard, Robert D. (1990). *Dumping in Dixie: Race, Class and Environmental Quality.* Boulder, CO: Westview Press. A pioneering study of the environmental impact on poor black communities in the U.S. South as a result of the siting of petrochemical factories, oil refineries, hazardous waste facilities, and other sources of industrial pollution.

Carson, Rachel. (1962). *Silent Spring.* Boston: Houghton Mifflin. The book that launched the modern environmental movement. Still a profound and relevant statement of the dangers posed by agricultural chemicals to the natural world and the human food chain.

Hannigan, John A. (1995). *Environmental Sociology: A Social Constructionist Perspective.* London and New York: Routledge. The essential ingredients of environmental sociology, Hannigan contends, are questions of risk, media, science, nature, regulation, postmodernity, and social movements. In this highly readable overview of the field, students are provided with a social-constructionist model for analyzing environmental issues that can form the basis for their own research projects.

Harrison, Kathryn, and George Hoberg. (1994). *Risk, Science and Politics: Regulating Toxic Substances in Canada and the United States.* Montreal and Kingston, ON: McGill-Queen's University Press. A comparative study of government regulation of toxic substances in two neighbouring countries. The authors present case studies of six controversial substances suspected of causing cancer in humans: the pesticides Alar and alachlor, urea-formaldehyde foam insulation, radon gas, saccharin, and asbestos.

Macdonald, Doug. (1991). *The Politics of Pollution: Why Canadians Are Failing Their Environment.* Toronto: McClelland and Stewart. A useful discussion of the rise of environmentalism in Canada, with a special focus on the politics of environmental regulation.

Mehta, Michael D., and Eric Ouellet, eds. (1995). *Environmental Sociology: Theory and Practice.* North York, ON: Captus Press. A contributed volume of original pieces by an assortment of Canadian environmental researchers. Included is David Cameron's "The Making of a Polluter: A Social History of Uniroyal Chemical in Elmira," which is summarized in this chapter. Other articles deal with "green" social theory, sustainable development, environmental risk, and the social bases of environmental concern.

World Commission on Environment and Development [The Brundtland Commission]. (1987). *Our Common Future: Report to the United Nations General Assembly.* New York: Oxford University Press. A much-cited examination of the relationship between economic development, Third World poverty, and global environmental problems.

CHAPTER SIXTEEN
Population

IN THIS CHAPTER YOU WILL LEARN THAT

- demography involves the study of population size, growth, distribution, composition, fertility, mortality, and migration; these population considerations have enormous consequences for social change, and social change has enormous consequences for demographic questions

- demography distinguishes between population states (size, distribution over space, and composition by various characteristics) and population processes (fertility, mortality, and migration); it is important to analyze how processes influence states and vice versa

- Malthus argued that populations have a tendency to grow more rapidly than other resources and that it is important to control the growth of population by reducing births; in contrast, Marx argued that economic and social conditions determine the rate of population growth and that proper social arrangements should be able to accommodate population growth

- the demographic-transition theory summarizes the history of population growth through three stages — stable, high, and stable — as birth and death rates decline; the phase of rapid population expansion, which occurs because death rates decline sooner and faster than birth rates, occurred in Europe from 1750 to 1970, while in Asia, Latin America, and Africa it has been taking place since 1950

- since Confederation, life expectancy in Canada has increased from 42 to 78 years because of increased standards of living, improvements in sanitation, and medical improvements; average births have declined from seven to two per woman, although the decline in fertility was not uniform, with the baby boom of 1946–66 representing a major exception to the downward trend

- the net balance between immigration and emigration accounts for 22 percent of population growth in Canada during this century; 16 percent of the Canadian population is foreign-born

- net migration in the period 1986–96 accounted for nearly half of Canada's population growth, as large numbers of Asians, Latin Americans, and Africans entered the country; controlling the level of immigration, and especially refugee arrivals, poses challenges in the context of demographic pressures at the world level

- Canada's population has grown rapidly since Confederation — twice as rapidly as the population of the world as a whole — but because of lower fertility, growth is now less rapid and there is considerable population aging, posing various challenges of adaptation, especially in the areas of education, labour force, health care, and pensions; at the same time, population movement has tended to be toward the western and southern parts of the country and immigrants have tended to concentrate in Toronto, Montreal, and Vancouver

RODERIC BEAUJOT
University of Western Ontario

■ INTRODUCTION

One of the most important features of any society is the number of people in it and the relative size of the various subgroups it contains. When populations grow or shrink, and when subgroups change in relative size, serious repercussions follow.

Consider English–French relations in Canada. For a long time, the French constituted about a third of the population. In response to heavy English immigration, French-Canadian society emphasized the importance of births for maintaining the relative power of the French element in the country. A Catholic priest called for *La revanche des berceaux* ("the revenge of the cradles)" — that is, for maintaining a high French birth rate as a means of securing the status of the French in the country. When Quebec fertility fell in the 1960s and the French-speaking population of Canada dropped to nearly a quarter of the total, the long-term accommodation within a single nation of the country's two charter groups was threatened.

Particularly problematic for Quebec was the eagerness of various immigrant groups to associate with the English minority of the province. In the early 1970s, there was even concern that French would no longer be the working language in the province of Quebec. Various accommodations have been made to this demographic change, such as the Official Languages Act, the policy on multiculturalism, the recognition of a distinct role for Quebec in immigrant selection, and the Quebec Charter of the French Language (Bill 101). The constitutional crises of the 1990s, particularly as they pertain to the concept of Quebec as a distinct society, indicate that Canada is still looking for ways to accommodate the changing demographics.

Canadian population change is having massive effects in other ways as well. Particularly apparent is the aging of the population. At first, the increase in the average age was attributable primarily to smaller numbers of young people; today, it is also affected by larger numbers of older people. The earlier stages of aging seemed relatively easy to accommodate. In a broad sense, adults were freer, given that they had fewer children to care for. These changes both maximized the proportion of the population that was at an employable age and freed women from family preoccupations, encouraging them to participate in the labour force. All these trends permitted an expansion of the social programs that depend on revenues from the taxation of employed persons (particularly health, education, social security, and pension programs).

However, at later stages of aging, it will no longer be the relative size of the population of labour-force age that will be growing. Instead, the proportion of Canadians over age 65 will rise from 1 in 10 to 1 in 4. This change will again require various social accommodations. Some observers have come to question whether we will be able to afford all our social programs. Others call for different forms of accommodation, such as greater individual responsibility for personal health, greater repayment for the economic benefits of government-subsidized education, a longer work life, lower pension benefits, and even the promotion of higher birth rates and increased immigration.

At the international level, a provocative book by Wattenberg (1987) entitled *The Birth Dearth: What Happens When People in Free Countries Don't Have Enough Babies?* notes that the nations he labels "modern, industrial, free and western" represented 22 percent of the world population in 1950 but will represent only 9 percent in 2025. Wattenberg argues that this relative demographic decline will bring about an erosion of military, economic, political, and cultural influence. Many other examples could be given of societies that are struggling to accommodate changing demographics, among them Lebanon, which is trying to accommodate the relative decline of its Christian population, and Germany, which is trying to adjust to increases in its immigrant population.

At the level of the total human population, some have proposed that the rapid growth of the human species represents in biological terms a catastrophic event for the planet, comparable to an ice age or a major meteoric collision. Biologists measure change over millions of years and, in this context, the human presence, which was once insignificant, can be seen as changing the very environment of the planet. Many call for sustainable development, and various world meetings sponsored by the United Nations are attempting to find ways to ensure that the sheer size of the human population does not endanger our viability on the planet.

These few examples illustrate the importance of studying population dynamics. This chapter will first consider the ways in which populations are studied. Various theoretical perspectives will be used to analyze the causes and consequences of population change. We will then consider two specific cases: world population growth and population change in Canada. The Canadian case will include the dynamics of mortality, fertility, and immigration, and their implications for the size, age structure, and geographic distribution of the population.

▲ THE STUDY OF POPULATION

People are born, they move around, and they die. When these events are added up for a number of people, demographers call them *fertility, migration,* and *mortality*. These events mark a person's life-course: Any short biography would certainly include when the person was born, where he or she lived, and when he or she died.

Although these events are clearly experienced by individuals, added together, they also demarcate the life-courses of societies over time. At the group level, fertility and immigration are the basic mechanisms through which populations, countries, societies, and communities are regenerated. These regenerative processes not only add numbers to the population, ensuring demographic continuity in the face of departures through death and emigration, they also change the character of the population and, consequently, of the society. The character of the population is changed in terms of age and sex structure, socioeconomic composition, cultural make-up, and regional distribution.

An understanding of society needs to take into account the nature of the population: How many people are there? How are they distributed over space? How many children are there? How many older people? How many have university degrees? How many have low incomes? How many are bilingual? And so on.

We also want to know something about these basic numbers for the purpose of *comparing* societies. For instance, at the time of Confederation in 1867, Canada's population was relatively small. At 3.5 million, it was about one-tenth the size of each of France and the United Kingdom; at an estimated 30.3 million in 1997, Canada is now half the size of each of those countries. If Canada had remained a relatively very small country, it probably would not have become part of the Group of Seven (G-7), the seven major Western industrial countries, or of any other major international organization.

The other side of the coin is this: It is by means of understanding the society that we are able to interpret trends in the vital events of births, deaths, and geographic movement. What is it that makes people want to have children? Why do people have fewer children now than they did in the 1950s? Why have abortions become more acceptable? What kinds of people find abortions acceptable, and under what circumstances? Why are there fewer deaths resulting from infectious diseases, and more from cancer? Why does migration in Canada tend to be to the west and to the south? Who tends to move and why? In attempting to answer these question, we need to know something about the demographic make-up of a society. Besides, the analysis of these basic questions tells us important things about the society.

Putting this discussion in the language of sociological methodology and statistics, population phenomena can be treated as independent or dependent variables. If we were to analyze the effect of population size, gross domestic product, and military might on the relative power of countries, we would be treating population size as an independent variable whose consequences we wanted to understand relative to the consequences of the other independent variables. But if we were to analyze the impact of income, education, and attitudes on the number of births, we would be treating fertility as a dependent variable, the causes of which we were seeking to understand.

▲ POPULATION AND POLICY

Given that demographic processes are fundamental to societies and their regeneration, society has a vested interest in ensuring that population dynamics operate to produce an overall net benefit (Demeny, 1988). All societies attempt to shape the decision-making framework of individuals in such a way as to promote this common benefit. With respect to fertility, behaviour that promotes reproduction will sometimes be encouraged and sometimes constrained. With respect to mortality, behaviour that will prolong a person's life in the society will be encouraged, and the society will often take some responsibility for the health and safety of its citizens. With respect to immigration, the society as a whole will typically establish structures, policies, and rules through which entry (and sometimes exit) are controlled in order to produce a social benefit.

There are a number of questions that interest the society as a whole. How many new members are to be added and by what means (through births or immigration)? How are the costs of these additions to be paid, and who receives the benefits? How should the costs and benefits of children be distributed among the families to which they are born and the larger extended family, the community, and the society as a whole? How are the costs and benefits of immigration to be distributed between, on the one hand, the immigrants themselves and their sponsoring families and, on the other hand, the receiving country, province, city, and community? To what extent are health and safety the responsibility of the individual or the surrounding society? These are among the policy questions that all societies must address. Policy orientations to changing demographics can take two forms: that of attempting to influence the course of demographic events or that of ensuring that the society makes the adjustments necessary to accommodate the population change.

Such policy considerations underline the importance of gathering accurate information. Censuses were first taken to enable rulers to tax their citizens and to determine the number of men available for military service. With the advent of the welfare state, it is particularly important for governments to have accurate and up-to-date information on the population whose welfare they are trying to enhance. It is crucial to know how given groups would benefit or suffer from given policies.

■ POPULATION STATES AND PROCESSES

Demography is the study of populations — their size, distribution, and composition — and the immediate factors causing population change (births, deaths, and migration). We are interested in the stock and the flow of population. The *stock,* or the state of the population, is a picture of the population at one time, including its size, its distribution over geography, and its composition in terms of a variety of characteristics, such as age, sex, marital status, education, language spoken at home, occupation, and income. The *flow,* or the population processes, involves changes in population from one time to another as a function of births, deaths, and movements of people. As noted earlier, in demography, these processes are called, respectively, fertility, mortality, and migration.

▲ LINKS BETWEEN POPULATION STATES AND PROCESSES

Population states and processes are dynamically interrelated. For instance, lower birth rates (a process) produce an older population (a state); conversely, an older population tends to have a lower birth rate.

Let us explore further the links between population processes and states, beginning with the impact of processes *on* states. A change in population

size — that is, a change from one state to a second state — is clearly a function of intervening births, deaths, **immigration,** and **emigration.** Births minus deaths is called **natural increase** (or decrease), and immigration minus emigration is called **net migration.** Thus, the basic equation for population at a given time is as follows:

$$P2 = P1 + B - D + I - E,$$

where *P2* represents the population at a given time; *P1,* the population at an earlier time (normally, the time at which a census is taken); *B,* the number of births in the interval; *D,* the number of deaths in the interval; *I,* the number of immigrants who arrived in the interval; and *E,* the number emigrants who departed in the interval.

For example, over the first nine decades of this century, net migration (more people coming than leaving) has comprised some 22 percent of Canadian **population growth,** with natural increase (more births than deaths) comprising the other 78 percent. However, in the period 1986–96, an estimated 42 percent of population growth was attributable to net migration. Were it not for migration, Canada's population growth during this period would have been well under 1 percent per year.

In considering the *distribution* of the population over space, the analysis becomes more complex. For one thing, international immigrants tend to settle in certain parts of the country more than in others. For another, **internal migration,** in terms of both places departed and destinations, is not evenly distributed throughout the country. Finally, regions may differ in fertility and mortality rates. For example, over the period 1931–61 in particular, higher birth rates in Quebec helped to maintain its relative size among the provinces of Canada. Today, differences in natural increase have little impact on the relative growth of regions, but trends in international and internal migration tend to increase the relative size of Ontario, British Columbia, and Alberta, and to reduce the relative size of the Atlantic provinces, Manitoba, and Saskatchewan.

Although changes in a society's *age structure* are complex to the extent that people's age is constantly changing, the change is at least systematic: Everyone ages by one year every calendar year. The age structure of a population is often depicted as a pyramid, with the youngest age groups at the base; males are represented on one side and females on the other. (See Figures 16.3 and 16.6 for examples of age pyramids.) All births occur at what demographers call "age zero" of the age structure, whereas deaths can occur at various ages, as can migrations. It is often thought that the increase in the proportion of older people in the population is attributable to the fact that people are living longer, making for more people at the top of the pyramid. However, it is births and the way they change over time, rather than deaths, that are most responsible for determining the shape of an age-structure pyramid. Deaths, being spread out over a range of ages, do not have as great an impact on the shape of the pyramid.

Other analyses of changes in population states follow the same pattern. Recall that a population stock, or state, is the picture of a given population at one point in time in terms of size, distribution, or composition. For instance, in analyzing changes in population *composition* by legal marital status (how many are single? married? widowed? divorced?), we must take into account births (which are all single), deaths by marital status, migrants by marital status, and changes in marital status (single to married, married to divorced or widowed, divorced or widowed to married). Similarly, an analysis of composition by levels of education must take into account how people change their education over time — a task that is not at all as simple as analyzing changes in age structure, where everyone ages one year at a time.

We have been considering how the population processes of fertility, mortality, and migration affect the population states of size, distribution, and composition. We could also consider how population states affect population processes. For instance, one of the reasons for the decrease in the number of births in Canada is that the composition of the population by marital status is currently characterized by a reduced proportion of young adults living in marital or cohabiting unions. As another example, the number of deaths in Canada is increasing not because death rates in given age groups are increasing, but because there is now a greater predominance of people at ages at which deaths are more common — in other words, because ours is an aging population.

Box 16.1 provides further examples of the importance of looking at population composition when considering future changes in Canadian society.

THEORETICAL PERSPECTIVES ON THE CAUSES AND CONSEQUENCES OF POPULATION CHANGE

This section reviews various theoretical perspectives on population change, focussing on those that explore the causes and consequences of change.

▲ THOMAS MALTHUS

The political economist Thomas Malthus (1766–1834) was the first to develop a systematic theory of population change and its relation to economic conditions (Malthus, 1798). He considered the causes of population growth to be grounded in human nature. On the one hand, because of the natural attraction between the sexes, along with what he called an "urge to reproduce," he thought there was a natural tendency for the population to grow — and to do so at such a rapid rate as to outgrow the available food supply. On the other hand, he saw two checks on population growth. One, which he called "positive," occurred through mortality, from causes such as famine, epidemics, wars, and plagues. The other, which he called "preventive," occurred through fertility, and could take two forms — "moral restraint," the postponement of marriage, and what he regarded as "vice," the prevention of births in marriage through abortion, infanticide, and other unacceptable methods of contraception.

Today, infanticide is condemned and there is enormous debate and conflict about abortion. For many people, even contraception is abhorrent: Some view it as a form of abortion (the "morning-after pill" is seen as killing a potential child); others see it as a serious health hazard (the birth-control pill, the IUD, and Norplant have all been linked to health problems). It is perhaps not surprising, then, that Malthus, an Anglican clergyman, argued for the delay of marriage until a young person was sufficiently established to have children, and for abstinence.

Although we may not like some of Malthus's moral values, he did have a clear view of the basis for population change. Populations grow if births outnumber deaths. If this growth strains the available resources, there are likely to be more deaths and/or fewer births. If births take place mostly in the context of marriage, the postponement of marriage or the use of contraception by married couples could be relied upon to produce fewer births.

Malthus thought that the consequences of population growth were fairly serious. He argued that, left unchecked, population growth would proceed in a geometric progression (2, 4, 8, 16), whereas resources would grow arithmetically (2, 4, 6, 8). What is key here is not whether there is precisely a geometric versus an arithmetic progression, but the basic conclusion that population has a tendency to grow more rapidly than do available resources, particularly the supply of food. As a consequence, population growth could be expected to produce poverty and misery.

Box 16.1
Demographics Tell the Story

Economist and demographer David Foot believes business and recreation trends and even societal value shifts can be predicted by looking at the number of people born in a time period and projecting the impact of their changing needs.

He focuses on one of the biggest bulges on the Canadian charts — the baby boom generation of 9.8 million people born between 1947 and 1966. They were a unique phenomenon, Foot said, since for most of this century, there has been declining family size as people moved off farms and into industrial areas.

There are subgroups. Younger boomers are 30 to 36 and popularly known as Generation X. This group has problems being at the back end of the boom. For example, their career paths are likely to be blocked by older boomers still 15 to 20 years from retirement.

Because there are a lot of them, they had trouble getting jobs through the 1981 recession. Those who did get jobs and bought houses found house prices began to drop soon after.

Foot believes the changing life stages of the boomers explain many social and economic trends.

"The rebellion of the '60s and '70s was the boomers going through the age when you are rebellious," he said. "The cocooning of the '80s was all about them going out to the suburbs to set up their nests and raise their families."

Two demographic factors partially explain the "downsizing" that has people worried about their jobs in both the public and private sectors, he said.

The first is that front-end baby boomers are now in their late 40s. Many are not satisfied at their job level and aspire to middle-management positions, but there are too few of those to go around. The second reality is that the boomers are moving out of their prime spending years and into prime savings years.

SOURCE: Rose Simone, "Demographics Tell the Story, Professor Says," *London Free Press*, July 12, 1996, p. C12. Reprinted with permission of Canadian Press.

Particularly in his early writings, Malthus did not hold out much hope for finding a solution to this problem. If for some reason the food supply increased more than the population did, people would probably get married earlier and have more children, so there would eventually be even more people living in poverty. He feared that if the conditions of the poor were improved (for instance, through a more equitable distribution of income), there would be even more population growth and thus a larger problem in the long term. He felt strongly that people had to absorb the consequences of their own actions, and he preached "responsible procreation" or "moral restraint" as a way of avoiding excessive growth.

Today, we often refer to Malthus's theory as the "Malthusian trap." Population is limited by the means of subsistence; continuous growth is not possible in a limited world. The "Malthusian solution" adopted by today's society is to encourage a reduction of births, both through later marriage and, especially, through the use of contraception, in order to avoid an increase in deaths. Malthus's contribution thus lay in his view of population growth as a serious problem that causes poverty, strains resources, and undermines efforts to improve society.

▲ KARL MARX

Karl Marx (1818–83) wrote extensively on economic, political, and social relations in society, but his writing on population was mostly in opposition to Malthus (Meek, 1971). Marx thought that there were

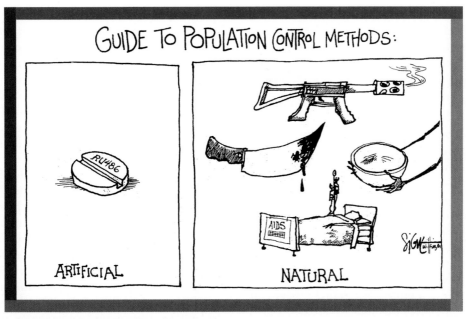

SOURCE: Signe Wilkinson (SIGNE)/USA. Reprinted with permission from IPS—Inter Press Service.

several stages in human history (slavery, feudalism, capitalism, and socialism) and that each stage was different in terms of the vested interests of given groups in society. Each stage had a unique "mode of production," or a way in which economic production was organized, and specific "relations of production," or relations among classes of people with different stakes in the production process. He also thought that each stage of human history had its own "laws of population." Stated differently, Marx considered that the dynamics of population growth derived from the "mode of production" and the "relations of production," as these worked themselves out in specific stages of human history.

Although Marx did not specify the "laws of population" for each stage of history, he did write about the population dynamics under capitalism. Specifically, he argued that the capitalist class had a tendency not only to become more powerful as it came to exercise increasing control over the means of production, but also to become smaller in size. In contrast, the working class, as it lost control over the product of its labour, had a tendency to get larger. He argued that workers were not paid the full value of their labour and that the "surplus value" they generated was appropriated by the capitalist class, allowing the latter to invest and become more dominant. Thus, the capitalist system depends on a "reserve army of labour."

Marx observed that the capitalist economy tends to experience periods of strong growth and periods of recession. More workers are needed during growth periods; during recession periods, those who are not needed are let go. Besides, surplus labour ensures that wages can be kept low in order to maximize the amount of "surplus value" that is extracted.

Because the capitalist system has become a world economic system, some of these dynamics have become evident at the global level. In particular, the richer countries are becoming smaller in relative size, and the system is becoming more dependent on cheap labour and raw materials from the rapidly growing populations of the Third World.

Marx concluded that problems of excess population were specific to the capitalist system. According to him, the problem was not that there were too many people, but that there were too many poor people, and they were impoverished as a result of the exploitation of workers. He proposed that, in a more equitable society, the problem would disappear. Contrary to Malthus, Marx felt that, with the proper economic and social arrangement — which he called "socialism" and "communism" — we would be able to produce all the food and other resources necessary to accommodate population growth. More people, he reasoned, should be able to create more wealth and more food.

Even if we do not agree with the specific "stages of human history" that Marx elaborated, and even if we question some of his conclusions regarding the "laws of population under capitalism," we may still be impressed by his view that, given certain economic and social arrangements, particular population dynamics will follow. In other words, if population dynamics are to be changed, it is first necessary to change basic economic and social arrangements. In

Marx's view, rapid population growth is not a cause of social problems, as Malthus argued, but a consequence of specific socioeconomic conditions.

▲ THE MALTHUSIAN–MARXIST DEBATE

The debate between advocates of Malthusian and Marxist thought on population has taken various forms. On the one hand, Ehrlich and Ehrlich (1990) argue that, given limited resources, rapid population growth will tear our world apart. On the other hand, Simon (1990) argues that people constitute the ultimate resource that stimulates economic growth. Clearly, Ehrlich and Ehrlich were inspired by Malthus's thinking, and Simon by that of Marx. Ehrlich and Ehrlich propose that rapid population growth, particularly at the world level and in poorer countries, is creating misery and poverty. Simon proposes that human capital is mainly what promotes economic growth and, consequently, that population growth increases our ability to solve the problems of hunger and poverty.

The Malthusian–Marxist debate has also been evident in Canada. Some scholars have argued that the dangers of population growth involve not only the strain it places on limited resources, but also its deleterious effects on the environment, including the possibility of global climatic change. Others have argued that population growth is good for Canada, because its population is small and a larger population would create more markets and more economic development. In short, some arguments point to the disadvantages of population size and growth, whereas others point to their advantages.

From Malthus, we learn that society needs to be concerned about its population, whether because growth is too rapid or because it is not rapid enough. In other words, questions of population are important to the welfare of societies, and it makes sense to implement policies that promote the evolution of the population in a direction that corresponds to the social benefit. From Marx, we learn that population dynamics are largely a function of socioeconomic arrangements, particularly of broadly defined economic structures. As the society changes, population dynamics also change. In order to understand population trends, it is essential to understand the underlying economic and social dynamics.

▲ HUMAN ECOLOGY

Human ecology is a broad perspective that embraces the subject of the causes and consequences of population processes. The study of ecology is basically the study of categories of organisms, or *populations,* in their environment — of how those populations gain their sustenance from the environment and, in so doing, how they introduce certain changes to that environment. Thus, the term *population* can be used for species other than humans. This reminds us of the similarity of the human species to other species, each of which needs to find its sustenance and niche in the environment.

In considering human ecology, however, we must take into account two major factors that do not apply to other species: In gaining their sustenance from the environment, human populations employ *organization* and *technology.* The ways in which humans organize themselves, and the technologies they develop, are central to understanding how they adapt to and influence the environment.

The dynamic interplay of these four basic considerations (population, organization, environment, and technology — POET for short) presents an overarching picture of population dynamics (see Figure 16.1). Each factor influences the others. For instance, historically, more rapid population growth has tended to follow the introduction of new forms of organization or new developments in technology. For instance, the urban revolution involved a new way of organizing human settlements that permitted considerable growth in population. Similarly, the Industrial Revolution involved major changes in technology that fostered population growth; particularly important in this regard were developments that allowed resources to be extracted more efficiently from the environment.

Changes in the environment, such as climatic changes, can also produce opportunities or hazards with respect to population. Some observers have argued that population pressure on the environment and technological developments can bring about environmental changes (as, for example, has

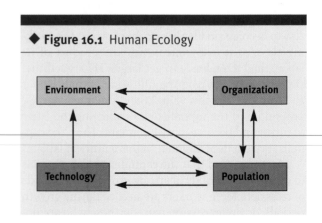

◆ **Figure 16.1** Human Ecology

the intensive use of fossil fuels) and, thus, changes in the potential for sustenance. Conversely, difficulties imposed by the environment can induce a population to find new forms of organization and technology that will enable it to survive and prosper — a process commonly known as "adaptation."

The human-ecology perspective highlights the fact that both benefits and problems can be associated with large numbers of people. Population growth can be seen as reducing average well-being because resources have to be shared with more people. In this view, larger numbers simply mean more competition for scarce resources. If there are more people, will there be enough jobs? If there are more old people, will there be enough services for them? With higher numbers come various forms of "crowding," which typically place people at a relative disadvantage in the competition for resources. In another sense, however, larger numbers mean greater strength, in that there are more people to deal with the existing problems. For instance, with more scientists, better and more efficient technologies might be developed to compensate for scarcities in natural resources. Crowding can also reinforce positive factors — larger cities, for example, offer more amenities of various kinds. Especially in a democracy, larger numbers can mean more political weight. The "grey power" groups, on the one hand, certainly realize that their numbers give them the strength they need to change social arrangements to their benefit. On the other hand, Quebec has been concerned that the decline in its relative share of the Canadian population reduced its relative weight in national decision making. In effect, these alternative assessments mirror the contrast between the Malthusian view — that with more people, there are more problems — and the Marxist view — that with the proper social arrangements, more people can bring more resources to solve the problems as they arise.

▲ THE DEMOGRAPHIC TRANSITION

One of the main demographic theories is that of the **demographic transition**. This theory has been used to summarize the historical demographic experience of societies of European origin over the past two centuries, as well as the more recent experience of many Third World societies. The basic elements of the theory are presented in Figure 16.2. Births and deaths per 1000 population are represented on the vertical axis; time is shown along the horizontal axis. Although the rates and dates vary by country, the pattern basic to all countries is a movement from an equilibrium of high birth rates and high death rates, through a transitional disequilibrium in which death rates begin to decline sooner than birth rates do, to

With more people living in metropolitan areas, various forms of crowding take place. This is average traffic for Toronto's Highway 401. SOURCE: Dick Hemingway.

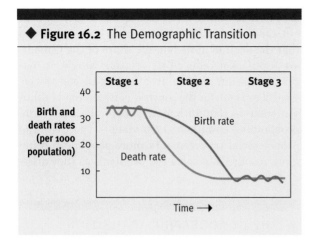

◆ **Figure 16.2** The Demographic Transition

a second equilibrium of low birth rates and low death rates. In the pretransition and post-transition states of equilibrium, there is little change in population size. The transition period, however, is characterized by a large increase in population size — sometimes as large as sevenfold.

Stage 1 of the demographic transition is one of high but fluctuating mortality and high fertility. Mortality is high because of poor nutrition, low standards of living, poor sanitation, and poor control over disease. Several reasons can be given for high fertility. The demographic argument proposes that, under conditions of high mortality (among infants and children, in particular), fertility needs to be high in order for the group to survive. The economic argument suggests that, because the family was the main economic unit in preindustrial society, children were important to parents both as producers and as a source of security for the future. The cultural argument focusses on ideas and values, suggesting that preindustrial societies did not consider deliberate family limitation to be appropriate behaviour.

In stage 2, mortality declines as a result of various agricultural, industrial, sanitation, and health innovations. Again, it is the interpretation of the fertility decline that has received the most attention.

There are two interpretations of the fertility decline, one economic, the other cultural. The economic argument notes that the economic and industrial transformation of society in the Industrial Revolution changed the role of the family — that is, most economic production came to be organized outside the family context. As a consequence, children became less valuable in family production, and the costs of raising them increased as they came to spend a larger portion of their lives in school. Stat-

ed differently, the economic role of children changed from that of producer to that of dependant. Later, social security replaced the family as the basic welfare net in the face of economic hardship, incapacity, and old age. With the expansion of the role of the state, the economic rationale for having children was reduced; family and kin groups became less important as guarantees of economic security.

The cultural explanation suggests that the idea of limiting births within marriage, along with the use of contraception, gained legitimacy over time. From this perspective, fertility changed as new models of the family and of appropriate behaviour became prevalent. The deliberate regulation of births within marriage was a new model of behaviour that spread across societies through cultural contact, first in Europe and eventually around the world.

Cultural barriers sometimes impeded the spread of the new models of behaviour. In Belgium, for instance, fertility declined faster in the French-speaking population than in the Flemish population. Similarly, for a long time, fertility remained higher among French Canadians than among English Canadians. Certain minorities, such as the Native peoples, resisted the penetration of different forms of behaviour, including the adoption of changed modes of fertility. In support of this cultural explanation, Van de Walle and Knodel (1980) note that the beginning of the fertility decline has occurred in a variety of different socioeconomic conditions, and that, once the decline starts, the process appears to be irreversible.

Stage 3, as shown in Figure 16.2, involves persistent low mortality with low but fluctuating fertility. Mortality is now under control, with fertility varying slightly with economic and cultural conditions. Depending on the economic and social climate, it may be considered more or less feasible (economically) and more or less appropriate (culturally) to have children.

The essence of the demographic-transition model is that decreases in mortality precede reductions in fertility and that populations move from relatively high and stable vital rates to relatively low and stable vital rates. In the process of the transition, the gap between births and deaths causes the population to expand considerably.

However, there are various debates regarding this model. For instance, some scholars have noted that fertility reductions can occur when standards of living are threatened. The early fertility declines in France may not have been a function of economic improvements and mortality decline, but rather of economic stagnation in a rural society. There are also cases in the Third World in which economic reversals appear to have accelerated fertility decline (Sinding, 1993).

Other discussions focus on the third stage, suggesting that a number of rich countries may have gone beyond stable low birth and death rates to a fourth stage, characterized by more deaths than births. The latter stage involves considerable population aging and the threat of eventual population decline in the absence of substantial immigration (Van de Kaa, 1987).

The most lively debate about the demographic-transition model pertains to the relative importance of economic versus cultural considerations. This discussion can be traced back to the Malthusian–Marxist debate. In some ways, however, the demographic-transition model brings into question both the Malthusian and the Marxist perspectives. Malthus would have to admit that, historically, improvements in standards of living and increases in the food supply did not induce people to have more children; on the contrary, fertility declined. Marx, for his part, would have to admit that demographic dynamics changed without a movement from capitalism to a new socialist stage of human history.

Focussing on different aspects of the demographic transition, however, both Marx and Malthus could argue that history also supports their perspectives. Marx would note in particular that fertility declined as a function of major economic and industrial transformations. Although it was not a revolution from capitalism to socialism, industrialization involved a significant change in the economic structure of society. Thus, as the economic context of people's lives changed, fertility declined. Malthus, on the other hand, might argue that his focus on ideas such as "moral restraint" and "responsible parenthood" helped to instigate new moral values, prompting people to take control of their reproduction and to deliberately limit family size. He would probably have less objection to specific methods of contraception. In other words, Malthus would subscribe to the cultural argument, noting that the diffusion of modern contraception has not only given people the means to limit their families but also promoted new values. According to these new values, it is appropriate to control conception, and small families are best.

■ POPULATION GROWTH AT THE WORLD LEVEL

Although necessarily vague, estimates suggest that the population of the world 12 000 years ago was in the range of 5 to 10 million people. The estimated number for 1998 is 6 billion (see Table 16.1). Where there was once one person, there are now a thousand. Growth has escalated dramatically over the past two centuries. It is estimated that world population reached its first billion around 1800, its second in 1930, its third in 1960, its fourth in 1975, and its fifth in 1987.

◆ **Table 16.1** Estimates and Projections of World Population, 10 000 B.C. to A.D. 2100 (in millions)

Year	World population	Regions of European origin plus Japan[a]	Less-developed regions[b]
10 000 B.C.	6	—	—
0	252	—	—
A.D. 1750	760	191 (25.1%)	569 (74.9%)
1950	2 516	835 (33.2%)	1 681 (66.8%)
1995	5 759	1 244 (21.6%)	4 515 (78.4%)
2025	8 472	1 403 (16.6%)	7 069 (83.4%)
2100	10 185	1 437 (14.1%)	8 748 (85.9%)

[a] Includes Europe, the former U.S.S.R., Japan, Australia, New Zealand, the United States, and Canada.

[b] Includes Africa, Asia (minus Japan and parts of the former U.S.S.R.), and South America.

SOURCE: Massimo Livi-Bacci, *A Concise History of World Population* (Cambridge, MA: Blackwell, 1992), p. 31; Thomas W. Merrick, with PRB Staff, "World Population in Transition," *Population Bulletin* 41, no. 2 (Washington, DC: Population Reference Bureau, 1986), p. 12; United Nations, *The Age and Sex Distribution of the World Population*, UN ST/ESA/Ser A/134 (New York: United Nations).

Human history can usefully be divided into segments characterized by different population-growth dynamics. Ten thousand years ago, people lived in *hunting-and-gathering* societies. It appears that growth dynamics in those societies were minimal, in part because of high mortality but also because births were spaced to ensure the survival of infants. Evidence from societies that until recently lived as hunters and gatherers suggests that the difficulty of finding soft food for children and the consequent need for long periods of lactation kept average births per women in the range of five or six (Howell, 1979).

The Agricultural Revolution, which began 10 000 to 12 000 years ago, involved the emergence of agriculture and the domestication of animals, allowing more people to be supported by the environment. It seems that, with a more secure food supply, there were fewer deaths. However, famines associated with climatic conditions were still prevalent, and increased population density fostered the spread of communicable diseases. The number of births probably increased as the availability of softer foods made shorter lactation periods possible.

The next period was that of European population expansion over the two centuries from 1750 to 1950. As seen in the demographic-transition model, this period of rapid population growth in countries of European settlement occurred largely because of a reduction in death rates, which was in turn attributable to the nutritional improvements afforded by agricultural innovations. Improvements in public sanitation followed, and the practice of medicine also started to have an effect. After about 1870, birth rates started to decline, and this ultimately slowed down European population growth.

The last period, which started around 1950 and will probably continue into the first two decades of the twenty-first century, might be called the period of Third World population expansion. Here again, death rates declined, in fact more rapidly than they had in the case of the European populations. This was also a function of improved living conditions, better sanitation, and improved medicine. It was largely after 1970 that birth rates started to decline in the developing countries, where the rate of population growth has just started to slow down. About a fifth of the world population has not yet entered (or has *just* entered) the fertility decline (United Nations, 1989). At the same time, an estimated 50 percent of women of childbearing age in the Third World now use contraception. In broad terms, half of the fertility transition has taken place, bringing the average births per woman down from six to four; the other half, which will bring that average down to two, has yet to occur.

It is useful to see the rapid population growth of the less-developed countries in a historical context. First, it is important to appreciate that this growth has been caused by reductions in mortality rather than increases in fertility. More precisely, in both the European and Third World expansions, growth has occurred because death rates fell sooner and faster than did birth rates. Second, it is noteworthy that, in some regards, the two population expansions have compensated each other. It is estimated that, in 1750, 25 percent of the world population lived in Europe, North America, Oceania, and Japan (that is, in the more-developed countries), whereas 75 percent lived in the remaining parts of Asia as well as in South America and Africa (that is, in the less-developed countries). By 1950, the population of the more-developed countries had risen to 33 percent of the world population, but today, it is back to 22 percent — a proportion comparable to that of 1750.

However, the future is likely to witness a continuation of the relative expansion of the population of the less-developed countries, which will intensify the demographic contrasts. According to the projections of the United Nations (1993), the European/Japanese population will drop to roughly 17 percent of the world population by 2025, and to only 14 percent by the year 2100.

As Figure 16.3 illustrates, the population of the less-developed countries is young and growing rapidly, whereas that of the more-developed countries is aging and growing much more slowly. It is significant to note that the larger, more rapidly growing population has a significantly smaller share of the world's economic product; moreover, it is the wealthy, smaller population that wields power in the world. From the perspective of such inequalities, demographic trends can be considered explosive. John Maynard Keynes, the father of modern economics, thought that big historical events are often caused by slow demographic processes. The differences in demographic dynamics between the less-developed and the more-developed countries are likely to bring about changes in international relations: It seems inevitable that the larger countries and regions will eventually come to have more power in defining our destiny.

Concerns about population growth led the United Nations to organize three World Population conferences (in 1974, 1984, and 1994), bringing together government representatives from countries around the world to deliberate on the action that needs to be taken to forestall potential disaster. The 1974 conference was characterized by heated debates between those who wanted all countries to

◆ Figure 16.3 Population Age Pyramids for Less-Developed and More-Developed Countries, 1985 and 2025

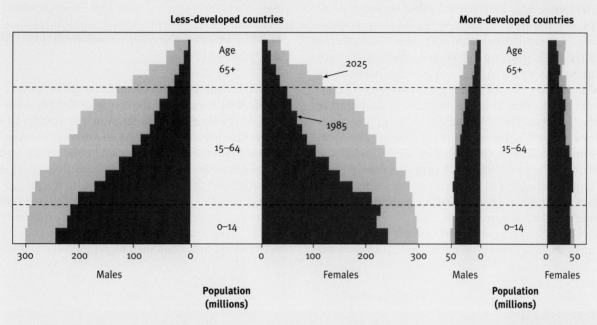

SOURCE: Thomas W. Merrick. with PRB Staff, "World Population in Transition," *Population Bulletin, 41* (2) (Washington, DC: Population Reference Bureau, 1986), p. 19.

commit themselves to lower birth rates and those who argued that birth rates would fall only as a consequence of economic development. The debate was effectively between Malthusian and Marxist views. Malthusians argued that, in order to reduce poverty, we must promote the use of contraception worldwide and work to reduce fertility. Marxists countered with the slogan "Development is the best contraceptive." In other words, they argued that it was only through development that fertility would decline significantly.

By 1984, there was more consensus among nations, on both the importance of the problem of population growth and the approach that should be adopted to deal with it. It was generally agreed that improvements in health and standards of living (through economic development) and a greater availability of contraception were both necessary, as mutually reinforcing strategies.

The 1994 conference faced strong pressures on four fronts in particular. Environmentalists, while recognizing that overconsumption and high standards of living are partly responsible for the growing stress on the environment, emphasized the dangers of population growth in this regard. Civil-rights activists argued against the coercive family plan-

ning that some governments have been imposing on their populations, and argued that family size should be a matter of individual choice. European countries in particular expressed concerns about massive international migration as a consequence of population pressures. Finally, media attention at the conference focussed on the abortion controversy. There

SOURCE: Ajit Ninan/India. Reprinted with permission from IPS—Inter Press Service.

were, however, strong elements of consensus in the final 1994 conference document. Population issues were clearly related to sustainable development. Clear principles were accepted that agreed that "all couples and individuals have the basic right to decide freely and responsibly the number and spacing of their children and to have the information, education and means to do so." Regarding international migration, the document speaks of enacting policies that would make migration a positive phenomenon for both sending and receiving countries, as well as for migrants themselves. For abortion, the document first says that "in no case should abortion be promoted as a method of family planning," and, later, that "in circumstances where abortion is not against the law, such abortion should be safe" (United Nations, 1995: 44).

Box 16.2 brings attention to some other important concerns connected with population growth.

■ COMPONENTS OF POPULATION CHANGE IN CANADA

▲ MORTALITY

We have witnessed remarkable changes in longevity and health care over the course of Canadian history. At the time of Confederation, the average **life expectancy** was 42 years. As an average, this takes into account the many infant and child deaths and the not-infrequent deaths in early adult years that characterized the latter half of the nineteenth century; a relatively small number of people lived into their 60s, 70s, or later at that time. A life expectancy of 42 is very low by today's standards. No country in the world today has such high mortality, and life

Box 16.2
Population Growth and Political Tensions

Two hundred years ago, as the eighteenth century was drawing to a close, observers of social and political trends in Europe were deeply troubled. A revolutionary tide, which had first surged in France in 1789, was spreading to neighbouring states, bringing down regimes from Italy to the Netherlands. . . .

Although the French Revolution had specific causes — for example, worsening state finances during the 1780s — many felt that there were deeper reasons for these social upheavals. One such was obvious to anyone who visited Europe's crowded cities or noted the growing incidence of rural underemployment: it was the sheer press of human beings, all needing food, clothing, shelter, and work in societies not well equipped to meet those demands, at least on such a scale. Countryside hovels teemed with young children. Town authorities grappled with a rising tide of homeless vagrants. In the larger cities, a floating population of tens of thousands of unemployed slept on the ground overnight and poured into the streets the next day. Jails, pauper houses, foundling hospitals, and lunatic asylums were packed with human casualties who had not yet arrived at their common grave. . . .

Three developments permitted the British people to escape the fate Malthus predicted for them. The first was emigration, . . . the second was . . . the Agricultural Revolution . . . the third was the Industrial Revolution. . . . Thus, "the power of population" was answered not so much by "the power in the earth" itself, but by the power of technology. . . .

There was, it is worth noting, another solution in Malthus's time to the problem of excess population, namely, internal unrest followed by external aggression. In France, popular discontents smashed an *ancien régime* that was less well structured than Britain in agriculture, industry, and commerce, and in its social framework and attitudes, to sustain rapid demographic growth. . . .

(continued)

Box 16.2
(continued)

Those same interrelated issues — overpopulation, pressure upon the land, migration, and social instability on the one hand, and technology's power both to increase productivity and to displace traditional occupations on the other — still confront us today, with a greater force than ever. In other words, we should see the demographic and economic conditions of the late eighteenth century as a metaphor for the challenges facing our present global society, two centuries after Malthus's ponderings. . . .

Although few, if any, of our political leaders appear willing to face the fact, the greatest test for human society as it confronts the twenty-first century is how to use "the power of technology" to meet the demands thrown up by "the power of population"; that is, how to find effective global solutions in order to free the poorer three-quarters of humankind from the growing Malthusian trap of malnutrition, starvation, resource depletion, unrest, enforced migration, and armed conflict — developments that will also endanger the richer nations, if less directly. . . .

[There is an] important implication of population change upon international security: the prospect of demographically driven social unrest, political instability, and regional wars. As noted earlier, behind many well-known historical upheavals — the outward thrust of the Vikings, the expansion of Elizabethan England, the French Revolution, Wilhelmine *Weltpolitik,* the turbulences that rack Central America and the Middle East today — the societies involved were experiencing population explosions, and often having difficulty in absorbing increasing numbers of energetic young men. Sometimes the unfulfilled expectations of a new generation exploded into violence and revolution. In other instances, those energies were diverted by nimble and ambitious political leaders into foreign adventures and conquests.

SOURCE: Excerpted from Paul Kennedy, *Preparing for the Twenty-First Century* (New York: Random House, 1993), pp. 3–4, 6–12, 34–35. Copyright © 1993 by Paul Kennedy. Reprinted by permission of Random House, Inc.

expectancy is below 45 years in only three countries: Afghanistan, Guinea, and Guinea-Bissau (Population Reference Bureau, 1996). In 1993, life expectancy in Canada reached 78 years; life expectancy was higher only in Iceland and Japan.

Between 1851 and 1931, life expectancy in Canada rose from 41 to 61. This improvement was largely a function of reductions in the prevalence of infectious diseases such as tuberculosis, pneumonia, diphtheria, scarlet fever, enteritis, and diarrhea. Although diseases struck at all ages, the very young were particularly vulnerable. In fact, the declining **infant mortality rate** was the most important factor contributing to the improvement in life expectancy. In 1831, 1 in 6 children did not survive their first year; in 1931 it was 1 in 14, and by 1993 only 1 in 160 children did not survive their first year.

The question of why infectious diseases have declined brings us to consider standards of living as well as medical knowledge. As a component of the standard of living, improved nutrition appears to have played an important role (McKeown, Brown, and Record, 1972). Poor nutrition not only makes us more susceptible to infection, but also increases the likelihood that infection will be fatal. Medical improvements in the treatment of infectious diseases have included preventive medicine, from knowledge about the importance of sanitation and improvements in the care and feeding of infants, to the development of effective vaccines.

Improvements over the period 1931–93 have also been impressive, raising life expectancy from 61 to 78 years. Today, the leading causes of death are degenerative diseases that affect individuals predominantly in the later decades of life. In fact, diseases of the circulatory system and cancer now account for 44 percent of the years of life lost through deaths before age 70 (Nagnur, 1986: 22–23).

At Confederation, average life expectancy was 42 years. In 1993, it was 78 years. The number of people 65 years and older in Canada is steadily increasing because of increased living standards, improvements in sanitation, and medical advances. SOURCE: Dick Hemingway.

The prospects for further improvement in life expectancy are difficult to predict. However, recent changes suggest that some earlier conclusions can be questioned. It was thought, for instance, that improvements in life expectancy would eventually slow down. However, improvements between 1976 and 1986 were greater than they had been in the previous decade. Second, the late 1970s and 1980s saw a turnaround in the life-expectancy gender gap. That gap had spread from a 2.1 year advantage for women in 1931 to a 7.3 year advantage in 1976. However, the gap has recently started to narrow — it fell to 6.2 years in 1993. Third, until 1971, there had been very little improvement in the mortality of adults, especially among those over the age of 50, but the past two decades have shown progress in this area as well.

In many areas of public policy, when a social problem is alleviated, the need to allocate resources to the problem declines. However, in the area of health and longevity, the opposite appears to be true: The higher the life expectancy of the population and the more successful the prevention of disease, the greater the need for services and resources to cope with the health problems of those who survive. Although people live longer, their additional years of life are not necessarily spent in good health.

With longer life come longer average periods of poor health and disability. Not surprisingly, therefore, there is currently much discussion about health budgets and the level of medical effort that should be expended to extend the life of the chronically ill.

▲ FERTILITY

There has also been a substantial long-term change in fertility, from about seven births per woman in the 1850s to fewer than two births in the 1980s and 1990s. Changes in fertility, however, have not been as uniform as changes in mortality. The baby boom of the period 1946–66 presented a major exception to the long-term trend. The analysis of fertility is also more complex than that of mortality: Whereas everyone dies (and dies just once), typically of an identifiable cause, some people have no children while others have several.

Changes in fertility in Canada over the period 1871–1995 are shown in Figure 16.4. Although the trend is not uniform, it does involve a long-term decline. Two fertility measures are shown on the same graph. One uses **cohort analysis,** following the life-paths of people belonging to the same **cohort** or who have shared a common temporal demographic experience. The other uses **period analysis,** counting the births of a specific period or year. **Cohort fertility** is the average number of births per woman for women of a given birth cohort, or a given year of birth. The *cohort completed fertility rate,* which is depicted in the graph, is the number of births per 1000 women for women of given birth cohorts who have completed their childbearing years. In Figure 16.4, the last few births for the youngest cohorts have been estimated, showing a level of 1900 births per 1000 women (or 1.9 births per woman) for the cohort of women born in 1954 (Dumas, 1996: 18).

The **total fertility rate** is called a "period" rate. It takes the rates of childbearing of women at the various childbearing ages in a given period or year, and adds them up over all the childbearing years. The result is a measure of what would be the average births per woman if the rates for one period or year represented the actual lifetime experiences of

women. The period rate has the advantage of being more current than the cohort completed fertility rate, but it may misrepresent the underlying reality. For instance, if women are postponing births but will have them later, the total fertility rate will be low compared with the ultimate cohort completed fertility rate. The cohort approach has the advantage of better representing the underlying reality, but the measurement is incomplete until the cohort has passed through the childbearing years. Therefore, it is important to use both measures and to appreciate the strengths and limitations of each.

The graph in Figure 16.4 shows that, during the baby-boom period (1946–66), the period rate was higher than the cohort rate. This was because the timing of births in people's lives was changing toward younger ages. The baby-boom period was unique in other ways as well. This was a time of sustained economic growth, with a consequent optimism about the future, and also a time of societal focus on family roles, especially for women. Since 1966, the period rate has been lower than the cohort rate

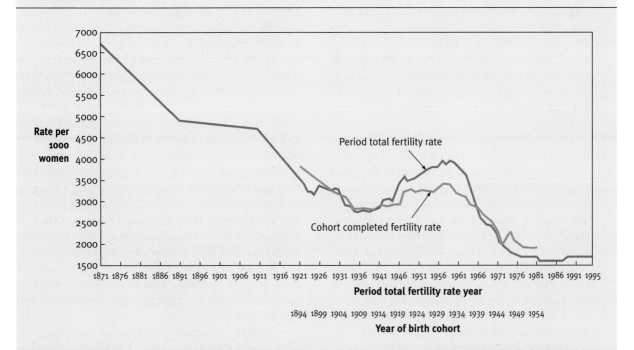

◆ **Figure 16.4** Period Total Fertility Rate for 1871–1995, and Completed Fertility Rate for Cohorts, 1894–1954, Canada

SOURCE: Anatole Romaniuc, *Current Demographic Analysis: Fertility in Canada: From Baby-boom to Baby-bust* (Ottawa: Minister of Supply and Services, 1984), pp. 121–22; Roderic Beaujot and Kevin McQuillan, *Growth and Dualism: The Demographic Development of Canadian Society* (Toronto: Gage, 1982), p. 54; Jean Dumas, *Rapport sur l'état de la population du Canada, 1990,* Statistics Canada, Cat. no. 91-209 (Ottawa Supply and Services Canada, 1990), p. 18. From R. Beaujot, *Population Change in Canada* (Toronto: McClelland and Stewart, 1991), with updates.

because women began to postpone births. The total fertility rate has been very stable at about 1.7 births per woman over the period 1977 to 1995.

The rate of 2.1 births per woman has traditionally been viewed as the level of **replacement fertility** — that is, the level of fertility at which one generation will be fully replaced by the next. Two births are needed to replace the parents and about 0.1 to compensate for the small number of deaths that occur before the next generation reaches reproductive age. Demographers speak of **population momentum,** whereby a population continues to grow for some time after fertility declines. Births continue to outnumber deaths because the demographic bulge in the population age structure is at reproductive ages. Thus, even though the generation constituting the demographic bulge is having fewer births than are needed for replacement, this generation is sufficiently numerous to ensure more births than deaths. In Canada, the current population momentum will continue for some time. In 1990, Statistics Canada projected that, if fertility remained constant at 1.7 births per woman, births would continue to outnumber deaths until 2020.

We can extend our discussion of the demographic transition, applying it to the Canadian case of low fertility, through a consideration of four sets of factors — proximate, economic, structural, and cultural:

- *Proximate,* or immediate, factors of lower fertility in Canada include higher age at marriage, a larger percentage of couples cohabiting and a smaller percentage marrying, more divorce, and, most important, the prevalent use of modern contraception.
- *Economic* factors include the value and cost of children in our time — specifically, their decreasing economic value as producers in the family unit and their increasing cost as dependants over a long period of time. Estimates suggest that three children, aged 10, 12, and 17, cost parents roughly $20 000 per year and reduce the standard of living of the family by 33 percent relative to that of a childless family (Dionne, 1989).
- *Structural* factors of low fertility in Canada involve broad changes in the political economy that have altered the productive and reproductive roles of women and men. In the "breadwinner model" of the family, the husband looks after economic production and the wife concerns herself with reproduction. Especially since the 1960s, however, the growth of the service sector has opened up many new economic opportunities for women. In addition to changing the economic aspects of the

relations between women and men, the increased participation of women in the paid labour force has made it more difficult to have children.
- *Cultural* factors include prevailing norms and attitudes defining appropriate behaviour. With respect to Canada in the twentieth century, we can speak of a greater concern for self-gratification and a greater freedom of choice in family-related matters, as evidenced by the growing acceptability of divorce, cohabitation, and childlessness. In particular, there may be a weakening of the consensus that marriage and childbearing are integral parts of the normal adult role.

▲ IMMIGRATION

In contrast to many other advanced industrial countries, Canada has a long history of policies and programs that encouraged immigration; consequently, immigration has contributed significantly to population change in this country. Over the course of this century, net international migration has accounted for some 22 percent of total population growth. This figure does not take into account the further impact of children born to immigrants. Fully 41 percent of Canada's population growth from 1966 to 1991 was a function of immigration and of births to these immigrants over the period (Duchesne, 1993). In 1991, 16 percent of the population of Canada was foreign-born, a higher proportion than that in any other major industrial country, except Australia and Israel.

In terms of trends and dynamics, I find it useful to divide Canada's history of immigration into four periods: 1861–95, 1896–1913, 1914–45, and 1946 to the present. (Figure 16.5 depicts both immigration and emigration from 1900 to 1996.) The period from just before Confederation to about 1895 saw more departures than arrivals. This was a time of depression in international trade, which undermined markets for Canadian raw materials. The earlier industrialization of the U.S. economy offered employment prospects that attracted residents of Canada, both recent immigrants to the country and native-born Canadians.

The year 1896 marked the end of the long period of international economic depression, as well as a turnaround in net migration to Canada. Although departures to the United States remained significant, the gains of the decade 1901–11 more than balanced the net loss experienced over the course of the previous four decades (Beaujot and McQuillan, 1982:

◆ **Figure 16.5** Annual Levels of Canadian Immigration and Emigration, 1900–1996

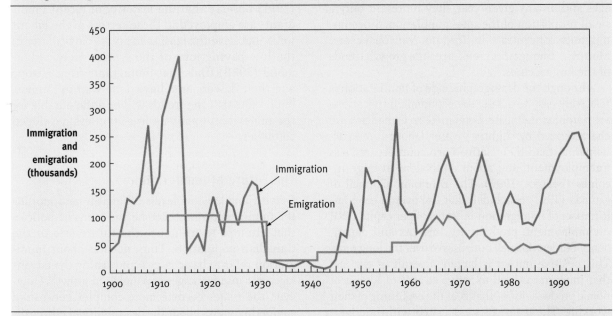

SOURCE: Jean Dumas, *Rapport sur l'état de la population du Canada, 1995*, Statistics Canada, Cat. no. 91–209 (Ottawa Supply and Services Canada, 1996), p. 2; Roderic Beaujot, K.G. Basavarajappa, and Ravi B.P. Verma, *Current Demographic Analysis: Income of Immigrants in Canada*, Statistics Canada, Cat. no. 91-527 (Ottawa: Supply and Services Canada, 1988), p.7. From R. Beaujot, *Population Change in Canada* (Toronto: McClelland and Stewart, 1991), with updates.

83). This development was attributable in part to active efforts by government to encourage settlement of the Canadian West and in part to the onset of industrialization. The years 1911–13 saw record arrivals of immigrants (300 000–400 000 per year), which have never since been surpassed (see Figure 16.5). The total for the period 1896–1913 was close to 3 million arrivals.

The onset of World War I marked an abrupt end to this first major wave of immigration. Although immigration picked up somewhat in the 1920s, the Depression of the 1930s and World War II make the whole period from 1914 to 1945 something of an interlude in immigration, with total arrivals numbering roughly 1.3 million.

The post–World War II period can be viewed as a second major immigration wave. Total arrivals between 1946 and 1996 amounted to 7.4 million. In 1962, there was a major change in immigration policy, in that the racial components of immigrant selection criteria were removed. Subsequently, the places of origin of immigrants to Canada became much more diverse. Fluctuations in immigration have followed the path of events both inside and outside the country. Directly following World War II, the arrival of refugees and war brides created a surge

of new arrivals. The high point of postwar immigration, in 1956–57, reflects the arrival of British subjects escaping the Suez crisis and of refugees fleeing Hungary before the Soviet invasion of that country. The dips in 1961 and again in 1983–86 coincided with downturns in the economy. The increase during the period 1986–93 was the outcome of a deliberate government program of "moderate controlled growth" in immigration levels. Using the title "Staying the Course," the 1997 annual immigration plan set the target at 195 000 to 220 000 admissions for 1997 (Canada, 1996).

As noted earlier, immigration has become highly diversified by ethnic origin since the 1960s. Whereas three-quarters of the immigrants to Canada came from Europe and the United States in the period 1946–67, in the period 1976–96 the proportion from Asia, Latin America, and Africa rose to more than two-thirds of the total. In 1991, 39 percent of the foreign-born population in Canada were born in Asia, Africa, or Latin America.

The Impact of Immigration

From a demographic point of view, immigration clearly contributes to population growth. However, it has only a small impact on a population's age structure, because immigrants arrive at a variety of ages and, in any given year, they represent only a small proportion of the total population. Since immigrants concentrate in Toronto, Vancouver, and Montreal, immigration reinforces the growth trends of the largest cities.

Although the demographic side of immigration is relatively easy to assess, the economic implications are harder to delineate. Foreign-born Canadians are characterized by slightly greater labour-force participation than their native-born counterparts, less unemployment, and about equivalent average incomes (Beaujot, 1996). The Economic Council of Canada (1991) concluded that the overall economic impact of immigration in terms of per capita GNP, unemployment, productivity, and tax and dependency burdens is small but positive over the long term. This positive impact is largely a result of the fact that immigrants tend to arrive at ages of high economic productivity — that is, at the beginning of their worklife. The main costs associated with immigration are encountered in the shorter term, specifically in relation to initial settlement and adjustment.

Other summaries of the economic impact of immigration are less optimistic. Seward and Tremblay (1991) observe that the majority of recent immigrants are employed in those sectors of the labour force that have the least security — particularly in the low-paying jobs of the service sector. Richmond (1988) finds that immigrants from Europe and their descendants have done well in Canada, but doubts that the trends will be as favourable for the more recent arrivals from the less-developed countries.

The Future of Immigration

Given Canada's low levels of fertility and mortality, immigration has become the focus of policies that attempt to influence the future size of the Canadian population. Thus, debates about immigration refer to basic issues concerning the advantages and disadvantages of population growth. However, the issues become more complex because of competing views about the desirability of ethnic diversity. In addition, pressures from the outside mean that questions of immigration are only partly sub-

Since Confederation, Canada's population has grown twice as rapidly as the population of the world as a whole. Immigrants, one of the main sources of growth, have tended to flow to the western and southern parts of the country. This photo shows Markham, a Toronto suburb, expanding into the countryside. SOURCE: Dick Hemingway.

ject to social policy. Clearly, immigration is a hot topic of debate. Its importance to Canada is emphasized by the fact that legislation requires the minister of immigration to make an annual "statement to Parliament" that outlines the government policy on immigration, including the anticipated level of admission.

The determination of an appropriate immigration level and its composition are clearly matters of values and politics. Research can shed some light on the past, but it is for the political community to decide what is best for the future and how immigration is to figure into that social vision. Weinfeld (1988) suggests that there are two predominant visions that apply to immigration. One view, which in its extreme version might be called "Fortress Canada," sees the country as well established and needing to protect its resources and its inheritance against destabilizing external forces. This perspective is apprehensive about a multiethnic society. In this view, tradition is preferable to change, and immigration policy should be cautious. As the total number of Third World immigrants and their descendants increases, Canadian society will continue to face significant challenges in seeking ways to avoid conflict between racial, linguistic, and cultural groups. A solution is simply to reduce the intake of immigrants. In opinion surveys, the majority opinion tends to be that immigration should be lower or, at least, that it should not increase (Angus Reid Group, 1989).

The alternative perspective, according to Weinfeld (1988), views Canada as a country that is young, rich, and, as yet, not fully developed. From this perspective, immigration is part of a process of nation building; ethnic variety and demographic growth are interpreted positively. As stewards of this large land and its resources, we might be seen as managing our endowment for the greater benefit of humanity and less for our narrow self-interest. An openness to the cultures of the world may be taken as a sociocultural and demographic challenge that would bring Canada into the modern international world, in which European-based societies are a declining component. Tepper (1987) proposes that societies that find ways to manage ethnicity and pluralism may well be in a stronger position to face future challenges in the interdependent world of nations.

Pressure from the Outside

Although we can debate the relative advantages of these alternatives, it is also important to recognize that international movements of population are not totally under Canada's control. It is estimated that there are some 125 million international migrants in the world, seeking to establish themselves in a favourable country, including some 19 million refugees (United Nations, 1995: 51, 55). It is clear that migration pressure at the global level will continue to be greater than the numbers that can be accommodated in receiving countries (Pacini, 1992).

These population displacements follow on various circumstances, including global economic restructuring and the break-up of the former Soviet Union. In addition, the very process of development brings with it various economic disruptions, uprooting people, especially in subsistence rural economies. Note that it was precisely when Europe was industrializing that large numbers of Europeans left the continent. Until World War II, the net movement was in fact from the North to the South — that is, from Europe to Africa, Latin America, and Asia. This migration obviously went hand in hand with political and economic domination, including the colonization of much of the South.

Now the tables are turned and the countries of Western Europe are trying to set up various legal fortifications against migration from Eastern Europe, Africa, Asia, and even Turkey, while the United States tries to control arrivals from Mexico and places south. It will be interesting to see the extent to which Canada follows the same path. Compared with European countries, Canada has a longer history of immigration policies and of building a multiethnic society. However, there is also a felt need to control a process that is very difficult to manage and regulate, let alone control.

▲ REFUGEES

It is difficult to estimate accurately the refugee component in past immigrant arrivals. Refugee arrivals started with the United Empire Loyalists, around 1776, and continued through to World War I with various groups including the Quakers, Mennonites, blacks, Doukhobors, Hutterites, Mormons, and Jews (Ziegler, 1988).

Some of the harshest controls on refugee arrivals were set in the 1930s and 1940s. Avery (1979) appropriately entitled his book *Dangerous Foreigners* to give a sense of the attitudes toward immigrants that prevailed at that time. A well-known case in point was Canada's refusal to allow Jews entry into the country just before World War II. In 1939, for example, the *St. Louis,* an ocean liner carrying 907 desperate German Jews, was refused entry into Canada and was forced to return to Europe. Abella and Troper (1982) reveal the extent of Canadian prejudice against Jewish immigration, even to the point of obvious persecution.

In the period immediately following World War II, Canada opened its doors to refugees from war-torn Europe. They were known as "displaced persons," and the tag "DPs" soon took on a negative connotation. Subsequently, the major refugee movements included Hungarians, Czechoslovakians, U.S. draft dodgers and deserters (though they were not admitted as refugees), Tibetans, Ugandan expellees, Chileans, and Indo-Chinese. Since 1978, the planning of immigration levels has taken anticipated refugees into account, and the source countries of immigrants have consequently become considerably more diversified. Total numbers of refugees are difficult to estimate for the earlier period, but in the post–World War II era, there have been roughly 700 000 refugee arrivals, representing about 10 percent of all immigrants (Nash, 1989: 125–27, and updates).

In the 1980s, Canada encountered the problem of people claiming refugee status after they had arrived in the country. (The standard procedure involves applying for refugee status from abroad.) As a signatory to the International Convention on Refugees, Canada is obliged to give safe haven to people who have left their country because of persecution. The problem thus became one of determining whether claims of refugee status were legitimate. The process has involved complex legal and administrative arrangements, which have resulted in a considerable backlog of claims. Although the public is generally supportive of accommodating refugees, there is also a sense that the system should not be abused. However, it is very difficult for a receiving country to control this process. The pressure on Canada is particularly strong because it allows refugees to settle permanently. Other countries that have signed the international accord provide asylum only on a temporary basis, in a sort of holding capacity, with limited prospect of gaining permanent status and citizenship.

■ CANADIAN POPULATION GROWTH: PAST AND FUTURE

Having analyzed mortality, fertility, and migration, we can now sketch the overall picture of population change in Canada. We will consider past growth patterns and prospects for the future, along with some of the broader implications of existing trends.

▲ GROWTH AND AGE STRUCTURE

In 1851, the population of Canada was 2.4 million; by 1997, it had grown to 30.3 million. This rate of growth is considerably faster than that of many other countries, including England and France, and that of the world as a whole.

The main components of Canada's shifting demographic situation today are low fertility, low growth, and population aging. These trends are setting parameters that differ in many respects from those that prevailed in the past. In the 45-year period between 1946 and 1991, Canada's population more than doubled. Most would interpret this change positively, noting that the baby boom and the immigration boom of the post–World War II period have permitted Canada to flourish. Projections made in 1946 did not foresee these fertility and immigration changes, and estimated that the population would reach a maximum of only about 15 million. It is arguable that the actual, strong growth of Canada's population has ensured more domestic control over resources, elevated the country's status among the nations of the world, and contributed to economic growth and social development.

Projections indicate that, unless there is a substantial increase in fertility, population growth will come to a halt during the 45-year period from 1991 to 2036, with immigration becoming the only component of growth after about 2020. During this period, the average age of the population will increase from 32 to 45 years, and the proportion of people aged 65 and older will rise from 1 in 10 to 1 in 4 (see Figure 16.6) (Statistics Canada, 1990). Because this scenario is significantly different from anything we have known in the past, it is difficult to anticipate the impact of such population change on Canadian society.

Some things are clear, however. The relative costs of health and public pensions will increase, whereas there may be some decline in the cost of education (Fellegi, 1988). What is less clear is the potential impact on the labour force. Although population growth has been slowing down since the 1950s, and although the population has been aging for a century, the labour force was not subject to the effects of these trends until very recently. The entry of the baby boomers and women into the labour force

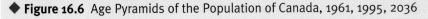

◆ **Figure 16.6** Age Pyramids of the Population of Canada, 1961, 1995, 2036

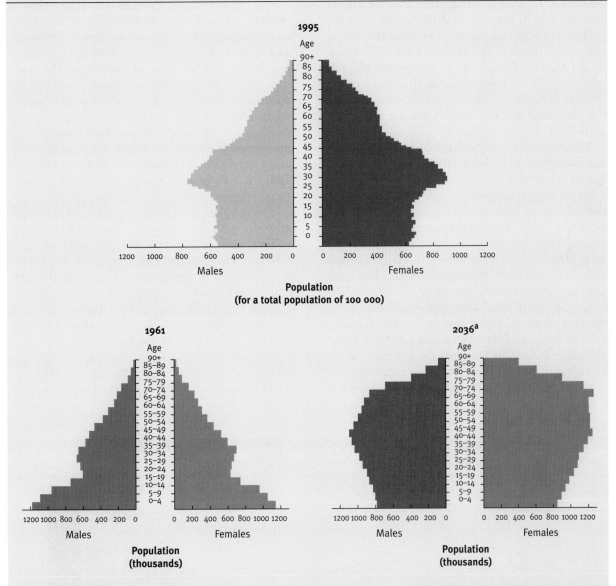

ᵃ Projections for 2036 are based on fertility of 1.67, immigration of 200 000 people per year, and emigration of 0.25 persons per 100 population per year.

SOURCE: Statistics Canada, *Postcensal Annual Estimates of Population by Marital Status, Age, Sex and Components of Growth for Canada, Provinces and Territories,* Cat. no. 91-210, Vol. 10 (Ottawa: Industry, Science and Technology Canada, 1992), p. 13; Statistics Canada, *Population: General Characteristics—Age Groups,* Cat. no. 92-542 (Ottawa. Supply and Services Canada, 1962), pp. 20-1, 20-2. From R. Beaujot, *Population Change in Canada* (Toronto: McClelland and Stewart, 1991), with updates.

caused its numbers to grow and resulted in a slight decline in the average age of labour-force participants. However, especially after the turn of the century, the growth of the labour force will be slower, and the average age of workers will rise. An older labour force might mean less unemployment and less need for new investments, but it might also mean less flexibility and lower productivity relative to labour costs.

▲ POPULATION DISTRIBUTION

In addition to looking at the overall growth of the population and its age structure, it is useful to consider its geographical distribution. Before the arrival of the Europeans, the greatest concentrations of Native peoples were in the St. Lawrence Valley and on the Pacific Coast (Careless, 1963: 18–21). The distribution that has emerged since the beginning of European immigration is quite similar. The analysis of population distribution is an important indicator of the relative attractiveness of the various parts of the country over time. In addition, the distribution of the population plays an important role in the regional dynamics of the country. (Figure 16.7 shows population growth for the provinces and the country during the period 1951–91.)

The Atlantic provinces have declined in relative size with the diminishing importance of wood and fish as export commodities and with the establishment of the St. Lawrence Seaway, which allowed the Atlantic provinces to be by-passed as a transportation route. The region has received few immigrants and has tended to be an area of net **outmigration**. As a consequence, the population is ethnically relatively homogeneous and has long-established roots in the region.

Quebec has received a considerable number of immigrants over the years. Montreal was a favourite destination, especially when it was viewed as Canada's major metropolis. However, the province has not always managed to retain its immigrants (especially those who were not French); it even lost some of its nonimmigrant population to the general westward movement in North America.

Ontario has made population gains through both immigration and internal migration. With its link to the Atlantic Ocean via the St. Lawrence Seaway and with its proximity to the rich farmland of southern Ontario and the mineral resources of the Canadian Shield, Toronto has become Canada's major metropolis. In 1951, Toronto was 18 percent smaller than Montreal; by 1991, it was 20 percent larger. Eight of Canada's 25 census metropolitan areas are located in southern Ontario, between Windsor and Ottawa. The immigration of the 1970s and 1980s has diversified the population in terms of racial origins.

The population of the Prairies has declined in relative size with the decreasing importance of its agricultural base. Alberta's oil resources, however, have provided growth potential. The harsh winter climate and lack of precipitation limit both the agricultural potential of the Prairies and their attractiveness for population settlement. The ethnic origins of the population are largely European, but nearly half are neither British nor French.

British Columbia has made continuous population gains because of the enduring importance of wood and mineral resources and the province's agree-

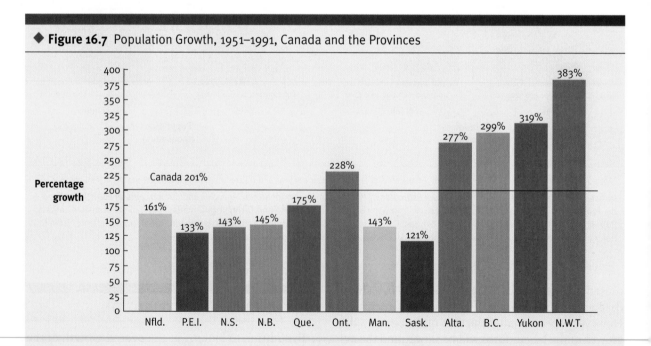

Figure 16.7 Population Growth, 1951–1991, Canada and the Provinces

SOURCE: Statistics Canada, *Annual Demographic Statistics, 1993*, Cat. no. 91–213 (Ottawa: Industry, Science and Technology Canada, 1994), p. 66. Reproduced by authority of the Minister of Industry, 1997.

SOURCE: Dave Anderson (ANDY)/South Africa. Reprinted with permission from IPS—Inter Press Service.

able climate. As a result of numerous arrivals from other parts of Canada and other countries, close to half the population was born outside the province.

The North represents a large part of the Canadian land mass but a very small part of the population. Defined as including the Northwest Territories, the Yukon, Labrador, and northern Quebec, the region had a population of only 140 000 in 1986, or 0.6 percent of the total national population (Maslove and Hawkes, 1989). It is a relatively young population, and 40 percent have aboriginal roots. Although the Yukon and the Northwest Territories are growing faster than other parts of Canada, they represent only 0.3 percent of the country's population.

■ OVERVIEW

The study of population starts with the processes of fertility, mortality, and migration; analyzes the immediate impact of those processes on population size, composition, and distribution; and, finally, considers the broader causes and consequences of demographic change.

At the level of the total world population, where we can ignore migration, we are currently observing very significant changes in mortality and fertility. Particularly impressive has been the change in mortality: In 1950–55, average life expectancy globally was 46.4 years; by 1990–95, it had risen to 64.7 years. Fertility has also declined, from an average of 5.0 births per woman to an average of 3.3 over the same period. The faster change in mortality than in fertility, as interpreted by the demographic-transition model, is the reason for the rapid growth in world population. Although the rate of growth reached a peak of 2.1 percent per year in the early 1960s, it remains very high by historical standards, at 1.5 percent per year. What is more, the net additions are at an all-time high of nearly 90 million persons annually (United Nations, 1995: 24).

A number of consequences and implications arise from these trends at the global level. Concerns persist about the high level of mortality in many countries (particularly the high level of infant mortality) and the variability in maternal mortality from country to country. According to the World Health Organization, the lifetime risk of dying from pregnancy or childbirth-related causes is 1 in 20 in some developing countries, compared with 1 in 10 000 in some developed countries (United Nations, 1995: 42). More generally, there is widespread concern for all people to have access to basic health care — a goal that can easily be undermined when a society supports expensive technological facilities that benefit the few and deplete resources that could subsidize basic care for the many. With respect to fertility, there has been much progress, with more than half of all women of childbearing age now using contraception. However, in some countries, the demand for contraception is higher than the supply, and in other places there is a need to encourage people to have smaller families.

More broadly, the rapid change in world population is accompanied by various concerns, ranging from the difficulty of enhancing standards of living in such large and rapidly growing populations, to the stress those populations place on the environment. As noted earlier, such concerns brought the United Nations to sponsor several international conferences to consider how the world is to deal with population questions. It has generally been agreed that development is key to bringing down the rate of population growth. Inspired in part by Marxist thinking, the World Population Plan of Action concludes that lack of development as manifested by "widespread poverty, unemployment, malnutrition, illiteracy, low status of women, exposure to environmental risks and limited access to social and health services . . . contribute[s] to high levels of fertility" (United Nations, 1995: 13). However, there is also a need to supply contraception and to promote the idea of smaller families. Recalling the concerns of Malthus, many international agencies and governments have come to conclude that it is essential to slow down population growth by deliberately promoting birth control. The closing address at a 1992 conference organized by the International Planned Parenthood Federation stated that "contraception is the best development."

Canadian trends also involve significant changes. Over the period 1951–93, life expectancy rose from 69 to 78 years, and average births per woman dropped from 3.5 to 1.7. Here, the fertility change is more rapid, and the reduction in the relative number of young people has brought about a considerable increase in the average age of the population. Earlier changes in mortality benefited mostly children and young adults, but, since 1971, older adults are also among those living longer. With longer life, however, come longer average periods of poor health, which can drain health-care funds.

Canada's fertility change is particularly significant since it implies that, over the long term, there will be more deaths than births. There are currently more births simply because of the large numbers of people who are still at reproductive ages. Low fertility is a function of effective contraception, but, more broadly, it is a function of the high cost of children (especially the opportunity cost in terms of parents' careers) and of the lower value that the culture has come to place on children relative to other sources of fulfilment in life. The issue might be raised — in fact, it has already been raised in Quebec — that the state should support childbearing by absorbing more of the costs of raising children and, especially, by making changes that would enable parents to have both productive and reproductive roles — that is, both to work and to raise children.

Given decreasing levels of natural increase, immigration has come to play a larger role in population change. Over the period 1986–96, 42 percent of population growth in Canada was a function of net international migration (the other 58 percent was the result of natural increase). Indeed, many people think of immigration as a way of compensating for declining fertility. Although immigration does support population growth, it can change the ethnic composition of the population dramatically and requires various forms of adaptation on the part of both immigrants and the receiving society. Canada must ensure that its immigrant groups do not become an economic underclass. Fortunately, compared with many other countries, Canada has a long history of public policies concerning the selection of immigrants and their integration into a changing society.

Clearly, population dynamics present both Canadian society and the world community with numerous serious challenges. ■

SUMMARY

1. The consideration of demographics — population size, growth, distribution, composition, fertility, mortality, and migration — is important to the study of societies as they change over time. Conversely, studies of changes or differences in fertility, mortality, and migration require sociological analysis.

2. Demography analyzes population states (size, geographical distribution, and composition by various characteristics) and population processes (fertility, mortality, and migration), their reciprocal influences, and their various determinants and consequences.

3. Malthus concluded that populations have a tendency to grow more rapidly than other resources and that it is important to control the growth of population by reducing births. Marx concluded that economic and social conditions determine the rate of population growth and that proper social arrangements should be able to accommodate population growth. Both of these perspectives are useful.

4. The demographic-transition model summarizes the historical tendency of populations to move from an equilibrium of high birth rates and high death rates to one of low birth rates and low death rates. Because death rates decline sooner and faster than birth rates, there is considerable population expansion during the course of the transition. In the European populations, the demographic transition occurred mostly over the period 1750 to 1970, whereas in Asia, Latin America, and Africa, it started only in the 1950s.

5. Since Confederation, life expectancy in Canada has increased from 42 to 78 years as a result of higher standards of living, improvements in sanitation, and advances in medicine. Degenerative diseases have replaced infectious diseases as the major causes of death. In the same period, average births declined from seven to two births per woman, though the decline in fertility was not as uniform as the decline in mortality (the baby boom of the period 1946–66 represented a major exception to the downward trend). Fertility will likely continue to fluctuate according to economic and cultural conditions.

6. Immigration has contributed considerably to Canadian population growth. The net balance between immigration and emigration is responsible for 22 percent of the population growth over the past century, and 16 percent of the current population is foreign-born. Net migration in the period 1986–96 accounted for close to half of the country's population growth. Immigration has brought significant ethnic diversity to Canada's population, including, since the mid-1960s, large numbers of arrivals from Asia, Latin America, and Africa. Controlling the level of immigration, particularly refugee arrivals, poses challenges in the context of demographic pressures at the world level.

7. Canada's population has grown rapidly since Confederation — twice as rapidly as the population of the world as a whole. Today, however, fertility is low, growth is less rapid, and the population is aging — a process that poses various challenges of adaptation, particularly in the areas of education, the labour force, health care, and pensions. At the same time, population distribution has tended to be very uneven, with different growth dynamics in the various regions. Movement has tended to be toward the western and southern parts of the country. In addition, immigrants have tended to concentrate in the three largest cities (Toronto, Montreal, and Vancouver). With the exception of Montreal, immigrants do not contribute to the relative size of the population of Quebec and the Atlantic provinces.

8. In terms of its population characteristics, Canada displays some unique features. Only 2.2 percent of the world population live in countries with a higher life expectancy than Canada's, and only 10.7 percent in countries with lower fertility. In other ways, Canada shares in the slower population growth and consequent population aging that typically characterize the more-developed countries and distinguish them from the younger and faster-growing populations of the developing world. Canada's relatively high and diversified immigration promotes a cultural mosaic that may help us to retain a common sense of destiny with the three-quarters of humanity that populate the less-developed countries.

QUESTIONS TO CONSIDER

1. Using the frameworks of Malthusian and Marxist theory, discuss the relationship between population size and environmental damage.
2. In the case of the Canadian demographic transition, do you think that economic or cultural arguments were more relevant?
3. Poorer countries typically have higher fertility than richer countries, and poorer people within any given country have more children than richer people, but the main reason middle-class people give for not wanting more children is that they cannot afford more. Moreover, the baby boom occurred during a period of economic expansion. Is the relationship between income and fertility positive or negative? What qualifications must be introduced in order to understand this relationship?
4. As minister responsible for immigration, what kind of a statement to Parliament would you make regarding the level and composition of immigration for the short-term future? Why?

GLOSSARY

cohort A group of people, observed through time, who share a common temporal demographic experience. For example, the birth cohort of 1960 is the people born in that year. There can also be marriage cohorts, university-admission-year cohorts, and so on.

cohort analysis Analysis that follows the life-paths of persons who belong to a given cohort. *Cohort fertility* and *cohort completed fertility* are cohort rates. Compare *period analysis*.

cohort fertility The average number of births per woman for women of a given cohort or year of birth. For cohorts who have completed their childbearing years, this becomes *cohort completed fertility*.

demographic transition The theory that the rate of population growth passes through three stages — stable, rapid, and stable — as fertility and mortality rates decline.

demography The study of populations, their size, distribution, and composition, and the immediate factors causing population change (births, deaths, and migration).

emigration The number of people leaving a country over a given period of time.

immigration The number of people moving into a country over a given period of time.

infant mortality rate The number of deaths of infants under 1 year of age per 1000 live births in a given year.

internal migration The movement of people within a given country. Generally, only movement across municipal boundaries is counted as internal migration; interprovincial migration is one kind of internal migration.

life expectancy Unless otherwise indicated, the term refers to life expectancy *at birth*. It is an estimate of the average number of additional years a person can expect to live, based on the age-specific death rates of a given year.

natural increase The difference between the number of births and the number of deaths in a population over a given period. Natural increase can be given in absolute numbers or as a percentage of the mid-year population.

net migration The difference between the number of immigrants and the number of emigrants in a population over a given period. Net migration can also refer to the net balance of internal migration (in-migration minus out-migration to a particular area).

out-migration The process of leaving an administrative subdivision of a country to take up residence in another subdivision of the same country.

period analysis Analysis of a population at a specific period in time. The total fertility rate and life expectancy are derived from data from one year and are therefore period rates. Compare *cohort analysis*.

population growth The change in population size over a specific period of time. For a given country, population growth is a function of natural increase (births minus deaths) plus net migration (immigration minus emigration).

population momentum The tendency of a population to experience natural increase even when the total fertility rate involves fewer than 2.1 births per woman, as a function of the high proportion of persons of childbearing age in the population.

replacement fertility A level of fertility that, if continued over a long period of time, would ensure the replacement of one generation of women by another generation of daughters who are themselves able to reach reproductive ages. Given that some deaths occur before women reach reproductive age, the total fertility rate of 2.1 is generally used as an indicator of replacement fertility.

total fertility rate The average number of children that would be born to a woman during her lifetime if she were to pass through all her childbearing years conforming to the age-specific fertility rates of a given year. It is an indicator of the level of childbearing in a population, measured in terms of births per woman.

SUGGESTED READING

Beaujot, Roderic. (1991). *Population Change in Canada: The Challenges of Policy Adaptation*. Toronto: McClelland and Stewart. An interpretation of population change in Canada, with suggestions of policy issues for discussion. Policy issues are raised in terms of either influencing population change or adapting to population change.

Charbonneau, Hubert. (1987). *Naissance d'une population*. Montreal: Les Presses de l'Université de Montréal. The beginnings of the French population in Canada are explored through an analysis of records of people who settled in this country in the seventeenth century.

Dumas, Jean. (Annual). *Report on the Demographic Situation in Canada*. Statistics Canada, Cat. no. 91-209. Ottawa: Industry, Science and Technology Canada. This annual publication gives data on the changing demographic situation in Canada and provides an analysis of some of the major observations. Each issue also focusses on a topic of special interest.

Foot, David K., and Daniel Stoffman. (1996). *Boom, Bust and Echo*. Toronto: Macfarlane Walter and Ross. This bestseller reflects on how the demographic shift, especially the changing age structure of the population, is transforming Canada's social and economic life.

Livi-Bacci, Massimo. (1992). *A Concise History of World Population*. Cambridge, MA: Blackwell. This book considers population throughout human history, and reviews the issues facing the world population in the late twentieth century. Questions of population and resources are addressed throughout.

Population Reference Bureau. (1991). *Population Handbook*. Washington, DC: Population Reference Bureau. A quick guide to population dynamics, focussing on definitions, methods of calculating various rates, and interpretive examples.

CHAPTER SEVENTEEN
Globalization

IN THIS CHAPTER YOU WILL LEARN THAT

- the end of the Cold War has not resulted in a unitary power centre for the world but in a new sense of the interdependence of all people and a perceived weakness of the nation-state
- the global may be seen as a new historical period or a level of social organization above and beyond the nation-state
- the world economy has become a single transnational system, but globalization may promote local economic activity rather than concentrate it in one or a few locations
- people travel and communicate across national borders so frequently that social relations have been lifted out of local contexts
- global images and information from the mass media enhance global consciousness and encourage the growth of new globalist social movements, such as the environmental movement
- global economic, political, and cultural forces impinge on people's everyday lives and can generate insecurity
- homogenization and fragmentation of social groups and individual consciousness are equally possible outcomes of globalization

MARTIN ALBROW
Roehampton Institute, University of Surrey

■ INTRODUCTION

In this chapter, you are asked to examine all the influences on you that originate in other parts of the world, and the way you relate to the world as a whole. Globalization works through practices that cross national boundaries and tie everyday life to worldwide processes. It may have begun with the expansion of the West, but globalizing influences are no longer unidirectional. Rather, the lifestyles that jostle with one another for your attention may seem bewildering in their variety.

The same may be said for global institutions. Whether regarding international politics after the end of the Cold War or the movements of international finance, national leaders face situations that seem unpredictable. This is attributable in part to the fact that individuals are now able to become directly involved in matters of global importance. We can express our concern for the world as a whole through movements for the environment, women's rights, human rights, and peace. The representatives of such movements literally knock on our doors. The global has become local. The food we eat, the vehicles we drive, and the news we see on television can equally be found anywhere in the world. Manufacturers and advertisers promote and take advantage of globalization to ensure that their products will find the largest possible market worldwide.

Sociologists find all kinds of contradictions in these changes. They find the world a smaller place, but one replete with unfamiliar things. The world may be unified, but peace is as far away as ever. Western ways pervade the world, but the West is less certain than ever about what those Western way are. Thus, globalization creates controversy among sociologists, as well as provoking public and political concern. Is it a process that can be stopped? Since much of sociology has developed within and for the benefit of the nation-state, does the discipline have to be seriously revised in view of globalization? Whatever the answers, globalization has become a key issue for the twenty-first century.

■ WHERE IS MY SOCIETY?

How do we best study social life? Should we consider human beings members of one society among many, with their lives bounded by that membership? Or should we take them to be part of an all-inclusive human society to which all people throughout the world belong?

Both of these alternatives have found advocates over the course of centuries of social thought. In sociology in the twentieth century, practical considerations have led us to favour the former. Sociologists have largely treated individuals as belonging to particular societies and, again for mainly practical reasons, have equated societies with the nation-state.[1]

The practical reasons for this preference are very much rooted in who pays for sociology. The discipline's main customer has always been the state, seeking to know about the conditions of life and the attitudes and aspirations of its own citizens, and wanting to train people in the analysis of its society.

The discipline's other major customer has been you, the student, seeking to discover your own place in society. Throughout the world, the nation-state has supported student education in some way, and has often served as a major potential future employer. The nation-state has provided broad foundations for your social life and involves you in its operation through citizenship.

As a result, every national society has its own textbooks in sociology and its own sociological professional associations, journals, and research projects.[2] Most of the major sociological theorists, however, have sought to offer a wider perspective — for Karl Marx, it was capitalism; for Max Weber, an overarching process of rationalization affecting all modern societies. Even Émile Durkheim, whose sociology was partly directed to the renewal of the society he loved (France), made it clear that the processes that threatened it were universal.

Very broadly, then, empirical and applied sociology have treated the nation-state and its citizens as equivalent to a distinct society and its individual members, whereas social theory has drawn our attention to wider social processes. This division of emphasis is becoming increasingly strained today, because worldwide social processes are transforming the relations of citizens and state, of individuals and societies. Consequently, we must begin to look at society in a different way.

This chapter considers the process of world social transformation that has come to be known as globalization. Globalization leaves no society untouched. Indeed, some have called it the process that makes the world a single place (Robertson,

1992: 64) or that binds the population of the world into a single society (Albrow, 1993: 248).

The consequences for sociological analysis are dramatic. Globalization removes the choice between thinking in terms of national societies and thinking in terms of world processes. Because of the latter, individuals increasingly "think globally" while "acting locally," as a currently popular slogan has it. They consider themselves to be part of a worldwide society, and their lives are influenced directly by events and processes that are happening far beyond state boundaries.

In this chapter, we will explore the way in which we can speak of a single world society. We will also identify the changes that have brought this state of affairs about. First of all, however, we must recognize that we are discussing not simply the changing world around us, but also a challenge to the way we analyze that world.

Globalization makes us question the idea of society itself (Giddens, 1990; McGrew, 1992). Think of society for a moment in a commonplace way — as a definite number of people who are conscious of their membership in a group that treats other people as outsiders; that is largely self-directing through state institutions, in which people share values and work within a common framework of law, education, and economic activity; and that occupies a territory known as "our country." Now ask yourself how the kinds of social activities described in Box 17.1 fit this definition of society. Ask yourself which "society" is reflected in the anecdote. The people, the images, the products, the projects, and the values do not appear to belong to any one country in particular. They are manifestations of social and economic systems that have no particular geographical location and in which any part of the world can figure.

Perhaps the world of national societies has been replaced by a multitude of societies of no particular national identity, or perhaps we simply have to treat the whole world as a single society.[3] But in that case, where are the boundaries? And what about membership? Society has changed drastically from our original conception of it. Perhaps we have nothing left that we can call "society" at all.

The questions just posed are not simply the concern of our imaginary student — they preoccupy sociologists and social theorists generally in the world today. Indeed, the prevalence of such issues makes this a time of profound inquiry into the nature of society.

Box 17.1
Where Is My Society?

You get up in the morning, turn on the TV, and watch a mob burn down a temple in India. You snatch a croissant and coffee and are about to leave the apartment when your landlord, who comes from Pakistan, calls and asks if you wouldn't mind buying some Basmati rice on your way home after class. You're unable to run the errand because you've arranged to go to a meeting of the Worldwide Fund for Nature, so you ask a friend to get the rice. He comes back with American rice because he is against the exploitation of child labour in India. You have a fierce argument with him because you can't afford to offend your landlord, since the rent is low and you are saving to go on vacation to Europe this summer. But the argument ruins your plans anyway, because you were going to travel with that very friend, who speaks good French. You regret this turn of events because you very much wanted to see your cousins in France. You telephone your uncle, who reminds you that he has already bought you a plane ticket, because it is cheaper to do so from there. It's all a mess, and you finish up on your own in a bar drinking a Budweiser and listening to a local reggae band.

■ FROM THE MODERN TO THE GLOBAL AGE

▲ UNIVERSALISM, IMPERIALISM, AND CAPITALISM

Globalization takes time. It is also the latest stage in a long development that has brought different parts of the world closer together. We can trace that development through history. Bringing the nature of society into question alerts us to questions of origins and historical development; in other words, it combines historical and sociological inquiry.

How have we come to the point where we can even conceive of a single world society? In response to this question, we might list all the events and inventions that have contributed to bringing people together: the wheel, script, printing, the compass, "discovering" America, the conquest of India, the colonization of Africa, the railways, and the world wars are only a few. We might also attempt to identify forces or impulses that have had an abiding influence over time. Three are notable: universalism, imperialism, and capitalism. Each of these forces is in its own way expansionary, and has led to changing the world; each has characterized Western civilization in particular.

These three forces are not features of the human condition everywhere and at all times. For instance, the oldest continuous civilization is arguably the Chinese, and it has not been characterized by any of them. On the contrary, the core values of its traditional culture were designed to maintain boundaries, tend ancestors, and reproduce sacred social relations. Much the same can be said of the Indian caste system.

Universalism, which seeks truths that apply to all times and places, has its roots in the philosophy of the ancient Greeks. It is the origin of modern science and is closely linked with mathematics. It finds order in chaos and seeks to include all human beings within its frame. Universalism subjects nature and humanity to an all-embracing rationality.

There are both ideal and material expressions of universalism. The notion that all human beings have fundamental rights and are equal in the sight of God is an ideal never attained in reality. "Men are born free but everywhere they are in chains," said Rousseau (1968 [1762]: 49). Material products, in contrast, can be made to universal standards in dimension and weight. Indeed, there is an International Standards Organization that provides such regulations.

Whether in law or science, philosophy or production, universalism involves the impetus to bring everything within a single frame of reference. Its inclusiveness leaves nothing untouched, and although it seems unthreatening as an abstract idea, it has often been accompanied in practice by forceful ways of making the world conform to a single pattern. Conceptual universalism has often been coupled with military imperialism — Bible and sword, Koran and scimitar, *Communist Manifesto* and tank.

Armed conflict is as old as history. However, the success of European countries and, later, the United States in imposing their pattern of institutions on the rest of the world has been unprecedented. With each imperialistic venture, the conquest had to be stabilized and the new regime had to be defended in turn; moreover, in each case, the combination of Western science and administrative rationality secured enduring gains for what has come to be known as the modern way of life.

The expansion of the West over the last 500 years could not have happened without ideas in combination with military force, but the motives behind it were often the quest for wealth, resources, and trade (J.A. Hall, 1985; Mann, 1986). From prehistoric times, the search for opportunities to exchange goods to mutual advantage has stimulated exploration and expansion. Indeed, the economic dynamism of the West arose out of a combination of trade and an expansionary state, with science and religion serving those ends (Wallerstein, 1974). The West developed the distinctive form of systematic production, consumption, means of exchange, and wealth accumulation known as capitalism. Like its partners, universalism and imperialism, capitalism is inherently expansionary, always requiring new markets simply to survive, always seeking to develop new ways of generating profit. At the beginning of the 1990s, with the collapse of state socialism in Eastern Europe, capitalism has finally become the unrivalled world economic system.

▲ THE OUTCOME OF MODERNITY

The Expansion of Modern Culture

The expansion of the West over the last 500 years coincides with what is called the "modern age." But the term *modern* is more than just the name of a time period; it is used to convey the quality of living that results when the new, the technically advanced, and the rational push traditional ways of doing things into the background. We refer in this sense to "modern culture" as well as "modern society."

The idea of culture takes in all the ways of acting and thinking that human beings learn from the previous generation, and all the means of communication — the languages and symbols — through which they express their needs and goals. It is an all-embracing concept. It also poses many of the same problems posed by the idea of society.

Anthropologists have long pointed to the distinctiveness of the cultures of preliterate peoples. They have depicted societies in which language, rituals, and customs make up a way of life that separates one group from another. It was similarly commonplace for historians from the eighteenth century to the recent past to point to the differences among national cultures in Europe, as well as to those between European and non-European cultures, such as the Chinese.

In contrast, the culture of the modern age, with its emphasis on rationality, science, and technology, appears to bring the world into a single frame of reference. The internal-combustion engine and the computer work in the same way in Tokyo as they do in New York, and bring with them similar consequences for ways of living. This phenomenon has been called the "logic of industrialism," and has been cited in evidence of what has come to be known as convergence theory — the idea that all societies are taking on the same characteristics (Kerr et al., 1960).

Modern culture appears to involve the worldwide extension of a dominant culture — that of the West. It even seems that the modern personality is a Western product (Elias, 1978, 1982; Inkeles, 1983). This impression is strengthened by the activities of Western states, which export their forms of administration to developing countries and make their aid dependent on the adoption of Western practices of management, education, and even family life. *Modernization* was the term used to describe efforts by the United States in particular, but by other advanced states as well, to bring Third World countries into the capitalist economic system.

These features of the modern age led Anthony Giddens (1990: 63) to say that "modernity is inherently globalizing." But this raises the prospect of a world without variety, of a uniform way of doing things from which there is no escape. From this point of view, it would seem that Max Weber's threatening vision of an advancing technical and economic machine trapping everyone in an iron cage has indeed become a reality (1976 [1904–5]: 181).

But not everyone has had so gloomy a view of the direction of modernity. The passage from Henry David Thoreau (1927 [1854]) in Box 17.2 shows how it was his sense of the huge variety in kind and place of origin of the world's products that made him feel like a world citizen. The "extent of the globe" inspired him to find unity in diversity.

So a single world might be the outcome of modernity in two quite different ways — as uniformity or as unity in diversity. Today, there is a widespread sense of a third possibility as well: The globe may become a place for many subjective worlds. Not just Thoreau's material goods, but our style of clothes, our music, and our cuisine come from all over the world and combine in an ever-greater variety of lifestyles. We may regard each combination of lifestyles as a different world; subjectively, that is the way each one feels. So much, then, for modern uniformity, or even for an ordered diversity.

But is this not chaos, even the end of modernity (Touraine, 1995)? We clearly need to examine the outcome of modernity more closely.

The Global Shift

As noted earlier, the forces of universalism, imperialism, and capitalism have been at work for centuries making a single world society. But the term *globalization* came into widespread use among social scientists and, later, in the mass media, only in the 1980s. This in itself suggests that the changes of the recent past are something other than the continuation of a long trend. They may reflect a more fundamental transformation.

Think of a project to complete all possible communication links worldwide. That was in effect the outcome of "the modern project." In other words, **modernity,** the expansion of Western rational methods and technology, reached its culmination when communication with all became open to all. When Marshall McLuhan (1962: 31) announced that the "new electronic interdependence recreates the world in the image of a **global village,**" he used the term *global* in a new way to highlight the worldwide direct communication, transmission, and reception of speech and images. The world, or many worlds, now entered one's own locality.

The advent of **globality** released the potential of each individual to think, act, and feel as a global citizen. In one's own locality, it suddenly made sense to relate directly to events in other parts of the world. One could telephone a family member living in another country or watch a hockey game on television that was being played in Moscow. One could campaign for the rights of indigenous peoples in the Amazon or make an investment in the Hong

Box 17.2
Citizen of the World

Commerce is unexpectedly confident and serene, alert, adventurous, and unwearied. It is very natural in its methods, withal, far more so than many fantastic enterprises and sentimental experiments, and hence its singular success. I am refreshed and expanded when the freight train rattles past me, and I smell the stores which go dispensing their odours all the way from Long Wharf to Lake Champlain, reminding me of foreign parts, of coral reefs, and Indian Oceans, and tropical climes, and the extent of the globe. I feel more like a citizen of the world at the sight of a palm-leaf, which will cover so many flaxen New England heads the next summer, the Manilla hemp and coconut husks, the old junk, gunny bags, scrap iron, and rusty nails.

SOURCE: Henry David Thoreau, *Walden, or Life in the Woods* (London: Chapman and Hall, 1927 [1854]), p. 103.

Kong stock exchange. Settled in one's downtown apartment, one could engage meaningfully in any of these activities.

When formerly independent human activities are linked to a global frame of reference, their nature changes. Thus, the woman in a Bangladesh village who made baskets for her family now makes baskets for money and a trader sells them in Vancouver. She was given start-up capital and free contraceptive products by the state, supported by international agencies, all wanting to discourage her from having more children. Even her daily personal and intimate life has apparently become part of a global framework.

It is not only the market forces of capitalism that transform lives. Agencies and movements work together to promote values that take the globe as their point of reference. For example, people who devote their careers to spreading the gospel of family planning are driven by the idea that there is a limit to the population size that the world can sustain. **Globalism** refers to values that make the fate of humanity and the earth the centre of their concern.

Increasingly, globalist values are replacing older universalist values and the political ideologies of industrial societies. The quest for equality and liberty, the secularized heaven on earth that inspired the revolutions of the eighteenth century and the Russian Revolution of 1917, has given way to a focus on improving the quality and conditions of life as lived.

One of the major elements of globalist con-

sciousness now is the vivid realization of the limits in time and space of living on a planet with finite resources. Moreover, once the world came to be seen as one place, it also came to be treated as a common and shared territory. Not far behind was the recognition that it was the *collective* products of human activity globally that were endangering the atmosphere, destroying the forests, and poisoning the oceans.

The global physical environment is now seen as a potent condition and casualty of any lifestyle. Ecology as a global concern focusses on the idea of sustainable development and the management of the world's resources (Sachs, 1993). Sociologists have correspondingly sought to adapt their thinking to take account of this changed social reality. For Ulrich Beck (1992), this has meant thinking of society in terms of response to risk rather than in terms of the distribution of wealth.

This change of outlook has been prompted by world events with far-reaching consequences. The oil-price rises of the early 1970s led Ralf Dahrendorf (1975) to reflect that modern expansion was over and the best we could look forward to was survival with justice. The idea of limits to growth (Meadows et al., 1972) is diametrically opposed to the assumptions of the modern project, which valued expansion above all else. For many people, events like the dropping of the nuclear bombs in 1945 and the dismantling of the Berlin Wall in 1989 signalled the end of old directions and the beginning of something new.

We should recognize the interconnectedness of these changes. Market forces, environmental impacts, communication technology, international politics, and social movements have become interdependent and have all globalized. We can call this a global shift (Dicken, 1992) since the globe seems to enter into each sector and into everyone's lives.

▲ THEORIZING GLOBALIZATION

Social scientists, politicians, and journalists now refer to the way the global affects both social systems and everyday life as "globalization." Compared with classic themes of sociology like social order, class conflict, elites, or bureaucratization, the concept of globalization is very new and in an early stage of theorization. It was not a focus for the founders of the discipline, even though they considered the world as a whole the proper frame of reference for sociology. In their day, the world presented itself as a world of nation-states, not as the place of a single human society.

However, sociologists of globalization today have built upon the classic approaches to theory. The major theorists all sought to show how changes in the wider society worked their way through people's social relations. To do this, they both developed the analysis of social relations and wove this analysis into an account of historical change.

We can follow suit. We can first show how the global now enters into the analysis of social relations. Then we can consider those changes in the recent past that have made the global level more important in our lives.

Let us begin by considering the issue of globalization in terms of **levels of analysis**. We can think of social life as made up of people interacting at three levels: households, communities, and nation-states. Each level is dependent on the others. For instance, the organization of household routines depends in part on how communities organize and schedule schools. Similarly, the state enters into relations between marriage partners in a household — for example, through property law and debates on sexual rights. In practice, all three levels of analysis only exist in and through the lives of individual people.

Now add a fourth level of analysis: global social organization. The inclusion of the global level is evident in discussions of the global becoming local, of worldwide organizations operating locally — for example, McDonald's and the Green Movement, each in its own way a global concern operating at the local level.

If you add a level of analysis, it is clear that you increase the complexity of theory. With only three levels of analysis, we needed to think only in terms of household–community, household–state, and community–state relations — that is, three possible interactions. With a fourth level, there are six possible interactions: global–state, global–community, and global–household, in addition to the other three (see Figure 17.1).

Now let us briefly consider globalization in the light of theories of contemporary social change. We have already mentioned an older theory, that of modernization. Proponents of this school of thought argue that modern society broke with traditional society in Europe sometime between the sixteenth and eighteenth centuries, primarily as a result of the force of industrialization. Ever since, modern culture and ways of living have continued to expand worldwide.

However, the plain fact is that old industries have declined rapidly over the past several decades. New service occupations have emerged, especially in the area of information technology. As a result, new theories of postindustrial society have been formulated, according to which manufacturing industry no longer plays a dominant role in shaping social structure (Bell, 1973; Touraine, 1971). In addition, theories of **postmodernity** argue that, contrary to modernist claims, society is culturally fragmented rather than homogeneous, lacking direction toward "progress" or any other single goal (Lyotard, 1984; Jameson, 1991). One analyst has even claimed that cultural homogeneity and unanimity of purpose never existed and that modernity was therefore always a myth (Latour, 1993).

Globalization has added another dimension to this debate (Waters, 1995). But should we regard globalization as a late stage of modern society? Or is it an aspect of postmodernity and of the general

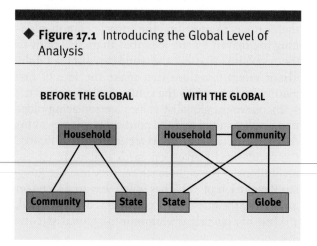

◆ **Figure 17.1** Introducing the Global Level of Analysis

BEFORE THE GLOBAL   WITH THE GLOBAL

Household   Household — Community

Community — State   State — Globe

fragmentation of society, as many postmodern writers declare? Or should we really be talking about a new historical epoch, beyond the modern, but not postmodern either — a **global age** (Laszlo, 1989: 48)? These questions belong to sociological theory conceived as the broadest possible inquiry into the history and development of human society.

Two of the most important contributors to the emerging sociological theory of globalization are Roland Robertson and Anthony Giddens. Both suggest that, as big structures change at the global level, so do people's daily lives.

Robertson (1992: 27) speaks of the **relativization** of selves and societies, the phenomenon whereby each changes in relation to the other in the context of a changing world system. Anthony Giddens (1990: 21–29) emphasizes the notion of **disembedding**: People increasingly put their faith in abstract systems that were organized over the course of decades, span thousands of kilometres, and involve millions of people. A good example is that of lending and exchange in worldwide economic relations.

A central difference between Robertson and Giddens lies in their causal ordering of events. Giddens considers modernity to be a *cause* of globalization. He thus focusses on how new technologies of communication have helped globalize the world. For Robertson, however, the causal sequence is the other way around: Modernity, he says, is the *result* of globalization. Thus, focussing on institutions of social order at the global level and values that focus on globality, Robertson traces their origins back at least 2000 years, long before the modern era.

Other scholars have added to the debate by arguing that both the modern and the postmodern eras are the outcome of globalization (Featherstone, 1995: 81–84; see Hirst and Thompson, 1996, for a critique). My own way out of this disagreement (Albrow, 1997) is simply to define the global age as the time when the global entered our lives as never before. From this point of view, the global age has replaced the modern age only in the last few decades. The transition has taken place not simply because people everywhere relate their lives to global forces and issues, but because they have generally lost confidence in the core feature of modernity — the idea that people's rational control of nature and society is increasing all the time. Knowledge societies (Stehr, 1994) are also risk or "nonknowledge" societies (Beck, 1992). The nuclear bombs dropped on Hiroshima and Nagasaki in 1945 brought this realization as never before: Great scientific achievement can destroy the world. We can now see the repercussions of this event as the beginning of the end for the modern age.

Let us now review different aspects of world social organization, including politics, the economy, social relations, and the media. We will find that globalization has not resulted in a predictable world order. On the contrary, it is taking us into an unknowable future.

■ ONE-WORLD POLITICS

▲ TOWARD A NEW WORLD ORDER?

The event that shook the world more than any other since the end of World War II was the dismantling, in 1989, of the Berlin Wall. The Berlin Wall represented the division of Germany and the rest of the world into two power blocs, led by the United States and the Soviet Union. The latter disintegrated soon after, in 1991, and its subject Eastern European regimes turned away from communism. Almost overnight, it seemed, a **new world order** had appeared.

No situation could better illustrate how paradoxical the consequences of achieving a goal can be. The Cold War — the struggle of Western powers to overcome the communist regimes of the Soviet Union and its allies — had been the dominant structural feature of world politics for half a century. But once it was over, the struggle seemed easier to manage than the victory.

It was not just a "political" event. The former confrontation between two state systems, capitalist and socialist, had important effects on the structures of the two societies. For a start, they were mobilized to meet their opponent's challenge by way of military preparation, industrial production, and ideological schooling. Loyalty to the state also meant loyalty to a way of life that distinguished one's own system from the system of the enemy.

Internal dissent was made more difficult by the conflict. Even in the West, where the idea of legitimate political opposition had long been institutionalized, there were tight limits on organizing opposition and challenging the premises of the society. Movements that protested aspects of government policy, such as opposition to the Vietnam War, were often labelled "unpatriotic." Coal miners on strike in the United Kingdom in 1984 were called "the enemy within." For many years, critics of capitalism in the West ran the risk of being accused of sympathizing with communism, because the Soviet system proclaimed the eventual collapse of capitalism.

The end of the Cold War has had a profound influence on national social structures. There is no longer a clear enemy against which states can organize; the military-industrial complex has lost much of its former political weight; political rhetoric has lost the option of targeting the subversive. The contradictions inherent in capitalism have become more obvious and are less easily attributed to malevolent outside forces. With the removal of the "enemy," the choice of fighting disappears. The system looms larger, and the choices at hand appear to be fewer.

The End of American Hegemony

The effects of the end of the Cold War have been felt most acutely in the United States. As the most powerful state in the West, it assumed the role of leader of the free world, exercising a controlling influence over its allies through the North Atlantic Treaty Organization (NATO) and, indirectly, over the Third World through the International Monetary Fund (IMF) and the World Bank.

There is now no credible external threat to match that which the Soviet Union represented, and, although the existence of nuclear weapons in the hands of unstable former Soviet states makes for an uncertain future and is a constant source of anxiety, those weapons are not aimed in any obvious direction. Thus, the former allies do not need the protection of the superstate.

For a brief period, there was talk of a "new world order," in which the United States would adopt the role of the world's police officer on behalf of the United Nations. The Gulf War appeared to offer that possibility. But, since then, the Bosnian conflict, Somalia, and Rwanda have proven to be intractable problems and have caused international efforts to lose credibility.

In the meantime, the United States' economic dominance, unrivalled since 1945, came to be threatened by Japan. Moreover, all signs indicate that, although the United States is still by far the world's single most powerful state, its scope for controlling events is diminishing all the time. Indeed, its current situation parallels that of previous historical great powers that fell as a result of "imperial overstretch" (Kennedy, 1988: 666).

It is symptomatic of the reigning confusion that a former U.S. government official should trumpet the worldwide "triumph" of liberal democracy as the "end of history" (Fukuyama, 1992)[4] at the same time that the Clinton presidential campaign focussed on the declining position of the United States in world affairs. In fact, the campaign invoked globalization as the underlying reason for the need to reassert national direction and energy. The future vice-president, Senator Al Gore (1992), called for leadership on the part of the United States to save the global environment, and the election was fought on the consequences of globalization for the internal structure of the country and for unemployment, urban deprivation, crime, and health within its boundaries. Meanwhile, as the United States looks to its own problems, many areas in the rest of the world appear to be moving further toward endemic strife as boundaries become unstable and older loyalties are reasserted.

Organizing the State in a Global World

If politics at a world level looks increasingly chaotic, it is because, as the possibility of a single power centre becomes less realistic, there is evidence of a process at work that appears to deprive states of sovereignty and that thereby reinforces the image of a world descending into disorder (Rosenau, 1989). It is not only the United States that feels less powerful; other states are also finding that they have less room to manoeuvre. To a large extent, this is attributable to the fact that the principle of order has moved to another level — namely, that of transnational relations.

Since the establishment of the United Nations, the institutionalization of activities between states and of activities that transcend state boundaries has proceeded almost without check. International civil servants provide assistance for and monitor activities as various as fishing and civil aviation, world health, and the control of drug trafficking. National officials co-operate across national borders and create new transnational forms of discourse.

Commentators such as Martin Jaques (see Box 17.3) link the decline of the nation-state to the process of globalization, often deploring the loss of national control. National politicians may even campaign on the issue. But what is happening is that state functions are being taken over by bodies operating at a different level. It is becoming obsolete to think of the "state" as represented by nation-states and their organs; we have to start thinking of state functions as being distributed among various organizations and agencies, from the United Nations, at one extreme, to the local community council, at the other.

Many have dreamed of the day when the United Nations might become a world government. If by that was meant that the people of the earth would come together to form a single nation-state, then it has obviously not happened. The United Nations can neither tax us nor put us in jail. But it and related agencies do monitor and regulate a huge number of functions that ultimately relate to and affect our behaviour.

Thus, while at one level the world focusses attention on the fragmentation of states such as the Soviet Union and Yugoslavia, at another it tends to overlook the accumulation of powers in organizations and agencies, often regionally based, that are not nation-states. One of the most obvious of these is the European Commission in Brussels, which acts on behalf of the fifteen member states that form the European Union (EU; called the European Community before November 1, 1993).

One very good reason for the lack of media attention on these developments is that the organizations involved in them are not democratically led. Elections are still held within nation-states. The European Parliament has no powers to pass laws or direct the European Commission, just as individuals do not have the right to elect representa-

tives to the United Nations. Insofar as there is a "new world order," it is bureaucratic, not democratic.

This draws our attention to the fact that classic theories of representative democracy have viewed the nation-state as the natural arena for its exercise (Held, 1991: 199). However, because of the impact of transnational forces, including multinational enterprises, the nation-state is losing its control over the destinies of individuals. Increasingly, individuals are looking to, and creating, a politics that has global reference, a politics that David Held (1995) sees as a new order of cosmopolitan democracy.

▲ HUMAN RIGHTS AND GLOBAL MOVEMENTS

Individuals may not have a vote as world citizens, but they do have the ability to influence the agen-

---

Box 17.3
Globalization as the Transformation of Society and Politics

Governments are simply not what they once were. Globalization in all its forms — production, investment, communications, and information — has greatly weakened the power of governments to control what happens within their own borders. And while economics and culture have gone global, politics, parties, and politicians remain determinedly and narrowly national.

But that is relatively old hat. What has not been sufficiently observed is the loss of power by governments and parties within their own societies. Over the postwar period, there has been a veritable explosion of civil society. We are aware that organizations and movements such as Friends of the Earth and Comic Relief have become far more important. But the point is not so much this or that body, but what lies behind them.

Growing prosperity and the rising importance of leisure have helped to transform the interests and identities available to people. We now make our own society to a far greater extent than was ever previously the case. The market is the metaphor which has come to express diversity and choice in the economic sphere, but the same has happened in the cultural domain with an expanding range of lifestyles and a plethora of organizations which express them.

Where once society was governed from a single point, the state, power is everywhere and nowhere, vested in each of us. In the days when governments were the source of authority, the commanding height of society to which citizens showed due respect and deference, their task was relatively easy. Now they are obliged to share power.

SOURCE: Excerpted from Martin Jaques, "Politicians Stand Still While the World Moves On," *The Times* (London), October 4, 1993.

as well. Thus, even as the great economic powers work to make the world a single market, they are apprehensive about the consequences. The United States fears Japanese competition. Newly industrializing countries threaten the industrialized countries. The fears of the latter have been prompted in part by studies that forecast growing unemployment in industrialized countries resulting from the new international division of labour (Fröbel, Heinrichs, and Kreye, 1980).

This theme continues into the 1990s. President Clinton convened a conference of the seven countries with the most powerful economies (the G-7) in Detroit on March 14 and 15, 1994, to address the conventional wisdom that globalization destroys jobs. The conference heard that the global spread of new production practices could have quite different consequences.

▲ GLOBAL PRODUCTION AND CONSUMPTION

The expansion of markets has been associated with the growth of megacorporations whose operations span the globe (Sklair, 1991). These transnational corporations (TNCs) seek both to diversify their activities into every area of the market and to develop goods that will sell everywhere in the world. These are not necessarily compatible objectives, and there is no sure way for a TNC to achieve world dominance. But for the largest TNCs, that has become the aim.

The idea of globalization first gained prominence in the marketing strategies of the TNCs. In the 1970s, Coca-Cola was the most prominent global product. In the 1980s, McDonald's became equated with the globalization process itself — as evidenced in phrases such as the "McDonaldization of everything" and in the use of the prefix "Mc" to denote any standardized activity that can be repeated anywhere (Ritzer, 1992). All TNCs had to develop global strategies for a world market.

Interestingly, the consequences have been twofold: Globalization does not work in only one direction, toward standardization; it may also lead to deliberate local adaptations. From the 1970s onward, firms have sought the right combination of a product standardized the world over yet marketed to appeal to different tastes in different cultures (Yip, 1993). Those cultures in turn respond in their own way to worldwide marketing.

Globalization produces all kinds of contradictory pressures for traditional societies. In order to succeed economically, they must attempt to capture world markets; at the same time, they are under pres-

sure to impose global standards in areas such as environmental conservation. Ancient cultures find themselves trying to resist Western penetration at the same time that they must try to develop an image that will help them sell goods worldwide.

Paradoxically, bringing the world together in one place to show its variety, as in a world exhibition, can give the opposite impression — that of **homogenization,** of repetitive sameness. Don Gifford (1990) has named this phenomenon the "Crystal Palace paradox" after the structure that housed the Great Exhibition in London in 1851 (see Box 17.4).

The world economy now has a very different shape from either Adam Smith's vision of a world of merchants and tradesmen or Marx's grim spectacle of a factory-based urban proletariat. Revolutions in the technology of production replaced the machine worker with the worker on the assembly line, who in turn is giving way to the robot. Developed methods of transportation and communication make it possible for finished products to be assembled anywhere in the world by firms whose offices and plants may be dispersed worldwide. Ownership of firms has lost national identity. Decision making can be conducted with the aid of fax and video-link technology by people located in different countries (Carnoy et al., 1993).

Such developments suggest that globalization does not mean a simple transfer of jobs to areas of low wages (Best, 1990; Oman, 1994). Flexibility has become a watchword in both management practices and production; the old methods associated with assembly-line production and strict hierarchies of managers and workers have given way to a "lean production" approach and new informational links between customers, firms, and component suppliers that now permit local production for local preferences. The globalization of the new information technology has thus encouraged the localization of production, and by reducing direct labour costs, it has prevented the dramatic outflow of jobs from the West to the East that was predicted in the early 1980s. "Post-Fordism," as this general organizational change is often called, also obscures the old divide between managers and workers. It does not, however, reduce power inequalities.

▲ GLOBAL MONEY AND POWER

International Capital

As with politics, economic activity, in becoming global, has also lost its centre. No longer is there a clearly dominant area of production in the world;

The idea of globalization first gained prominence in marketing strategies in the 1970s. In the 1980s, companies like Coca-Cola and McDonald's expanded into non-Western countries in order to find new markets. In the 1990s, Kellogg's markets products in over 160 countries. Basmati Flakes cereal was first produced by the plant in Tajola, India, in 1992. SOURCE: Reproduced with permission of Kellogg's Co.

there are now many important areas. Even if Japan is the most prominent new manufacturing nation, it is threatened by competition from the developing Asian economies of Korea, Taiwan, Singapore, Thailand, and, in the longer run, China. Moreover, Japanese corporations themselves have established plants that employ Japanese methods in North America and Europe. Everywhere, governments feel bound to encourage foreign direct investment. This is bringing Asian wage levels closer to North American and Western European levels. (See Figure 17.2.)

Nowhere is the loss of independence of national economies demonstrated better than in the sphere of financial capital. At one time, money for investment in a given national economy came predominantly from within that country, and the stock exchanges traded in stocks and shares of companies based in that country. But now, more than half the value of shares traded in London, for instance, are for overseas stocks. Furthermore, the major investors are no longer individuals; banks, insurance compa-

nies, and pension funds now conduct more than half the trading in all the major investment centres. These organizations are prepared to invest anywhere in the world.

Governments themselves, having promoted the freeing of financial markets, now find that they have to follow the dictates of those markets. Increasingly, they find themselves limited in their taxation policies, because capital can move to countries with favourable tax regimes and the rich can move easily to escape high individual tax bills.

Global Cities

The great financial centres are global in terms of both the activities they finance and the people who do the financing (King, 1990; Sassen, 1991). Although these centres are located within nation-states, their operations are largely independent of national control and the transactions conducted in them are part of the global economic system.

Box 17.4
The Crystal Palace Paradox

The variety of exhibits was so impressive, their sheer quantity so overwhelming, that even the most studious mind couldn't hope to take it all in. By a sublime law of paradox, this rich variety disappears off one end of the spectrum and reappears as an elaborately homogenized sameness at the other. The Crystal Palace ushered in the vision of sameness in variety that our grandparents faced in the Sears, Roebuck Catalog and that we face daily in supermarkets and shopping malls and on the television set and the flood of mail-order catalogs, the wish books that clutter the daily mail. In this world of homogenized variety, tourism becomes an endless shopping trip, the quest for the grail of something completely different. The national boutique-supermarket-mall dissolves its boundaries to include overseas and urges on us the paradox of that democratic torrent of mass-produced variety and uniqueness that adds up to more than we can comprehend of the homogenized one-and-the-same.

SOURCE: Excerpted from Don Gifford, *The Farther Shore: A Natural History of Perception* (New York: Atlantic Monthly Press, 1990), pp. 129–30.

◆ **Figure 17.2** Wage Changes Adjusted for Price Changes, by Region, 1995–2005

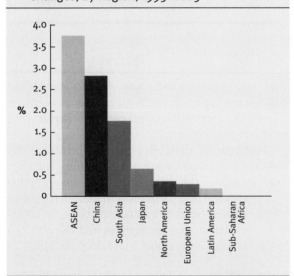

Note: Wages in Asia (especially in the ASEAN countries of Thailand, Singapore, Philippines, Indonesia, and Brunei) will converge with those in North America and the European Union over the next decade, but wages in Latin America and Sub-Saharan Africa will diverge from North American and Western European wage levels.

SOURCE: Adapted from United Nations Development Program, *World Development Report 1995: Workers in an Integrated World* (New York: Oxford University Press, 1995), p. 57.

Thus, although London is the capital city of a state whose economy is relatively minor in today's world league, it is the world's largest foreign-exchange transaction centre, as well as being second only to Tokyo as a banking centre. But the banking conducted in this centre is not predominantly British; it is dominated by Japanese and U.S. banks.

Cities such as London, New York, and Tokyo are not simply centres for financial transactions. They are places people live in and visit (Budd and Whimster, 1992). But more and more of the people who stay there look to the rest of the world for both their personal ties and their business interests. Similarly, these cities hold a strong attraction for people from the rest of the world. For these reasons, they have come to be called **global cities**.

An International Elite

The globalization of capital is not simply a matter of large organizations gaining ever-increasing control over the world's economy. With globalization, the chances for people to accumulate vast personal fortunes have also increased. For example, in 1992, the Hungarian financier George Soros gained more than a billion dollars in speculating on the devaluation of the British pound.

Financiers and executives of multinational enterprises think of the world as their market. They are also prepared to place and spend their personal fortunes anywhere in the world. They may divide their time among several residences in different countries, and they enjoy a lavish, "jet-setting" lifestyle. It should be noted that, today, it is not only capitalists who live in this style. The senior employees of international organizations have also become used to a lifestyle in which they may be posted anywhere in the world and are rewarded in a way that sets them apart from the local population.

Globalization has also affected the lives of sports and media stars: Their fame is directly dependent on catering to a world audience, and they must travel widely to cultivate their markets. They take part in global tournaments and concert tours, and may maintain residences in various places in the world.

In the 1950s, American sociologist C. Wright Mills (1956) made an enormous impact with his book *The Power Elite,* in which he explored the connections between money, politics, and fame in the United States. What he observed then with respect to a single country can now be found at the global level.

The members of the **international elite** speak English as their primary language, but are often bilingual; spend leisure time together; intermarry; send their children to international schools; and often have more than one nationality (Van der Pijl, 1989). Whether this elite has the capacity or the collective will to exercise power on behalf of the world as a whole, as well as in its own interests, is a great open question.

■ SOCIAL RELATIONS WITHOUT FRONTIERS

▲ TIME, SPACE, AND TRAVEL

Members of the international elite can cross the boundaries of nations and cultures with ease. Distance is not a major obstacle to their social relations. But they are not alone in being able to overcome what used to be insuperable barriers of time and space. Modern means of transportation allow people and goods to travel once-unthinkable distances; telephones make it possible to talk to someone on the other side of the world; satellites beam images worldwide; recording technology enables us to preserve the voices and images of people from the past. All this amounts to what has been called **time–space compression** (Harvey, 1989: 241), which has led us to perceive the world very differently from the way our predecessors perceived it. Places that were once remote have come within our reach; the past has become familiar to us.

The possibilities of travel and communication over long distances increased throughout the modern period. Improvements in navigation made possible the sea voyages that led to the expansion of Europe at the beginning of the modern era. Later, trains, automobiles, and planes appeared in quick succession, opening up travel in previously unimaginable ways for millions of people (see Table 17.1).

These changes have had consequences for the economy and culture. Possibilities for the transportation of goods have revolutionized world trade. The possibility of separating home and workplace has changed both production methods and the shape of human settlement. Finally, what now claims to be the world's largest industry, tourism, has developed on the basis of cheap means of transportation for the masses.

These developments in transportation must be related to the development of distance communications. In the nineteenth century, a worldwide postal system made it possible to send a letter from New York to London and get a reply within a month. Facsimile machines now make it possible to send a letter in minutes. There is now an international telephone

◆ **Table 17.1** World Air Transport, 1950–1992

Year	People (billion passenger kilometres)	Freight (million ton kilometres)
1951	35	0.9
1956	71	1.5
1961	128	2.4
1966	230	5.6
1971	494	13.2
1976	762	21.4
1981	1119	30.9
1986	1452	43.2
1991	1842	58.5

SOURCE: Adapted from Lester R. Brown, Hal Kane, and Ed Ayres, *Vital Signs: The Trends That Shape Our Future* (New York: W.W. Norton, 1993), p. 91. Copyright © 1993 by Worldwatch Institute. Used by permission of W.W. Norton & Company, Inc.

network that allows direct dialling between individual numbers in most of the countries of the world at a cost accessible to the mass of telephone subscribers. And scores of millions of Internet users are now able to send each other text, images, and sounds — all virtually instantly.

Taken together, developments in travel and telecommunications have transformed personal relationships as well as business practices and leisure activities. Consider, for example, the effects of modern-day travel. If we travel to another country, we are free to return home whenever we please; the Quaker Pilgrims, in contrast, had to assume that they would never again see the families they had left behind. Today, we can stay in close contact with our families by telephone. In fact, we can have family and friends in several countries, and remain "close" nonetheless. That may be important for financial as well as emotional reasons. People are freer to travel because it is so easy to stay in contact.

Thus, the personal interactions that once had to be conducted within a relatively small territory can now span the globe. Because of the dramatic reduction in the time it takes to communicate across space, relationships can be maintained irrespective of physical distances between people. As noted earlier, Giddens (1991) called this phenomenon disembedding — the lifting of social relations out of local context.

The consequences of the communications revolution for interpersonal relationships have not yet been fully documented. People have certainly been freed from many of the territorial and nation-state constraints that had previously been taken for granted. In that sense, the effects of the new technologies are political as well, constituting another element in the loosening of nation-state control. But, in yet another paradox of globalization, advanced communications technology simultaneously facilitates surveillance of people by the state.

The results of time–space compression can be contradictory. Although we have greater access to more people and places, familiar things tend to disappear more quickly. The faster pace of life is linked to the speed with which things pass away: Our contacts with people and things have become more ephemeral. Although opportunities to find the best of everything may have increased, the best, by definition, can be found in just one place in the world. Both worldwide fame and ease of travelling promote the development of unique world centres such as Hollywood for films, Silicon Valley for computers, and the Parisian Left Bank for philosophy — this is known as the "Mecca effect," Mecca being the place revered above all other places by Muslims. Although ease of travel may make location immaterial, it may also cause physical space to be guarded more jealously than ever. We will encounter similar paradoxes in the following discussion of migration and tourism.

Migration

The ease of travel and of maintaining communication over long distances has made migration less harrowing. At the same time, the globalization of the world's economy has opened up greater possibilities to move from one country to another in search of work (Castles and Miller, 1993).

The stresses that have arisen from the globalization of politics have caused growing numbers of people to try to flee their countries. The availability of advanced means of travel has facilitated these attempts. Consequently, the number of refugees throughout the world has been increasing steadily in recent years. For example, thirteen years of war in Afghanistan resulted in about 6 million people leaving that country, and, in 1991, turmoil in Eastern Europe following the dissolution of Soviet power led to 28 000 Albanians seeking in vain to enter Italy in one weekend (Brown, Kane, and Ayres, 1993: 100).

The twin impact of growing numbers of immigrants and refugees is especially evident in Germany. In 1990, there were more than 5 million foreign residents in the federal republic, constituting 8.2 percent of the total population. They were made up of both long-resident immigrant workers, primarily from Turkey, and refugees from the collapsing Eastern European regimes. By 1993, there had been numerous outbreaks of violence against immigrants and refugees alike.

Whether searching for work or fleeing political oppression, foreigners in a new country look to people of similar origin for mutual support. In doing so, they create the circumstances that allow them to bring up families in their own cultural traditions. This pattern can pose a problem for nation-states, which usually set state education standards, marriage laws, and health and employment requirements.

States have increasingly been pursuing policies of **multiculturalism** in an attempt to reduce tensions among the various ethnic groups within their borders. This trend, coupled with the relative ease with which members of immigrant groups can maintain contact with their countries of origin, has meant that ethnic identity can more easily be maintained abroad and that it can be separated from territory.

The various minorities in different countries belong to worldwide ethnic or racial communities and, increasingly, do not expect to return to a homeland. For instance, Poles living outside of Poland make up what they call "Polonia" and are almost as numerous as Poles in Poland, to which few expect to return to live. But, as an ethnic group, they maintain close contact with one another through social networks and organizations throughout the world.

Immigration always reflects the situation in the wider world. Two factors determine the composition of an immigrant population — who the host country will accept and who seek to enter. Canada's inflow of immigrants reflects as much the increasing diversity of the world flow of migrants as it does immigration policy. By 1969, 80 percent of arrivals in Canada came from 22 countries; in 1988, the same percentage came from 37 countries (Basavarajappa, Beaujot, and Samuel, 1993). Table 17.2 shows how the distribution of immigrants in Canada is increasingly coming to reflect the population proportions of the world as a whole. The mosaic is becoming global. Figure 17.3 illustrates the same process in different regions of the world.

Tourism

Travel for noneconomic reasons has deep roots in history. The political envoy figures in the earliest historical accounts. In the premodern period, pilgrims often travelled hundreds of kilometres, inspired by the hope of salvation. The medieval wandering scholar was the forerunner of the modern scientific conference. The Grand Tour of the eighteenth century was designed to educate the young men of the European aristocracy.

To a large extent, these early forms of travel attested to the supranational nature of cultural and political ties. Often, their purpose was to seek historical relics of common culture. Early travel was undertaken in full awareness of the wider community of human beings. In short, it was an early intimation of the possibility of world society.

Modern tourism is an industry that mass-produces intimations of the possibility of access to historic roots and cultural diversity (MacCannell, 1976). It promotes fantasies of personal fulfilment against the backdrop of images of exotic places. At the same time, it reproduces the comforts of modern furnishings, sanitation, and cuisine, which make the experience predictable in any setting.

Tourism thus operates at two levels. It brings quite disparate cultures into contact and promises the experience of otherness, while producing a standard tourist environment recognizable anywhere in the world. The search for difference generates global sameness.

▲ THE GLOBAL VILLAGE

News and Risk

Advances in communication technology have made it possible to transmit voice and image instanta-

♦ **Table 17.2** Percentage Distribution of Immigrants into Canada by Place of Birth, 1946–1991

Year	Europe	U.S.A., Australia, Other	Latin America	Africa	Asia
1946	79.4	18.7	0.8	0.3	0.8
1951	92.3	4.9	0.5	0.2	2.1
1956	88.5	6.9	1.2	0.8	2.5
1961	75.8	15.8	3.0	1.8	3.6
1966	75.3	9.8	4.1	2.6	8.1
1971	42.8	20.5	13.5	3.0	20.3
1976	32.6	11.6	17.8	6.0	31.9
1981	34.1	8.6	12.3	4.8	40.1
1986	22.7	7.7	21.6	5.2	42.8
1991	20.8	4.2	16.0	7.0	52.0

SOURCE: Adapted from K.G. Basavarajappa, R.P. Beaujot, and T.J. Samuel, *Impact of Migration in the Receiving Countries: Canada* (Geneva: International Organization for Migration, 1993), p. 44.

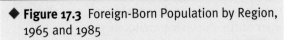

◆ **Figure 17.3** Foreign-Born Population by Region, 1965 and 1985

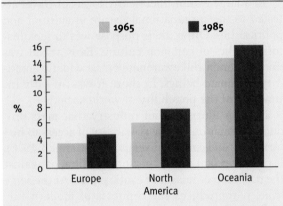

Note: The integration of the world economy between 1965 and 1985, combined with the ease of international travel, has led to increases in the foreign-born populations of the Western industrial nations.

SOURCE: Adapted from the United Nations Development Program, *World Development Report 1995: Workers in an Integrated World* (New York: Oxford University Press, 1995), p. 65.

neously to any part of the world. Television and radio program producers do not feel compelled to take advantage of these technical possibilities for their own sake. But the opportunity to do so is always there, waiting for the suitable motive.

Globalist values provide just the kind of motive that finds the new technology appropriate and that can overcome local resistance to the introduction of that technology. If the cause is big enough, it is possible to network an event or a program throughout the world, reinforcing the global message. But the promoters of the cause have to work at disseminating information about it. They have to make the linkage between fighting world famine, an all-star rock concert, and a satellite television transmission. Globalism — the adoption of values that apply concretely to people all over the world — does not sweep all before it.

Even those who have no commitment to globalist values find that global events nonetheless impinge on their lives and that global information is relevant to them. For example, the assassination of President Kennedy in 1963 was shattering for people in the United States, but it also sent a shudder throughout the globe, largely because of the political interdependence of the world during the Cold War period. Even those who were opposed to Kennedy were affected, faced with the possible consequences of sudden global uncertainty. It has often been said

that the death of Kennedy was unique in the pervasiveness of its impact: Everyone who lived through it can remember what they were doing when they heard the news.

The objective interdependence of the world combines with the scientific knowledge of the modern period to produce what Ulrich Beck (1992) has called "global risk." Science has not only produced innovations that have worldwide application, it has also become aware of the consequences of their use for the world. For example, one product of nuclear physics is the nuclear reactor, which provides energy for industrial and everyday uses. Scientists are able to predict the likelihood of an accident involving a reactor, the amount of radio-active fall-out that could be expected from it, and the consequences it would have for the health of both the current population and future generations. Safety measures are in place to prevent such accidents or, if they occur, to minimize their consequences. Such preparedness for the anticipated consequences of one's actions is called "reflexivity."

Globalized conditions of life involve becoming attuned to global risk. An awareness of global risk as ever-present was sustained during the Cold War by the rhetoric of the opponents and the activities of the peace movement, which sought the destruction of nuclear weapons. A worldwide interest in peace then transcended boundaries and patriotic commitments. News items about nuclear tests and the protests organized against them gained worldwide interest.

Although the risk of accidental nuclear holocaust remains, people have been less preoccupied with it since the end of the Cold War. The destruction of the ozone layer and the danger of global warming have attracted more attention. The world's ecology has become a matter of concern to individuals. Many who were involved in the peace movement have since transferred their commitment to the ecological movement, a current worldwide focus of concern.

Viewing risk globally takes place at both the individual and the organizational level. Individuals may accord great weight to the future of the planet even if the risks during their own lifetime are minuscule. Their commitment is a matter of values. Large organizations think in terms of global risk for several reasons. The attitudes of millions of individuals are important to the extent that they create a vast market for new products. Corporations thus take both individuals' values and the objective global risks into account in conceiving and selling such new lines as "green" products. Other kinds of corporations consider the chances that global warming will alter objective conditions. Thus, the largest reinsurance company in the world, Munich-Re, has increased its premiums for customers with property in low-lying regions.

In recent years, there has been an increasing amount of news coverage of global risks. A hurricane, such as Hurricane Andrew in the West Indies and Florida in 1992, produces dramatic images, which it is now technically feasible to transmit worldwide on channels such as CNN. In addition, natural disasters have major consequences for the world insurance market, because the risks are so extensive that they have been distributed among insurance providers worldwide. Thus, such events are news at many levels.

The current global scope of the media and the correspondingly vast market to which they extend make them attractive commercial prizes. Consequently, worldwide multimedia conglomerates, such as Rupert Murdoch's News Corporation, are being built up, incorporating a mix of television, radio, film, and publishing companies. Those who fear that globalization implies homogenization see the threat of worldwide cultural domination in this growth of global media giants. They take no comfort in the fact that Microsoft president Bill Gates has lately turned his attention to buying large blocs of shares in major North American cable companies.

The threat of global political domination by media conglomerates is also feared, since the capacity to influence opinion worldwide is now open to them, whereas it is beyond the scope of political leaders working within the confines of nation-states. A global cultural hegemony exercised by media moguls is not what those who want a peaceful world order have advocated.

Fame and Fashion

Global media enhance the possibility of global fame. In the 1920s, the movies made Rudolph Valentino a household name, as they did Marilyn Monroe in the 1950s. In the 1960s, the vinyl sound-recording disc gave the world Elvis Presley and the Beatles. In the 1980s, the video-recording tape provided Madonna and Michael Jackson, entertainers in sight and sound.

Music and film appear to obey the same laws of concentration of production that hold for material goods. The massive size of the English-speaking market, ownership of advanced technology, and access to the capital needed to launch a product on the worldwide market combine to facilitate U.S. domination of a mass culture that threatens the survival of distinct national cultures. Even if the political

domination of the United States no longer seems assured, the American superstar appears to exercise another kind of hold on the world.

However, homogeneity is not a necessary outcome of advances in media technology. A visitor to Eastern Europe or China in the 1970s would have heard completely homogenized — indeed, identical — messages broadcast into houses, streets, and fields by means of quite primitive radio communication. The content of those broadcasts was under tight political control. Conversely, governments today can actively promote national culture to counteract homogenization (usually Americanization). The Canadian government, for example, set up Telefilm Canada to produce television programs that have local appeal but that are also able to attract international sales. Although financial constraints have often put the survival of such efforts in doubt, new computerized production technologies hold out the hope for inexpensive local production that will enable local programming to compete successfully for audiences (Perlmutter, 1993).

New technology even makes it possible for individuals to generate their own media products. People make video recordings of their own activities, create their own travel films and Web pages, take part in interactive television programs from their own homes, and perform popular songs with full instrumental backup before audiences. The technology that facilitates the latter, called karaoke, allows for a form of individual participation in mass culture that bears a certain stamp of Japanese culture — namely, that culture's predilection for customized products. One might argue, however, that, despite allowing for a kind of individual expression, karaoke simply standardizes tastes around commercially promoted world (largely American) music. After all, Japanese karaoke singers delight in singing in English.

There is a more substantial criticism of the homogenization thesis that focusses on the contemporary fragmentation and diversification of cultural expression. Let us consider the case of fashion. Although the penetration of American mass culture into national cultures may weaken the hold of nation-states on their citizens, this intrusion is not the only source of cultural change. Today, national cultures are open to influences from all over the world. Top fashion designers often combine different ethnic elements in a single outfit or even a single article of clothing. American blue jeans may have acquired universal appeal, but students today often combine them with a shirt from India or a sweater from Guatemala and a Jamaican cornrow hairstyle.

Interracial and interethnic marriages have increased dramatically in recent years. In order to dramatize this phenomenon, the editors of *Time* magazine used computer "morphing" to illustrate the various combinations of offspring that might result from the mating of seven men and women of various ethnic and racial backgrounds. *Time* suggests that this chart is a preview of the faces of the multicultural society that is likely to emerge in the twenty-first century. SOURCE: Ted Thia/Time Magazine. Computer morphing by Kin Wah Lam. Design by Walter Bernard and Milton Glaser.

Clothes and hairstyles are only one form of cultural expression that permits a blending of ethnic themes and individual choice. Food is another. Not only is it possible to choose from Indian, Italian, Chinese, French, Mexican, Caribbean, Middle Eastern, and many other ethnic foods in most major cities today, but the food people prepare for themselves at home is increasingly characterized by a mix of recipes and ingredients from different culinary traditions.

In general, the intensification of communication worldwide, the enhancement of possibilities for travel, and the globalization of the economy actually permit individuals to make an increasingly personalized choice from among the diverse cultural resources available to them. The fragmentation of culture leaves people free to make up their own minds, choose their own style, find their own identity. As a result, old identities are replaced by new, original ones that some observers have termed *hybrid* (S. Hall, 1992: 310–14). We can therefore set against homogenization the apparently equal and opposite tendency of **hybridization**. Each is directly related to the overall process of globalization, and both seem to be in equal evidence in the world today. Which one we choose to deplore and which to applaud depends more on personal values than on the objective predominance of the one over the other. In other words, globalization does not present us with a case of building a "world-nation" on the historical model of the building of nation-states.

We can contrast the current situation with that of earlier times, when the building of the United States was the prime example of creating national identity. American identity was created in a "new" territory and in the context of an outside environment of existing nation-states. Today, we are witnessing the multiplication of new identities *within* existing nation-states. Consequently, there is no reason to think that the outcome will be the same.

Indeed, Anthony Giddens (1991: 5) suggests that globalization forces individuals into a process of self-inquiry, because the fundamental indeterminacy of the world around them creates anxiety and ontological insecurity: "The more tradition loses its hold, and the more daily life is reconstituted in terms of the dialectical interplay of the local and the global, the more individuals are forced to negotiate lifestyle choices among a diversity of options."

Thus, globalization engenders choice and uncertainty quite as much as it promotes sameness. The traditional idea of home as a private place bounded in material and nonmaterial ways from outside influences gives way to an image of it as a cultural site, an arena of discretionary consumption, wired to receive global messages (Putnam, 1993). In this respect, the idea of globalization easily merges with the notion of a postmodern culture (Harvey, 1989; Jameson, 1991) — no single style dominates; a confusion of images from different parts of the globe come together in one place.

■ TOWARD WORLD SOCIETY?

Even if globalization does not signal a new age, its main theorists view it at least as a fundamental transformation of the old one. If that is the case, we can expect sociological concepts to undergo a fundamental change as well — a discomfiting prospect for those who have become accustomed to them. Sociology originates in the modern age; if the modern changes, so must the discipline.

Take an idea such as community. It has long held a key position in sociological theory. In the late nineteenth century, the small rural community in which everyone knows everyone else was regarded as a point of departure against which the cities and associations that developed later, in industrial society, could be compared. Then it was recognized that cities could also contain within them familiar localities, neighbourhoods, and milieux in which people also felt at home with one another. The notion of "belonging" was thus removed from the rural. But if one takes into account the attachments that people feel to those who are distant from them — particularly the attachment migrants feel for family and compatriots in their homeland — one recognizes that "belonging" does not depend on being in the same place. For this reason, Benedict Anderson (1986) suggests that we recognize nations as "imagined communities" that are not essentially linked to a territorially based nation-state. The nation is not the only concept that has to be revised when we separate place from social unit. Since globalization involves this separation, it has consequences for a whole range of sociological concepts (Albrow et al., 1994).

Suppose we find the lifestyles of a group of people congenial and we join with them for that reason. People who relate to each other out of shared private interests and consumption patterns form what Robert Bellah and his colleagues (1985: 71–75) call a "lifestyle enclave." Young people, in particular, group together on the basis of lifestyle. A recurrent theme in Douglas Coupland's *Generation X* (1991) is

Box 17.5
Global Lifestyles

In his acclaimed first novel *Generation X,* Canadian author Douglas Coupland finds many ways of depicting the confusions and uncertainties of living in a globalized culture. Coupland has one of his three central characters, Andy, mock a younger brother who lives at home, wants to work in a big corporation, and spends all his money on clothes:

> How cliquish are these *Global Teens?* It really boggles. Not one of them can go to Waikiki for a simple one-week holiday, for example, without several enormous gift-laden send-off parties in one of three classic sophomoric themes: Tacky Tourist, Favourite Dead Celebrity, or Toga. And once they arrive there, nostalgic phone calls soon start: sentimental and complicated volleys of elaborately structured trans-Pacific conference calls flowing every other day, as though the jolly vacationer had just hurtled toward Jupiter on a three-year mission rather than six days of over-priced Mai Tais on Kuhio Street.
>
> They're nice kids. None of their folks can complain. They're *perky.* They embrace and believe the pseudoglobalism and ersatz racial harmony of ad campaigns engineered by the makers of soft drinks and computer inventoried sweaters. (p. 106)

But Andy has his own problems with the global. He lives adrift with Claire and Dag in the California desert, looking for a different kind of life, but remaining dependent on the casual "Mcjobs" that the global economy supplies. When he leaves for Mexico, his Volkswagen, containing its two dozen bottles of Evian water, is surrounded by locals in their Hyundais. He is caught in what Coupland calls "terminal wanderlust":

> A condition common to people of transient middle-class upbringings. Unable to feel rooted in any one environment, they move continually in the hopes of finding an idealized sense of community in the next location. (p. 171)

SOURCE: Excerpts taken from Douglas Coupland, *Generation X: Tales for an Accelerated Culture* (New York: St. Martin's Press, 1991), pp. 106, 171. Copyright © 1991 by Douglas Coupland. Reprinted by permission of St. Martin's Press Incorporated.

the quest for a new style in a globalized world (see Box 17.5). Older people also seek out lifestyle companions, as exemplified by the large numbers of people who migrate to Florida on retirement. They do gather together in one place, but on a quite different basis from traditional communities.

The other side of the coin is that people living in a locality may have little to do with each other. This is just what gives rise to the lament for lost community and the communitarian movement to renew American society inspired by the sociologist Amitai Etzioni (1994). But if people find their meaningful ties at a distance, loss of local community may matter little to them. Indeed, John Eade (1997) has identified new local social processes as global

in extent. Through computer linkages, for example, we find new "socioscapes" in the city, people co-existing in a single place but engaged in social relations at a distance, familiar milieux that extend far beyond the locality to the ends of the earth.

Now consider the kind of belonging that brings people together on a computer network. People who share an interest today can communicate instantly worldwide not just by telephone and fax but also by computer, over the Internet. They can use the Net to discuss business, scientific research, political views, sex, or rare birds. Indeed, there is no limit to the number of people or topics that can be involved. This new form of community is known as the **telecommunity** or *virtual community.*

In sum, globalization involves the transformation both of our lives and of the way we talk about them, both in everyday language and in sociological terms. It is up to the discipline to consider also whether globalization transforms the very idea of society, the most general concept on which sociology has traditionally been centred.

On the basis of the foregoing discussion, three alternative views of the future of society are possible. One is that the fragmentation of modern life and the transformation of the nation-state that goes with it involve the disintegration of society itself. This is a radical view that often inspires strenuous political and religious debate. The second alternative suggests that the new forms of life and relationships developing in a globalized world make the idea of society, which has been so closely associated with the nation-state, obsolete and in need of replacement (see Mann, 1986; Bauman, 1992). The third possible view is to accept that the relationships that bind people can now crisscross the globe and that the institutions we depend on are worldwide in scope. This view allows us to argue that we can retain the idea of society if we revise it to take account of world society (see Albrow, 1990; Archer, 1991).

Each of us should consider which of these alternatives our understanding of globalization leads us to accept, bearing in mind that our choice is likely determined by our subjective reactions to the changes implied by globalization. My own choice among the three alternatives is the third one — but that tells you as much about me as about globalization. Projecting an idea of society on to the world as a whole effectively resumes a tradition that is as old as social thought itself and was interrupted by the modern limitation of society to the boundaries of the nation-state. It emphasizes the inherently social nature of human beings and affirms the potential of social relationships to cross artificial limits of time and space set by political authority. World society in this sense is not a larger and more comprehensive version of the nation-state; it is the sum total of the relations between human beings as they develop throughout the globe, and it leaves the prospective shape of those relations open. We can only guess at future social arrangements. At least we can safely say that, as long as people are allowed to travel and communicate freely worldwide, the diversification of this world society — the continuous formation of new groups and social arrangements of all kinds — will continue. ■

SUMMARY

1. Whereas the West expanded to take in the whole world, globalization is the transformation of the world as a whole.

2. Globalization may be seen as ushering in a new historical period and as creating a level of social organization beyond that of the nation-state.

3. The end of the Cold War has resulted not in a unitary power centre for the world, but rather in a new sense of interdependence and a perceived weakness of the nation-state.

4. Although the world economy has become a single transnational system, globalization may nonetheless promote local production.

5. The people of the world travel and communicate across national borders as never before, lifting social relations out of their local contexts.

6. Global images and information from the mass media enhance global consciousness and facilitate the development of new globalist social movements.

7. Globalization can impinge on people's everyday lives in ways that create anxiety and insecurity, and cause them to re-evaluate their identity and lifestyle.

8. Homogenization and hybridization are equally possible outcomes of globalization.

9. Globalization challenges existing conceptions of society, compelling us to devise more suitable alternatives for the twenty-first century.

QUESTIONS TO CONSIDER

1. What do you consider to be the forces underlying globalization? Will they continue to have an impact in the future, and are they more likely to produce order or disorder in the world?
2. What are the effects of globalization on democratic participation? Do people have more or less control over their national governments as a result?
3. Think of the different ways in which globalization could affect employment in Canada. Are your job prospects better or worse as a result?
4. Why do people choose to watch foreign programs and to take holidays abroad? Do these and similar choices undermine national culture?
5. On the basis of what you know about globalization, do you
   a. think it means that society is disintegrating?
   b. regard the idea of society as outdated?
   c. prefer to think in terms of world society or of other possible outcomes for society?

GLOSSARY

disembedding The act of lifting social relationships out of local settings and maintaining them over indefinite times and distances.

global age The contemporary period of history when the globe is relevant to both everyday lives and social units of all sizes.

global cities Cities, such as London, New York, and Tokyo, that are centres of activity for the global economy, with an importance extending far beyond the boundaries of the nation-states in which they are situated.

global village Refers to the immediate experience of sights and sounds from anywhere in the world when transmitted by electronic media.

globalism An orientation to values that identify the world as the focal point of concern.

globality The quality of relating to or deriving from the world as a whole.

homogenization The removal of all differences.

hybridization The combination of two or more different influences or types in a single entity.

international elite The people who have the greatest amounts of power, wealth, or fame in the world and who put them to use with relative disregard for national boundaries.

levels of analysis Differing degrees of scale and scope in social organization.

modernity The complex of features that has distinguished Western cultures and societies over the last 300 or 400 years; it includes, above all, rationality, individualism, and the quest for improvements and novelty.

multiculturalism The policy that treats different cultures as having the right to equal treatment.

new world order The idea that, with the end of the Cold War, the world was free to devise a new set of principles for international relations that would be consensual and predictable.

postmodernity Also, "the postmodern"; a term used widely in the arts, literature, philosophy, history, and the social sciences during the last 40 years to refer either to contemporary alternatives to modernity or to what may come after it. (The term *postmodernism* refers to the ideas and practices of movements, usually literary or artistic, that aim to develop such alternatives.)

relativization The process of altering the way the nature of a thing is perceived by considering it from a different standpoint.

telecommunity A community in which relationships are maintained at a distance through telecommunications.

time–space compression The effect of processes that speed up the pace of life and seem to shrink the space that surrounds us.

universalism The doctrine that human existence depends on principles that hold for all times and places.

SUGGESTED READING

Archer, M. (1991). "Sociology for One World: Unity and Diversity." *International Sociology, 6,* 131–47. A reprint of the presidential address delivered to the Twelfth World Congress of Sociology, held in Madrid in 1990, which took "sociology for one world" as its theme. Archer provides the authentic flavour of heated scholarly debate, in particular attacking a relativism that would see sociology disintegrate and advocating an international sociology concerned with "the integration of diversity."

Brecher, J., J. Brown Childs, and J. Cutler, eds. (1993). *Global Vision: Beyond the New World Order.* Boston: South End Press. Thirty-two brief essays by a worldwide selection of authors, amounting to what the editors call "a manifesto for globalization-from-below" and a critique of "globalization-from-above" by multinational corporations and the world's richest countries.

Brown, L.R., H. Kane, and E. Ayres. (1992, 1993). *Vital Signs: The Trends That Shape Our Future.* New York: W.W. Norton. A Worldwatch Institute annual publication tracking global trends, with tables for key indicators and commentary on food, agriculture, energy, the atmosphere, the economy, transport, and social and military matters.

Coupland, D. (1991). *Generation X: Tales for an Accelerated Culture.* New York: St. Martin's Press. This is a first novel by a Canadian author in which three characters in their 20s experiment in their lives and imaginations with the paradoxes of contemporary culture. Look for the global themes and symbols in it.

Giddens, A. (1990). *The Consequences of Modernity.* Stanford, CA: Stanford University Press. Based on lectures at Stanford University in 1988, this is an ambitious interpretation of the direction of modernity, linking globalization to transformations in temporal and spatial organization of social relations, and to risk, trust, and personal security.

Robertson, R. (1992). *Globalization: Social Theory and Global Culture.* Newbury Park, CA: Sage. Based on a series of essays and commentaries dating from 1985 by the scholar who first argued that the concept of globalization should occupy a key place in general sociological theory.

NOTES

1. Robert Nisbet (1993: 626) provides an exception to this view when he writes: "Probably the most frequent use of the word [*society*] today is in reference to the totality of human beings on earth together with their cultures, institutions, skills, ideas and values."

2. In 1986, the International Sociological Association established its journal *International Sociology* (London: Sage) to balance this situation; similarly, in 1990, the World Congress of Sociology in Madrid addressed the theme "sociology for one world: unity and diversity."

3. Examples of a developed concept of world society are contained in Burton (1972) and Pettman (1979).

4. Francis Fukuyama was deputy director of the U.S. State Department's Policy Planning Staff.

CHAPTER EIGHTEEN
Deviance and Crime

IN THIS CHAPTER YOU WILL LEARN THAT

- deviance and crime are relative; that is, what is defined as deviant or criminal and the ways people react to deviance and crime depend on the circumstances of time and place, and are subject to conflict and change
- definitions of deviance and crime are the outcome of political processes and power relations in which different groups compete to define right and wrong; conflicts over status, the means of production, and knowledge have each been seen as a source of this competition
- sociological explanations of deviance can be grouped into two types: those that identify the social factors that motivate people to engage in deviance and those that identify the social factors that fail to control or prevent deviance
- there are many consequences of deviant behaviour and defining deviance, both for the deviant and for those reacting to deviance; some of these consequences are positive, some are negative, and many are unintended and counterintuitive
- deviance, crime, and social control are unequally distributed within and among societies; Canada has relatively high rates of crime compared with many other industrialized countries, and also incarcerates people at higher rates than most other industrialized countries

ROSEMARY GARTNER
University of Toronto

■ INTRODUCTION

When you hear the word "deviant," what images come to mind? If you are like most people, you think of someone who is evil, immoral, criminal, insane, or highly eccentric — a person at the margins of society. How would you react, then, to a textbook on deviance that includes a chapter on petting, reading erotic literature, and coitus among Canadian college students? A widely used Canadian textbook published in 1968 featured such a chapter (Mann, 1968). It would be easy to dismiss the author's definition of these behaviours as deviant by saying that the book is out of date, that times and attitudes about sex have changed. In fact, it is exactly those kinds of changes in people's attitudes to different behaviours that are at the centre of the sociological study of deviance.

Consider another type of behaviour that has been defined as deviant at some times but not at others: the physical punishment of children. In August 1930, the principal of Prince Arthur School in Moose Jaw, Saskatchewan, had his conviction for assaulting a pupil overturned on appeal by District Court Judge Ouseley. Ouseley found that the pupil, a 10-year-old girl, had suffered "black and blue marks and weals" from the whipping she received from the principal. Nevertheless, he ruled that the whipping had been "administered on that part of her anatomy ... specially designed by nature for the receipt of corporal punishment," that the girl was a "disobedient and provoking pupil," and that the punishment, being no more than a "wise, firm, and judicious parent would use," was proper and within the law (*R. v. Metcalfe*, 1927).

Compare this case with that of Don Wierenga of Lacombe, Alberta, who pleaded guilty to assaulting his 11-year-old daughter and was given a one-year suspended sentence in June 1996. Wierenga admitted that he had spanked his daughter "six to ten times on the bottom with his open hand" after she had a series of arguments with her stepmother (Woodard, 1996). The judge ruled that Wierenga's use of force was criminal because it was excessive in the circumstances. The *Wierenga* decision attracted widespread attention and controversy, including criticism from the Reform Party, which argued that the decision whether to use corporal punishment is best left to parents. Perhaps you agree. But whether the judgements in these two cases were right or wrong is not what makes them interesting to a sociologist of deviance. They are so-

ciologically interesting because they illustrate both how definitions and perceptions of deviance change over time, and how disagreements often arise over those definitions.

Deviance, then, is relative. Although common sense would tell us that deviance involves breaking rules, those who study deviance remind us that rules change and that people often disagree with the rules. Moreover, breaking rules doesn't always get one labelled a deviant, and sometimes people are labelled deviant without breaking any rules. Understanding deviant behaviour requires us to look at the people and organizations who define and react to deviance — the rule-makers and the rule-enforcers — as well as at those who break the rules.

In this chapter, we will discuss where rules about deviance come from and why people break them. We will also discuss some of the consequences of rule breaking, both for the deviant and for the wider society. Finally, we will look at patterns of deviance and crime in Canada, and recent changes in crime

Social diversions are the lifestyle variations that help make our lives more interesting and, at times, more exciting: the fads and fashions of speech, appearance, and play. SOURCE: Dick Hemingway.

and social control around the world. A central theme of this chapter is that deviance is not simply about marginal people and odd behaviours. Studying how deviance is defined and how people react to it tells us about how a society is organized; how power, privilege, and resources are distributed; and how social order is achieved. Deviance and crime, then, are at the heart of the struggles every society goes through in organizing its social life.

■ DEFINING DEVIANCE AND CRIME

Deviance is not the same as nonconformity, or the violation of social rules or norms. All of us are non-conformists at one time or another in our lives, but few of us are ever labelled deviant or formally punished for our nonconformity. Nonconformity becomes deviance when it produces a negative social reaction and concerted public efforts to change or punish the behaviour or person. These efforts are what sociologists call **social control**. As the public expression of right and wrong, social control takes many forms. Informal social control occurs in interactions among individuals and includes expressions of disapproval, avoidance, and the many other ways we try to communicate and enforce standards of appropriate behaviour in our everyday lives. All of us have been stopped from doing something by an internal voice asking, "What would others think?" That is informal social control in action. It is most effective at preventing deviance when it works through self-control.

When informal social control is ineffective, society falls back on formal methods — the controls exerted by the state through official organizations and agents, such as the criminal-justice system, and by some professional groups, such as social workers and psychiatrists. In contrast to informal social control, formal social control relies largely on the external control of people after they have been defined as deviant. Organizations and agents of formal social control do much more than react to deviance, however. As we will see, they also are actively involved in determining which behaviours and people should be classified as deviant and in deciding how different types of deviance should be dealt with.

Deviance is defined by social control — in other words, by the reactions to it. Those reactions can be more or less severe, depending on how serious the deviance is thought to be. Being gossiped about and shunned by your friends for engaging in adultery may feel like harsh informal social control; being stoned to death for engaging in adultery — a punishment currently prescribed by law in Afghanistan — is obviously a much more severe and formal reaction. One way to predict the severity of the reaction to a deviant act — and thus the seriousness of the deviance — is to measure the number of people who feel threatened by the act, the intensity with which they feel threatened, and the power they have to invoke formal social control against the act. The more consensus there is among the reactors, the more intensity they display in their reactions, and the more power they are able to deploy in response, the more serious the deviance is considered to be. The fact that the same act can be treated as an indiscretion in some societies and as a capital crime in others shows that deviance is not simply a characteristic of behaviours, but exists in the territory between behaviours and the reactions to them.

Crime is a special case of deviance, defined by social norms that are formalized in criminal law. The norms enshrined in the criminal law tend to have

This 1936 movie poster illustrates how relative deviance really is. It suggested that people will go insane from smoking marijuana. SOURCE: *Reefer Madness,* 1936. Directed by Louis Gasnier.

greater consensus than the norms defining other forms of deviance. For example, when people are asked to rate the seriousness of different kinds of deviant acts, criminal acts — such as murder — are consistently rated as more serious and deserving of harsher punishment than noncriminal deviance (Wolfgang et al., 1985). On the surface, the consensus regarding crimes like murder may seem obvious and natural to you. But, like other forms of deviance, crime — even in its most serious forms — is also relative. Virtually all Canadians would say that the intentional killing of one person by another should be treated as a serious crime. But how many would say that euthanasia, the death penalty, killing by soldiers during war, or fatal shootings by police — all of them instances of intentional killing — should be treated as serious crimes? Consider how many people disagreed with the second-degree murder conviction of Robert Latimer for the killing of his disabled daughter (see Box 18.1). Conversely, many people feel that the criminal law on homicide should apply to a wider array of acts, such as deaths caused by workplace "accidents" or abortion. In other words, even the most serious forms of deviance in a society are the subject of conflicting opinions and changing social reactions.

Box 18.1
Should Robert Latimer Go Free?

It is the day after a second jury has found him guilty of second-degree murder, and Robert Latimer is relaxing with relatives at his modest farmhouse in Wilkie, Saskatchewan. Parked across the tidy yard is the half-ton Chevy pickup, the one he filled with deadly carbon monoxide fumes to end the life of his severely disabled 12-year-old daughter, Tracy, on October 24, 1993. While he may be relatively isolated on his 1,280-acre canola and wheat farm, Latimer is at the centre of an emotional public debate that is addressing thorny ethical and philosophical questions about the fairness of the Canadian legal system, the value of a human life, the meaning of pain and suffering, and the morality of mercy killing. Is Latimer a merciful father? A cold-blooded murderer? "Canadians are feeling ambiguous," says University of Manitoba ethicist Arthur Schafer. "They are sending a loving man and a decent father to spend the next 10 years of his life living in a cage which will destroy him, his family and farm," states the ethicist. "But if pain really can't be relieved in any other way, killing can sometimes be an act of love."

Many people sympathize with Latimer. "Public support has been fantastic," Latimer says. Contributions have reached $90,000, funds that helped defray Latimer's mounting legal costs. After the guilty verdict was announced in court, several jurors were clearly shocked to learn it meant a life sentence with no access to parole for at least 10 years. Some gasped and covered their mouths with their hands, and two began to cry. The jury then made an unusual — and likely unenforceable — recommendation: that Latimer be considered for parole after just a year.

But many disabled rights activists see it another way entirely. They are furious that the legal system would even consider leniency for Latimer. "What that says is that it's all right to kill your child with a disability because she may encounter some discomfort," says Pat Danforth, a spokesman for the Council of Canadians with Disabilities. Alarmed by the perceived threat to people with disabilities, the organization mounted a national campaign after Latimer's first trial. Although many advocates for the disabled felt relieved after last week's guilty verdict, some believe Latimer is getting off too easily. Julian Bodner, a Saskatoon lawyer with cerebral palsy, says he should have faced an even more serious charge. "It's almost a mockery," rails Bodner. "Given the confession, and its validity, this should be first-degree murder."

SOURCE: Excerpted from Sharon Doyle Driedger, "Should Latimer Go Free?" *Maclean's*, November 17, 1997, pp. 13–14. Reprinted with permission.

■ WHERE DO DEFINITIONS OF DEVIANCE AND CRIME COME FROM?

To understand where definitions of deviance come from and why they are often so flexible, we must look at the processes through which they are created. These processes involve different groups and institutions sometimes co-operating and sometimes competing with each other to articulate the norms and expectations for behaviour for the rest of society — in other words, to define the boundaries of the moral order. Efforts to define deviance — or **moral crusades** — are initiated by individuals and groups who act as moral crusaders or claims-makers. In this role, they actively create deviance definitions by making claims that a behaviour or a condition violates fundamental moral standards and requires formal recognition and intervention.

A recent example of a moral crusade is the campaign by Mothers Against Drunk Driving (MADD) to educate the public about the costs of drunk driving, to stigmatize those who drink and drive, and to increase the criminal penalties for drunk driving. The success of MADD's campaign, like that of many other moral crusades, reflects the group's ability to gain the support of the media and various politicians, through which changes in both legal and popular definitions of drunk driving were changed. Moral crusades are not always successful, however. Anti-abortion groups, for example, have failed to garner sufficient support to have abortion defined again as a serious form of deviance and criminalized. The success of a moral crusade depends on the extent to which claims-makers can enlist the support of groups with political and economic power, including, and especially, the state's official rule-makers (e.g., legislatures) and rule-enforcers (e.g., courts).

We are still left with the question of why moral crusades occur. A common-sense response is that claims-makers are the first to recognize the harm in the behaviours or conditions they seek to define as deviant and take it upon themselves to educate the rest of society. But this answer fails to recognize that many behaviours defined as deviant are of questionable or limited harm (e.g., bestiality) and that many harmful behaviours are not defined as deviant (e.g., having a high-fat diet). The common-sense response also is not very good at accounting for why moral crusades often meet with resistance and why the process of defining deviance is therefore often fraught with conflict. What explains this conflict? Sociologists of deviance take different views on the sources of conflict associated with the process of defining deviance, but all agree that power relations and political processes are central features of this process.

▲ THE STATUS-CONFLICT PERSPECTIVE

One answer to the question of why defining deviance is characterized by conflict can be found in the **status-conflict perspective,** which found its first expression in the work of Max Weber and was further developed by Vold (1958) and Turk (1969). According to this perspective, the variety of social, economic, political, ethnic, religious, and professional groups that characterize modern societies continually compete with each other for status and influence. Among the outcomes they compete for is control over definitions of right and wrong, deviance and conformity. The law, especially the criminal law, is an important target of these struggles because of its power to define and punish deviance. The rewards of being a winner in these struggles are many. Winning groups can advance their interests over losing groups, thereby gaining greater access to power, resources, and authority. By controlling definitions of deviance, winning groups accomplish at least two goals. First, they legitimate their moral standards and hence their claims to moral authority over losing groups. Second, they can determine the types of social controls applied to deviance — and, in turn, affect the demand for different professions and occupations, such as social workers, physicians, and criminologists, and for different social-control bureaucracies.

From the status-conflict perspective, struggles over the defining of deviance and social control are ultimately about symbolic politics and the social construction of perceived reality. By shaping and passing laws, even laws that are unenforceable or underenforced, groups enhance their moral authority, a form of power that is more subtle, less costly, and more effective in the long term than overt, coercive power.

The central themes of the status-conflict perspective can be seen in Erickson's (1996) analysis of the criminalization of psychoactive drugs in Canada during the last century. At the beginning of the twentieth century, psychoactive drugs (such as opium, heroin, and cocaine) were widely available in Canada and commonly used, most often in the form of patent medicines. Users were rarely stigmatized. Within two decades, use of many psychoactive drugs was criminalized and subject to severe penalties, including long prison terms with hard labour and whipping. This dramatic change resulted from a concerted campaign by various interest groups and politicians, especially Mackenzie King. To justify the crackdown on some psychoactive drugs, moral crusaders cited the dangers they posed to physical health. But, as Erickson notes, these definitions of dangerousness were socially constructed by the moral crusaders, rather than based on scientific evidence. The true motivations behind the campaign included cultural and economic antagonism toward Asian immigrants (some of whom brought a new form of drug use — opium smoking — to Canada). Because these immigrants were willing to work for lower wages than working-class whites were demanding, they were strongly resented by white workers. In addition, certain occupational groups supported the campaign, in part out of a desire to strengthen the power base of government bureaucrats. The ultimate consequences of the campaign were the control and criminalization of less-powerful cultural groups in the interests of more-powerful groups.

▲ THE CLASS-CONFLICT PERSPECTIVE

Another explanation for the conflict that characterizes the definition of deviance comes from **Marxist theories,** which locate the source of these conflicts in struggles to control the means of material production in society (Taylor, Walton, and Young, 1973; Quinney, 1977). From a Marxist perspective, the economic organization of a society determines both the types of deviance it experiences and the types of social controls used to control deviance. The main groups with competing interests are social classes, defined by their relation to the means of economic production. Unlike the status-conflict perspective, which sees various cultural and interest groups sometimes competing and sometimes co-operating, sometimes in ascendance and sometimes in decline, Marxist theories see the relationship between social classes as being much more fixed. Capitalist society is characterized by a continual struggle between the more-powerful capitalist class and the less-powerful working class. One resource that the capitalist class uses in this struggle is the criminal law and its associated agencies of social control.

According to Marxist theories, the types of behaviour and people defined as deviant and criminalized in any particular society can be predicted from the nature of the economic organization of the society. In capitalist societies, definitions of deviance will be biased against those who challenge the capitalist order. This prediction is the basis for Spitzer's (1975) examination of how the contradictions of capitalism produce both certain types of problem populations and characteristic techniques for regulating and managing them. A basic contradiction of capitalism is that it depends on a surplus supply of labour, or a pool of readily available workers whose excess numbers help keep the cost of wages down. But this same surplus-labour pool can cause problems for capitalism if workers, frustrated with low wages and regular periods of unemployment, start to question the legitimacy of the economic order and withdraw their support from it. To prevent people in this group, which Spitzer calls "social dynamite," from undermining the capitalist system, the law is used to define many of their behaviours as criminal. Social dynamite presents a direct and active threat to capitalist relations of production and domination, and includes "youthful, alienated, and politically volatile" lawbreakers and radicals.

The contradictions of capitalism produce a second type of problem population, which Spitzer calls "social junk." In this group are people who are unable to function in a competitive labour market because of age or disability. In contrast to social dynamite, social junk poses a threat to capitalism that is more indirect, passive, and economic. Their dependence and vulnerability require the state to spend considerable time and money regulating and managing them through therapeutic social controls, such as medical and welfare agencies. As this example shows, Spitzer, like other Marxist theorists, sees the processes of both lawmaking and lawbreaking as part of the perpetual struggle between classes for economic advantage.

▲ THE KNOWLEDGE–POWER PERSPECTIVE

Recently, there has emerged a third perspective on the creation of definitions of deviance — the **knowledge–power perspective**. It is associated with postmodernism and discourse analysis, and sees language and communication systems as the most important sources of social control, and hence of definitions of deviance. In this view, society is stratified not by hierarchies based on status or class, but by hierarchies of knowledge. Knowledge and the languages that express it are intimately linked to power, especially the power to construct definitions of right and wrong, good and evil. Different groups compete to develop discourses or ways of representing reality that treat certain types of knowledge as more valid than others.

Accordingly, the most fundamental conflicts in modern society emerge over knowledge and the ways it is produced and legitimated through the media, technology, and scientific expertise. The law is a particularly effective knowledge system, in part because the language and rituals it uses disguise how it produces and reinforces power. Far from being a neutral body of principles, the law is political, flexible, and subject to interpretation, which is why many groups attempt to use it to advance their interests. Law has the ability to make socially contested and constructed knowledge appear natural, commonsensical, and incontestable.

The connection between power and knowledge is expressed in the idea that everything we know to be true is shaped by relations of power in which we all participate. This theme runs through Michel Foucault's analyses of mental illness, criminal punishment, and sexuality. For Foucault, the ways we have of knowing things — through classifying, codifying, naming, and so on — limit what we can know about our world and reflect the systems of domination that surround us. In his work on the emergence of the prison in the early nineteenth century, Foucault (1979) links the rise of reason, science, and democracy to less physically repressive but more extensive techniques of discipline, surveillance, and punishment. With new forms of knowledge about people based in the human sciences came new ways of exercising power over people. Scientific discourses conceived of deviants as people needing control and provided the justification for controlling them through rehabilitation and institutional discipline.

In a recent application of some of these ideas, Menzies describes how a psychiatric-assessment unit in Toronto assembled expert knowledge on troublesome people from police and clinicians. These expert narratives were presented in a scientific language of discovery and diagnosis and used in court to transform the patient-defendants into sources of danger. Once diagnosed as dangerous, the patient-defendant became a "recyclable commodity for distribution and consumption" (Menzies, 1989: 209) by a network of medical and legal institutions. In this approach to the construction of deviance, then, both deviance and social control are the by-products of hierarchical systems of knowledge and power.

Although each of these perspectives identifies different sources of the conflicts that produce definitions of deviance, they share important as-

sumptions. Each sees social control not as a natural reaction occurring after a deviant act is committed, but as part of the social process that defines and produces deviance. Each recognizes that there is often widespread agreement that some behaviours are deviant because they are harmful to individuals and to society. But each perspective also argues that these perceptions about deviance and the harms it causes are themselves socially constructed.

Finally, all three perspectives agree that controlling the process of defining deviance is very different from controlling deviant behaviour. Indeed, many moral crusades are aimed not so much at eliminating as at regulating a particular type of behaviour, and aimed less at changing and more at managing particular types of people. At least two reasons have been offered for these apparently modest goals. The first is self-preservation: Without the deviance they are campaigning against, moral crusaders would lose their sense of mission and reasons for action. The second is moral crusaders' awareness of the limits on their ability to eradicate deviance. Behaviours that are defined as deviant are, after all, typically rewarding for those who engage in them. Consequently, even successful efforts to change the definition of a behaviour from conventional to deviant rarely put an end to it.

WHY DO PEOPLE BEHAVE IN WAYS THAT LEAD THEM TO BE DEFINED AS DEVIANT?

How can we explain deviant behaviour? Dozens of sociological explanations of deviance have been proposed, but they can be grouped into two basic types, each of which makes very different assumptions about the nature of human behaviour. One set of explanations asks the question, "Why do people engage in deviance?" and answers it by identifying social factors that motivate or push people toward deviance. We will call these **motivational theories of deviance**. The other set of explanations asks the question, "Why doesn't everyone engage in deviance?" and answers it by identifying social factors that control or prevent people's deviance. These are typically called **control theories of deviance**. Let's consider how these theories have accounted for deviant behaviour.

▲ MOTIVATIONAL THEORIES

Strain Theory

One of the best-known examples of a motivational theory of deviance is Robert Merton's strain theory (Merton, 1938). For Merton, motivation to deviate lies in society, not in individuals: "social structures exert a definite pressure upon certain persons in the society to engage in non-conforming rather than conforming conduct" (Merton, 1957: 32). Some societies have higher rates of deviance than others because their cultures value certain achievements but their social structures fail to provide many people with legitimate ways to attain these valued goals. For example, in North America children learn at home, at school, and from the media to value economic achievement and the status that comes with it. From an early age, we see others evaluated on the basis of what they own or what they can buy. At the same time, the structure of North American society limits many people's opportunities for economic success. A high-paying job and a college education are out of many people's reach.

This lack of fit between cultural goals and social structural opportunities — or what Merton, following Durkheim, called **anomie** — means that many people feel strained because they are unable to achieve what they have been taught to value. In response to this strain, people react in a variety of ways. Some, indeed most, continue to conform despite the strain they feel. Others choose deviance in a variety of ways: by dropping out of conventional society and withdrawing from the competition over cultural goals; by abandoning the goal of success, but ritually following or overconforming to the rules; by rebelling against convention and supporting alternative goals and means; or by finding alternative but illegitimate ways to achieve cultural goals. This last deviant adaptation — Merton called it **innovation** — is the one most likely to lead people to commit economic crimes, such as burglary, forgery, or selling drugs.

For Merton, each of these deviant adaptations is a normal reaction to the lack of fit between cultural goals and approved means. Deviants, then, are not sick, evil, or stupid people. They are simply responding unconventionally to a contradiction that exists in conventional society. The fact that poor people are overrepresented among those arrested and convicted of crimes, Merton concluded, reflects not individual pathology but the lack of legitimate opportunities for success.

Merton's portrayal of the lower class as particularly prone to criminal and deviant behaviour drew a strong critical reaction from many sociologists. Official statistics on crime, these critics argued, reflect discriminatory practices as much as actual behaviour. For example, police pay greater attention to muggers and shoplifters than to tax-evaders. Moreover, the poor are less able to keep their deviance out of public view. When they suffer from mental illness, drug addiction, or alcoholism, they cannot afford the kinds of private care and treatment that wealthier people can.

Decades of debate and research on the relationship between class and crime or deviance suggest that Merton did overplay the extent to which crime and deviance are concentrated in the lower class. When people are asked in self-report studies about their involvement in various forms of delinquency and crime, class differences (particularly among young people) are small or nonexistent, especially for less serious forms of crime (Weis, 1987). However, serious violent crimes, such as homicide, armed robbery, and assault, do appear to involve disadvantaged people — both as victims and offenders — at higher rates (Sampson and Lauritsen, 1994). The economically disadvantaged are also overrepresented among the mentally ill, alcohol and drug abusers, and those who commit suicide (Palmer and Humphrey, 1990).

Nevertheless, official statistics on crime and statistics from public agencies that deal with various types of deviance tend to exaggerate class differences. Research has shown that some of the class difference in official crime statistics results from greater surveillance of lower-class communities by police (Hagan, Gillis, and Chan, 1978). Official crime statistics also feature street crimes, and not the kinds of white-collar, corporate, or political crimes that are committed by those higher in the class structure. So, as John Braithwaite (1981: 47) has noted, the relationship between class and crime "depends entirely on what form of crime one is talking about."

Merton's strain theory, then, is perhaps less useful for understanding the motivations for deviance among those with access to legitimate means to success than for understanding the deviant motivations of the disadvantaged. To explain deviance among the powerful as well as the powerless, we can turn to another set of motivational theories.

Learning Theories

A second variant of motivational theory contends that, just as we learn to play hockey or to enjoy country and western music, we learn to engage in deviant behaviour. Like strain theory, learning theories see deviance as a normal and socially formed response to one's environment. They also regard a particular context as necessary to provide deviant motivations. Where learning theories differ from strain theory is in their focus on individuals and how they influence each other, rather than on society and how it influences individuals.

The best-known version of learning theory is Edwin Sutherland's theory of **differential association** (Sutherland, 1939). Like other critics of Merton's strain theory, Sutherland pointed out that strain could not predict with any precision how people under strain would respond. Would they conform or deviate? And if they deviated, would they become wifebeaters, drug-users, or terrorists? To understand how and why people choose any particular deviant activity, Sutherland directed his attention to people's particular learning histories and environments. Throughout our lives, each of us is surrounded by people with attitudes, values, and behaviour patterns that sometimes encourage and sometimes discourage deviance. Whether you engage in any particular type of deviance depends on the relative mixture of these prodeviant and antideviant influences. Deviance occurs, says Sutherland,

because one has experienced more prodeviant influences. If you choose to become a car thief, it is because you have learned from others that it is acceptable to steal cars; and you have learned which cars are easiest to steal, how to break into them, how to avoid the police, and how to justify your activities to others.

A distinctive feature of differential-association theory is its ability to account for deviance at all levels of society. Indeed, Sutherland (1949) applied the theory in his landmark study of white-collar crime. White-collar criminals, according to Sutherland, are like street criminals in that they often express contempt for the law, share a culture that rewards rule breaking, and associate with others from whom they can learn both the skills and the rationalizations needed to carry out their crimes.

The idea that engaging in deviance requires learning rationalizations that protect one from the moral challenges of conventional society was developed further in the work of Sykes and Matza (1957). Because deviants live and learn in both conventional and deviant worlds, they rely on what Sykes and Matza called **techniques of neutralization** to reconcile the two worlds. These techniques are rhetorics or vocabularies that nullify guilt and the blame of others. Deviants use them to deny personal responsi-

Much urban grafitti are creative expressions of juvenile-delinquent subcultures. SOURCE: Dick Hemingway.

bility for their actions, condemn those who pass judgement on them, claim their victims deserved what they got, or deny that they caused any real harm. If these sound familiar to you, it is because you have probably used the same techniques to excuse your own misbehaviour. As learning theorists point out, we all learn some techniques that are favourable to deviance.

Subcultural Theories

A third type of motivational theory combines elements of both strain and learning to explain deviance, especially delinquency among lower-class youths. For these **subcultural theories,** lack of access to legitimate opportunities, and thus strain, is a common condition of adolescents' lives. Youths respond to this strain not as isolated individuals, but collectively by forming deviant subcultures. In Albert Cohen's (1955) subcultural theory, this collective response is apparently irrational and malicious behaviour, such as vandalism, truancy, stealing and then destroying property, and fighting — acts that allow youths to reject values of a middle-class world that they feel has rejected them. Learning plays an important role in the subculture developed by these youths because they respond to strain collectively. Youths choose others like themselves as their reference group, rather than middle-class role models, and, by interacting with each other, learn to define their behaviours according to an alternative, deviant set of values and attitudes.

In Cloward and Ohlin's (1960) subcultural theory of delinquency, lower-class youths not only lack access to legitimate opportunities for success, they also may find that illegitimate opportunities for success are not widely available, depending on the type of neighbourhoods in which they live. In some lower-class neighbourhoods, criminal role models and organizations may be plentiful, providing youths with a chance to learn and put into practice the skills and attitudes necessary to be successful at crime. In other neighbourhoods, however, these types of criminal opportunities may be lacking. In the latter case, youths may become involved in violent gangs as a way of achieving status; or they may retreat into drug-using gangs as a way to relieve the strain from having neither legal nor illegal ways to get ahead. The type of delinquent subcultures that develop, then, depend on access to, and interaction with, a learning environment.

A common theme uniting strain, learning, and subcultural theories is that, for deviance or crime to occur, some kind of motivating influence must be present. Motivational theories assume that, in the absence of such influences, people would rarely misbehave. This contrasts sharply with the assumptions of control theories, the second type of explanation of deviance.

▲ CONTROL THEORIES

Control theories find deviance and crime easy to explain: They are rewarding. Stealing is a fast way to make money; getting drunk or high, or having adulterous sex, can be easy ways to feel good; trashing a subway platform is risky fun. The question then, for control theories, is why most of us play by the rules most of the time. (The fact that all of us break the rules at times is, of course, completely consistent with control theories.) For control theories, deviance and crime occur because of the absence of some kind of control.

Youths in a deviant subculture commit acts that allow them to reject the values of the middle-class world that they feel has rejected them. SOURCE: Mug Shots/First Light.

In one of the most influential versions of control theory, Hirschi (1969) argued that juvenile delinquency results from the lack of strong bonds to conventional social institutions. Adolescents with few attachments to their parents, teachers, or other conventional role models, with little commitment to family, school, or other conventional institutions, with weak beliefs in conventional values, and with little involvement in conventional activities are free to act on their deviant impulses. Those with strong bonds to conventionality, on the other hand, will not want to risk breaking the rules. Have you ever stopped short of cheating or stealing or lying because you didn't want to hurt your parents or your chances of getting into college? Your deviant impulses were controlled or contained by your social bonds.

In another version of control theory, Gottfredson and Hirschi (1990) identify self-control as the key to conformity. People with low self-control will try to get what they want quickly, easily, and without thinking about others; and if doing so involves excitement and risks, so much the better. As you might expect, behaving in this way often means breaking rules or failing to fulfil conventional responsibilities — in other words, being deviant. Weak self-control, then, frees people to gamble, drink and drive, bribe officials, and do just about anything else that provides quick and relatively effortless gratification.

Concepts from control theory have also been used by Hagan, Simpson, and Gillis (1987) to explain the gender difference in delinquency. Families exert greater control over girls than boys by socializing girls to avoid risks and by supervising them more closely. In contrast, boys are encouraged by their families to take risks and be independent. As a result, boys are freer to engage in delinquent acts than are girls.

Early childhood socialization — the ways in which parents reward and discipline their children's behaviour and the extent to which they develop affectionate bonds with them — is critical to all control theories. Families are the major source of the controls that prevent deviance. If those controls are developed early in life, children will not be as susceptible to the deviant influences of peers, nor will they respond to strain with deviance. Without those controls, however, neither deviant influences nor strain is needed for deviance to occur.

Explanations of deviance that emphasize motivations and those that emphasize controls help us to understand why deviance and crime occur. They do not, however, pay much attention to what consequences follow. Sociologists have identified a number of consequences — some obvious and some not so obvious — of defining deviance.

■ THE CONSEQUENCES OF DEFINING DEVIANCE

If asked to think about the consequences of deviance and crime, most people would probably conjure up negative images of pain, anger, harm, conflict, and so on. Many types of deviance and crime obviously have such consequences, both for the persons defined as deviant and for those affected by their actions. But the effects of defining deviance are more varied, far-ranging, and complex than this. Effects are both positive and negative, and they are felt by those defined as deviant as well as by those who define deviance.

▲ CONSEQUENCES FOR THOSE WHO DEFINE DEVIANCE

The notion that deviance and crime could have benefits for society was an important theme of Émile Durkheim's work. Since deviance and crime occur in all societies, Durkheim (1938 [1895]) reasoned, they must serve some positive social function. One benefit a society gains from rule breaking by its members is increased social solidarity or integration. Serious violations of a group's rules typically bring people together in collective expressions of outrage and loss, and remind them of their common values. The killing of fourteen women engineering students at the University of Montreal in 1989 was a tragedy felt throughout Canada. Both the immediate response and the continuing commemoration of the killings have brought together Canadians of all sorts in a common condemnation of violence against women.

Another social benefit of deviance is the clarification of a group's moral boundaries. In defining and confronting deviance, a group highlights its standards of right and wrong to its members. The "No Means No" campaign sent a message to both women and men that sex without consent is rape. As in other cases of defining deviance, this campaign drew a clear distinction between acceptable and unacceptable behaviour in an area of conduct prone to interpretational disagreement. When, as is inevitable, someone ignores the message that "no means no" and is charged with sexual assault, the public definition of his behaviour as deviant serves another social function. It allows those who follow the rules to feel virtuous and reinforces their conformity by reminding them of the costs of rule breaking.

Durkheim stressed another social benefit of deviance. Societies need deviance, he said, to keep them flexible and to allow them to adapt to a changing world. When people test society's rules by challenging them, they provide an opportunity to consider whether the rules should be changed. In the 1970s and 1980s, Henry Morgentaler regularly performed abortions in Quebec abortion clinics, not hospitals, and performed them on demand — without the approval of a therapeutic abortion committee, as required by law. He was prosecuted for doing so, but twice acquitted by juries, even though he admitted breaking the law and even though there was no legal defence available to him. After the second acquittal, the government gave up prosecuting him. Abortion on demand in specialized clinics became legal.

With these functions of deviance in mind, it is easier to see how Durkheim and others could argue that deviance and crime are not only inevitable, but integral to and useful for social order. Yet deviance also has clear costs or dysfunctions for society. Too much of it can lead to chaos and conflict, undermining the stability of the society. No society can afford to spend too much of its time, energies, and resources on defining and punishing deviance. But even moderate levels of deviance incur social costs. For example, in his examination of the ironies of social control, Gary Marx identifies a number of ways in which efforts to control deviance actually produce more of it. An excerpt from his analysis in Box 18.2 outlines one way in which social-control efforts by authorities contribute to rule breaking.

▲ CONSEQUENCES FOR THOSE DEFINED AS DEVIANTS

An entire theoretical perspective focusses on the consequences of defining deviance for people defined as deviant. The **labelling perspective** is organized around the surprising idea that societal reactions to deviance are an important *cause* of deviance. Rather than looking at the events and conditions in people's lives before they are defined as deviants, the labelling perspective directs attention to what happens after someone has been singled out and labelled a deviant (Becker, 1973; Lemert, 1967). It is the people who react to deviance, and the character and

Box 18.2
An Irony of Social Control

By taking enforcement actions, authorities [may] unintentionally encourage rule breaking. . . . [The] very process of social control directly triggers violations. High-speed chases offer an all too tragic example. They result in injuries, in death, and often in manslaughter charges against persons who, in the absence of the chase, might have faced minimal or no charges.

[Another] consequence of strong enforcement actions can be to change the personnel and social organization of those involved in illegal activities. For example, stepped-up enforcement efforts with respect to heroin and cocaine appear to have moved the drug traffic away from less sophisticated and skilled local, often amateur, groups to more highly skilled, centralized, better organized criminal groups. The greater skill and sophistication of those now drawn into the activity may mean the development of new markets. Increased risks may mean greater profits, as well as incentives to develop new consumers and markets. The more professional criminals are more likely to be able to avoid prosecution and are in a better position to induce police corruption.

SOURCE: Gary Marx, "Ironies of Social Control: Authorities as Contributors to Deviance through Escalation, Nonenforcement, and Covert Facilitation," *Social Problems, 28* (1981), pp. 222–24. © 1981 by the Society for the Study of Social Problems. Reprinted with permission.

consequences of their reactions, that concern the labelling perspective. The audience includes agents of formal social control (such as police or psychiatrists), significant others in the labelled person's life (such as family members and friends), and members of the society at large, whose disapproval of the deviant act is typically known to the labelled person.

As we have already noted, virtually all of us, at one time or another, engage in deviant behaviour, even deviance serious enough to get us in trouble with the law. Typically, these acts — which are caused by accident, by pressure or encouragement from others, by lapses in conscience or judgement, and so on — are hidden or occasional, so they can be ignored or explained away by ourselves and others. This **primary deviance** (Lemert, 1967) can turn into **secondary deviance** if it becomes public and the person becomes the target of a strong and enduring negative reaction by others. Public disapproval can take many forms: Family and friends may turn away, employers may become ex-employers, and agents of formal social control may treat you as if your deviant behaviour is the key to who you really are. Eventually, deviance may become your **master status**: Your statuses as a university student, a son and brother, and a musician will matter little in comparison to your status as a deviant. When, as a consequence of all this, you come to define yourself as essentially and indelibly a deviant, secondary deviance has occurred. In the final stage of this process, you have become what you were defined as: Your commitment to your deviance increases as your claims to conventionality are lost or denied. As "Ken," a young man convicted of passing a bad cheque, said: "What the hell — if I'm going to be named a criminal I might as well be one" (Frazier, 1976: 136). This is the self-fulfilling prophecy of the labelling process and demonstrates how reactions to deviance are one of its important causes.

The process by which reacting to deviance can stabilize and reinforce deviance has been described in studies of mental patients, homosexuals "outed" in the early 1960s, adolescent "troublemakers," the physically handicapped, and public drunks (Becker, 1964; Chambliss, 1973; Scott, 1969; Spradley, 1970). But, as some of these studies show, it would be a mistake to see those defined as deviants as simply passive, compliant subjects. They frequently resist or challenge the deviant label, sometimes individually and sometimes collectively. Faced with the stigma and rejection caused by a deviant label, some fight back by denying the deviance of their actions or questioning the motivations of reactors. Gerald Hannon, a journalist, college teacher, and gay prostitute in Toronto, is an example. The target of public condemnation for advocating sex between adult males and underage boys, Hannon has responded by condemning mainstream religion, heterosexual nuclear families, and what he sees as a "sex-negative culture" — and has earned support from civil libertarians, many of whom find his message shocking but defend his right to express it (Martin, 1996).

The shared experience of being labelled can also bring deviants together in collective responses. In recent years, many different types of stigmatized people have formed voluntary organizations to provide support and positive recognition for their nonconformity, to educate the public, and to challenge discriminatory policies — in other words, to alter the definition of deviance and limit the negative social consequences of their behaviour or condition. For example, organizations like the National Association to Advance Fat Acceptance, the Living Large Club, and the Ample Opportunity Group urge their members and the wider public to question the social intolerance of obesity (Findlay, 1996). Similarly, some smokers are aggressively contesting their stigmatization by setting up a Smokers' Home Page on the World Wide Web that includes a series of articles denouncing smoking restrictions and urging bloc voting by smokers, who have more numerical clout than many other lobbying groups.

These kinds of collective responses have positive consequences for deviants. The recognition of shared experiences of rejection can bring otherwise isolated and perhaps self-blaming people together. Whether or not such groups are able to alter how their members are perceived by the wider public, they at least can counter some of the more damaging consequences of social condemnation. As with the moral crusades to define deviance discussed earlier, campaigns by deviant groups to eliminate deviant definitions will succeed to the extent that they marshall political support and favourable media attention. Both constructing and repudiating definitions of deviance, then, involve power struggles and symbolic politics.

■ PATTERNS OF DEVIANCE AND CRIME

My discussion of where definitions of deviance and crime come from and why people behave in ways that get them defined as deviant suggests that rates of deviance and crime should vary among social groups in a given society as well as among societies. Docu-

Rates of deviance and crime vary among social groups in society as well as among societies. Documenting such variation with any accuracy is not easy, however, because of the hidden nature of much deviance and the political nature of defining deviance. SOURCE: Seb Janiak/The Image Bank.

menting such variation with any accuracy is not easy, however, because of the hidden nature of much deviance and the political nature of defining deviance. If deviance becomes the target of formal control, it can be documented through the statistics produced by official control agents and organizations. These statistics are affected by more than just deviant behaviour, however. Control agents and the wider public make decisions about which deviant acts or persons to report and which to ignore. So, for example, if public intolerance of young "troublemakers" increases, official statistics on youth crime may indicate an increase not because there is more of it, but because more of it is reported to police (Tanner, 1996).

Those who study deviance, aware of the limitations of official statistics, often rely on other information sources. Surveys that ask people to report on their own involvement in deviance or on their experiences as victims of crime produce results that are closer to the actual behaviours, and so avoid many of the problems associated with official statistics. But survey data, like official statistics, are affected by people's willingness and ability to reveal their own or others' deviance. Indirect measures of deviance can avoid many of these problems. Examples include statistics on deaths due to cirrhosis of the liver as a measure of alcohol abuse, or statistics on sales of medical syringes as a measure of intravenous drug use.

Thus, how we count deviance and what we know about it are the outcomes of a social and political process. Although it is important to keep in mind that all sources of information on deviance are imperfect, combining information from many sources does permit greater confidence in our depiction of deviance. This means that we have a better idea of the extent and nature of some kinds of deviance than others, because some kinds of deviance can be documented through a variety of sources. Let's turn to what we know about one of the best-documented types of deviant behaviour: crime.

▲ CRIMINAL BEHAVIOUR IN CANADA

Is Canada in the 1990s particularly crime-prone? The answer depends on whom you ask, what type of crime you're referring to, and what you're comparing it with. Many Canadians think there is more crime in Canada now than in the recent past. In a 1993 nationwide survey, almost half of all respondents said they thought crime in their neighbourhoods had increased over the last five years, and 27 percent (up from 25 percent in 1988) said they felt unsafe walking alone in their neighbourhoods after dark (Gartner and Doob, 1994).

When asked in the same survey about their experiences of criminal victimization, however, Canadians did not report higher rates of victimization from assault, theft, robbery, or break and enter in 1993 than they had in 1988. Moreover, the most recent official crime statistics indicate that the violent-crime rate declined for the fourth year in a row in 1995, when the homicide rate reached a 26-year low; and the 1995 property-crime rate stabilized after declining steadily between 1984 and 1994 (Canadian Centre for Justice Statistics, 1996b). Still, the total violent-crime rate rose annually for fifteen years before 1991, and this increase may have fuelled public fears. The vast majority of this increase, however, was in minor assaults — a category of crime notoriously subject to changes in both the reporting behaviour of the public and police charging practices.

Although Canadians do not appear to be at greater risk of criminal victimization in the 1990s compared with the 1970s or 1980s, they are at greater risk than citizens of many other industrialized nations. Victimization surveys (see Figure 18.1) indicate that rates of theft, burglary, and contact crime (assault, robbery, pickpocketing, and sexual incidents) are higher in Canada than in several European countries. The risk of being a victim of homicide is also greater in Canada than in several other developed nations, though substantially less than in many Eastern European nations (see Table 18.1). As these homicide data suggest, crime in Canada remains distinct from crime in the United States in at least one important respect. Although Canadians are about as likely as Americans to be the victims of burglaries, larcenies, and car thefts, they are much less likely than Americans to be the victims of serious violent crime, such as aggravated assault, robbery, and murder (see Table 18.2).

Crime is unequally distributed within societies, as well as among societies. In Canada, crime rates have historically been lower in the eastern provinces and Quebec than in the western provinces, and highest in the Yukon and the Northwest Territories. Women, urban dwellers, and young Canadians report higher rates of personal victimization than do men, rural dwellers, and older Canadians (Gartner and Doob, 1994). Males, however, commit a disproportionate number of violent and property offences. Criminal offenders also tend to be younger than the

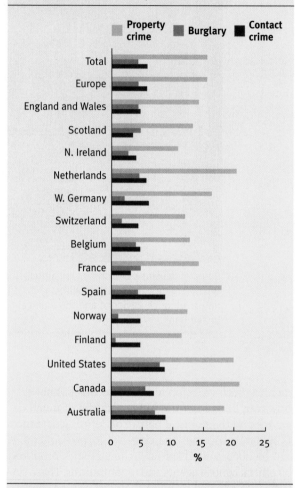

◆ **Figure 18.1** Percentage of People Reporting Property-Crime, Burglary, or Contact-Crime Victimization in Year prior to Interview

SOURCE: Jan J.M. van Dijk, Pat Mayhew, and Martin Killias, *Experiences of Crime across the World* (Deventer, Netherlands: Kluwer, 1991), p. 40. Reproduced with permission.

general population. In 1995, the median age of those accused of property crimes was 24, and those accused of violent crimes was 29 (Hendrick, 1996).

Aboriginal Canadians are also overrepresented among many types of crime victims and offenders. For example, indigenous peoples (including Inuit and Métis) constitute about 2 percent of the Canadian population, but about 15 percent of all homicide victims (Canadian Centre for Justice Statistics, 1996b). Because most homicides are intraracial (about 85 percent of aboriginal victims are killed by aboriginal offenders), a disproportionate number of suspects are aboriginal as well. Native people account for about 18 percent of all persons ar-

◆ **Table 18.1** Homicide Death Rates for Men and Women, 1992–93

	Male victims (per 100 000 male pop.)	Female victims (per 100 000 female pop.)
Russian Federation	49.5	13.5
Estonia	44.6	9.3
Mexico	33.9	3.7
Lithuania	20.0	5.7
Ukraine	18.0	5.7
United States	16.7	4.4
Belarus	15.9	5.7
Bulgaria	8.2	1.8
Italy	5.7	0.7
Hungary	5.2	3.1
Finland	4.7	2.0
Poland	4.0	1.4
New Zealand	3.2	1.6
Canada	**2.9**	**1.4**
Czech Republic	2.8	1.6
Australia	2.1	1.3
Portugal	2.1	1.0
Greece	1.9	0.7
Sweden	1.8	1.0
Norway	1.6	0.6
Denmark	1.5	0.9
Israel	1.5	0.7
Germany	1.4	1.0
Hong Kong	1.3	1.1
France	1.3	0.7
United Kingdom	1.2	0.6
Japan	0.8	0.5

SOURCE: World Health Organization, *World Health Statistics Annual, 1994* (Geneva: WHO, 1995).

rested for homicide. Canadian police do not systematically collect information about the ethnicity of those charged with crimes except criminal homicide, so it is more difficult to document the involvement of aboriginals in other crime. It is clear, however, that aboriginals are overrepresented among those serving time in Canada's jails and prisons. In 1994–95, aboriginals accounted for 17 percent of persons sentenced to provincial custody and 13 percent of those sentenced to federal custody (Canadian Centre for Justice Statistics, 1996a); in Saskatchewan, fully 71 percent of those admitted to provincial custody were aboriginal.

There are at least two ways to explain these patterns. Aboriginals may be at higher risk of incarceration because they engage in the kinds of behaviours that put them in conflict with the law. Although crime statistics by race are not collected for most crimes, the homicide data cited above support this explanation. In addition, other evidence suggests that aboriginal Canadians are exposed to many of the correlates of criminal behaviour — such as alcohol abuse, history of sexual abuse, family disruption, and unemployment — at much higher rates than other Canadians (Frideres, 1996). These and other indicators of strain and weak social bonds — such as high rates of suicide and depression among aboriginals — would predict greater involvement of aboriginals in crime.

The overrepresentation of aboriginals in the criminal-justice system could also be due to discrimination in the creation and application of criminal definitions. This possibility has been investigated in a series of federal and provincial inquiries, which have concluded that "systemic" or "institutional" racism is responsible for at least part of the aboriginal over-

◆ **Table 18.2** Crime Rates for Canada and the United States, 1995

	Canada (per 100 000 pop.)	United States (per 100 000 pop.)
Murder and non-negligent manslaughter	2.0	8.2
Robbery	102.4	220.9
Aggravated assault	93.6	418.3
Burglary	1320.3	987.6
Larceny	2909.1	3044.9
Motor-vehicle theft	552.4	560.5

SOURCE: Canadian Centre for Justice Statistics, *Canadian Crime Statistics: 1995*, Cat. no. 85-002 (Ottawa: Statistics Canada, 1996). Reproduced by authority of the Minister of Industry, 1997; Federal Bureau of Investigation, *Uniform Crime Reports, 1995* (Washington, DC: U.S. Government Printing Office, 1996).

representation (Cawsey, 1991; Manitoba, 1991). According to one provincial commission, other visible minorities are also adversely affected by systemic racism in the operation of the criminal-justice system (Commission on Systemic Racism in the Ontario Criminal Justice System, 1995). Perceptions of racial bias in the enforcement of laws are one of the reasons that visible-minority communities have opposed the collection of official crime statistics by race (Wortley, 1996); these groups argue that such statistics, if used in an uninformed fashion, could be used to justify discriminatory attitudes and practices both in and outside the criminal-justice system (Doob, 1991). In contrast, those in favour of collecting crime statistics by race argue that such statistics could be used to challenge racist explanations of crime and document discriminatory treatment by the criminal-justice system. Nevertheless, because such statistics are not currently collected in any systematic manner, it is impossible to examine patterns of criminal victimization or offending among different racial or cultural groups in Canada.

▲ CRIME AND SOCIAL CHANGE

If the explanations for people's deviant behaviour discussed earlier have validity, we would expect to see changes in crime rates accompanying other kinds of social changes — especially social changes that might affect levels of criminal motivation or social control. Let's consider two types of social change and their effects on criminal behaviour.

Crime in Eastern Europe

The transition from communism to capitalism has brought with it radical changes in the economies, politics, social life — and crime rates — of many Eastern European countries. Although criminal statistics from the former communist countries were and continue to be of questionable reliability, observers agree that crimes of all types have increased throughout Eastern Europe. Organized crime in all its manifestations — from fraud and bribery of officials to contract killings, black marketeering, and drug smuggling — is flourishing (Handelman, 1995). Underpaid police and other official control agents are succumbing to the temptations of crime. Police in Poland have been arrested for everything from cooperating with car thieves to distributing stolen whisky (*The Economist*, Mar. 11, 1995: 54). Much of the new wave of crime is international in scope and involves complex criminal conspiracies that span continents and extend into Canada (Crane, 1996). But even common crimes by individuals — homicides, armed robberies, thefts — appear to be increasing. Hungary, the Czech Republic, Poland, and many countries formerly part of the Soviet Union have all reported dramatically higher rates of serious violent crimes in the 1990s compared with the 1980s (Myers, 1996). Paralleling these trends in crime are rising rates of suicide and drug addiction in many of the same countries.

Explanations offered for this wave of crime and deviance should sound familiar to you. Observers cite rising unemployment and poverty, leading to a growing gap between rich and poor, a weakening of formal controls with the collapse of repressive governments, and material and political expectations increasing faster than they can be met — in short, a potent combination of escalating motivations and diminishing controls. Still, the crime rates of many Eastern European nations remain lower than those in the United States, and there are signs that crime rates are stabilizing in some of the former communist countries.

Crime and Changing Gender Stratification

As noted in Chapter 8, one of the most influential social changes of the last century has been growing awareness and lessening of many forms of gender inequality. In the 1970s, some criminologists argued that this change in gender stratification could reduce the long-standing gender gap in crime (Adler, 1975). Put crudely, women's liberation might mean women would catch up to men in their criminal behaviour as women's access to less-traditional roles expanded, the stresses associated with these new roles increased, and the controls over women's activities decreased. This expectation has found little support in research: A large gender gap persists in most crimes, especially the kinds of serious violent crimes traditionally dominated by men (Steffensmeier and Allan, 1991). In Canada, for example, the ratio of males to females charged with murder has remained at about 7 to 1 for at least the last 25 years. Changes in gender stratification are, however, related to one aspect of women's involvement in crime — as victims, not offenders. In developed nations since World War II, as women have moved into the labour force in unprecedented numbers, they have also taken on less-traditional domestic roles — by having more children out of wedlock, marrying later, and divorcing more often. This shift toward less-traditional gender roles for women has affected their risks of homicide victimization in complex ways (Gartner, Baker, and Pampel, 1990). In countries where women's status is relatively low, women's risks of homicide have increased with these changes. However, in countries where women's status is relatively high — such as Canada — women's risks have not increased relative to men's risks as women have assumed less-traditional roles. In fact, in Canada, the gender gap in homicide victimization has grown substantially since the early 1970s (see Figure 18.2).

As both the recent crime waves in Eastern Europe and the changing risks of women illustrate, major social, economic, and political transformations can have both profound and complex effects on patterns of crime and deviance in a society. Not surprisingly, such transformations also affect patterns of social control.

■ PATTERNS OF SOCIAL CONTROL

Until recently, families, communities, and the church were the major sources of social control; serious rule breaking was responded to with physical, and, to our eyes, often horrific punishment. Before the seventeenth century, centralized states either did not exist or were too weak to sponsor the institutions of formal social control that predominate in modern societies. With the growth of market-based economies and industrialization — and the growth of a dependent working class that accompanied them — state-based formal social controls emerged. The most obvious examples of these formal controls are the confinement institutions — prisons, asylums, poorhouses, and so on — which emerged in the seventeenth century. These were places of residence and work where those unable or unwilling to work or conform to other rules were isolated from the outside world, closely watched, and continuously regimented by impersonal agents of control. Punishment based on physical pain shifted to punishment based on deprivation and discipline.

Confinement institutions remain one of the favoured responses to deviance and crime today in Canada and most other industrialized nations. But throughout the twentieth century, these institu-

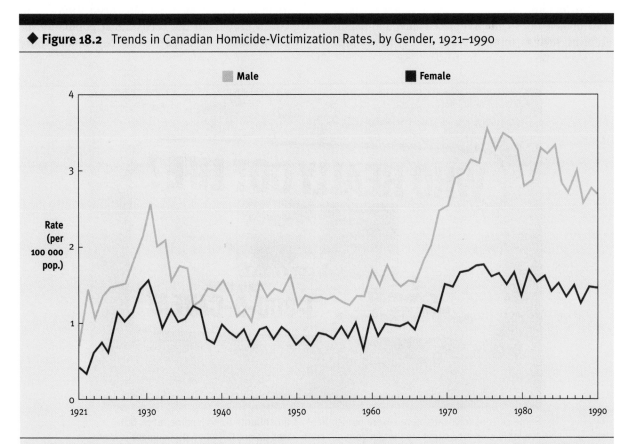

◆ **Figure 18.2** Trends in Canadian Homicide-Victimization Rates, by Gender, 1921–1990

SOURCE: Rosemary Gartner, "Homicide in Canada," in J.I. Ross, ed., *Violence in Canada: Sociopolitical Perspectives* (Don Mills, ON: Oxford University Press, 1995), p. 201. Reproduced with permission.

tions have been the target of criticism — for their inefficiency, costliness, repressiveness, and failure to rehabilitate. The 1960s and 1970s saw growing support for alternative methods of control through decentralization, deinstitutionalization, and decriminalization. The goal became shifting control to local governments and community agencies, closing down large-scale institutions, and eliminating criminal sanctions for victimless crimes, such as sodomy and public drunkenness. This move away from confinement was parallelled by the ascendance of the medical model of deviance and a therapeutic approach to social control. Over the twentieth century, many forms of deviance and crime have been medicalized — in other words, defined as illnesses in need of treatment, rather than sins in need of punishment. Professional groups — psychiatrists, social workers, psychologists — have urged this redefinition of deviance and its solution through psychological adjustment and community-based care, rather than through physical discipline and confinement.

Whether these new forms of social control are less coercive and repressive than older forms, as their advocates claim, has been the subject of much debate. In addition, some argue these new forms of control have not so much replaced older and harsher forms, such as imprisonment, as they have added to them, widening the social control net to capture people who might otherwise have avoided formal social controls (S. Cohen, 1985). Patterns in the use of confinement in recent years in Canada suggest a complicated picture, but one that at least partly supports this view. For example, hospitalization for mental disorders was the preferred treatment until well into the 1950s in Canada. Since then there has been a dramatic shift toward deinstitutionalization of mental patients. In the last twenty years, the number of psychiatric hospitals in Canada has decreased from almost 60 to fewer than 20; and the number of patients admitted to these hospitals each year has dropped from about 50 000 to well under 20 000 (Health and Welfare Canada, 1977, 1991, 1994). At the same time, hundreds of community-care facilities have been established that serve thousands of clients a year, many of whom would, but some of whom would not, have been admitted to psychiatric hospitals in earlier years.

The correctional system, in contrast, does not show a similar trend toward deinstitutionalization. Since the early 1980s, the population of those serving sentences in federal and provincial jails and prisons has increased by 50 percent, with about 34 000 people in custody in 1994–95 (Reed, 1996). The greatest growth in the correctional population in the last fifteen years, however, has been among those

Some citizens advocate more severe punishment as an antidote to high crime rates, but available evidence suggests that, in general, crime rates do not fall when punishment is more severe. SOURCE: Dick Hemingway.

supervised within the community — that is, those on parole or probation. The increase in the correctional population has occurred for both adults and youths and is most evident in recent years. For example, from 1990 to 1995, the total adult correctional caseload — which includes those in custody on sentence or remand, on probation, and on conditional release — grew from 127 609 to 154 238 (see Table 18.3).

Canada is not alone in sending more people to prison than ever before. Prison populations have been increasing in many Western nations, especially the United States, and experts expect this trend to continue. Canada is unusual, however, in the rate at which it imprisons people. Currently, there are about 150 persons incarcerated per 100 000 adults in Canada. Although this is less than one-third of the incarceration rate in the United States, it is higher than the rate of any European nation for which figures are available, except Romania and Russia. The expansion in prison populations has many experts concerned, both because it is not directly related to changes in crime rates and because it has no natural limits — in other words, there is an unlimited reservoir of people and acts that could be defined as deserving imprisonment. As one observer (Christie, 1993: 166) has noted, the crime-control system "is a system of production of vital importance to modern societies. It produces control. In this perspective, the problem arises: when is enough, enough?"

One possible limit on the willingness to use imprisonment is its cost. Canada spends $2.5 billion per year on adult and youth corrections; to keep a person in prison for a year in Canada costs about $44 000. As governments search for ways to cut public spending, other, less-expensive modes of social control are likely to develop, such as electronic monitoring of convicted criminals. Some countries, like the United States, remain committed to imprisonment, but are experimenting with privately run prisons — even to the extent that some states now administer capital punishment through private contractors. Privatization is also apparent at other stages of formal social control. Perhaps as much, or more, policing is now done through private security as through public law enforcement in many countries, including Canada; and the number of people employed by private police agencies equals or exceeds those employed by public police agencies (Shearing, 1992).

Some observers see private entrepreneurs joining with the state to extend social control through new, technically sophisticated, and better-disguised techniques. Gary Marx (1995), for example, describes a **maximum-security society** characterized by "softer" social-control processes where the role of human agents is reduced and control is achieved at a distance. In this maximum-security society, deviance and crime will be engineered away by controlling the physical environment, rather than people. Think of subways with graffiti-resistant metals, malls playing classical music to discourage disorderly congregations of teenagers, remote surveillance cameras, or the anticarjacking mannequins that drivers can place in the passenger seats of their cars.

Whether these new techniques of control will replace or merely add another layer to existing formal controls, like prisons, is unclear. Some fear the new strategies will create an Orwellian future of more powerful and intrusive state control over our lives, whereas others see technological advances providing control that is less discriminatory, more effective, and more accountable. The reality, as Marx argues, is likely to be somewhere between these two

◆ **Table 18.3** Trends in Canadian Adult Correctional Populations

	1990–91	1991–92	1992–93	1993–94	1994–95
Custody sentenced	24 470	25 712	26 477	27 573	28 318
Custody remand	4 711	4 947	5 111	5 130	5 378
Probation	82 091	93 314	100 386	102 402	99 910
Conditional release	16 337	18 094	19 192	19 001	20 632
Total	127 609	142 067	151 166	154 106	154 238

SOURCE: Canadian Centre for Justice Statistics, *Adult Correctional Services in Canada, 1994–95*, Cat. no. 85–211 (Ottawa: Statistics Canada, 1996), p. 8. Reproduced by authority of the Minister of Industry, 1997.

extremes. New technologies of control will not address the social inequalities that cause crime and deviance, and may even reinforce them if only the well-off can afford the technology. But these new technologies may also be more democratic, capturing the deviance of the powerful and the disadvantaged equally. (Photoradar to control speeding is an example of such a democratic technique, which may explain much of the public's resistance to it.)

Certainly, as we move into the twenty-first century, we can expect some unintended consequences from new forms of control, including the emergence of new, and perhaps more serious, forms of crime and deviance. Carjackings sprang up as a reaction to tougher security systems that made cars harder to hotwire; so we should not be surprised if bank robbery by means of computer replaces bank robbery by force as bank security systems become more sophisticated. Once again, we see how intimately social control and deviance are related, with social control being an important cause, and not just a consequence, of deviance. ■

● SUMMARY

1. Deviance is relative. In other words, what is defined as deviance, as well as the way people react to deviance, depends on social circumstances. Even what you may consider to be serious deviance is subject to conflicting opinions and changing social reactions. This means that deviance exists in the territory between behaviours and reactions to them.

2. Crime is a special case of deviance and is defined by social norms that are formalized in criminal law. The vehicle of response to crime is formal social control, such as the criminal-justice and correctional systems, whereas the vehicle of response to noncriminal deviance is informal social control, such as gossip, avoidance, and other forms of disapproval. There tends to be wide — though certainly not complete — agreement that crime is wrong but less agreement that noncriminal forms of deviance are wrong.

3. Deviance is defined through a political process that typically involves struggles between competing groups over status, resources, and knowledge. Although there is often some relationship between the harm that a behaviour causes and the likelihood that the behaviour is defined as deviant, many harmful behaviours are not defined as deviant and some behaviours defined as deviant are not harmful.

4. Sociological explanations of deviant behaviour can be grouped into two types. Motivational theories of deviance address the question, "Why do people engage in deviance?" and answer it by identifying social factors that push people toward deviance. Control theories of deviance address the question, "Why doesn't everyone engage in deviance?" and answer it by identifying social factors that stop people from acting on their deviant impulses.

5. Defining deviance can have both positive and negative consequences for those reacting to, and for those engaging in, deviance. For those reacting to deviance, some of the positive consequences are increased social solidarity and feelings of virtuousness. For deviants, one of the negative consequences is the escalation of deviance.

6. Rates of serious crimes, such as murder and robbery, have not increased in Canada in recent years, although public fears of crime have increased. Canadian citizens are victims of serious violent crime at lower rates than citizens of the United States, but at higher rates than citizens of other developed democracies. Aboriginal Canadians are at particularly high risk of involvement in criminal homicide, both as victims and offenders. They are also overrepresented among those incarcerated in Canadian prisons and jails. This overrepresentation has been attributed in part to systemic racism in the criminal-justice system.

7. Crime rates are often affected by major social changes. For example, with the transition from communism to capitalism in Eastern Europe, crime rates have risen sharply. Changes in gender inequalities, on the other hand, have not been accompanied by a reduced gender gap in criminal offending. Men still greatly outnumber women among offenders.

8. Many new forms of social control that are technically sophisticated, disguised, and less dependent on human agents have been introduced in the last decade. Nevertheless, Canada continues to rely heavily on incarceration to control crime. Rates of incarceration have been increasing rapidly in Canada and many other countries, a trend that has been criticized by a number of experts.

● QUESTIONS TO CONSIDER

1. Think of a behaviour that, during your lifetime, has gone from being considered deviant to nondeviant, or vice versa. What explains this changing definition? Have any individuals, lobby groups, or professions been involved in changing the definition of the behaviour?
2. Most of us, at some time in our lives, have engaged in behaviours that violate the law. How would the different explanations of deviance discussed in this chapter explain your rule-violating behaviour? Which explanation appears most consistent with your experience and why?
3. Do you agree that deviance, since it occurs in all societies, must be functional? Can you think of an instance or type of deviance that serves no social function?
4. What kinds of social policies to control deviance and crime would be consistent with the labelling perspective on deviance? Are the recent trends in social control that are discussed in this chapter consistent with the kinds of policies the labelling perspective would support?

● GLOSSARY

anomie According to Robert Merton, a social condition in which there is a gap between the cultural goals people are taught to aspire to and the social-structural means available to achieve those goals.

control theories of deviance Explanations that emphasize the factors that prevent people from acting on deviant impulses.

differential association The process by which people learn deviance through exposure to more definitions favourable to deviance than definitions unfavourable to deviance.

innovation Robert Merton's term for the type of adaptation to strain that involves seeking illegitimate means to achieve legitimate goals; it encompasses most types of money-making crimes.

knowledge–power perspective According to this perspective, definitions of deviance emerge from competing discourses and knowledge systems that reflect wider systems of domination.

labelling perspective An approach to the study of deviance that emphasizes that rule making and rule enforcement — in other words, the definitions of and reactions to deviance — are often important *causes* of deviance.

Marxist theories These theories argue that definitions of deviance emerge from struggles among social classes to control the means of material production in a society.

master status A status that stands out above all others; deviance is often a master status, overshadowing other statuses in the eyes of people who interact with the deviant.

maximum-security society The growing importance in contemporary society of softer social-control processes that control at a distance, with technology, and with less human contact.

moral crusade An organized campaign to discredit an activity or a group of people so that it becomes viewed as deviant and deserving of stigma.

motivational theories of deviance Explanations that emphasize the factors that push or encourage people toward deviant behavior.

primary deviance Deviance that occurs for any of a variety of reasons, but that does not lead one to be labelled a deviant or to see oneself as a deviant.

secondary deviance Deviance that occurs after one has been labelled a deviant and starts to view oneself as a deviant.

social control The various means used by members of society to ensure conformity to norms and to punish violations of norms.

status-conflict perspective This perspective argues that definitions of deviance emerge from struggles between different cultural and interest groups to gain status and moral authority.

subcultural theories Explanations of deviance that assume that deviance occurs when those who are subject to strain collectively develop values and beliefs that encourage or reward deviant behaviour.

techniques of neutralization A set of rationalizations used by people who break rules to excuse their behaviours and to protect themselves against guilt and the blame of others.

● SUGGESTED READING

Downes, David, and Paul Rock. (1995). *Understanding Deviance: A Guide to the Sociology of Crime and Rule Breaking.* 2nd ed. Oxford: Clarendon Press. A thorough overview of classic and contemporary perspectives on deviance, with chapters on feminist criminology and on deviance and social policy.

Goode, Erich, and Nachman Ben-Yehuda. (1995). *Moral Panics: The Social Construction of Deviance.* Oxford: Cambridge University Press. To illustrate one of the ways in which deviance is created through social reactions, the authors focus on moral panics and discuss how this concept applies to the Renaissance witch craze as well as to drug panics in the United States and Israel in the 1980s.

Sacco, Vincent F., ed. (1992). *Deviance: Conformity and Control in Canadian Society.* Scarborough, ON: Prentice Hall. An excellent introductory essay on the study of deviance and control is followed by a series of chapters by Canadian scholars on various forms of deviance, including political deviance, commercial crime, drug use, and street prostitution.

Silverman, Robert A., James J. Teevan, and Vincent D. Sacco, eds. (1996). *Crime in Canadian Society.* Toronto: Harcourt Brace. An overview of Canadian criminology, with sections on defining and measuring crime, theories of crime, and recent research on patterns of crime in Canada. Current topical issues, such as collecting crime statistics by race, the battered-wife defence, and crime and immigration, are covered in separate chapters.

CHAPTER NINETEEN
Social Movements and Politics

IN THIS CHAPTER YOU WILL LEARN THAT

- people sometimes riot, petition, strike, and take other forms of collective action in order to correct perceived injustices: when they do so, they are participating in social movements
- people are more inclined to rebel against the status quo when they are bound by close social ties to many other people who feel similarly wronged; when they are sharply socially separated from the people whom they regard as the source of the injustice; and when they have the time, money, and other resources needed to protest
- in order for social movements to grow, members must make the activities, goals, and ideology of the movement congruent with the interests, beliefs, and values of potential recruits
- the history of democracy may be viewed as a struggle for the acquisition of constantly broadening citizenship rights
- the level of democracy in a society depends on the capacity of citizens to influence the state through their support of social movements, political parties, and other groups; that capacity increases as power becomes more widely distributed in society
- the degree to which power is widely distributed influences the success of particular kinds of parties and policies
- paradoxically, the process of globalization alters the character of politics by simultaneously unifying and fragmenting nation-states and forms of collective action

ROBERT J. BRYM
University of Toronto

■ INTRODUCTION

When I was in Grade 11, I was shocked to learn one day that $H_2O + SO_2 = H_2SO_3$. In order to appreciate why a 16-year-old schoolboy should have been alarmed to hear that water combined with sulphur dioxide produces sulphurous acid, you have to know where I lived: in Saint John, New Brunswick, about 100 m downwind of one of the larger pulp and paper mills in Canada. Acrid waves of sulphur dioxide billowed day and night from the mill's imposing smokestacks. The entire city was blanketed in the gas. As was true for other Canadian towns graced by pulp and paper mills, Saint John's pervasive rotten-egg smell was a subject of derision by outsiders and residents alike. But, for me, contempt turned to near-panic when I realized that we were being poisoned by the fumes. Suddenly, it was clear why many people I knew — and especially people living near the mill — woke up in the morning with a kind of "smoker's cough." By the simple act of breathing, we were causing the gas to mix with the moisture in our bodies and form an acid that our lungs tried to expunge, with only partial success.

Twenty years later, in the late 1980s, I read the results of a medical research report showing that residents of Saint John suffer from rates of lung disease, including emphysema and lung cancer, significantly above the national average. But even in 1968 it was evident that there was a serious problem in my home town. I therefore hatched a plan. Our high school was about to hold its annual model parliament. The event was notoriously boring, partly because, year in, year out, virtually everyone voted for the same party, the Conservatives. Saint John was, after all, founded by antirevolutionaries — Americans who remained loyal to the British crown and fled the new republic during the American Revolution. It had been a bastion of conservatism ever since. But here was an issue, I thought, that could turn things around. The pulp and paper mill was owned by K.C. Irving, a magnate so powerful that his companies were said to control 40 percent of New Brunswick's economic output. *Forbes* business magazine in the United States annually ranked Mr. Irving among the very wealthiest men in the world. I reckoned that once I told my fellow students the political implications of the fact that $H_2O + SO_2 = H_2SO_3$, they would quickly rise to arms and demand the closure of the mill until such time as Mr. Irving could guarantee a clean operation.

Was *I* naïve. As head of the tiny Liberal party, I was obliged to address the entire student body during assembly on election day in order to outline the party platform and mobilize votes. When I got to the part of my speech explaining why K.C. Irving was our enemy, the murmuring in the audience, which had been growing like the sound of a hungry animal about to attack its prey, erupted into loud "boos." A couple of students rushed the stage. The principal suddenly appeared from the wings and commanded the student body to settle down. He then took me by the arm and informed me that, for my own safety, my speech was finished. So, I discovered on election day, was our high school's Liberal party. And so, it emerged, was my high-school political career.

This incident troubled me for many years, less because of the embarrassment it caused me than the puzzles it presented. Why didn't my fellow students rebel? Why did they continue to support an arrangement that was enriching one man at the cost of a community's health? Why weren't they enraged? Couldn't they see the injustice? Other people did. Nineteen sixty-eight was not just the year of my political failure at Saint John High School. It was also the year that student riots in France nearly caused the fall of the government of Charles de Gaulle; the year in which the suppression of student strikes by the Mexican government left dozens of students dead; the year in which American students at Berkeley, Michigan, and other universities fought with unprecedented vigour for free speech on their campuses, an end to U.S. involvement in the war in Vietnam, increased civil rights for American blacks, and an expanded role for women in public affairs.

I didn't know it at the time, but by asking why students in Paris, Mexico City, and Berkeley rebelled while my fellow students in Saint John did not, I was raising the single question that, perhaps more than any other, animates the study of social movements and political sociology. What social mechanisms allow some people's demands to get articulated, modified, and implemented, and other people's demands to be ignored and suppressed? Said differently, who gets what and under what social circumstances? This is the main issue addressed by this chapter.

In order to answer this question, I have divided the chapter into three main sections:

1. I will first discuss the conditions underlying the formation of **social movements,** or enduring collective attempts to change part or all of the social order by means of rioting, petitioning, striking, demonstrating, and establish-

The history of democracy may be viewed as a struggle for the acquisition of constantly broadening citizenship rights. The level of democracy in a society depends on the capacity of citizens to influence the state through their support of social movements, political parties, and other groups. SOURCE: Larry Fisher/Masterfile.

ing pressure groups, unions, and political parties. We will see that an adequate explanation of protest against the status quo requires the introduction of a set of distinctively sociological issues. These concern (a) the distribution of power in society and (b) the "framing" of political issues in ways that appeal to many people. I will support my arguments by drawing mainly on the experience of some important Canadian social movements. This exercise will also give you a sense of how and why the character of social movements has changed in the course of this century.

2. Next I will discuss how social movements are sometimes transformed into **political parties,** or organizations that seek to control state power. We will see that different political parties tend to support different public policies. We will also see that, under some circumstances, different public policies tend to appeal to different groups of citizens. My analysis of these points will lead me to emphasize that the victory of one political party or another often has far-reaching consequences for different groups of citizens. I will draw on studies of the political sociology of Canada and other countries to make my case.

3. Finally, I will make some observations about the character of politics and social movements as we enter the twenty-first century. In particular, in the context of discussing the impact of globalization on Canada, I will offer a sociological commentary on where we stand politically and where we might be headed.

■ SOCIAL MOVEMENTS

▲ BREAKDOWN THEORY

How, then, does an individual's frustration sometimes get turned into a collective sense of injustice? One answer, first proposed two centuries ago, is that a collective sense of injustice grows when people experience widespread social and/or psychological breakdown.

The **breakdown theory** of social movements first arose in the wake of peasant migration to Europe's cities in the late eighteenth and early nineteenth centuries. Particularly in France, conservative and aristocratic social thinkers were appalled by what they thought they saw. In rural Europe, they said, peasants were constrained by the rigid demands of the church, the rigours of traditional community life, and the strict social hierarchy that taught everyone their place in the world. But in the cities, they continued, God-fearing and obedient peasants were transformed into dangerous "rabble," a disorganized "mob" that escaped the constraints of church, community, and class structure. Once converted into urbanized workers, the peasants allegedly lost faith in God. They suffered moral corruption. They often engaged in criminal activities. They sometimes committed suicide. And, worst of all (according to the conservatives), they frequently took part in collective violence against authorities, expressing dissatisfaction with their lot by demonstrating, striking, and rioting for more bread, more jobs, more pay. All this, according to the conservative social thinkers of the day, resulted from the breakdown of traditional authority, the collapse of established forms of social organization, and the erosion of personal constraint.

There are modern forms of breakdown theory too. For example, in the 1960s, it was proposed that people rebel when many of them experience **relative deprivation,** or an intolerable gap between the social rewards they feel they deserve and the social rewards they expect to receive (Davies, 1969; Gurr, 1970). (Social rewards are widely valued goods, such as money, education, security, and prestige.) According to this school of thought, people are most likely to rebel when rising expectations brought on by rapid economic development and urban migration are met by a sudden decline in social rewards received due to economic recession or war. Other analysts emphasized the breakdown of social rather than personal stability as the main condition underlying the emergence of social movements — the collapse of mechanisms of social control during times when value conflicts, catastrophic events, or other disruptions cause severe "social strain" (Smelser, 1963). In essence, these arguments are little different from the 200-year-old view that people will rebel if traditional forms of social organization and authority fail to keep expectations in check.

Sociological research does not lend much support to the breakdown theory. Most impressively, Charles Tilly and his associates (Lodhi and Tilly, 1973; Tilly, 1979; Tilly, Tilly, and Tilly, 1975) studied social movements in France, Italy, and other Western European countries between 1830 and 1930. By systematically reading newspaper and government reports, they collected data on the number, size, duration, and purposes of strikes and demonstrations throughout the century. In addition to measuring collective unrest in this way, they gathered data on crime rates (which they regarded as an indicator of individual or noncollective unrest) and urban-growth rates (which they regarded as an indicator of the speed with which the rural social order was breaking down). The breakdown theory would have been supported if they had found that rates of urbanization, collective protest, and crime fluctuated together. But they did not. Throughout the nineteenth century and into the twentieth, collective protest did not increase in the wake of mounting social breakdown and crime. Nor did it decrease in peaceful periods marked by less breakdown and crime.

Theories that emphasize social and personal breakdown as the main causes of social-movement formation typically regard movement members as "marginal" people who lack social ties to communities and associations. From this point of view, social movements are as socially disorganized as the larger social and personal conditions that give rise to them. We have already met the socially marginal type in the uprooted peasant who makes his or her way to the supposedly disorganized city and there becomes an urban rebel. In addition, breakdown theorists often brand movement leaders "outside agitators" who stir up otherwise contented citizens.

Again, research demonstrates that breakdown theory is on shaky ground in characterizing movement members and leaders as socially marginal types. In fact, research shows that movement members and leaders usually have strong ties to some types of community organizations. For example, the Co-operative Commonwealth Federation (CCF) of Saskatchewan was a radical farmers' and workers' movement and political party that originated in the early 1930s and first formed the provincial government in 1944. Today's New Democratic Party (NDP) grew out of the CCF. Sociologists have shown that the early members and leaders of the CCF were often key figures in consumer co-operatives and trade unions before they got involved in the movement. These people were socially unattached to establishment or elite organizations. They were, however, very well connected to their communities and to farmers' and workers' social organizations (Lipset, 1968 [1951]).

I conclude, as most sociologists have, that breakdown theory is not a very useful approach for understanding how individual grievances get generalized and become the driving force behind social-movement formation. A second approach, known as solidarity theory, is considerably more useful in that regard. However, as we will see, it fails to provide a completely satisfactory answer to the question of why people sometimes rebel.

▲ SOLIDARITY THEORY

If breakdown theory of social movements originated in conservative thought, **solidarity theory** traces its pedigree to the socialism of Karl Marx. Marx, you will recall, predicted that capitalism would drive inefficient business owners into bankruptcy and peasants into the cities (for synopses of Marx's ideas, see Chapters 1, 7, and 20). According to Marx, these two groups of people would find jobs as urban industrial workers. He predicted, moreover, that competitive pressures would cause successful capitalists to create larger and larger factories. There, huge masses of workers would become aware of their common interests. They would also become aware of their common enemy: the increasingly wealthy owners, from whom they would be separated by a vast

Karl Marx predicted that capitalism would drive business owners into bankruptcy and peasants into the cities. Marx thought that in the cities huge masses of workers would become class-conscious and solidarity would be born. SOURCE: Diego M. Rivera, *Parade in Moscow* (1956). 135.2 x 108.3 cm. Collection Banco National de Mexico, Mexico City. Reproduced with permission of the bank.

social, economic, and political gulf. As a result of these developments, Marx expected workers to form a social movement to further their aims. That social movement, he believed, would spawn radical trade unions and socialist political parties. Expecting the number of industrial workers to grow and the number of capitalists to decline, Marx felt that the workers' movement would eventually become powerful enough to overthrow the existing social order and create a prosperous and egalitarian society governed by human need rather than the profit motive.

Although many of Marx's predictions turned out to be inaccurate, three useful sociological generalizations have been derived from his ideas. First, it is now generally accepted that social movements are new social organizations that emerge to rectify perceived injustices. They are forged in circumstances that create social solidarity, such as the conditions that bound workers together in the large factories of Marx's theory. Moreover, they give rise to new organizational forms, such as the radical trade unions and socialist political parties that Marx wrote about. Second, most analysts concur that social movements are more likely to emerge where opposing groups are socially **segmented,** or separated by large economic inequalities and memberships in different social organizations. Third, it seems that as members of a social movement become more powerful relative to their opponents, social conflict usually intensifies. Indeed, if it becomes powerful enough, a movement may dislodge its opponents from positions of authority. Logically speaking, however, nothing prevents the opposing parties from reaching a compromise rather than engaging in a violent winner-take-all conflict.

Sociologists have extended these ideas in various ways. One extension takes the form of **power-balance theory**. Proponents of this theory think that social-movement formation and success depend on how powerful authorities are compared with partisans of change (Brym, 1979; Gamson, 1968; Korpi, 1974). **Authority** is power that is widely viewed as legitimate, and **authorities** are people who occupy the command posts of legitimized power structures. **Partisans of change** are people who have little influence on legitimized power structures. They form social movements in order to influence such structures from the outside and gain legitimacy for their goals. A second extension of Marx's ideas takes the form of **resource-mobilization theory**. Proponents of this theory argue that social movements crystallize and succeed in achieving their goals to the degree that they have access to scarce resources, such as money and effective communication facilities

(Jenkins, 1983; McCarthy and Zald, 1977; Oberschall, 1973; Tilly, 1978). In the discussion that follows I present a composite sketch of these two theories.

The **power** of a group is its ability to impose its will on other groups (Weber, 1946 [1922]: 180). That capacity depends on its size, level of organization, and access to scarce resources (Bierstedt, 1974). These three determinants of group power are listed in ascending order of importance. A big group is more powerful than a small group if the two are alike in all other respects. However, smaller, well-organized groups are often more powerful than larger, poorly organized ones. And groups that also have the resources to impose their will by force, to buy support, and, most important, to convince others of their ideas through the use of mass media, systems of religious belief, and the like are the most powerful of all.

The likelihood of a social movement emerging depends on the ratio of authorities' to partisans' power. The higher the **power ratio** — the greater the power of established authorities compared with that of partisans of change — the less likely it is that a social movement will emerge. But if the relative power of partisans increases — if the value of the power ratio falls — the likelihood of social conflict and social-movement formation increases. A fall in the power ratio to a value of 1 or less indicates that partisans of change have become more powerful than established authorities. Under such circumstances, a **revolution** takes place. A revolution is a violent and rapid upheaval in which partisans of change assume positions of authority and substantially alter the social, economic, and political organization of society in their favour. Figure 19.1 illustrates how the intensity of conflict varies with the power ratio.

Bearing these theoretical principles in mind, and thinking back to 1968, it is evident why I failed to mobilize my classmates against K.C. Irving. Irving's power was so vast that most New Brunswickers

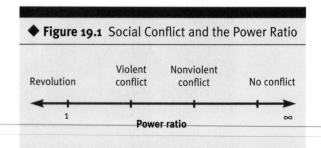

◆ **Figure 19.1** Social Conflict and the Power Ratio

Note: As the ratio of authorities' to potential partisans' power falls, the rate and intensity of conflict increase.

could not even conceive of the need to rebel against the conditions of life that he created for them. His control of resources was pervasive. Not only did he own most of the industrial establishments in the province — the oil refinery and its network of gas stations, the dry docks, the pulp mills, the mines, the logging operations. Every single daily newspaper, most of the weeklies, all of the TV stations, and most of the radio stations were his too. There were few sources of information that Irving did not control. Little wonder that one rarely heard a critical word about his operations and nearly everyone believed that he was the great provider. It was also widely believed that he could virtually make or break provincial governments single-handed. Should one therefore be surprised that mere high-school students refused to take him on?

In their conservatism, my fellow students were only mimicking their parents, who, on the whole, were as powerless as Irving was mighty. New Brunswick had an underdeveloped economy. On average, its citizens' incomes were among the lowest in the country and their unemployment rate was among the highest. Moreover, while Marx had envisaged a sturdy proletariat gaining in solidarity and organization as its members converged in giant factories, New Brunswick, for all of Irving's investment, was only semi-industrialized. Many of its citizens were poor farmers, fishers, and loggers, and its industrial workers were relatively un-unionized and employed in relatively small enterprises. Poorly organized and lacking resources, ordinary New Brunswickers simply did not have the time, money, and organizational experience necessary to engage in political conflict. They could hardly be expected to respond positively to radical political ideas (Brym, 1979). Solidarity theory helps us see why. And, as we will see shortly, it also helps explain why some social movements do emerge and achieve their goals.

▲ FRAMING DISCONTENT

One sociological lesson that I learned from my ill-fated 1968 model parliament was that misery does not always love company. That is, one person's sense of suffering is not necessarily shared by others. I was right to think that our being poisoned by sulphur dioxide was an objective fact. I was wrong to think that objective facts about suffering are always or even often translated into common feelings of injustice that can serve as a basis for recruiting people into social movements. My classmates believed that K.C. Irv-

ing's pulp and paper mill, as well as his myriad other industrial establishments, gave many New Brunswickers jobs. That was an objective fact too, and one that they regarded as more important for their lives and the lives of their families than the pollution problem I raised. As people almost always do, my classmates acted *subjectively* — that is, in accordance with their culturally grounded *interpretation* of the facts.

These observations suggest that an adequate explanation of social-movement formation and success requires more than an analysis of objective social-structural conditions, such as the balance of power between contending parties. From time to time, the crystallization of some social movements strikes trained observers by surprise. Occasionally, the failure of an aggrieved group to press its claim is equally unexpected. And movements that do emerge meet with varying degrees of success. It seems, therefore, that something lies between (1) the social-structural conditions that facilitate the first expression of grievances by members of a new social movement and (2) the recruitment of a substantial number of movement members. Sociologists call that "something" **frame alignment** (cf. Goffman, 1974; Snow, et al., 1986). Frame alignment is the process by which individual interests, beliefs, and values either become congruent and complementary with the activities, goals, and ideology of the movement or fail to do so. Thanks to the efforts of scholars operating mainly in the symbolic-interactionist tradition (on which see Chapters 2 and 20), frame alignment has recently become the subject of sustained sociological investigation.

There are four frame-alignment processes that can occur when social movements try to recruit new members: bridging, amplification, extension, and transformation (Snow et al., 1986). **Frame bridging** is the process by which social movements reach out to other organizations that are thought to contain people who may be sympathetic to the movement's cause. For example, an antinuclear movement may use the mass media, telephone campaigns, and direct mail to appeal to feminist, antiracist, and environmental organizations on the assumption that they are likely to have members who would agree, at least in general terms, with the antinuclear platform.

Frame amplification involves identifying and idealizing values that have so far not featured prominently in the thinking of potential recruits. It also involves clarifying and elevating the importance of positive beliefs about the social movement and what it stands for. For example, in their efforts to win new recruits, movement members might try to emphasize the seriousness of the movement's purpose.

They might try to clearly and convincingly analyze the causes of the problem that the movement is trying to solve, or they might emphasize the likelihood of the movement's success. By doing so, they might increase the movement's appeal to the potential recruit and win him or her over to the cause.

Frame extension involves the stretching of a movement's objectives and activities in order to win recruits who are not initially sympathetic to the movement's original aims. This may involve a "watering down" of the movement's ideals. Alternatively, movement leaders may decide to take action calculated to appeal to nonsympathizers on grounds that have little or nothing to do with the movement's purpose. When rock, punk, or reggae bands play at nuclear-disarmament rallies or gay-liberation festivals, it is not because the music is directly relevant to the movement's goals, nor is it just because movement members want to be entertained. The purpose is also to attract nonmembers. Once attracted by the music, however, nonmembers may make friends and acquaintances in the movement and then be encouraged to attend a more serious-minded meeting during which frame amplification can take place.

Frame transformation is the final framing process. It involves a radical and often sudden change of perspective on the part of people who are unsympathetic and perhaps even antagonistic to a social movement. For example, in the late 1960s and early 1970s, members of the women's movement often held "consciousness-raising" sessions. Members might convince friends, including homemakers with little or no interest in feminism, to attend just one such session out of a sense of personal obligation. At these meetings, a range of everyday problems — such as never having enough time to complete one's housework — might be discussed. But rather than proposing the usual solutions, such as time-saving cleaning techniques and quick-fix recipes, guests would be presented with a radically different kind of analysis. Rather than blaming the homemaker for her inefficiency, movement members shifted the blame for making housework entirely the woman's responsibility to the system of gender relations. This kind of analysis sometimes struck the guest like a thunderbolt. Suddenly, women might see themselves as victims rather than causes of a problem, and uncomfortable aspects of life that seemed inevitable might suddenly appear changeable. Such a rapid shift in interpretation was sure evidence that frame transformation had occurred.

Frame-alignment theory usefully supplements solidarity theory. Solidarity theory focusses on the broad social-structural conditions that facilitate the emergence of social movements: how social groups get segmented, how social solidarity grows among the discontented, how shifts in the balance of power between authorities and partisans of change affect levels of social protest. Frame-alignment theory focusses on the face-to-face interaction processes that help determine a movement's degree of success: the daily strategies employed by movement members to recruit nonmembers who are like-minded, apathetic, or even initially opposed to the movement's goals.

What solidarity and frame-alignment theories lack is an appreciation of how the sociological character of social movements has changed over time. We now turn to an analysis of some twentieth-century Canadian social movements. This analysis will illustrate how the concepts introduced above are used by sociologists. It will also help you develop a better historical sense of our subject matter.

■ SOCIAL MOVEMENTS IN TWENTIETH-CENTURY CANADA

▲ THE FARMERS' MOVEMENT

A century ago in Europe, the largest and most influential social movement — the French called it *the* social movement — consisted of industrial workers. In Canada, however, the development of the workers' movement was delayed, because Canada was a late industrializer. Farming was the most important sector of the Canadian economy until well into the twentieth century, especially on the Prairies. As a result, the most important pre–World War II Canadian social movement consisted mainly of Prairie farmers. They believed that they were being exploited by rich business owners and the federal government in the East. They took collective action to correct the perceived injustice.

Montreal and Toronto financiers and industrialists were the main backers of Confederation. They were keen to see the West settled by European immigrants, who could establish both a market for Eastern-produced manufactured goods and an agricultural region whose exports would provide revenue for the new Dominion. Consequently, they succeeded in getting the federal government to place high tariffs on manufactured goods. That protected Eastern manufacturers from foreign competition. It also made the ploughs, tractors, clothing, and other finished goods needed by Western farmers more expensive. Furthermore, the federal government set low freight rates for shipping grain out of the West and shipping manufactured goods in. That stunted Western economic development, helping to lock the West into the position of an agricultural frontier. Finally, the availability of credit was controlled by Eastern banks and the marketing of grain by a subsidiary of the Canadian Pacific Railway, with its head office in Montreal. Farmers persistently complained that farm loans were too expensive and grain prices too low. They blamed that state of affairs, once again, on Eastern business interests.

Because of the conditions just described, Western farmers soon came to view their region as an internal colony of Canada. Solidarity theorists would agree that Prairie farmers were not just disadvantaged but highly segmented from the East. It is also clear that the farmers constituted a large group living in a region with an unusually homogeneous class structure. As a result, an angry farmer could easily see that many other people faced identical problems, had the same interests, and faced the same enemies. These were ideal structural conditions for social-movement formation.

In 1906, Prairie farmers decided to take collective economic action. They established a company to collect wheat in their own grain-elevator system and sell it directly to the central wheat exchange. This eliminated the function and profits of the Eastern-owned grain-elevator system and increased farmers' revenues. In the following years, a whole series of marketing and consumer co-operatives were established in order to reduce costs of production and increase incomes. As solidarity theorists would emphasize, the creation of Prairie co-operatives turned farmers into a highly cohesive group and gave them important organizational experience that would prove useful in the coming decades when their actions turned political.

The politicization of the farmers' movement began in the 1910s, when wheat prices fell on the world market and freight rates and the cost of manufactured goods rose. Caught in a cost–price squeeze, the farmers decided that they should try to influence the federal government to lower the tariff on manufactured goods, buy grain that could not be immediately sold, and set a floor price for wheat. However, their first major attempt to enter politics in the 1920s was not very successful, partly because they were uncertain whether they should remain independent of existing political parties or try to influence the ruling Liberal party from within.

It was during the height of the Great Depression that farmers firmly chose the path of political independence. In Regina, Saskatchewan, in 1933, the CCF, a democratic-socialist alliance between organized farmers and a smaller group of unionized industrial workers, was created. The CCF aimed to decrease social inequality by expanding the state's role in economic planning. It issued an eloquent and stirring statement, "the Regina Manifesto," that serves as a model of frame amplification (see Box 19.1). The Regina Manifesto clearly defined the nature of the problems that beset working Canadians, appealed to people's sense of justice and traditional democratic values, and emphasized the ability of the movement to win state power. It helped recruit many converts to the cause.

In addition, frame extension was used to win new recruits to the movement. Most Saskatchewan farmers were landowners, and the CCF's socialist idea that land should be government-owned sounded like robbery to them. In order to appeal to a wider base of supporters, the CCF had to water down its radicalism, particularly on the land-ownership question. By presenting itself as a champion for the reform and humanization of the capitalist system rather than a Marxist-style movement — an advocate of unemployment insurance, medicare, and low tariffs rather than state ownership of the means of production — the CCF went on to win new adherents throughout the 1930s.

Nonetheless, the CCF was unable to win a provincial election until a key resource was entered into the political mix. During the Great Depression, many farmers were just too destitute to care much about politics, let alone invest the time and energy to get involved in the movement. As solidarity theorists would predict, however, when the Depression ended in 1939 and the economy picked up, more time and money were available to farmers for political activity. They then flocked to the CCF. In 1944, the CCF became the first socialist-influenced government in Saskatchewan and in North America. It continued until 1961 to be an important force for change on the left wing of the Canadian political spectrum, both provincially and federally.

▲ THE WORKERS' MOVEMENT

By 1961, Canada was no longer just a granary (and a fishery and a woodlot) to the world. Fewer than 1 in 10 Canadians were farmers. Nearly 7 in 10 worked for a wage either in industrial "blue-collar" occupations or "white-collar" service jobs. In order better to reflect the shape of the changing class structure, the CCF reinvented itself in 1961. To-

Box 19.1
Frame Amplification: "The Regina Manifesto" of 1933

The CCF is a federation of organizations whose purpose is the establishment in Canada of a Co-operative Commonwealth in which the principle regulating production, distribution and exchange will be the supplying of human needs and not the making of profits.

We aim to replace the present capitalist system, with its inherent injustice and inhumanity, by a social order from which the domination and exploitation of one class by another will be eliminated, in which economic planning will supersede unregulated private enterprise and competition, and in which genuine democratic self-government, based upon economic equality, will be possible. The present order is marked by glaring inequalities of wealth and opportunity, by chaotic waste and instability; and in an age of plenty it condemns the great mass of people to poverty and insecurity. Power has become more and more concentrated into the hands of a small irresponsible minority of financiers and industrialists and to their predatory interests the majority are habitually sacrificed. When private profit is the main stimulus to economic effort, our society oscillates between periods of feverish prosperity in which the main benefits go to speculators and profiteers, and of catastrophic depression, in which the common man's normal state of insecurity and hardship is accentuated. We believe that these evils can be removed only in a planned and socialized economy in which our natural resources and the principal means of production and distribution are owned, controlled and operated by the people.

SOURCE: "The Regina Manifesto," adopted at the First National Convention of the CCF, Regina, Saskatchewan, July 1933. Reprinted in Walter D. Young, *The Anatomy of a Party: The National CCF, 1932–61* (Toronto: University of Toronto Press, 1969), pp. 304–305. Reprinted with permission.

gether with the Canadian Labour Congress, the country's biggest trade-union umbrella organization, it created the NDP. In this manner, the left-wing social movement that began in rural Saskatchewan went to town in order to mobilize the largest disadvantaged group in the country: the working class.

The NDP was only modestly successful. Since 1961, it has formed provincial governments several times in British Columbia, Saskatchewan, and Manitoba, and once in Ontario. But in every federal election since 1961, Canadian workers gave more support to the Liberal party than to the NDP. And after winning a record 43 seats (14.6 percent of the total) in the 1988 federal election, the NDP was reduced to a mere 9 seats (3.1 percent of the total) in the 1993 federal election and 21 seats (7.0 percent of the total) in the 1997 federal election (see Figure 19.2).

Political scientists frequently say that one of the biggest problems faced by the NDP, and the CCF before it, was the Liberal party, which often took ideas from the left, made them part of the Liberal plat-

form, and thereby won the support of most Canadian workers. Sociologists would say that the Liberals have been masterful practitioners of frame extension. The Liberals could well afford to put CCF-NDP ideas into practice. For three decades after the end of World War II, Canada witnessed rapid economic growth. During that time, the Liberal party implemented unemployment insurance, medicare, government pensions, a greatly expanded system of accessible higher education, and other features of the modern welfare state that blue- and white-collar workers strongly favoured.

From a broad, historical perspective, the post–World War II period of growth in the welfare state is best viewed as a struggle for citizenship rights. More precisely, it was the third stage in a 200-year international struggle aimed at enlarging the rights of citizens. All nation-states specify the rights and obligations of their citizens. They do not, however, do so once and for all. In different eras, different classes and groups have gained enough power to ex-

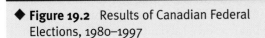

◆ Figure 19.2 Results of Canadian Federal Elections, 1980–1997

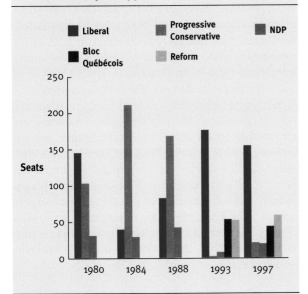

Note: In addition to the results shown here, one independent was elected in the 1984, 1993, and 1997 elections.

SOURCE: Adapted from "Distribution of House of Commons Seats at General Elections, by Political Affiliation, Canada, Provinces and Territories, http://www.StatCan.CA/Documents/English/Pgdb/State/Government/govt10.htm (September 21, 1996); Edward Greenspon, "Liberal Unity Agenda Part of Election Debris," *The Globe and Mail*, June 3, 1997, pp. A1, A16.

pand citizenship rights in ways that suit their own interests. Citizenship rights have thus changed as new classes and other groups have forced themselves on to the political stage. For example, in the eighteenth century, the fight for **civil citizenship** — the right to free speech, freedom of religion, and justice before the law — was fought and won by wealthy British property owners. Civil citizenship was simultaneously extended to Britain's colonies, including what was later to become Canada. In the nineteenth century, the fight for **political citizenship** — the right to run for office and vote — was fought and won by the male middle class and the more prosperous strata of the working class. Early in the twentieth century, these rights were won by women and less-prosperous workers. For most of the twentieth century, the main struggle was for **social citizenship** — the right to a certain level of economic security and full participation in the social life of the country. The main champions of social citizenship have been blue- and white-collar workers (Marshall, 1965).

Through their support of political parties and trade unions, by means of voting, striking, demonstrating, and meeting with public officials, the in-creasingly numerous and materially better-off class of blue- and white-collar workers successfully struggled for social citizenship in the post–World War II era. Workers pushed Canadian governments to ever-higher levels of public-welfare spending. Governments borrowed large sums of money to finance the growth of the welfare state, counting on continued rapid economic growth to pay off the debt.

Then came the 1970s. By the middle of that decade, it was evident that the spending spree was about to end. Economic growth began to lag. Unemployment and inflation both rose. Soon, governments were strapped for funds. They first had to borrow money to maintain social programs. Then they had to borrow just to pay interest on the existing debt. By 1995, the federal government debt stood at $541 128 000 000 — well over half a trillion dollars — and interest payment on the debt was the biggest single expense in the annual budget (Statistics Canada, 1996). Under pressure of the debt, the welfare state ceased to grow. In the early 1990s, it began to shrink as governments started to cut services (Myles, 1995). In addition, many government-owned businesses were privatized in order to raise revenues.

The shrinking of the welfare state and the decreased involvement of government in the economy decreased the standard of living of Canadian workers. The **restructuring** of the global economy undertaken by a reinvigorated capitalist class had the same effect. Restructuring involved (1) removing barriers to free trade and free capital movement, (2) breaking up the production process into separate parts and locating each part where it could be carried out most cheaply and efficiently, (3) using advanced computer technology in the production process, and (4) hiring fewer full-time workers and more part-time, seasonal, and contract workers. Each of these innovations caused or threatened job losses to full-time workers and, therefore, dampened the vigour of the workers' movement. For example, big business owners recognized that by making investment capital more mobile internationally, they would be free to locate their operations or parts of their operations wherever taxes and wages are lowest and labour supplies are best suited to company needs. Workers, however, are not very mobile internationally. They are rooted in local communities and anchored by family ties. As a result, when faced by the threat of capital flight, they are forced to compete for jobs and attract investment by keeping their wages as low as possible. Some Canadian factory owners have moved their operations to the United States, Mexico, and other countries to take advantage of lower labour costs; many more have prevented wage rates from rising in Canada by virtue of an implied or explicit threat to relocate. The use of high technology in the workplace, combined with the switch to nontraditional forms of employment, caused additional full-time job losses and implied the threat of still more losses unless workers made material sacrifices. As a result, Canadian workers are worse off now than they were twenty years ago in terms of both wages and state benefits.

Solidarity theory leads us to expect that the strengthened position of employers and the weakened position of workers since the mid-1970s ought to be reflected in less protest action by the workers' movement. For example, we might expect growth in union membership to have declined and strikes to have occurred less frequently. Figures 19.3 and 19.4 show this to be the case. Consider strikes first. By withholding their labour, workers have historically been able to extract higher wages and better working conditions from their employers. In the 1970s, Canada was in fact the most strike-prone industri-

alized country in the world, and in the first half of the 1980s it still ranked second only to Italy (Ward, 1981; International Labour Organization, 1987). Since 1974, however, the number of strikes that have taken place in Canada per 100 000 workers has fallen. Now strikes are relatively rare events. In 1974, there were nearly sixteen strikes for every 100 000 nonagricultural workers in Canada. In 1995, there were just over three strikes per 100 000 nonagricultural workers (see Figure 19.3). Workers, recognizing their poor bargaining position in the light of economic restructuring and a shrinking welfare state, are increasingly loath to strike. Data on union membership tell a similar story. The proportion of unionized nonagricultural workers, or *union density,* increased steadily from about 7 percent in 1911 to about 38 percent in 1978. Thereafter, growth stagnated and union density has decreased somewhat in recent years (see Figure 19.4). Thus, the workers' movement has been on the decline for roughly two decades.

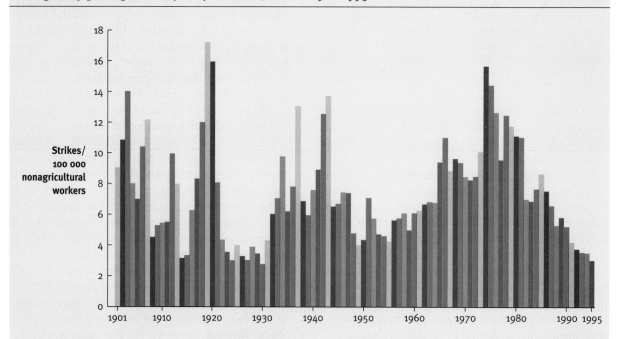

◆ **Figure 19.3** Weighted Frequency of Strikes, Canada 1901–1995

Note: "Weighted frequency" is the number of strikes per 100 000 nonagricultural workers. Estimates for the number of nonagricultural workers for the periods between the 1901, 1911, and 1921 censuses have been interpolated.

SOURCE: Adapted from *Strikes and Lockouts in Canada 1968*, Cat. no. L2-1/1968 (Ottawa: Economic and Research Branch, Canada Department of Labour, 1970), pp. 12–13; *Strikes and Lockouts in Canada 1985*, Cat. no. L160-2999/85B (Ottawa: Supply and Services Canada, 1985), p. 9; special tabulation of strikes statistics for 1986–95 prepared by the Workplace Information Directorate, Human Resources Development Canada, Ottawa; *Labour Organizations in Canada 1972*, Cat. no. L2-2-1972 (Ottawa: Economics and Research Branch, Canada Department of Labour, 1973), pp. xxii–xxiii; *1994–1995 Directory of Labour Organizations in Canada*, Cat. no. L2-2-1995 (Ottawa: Supply and Services Canada, 1995), p. xiii; *Fifth Census of Canada, 1911*, Vol. VI (Ottawa: Census and Statistics Office, Department of Trade and Commerce, 1915), Table 1, p. 3.

◆ **Figure 19.4** Percentage of Nonagricultural Workers Unionized, Canada 1911–1994

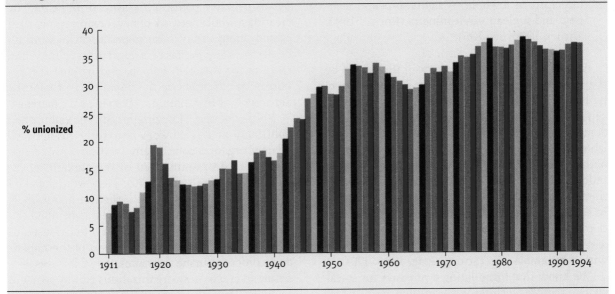

Note: Estimates for the number of nonagricultural workers for the periods between the 1901, 1911, and 1921 censuses have been interpolated.

SOURCE: Adapted from *Labour Organizations in Canada 1972*, Cat. no. L2-2-1972 (Ottawa: Economics and Research Branch, Canada Department of Labour, 1973), pp. xxii–xxiii; *1994–1995 Directory of Labour Organizations In Canada*, Cat. no. L2-2-1995 (Ottawa: Supply and Services Canada, 1995), p. xiii; *Fifth Census of Canada, 1911*, Vol. VI (Ottawa: Census and Statistics Office, Department of Trade and Commerce, 1915), Table 1, p. 3.

Does this mean, as some analysts say, that the workers' movement will soon go the way of the farmers' movement (Clark and Lipset, 1991)? I will argue in the concluding section of this chapter that such an interpretation is probably not warranted. For the moment, however, I want to round out my discussion of the history of social movements in twentieth-century Canada by turning to so-called new social movements.

▲ NEW SOCIAL MOVEMENTS

When sociologists speak of **new social movements,** they have in mind the antinuclear movement, the women's movement, various antiracist movements, the environmental movement, and the movement for gay and lesbian rights (Melucci, 1980; 1995). Despite their diverse aims, these movements share five characteristics:

1. Although some of them originated as much as a century ago, they assumed their present form in just the last three or four decades.

2. With the exception of the environmental movement in continental Western Europe, they have tended not to form separate political parties.

Instead, they have fought their battles mainly within established parties or outside the political system.

3. They tend to attract a disproportionately large number of highly educated people in the social, educational, and cultural fields: teachers, university professors, students, journalists, social workers, artists, actors, writers, and the like (Brint, 1984; Rootes, 1995). That is because people in these occupations work outside the business community, which is often hostile to their interests; because in their work they often get personally involved in their clients' problems, sometimes to the point of becoming their advocates; and because their higher education exposes them to radical ideas and makes those ideas appealing.

4. New social movements have an uneasy relationship with older social movements, and this uneasiness sometimes erupts into open conflict.

5. They have carried the struggle for citizenship rights to a fourth stage, one that I would like to call the stage of **universal citizenship**. That is, the new social movements wish to extend citizenship rights to all adult members of society. Some of them therefore promote the rights of groups that have been excluded from full social

participation on the basis of gender, sexual orientation, or race. Others promote the rights of humanity as a whole — rights to peace, security, and a clean environment (Roche, 1995; Turner, 1986: 85–105).

All five of these features are well illustrated by the women's movement, the origins of which may be traced back to the late nineteenth century. A century ago, women began to play a smaller role in domestic and farm work and started to enter the paid labour force in significant numbers. Possessing more of their own economic resources, they became more independent-minded. They began to realize that they might free themselves of oppressive authority in the home. They also started to understand that there was nothing inevitable about their receiving less pay and working in worse conditions than men with comparable jobs (Strong-Boag, 1986: 179).

We know that formulating a program for social change requires such resources as time, money, and education. It should therefore come as no shock that the "first wave" of the women's movement was composed of highly educated professionals. A group of women with just that social profile established the Canadian Woman Suffrage Association in Toronto in 1883. By means of demonstrating, petitioning, and gaining the support of influential liberal-minded men, they won the right to vote for women federally in 1918, in all provinces but Quebec by 1925, and in Quebec in 1940.

Along with the right to vote, women won the right to run for public office. They immediately exercised that right, running mainly on the CCF and Liberal party tickets. A woman was first elected to provincial office in Alberta in 1917 and to the federal parliament in 1921.

In provincial legislatures and the federal parliament, women sought institutional reform through government action. Specifically, they pursued more equitable pay for women, easier access to higher education, protection from domestic violence, and a fair share of family assets and child support in the event of divorce or desertion. But progress was slow on all these fronts. That was partly because women's representation in the country's legislatures remained meagre. Even as late as the federal election in 1993, women composed just 18 percent of federal MPs, and some female MPs were by no means advocates of women's rights (Bashevkin, 1986; see also Chapter 8).

Because of this slow progress, feminists developed a strategy in the 1960s and 1970s that was oriented less toward established political institutions and more toward grass-roots action. The new strategy sought to achieve change not just "from above," by means of party politics, but also "from below," by creating a whole network of new organizations, such as study groups, consciousness-raising circles, women's book stores, rape-crisis centres, abortion clinics, and shelters for battered women, and by creating opportunities to publicize the importance of feminist aims, such as International Women's Day marches.

It was not only slow progress on the established political front that led women to create this network of new organizations. Many "second-wave" feminists were deeply involved in the student movement of the 1960s and 1970s. They were appalled to discover that, despite much rhetoric about liberation and equality, it was men who controlled the student movement and men who often refused to allow feminist issues to become part of their agenda. In order to pursue their aims, they felt it was necessary to create new organizations run by women.

Today, then, the women's movement operates at both the grass-roots level and within established political organizations to achieve its aims. It also contains internal divisions. Liberal feminists believe that women will be able to participate fully in society if they achieve equality of opportunity with men. Therefore, they advocate policies aimed at pay equity and the elimination of gender discrimination in the workplace. Radical feminists hold that male domination is rooted in the family. They champion free and safe contraception and abortion, an equitable division of domestic labour, and the like. Socialist feminists maintain that legal equality is not enough to ensure that women can participate fully in society. In addition, they argue, the state should provide affordable and accessible day-care facilities and other services. These services, they say, could alleviate the economic burdens that prevent most women, especially those in the working class, from taking full advantage of available opportunities for education and employment (see Chapter 20). Thus, despite their different emphases, all three feminisms share a strong desire to see members of a previously marginal group expand their citizenship rights and become full participants in society.

Some social scientists argue that old social movements were grounded in materialistic values. Farmers, for example, demanded lower tariffs; workers, higher wages. But, they continue, most people in the advanced capitalist countries now have their materialistic needs filled. Therefore, they conclude, new social movements are grounded in "postmaterialist" values and "identity politics," such as gay men wanting to have homosexuality recognized as a legitimate identity and way of life (Inglehart, 1990). Quite apart from the dubiousness of the claim that most Canadians are satisfied materially when unemployment stands at nearly 10 percent and the average family's purchasing power has been falling for more than two decades, I believe that this interpretation misses what is really historically significant about new social movements. They are every bit as materialistic as earlier movements in their desire to expand their members' citizenship rights. But, as the foregoing analysis of the women's movement suggests, it is the *universalizing* of citizenship claims to include previously marginal groups and society as a whole that, among other characteristics discussed above, distinguishes new social movements from old.

■ MOVEMENTS, PARTIES, STATES, AND DEMOCRACY

▲ SOCIAL MOVEMENTS AND THE STATE

There are, or there can be, three stages in a **social-movement life cycle**:

1. As we have seen, if social-structural conditions permit, and if activists can frame grievances in culturally appealing ways, discontent becomes collective and movements enter their first phase of development, which may be called *crystallization.*
2. If movements succeed in building up a stable membership and organizational base, they usually move from an exclusive focus on short-lived actions, such as demonstrations, to more enduring and routine actions, including running for public office and establishing a publicity bureau. This is the second phase of movement growth, often called *bureaucratization.* When a movement bureaucratizes, it hires movement professionals to work full-time on various movement activities. Moreover, its tactics and even its goals may moderate as movement professionals develop a vested interest in the stability of operations and in the security of their jobs.
3. On the one hand, movements may never bureaucratize. They may be repressed by their opponents. Early on, their leaders may be co-opted and deradicalized by being brought into the ranks of the authorities. On the other hand, movements that do bureaucratize may succeed

in making their goals and values part of the everyday lives of most members of a society. This occurs when a movement's goals become widely accepted by existing authorities or when the movement removes old authorities from office and becomes the dominant force in society. In either case, we may speak of the *incorporation* of social movements into established practice as a social movement's third stage.

Thinking about the three stages of the social-movement life cycle highlights something that may not be at all obvious: The effects of past collective unrest are, to varying degrees, embedded in aspects of our everyday lives that we are likely to take for granted. What could be more routine than a woman enrolling in a university, or a clerk joining a union, or a miner voting on election day, or a teenager taking the household recycling bin to the curb early Tuesday morning, or a gay couple walking hand in hand down a busy urban street? Yet, behind each of these everyday actions — and many more — lie years of protest and conflict that finally succeeded in legitimizing formerly unaccepted and even illegal actions. One of the most remarkable things about so much of the content, organization, and tempo of your life is that it is not natural and not the result of people quietly sitting and reaching a consensus on how things should be done. It is the result of collective conflict, some of it bloody.

Since so much social-movement activity is aimed at changing laws and government policies, the **state** is one of the most important repositories of past collective conflict. It embodies in its organizations and practices the history of a country's discontent.

The state is a set of institutions that formulate and implement a country's laws, policies, and binding regulations (see Figure 19.5). In democratic countries such as Canada, the government is formed by the elected members of the political party that wins most seats in a general election. The Canadian government is composed of the head of the party, who becomes prime minister, and the cabinet ministers he or she selects to advise him or her. It is the job of the government to initiate policies, propose laws, and see that they are enforced, which is why the government is also called the *executive branch* of the state. Proposed laws are turned into operating statutes by the *legislature,* which consists of all the people elected to parliament. It is the responsibility of the *judiciary* or court system to interpret laws and regulations — that is, to determine in contentious cases whether and how particular laws and regulations apply. Implementation of laws is undertaken by the state's *administrative apparatus* or bureaucracy. If laws are broken or the state's security is jeopardized, it is the role of the *coercive apparatus* — the police and military — to enforce the law and protect the state.

The state, then, is a set of institutions that exercise control over society. But individuals in **civil society,** the private sphere of life, also exercise control over the state through a variety of organizations and institutions (see Figure 19.5). We have already seen in some detail how social movements may influence the state. In addition, the mass media keep a watchful and critical eye on the state and thus help keep the public informed about the quality of government. Interest groups or "lobbies" are formed by trade unions, manufacturers' associations, ethnic groups, and other organizations to advise politicians on their members' desires and to remind politicians how much their members' votes and campaign contributions matter. And political parties regularly seek to mobilize voters as they compete for control of government.

▲ HOW DEMOCRATIC? THREE THEORIES

How democratic are the arrangements just described? Do the interactions of state and civil society ensure that every Canadian citizen has a roughly equal say in the determination of laws and policies? Or, as George Orwell asked in *Animal Farm,* are some citizens more equal than others? Do we, as Abraham Lincoln claimed for the Americans, enjoy "government of the people, by the people, for the people"? Or is it more accurate to say, along with one wag, that we suffer from "government of the people, by the lawyers, for the business owners?" These are among the chief questions asked by sociologists who study the state and its operations. It is now time to consider them in greater detail.

Three main theories have been developed to account for the relationship between state and civil society.

◆ **Figure 19.5** The Institutions of State and Civil Society

THE STATE

- **Legislature** (parliament: makes laws)
- **Executive** (government: initiates laws)
- **Judiciary** (courts: interpret laws)

- **Administrative apparatus** (bureaucracy: implements laws)
- **Coercive apparatus** (police, military: enforce laws)

Two-way control

CIVIL SOCIETY

- **Political parties**
- **Interest groups**
- **Mass media**
- **Voluntary associations**

Social movements

The Assembly of First Nations, which represents 633 Native groups, demands that aboriginal Canadians have the right to formulate their own laws and rejects some Canadian laws. Here, aboriginal peoples protest certain taxes outside a government office. SOURCE: Dick Hemingway.

1. According to **pluralist theory,** we live in a heterogeneous society with many competing interests and centres of power. For example, the interests of people who control schools are often different from the interests of people who control provincial governments. Teachers may want school budgets to grow, politicians may want them to shrink. Indeed, even within one social institution, there are likely to be competing interests. In the economy, for example, oil exporters may want free trade with the United States so that they can increase exports, while clothing manufacturers may oppose free trade because they are afraid of foreign competition. Because there is such heterogeneity between and within institutions, no one group is able to control politics. Instead, say the pluralists, all voters and interest groups influence the political process. Sometimes one category of voters or one set of interest groups wins a political battle, sometimes another. In the long run, however, pluralism ensures democracy because no one group of people is always able to control politics. The best-known Canadian application of this theory is John Porter's famous *The Vertical Mosaic* (1965).

2. Theorists supporting **elite theory** do not deny that there are competing interests within and between institutions, nor do they deny that voters and interest groups are free to influence the political process. They insist, however, that well-to-do people have much more political influence than others. It is mainly the well-to-do who have the time, money, and organizational resources to run for office, and it is mainly the well-to-do who contribute money directly to political parties (see Table 19.1). More generally, people from higher classes tend to predominate in dominant institutions and they are usually in basic agreement about the most important issues confronting a society. Canadian elite studies thus show that roughly 40 percent of senior executives and members of the boards of directors of large corporations, senior federal and provincial politicians, and senior federal bureaucrats were born into the wealthiest 10 percent of Canadian families. Hardly any of them were born into industrial working-class families (Brym, 1989; Clement, 1975; Olsen, 1980). Moreover, elite members from wealthy-class origins are linked not just by class interest but by a host of social ties. Unlike the vast majority of Canadians, they tend to have been educated at private schools, belong to expensive private clubs, and sit on the boards of hospitals and charitable foundations. Elite theorists conclude that social ties and class interests enable well-to-do elite members to form a cohesive group that controls politics; society is therefore much less democratic than we are often led to believe.

3. Pluralists assume that all major groups in society have approximately equal power. Elitists assume that members of the upper class have most power. Both assume that the distribution of power in society does not change much over time. However, even casual observation suggests that all of these assumptions are problematic. After all, change in government occurs often and it frequently reflects change in the classes and groups that control the state. For example, when a Western European labour government loses an election to a conservative party, trade unionists and blue- and white-collar workers usually lose out to professionals and business owners. This is reflected both in the social composition of the political elite and in the kinds of policies adopted by the new government. An adequate theory of democracy must be able to account for such political change, and it must therefore free itself of the assumption

◆ **Table 19.1** Federal Political Contributors per 10 000 Tax Filers, by Income and Region, Canada, 1988

Annual income	Atlantic	Quebec	Ontario	West	Canada
<$25 000	21	17	34	80	42
$25 000 < $50 000	126	73	126	253	150
$50 000 < $75 000	429	242	304	467	353
$75 000 +	1149	679	790	964	830

SOURCE: Jeffrey Frank, "Voting and Contributing: Political Participation in Canada," *Canadian Social Trends*, Cat. no. 11-008, Winter 1992, pp. 2–6. Reproduced by authority of the Minister of Industry, 1997.

that the distribution of power in society is fixed. Power-balance theory, which we encountered in our discussion of social movements, does just that. Proponents of power-balance theory argue that the degree to which a political system is democratic depends on how power is distributed in a given place and time. Accordingly, power-balance theorists measure variations in the social distribution of power. They then show how those variations are reflected in the successes and failures of different political parties and the rejection and adoption of different state policies. Along with the pluralists, they recognize that society is truly democratic only when power is relatively widely distributed, for it is only then that citizens can take full advantage of their political rights and expand their social rights. They concur with the elitists that society is not very democratic when power is highly concentrated in the hands of a few wealthy citizens. But by treating the distribution of power as a variable, they improve our understanding of the relationship among power, parties, policies, and democracy. Let us now see in greater detail how power-balance theorists do their work by examining class voting and public policy in Canada from a comparative perspective.

▲ THE SOCIAL BASES OF LABOUR PARTIES AND POLICIES: CANADA IN COMPARATIVE PERSPECTIVE

Studies of voting in Canada have repeatedly found that social class is only weakly associated with voting for different parties (Clarke et al., 1996: 53, 97). Said differently, people's class position, as measured by annual income, has little influence on their tendency to vote for one party or another. For example, neither workers with modest incomes nor poor people tended to vote disproportionately for the NDP, Canada's democratic-socialist party.

The political expression of class difference is weak in Canada partly because regional and linguistic divisions have absorbed the attention and energies of citizens and politicians since Confederation. The conflict between Quebec and the rest of Canada has been especially important in this regard. But that is not the whole story. Interestingly, Canadian workers *have* tended to vote disproportionately for the NDP if they reside in areas where union membership is widespread and the NDP has previously formed a gov-

ernment (Brym, Gillespie, and Lenton, 1989). This pattern is repeated in other nations. In countries such as Sweden and Norway, which have high levels of union membership and where democratic-socialist parties have formed national governments, class voting is much more widespread than it is in countries of low union membership and weak democratic-socialist parties, such as Canada and the United States (Korpi, 1983).

If power-balance theorists are right, the implications of this pattern ought to be profound. The exercise of citizenship rights by lower-class citizens — their tendency to vote, their ability to run for office, their capacity to influence public policy — ought to be greater where they have more access to political resources; in other words, where they are relatively powerful. It follows that Sweden should be considered more democratic than Canada. True, citizens of both countries are legally free to vote and influence their governments. But because lower classes are more powerful in Sweden, power-balance theorists would expect Swedes' legal right to vote and influence governments to be turned into real political influence on a wider scale.

In order to see whether the power-balance theory is valid, examine Table 19.2. There, eight industrialized countries are compared along five dimensions. First, note that the eight countries are divided into three groups: those where workers have high, moderate, and low power in the market and in politics. Next, observe that voter turnout decreases as we move from countries of type 1 to countries of type 2 to countries of type 3. As power-balance theory suggests, more citizens are able to take advantage of their right to vote where working classes are more powerful. Finally, observe that there is more economic inequality as one moves from countries of type 1 to countries of type 2 to countries of type 3. In other words, the state is forced to redistribute more income to the less well-to-do where working classes are more powerful, again as power-balance theory suggests. Studies of public pensions and other welfare benefits in industrialized countries reach similar conclusions about the effect of working-class power on the distribution of social rewards in society (e.g., Myles, 1989 [1984]).

In general, we may say that when and where lower classes are more powerful, political and social citizenship rights are exercised more fully. In other words, where power is widely distributed, there is more democracy and lower classes are materially better off. I conclude this section by emphasizing an important implication of this argument: Since women

◆ **Table 19.2** Working-Class Power, Voter Turnout, and Income Inequality in Eight Industrialized Countries

Country	Power in the market: average % unionized	Power in politics: average weighted cabinet share	% voter turnout	Income inequality	
				% of total income to richest 10%	% poor
1. Sweden, Norway	59	High	86	22	4
2. United Kingdom, Australia	47	Moderate	84	24	8
3. France, Canada, United States, West Germany	28	Low	75	28	11

Note: All percentages are rounded. Average % unionized = average percent of nonagricultural workers unionized, 1946–76. Average weighted cabinet share = the proportion of seats in each cabinet held by socialist parties weighted by the socialist share of seats in parliament and the duration of the cabinet, 1946–1976. Percent voter turnout = average percent of eligible voters voting in federal elections, 1980s. Percent top decile = percent of total national income going to the top 10% of income earners, 1960s and 1970s. Percent poor = percentage of the population living in relative poverty according to OECD standards with poverty line standardized according to household size, 1960s and 1970s.

SOURCE: Adapted from Jeffrey Frank, "Voting and Contributing: Political Participation in Canada," *Canadian Social Trends*, Cat. no. 11-008, Winter 1992, pp. 2–6; Walter Korpi, *The Democratic Class Struggle* (London: Routledge and Kegan Paul, 1983), pp. 40, 196.

are disproportionately concentrated in low-income, low-status jobs (see Chapter 8), they benefit more than men when power is broadly distributed. Thus, in countries like Sweden and Norway, the ratio of women's to men's earnings is considerably higher than in countries like Canada and the United States, parental benefits are superior, and child-care facilities are more widely available and affordable (O'Connor, 1996).

■ GLOBALIZATION AND THE FUTURE OF SOCIAL MOVEMENTS AND POLITICS IN CANADA

In many respects, the world is a more unified political, economic, cultural, and social system than it was just a few decades ago. Instantaneous international communications, giant multinational corporations, and increasingly powerful transnational organizations such as the United Nations and the European Union tie people from different countries together, give them more in common, and promote a new global consciousness. Paradoxically, however, the forces that are unifying and homogenizing the world simultaneously fragment it. As transnational entities grow, the authority of the old nation-state erodes. This creates opportunities for various ethnic and religious groups to form movements of ethnic exclusion, national liberation, and militant religious expansion (Barber,

1996). The twin processes of homogenization and fragmentation are commonly known as **globalization** (see Chapter 17).

The breakup of the former U.S.S.R. and the former Yugoslavia, the inability of many weak African states to govern their multitribal populations, the independence movements in the Basque region of Spain, East Timor in Indonesia, and northern Italy all indicate the eroding sovereignty of old nation-states and the growth of ethnic, national, and religious movements. The fragmenting effects of globalization are felt in Canada too; the breakup of the country is a real possibility early in the new century.

Free trade with the United States and Mexico has made north–south commerce the lifeblood of the Canadian economy. At the same time, the erosion of federal welfare programs has left the central government with few services to provide, weakening the East–West ties that bind the provinces together. In this context, Quebec has led a successful provincial struggle to gain authority to tax and provide services. As a result, Canada is already one of the most decentralized states in the world. Quebec's second referendum on independence, held in 1995, came within 1 percent of the majority needed to permit a declaration of independence. A third referendum on independence is expected before the year 2000.

Since 1867, the Quebec issue has dominated the political agenda in this country. The regional/linguistic cleavage between Quebec and the rest of Canada has limited the degree to which economic problems have been expressed in class terms. Decentralized, linguistically distinct union organiza-

The sovereign power of nation-states declines as they become part of larger political entities, such as those created by the Canada–U.S. Free Trade Agreement and the North American Free Trade Agreement. SOURCE: Dick Hemingway.

tions have prevented workers from speaking with one voice, and political parties have failed to define economic troubles as class issues. It follows that if Quebec does separate, regional/linguistic cleavages will decrease in the rest of Canada and class voting is likely to increase (Brym, 1992).

This is not the only way in which globalization may revive the dormant labour movement in this country. As you know from our earlier discussion, the globalizing forces that led to economic restructuring weakened the Canadian labour movement for more than two decades beginning in the early 1970s. But restructuring also placed some workers in strategically sensitive positions, thus effectively increasing their bargaining power. For example, General Motors (GM) restructured by having plants located in different parts of North America specialize in different product lines; producing parts only as immediately needed, thus keeping inventory costs down; and "outsourcing," or contracting outside

firms to produce parts for less than it would cost GM to make them internally. All of these innovations enabled GM to cut the size of its workforce — so much so that the auto workers were eventually motivated to strike in 1996 for fear of additional job losses. But they felt able to force GM's hand because the corporation was much more delicately organized than it was before restructuring. With small inventories and highly specialized production facilities, a shutdown of one plant in St. Catharines, Ontario, quickly threatened the entire North American operation of one of the world's largest corporations. Paradoxically, new production processes that shrank the workforce, kept its wages low, and halted its unionization also gave auto workers more power because the new system of production was more sensitive to disruption than the old system was.

Significantly, the now conventional response to union militancy — threatening to locate operations elsewhere — will be less of an option in the twenty-first century. That is because heavy investment in low-wage areas today is causing a convergence of living standards between North America and Western Europe, on the one hand, and parts of Latin America and all of Asia, on the other (United Nations Development Program, 1995: 57). The United Nations expects global poverty to be virtually eliminated in the next century, and the increasing size, organization, and prosperity of workers in less-developed regions of the world will strengthen the bargaining power of employees everywhere (Stackhouse, 1996).

Separatism and the reinvigoration of the labour movement are two of the main expressions of discontent that may colour Canadian politics in the coming decades as a result of globalization. A third political growth industry that is likely to be fuelled by globalization is the spread of new social movements. I can best illustrate this point by coming full circle and returning to the anecdote with which I began this chapter.

In 1991, I was invited to give a guest lecture at the University of New Brunswick. Following my talk in Fredericton, a friend drove me 100 km south to Saint John. I hadn't been back to my home town in years, and as we entered the city limits I vaguely sensed that something was different. I wasn't able to define the change precisely until we reached the Irving pulp and paper mill. As we approached my 1968 nemesis, it suddenly became obvious: The rotten-egg smell was virtually gone. I discovered that in the 1970s a local woman whose son developed a serious case of asthma took legal action against Irving and won. Irving was subsequently required by law to install a "scrubber" in the mill's main smokestack in order to remove most of the sulphur dioxide emissions. By the early 1990s, the federal Department of the Environment was also putting pressure on Irving to purify the polluted water that poured out of the plant into the St. John River and the Bay of Fundy. Apparently, local citizens and the environmental movement had caused a deep change in the climate of opinion, influencing the state to force Irving to spend many millions of dollars in a huge cleanup effort. It took decades, but what was political heresy in 1968 was established practice in 1991, making it crystal clear what the great German political sociologist Max Weber meant when he called politics "the slow boring of hard boards."

The incident in Saint John also drove home for me one of the main effects of globalization on so-cial movements and politics. Local ecological problems are now commonly seen to have worldwide implications for the environment and they lead to global political action: When Indonesian loggers destroy their rain forests to make toothpicks for Japanese diners, the oxygen balance of the entire planet is upset and environmentalists in the Netherlands take to the streets. When an isolated schoolboy cried foul in 1968, nobody heard; a few years later, a mother's cry initiated a whole chain of political events because it was amplified by the voice of a global movement. In general, globalization helps to ensure that many new social movements — not just the environmental movement, but the women's movement, the movement for gay and lesbian rights, and so on — transcend national boundaries and promote universalistic goals. ■

SUMMARY

1. Research does *not* suggest that participation in social movements is associated with the degree to which social control has broken down or expectations have been inadequately constrained.

2. Research does suggest that people are more inclined to rebel against the status quo when they are bound by close social ties to many other people who feel similarly wronged; when they are sharply socially separated from the people whom they regard as the source of the injustice; and when they have the time, money, and other resources needed to protest.

3. The structural conditions underlying the formation of social movements may conveniently be expressed as a power ratio — the distribution of power between authorities and potential partisans of change. As the power ratio falls from a high value, collective protest is more likely; as it falls further, violence is more likely; and as it approaches a value of 1, revolution is likely.

4. In order for social movements to grow, members must engage in frame alignment, making the activities, goals, and ideology of the movement congruent with the interests, beliefs, and values of potential recruits.

5. The history of democracy may be viewed as a struggle for the acquisition of constantly broadening citizenship rights — first the right to free speech, freedom of religion, and justice before the law; then the right to vote and run for office; then the right to a certain level of economic security and full participation in the life of society; and, finally, the right of marginal groups to full citizenship and the right of humanity as a whole to peace and security.

6. Democracy involves a two-way process of control between the state (the set of institutions that formulate and implement a country's law, policies, and binding regulations) and civil society (the private sphere, consisting of social movements, political parties, and so on).

7. The level of democracy in a society depends on the capacity of civil society to influence the state through citizen support of social movements, political parties, and other groups. That capacity increases as power becomes more widely distributed in society.

8. The degree to which power is widely distributed influences the success of particular kinds of parties and policies. Widely distributed power is associated with the success of labour parties and redistributive policies.

9. Paradoxically, the process of globalization alters the character of politics by simultaneously unifying and fragmenting nation-states and forms of collective action.

QUESTIONS TO CONSIDER

1. Have you ever participated in a social movement or been actively involved in a political party? If so, explain how your political choices (e.g., which party you joined, your level of participation, and the timing of your recruitment) were influenced by the sociological factors discussed in this chapter. If not, explain how the sociological factors discussed in this chapter influence you to remain politically inactive.

2. How would you achieve a political goal? Map out a detailed strategy for reaching a clearly defined aim, such as a reduction in income tax or an increase in university funding. Whom would you try to recruit to help you achieve your goal? Why? What collective actions do you think would be most successful? Why? To whose attention would these actions be directed? Why? Write a manifesto that frames your argument in a way that is culturally appealing to potential recruits.

3. Do you think that social movements will be more or less widespread in the twenty-first century than they have been in the twentieth? Why or why not? What kinds of social movements are likely to predominate?

4. Do you think that the twenty-first century will be more or less democratic than the twentieth? Why or why not?

GLOSSARY

authorities People who occupy the command posts of legitimized power structures.

authority Power that is widely viewed as legitimate.

breakdown theory The theory that suggests that social movements emerge when traditional methods of social control operate ineffectively and people's expectations are not held in check.

civil citizenship The perspective that recognizes the right to free speech, freedom of religion, and justice before the law.

civil society The private (nonstate) sphere of life.

elite theory A theory that maintains that well-to-do people consistently have much more political influence than people who are less well-to-do, and that society is therefore not as democratic as it is often portrayed.

frame alignment The process by which individual interests, beliefs, and values either become congruent and complementary with the activities, goals, and ideology of the movement or fail to do so.

frame amplification The process by which social movements identify and idealize values that have so far not featured prominently in the thinking of potential recruits. The process also involves clarifying and elevating the importance of positive beliefs about the movement and what it stands for.

frame bridging The process by which social movements reach out to other organizations that are thought to contain people who may be sympathetic to the social movement's cause.

frame extension The process by which a social movement's objectives and activities are stretched in order to win recruits who are not initially sympathetic to the movement's original aims. This may involve a "watering down" of the movement's ideals.

frame transformation A radical and often sudden change of perspective on the part of people who are unsympathetic and perhaps even antagonistic to a social movement.

globalization The simultaneous homogenization and fragmentation of the world resulting from the growth of instant international communications, giant multinational corporations, and powerful transnational organizations.

new social movements Post-1950s movements that attract a disproportionately large number of highly educated people in the social, educational, and cultural fields; fight their battles mainly inside established political parties or outside the political system; have an uneasy relationship with older social movements; and universalize the struggle for citizenship.

partisans of change People who have little influence on legitimized power structures and who form social movements in order to influence such structures from the outside and gain legitimacy for their goals.

pluralist theory The theory that holds that there are many competing interests and centres of power in society and that no one interest or power centre predominates in the long run.

political citizenship The perspective that recognizes the right to run for office and vote.

political parties Organizations that seek to control state power.

power The ability of an individual or a group to impose his, her, or its will on other individuals or groups. Group power is determined by group size, organization, and access to coercive, material, and normative resources.

power-balance theory The theory that suggests that social-movement formation and success depend on how powerful authorities are compared with partisans of change. It also holds that societies with widely distributed power are more democratic and more egalitarian than societies with narrowly held power.

power ratio A measure of the power of authorities relative to the power of potential partisans.

relative deprivation An intolerable gap between the social rewards people feel they deserve and the social rewards they expect to receive.

resource-mobilization theory The theory that holds that social movements crystallize and succeed in achieving their goals to the degree that they have access to scarce resources, such as money and effective communication facilities.

restructuring A business process that involves removing barriers to free trade and free capital movement; breaking up the production process into separate parts and locating each part where it can be carried out most cheaply and efficiently; using advanced computer technology in the production process; and hiring fewer full-time workers and more part-time, seasonal, and contract workers.

revolution A violent and rapid upheaval in which partisans of change assume positions of authority and substantially alter the social, economic, and political organization of society in their favour.

segmentation The separation of groups by large economic inequalities and memberships in different social organizations.

social citizenship The perspective that recognizes the right to a certain level of economic welfare security and full participation in the social life of the country.

social movement A collective attempt to change part or all of the social order by means of rioting, petitioning, striking, demonstrating, and establishing pressure groups, unions, and political parties.

social-movement life cycle A three-stage process that begins with the crystallization of an organization, continues with its bureaucratization, and ends with its incorporation into the larger society.

solidarity theory The theory that suggests that social movements are more likely to emerge if potential members are bound together by a pre-existing network of dense social ties. It also suggests that social movements are new social organizations that bind aggrieved individuals together and turn them into self-conscious groups.

state A set of institutions that formulate and implement a country's laws, policies, and binding regulations. The state consists of an executive branch, which initiates laws; a legislative branch, which makes laws; a judicial branch, which interprets laws; an administrative apparatus, which implements laws; and a coercive apparatus, which enforces laws and protects state security.

universal citizenship The perspective that recognizes the right of marginal groups to full citizenship and the rights of humanity as a whole.

SUGGESTED READING

Barber, Benjamin R. (1996). "Jihad vs. McWorld." In Robert J. Brym, ed., *Society in Question: Sociological Readings for the 21st Century* (pp. 193–99). Toronto: Harcourt Brace. A compelling analysis of the fragmenting and globalizing forces affecting political life today.

Brym, Robert J. (1989). "Politics." In Robert J. Brym with Bonnie J. Fox, *From Culture to Power: The Sociology of English Canada* (pp. 57–79). Toronto: Oxford University Press. An overview of major themes and research in Canadian political sociology.

Kimmerling, Baruch, ed. (1996). "Political Sociology at the Crossroads." *Current Sociology, 45* (1), 1–222. An up-to-date assessment of the state of political sociology around the world.

Tarrow, Sidney. (1994). *Power in Movement: Social Movements, Collective Action and Politics.* Cambridge, UK: Cambridge University Press. Synthesizes resource-mobilization and framing theories and underlines the importance of political structures in shaping discontent.

Turner, Bryan S. (1986). *Citizenship and Capitalism: The Debate over Reformism.* London: Allen and Unwin. A theoretically sophisticated analysis of the growth and universalization of citizenship rights.

Part Six THEORY AND METHOD

SOCIOLOGICAL THEORIES WERE FIRST PROPOSED

IN THE NINETEENTH CENTURY TO PROVIDE SECULAR

ACCOUNTS OF RAPID SOCIAL CHANGE. BY THE

EARLY TWENTIETH CENTURY, SYSTEMATIC METHODS

FOR EMPIRICALLY TESTING HYPOTHESES WERE

BEING INTRODUCED. BOLD IMAGINATION AND

RIGOROUS LOGIC ARE REQUIRED TO FORMULATE

THEORIES AND TEST HYPOTHESES.

CHAPTER TWENTY
Sociological Theory

IN THIS CHAPTER YOU WILL LEARN THAT

- sociological theories make statements about existing features of society and explain how some aspects of society affect other aspects
- one cannot do sociological research without sociological theories; indeed, much sociological research is conducted in order to evaluate or test the validity of theories
- sociological theories were first proposed in nineteenth-century Europe to provide secular accounts of rapid social changes and the experiences of neglected social groups
- major theoretical schools include functionalism (which views society as an integrated, consensual whole); conflict theory (which regards society as constantly changing because of the struggles that take place between different groups trying to advance their interests); symbolic interactionism (which examines the ways people derive meaning from their social settings); and feminism (which argues that male domination shapes all social processes and our knowledge of those processes)
- middle-range theories are sets of tendency statements about specific social processes; they can be tied together in the framework of more comprehensive theories, such as functionalism, conflict theory, and feminism

KEN S. MENZIES
University of Guelph

■ INTRODUCTION

Gossips tell you everything. They tell you who is getting married, who lost their job, and who had two helpings of pie last night. At their best, gossips portray social life as a series of joys and sorrows. At their worst, gossips present life as soap opera. Sociological theory enables us to go beyond gossip. It tells us what to look for and how facts fit together to give understanding.

In this chapter I begin by examining the nature of theory. I then discuss why people became interested in developing explicit sociological theories in the nineteenth century. Some theorists were concerned most with social order — how to stabilize the newly emerging industrial society. Other theorists were committed to changing the new social order radically. Their answers about how to create stability and change have had a major impact on most subsequent theory. From the former has developed the functionalist or order approach, and from the latter the conflict or change theory.

Other theorists have been concerned more with specific social processes than with society's overall stability or potential for change. For example, symbolic interactionists focus on how people imbue their social worlds with meaning, while ethnomethodologists focus on how people produce "objective reality" by their procedures for making actions "accountable." Focussing on causal sequences, middle-range theorists help us understand much about the complex interplay of diverse social tendencies. However, they have found it difficult to build a unified, comprehensive theory of society. Comprehensive theories, such as functionalism and conflict theory, despite their weaknesses, can bring middle-range theories together. I illustrate this point with another comprehensive sociological theory, feminism. Feminist theory recognizes the sources of stability of the male-dominated social order, yet is committed to changing that order.

■ THE NATURE OF THEORY

Having a theory is like having read the last page of a mystery. When you know who the murderer is, your perception of events changes — an assertion becomes a lie, the second cup of tea acquires deadly significance. Theories are similar. They tell you what is important and how it fits together. Theories provide the categories with which you look at the world. Thus, theories determine what you can see. **Facts** are correct observations in the categories of your theory.

In formal terms, a **theory** is a set of claims about what exists and the interconnection among existing phenomena. A theory identifies the key features of a social process that shape other important aspects of the social process. For example, feminist theory asserts that patriarchy, a male-dominated society, is the basic social reality. Because of patriarchy, beauty is more important for women than for men. Men's power and economic dominance enable them to impose their ideas of what women's appearance should be. Thus, from a feminist perspective, if you look only at women's biology, eating patterns, and energy-expending activities, you will not understand women's body shape or eating disorders like anorexia or bulimia, which result from women's attempts to conform to their idealized body shape. Women's bodies are, in effect, not their own but rather, according to feminist theory, part of patriarchal society (Brown and Jaspers, 1993).

In societies governed by tradition, people know the social possibilities they will encounter. They feel no need for sociological theory. Tradition teaches them which social features are linked. In contrast, in Canada today, previous patterns of events are often poor guides to the future. For example, if one predicted average family size on the basis of 1921's trends, one's prediction for 1998 would be more than double the 1998 reality. By linking different social features, theory enables us to understand new social possibilities.

A theory about welfare benefits illustrates this claim. Piven and Cloward (1971) suggest that generous welfare benefits are the state's response to civil disorder. Welfare increases in response to the poor's power to disrupt society. If this theory is correct, the level of welfare in Canada in the next century will depend on the elite's perception of the level of welfare that is needed to keep the poor politically quiet. By linking welfare and political disorder, this theory provides a different perspective on welfare in Canada from one that sees welfare as a response to need.

Theory is not simply a detached understanding of events that shape our lives. It often influences these events. For example, in the early 1970s, some social scientists (e.g., Kasselbaum, Ward, and Wilner, 1971) theorized that rehabilitation techniques such as group counselling would be ineffective in prison. They argued that the prison setting precluded two conditions necessary for group counselling to be effective. First, prisoners do not feel secure discussing their feelings. Second, prison undermines mutual acceptance among group members. As a result, group counselling and similar techniques are ineffective in rehabilitating prisoners. This argument received convincing empirical support from an article that reviewed numerous studies of rehabilitation in prison (Martinson, 1974). Its basic conclusion was that nothing works. This evidence, and the theoretical analysis that made sense of the evidence, cut into support among the public, court officials, and prison administrators for rehabilitation. The decline in support for rehabilitation in the late 1970s and early 1980s was a response to more than changing theoretical views. It was part of a growing loss of faith in the government's ability to attain public-policy objectives. The theory that questioned rehabilitation's effectiveness was also a response to this trend, and it strengthened the trend.

Everybody theorizes, though some people deny they do. Some theories are implicit, other explicit. Consider the claim that we do not need to theorize about criminals in order to respond to them, and that all that is needed is common sense. Common sense says: "Get tough." This common sense, however, is an implicit theory: Deterrence works. Nobody denies that a police officer in a front of a bank deters bank robbers, but getting tough on criminals is more complex than this. It involves more police, fewer legal safeguards, and longer prison sentences. Substantial increases in the number of public and private police in Canada in the last twenty years have not reduced the reported crime rate. In the United States, crime rates have soared as the imprisonment rate has risen to one of the world's highest. The deterrence theory that underlies a tough response to crime has to talk about criminals' perception of their chance of being caught, their fear of imprisonment, and how these deterrents are affected by court delays. By covering up these concerns under the guise of common sense, advocates of tough policies on crime fail to consider what their position really claims.

Once a theory has been stated clearly, it has to be tested against the evidence. If theory is to inform our lives and influence where society is heading, it is important to be able to judge how good a theory is.

▲ THEORY AND IDEOLOGY

Because theory draws attention to certain features of what exists and how those features are inter-

connected, it tells researchers what to expect. If researchers find what they expect, the theory is confirmed, at least for the time being. Researchers gain confidence that their theory, having passed one test, will pass again when applied to a different sector of the same society or another society. (As you will know from your own experience, passing tests gives you confidence that you are studying well, but does not guarantee that you will pass again.) If researchers find that the theory is not supported by the data, they are faced with a problem. Several responses are possible. They can reject the theory and test another one. Alternatively, they can keep the theory and provide an account of why it did not work in this particular case. Ideally, after reformulating the theory, researchers retest it to identify a class of cases that the theory does not fit. Exceptions do not prove rules; exceptions require new rules that cover the old cases and the exceptions, or that exclude the exceptions on a consistent basis. A third legitimate response is simply to acknowledge that more work is needed. The researchers admit that the theory has failed this test. However, they do not know of, or cannot make up, a better theory.

Yet another choice exists. Analysts can ignore the data and stick confidently to their theory. When people refuse to have their understanding affected by research, they have an **ideology**. Both scientific theories and ideologies tell you what exists and the interconnections among the important aspects of reality. The difference between them lies not in what they claim, but in how people treat discrepancies between explanations and perceptions of reality. Ideologists ignore them; scientists acknowledge them. For example, Marxism can be a theory or an ideology. If people modify their Marxism in the light of new data, they are theorists. If they stick to it in the face of discrepant evidence, they are ideologists. Most sociologists are part scientist, part ideologist.

Having clarified what theory is and how to judge a theory in terms of the evidence, it is possible to consider why people first became interested in formulating good sociological theories. This occurred in Europe in the eighteenth and nineteenth centuries as modern industrial society emerged.

■ THE RISE OF SOCIOLOGICAL THEORY

In medieval Europe, the social order was seen as God-given and fixed. The Protestant Reformation in the sixteenth century raised questions about exactly what God had given. By the nineteenth century, religious tolerance, although qualified in many ways, had become extensive enough to make it difficult to accept one's own religion as the definitive answer to life's problems. Religion's decline left an opening for alternative accounts of society.

Science not only contributed to the decline of religion, it was increasingly accepted as an account of the world in its own right. Throughout the seventeenth and eighteenth centuries, science expanded to explain more and more of the natural order. In the nineteenth century, Darwin's theory of evolution, which asserts that humans and monkeys have a common ancestor, expanded science yet further to provide an account of human origins (Greene, 1959). Scientific experiments strengthened science's claim to explain reality. Demonstrated success lent science prestige. Sociology accepted the scientific method and sought to use it to provide an account of society as an alternative to religion's traditional account of the social order.

Auguste Comte (1798–1857) is usually identified as the first sociologist. In 1839, he was the first person to use the term "sociology." The word sociology has two roots: *socio,* from the Latin for "society," and *logy,* from the Greek for "study on a high level." Comte advocated the study of society on what he saw as the highest level — the application of the methods of natural science to society. Although his actual social analysis is now largely discredited, he is important because he clearly advocated a scientific approach to understanding society rather than a religious approach.

Slow change made the medieval social order appear natural and inevitable. Change occurred slowly enough for people to incorporate it into "God's plan." By the nineteenth century, however, the rate of change had accelerated. Urbanization increased dramatically. For example, London's population rose from 1 million in 1800 to more than 4 million in 1900. The number of people who earned their living from the land declined, while the number who worked in manufacturing jobs in appalling conditions grew. Despite these conditions, by the late nineteenth century, the general standard of living in Europe was rising. Sociological theory had much to explain.

Social change in nineteenth-century Europe heightened awareness that people's experiences mattered to society. For example, the Napoleonic wars were fought with large conscript armies instead of small professional armies, as in the eighteenth century. Masses of men had to be convinced that their social order was worth killing for and being killed for. Moreover, people's experiences expanded as railways moved people and goods throughout Europe. Much more than before, Europe was one market. The price of wheat in the Baltic region might influence the outbreak of food riots in the south of France. The spread of democracy meant that more people's views became politically relevant. The suffragette and temperance movements of the late nineteenth and early twentieth centuries brought women's experience and concerns to male-dominated public consideration. An account of society that stressed only royalty and the aristocracy became too narrow. Sociological theory faced the challenge of analyzing a wider range of human experience than the old chronicles of kings and queens.

The sociological theory that arose to account for the emerging society and its diversity of people was shaped by three major historical events: the Enlightenment, the French and American revolutions, and the conservative reaction to the French Revolution.

The Enlightenment was an eighteenth-century intellectual movement centred in France. Its key thinkers were Montesquieu (1689–1755) and Rousseau (1712–78). They had faith in the power of men's reason to build a better world. (Women were seen as naturally inferior to men and to be ruled by fathers or husbands.) Enlightenment thinkers attacked the hereditary privileges of the aristocracy as irrational. They viewed religious beliefs as ignorant superstition. They believed that once society was freed from the weight of irrational hereditary privilege and superstition, people could move toward perfection.

The Enlightenment provided much of the intellectual inspiration for the French Revolution (1789–99) and Napoleon's rule (1799–1815). The French Revolution showed that a social order could be quickly and violently overthrown. Both the French and American revolutions showed that a society without hereditary privilege was possible.

The French Revolution, particularly its violence, inspired a conservative reaction, which fed on fears that urbanization and industrialization would lead to the breakdown of society. Instead of rejecting the medieval world for its feudal privilege and superstition as the Enlightenment thinkers did, the conservative reaction admired the Middle Ages as a time of social and cultural unity. The conservative reaction wanted to recreate this social and cultural unity in a modernized form so that it would be appropriate for a society based on science and industry.

The Enlightenment, the French Revolution, and the conservative reaction led to two main types of sociological theory. "Order theorists" developed

functionalism, or order theory, which was built particularly on the conservative reaction to the French Revolution. They wanted an understanding of society that would help society adjust gradually to the social order that they saw emerging. They recognized that conflict existed in their own society, but they believed that a relatively conflict-free society was possible in a form similar to the emerging industrial society. In their view, attempts at radical change or revolution were destructive because they could not cope satisfactorily with the complexity of interconnections among the components of society. For these theorists, the fundamental question was: "How is social order possible?"

Conflict theorists, in contrast, started with the Enlightenment's faith in human perfectibility. The French Revolution gave them faith that radical change was possible. They believed that their society was so inegalitarian and destructive of human potential that radical social change was the only solution. Social inequalities and injustice generated conflict. This conflict would provide the impetus, they believed, for fundamental social changes that would benefit most people. Their basic question was: "What are the fundamental social conflicts in society?" They felt that once these conflicts were identified, it might be possible to help generate a revolution.

The answers of the first order and conflict theorists to the question of how social order and change are possible have influenced much subsequent sociological theorizing. Consequently, I discuss next the classic initial formulation of order theory — Durkheim's. After treating the modern functionalist version of order theory, I discuss the classic conflict theorist — Marx — and then contemporary conflict theory. Although Marx (1818–83) did his writing before Durkheim (1858–1917), it is helpful to outline an analysis of social order before considering how that order may change.

■ ORDER THEORY

▲ ÉMILE DURKHEIM

Émile Durkheim believed that social order and substantial consensus in society were fundamental goals of society. Without these, he argued, human happiness and satisfaction are impossible. Satisfaction and feelings of self-worth come from activities that a person has learned to value in conjunction with

other people, not from the activities in themselves. For example, running a four-minute mile is tiring and leaves one gasping for breath. However, it is satisfying because one knows that one has achieved a highly valued standard of excellence in running.

Durkheim asserts that **social facts** exist. Social facts are features of human activity that emerge or become apparent only when the activity is considered in relation to other activities, not when the activity is considered in isolation from its social context. For example, **norms** are social facts. Norms are social rules that people believe they and others should follow. Consequently, norms constrain people's choices. People must follow the norms, hide their

Émile Durkheim (1858–1917) was the first professor of sociology in France and is often considered to be the first modern sociologist. Particularly in *Rules of Sociological Method* (1895) and *Suicide* (1897), he argued that human behaviour is shaped by "social facts," or the social context in which people are embedded that defines the opportunities and constraints within which they must act. Durkheim was keenly interested in the conditions that promote social order in primitive and modern societies, and he explored this problem in depth in such works as *The Division of Labour in Society* (1893). SOURCE: Reproduced by permission of the Bettmann Archive.

actions, or face the consequences of being identified as deviants. Thus, social facts are coercive: People must take into account the responses of others in deciding what to do. One cannot ascertain whether an action follows a norm or deviates from it by looking at the action in isolation. The fact that an action follows a norm emerges only when the action is considered in its social context. Because the emergent properties of actions are important, Durkheim argues that social facts constitute an appropriate, separate topic of study. In Durkheim's view, sociology is the study of social facts.

For Durkheim, the central social fact about primitive societies, or those like aboriginal societies in Canada before the European invasion, is that they were characterized by *mechanical solidarity* (see Table 20.1). This means that everybody did basically similar work. The social bond was provided by religious and moral ideas held in common by most people. Rule-breakers were punished severely.

Modern society for Durkheim, in contrast, is characterized by *organic solidarity* (see Table 20.1). Just as the roots, stem, and leaves of a plant are interdependent and contribute to the plant's well-being, so too is modern society an organic unity. People do specialized work and are dependent on society's organization to fit their activities together. A complex division of labour bonds people to each other. Most laws regulate how the parts fit together. For example, the Landlord–Tenant Act spells out how tenants may compel landlords to do needed repairs by withholding rent money. Thus, the law aims to restore the situation to what existed before the land-

lord failed to do the needed repairs. Penal laws and repressive sanctions exist, but regulate fewer activities than co-operative laws.

Durkheim did not believe that the France of his time was an organic unity. France was only part way through the transition to a fully organic society. This incomplete transition made France somewhat "anomic." **Anomie** is the absence of norms. Fearful of social unrest, especially socialist-inspired class conflict, Durkheim argued that social solidarity and moral unity are possible in an industrial society despite the existence of classes. In his view, industrialists and workers have common interests. The division of labour makes everybody dependent on the efficient organization of production. Durkheim thought that an appropriate moral code was needed to achieve a fully organic society. This code would be based on the premise that people should be rewarded for their abilities. He drew the radical conclusion that a just society required the elimination of inheritance. Only after the elimination of inheritance would people be rewarded strictly for their own abilities.

Durkheim's views of both primitive and modern societies are problematic. "Primitive" people are much more interdependent than he suggests. Many "primitive societies" require restitution, not harsh repression, for serious moral offences. For example, a murderer might work as a slave for a murdered man's clan for seven years, or pay for the offence with several head of cattle. Moreover, Durkheim's view of organic societies ignores that there are real differences of interests among different groups in so-

---

◆ **Table 20.1** Mechanical and Organic Solidarity Compared

Mechanical solidarity	Organic solidarity
Based on resemblances	Based on the division of labour
Little interdependence:	High interdependence:
Weak social bonds	Strong social bonds
Low population and moral density	High population and moral density
Penal law	Co-operative law
Repressive sanctions	Restitutive sanctions (penalties that restore what existed before the offence)
Absolute collective authority	Possibility of individual initiative
Religious	Secular
Collective conscience places high value on interests of society as a whole	Collective conscience places high value on individual dignity, equality of opportunity, and social justice

SOURCE: Based on Émile Durkheim, *The Division of Labour in Society,* trans. W.D. Halls (New York: Free Press, 1965 [1893]).

ciety, even if they also share common interests. All societies thus have some anomie and conflict. The state of "transition" is permanent! Nevertheless, Durkheim's view of modern society is important. The specialized roles and complex division of labour in a modern society lock people into dependence on social organization and some amount of social consensus. Successful social change requires constant organization of complex social interdependencies. A successful revolution is difficult to organize, as the current problems of social breakdown in the former Soviet Union illustrate.

Durkheim analyzes activities in terms of their functions. The function of an activity is its contribution to the social whole. For example, he asks: "Why can society not eliminate crime? Surely enough effort is put into fighting crime." His answer is based on the social functions of crime and punishment. He argues that punishing an action functions to assert the group's values and solidarity in the face of a threat. Calling an action "criminal" functions to define the limits of acceptable behaviour in society. If little occurs that is unacceptable, society will strive to do better, and what is criminal will be redefined. Because some variation in human activity is always present, some actions will always be less valued than other actions. These less-valued acts will be called crime. In a community of saints, failing to say "thank you" would be criminal. If, however, too many people commit a certain crime, society may be forced to broaden its definition of acceptable behaviour. Otherwise, society will waste too many resources fighting the crime. For example, in the 1950s, about half the people sent to prison in Ontario had been arrested for drunkenness and subsequently defaulted on their fines. With the increase in alcohol consumption, and the prevalent view of alcoholism as a disease, being drunk in public is becoming largely decriminalized (Mahon, 1992: 142–69). The offence that concerns society now is drinking and driving.

Durkheim's theory has given modern functionalists an image of society as an interdependent social order. Different activities function in different ways to maintain social order. Modern functionalists accept Durkheim's assertion of a social level of analysis as sociology's unique domain.

▲ TWENTIETH-CENTURY FUNCTIONALISM

During the Depression of the 1930s, a quarter of the workforce in Canada and the United States was un-

employed. Sociologists became acutely aware of how precarious modern societies are. In the decades following World War II, the North American standard of living rose steadily. For most people, society seemed good. A theoretical solution to the problem of order like Durkheim's — one that stressed integration, consensus, and stability — fit the temper of the times. Sociologists in the United States, particularly during the 1940s and 1950s, clarified, developed, and applied Durkheim's functionalist framework.

Functionalists contributed to an understanding of society by placing numerous beliefs, activities, and institutions in a wider social context. Their analytical method took the following form:

1. Identify something that in isolation seems strange.
2. Show how it fits into a larger social whole by contributing to social stability.

For example, Davis and Moore (1945) asked why societies in general, and the United States in particular, are stratified. They found it puzzling that while Americans claim to believe in equality, some Americans have more prestige than others. Their functionalist analysis started with the claim that some jobs are more important to society than others. The talent to do these jobs well is scarce. High prestige and salaries ensure that talented people are motivated to undergo sacrifices, such as prolonged and expensive education, in order to fill socially important jobs. For example, doctors have high prestige and earn more than garbage collectors. This stratification exists, they argued, because the ability to doctor well is scarce and important to society.

To solve the problem of how social order is possible, Talcott Parsons (1902–79), an American sociological theorist, argued that shared values and beliefs are needed. He claimed that only when people define situations similarly and value doing the same things in these commonly defined situations can social order be maintained. There are many functional ways of ordering a society. For any particular society to exist, most people must share the values that support the particular social order. According to Parsons (1951), the importance of common values implies that Durkheim was right to insist on a social level of analysis. The sharing of values and meaning cannot be discovered if acts or individuals are examined in isolation from their social context.

Functionalists believe that people come to accept common values and meanings through socialization. Each society moulds its members to fit its values and norms. In the process of socialization, a society or a group within a society imparts to its unsocialized members (e.g., children) the ways of acting required to be effective group members. Through this process these members become social beings — they are socialized.

Functionalism is a theoretical solution to the problem of order that stresses integration, consensus, and stability. The turbulence of the 1960s showed, however, that functionalism's basic image of society was implausible. An increasing awareness of poverty, racism, sexism, and rising unemployment made clear that society was not functioning to meet all the needs of its members. The conservative social-policy implications of functionalism were unacceptable to many people who saw fundamental change as necessary. Criticisms of functionalism gained acceptance:

1. It has an oversocialized view of people. People fit into society with unrealistic ease in functionalist theory. Although some minimum of agreement must exist among many people for a group to be a society, functionalism cannot explain why so many people are opposed to, apathetic about, or in conflict with so many societal values.

2. Social change often comes from within a society. For example, feminism arose as a response to internal social factors, such as the concern in the 1960s with equality and civil rights and rising female labour-force participation.

The basic criticism of functionalism is that it solves the problem of order too well. In accounting for the conditions that make society possible, it ignores too much instability, conflict, and lack of fit among society's parts.

Before I turn to theories that make conflict central to their analysis, I will examine a major attempt, Merton's, to make functionalism flexible so as to avoid these problems.

The basic criticism of functionalism is that it solves the problem of order too well by dismissing conflict in society. In accounting for the conditions that make society possible, functionalism ignores all forms of instability or inequality. SOURCE: Brian Jones, *The Centre of the Universe* (1992). Oil on canvas, 9 x 6 feet. Photo courtesy of Nancy Poole Studio, Toronto. Reproduced with permission of the artist.

▲ MERTON'S ADAPTATION OF FUNCTIONALISM

Robert Merton (b. 1910) recognized the conservative bias in functionalism. Well before functionalism fell into disfavour, Merton provided options for functionalism in an article entitled "Manifest and Latent Functions" (1968 [1949]). Functions may be manifest (known to the participants) or latent (not known to the participants). Activities may be functional (tending to support the social structure), dysfunctional (tending to change the social structure), or a mixture of functional and dysfunctional. In addition, for any functional activity, there may be functional alternatives. Social "needs," according to Merton, can be met in many ways.

Merton's classification of functions is widely used (see Box 20.1). However, it allows for all logical possibilities. People may be aware or unaware of the activity's consequences. The consequences may support, somewhat support, or not the support the status quo. Something else might have these consequences. This makes for good description, but poor theory. A theory, as you know from our earlier discussion, identifies the key features in a situation and how these shape the rest of the social process. Theoretical explanations show how *particular* social features provide *specific* consequences rather than some other result. If *all* possibilities are admitted, we do not know how the social process is shaped. Therefore, Merton's attempt to produce a flexible functionalist theory does not succeed.

I will now examine an approach that makes conflict central to its account of society.

■ CONFLICT THEORY

▲ KARL MARX

Karl Marx was influenced by each of the three factors that I identified earlier as influencing nineteenth-century sociological theory. From the Enlightenment, he accepted a faith in human perfectibility. The French Revolution showed him that substantial social change is possible. Finally, from the conservative reaction to the French Revolution, he learned the importance of understanding social institutions as parts of a larger whole. These influences produced a revolutionary theory. Many disciplines, including sociology, are indebted to him.

BOX 20.1
A Functionalist Analysis of a Diet Group

For most women in the profit-making diet groups that Natalie Allon (1975) studied, the groups were a failure. The women lost no weight. Diet groups keep going, Allon suggests, because they provide stigmatized women with several social services. The women let off steam about the frustrations of being fat in a world that values thinness. They express sociability in a situation where everybody is overweight. In addition, the women exchanged recipes and the names of good places to shop for clothes for the fuller figure. The basic latent function of the diet groups is "the legitimation of venting multiple and ambivalent negative and positive feelings about oneself" (p. 68). In other words, by providing a space where the women can express the joys and frustrations of their lives, the group preserves itself. What do you think would happen if this latent function became manifest? Can you think of a functional alternative to a for-profit diet group?

source: Based on Natalie Allon, "Latent Social Services in Group Dieting," *Social Problems,* *23* (1) (1975), pp. 59–69.

Marx saw people in Europe as **alienated**. By "alienated" he meant that people could not reach their full human potential. Their potential was denied by the control that others exercised over their work. They were exploited: Their work was controlled by others for the benefit of these others (the exploiters). Exploitation denies people the opportunity to work together co-operatively and overcome their alienation.

In Marx's view, society was built not on co-operative relationships but on inequality and exploitation. He wanted to help build a society without exploitation. He saw nineteenth-century Europe as moving toward a capitalist society with two main classes, the exploiters and the exploited. The exploiters are the **bourgeoisie,** the owners of the means of production: factories and the ability to finance commercial activities. The exploited class are the **proletariat.** They have to sell their labour to survive. Using the categories of economic theory, but focussing on owners of capital and nonowners, Marx showed how exploitation occurred (see Box 20.2).

This exploitive capitalist social order is unstable, Marx argued. As competition forces the bourgeoisie constantly to improve technology, the capitalist mode of production is undermined. Better machin-ery requires fewer and fewer firms to produce the same quantity of goods as before. Consequently, the bourgeoisie declines in number and the proletariat grows. Capitalism rests on a basic contradiction. Production is social — it requires the work of many people. However, appropriation is private — one relatively small group of people claims the profits. Eventually, this contradiction will be massive enough to induce a revolution. Then, people can create the classless society.

In Marx's view, the economic base of a society shapes its superstructure — its political, religious, legal, and other noneconomic institutions. The class with economic power moulds all social institutions to reinforce its power. For example, Christianity's promise of rewards in an afterlife distracts attention from injustice in this life. Religion is "the opium of the people" (Marx, 1972 [1844]: 12). Many people believe that Marx overemphasizes economic factors and downplays superstructural factors. Others dispute the interpretation that Marx sees economic factors as fundamental.

According to Marx, social order prevails as the dominant class represses most people's potential through a mixture of force and shaping social institutions to support their dominance. However,

Karl Marx, the father of conflict theory, saw people in late-nineteenth-century Europe as alienated — people who could not reach their full human potential. He felt that their potential was denied by the control that others exercised over their work. SOURCE: Maria Gabankova, *FREEDOM — BOUND,* from *Body of Dust.* Acrylic, 6 x 3 feet. Reproduced with permission of the artist.

Box 20.2
Depression Hits Robinson Crusoe's Island

"Friday," said Robinson Crusoe, "I'm sorry, I fear I must lay you off."

"What do you mean, Master?"

"Why, you know there's a big surplus of last year's crop. I don't need you to plant another this year. I've got enough goatskin coats to last me a lifetime. My house needs no repairs. I can gather turtle eggs myself. There's an overproduction. When I need you I will send for you. You needn't wait around here."

"That's all right, Master, I'll plant my own crop, build up my own hut, and gather all the eggs and nuts I want myself. I'll get along fine."

"Where will you do all this, Friday?"

"Here on this island."

"This island belongs to me, you know. I can't allow you to do that. When you can't pay me anything I need I might as well not own it."

"Then I'll build a canoe and fish in the ocean. You don't own that."

"That's all right, provided you don't use any of my trees for your canoe, or build it on my land, or use my beach for a landing place, and do your fishing far enough away so you don't interfere with my riparian rights."

"I never thought of that, Master. I can do without a boat, though. I can swim over to that rock and fish there and gather seagull eggs."

"No you won't, Friday. The rock is mine. I own offshore rights."

"What shall I do, Master?"

"That's your problem, Friday. You're a free man, and you know about rugged individualism being maintained here."

"I guess I'll starve, Master. May I stay here until I do? Or shall I swim beyond your offshore rights and drown or starve there?"

"I've just thought of something, Friday. I don't like to carry my garbage down to the shore each day. You may stay and do that. Then whatever is left of it, after my dog and cat have fed, you may eat. You're in luck."

"Thank you, Master. That is true charity."

"One more thing, Friday. This island is overpopulated. Fifty percent of the people are unemployed. We are undergoing a severe depression, and there is no way that I can see to end it. No one but a charlatan would say he could. So keep a lookout and let no one land here to settle. And if any ship comes don't let them land any goods of any kind. You must be protected against foreign labour. Conditions are fundamentally sound, though. And prosperity is just around the corner."

SOURCE: Mary Attersbury, "Depression Hits Robinson Crusoe's Island," in Joyce L. Kornbluh, ed., *Rebel Voices: An I.W.W. Anthology* (Ann Arbor, MI: University of Michigan Press, 1964 [1932]), pp. 369–70.

this exploitative structure is unstable. Eventually, the exploited class, the majority, will overthrow their exploiters. Marx (1904 [1859]: 11–12) described the process by which exploitation and revolution occur as follows:

In the social production of their life, men enter into definite relations that are indispensable and independent of their will, relations of production which correspond to a definite stage of development of their material productive forces. The sum

Karl Marx (1818–83) was a revolutionary thinker whose ideas affected not just the growth of sociology but the course of world history. He held that major socio-historical changes — in modes of economic production, forms of political rule, and systems of governing ideas — are the result of conflict between society's major classes. In his major work, *Capital* (1867–94), Marx argued that capitalism would produce such misery and collective strength among workers that they would eventually take state power and create a communist society in which production would be based on human need rather than profit.
SOURCE: Reproduced with permission of Canapress Photo Service.

◆ **Figure 20.1** Marx's Conflict Theory

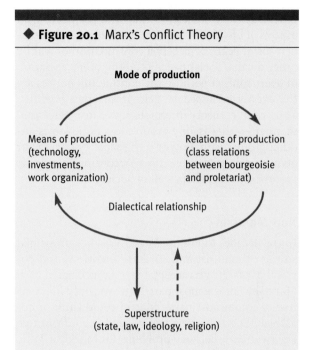

"In the social production of their life, men enter into definite relations that are indispensable and independent of their will, relations of production which correspond to a definite stage of development of their material productive forces. The sum total of these relations of production constitute the economic structure of society, the real foundation on which rises a legal and political superstructure and to which correspond definite forms of social consciousness. . . . At a certain stage of their development, the material productive forces of society come in conflict with the existing relations of production, or — what is but a legal expression for the same thing — with the property relations within which they have been at work hitherto. From forms of development of the productive forces these relations turn into their fetters. Then begins an epoch of social revolution."

SOURCE: Quotation from Karl Marx, *A Contribution to the Critique of Political Economy,* trans. N. Stone (Chicago: Charles H. Kerr, 1904 [1859]), pp. 11–12. Reprinted with permission.

total of these relations of production constitute the economic structure of society, the real foundation on which rises a legal and political superstructure and to which correspond definite forms of social consciousness. . . . At a certain stage of their development, the material productive forces of society come in conflict with the existing relations of production, or — what is but a legal expression for the same thing — with the property relations within which they have been at work hitherto. From forms of development of the productive forces these relations turn into their fetters. Then begins an epoch of social revolution.

Figure 20.1 illustrates the dialectical relationship between the means of production, the relations of production, and the superstructure that characterizes the capitalist social order.

Marx's vision of social order and social change based on power, especially economic power, has inspired modern conflict theory.

▲ MODERN CONFLICT THEORY

Two modern varieties of conflict theory are neo-Marxism and conflict theory. Both see conflict or the potential for conflict as normal and permeating all aspects of life. From the point of view of conflict theory, social peace is merely a continuation of war by other means. Social peace is a temporary cessation of overt conflict because the contending parties are too evenly balanced to gain from open hostility. Thus, conflict theory interprets power in a "zero-sum" manner — that is, one group's loss of power is another group's gain. **Power** is the capacity to get your own way despite opposition. According to conflict theorists, power shapes all of society.

Neo-Marxism

In the decades following World War II, Europe had strong communist and socialist traditions and political parties. It was acceptable to be associated with Marxism. For the most part, however, only Marxists free of communist party control could think innovatively. Such thinking was needed to confront two key twentieth-century problems for Marxists: Why was the Soviet Union not a model society? Why has a communist revolution not occurred in advanced capitalist societies as Marx anticipated? Neo-Marxists have tried seriously to answer these problems. Some neo-Marxists assert that they are simply reclaiming the old Marx from misinterpretation.

Russia's 1917 Revolution was made in Marx's name. Many were sympathetic to the massive communist social experiment. After Khrushchev's 1956 "secret" speech denouncing Stalin and his crimes and the publication in 1973–75 of Solzhenitsyn's *The Gulag Archipelago* — a study of Soviet forced-labour camps — it became clear, even to committed left-wingers, that the Soviet Union and other communist countries were not workers' paradises. Those who had made a revolution in Marx's name had turned an egalitarian dream into an inegalitarian nightmare.

Milovan Djilas, a senior communist party official who became Yugoslavia's most prominent prisoner, offered an analysis of the problem in *The New Class* (1957). He suggested that the communist party members collectively controlled the means of production. This collective control made them the new dominant class that exploited the rest of society. Neo-Marxists have extended Djilas's analysis. Communist societies can be seen as state capitalist societies. Instead of numerous monopoly or oligopoly capitalist enterprises as in modern capitalism, communist societies have only one capitalist — the state.

The second main problem for neo-Marxists is capitalism's strength in the West. They suggest that capitalism's strength may be explained in part by its imperialism. The West has found new markets and new people to exploit in the Third World. The gains from exploiting those nations enable Western capitalists to buy off their proletariats. Meanwhile, in the Third World, societies and economies that worked reasonably well in relative isolation have become part of one capitalist world order. "Undeveloped" societies become underdeveloped societies (Frank, 1969). Instead of being societies that could work and possibly change on their own, Third World societies are now trapped at the bottom of an international world order.

Conflict Theory

As radicalism and rising unemployment in the 1960s undermined the conservative functionalist view of society, many sociologists adopted a conflict perspective. They accepted conflict or the potential for conflict as ubiquitous, but rejected what they saw as Marxism's excess intellectual baggage — in particular, its stress on economic factors. In addition, conflict theorists tended to lack the Enlightenment's and Marx's faith in human perfectibility. Nazi concentration camps had shown how inhumane people could be. The failure of communism, fascism, national independence, and wars on poverty to deliver the gains that their supporters had promised generated cynicism and scepticism about the possibilities of social engineering.

In *Class and Class Conflict in Industrial Society* (1959), Ralf Dahrendorf (b. 1929) presented his theory as an alternative to functionalism (see Table 20.2). Society, he suggests, is made up of **imperatively co-ordinated associations**. In any association, people with power use it to dictate how activities are arranged. Thus, the powerful pursue their own interests. Those lacking power have common interests. If conditions are suitable, those at the bottom may organize and pursue those interests. Thus, the possibility of conflict and change is always present.

Randall Collins (b. 1941) focusses on power and the resources that create power. In *The Credential Society* (1979), for example, he examines how education is a resource that elites use to preserve their power and values. Education creates status groups; it gives people a pseudo-ethnicity. The primary gain from education, he argues, is elite culture. Job skills are secondary and largely learned on the job. For example, firms hire business-school graduates because attendance at business school indicates that one accepts probusiness values. Business schools develop these values. Choosing graduates of business schools enables the economic elite to reproduce its own values and culture. People committed to current busi-

---

♦ **Table 20.2** Assumptions of Conflict Theory and Functionalist Theory Compared

Conflict theory	Functionalist theory
Change is ubiquitous	Society is relatively stable
Conflict is ubiquitous	Society is well integrated
Everything contributes to change	All is functional
Society rests on the coercion of some by others	Society is based on value consensus

SOURCE: Based on Ralf Dahrendorf, *Class and Class Conflict in Industrial Society* (Stanford, CT: Stanford University Press, 1959), pp. 161–62.

---

ness values are then trained on the job to be good business people. Their success legitimates the values of business schools to the rest of society.

Conflict theory's basic problem is the mirror image of functionalism's. By asserting the predominance of social order based on domination or conflict and instability, conflict theory loses the ability to explain genuine consensus and harmony. Conflict theory's social-policy implication is change. However, conflict theory will analyze any new social order as needing change! With no capacity to suggest solutions, conflict theory becomes a perpetual critique of society. When people seek constructive alternatives, conflict theory is of limited use.

▲ VALUES AND MEANINGS IN CONFLICT THEORY AND FUNCTIONALISM

Functionalism and conflict theory offer **structural** accounts of society. That is, they focus on the impact of patterns of social relations on behaviour, and see people as shaped by social structures. Thus, both theories imply that, in similar social structures, people will have similar values and attribute similar meanings to activities. The plain fact is, however, that people can create very *different* meanings in similar situations. Therefore, theorists need to take the meaning of activities as problematic and requiring investigation in its own right. In addition, both theories tend to reject values as an independent source of human action. For functionalists, values bind people to the status quo, and for conflict theorists, values are a smoke screen for the interests of the powerful. Consequently, neither approach can explain why people act on values to change society if this change is not in their own interest. Yet this sometimes occurs. Marx, for example, was an intellectual who acted on behalf of the proletariat.

Thus, to have an adequate account of society, it is necessary to have a theory that considers values and meanings to be significant factors in social action. The first important sociological theorist to do this was Max Weber.

▲ MAX WEBER

Max Weber advocated ***Verstehende* sociology**. *Verstehende* sociology holds that the meaning of an activity is important to an understanding of its effects. An action's meaning is not inherent in it. For example, in eating bread, people may be relieving hunger, establishing social intimacy, or taking communion. To understand what meaning an action has for the people who perform it, we must learn about its context. In addition, we must develop empathy. The action's meaning affects its consequences. Consequently, Weber argues that social stability and social change can be understood only if we examine both the meanings of actions and their causal impact.

Weber's *The Protestant Ethic and the Spirit of Capitalism* (1958 [1904–5]) shows his concern with blending meaning and causal impact. He argues that a variety of material conditions (e.g., technology, navigable rivers) were required for the rise of capitalism in sixteenth- and seventeenth-century Europe. On their own, however, these factors were insufficient. The development of Protestantism, especially Calvinism, was also needed. This claim, initially, goes against common sense. Early forms of Protestantism were other-worldly and disdainful of material goods. Protestantism was dedicated, however, to the active mastery of the world in God's name. Religiously committed people did not have to become priests or join monasteries. People could find their calling — their vocation — in many walks of life. In the Protestant view, it was their respon-

Max Weber (1864–1920) was Germany's greatest sociologist. He profoundly influenced the development of the discipline internationally. Engaged in a life-long "debate with Marx's ghost," Weber held that economic circumstances alone do not explain the rise of capitalism in the West; as he showed in *The Protestant Ethic and the Spirit of Capitalism* (1904–5), independent developments in the religious realm had unintended, beneficial consequences for capitalist growth in some parts of Europe. He also argued that capitalism would not necessarily give way to socialism. Instead, he regarded the growth of bureaucracy and the overall "rationalization" of life as the defining characteristics of the modern age. These themes were developed in *Economy and Society* (1922). SOURCE: The Granger Collection, New York.

sibility to help remake the world as God wished. They believed that God hated waste and sloth. Protestantism encouraged people to make the world work more rationally and systematically in the service of the Lord. Systematic good works could not force God to reward the individual. They could, however, be taken as a sign that a person was one of the "elect," and therefore Heaven-bound. Consequently, good works gave psychological reassurance that a person was saved. A systematic, rational approach to an economic calling meant that a person constantly acted as a calculating capitalist, not a follower of economic tradition. Material success was not valued in

itself, so wealth was reinvested rather than spent on conspicuous consumption. Thus, Protestantism and its consequences for the conduct of people's lives were important factors in the rise of capitalism in Europe.

According to Weber, once capitalism was established, its religious underpinning became irrelevant. The capitalist approach to economic activity — in particular, its constant calculation of profit — facilitated the rise of bureaucracy. Formal, rational, bureaucratic ways of doing things came to permeate commerce, state administration, and the military. The tremendous efficiency of bureaucracy in these areas entrenched bureaucratic modes of management, and made bureaucracy an important force in the shaping of modern society.

Weber's concerns underlie several forms of contemporary theory. For example, symbolic interactionists focus on how people maintain and change the meanings of their social world, while ethnomethodologists examine how people's actions in particular social settings produce a seemingly objective external world. Middle-range theorists provide causal analyses of specific social processes. I turn first to symbolic interactionism and ethnomethodology and then middle-range theories, before discussing how these theories may be synthesized.

■ SYMBOLIC INTERACTIONISM

Symbolic interactionists understand people in terms of their meaningful actions. Herbert Blumer (1900–87), who coined the term **symbolic interactionism** in 1937, strongly rejected behaviourism and its assumption that a particular external stimulus produces a particular personal response. Instead, the response produced by a stimulus depends on how the stimulus is interpreted, he argued. The response that a stimulus produces cannot be determined until we know how the people we are observing interpret that stimulus. This view is incorporated in the three basic principles of symbolic interactionism enunciated by Blumer (1969: 2):

1. Human beings act toward things on the basis of the meanings that things have for them.
2. The meanings that such things have for a person are derived from, or arise out of, the social interaction one has with one's fellows.
3. These meanings are handled in, and modified through, an interpretive process used by the person in dealing with the things he or she encounters.

My experiences with snakes illustrate these principles. During my teenage years, I lived in what was then called Malaya, where some snakes were poisonous. If I saw a snake, I moved rapidly away (principle 1). Everybody else did so. The meaning of snake as dangerous was thereby solidified (principle 2). Shortly after returning to Canada, I had a summer job as a camp counsellor. While leading a canoe trip in northern Ontario, one of my young campers found a garter snake and threw it into my tent. The tent collapsed as I tried to exit through the back. Laughter ensued. My campers knew that no poisonous snakes existed in the area. I realized that my definition of snake had to change — and fast (principle 3). Just as I suspected, several hours later, another garter snake landed in my tent. I stayed calm.

Weinberg's (1996) analysis of the moral meaning of public heterosexual nudity at nudist camps also illustrates symbolic-interactionist principles. In nudist camps, nudity and sexuality are unrelated. People interpret exposing the human body as promoting natural pleasure and a feeling of freedom, not as being "indecent" (principle 1). This interpretation of nudity is maintained, Weinberg argues, by excluding, or substantially excluding, single men; a rule of no staring at the body; focus on the face; no sexual talk, with "sexual" being defined more widely than in the rest of North American society; no bodily contact and often no dancing; and no unnatural attempts to cover the human body. These interaction patterns, Weinberg argues, allow nudists to maintain the meaning of nudity as asexual (principle 2). However, their low threshold of acceptance of anything remotely sexual shows how hard a marginal group must work to sustain its meanings and betrays nudists' awareness of the moral meanings of clothed society (principle 3).

Symbolic interactionism has developed a variety of concepts to highlight the complexity of social processes involved in the creation, change, and stabilization of meaning. For example, stigma is defined as "the situation of an individual who is disqualified from full social acceptance" (Goffman, 1963: 1). Thus, stigma is not a characteristic of an individual, but of interaction among people. Stigmas may be visible or invisible. An invisible stigma may be hidden, but, if it becomes known, it is capable of discrediting the individual.

Laslett and Warren (1975) applied these concepts in their study of a for-profit weight-loss group, most of whose clients are female. Unlike in societies where being overweight is a sign of wealth and status, in our society being overweight is a visible stigma. The evidence shows that overweight people are perceived as weak-willed and less attractive and, thus, less qualified for full social acceptance. Recognizing this, the diet group divided the world into civilians (the "naturally" slender) and the overweight. They regarded overweight people's identity as permanent — they are "foodaholics." By following the diet group's guidelines, however, the members were led to believe that their stigma could be rendered invisible. Nevertheless, group members who lost weight felt that they remained overweight people who could now pass as thin people. They did not think of themselves as true civilians. Laslett and Warren concluded that deviant or stigmatized identity and deviant behaviour need not coincide. Some conformists persist in seeing themselves as deviant.

Symbolic interactionism's strength lies in its exploration of people's worlds "from the inside." It sensitizes us to nuances of meaning in people's actions. But symbolic interactionism's weaknesses also flow from its focus on people's own accounts of what is happening to them. First, people often do not understand what is happening to them. For example, in one weight-loss group studied by Laslett and Warren, the average weight loss was near zero. That their effort to lose weight did not work in reality shows that people's intentions and the consequences of their actions can differ. Both meaningful actions and causal sequences must be examined to fully understand human activity, as Weber emphasizes. Second, people often see themselves as freer than they are. This leads them to underestimate how the power of others constrains their choices. Symbolic interactionism consequently tends to ignore power. In addition, people underestimate how extensively their background shapes their choices. For example, most Canadians claim to "choose" their spouse freely on the basis of love, but they usually marry somebody from their own ethnic group and socioeconomic background.

ETHNOMETHODOLOGY

The basic claim of **ethnomethodology** is that "the activities whereby members produce and manage settings of organized everyday affairs are identical with members' procedures for making these affairs accountable" (Garfinkel, 1967: 1). Such accounting procedures are seen as requiring endless adjusting to new social contingencies. Ethnomethodologists see people as producing a world that seems objective and independent of themselves through their ways of accounting for, justifying, explaining, and rationalizing their actions in particular situations.

These insights have led ethnomethodologists to criticize official statistics that many sociologists rely on for data. Official statistics are seen as practical accomplishments in particular social settings, not objective reflections of an external reality. For example, in his critique of the use of suicide statistics, Douglas (1967) noted that people rarely observe suicide directly. Instead, deaths must be interpreted as suicides for certain practical purposes (e.g., insurance claims, avoiding embarrassment to families) by coroners. Coroners' understanding of who is likely to commit suicide informs their routine practices in certifying some deaths as suicide. Sociologists since Durkheim (1966 [1897]) have argued that single and divorced people are more likely than married people to commit suicide because they are more isolated and anomic. Coroners incorporate this understanding into their routine determinations of cause of death. Thus, they are more likely to account for a death as a suicide if they know that the deceased was a single person or divorced. This accounting, in turn, makes the official suicide statistics used by many sociologists suspect as independent evidence for theories.

Ethnomethodology has demonstrated the immense work that goes into the construction of what passes as social facts for most people, including other sociologists. However, many critics of ethnomethodology claim that ethnographies of particular constructions of meaning are just one-off descriptions of unique situations. These descriptions are not generalizable and they lack testable generalizations about social processes. This criticism has led many sociologists to turn to middle-range theories in order to analyze particular social processes. Let us consider middle-range theories next.

■ MIDDLE-RANGE THEORY

A **middle-range theory** makes causal claims about specific social processes. A typical and well-supported middle-range theory is that utilitarian attitudes toward drinking (as compared with convivial or ritual attitudes) promote alcoholism (Bales, 1962). Convivial attitudes are those that see alcohol consumption as an appropriate part of social gatherings (e.g., wine with family dinner). Ritual attitudes support alcohol consumption as part of religious cere-

monies. Utilitarian attitudes say that alcohol is useful — it can help people relax or facilitate fun at a party. In short, this middle-range theory claims that if you use alcohol to relax or have fun, you are at substantial risk of abusing alcohol.

Middle-range theories identify a small set of social forces acting in a situation. But these social forces may be overwhelmed by other social forces. Consequently, middle-range theoretical claims should be formulated as **tendency statements**. Tendency statements have the form: "Whenever A is present, B will also be present in the absence of interfering conditions," or "Whenever A is present, there is a tendency for B also to be present" (Gibson, 1960: 18). Thus, the claim that A tends to cause B does not imply that A is always followed by B. For example, in the theory of alcohol use, an educational campaign about the dangers of using alcohol to relax might block the tendency of utilitarian attitudes to generate high rates of alcoholism. It is possible that, in a particular society, A is normally blocked from affecting B so that A is not usually followed by B. Constructed in this way, middle-range theories are sets of tendency statements.

Middle-range theories recognize the complexity of the social world that almost all research reveals. This strength is particularly apparent when middle-range theories are formulated as sets of tendency statements. This alerts us to several points:

1. Because a wide variety of factors affect A's tendency to cause B, sociologists need to collect data on numerous factors to assess the impact of a particular factor. Consequently, most sociological research needs to be **multivariate**. That is, it must use many variables.
2. Sociologists need to read the literature. To know what may interfere with A's tendency to cause B, they need to know about past research. Their own research results cannot be interpreted in isolation.
3. Because any research has to be interpreted in the context of other findings, theoretical claims, even if supported by a study, will always be debatable.

To analyze a whole society or a substantial sector of it, middle-range theories may be brought together in three ways. The first is based on the view that the social world is composed of a diversity of social forces. These may reinforce each other, cancel each other out, partially cancel each other out, or combine to form new types of social forces. Thus, sociologists must build up an analysis of society piece by piece. They trace the interplay of some particular combination of social forces in producing order and change. Then, they consider other social forces, and the analysis becomes more complex. The problem with this approach is that it may become too complex. For example, Canadian alcoholism rates are influenced by a host of obvious directly relevant variables, such as attitudes to drinking, images of masculinity and femininity in relation to drinking, and the price of alcohol. After an analysis of direct influences on alcoholism is produced, large-scale social changes that might influence alcoholism rates must be considered. Such changes might include changing patterns of immigration or the possible rise of some new form of Puritanism. So many factors may be relevant that the analysis may be overcome by its complexity. Consequently, this approach to combining middle-range theories works best when the analysis can be restricted to a limited sector of society and the social forces internal to it.

Merton (1968 [1949]: 39–72) advocates a second approach. He suggests that middle-range theories are a way station between raw data and an eventual, comprehensive, unified theory of society. This position rests on a faith in some underlying unity of the social world that has yet to be discovered. However, little progress has been made thus far on a unified theory of society that is empirically adequate. If one rejects the view that there is one theory of all social processes because society is not of one piece, "middle-range theory" cannot be a step toward a nonexistent destination. Thus, Merton's approach to combining middle-range theories fails and the term "middle-range theory" is inappropriate.

The third approach to integrating middle-range theories is to use an existing overall interpretation of society, such as conflict theory. The overall theory provides the logic that brings together several middle-range theories. To illustrate this, I will now outline another overall interpretation of society, feminism, and show how it may be used to bring a variety of middle-range theories together.

■ FEMINISM

After a long period of development just below the threshold of general public awareness, feminism burst forth in the late 1960s, first as Women's Liberation, then as **feminist theory**. Feminism's central claim is that the basic structure of society is **patriarchal,** or male-dominated. Consequently, feminism insists that what has been taken as universal experience is, in fact, just male experience. It follows that theories based on, and framing, this experience are also male theories. According to feminists, our knowledge is man-made in two basic ways. First, it is largely produced by men. Second, even when women research and theorize, men are the gatekeepers of ideas. Men control almost all educational institutions, research funds, and publishing opportunities. Consequently, men decide what will pass as knowledge. Thus, even when women do the research and theorizing, male agendas and assumptions dominate the results.

Many feminists show how man-made knowledge disadvantages women. For example, Broverman et al. (1970) questioned psychiatrists, psychologists, and social workers in the mental-health field about their image of male and female social roles. Their results show that male and female workers in the mental-health field identify the characteristics of socially competent adults with those of social competent *men*. They also noted, however, that women are viewed as socially competent only when they do *not* act like socially competent adults. For example, a socially competent adult (i.e., male) behaviour is to be assertive, but women are commonly regarded as competent when they are *not* being assertive. Thus, male and female mental-health workers believe that the appropriate behaviour for women is nonadult, devalued behaviour.

A basic feminist claim is that "the personal is the political." This means that patriarchy shapes all social relationships, even the most intimate. Feminists emphasize consciousness raising to counter patriarchy. They argue that when people's consciousness is raised, small, seemingly private personal choices are seen actually to be reflections of a male-dominated society. Patriarchy rests on both men's dominance in the public sphere of society (e.g., the economy, law, politics) and the reproduction of this dominance in the detail of the private sphere (in the household). Resistance in the private sphere is often met with male violence (e.g., wife battering). Feminists argue that this violence, through its enforcement of male power in the private sphere, underpins male public-sphere dominance.

Feminism distinguishes sex from **gender**. Sex is biologically given, while gender is socially constructed, usually as a dichotomy, to which men and women may conform, and by which they are usually judged. For example, "childbearer" is a sex role, while "moth-

Margrit Eichler is a leading feminist theorist in Canada and has developed a worldwide reputation. She is best known for her work on feminist methodology, family policy, and social stratification. She believes that although feminists have helped bring about a sociology that is much more woman-centred than the sociology that existed 25 years ago, the objective of many feminists — the creation of a nonsexist sociological theory — has not yet been achieved. Her major works include *Nonsexist Research Methods: A Practical Guide* (1987) and *Families in Canada Today* (1988). SOURCE: Margrit Eichler.

er" is a gender role. The patriarchal nature of our society makes gender relations unequal relations. However, because they are gender relationships and not sex relationships, they can be changed.

Almost all feminists see society as patriarchal, knowledge as man-made, and gender as permeating everybody's activities. Beyond these basics there is considerable disagreement. Modern feminists may be liberal, Marxist, or radical (Tong, 1989).

▲ LIBERAL FEMINISM

Liberal feminists have documented the extensive inequalities affecting women in modern societies. Arguing that there are no relevant biological differences holding women back, they have searched for barriers to women's equality in differences between men's and women's socialization and in barriers to attainments in the public sphere (e.g., discrimination). They advocate policies for overcoming these barriers, such as affirmative-action programs for hiring and promoting women. In addition, to ensure that women's work is properly valued, they favour pay-equity plans. These plans compare male and female jobs in terms of working conditions, responsibility, training required, and other factors. These factors are then weighted and the wages of predominantly "female jobs" are recalculated to be the same as comparable "male jobs."

Liberal feminism seeks equality of opportunity for women and men in a society that is hierarchically ordered and similar to our present society. Because it accepts the status quo except as it affects women's equality of opportunity with men, liberal feminism underlies most popular feminist analyses and political actions that generate concrete, short-run political gains. However, as the liberal-feminist analysis of the barriers to women's equality advances, it is becoming clear that a society where most men and women enjoy equality of opportunity will have to be substantially different from our current society. For example, men would have to be much more involved in child rearing than they are currently. Increasing men's involvement would require substantial alteration in the relationship between paid work and the family. Thus, liberal feminism's acceptance of our current social structure and its commitment to male–female equality are in constant tension. Consequently, most academic feminists consider the changes that liberal feminists want to be worthwhile objectives but insufficient in themselves to generate equality.

▲ MARXIST FEMINISM

In the view of Marxist or socialist feminists, there are two separate but intertwined sources of women's oppression — capitalism and patriarchy — and both need to be overthrown to free women. Patriarchy predates capitalism but now each supports the other. Capitalist patriarchy is characterized by a virtually total separation of domestic and child-rearing tasks from "productive" labour. This separation helps ensure women's dependence on men in marriage. Cheap female labour helps perpetuate the dominance of men and the capitalist class. It also forces women into marriage. The gender divisions among workers help perpetuate the dominance of capitalists (Hartmann, 1984).

Marxist or socialist feminists understand the rise of the welfare state in terms of a shift from familial to social patriarchy. In familial patriarchy, power and authority over women is exercised largely by individual men in the home. In social patriarchy, power and authority over women resides in the laws and institutions of the state. In the latter situation, welfare legislation, instead of freeing women from poverty, regulates many aspects of women's lives. For example, the law defines what counts as cohabiting, which in turn determines who may receive social assistance (Ursel, 1992). A major strength of Marxist feminism is its ability to provide interpretations of macro or large-scale social change. However, these interpretations may be faulted for ignoring other sources of women's oppression, such as race or sexual orientation.

▲ RADICAL FEMINISM

Radical feminists think that the root of male power lies in the family, not the economy. In their view, the subordination of women and children in the family is the prototype and foundation of all subordination, including class subordination. Women's central role in raising children is crucial in creating deep-seated gender differences in personality that perpetuate gender inequality. On the one hand, the fact that raising children is almost exclusively a female gender role leads most women to want to be mothers and to be capable of raising children. On the other hand, the same fact leads most men to devalue women and to expect women to serve them. According to radical feminism, only male involvement in infant care can undermine the hierarchical gender division.

Radical feminists analyze women's experience to show how it is distorted by men. For example, Mary Daly (1978: 14–17) says that the term "hag" originally affirmed the wisdom and experience of old women, but then was turned by men into a term of derision. Critics of radical feminism argue that it assumes a universality or homogeneity to women's experience that ignores the diversity of women's experience produced by factors such as class and education.

▲ FEMINISM: WHERE NOW?

Feminists have shown that male–female gender inequality permeates human life in the workplace, politics, and the family. Feminist theory has led to important social-policy recommendations, including concern about (1) male violence (e.g., wife abuse, rape), which supports patriarchy; (2) the implications of all policies on women; and (3) the need to have women make policy, especially where the issues involve women. Feminist theory also generally views men as sufficiently free and powerful to change society. The more extreme forms of feminist theory, however, tend to see all men only as oppressors of women. Such a view overlooks the variation in men's actions. For example, men's participation in housework and child rearing varies considerably, as I will discuss in the next section.

Feminism has raised some difficult and still unresolved questions for those committed to an egalitarian society. For example, if gender tends to be constructed on the basis of sexual differences, then what types of gender construction are compatible with an egalitarian society? Alternatively, should people who wish to achieve an egalitarian society strive to be androgynous and to overcome a tendency to construct gender on the basis of sexual differences (Phillips, 1992)?

▲ FEMINISM AND MIDDLE-RANGE THEORY

The household division of labour in Canada favours men. A study in Calgary, for example, found that women who worked full-time and had a child under age 6 spent only slightly less time at paid work than their husbands, but did about three-quarters of the household chores and child care (Lupri, 1991). Men spent 61.5 hours per week at paid work, child care, and household chores, while women averaged 83.5 hours per week. Feminist theory argues that male domination of the public sphere gives men the ability to devalue housework and child care. Men's typically higher wages gives men the power to force women to do most of the housework and child care. But while feminist theory is a good explanation of the general pattern, it needs elaboration to explain the variation that exists in the household division of labour. Some men do more household chores and child care than others. To explain this variation, feminists use a variety of middle-range theories interpreted in terms of feminist theory.

Research in Canada and the United States shows that men do more housework and child care if (1) there is more than one child; (2) there is no child (particularly a daughter) old enough to assume some housework responsibilities; (3) their wives are employed at paid work full-time as opposed to part-time;

(4) their wives' income approaches their own (Hoffman, 1989); (5) their wives' job status is high (Moore and Sawhill, 1984); and (6) their sex-role orientation is one of "liberated masculinity," which means that they have an open, nontraditional style of being male (Nett, 1988: 224). Some of these results fit under a resource approach to household division of labour: As people contribute more resources to the household (e.g., job status, income), they do less of the less-valued work. Other data show that attitudes do affect behaviour; sex-role orientation matters.

Feminist theorists would interpret resources in terms of relative power. For example, the wife would be seen as having more power if she had a full-time paid job, because this would give her increased financial independence from her husband. Under these circumstances, divorce is a more realistic option. Having fewer children also gives her more power because it, too, makes divorce a more realistic option. Feminists would see the wife's income and job status in terms of their relative contribution to the household's economic and social status. As her contribution increases, so does her power. Her increased power allows her to mitigate some of the usual effects of patriarchal society and have her husband do more of the housework. Feminists would interpret the impact of male sex-role orientation as indicating the possibility of change as feminism grows stronger. Feminist theorists would insist, however, on putting all variation in household division of labour into the wider context of patriarchal society. For example, feminists would point out that while dual-career families had the most internally equal division of labour, these families achieved this equality by paying another woman to do housework or child care. The equality of some women is gained at the expense of other women (Hertz, 1986). In addition, feminist theorists would emphasize that even when men spend more time doing housework and child care, the chief responsibility for housework and child care usually remains with the women (Luxton, 1986).

Synthesizing numerous middle-range theories on a topic through a comprehensive theory such as feminism has several advantages:

1. The strengths and weaknesses of the more comprehensive theories are known. This helps us formulate a preliminary evaluation of the synthesis of the middle-range theories.
2. The analysis is simplified. As I noted earlier, when numerous middle-range theories are used to analyze the interplay of social forces acting on some sector of society, the analysis may be overwhelmed by complexity. Simplification allows for comprehension.
3. Today's multivariate research usually reveals a rich diversity of human activity. On their own, comprehensive theories tend to oversimplify human activity and thereby deny its complexity. Synthesizing middle-range theories with a comprehensive theory enables sociologists to acknowledge more fully the wide variety of human activity.
4. A comprehensive theory can suggest ways of extending the analysis. For example, the feminist view of knowledge as man-made could lead to a reconsideration of what counts as doing housework and how the current definition of housework is maintained.

■ THE FUTURE OF THEORY

Using middle-range theories, sociologists have imposed some order and understanding on a wide variety of research results from different sectors of society. Unfortunately, nobody has yet succeeded in building an empirically adequate theory of society from a variety of middle-range theories. However, these middle-range theories have been brought together with overall theories of society such as functionalism, conflict theory, and feminism. Because many of the strengths and weaknesses of these more comprehensive theories are known, the resulting analyses can help us gain a better and less ideological understanding of stability and change in Canada in the twenty-first century. ■

● SUMMARY

1. Sociological theories are claims about what exists and how key features of a social process determine other aspects of the social process.
2. Sociology and sociological theory arose in nineteenth-century Europe to provide a secular account of rapid social changes and the experience of neglected social groups.
3. Functionalism sees society as an integrated, consensual whole. It solves the problem of order too well.

4. Conflict theory sees society as constantly changing. It solves the problems of change and conflict too well.

5. Symbolic interactionists see people as maintaining and changing meaning; ethnomethodologists see a seemingly objective world produced by people's accounting procedures.

6. Middle-range theories are sets of tendency statements about specific social processes. Because tendency statements have to be interpreted in the light of previous research, they are always debatable.

7. Feminism sees patriarchy as shaping all social processes and our knowledge of that process. Although feminist theorists have developed a good critique of society as male-dominated, they have not created a nonsexist sociological theory that fully incorporates women's experiences.

8. Middle-range theories can be brought together by more comprehensive theories, such as functionalism, conflict theory, and feminism.

QUESTIONS TO CONSIDER

1. Formulate an original theory. (Do not worry if it is implausible.) What features of social life does your original theory identify as causes of other features of social life? How would you go about testing your theory?

2. What is the implicit theory in: "What schools need to do is concentrate on basics"?

3. What are the similarities and differences between functionalist, symbolic-interactionist, and feminist accounts of overweight people and how people may respond to being overweight?

4. What are the middle-range theories in an analysis given in another chapter of this text?

5. What is the most appropriate comprehensive theory for the analysis you clarified in question 4? Why?

GLOSSARY

alienation The state of being unable to reach full human potential.

anomie The absence of norms.

bourgeoisie The class of owners of the means of production.

conflict theory A theory that sees conflict and change as constantly present and possible.

ethnomethodology A theory that sees people as making actions "accountable."

facts Correct observations in terms of a conceptual scheme.

feminist theory A theory that sees patriarchy as dominating all social processes.

functionalism A theory that views society as consensual and composed of mutually supporting parts. Also referred to here as order theory.

gender A socially constructed identity based on an individual's biological sex.

ideology A set of claims about how society works that are not open to disproof.

imperatively co-ordinated associations Groups within which the powerful pursue their interests by dictating to the powerless.

middle-range theory A limited set of causal claims about a specific social process.

multivariate Using many variables.

norms Rules that people in a particular society believe they and others should obey.

patriarchy A male-dominated society.

power The capacity to get your way despite opposition.

proletariat The class of people who must sell their labour to survive.

social facts Features of human activity that become apparent only when considered in relation to other activities. Durkheim argued that social facts are coercive and that they constitute the proper focus of sociology.

structural Describing theories that focus on patterns of social relations.

symbolic interactionism A theory that sees people maintaining and changing meaning.

tendency statements Claims of the form that A will produce B unless something else interferes.

theory A set of claims about what exists and the interconnections among existing phenomena.

Verstehende **sociology** Sociology that holds that the meaning of an activity is important to an understanding of its effects.

SUGGESTED READING

Giddens, A. (1971). *Capitalism and Modern Social Theory.* Cambridge, UK: Cambridge University Press. Despite the title, this is a presentation of Marx, Weber, and Durkheim. It is an influential and sophisticated interpretation of these thinkers. Although the book is not an easy read, sorting it out will prove rewarding. In this chapter I have followed Giddens's interpretation of Marx, Weber, and Durkheim.

Jaggar, A., and P. Rothenberg, eds. (1984). *Feminist Frameworks: Alternative Theoretical Accounts of the Relations between Women and Men,* 2nd ed. New York: McGraw Hill. This book presents selections from conservative (nonfeminist), liberal, traditional Marxist, socialist, and radical-feminist theory. It is a useful collection that includes many classics.

Menzies, K. (1982). *Sociological Theory in Use.* London: Routledge and Kegan Paul. This book distinguishes between the theories that theoreticians discuss and the theories that researchers use. Its strength is its formula statements of theories and numerous examples of how theories are actually applied.

Ritzer, G. (1988). *Contemporary Sociological Theory,* 3rd ed. New York: McGraw Hill. After outlining how the major varieties of theorizing developed, particularly in the period immediately following World War II, Ritzer provides an extensive and balanced coverage of recent efforts at synthesis.

Whelehan, D. (1995). *Modern Feminist Thought: From Second Wave to Post-Feminism.* New York: New York University Press. This book shows the diversity of feminisms that exist. The author outlines not only liberal, socialist, and radical feminism, but also lesbian and black feminism, and then presents the responses of feminisms to various social and intellectual challenges in the 1980s and 1990s.

Zeitlin, I. (1990). *Ideology and the Development of Sociological Theory,* 4th ed. Englewood Cliffs, NJ: Prentice Hall. This book provides a good introduction to the major classic sociologists and a variety of eighteenth- and nineteenth-century writers who influenced them.

CHAPTER TWENTY-ONE
Research Methods

IN THIS CHAPTER YOU WILL LEARN THAT

- science is one of several sources of knowledge in the modern world and, like other sources of knowledge, it can be wrong; but, unlike other ways of knowing, science uses methods of gathering theoretically relevant information that are designed to minimize error

- research methods are used by sociologists to gather evidence in order to test theories about recurring patterns of human activity; underlying these techniques are a variety of assumptions about the nature of facts, objectivity, and truth

- in comparison with the evidence available to natural scientists, an added complexity confronts social scientists: humans assign meaning to their actions and interpreting meaningful action is very complicated

- sociologists have devised many useful methods of obtaining evidence about the social world, including experiments, surveys, participant observation, and interviewing

- good sociological research adds to our knowledge of the social world, expanding opportunities and options by helping to solve social problems

NEIL GUPPY
University of British Columbia

■ INTRODUCTION

Social research involves the systematic study of the social world. The systematic nature of sociological study comes, in part, from the methods sociologists use to study society. Basic to such study is the collection of evidence. However, only evidence relevant to theoretical ideas, and even then only evidence collected according to established principles, is useful in social research. Systematic study integrates both sound theory and careful methods.

This chapter introduces you to the principles of research methods. I begin by outlining some basic assumptions involved in social-science research, including assumptions about personal values or bias, the nature of facts, and the sources of knowledge. Next I introduce the idea that the subject matter of the social sciences, people, differs from the objects of inquiry in the natural sciences (e.g., molecules, plants). People studying people adds complexity to social research. This is especially the case because social behaviour is meaningful. That is, people interpret their own behaviour and the behaviour of others by trying to establish meanings. This complexity has led to the development of various methods of social research, and I review these techniques of research in the final section of the chapter. Methods of observation and questioning lie at the heart of much research, and I review the strengths and weaknesses of each of these approaches.

■ PERSPECTIVE

At age 47, Gwen was told she had cancer. A malignant tumour had been found in her left breast. Knowing that breast cancer was a major cause of death among women, Gwen and her family were immediately concerned about how long she might live. Her anxieties were mildly relieved when she learned that the malignancy had been detected early and that the nodule was not among the severest pathological grades. Her doctors also said that her chances of survival were significantly improved because she had a large, supportive network of friends, relatives, and neighbours. In other words, beyond medical pathology, she learned of an important causal link between *social structure* and *personal situation*.

Nancy Waxler-Morrison, a sociologist at the University of British Columbia, has worked as part of a team showing that "several characteristics of the women's friendship and social network, her marital status and employment status are significantly and independently related to survival" (Waxler-Morrison et al., 1991: 180). That is, quite apart from any medical factors affecting survival, social-support networks (part of social structure) have a unique, positive effect on life expectancy. This research, typical of much sociological investigation, shows that our lives reflect the contexts of our social experience. Care and rigour must be exercised in such research to conclude with confidence that social context affects life-chances, especially in this example, where the effect of social support must be shown to be independent of medical or pathological factors.

▲ THE PURPOSE OF SOCIAL RESEARCH

Waxler-Morrison's research nicely illustrates the purpose of sociological investigation. Put simply, good social research aims to better the human condition; it aspires to enlarge the scope of human freedoms. Waxler-Morrison strove to do this by demonstrating the importance of networks of social support to human well-being. She did not set out to prove this was the case; she wanted to know whether or not social networks were beneficial.

Science is a social process whose products are knowledge and understanding. As a social process, however, science is open to abuse and fraud. Under the guise of furthering knowledge, prisoners have been subjected to what were called medical experiments. Scientists have fabricated findings to win fame and fortune. There is also debate about whether scientific work has, in fact, improved the human condition. For example, were the physics experiments that lay behind the first nuclear bomb progressive — did they better the human condition? The purpose of social research, to better the human condition, is an ideal goal, a lofty principle open to exploitation. As stated in Chapter 1, however, the hope is that through greater scientific knowledge and understanding we will all be led "a little farther away from the mud outside the cave." Social research, in other words, seeks to demystify the world in which we live.

Social-science research requires that the current state of affairs be properly described. We would want to be certain, for example, that women in more supportive networks actually had higher survival rates. Beyond correctly recounting or displaying something, we need to explain or understand how or why something occurs. Waxler-Morrison speculates that women in larger networks are less isolated, interacting with and assisting others more. It is this helping activity that facilitates personal survival (i.e., not just the receipt of help, but also the giving of help is important). Finally, if the human condition is to improve because of sociological investigation, research findings must eventually be turned into action or social policy. In the case of health and social support, the research findings have led to the development of various social-support programs.

In this chapter, I explore the methods sociologists use, and the assumptions they make, in reaching conclusions about the social world. I begin by exploring some key suppositions we make in doing scientific work. What constitutes evidence? Why is evidence important? Where does theory fit? After reviewing some of these basic issues, I turn to the actual conduct of sociological research. How is evidence gathered? How are theoretical ideas tested with the use of evidence?

■ SOCIAL-SCIENCE METHODOLOGY

▲ WAYS OF KNOWING/SOURCES OF KNOWLEDGE

Improving the human condition requires knowledge. Science is about the pursuit of knowledge. Nevertheless, there are many ways of knowing. Personal knowledge has many sources. Many people believe, at various times in their lives, that their parents are either the best or the worst parents around. We form this judgement despite having only scanty knowledge of other parents. Similarly, many Canadians believe in God, yet very few would claim any first-hand experience in dealing with God. Furthermore, we have all had experiences where we learned that something we "knew" turned out to be wrong. My 8-year-old daughter is convinced that the "sun rises and sets"; only later in life will she consider that our common phrasing is in error and that the apparent motion of the sun is due mainly to the earth's rotation. From where does our "knowledge" of the world come?

Here are four different sources of knowledge:

• *Common sense.* Common sense is the impressive collection of accumulated, shared personal experience. It is collective wisdom distributed among

people; the basis of that knowledge is seldom questioned. For example, it just makes sense to us that sexual intercourse between brothers and sisters is wrong (although apparently not all cultures share this common sense).

• *Religious faith/mysticism.* Many people believe in the teachings of God or Allah, but few people claim direct experience or interaction with either. Religious truths have been handed down over the centuries, their sacred versions of right and wrong protected by prophets or leaders zealously guarding against revisionism.

• *Expertise/authorities.* Experts offer "correct" answers. Garage mechanics tell us the fuel pump needs replacing and medical authorities advise us that our gall bladder needs removing. We trust in this specialized knowledge because it is complex and it is given by acknowledged experts.

• *Science.* Science produces knowledge based on direct, systematic, reproducible observation. Scientific information is based on reason and evidence.

These ways of knowing share many attributes. First, we all believe strongly in information coming from more than one of the sources listed above. We all habitually rely on common sense and experts, and scientific and religious knowledge underlies much of Canadian culture. These knowledge systems also share a second important characteristic: Each can be wrong. No system of knowledge invariably produces truth, unerringly generating eternal accuracy.

This latter observation is especially important in a chapter on research methods. Science does not establish permanent, universal truth, even though truth is the goal scientists pursue. The history of science easily explodes the myth that science is about eternal truth. Scientific practice once routinely accepted that light travelled only in waves, much like sound. Now we think that view erroneous (although we must hold open the view that it was indeed correct, and that we are now wrong). Schizophrenia may prove to have a genetic component, although for a long time this idea was mocked in scientific circles. Currently, we believe that most cancers are not viral in origin, but that claim may also be shown to be false in the future. All of this is to say that science, just like common sense or expert knowledge, can be wrong.

Although science shares much with these other knowledge systems, two features of science set it apart from common sense and religion. First, science rests on the principle of open, public display. Not only the results of science, but also the precise methods of obtaining those results, must be open to others. Second, science encourages criticism and scepticism, especially through practices of competition, where a reputation can be won by demonstrating error or misinterpretation. Neither public display nor critical scepticism makes scientific practice immune from error, but both practices make scientific knowledge different from other forms of knowledge. And, of course, both public display and critical scepticism are ideals not fully realized in practice, although the history of science shows that both are institutionalized practices that strongly affect research.

▲ OBSERVATIONS ARE FACTS — NOT!

A common misconception is that science is founded on facts derived from direct observation. But the bedrock of science is not and cannot be observational fact. Observations depend on expectations formed by experience.

In Charles Dickens's *Hard Times,* Mr. Gradgrind demands facts — "What I want is Facts.... Facts alone are wanted in life." Contrary to the popular saying, though, facts do not speak for themselves. Millions of people have crossed many rivers and seas, but Moses' crossing of the Red Sea or Jacques Cartier's voyage across the Atlantic are significant historical facts. That you and I have crossed many bodies of water, let alone any one in particular, is not likely to get much historical ink. Facts do not exist independently of observers. Mr. Gradgrind could have collected a lifetime of facts, but they would have done him, or anyone else, little good. Science is not a collection of facts. It is, however, among other things, a method of collecting facts.

Facts are bits of evidence, information that you or I can verify using our senses. Since trillions upon trillions of bits of human activity might be taken as facts, how do we select what should count as evidence? How do sociologists avoid random, idiosyncratic, fact gathering? Sociological theory provides guidance for the hunting and gathering of facts. Evidence is gathered to test ideas, hunches, or theories. Only selected bits of human activity are used as evidence. Those selected bits are chosen only because they relate to a sociologist's hunch about how the world works.

Waxler-Morrison was not interested in everything in the lives of the women she studied. Through previous reading and observation, she had come to think that the life expectancy of women diagnosed as having breast cancer was related to their social circumstances as well as to their medical pathology. Given that hunch, she searched systematically for evidence that would show her whether or not life expectancy was related to the social resources on which an individual could draw. In making comparisons among the women she studied, she searched for evidence that would refute or support her claim. She also had to be very cautious that her "facts" (i.e., her evidence) were not "artifacts" — that is, figments or creations of her own making. Research methods are designed to reduce the likelihood that we are dealing in artifacts, while enhancing the likelihood that we have reproducible evidence.

Not all hunches qualify as scientific, however. Scientific claims are only those that can be refuted. Specifying observations or evidence that would contradict a hunch must be possible. This principle — the principle of falsifiability — is a key feature of scientific practice. Importantly, this does not mean that ideas that are unobservable are useless for science (e.g., we cannot observe gravity directly). The idea of gravitational attraction helps us understand forces, but this is a metaphor for how we think the world actually operates. We see the results of a process we call "gravity," but we do not see, in any literal sense, the direct force of gravity (just as we cannot see time). Nevertheless, time and gravity are convenient ideas that help us understand our world.

The principle of falsifiability suggests another caution, however. Useful scientific claims must not be true by definition (i.e., tautological). For example, in claiming "only the fittest survive," I can never be proven wrong if I define fittest as those who survive. No observation could disprove or falsify my claim, because you could repeatedly observe fit survivors. By definition, anyone who did not survive could not have been fit.

▲ OBJECTIVITY

Personal intuitions play a major role in all of science, whether natural, medical, or social. Scientific work requires subjectivity. The flair of human imagination and creativity is the most fundamental aspect of science. The drudge work of science is much like following a recipe book in cooking — a series of steps in a scripted process. The creative spark of science comes from people's insights, from their personal ingenuity or originality. As Albert Einstein once remarked, 90 percent of scientific work comes in asking the right question.

Furthermore, scientists cannot be neutral, unemotional beings like Mr. Spock of the old *Star Trek* fame. Scientists are human, and humans have many biases and deeply held beliefs. Since human beings cannot be robots, acting without feeling or emotion, a scientific method of marshalling evidence is used. This method helps guard against personal bias, although no set of rules can prevent cheating or distortion.

Among the rules of scientific method working to enhance **objectivity** and eliminate personal bias are critical scrutiny and full disclosure. Scientists must report not only their observations, but also exactly how and where the observations were made. The ideas of replication, reproducibility, and falsifiability are key. Other scientists must be able to replicate the research design and make similar observations. Thus, values or subjectivity always influence scientific work. What the rules of scientific method provide is a method to help filter out personal bias or distortion from individual values.

▲ NATURAL VERSUS SOCIAL SCIENCE

The science practised by chemists and the science practised by sociologists share many elements. The idea of a single scientific method, applicable both in chemistry and sociology, has a certain appeal. In both the natural and social sciences, research methods help in understanding and explaining why certain patterns emerge. Furthermore, values are important in this process because these values underlie the creative imagination so central to scientific puzzle solving. Values also have the potential to bias or distort observations, and both the natural and the social sciences must guard against distortion. If the scientific method is defined as a set of practices or procedures for testing the validity of knowledge claims, both chemists and sociologists could be seen as "doing" science.

There is, however, a profound difference between the subject matter of the natural and the social sciences: Bacteria don't blush. This phrase neatly captures a key distinction between the research methods of chemists and those of sociologists. Human beings are conscious and creative; we can think, act, reason, and decide. We are, as Anthony Giddens (1984) phrases it, "knowledgeable actors." As sociologists, we study "ourselves" — that is, our contemporaries and our peers. Bacteria, having no knowledge of social norms, do not blush when exposed to the beam of an electron microscope. Bacteria cannot think, act, reason, and decide; they cannot consciously control their surroundings or reactions in the same way human beings can.

Just what this difference in subject matter means for sociologists and chemists is still a matter of debate. Perhaps the single most important difference is that sociologists study **meaningful action** — that is, activities that are meaningful to the people involved. For example, bacteria may not blush when studied, but people often react self-consciously when they know they are being observed.[1] To study love, friendship, or charm depends on learning something about the meanings people ascribe to their actions. This has advantages and disadvantages for sociologists. Unlike chemists, we can ask questions of the people whom we study (bacteria don't talk either!). But this advantage can also be a disadvantage. Interpreting people's answers is not easy.

Because of this difference in subject matter, sociologists have developed an array of methods to help them understand and explain human activity. Since asking questions has advantages and disadvantages, good sociological research either employs a variety of ways to ask questions or relies on observational techniques to aid in understanding and explanation.

■ METHODS OF SOCIAL RESEARCH

▲ EXPLANATION

Sociologists have shown repeatedly that the years of schooling people typically receive is strongly influenced by the family backgrounds from which they come. Children raised in poverty tend not to go as far in school as do children from upper-class families. Although this research demonstrates a link between family background and educational attainment, this link is, as I have reported it, descriptive, not explanatory. I have offered no reason *why* this relationship between family origin and educational destination exists. It is true that I have noted a potential cause (family origin) and an effect (amount of schooling), but I have failed to provide any mechanisms through which this implied causal process might operate. An **explanation** would be judged adequate only if it could show how family resources actually influence educational outcomes.

The mere association or correlation between social origin and educational attainment does not prove causality. The relationship between smoking and lung cancer is a good example of the rule that *correlation does not prove causation.* Smoking has long been linked to lung cancer, but only in the past two decades have we learned more about the causal mechanisms underlying this correlation. Cigarette companies, especially, have argued long and loud that the presumed connection was **spurious,** that something other than smoking caused lung cancer (see Box 21.1). Accumulated evidence and a more precise notion of the underlying modes of transmission have established that the original correlation is causal.

There are several ways that we might try to explain the link between family and schooling. An obvious factor is money. Although public schooling is free, costs are incurred for field trips, exchanges, international tours, postsecondary education, and a host of other events. Children living in poverty may remain in school for fewer years than their upper-class peers because of these costs. Money seems to be a partial explanation for the link, but other factors may be at work as well. Many skills and values taught in school may be more readily grasped by children from upper-class families, not because these children are smarter than are children living in poverty, but because the home environments of the children may expose them to different skills and values. The classroom climate may be more like the climate of the upper-class home (e.g., abstract word games are valued, reading and music are prized) and these children may therefore be advantaged.

The first explanation is largely about money and material resources. The policy implications of this explanation point to eliminating or reducing the costs of schooling. This has been accomplished in large measure in Canada. However, even when the costs of postsecondary education have also been reduced (e.g., in Quebec and Newfoundland), social-class disparities in educational attainment have remained. The second explanation points to cultural factors in the home (e.g., reading) as a reason for the family–school link. This explanation has influenced policies related to compensatory education, such as Head Start and After Four, educational programs designed to help disadvantaged children by giving them educational enrichment.

We explain something by showing how or why a cause has a certain effect. The mechanisms by which causes have effects are essential for adequate explanation. Perhaps the cardinal lesson regarding explanation is that there is hardly ever a single explanation — *the* explanation — for anything. Because multiple causes are involved in social-scientific explanations, a single, unitary cause or explanation is rarely sufficient. Sociologists search for the multiple factors that can help explain some particular state of affairs. So, in the family–school example, although only two explanations for the link are mentioned here, other explanations may also be tested and refined as sociologists attempt to see how equality of educational opportunity might be attained.

▲ UNDERSTANDING

Sociologists must not be content merely to offer explanations for why a particular relationship exists. These explanations are often sterile unless they also address the meaningfulness of human activity. People make the social world go round, and in doing so they give meaning to their actions and to the actions of others. A failure to address these meanings would leave sociology underdeveloped.

It is no simple matter, however, to understand what someone or some group means by their actions or utterances. One way to think about **understanding** is as follows. The first time I saw a traditional Greek dance, I was unable to follow the patterns of movement or appreciate the symbolism of certain motions. Similarly, the first time I watched a cricket match, I could not fathom what was happening. To the extent that I have come to understand either of these complex social activities, I have learned *how to proceed with the activity.* To understand a Greek dance or a cricket match means being able to participate fully in the activity, knowing what others mean by their actions and utterances, and knowing how others will interpret our actions and utterances.

A fundamental social process, called "taking the role of the other," nicely captures this idea of understanding. By imagining yourself in the role of another, you come to appreciate someone else's point of view. You come to understand, to reflect upon, his or her ideas and issues. I do not mean that you must become Caesar to understand him; that would be impossible. Instead, sociologists focus on the web of relations in which people interact, paying attention to how people understand and interpret the views of others. They pay attention to "the definition of the situation," to the meanings of the people involved.

Erving Goffman's work in an "insane" asylum is a good illustration of sociological understanding (Goffman, 1961). Goffman was not interested in getting inside the heads of the mental patients to learn what and how they thought about things. Rather, he was interested in how the patterns of social activity in the asylum were organized. He

Box 21.1
Correlation and Causation

Where fires cause much damage, many fire trucks usually gather. This is a correlation; a lot of damage tends to go along with many trucks, while minimal damage tends to draw only a few trucks. This simple illustration makes the point that correlation does not prove causation. Consider the diagram below. The curved, double-headed arrow depicts the correlation between the amount of damage and the number of trucks on the scene. The single-headed, straight arrows show the direction of causation. The size of the fire is a common prior cause of both other variables.

Causality is controversial because it often involves something we cannot observe directly. For example, until very recently, no one could see lung cancer being caused by smoking. We inferred that conclusion from assembled evidence that fit with theoretical conjecture.

◆ An Example to Illustrate that Correlation Does Not Prove Causation

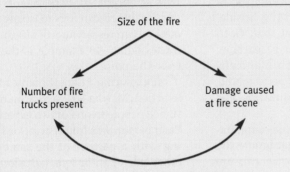

Women living in poverty eat less nutritious meals and consequently are more likely than better-off women to have premature babies. But not all women living in poverty have premature babies. There is a correlation between poverty levels and the incidence of premature births, and nutrition level has been identified as a key causal stimulus. Notice, however, that living in poverty does not guarantee premature births. Living in poverty only raises the probability that a mother will have a premature baby.

In a causal relationship, a change or variation in one thing produces a change or variation in another. If four basic conditions are met, causality may be established. First, two variables must be associated or correlated. Consider two variables — the likelihood of premature births and poverty. Premature births must be more likely to occur among poor women than among women who are not poor if a causal relationship exists. Second, the independent variable must precede the dependent variable in time. Establishing that a woman is poor while she is pregnant confirms the causal ordering or temporal sequencing of the variables. Third, the original association must not disappear once the effects of other variables on the dependent variable are examined. We need to verify that we have not made a false inference or a false reading. Does the causal process really go from poverty to poor diet to premature babies? Could it be that stress, and not poverty, is the causal agent? It may be that poor women are under more stress and that stress, not poverty, increases the likelihood of premature births. The initial causal relation between poverty and premature births would be spurious — that is, false, like the spurious causal relationship between the number of fire trucks at a fire and the amount of damage at the fire scene — if stress was determined to be the operative factor. Finally, we must offer a *theoretical* account of how one variable causes another. We must illustrate the mechanism(s) through which causation operates. This theoretical reasoning also enables us to establish which variables are important to examine when we test to see whether a causal relation might be spurious. In the example, we theorize that poverty affects nutrition, which in turn affects the likelihood of premature birth.

came to see the mental hospital from the patients' point of view. By dispensing with the medical categories and scientific labels assigned to individual patients, Goffman began to understand the ways in which patients worked co-operatively to produce a coherent social structure. He learned to appreciate how the patients defined the routine activities of the asylum, and how they coped with institutional procedures that denied them privacy and stripped them of their personal identities (e.g., by issuing institutional clothing and removing personal objects).

Goffman (1961: 129) also learned about what he calls the "careers" of mental patients: "Persons who become mental-hospital patients vary widely in the kind and degree of illness that a psychiatrist would impute to them. . . . But once [in treatment] they are confronted by some importantly similar circumstances and respond to these in some importantly similar ways. Since these similarities do not come from mental illness, they would seem to occur in spite of it." Although social life on the "inside" might seem unique or even bizarre at first, Goffman argues that anyone, patient or researcher, would, in time, come to find it much like many other communities in which one has participated, possessing an identifiable social organization and rhythm of activity.

Returning to the education example, explanations of high-school drop-out rates that ignore the attitudes and values of drop-outs themselves are one-sided. An appreciation of the experiences of drop-outs is essential to a more complete account of the schooling process. Especially important here is the resistance of students to authority, often expressed through music and clothing. This resistance is not some idiosyncratic expression of random individuals, but represents part of a youth subculture that must be understood by anyone who wants to alter the schooling process to make it a better environment. How young school resisters define the situation of schooling is important to a full appreciation of dropping out.

Understanding and explanation work together. While explanations of dropping out that ignore student values are deficient, merely reporting the stories of young resisters would be equally vacuous. A full appreciation of dropping out, or of any other social activity, requires both understanding and explanation. Often these activities are pursued by different researchers and their combined results contribute to fruitful research programs leading to social change.

■ TECHNIQUES OF SOCIAL RESEARCH

Sociologists have developed a variety of techniques to gather evidence. I will review three of the most important: experiments, survey research, and observation studies. As you read my accounts of research procedures, keep asking yourself: How do sociologists go about developing insights about, or knowledge of, the social world? How do they come to know what they claim to know? What methods do they use and how believable are the results generated by these methods?

▲ EXPERIMENTS

Experiments are the hallmark of scientific research and are commonly, though inaccurately, equated with science itself. Experiments are useful because they enable researchers to isolate causes. By no other method can researchers determine so precisely what causes what. An example is the best way to illustrate the point.

In exploring how ethnicity influences social interaction, Martha Foschi and Shari Buchan (1990) assigned people to one of two experimental conditions. Each person was told that he or she would be working with a partner of the same sex seated on the other side of an opaque partition. Their task was to make judgements about the relative sizes of graphic images. After seeing two contrasting images, but before finally selecting the one they felt contained the most white space, people were told of their partner's choice. Foschi and Buchan wanted to know whether the ethnicity of a partner would affect a person's likelihood of sticking with their own selection or switching to their partner's choice. Many people change their mind when they hear what decisions others have made. Foschi and Buchan were keen to see whether the likelihood of a person changing their mind depended on the ethnicity of the other person.

In one case ("condition one") the partner was described as East Indian, while in the second case ("condition two") the partner was described as English Canadian.[2] Because the experimenters wanted to examine the effects of ethnicity on personal judgements, they had to ensure that the only difference between conditions one and two was the partner's ethnicity. They could not, for example, let the participants meet their partners because that would expose them to more than just the partner's ethnicity (e.g., the partner's demeanour, clothing, height). All of the participants in the experiment were of European ancestry, but their "partners" were either East Indian or English Canadian. How could the experimenters subtly inform people of their partner's ethnicity, without arousing suspicion?

Foschi and Buchan developed a clever solution. First, they asked the participants to complete a short questionnaire. Then, under the guise of wanting to let the participants know something about their partners, the experimenters gave everyone their partner's completed questionnaire. In fact, each participant received a questionnaire that Foschi and Buchan had previously completed. By design, only two fictitious partners existed and they differed only by surname (Edwards or Sidhu), country of birth (Canada or India), and language (English or English/Punjabi). Apart from those three attributes (i.e., the difference between conditions one and two), every person in the experiment received identical descriptions of their partner (e.g., same age, level of schooling, place of residence).

The experimental results suggested that men were less likely to be influenced by East-Indian than by English-Canadian partners. Women did not systematically change their judgements according to their partner's ethnicity. The common attribute among men who were less influenced by their partner was their partner's ethnicity. The experimenters were confident that ethnicity was the only factor distinguishing the two groups because each man in the experiment was randomly assigned to one of two conditions — an English-Canadian or an East-Indian partner.

Random assignment or **randomization** lies at the heart of experimental design. Using a random procedure (e.g., flipping a coin, rolling a die), people in an experiment are assigned to an experimental condition on the basis of chance. If the flipped coin comes up heads, a person is automatically placed in experimental condition one; if the coin comes up tails, the person is assigned to condition two. Although individual participants will differ with respect to age, sex, weight, and so on, the two experimental groups will contain an approximately equal number of women and men; the average age of the two groups will be similar; and so on. This group similarity is accomplished by random assignment. Foschi and Buchan used random assignment to ensure that the only difference between conditions one and two was the partner's ethnicity.

For women, the partner's ethnicity made no difference. The treatment condition — East-Indian or English-Canadian partner — had no effect on the judgements women made. Exactly why men were influenced by ethnic cues and women were not remains open to debate. Foschi and Buchan suggest that women might be less prejudiced than men, perhaps because women have more frequently themselves been the victims of discrimination. The experimenters were quick to add, however, that there could be other, more likely explanations. In particular, they surmised that women may have been more likely than men to believe that ethnicity was of no relevance to a person's ability to make judgements about the visual images.

By dissecting the Foschi and Buchan experiment, we can examine more carefully the key design features of an experiment. The researchers began with a **hypothesis** — an unverified but testable knowledge claim about the social world. In the example, the experimenters hypothesized that ethnicity affects behaviour in social interaction. In more formal terms, Foschi and Buchan (1990: 5) "predicted different perceptions of competence and resulting behaviour for White subjects performing a task with a partner, depending on whether the partner was White or East-Indian."

To test this hypothesis, Foschi and Buchan examined the relationship between two **variables**. A variable is a measurable concept that can have more than one value. Age is a concept we use in talking about how long someone has lived. For newborns, age is measured in weeks or months, but for everyone else it is measured in years. One variable studied by Foschi and Buchan is ethnicity. They designed the experiment so that ethnicity could have one of two values: East Indian or English Canadian. In this experiment, ethnicity is the **independent variable,** which is presumed to affect other variables. Differences in this variable are hypothesized to affect a second variable, the **dependent variable**. In the experiment by Foschi and Buchan, the dependent variable is the amount of influence a person will accept from his or her partner. It was measured by the frequency with which people changed their initial judgements after learning of their partner's choice.

Nevertheless, how do Foschi and Buchan know that only a partner's ethnicity and not another factor, such as a partner's age or social class, influence judgements? They are confident of their conclusion because, by design, they know that only the ethnicity of the fictitious partner differed between conditions one and two. Apart from ethnicity, partners were identical. Could it not be, however, that the people making the judgements differed? After all, no two people are alike and perhaps this fundamental vari-

Before diving into social research, one must first develop hypotheses — testable knowledge claims about the social world. The outcome of hypothesis testing by means of research helps determine the validity of theories. SOURCE: Dick Hemingway.

ation was at work in the experiment. For example, perhaps the people in condition one (East Indian) were older than the people in condition two (English Canadian), and older people may reject their partner's influence more often. Foschi and Buchan eliminated this possibility by randomly assigning people to one or the other treatment condition. Randomization, as I explained earlier, is a procedure used in experiments to assign people to experimental conditions on the basis of chance. Because participants cannot choose which treatment condition to enter (i.e., they cannot self-select), the groups can be made alike.

Sociology experiments of the type conducted by Foschi and Buchan are relatively rare, in large part because many social processes that interest sociologists are not amenable to laboratory testing. Ethical and practical problems limit the use of laboratory experiments. Furthermore, we must be cautious in generalizing the results of laboratory experiments to nonlaboratory situations. This latter concern is tech-nically expressed as a problem of **external validity,** or the degree to which experimental findings remain valid in a nonlaboratory situation. External validity is often low; relationships discovered in sociological experiments do not always hold in more "real-life" settings because these settings differ in many ways from the laboratory. Still, the relevance of laboratory findings is an empirical question. There is reason to be cautious about generalization, but often findings from the laboratory apply in other real-life contexts.

As I mentioned earlier, when people know they are being studied, they often become self-conscious. The very fact of being studied may influence their behaviour. This was demonstrated in productivity experiments conducted by Roethlisberger and Dickson (1939) at the Western Electric Company's Hawthorne factory. They found that productivity (the dependent variable) increased when they brightened the lighting, but then also increased when they dimmed the lighting. The researchers realized that people worked harder because the research team was studying them. Productivity increased in response to the researchers' presence rather than because of any other changes they introduced. Social scientists have subsequently used the term **Hawthorne effect** when referring to changes in people's behaviour caused by their awareness of being studied. Bacteria don't blush because the Hawthorne effect does not operate in the natural sciences.

Field experiments have been used in sociology in an attempt to avoid some of the problems of laboratory experiments, especially problems of external validity. A good example of a field experiment is one undertaken in Toronto by Effie Ginsberg and Frances Henry (1985). They investigated the extent of job discrimination faced by people of different ethnic backgrounds. In one study, they sent actors, one black and one white, to apply for advertised job vacancies. The actors were given similar credentials and were trained to make their job-search behaviour as identical as possible. The researchers wanted to test the hypothesis that racial discrimination existed in the Toronto labour market. Their independent variable was the race of the job applicant and their dependent variables — their measures of discrimination — included the number of interviews granted and/or job offers made to each actor. They found evidence supporting the discrimination hypothesis, with whites having a 3-to-1 advantage over blacks in job offers (for discussion of a similar, more recent test of this hypothesis, see Reitz, 1993: 35).

The field experiment, conducted in a natural as opposed to a laboratory setting, reduces problems of artificiality. However, Ginsberg and Henry could explore only a limited range of jobs and were unable to focus on other urban centres, where discrimination may be more or less of a problem. Sociologists have had to develop other techniques to include larger populations.

▲ SURVEY RESEARCH

The social survey is the primary means of collecting social-science evidence. Researchers collect information using surveys by asking identical questions of a sample of people. Political pollsters, market researchers, labour unions, governments, and university researchers all rely heavily on survey-based knowledge. Survey research is so useful because it provides a method of systematically comparing answers to identical questions from a large sample of people, and allows researchers to generalize the results to the larger population from which the sample was chosen. Questions can be posed either on a **self-administered questionnaire** or through a personal **interview**.

Rhonda Lenton (1990) used survey research to investigate parents' aggression toward their children. Because of strong taboos against child abuse, asking questions about abusive behaviour is very difficult. The privacy surrounding child discipline makes observation or experiments inappropriate. Furthermore, asking blunt questions about "smacking your child" is unacceptable. Just as many alcoholics deny they have a drinking problem, many child abusers think of themselves as "strict disciplinarians." Parents use different strategies to influence their children, and Lenton wanted to examine the full range of this behaviour. Therefore, she chose to use a survey in which parents could be questioned by experienced and trained interviewers. She included questions covering an array of child–parent interactions, from praising and positive modelling through withholding privileges and love to spanking, slapping, and hitting.

A key problem facing Lenton was whether her questions about aggression and discipline would really measure child abuse. Child abuse is a theoretical concept. You and I may use the same term to mean different things. What types of maltreatment ought to be considered as child abuse? Lenton (1990: 159) defines child abuse as "any act, excluding sexual mistreatment [which she separated as sexual abuse], carried out by a parent ... that has the intention of, or is perceived as having the intention of, hurting a child." The idea of intention is tricky here. Lenton wanted to include as "abuse" any act that a parent understands may hurt the child. To mea-

sure abuse, she asked parents whether they had done any of the following, ever, and in the past year: yell at a child, ridicule a child, withdraw emotionally from a child, hit a child with an object, withhold food from a child, and 24 other actions. Do these items provide an indication of what Lenton defines as child abuse? That is, are these valid indicators? **Validity** refers to accuracy or relevancy. Lenton's measurement of child abuse is valid to the degree that the items she uses as measures of abuse actually measure abuse as she defines it theoretically.

Lenton interviewed each parent and child separately. Each family member was asked to complete a child-discipline questionnaire, on which each of the 29 abuse items were listed. This sheet was completed privately and handed to the interviewer in a sealed envelope. By comparing the responses of all family members, Lenton could determine the consistency with which abuse was reported by different family members. This gave her confidence in the **reliability** of her measure. **Measurements** are reliable if they are consistent or repeatable. If different measures or indicators of the same concept give similar results, the measurements are reliable or, in other words, internally consistent.

Lenton faced another problem when selecting the families to include in her study. She wanted families from across the spectrum of child discipline and, of course, she needed families with children. No publicly available list of such families exists. Lenton selected a random sample of Toronto families from the telephone directory. After first phoning to ensure that children lived in the household, members of the research team visited each eligible address to ask for permission to interview spouses and children.

Surveys always involve the selection of **samples**. Lenton's research team could never have interviewed all Toronto families (a complete enumeration of all families would be a *census*), nor would the expenditure of time and money have been efficient. Although the entire population could not be interviewed, it is this larger population about which Lenton wished to draw conclusions. To use a different example, in doing research on urban household waste, interviewing all city dwellers is both unnecessary and impractical, even though the intention might be to use survey results to help design city policy. Information obtained from a subset of the population, the sample, is used to represent the views and characteristics of everyone. For this reason, the survey sample must represent the population. Samples selected using rules of chance or probability provide random samples. These random samples give surveys better external validity than experiments.

Samples must represent the larger population from which they are drawn. For example, one or even a few kindergarten classes cannot be taken to represent all kindergarten classes, because not all kindergarten classes are alike. They vary in size, the ratio of boys to girls, and so forth. Therefore, if we wish to generalize about social processes common to all kindergarten classes, we need to select a number of classes for study. Because we cannot afford to study all kindergarten classes, we need a representative sample. Probability samples that rely on random processes for their generation are the most likely to yield samples that represent the population.

Exactly how many kindergarten classes or, more generally, how many units must be included in a sample is a complex question. The precise answer depends mainly on the amount of variation or heterogeneity in the population and the degree of accuracy required in the study's conclusions. If you need very accurate results, you need larger samples. Likewise, if the population is very variable, you need a larger sample to reflect that heterogeneity adequately. In studies of the Canadian electorate, very accurate forecasts of voting can be achieved with a random sample of about 1200 voters. The mathematical laws of probability can be used to generate efficient sample sizes.

Selecting samples is not as easy as it might seem. How would you go about selecting a random sample of students in your faculty? Distributing questionnaires in classes would be one method, but many students do not attend every class. Students who attend regularly are, by definition, different from those who attend infrequently. A sample of students present in classes would therefore be biased. Registration lists give an approximation of the student population, but these lists are never perfect. Students drop out as the term progresses, while others change their addresses and phone numbers. If you were studying student retention or student financial needs, the people who might be hardest to find might be the very people to whom it is most important to speak. Even with this severe limitation, however, student lists maintained by the registrar might be the best alternative available. The list from which a sample is selected is called the sampling frame. This frame must come as close as possible to including everyone in the population.

Researchers collect information using surveys by asking people in a representative sample a set of identical questions. People interviewed on a downtown street corner do *not* constitute a representative sample of a country's adults. That is because the sample does not include people who live outside the urban core, underestimates the number of disabled and elderly people, does not take into account regional diversity, and so on. SOURCE: Dick Hemingway.

Recently, market-research firms have been making greater use of telephone interviews in conducting their surveys. These firms usually rely on *random-digit-dialling* procedures to establish random samples. They select "banks" (i.e., lists) of working telephone numbers (e.g., 902-424-79xx), and let the computer randomly dial the last, or the last two, numbers. This method, used by Statistics Canada in some of its surveys, provides a random sample of households, including households with unlisted telephone numbers. Two important refinements are used. First, some households have more than one telephone number and their chances of inclusion are therefore increased. Statistics Canada asks respondents how many working telephone numbers there are in a house so that it can correct for this small bias. Second, the person who is interviewed in the house must also be randomly selected (because, for example, women are more likely than men to answer the phone even when both are at home). One popular strategy for obtaining a random sample of household members is to interview the person who has had the most recent birthday.

Telephone surveys require that people be interviewed. An alternative to telephone interviewing is the use of self-administered questionnaires, which can be either mailed or delivered to members of the sample. Mailing questionnaires to people and handing them out to groups (e.g., students in a classroom, patients in a clinic) are less expensive than telephone interviewing. However, questionnaires lack the personal touch of interviewing. In an interview, misunderstandings can be clarified and responses can be expanded upon. This cannot be done with self-administered questionnaires. Questionnaires work best with what are called close-ended questions, like those on multiple-choice exams, to which there are a limited number of set answers. Interviews, especially face-to-face as opposed to telephone interviews, allow for more open-ended questions, where respondents can be encouraged to elaborate their responses to ensure that they are properly understood. Lenton, for example, chose to use personal interviews because she thought that the subject matter was best handled with face-to-face interaction. Notice, however, that she incorporated a short questionnaire on disciplinary techniques because she thought the questionnaire would be less threatening to people in that it was more anonymous.

Once Lenton had established her sample and pretested her research strategy to ensure that she would obtain usable information, she set out to gather evidence that would allow her to evaluate the merits of three different hypotheses. A "cycle of violence" hypothesis holds that practices of child abuse are handed down from generation to generation. A "social-situational" hypothesis maintains that abusive parents may be reacting to stress and that stress itself may be linked to a family's socioeconomic status. Finally, a "cultural" hypothesis stresses that it is the attitudes of the family toward corporal punishment that best differentiate between the use of aggressive and nonaggressive behaviour in child discipline. Her research was designed to yield evidence that would help her decide which hypotheses were wrong. No researcher designs the definitive test of alternative explanations. After analyzing the data, Lenton (1990: 176) concluded that "parents are inclined to use the disciplinary repertoires they learned when they were children — but only as long as certain current structural conditions are consonant with these repertoires." In particular, she pointed to structural conditions such as unemployment in the family and low family income. To the extent that these structural conditions can be eliminated or reduced, the "cycle of family violence" can be arrested.

I mentioned earlier that the ability of sociologists to ask questions of people has both advantages and disadvantages. Lenton's work illustrates this. The physical punishment of children in the privacy of the home represents social activity that is not easily studied by any sociological method. Yet, as Lenton argues, child abuse is a public issue, not a private matter. By asking questions of people she was able, first, to describe the extent of physical aggression used to discipline children and, second, to explain why some families were more likely than others to use physical discipline. The disadvantage of asking questions of people, especially questions that people may find threatening, is that people may distort their responses. For example, Lenton found that in over 75 percent of all families, children had been spanked or slapped in the previous year. Given current social norms about child abuse, this estimate of physical discipline is more likely to be an underestimate than an overestimate of such activity. If, however, different social classes subscribe to these norms to different degrees, people's responses to the 29 disciplinary measures might have altered. Lenton herself anticipated this criticism and asked people not just about their behaviour, but also about their attitudes. She was therefore able to examine whether different social classes held different norms about child discipline.

This distinction between attitudes and behaviours, or words and deeds, is important. I always intend to give more money to charity than I do. Most people believe that littering is irresponsible, but most people still litter sometimes. When you read research that focusses on people's attitudes, remember that thought is not easily translated into action. This distinction goes beyond the asking of questions to issues of policy as well. Too often, people think that changing attitudes will solve social problems — if only people knew more, they would act more responsibly. A broken New Year's resolution is but one simple reminder of how often good intentions fail to translate into good deeds, no matter how aware we might be of the consequences.

Interpreting the answers that people give to researchers' questions is complicated by more than this behaviour–attitude distinction. In asking people questions, either in interviews or on questionnaires, we must be careful about making assumptions (Gray and Guppy, 1993):

- *Do not assume that people understand what you are asking.* Language is notorious for its ambiguity. How many friends did you see yesterday? This question may look simple at first, but people will differ in their understanding of "friends" and others will take "see" in the most literal way. The same words may mean different things to different people. Asking about family members requires care because some people will include only immediate family, and others will include extended family members.
- *Do not assume that people know the answer to questions.* Most people do not want to appear ignorant when asked a question. This was illustrated nicely in a study of the prestige of occupations by Peter Pineo and John Porter (1967). They asked people to rate the prestige of two fictitious jobs, archaeopotrist and biologer. Most respondents co-operated and assigned these nonexistent jobs a prestige rating. When asked about their attitude on some issue, many people feel they must respond, even if they have no opinion on the topic or only a weakly formulated view.
- *Do not assume that people will admit the answer to themselves.* Alcoholics frequently claim that they can "quit any time." They refuse to admit that they are addicted. Similarly, child abusers may define themselves as strict disciplinarians. People routinely deceive themselves, sometimes only in minor ways, but "admitting the truth to ourselves" is a problem. Sometimes we will admit these things more freely to strangers than to ourselves or our friends, but sometimes we admit these things to no one, including ourselves.
- *Do not assume that people will give valid answers to others.* People feel better about themselves when they are seen in a favourable light. In asking questions of people, researchers face the potential problem of "social desirability," because respondents may only give answers that reflect well on themselves. "What type of work do you do?" — "Oh, I'm in public relations." Such a response could come from people working as telephone receptionists, tourist guides, or corporate representatives.

Sociologists use many techniques in asking questions to gather valid and reliable evidence. For example, they will ask several questions rather than relying on only a single question; use supplementary questions to expand upon or clarify answers; and test questions before using them to improve any wording that is unclear or misleading. Many more techniques are set out in *Asking Questions* (Sudman and Bradburn, 1982).

Survey researchers do not focus only on individuals, although it is individuals who respond to survey questions. For example, it is possible to survey organizations, groups, corporations, electoral ridings, or job vacancies. Although people answer survey questions, the questions may apply to a unit or group of which someone is a member. Sandra Burt (1990) studied women's organizations using a survey to gather information about how various women's groups were organized (e.g., their size, authority structure, networks). She mailed questionnaires to each group, asking that a knowledgeable person answer all of the questions. Fiona Maybin (1993), in a study of job-search procedures, interviewed personnel officers about the characteristics of recent job vacancies. Among other questions, she asked how the vacancy was advertised, how many people applied, and how long the vacancy had existed. Several people she spoke with reported on more than one vacancy.

I am making two points here. First, surveys can focus on different units of observation (individuals, corporations, countries, etc.). Second, individuals can act as informants to report information that pertains not to themselves but to some group or unit about which they have information. People can, for example, report on individual events (e.g., job vacancies), family composition, or corporate policy. Although each of these represents different units of observation, individuals are still answering the questions.

▲ OBSERVATION STUDIES

Another method commonly used by sociologists to gather information is observation. Sometimes sociologists act as outside observers, at other times as insiders or **participant observers**. The obvious advantage of observation is that sociologists can see what people actually do, rather than relying on reports of what people say they do. The disadvantage is that gaining access to private actions or events can be difficult. For example, Lenton might have tried to observe parents disciplining their children rather than relying on what parents told her they did. But entering the privacy of people's homes to make such observations would have been difficult. Furthermore, her presence may have influenced the type of discipline parents used (the Hawthorne effect).

In observation studies, examining the intentionality of social action is especially important. Max Weber (1949 [1904, 1905, 1917]) was one of the first sociologists to address the issue of intention as a problem of social research. Weber argued that our interactions with other people draw upon meanings. For example, the clothing we choose to wear speaks to others. All of us are conscious of intentionally dressing in certain ways to impress others. We attribute meaning to bow ties, jack boots, Laura Ashley scarves, and baseball caps. None of this is done innocently, because what we wear helps define who we are. Skateboarders, for example, dress in a particular style; they wear a uniform of sorts. Making social life intelligible is part of what Weber thought sociologists must address. To understand skateboarding, it is essential to see how skateboarders "define the situation." It is important to learn about their culture and to understand their systems of meaning. The aim of such research is not to explain the behaviour of skateboarders from an outside point of view, but to investigate their shared values and beliefs — their "worldview."

Weber maintained that causal logic can be used to accomplish some of what sociologists wish to do. He thought, however, that sociology also had to make intelligible the subjective basis on which social action rested. Weber used the German word *Verstehen,* or understanding, to refer to this mode of sociological analysis. To understand the meaning of social action requires being able, at least in principle, to participate in the social activity of which the action is a part. An example is the best way to illustrate such participant observation.

Peter Rothe manages a research evaluation unit for the Insurance Corporation of British Columbia (ICBC). In this capacity, he does research that will help the corporation manage its public responsibilities, including safety promotion, risk-avoidance training, and driver education. Rothe is adept at rattling off statistics relating to vehicular mileage, traffic fatalities, weather conditions, risky behaviour, and road conditions. As a sociologist, he is also aware that a statistical portrait of road safety is only part of the picture. In particular, he became interested in long-distance truck driving, one form of road transportation that was significant to the corporation's activities. Trucking is a risky business, and Rothe wished to learn, from a trucker's perspective, the social conditions that demand risky driving.

Given his position with ICBC, Rothe knew a great deal about trucking before he began his study. He knew less, however, about how truckers themselves "defined the situation." How did truckers work with, and around, the rules and regulations that police forces, insurance companies, highway departments, car and truck manufacturers, motor associations, and policy regulators had created? As Rothe (1991: 2) phrased it, he was interested in "the meanings truckers assign to various facets of their driving lives, their regard for risk and safety and their observable behaviours on the road." From his policy role, he thought that by appreciating the role of the truck driver, he could act more effectively in promoting public safety.

In his study, Rothe logged thousands of kilometres with truckers, listening to their stories, observing their behaviour, and participating in their groups. The primary responsibility of truckers is the movement of goods between destinations; that is how they earn their livelihood. Owner-operator truckers make their profit by moving as much freight as quickly as possible with as little stress on the equipment as is feasible. The rapid increase in competition in recent years (because of the government deregulation of trucking) has meant declining profits and longer hours of work for truckers. Public safety, once a major concern, has declined in importance as economic competition has promoted concerns about livelihood to the front rank.

How do truckers cope with this double burden of making a living and public safety? Most truckers with whom Rothe spoke took safety seriously. Vehicle inspections were fairly routine and defensive-driving practices common. At the same time, though, he witnessed widespread use of drugs and alcohol, neglect of laws aimed at preventing drivers from continuing to drive for extended periods without breaks, and blatant disregard for truck maintenance. For example, he recounts the tale of accompanying a trucker who hauled 35 000 kg of flour from

Elkhead, Oregon, to San Jose, California, in 20 hours. The first few hours passed uneventfully, but as nightfall approached Rothe discovered he was driving in a truck without lights. The truck's driver, Dale, considered the problem "no big deal. . . . Besides, we're safe, there's a moon rising." Rothe left the truck just before midnight, with Dale high-balling it to San Jose to meet his deadline, lights or no lights. Rothe was left to ponder how truckers could accept such risky practice as part of the job.

During his study, Rothe came to understand how the pressures of making a living led truckers to adopt an ideology of rugged individualism. He repeatedly witnessed the determined individualism of truckers, men and women who demanded the right to control their own lives. "Fatigue, sure it's a problem," but truckers thought they were the best judges of how much rest or sleep their own bodies required. "Front-axle brakes, sure they might work for some people," but experience, not brakes, was what got real truckers out of trouble. In other words, most truckers felt that their know-how, their experience, was a better standard than the results of scientific study (on braking distances) or policy regulators (on the need for rest breaks). This suggests that working with truckers to enhance safety is likely to be a more beneficial strategy than imposing rules and regulations, since the latter strategy would alienate truckers and increase their determination to "beat the system."

Rothe was able to gain an understanding of the pressures of trucking work by participating in the activity. By travelling with truckers, he acquired an in-depth appreciation of their work. As a participant observer, he was able to ask many questions of many different drivers, gradually accumulating a sociological portrait of how the social forces of the transportation industry influenced truckers, and how truckers in turn reacted to or resisted many of those social forces. As his study progressed, Roche was able to refine his understanding. He could cross-reference his observations by seeing how other truckers reacted to each new insight he gained, thereby increasing both the reliability and validity of his impressions.

As with experiments, the external validity of participant observation can be problematic. How confident can Rothe be that his conclusions are not dependent upon the impressions he formed from the small number of truckers with whom he rode? The intensive, in-depth nature of participant observation makes generalizability problematic. The key trade-off is between the richly textured, "thick description" of participant observation and the insularity of detailed study of one or a few settings. Unlike survey researchers, participant observers do not select different sets of random individuals or groups. The groups or settings they investigate are purposively chosen, sometimes because of easy access. For example, Rothe did not randomly choose truckers to accompany. He made arrangements to ride with drivers as and when he could.

To increase the generalizability of his results, Rothe arranged to ride with as many different truckers as possible. In addition, he tried to ride with truckers involved in many types of trucking (e.g., owner-operators, company drivers, single-route drivers). Furthermore, Rothe relied on a variety of other methods to supplement his study. In addition to participant observation, he conducted formal interviews with fleet managers, dispatchers, driving-school instructors, weigh-scale attendants, and so on. He also presented some data derived from survey research and detailed reading of various trucking-policy discussions (e.g., in government reports, trucking association newsletters). Rothe relied principally on participant observation, but he used a variety of other methods to supplement his basic research.

Rothe's type of account, often termed an **ethnography,** portrays a culture from its members' points of view. There are potential pitfalls of which Rothe had to be aware. First, how much did his presence as a participant observer influence his findings? Did people act differently when he was not around? In principle, there is no way of answering this question, although participant observers have tried to account for the effect of their presence in various ways. Some researchers conceal their research role; in effect, they try to be known to the other participants as one of them, rather than as a researcher (the ethics of this are dicey). Other researchers report that, with time, participants' awareness of their presence fades and they are treated as a member. Notice that this problem of presence is the Hawthorne effect in another guise. Whether in survey research, experiments, or observation studies, the researcher's presence can distort the domain of investigation. Researcher presence may undermine validity, and that is one reason it was so important for Rothe to use multiple techniques in an effort to ensure that his insights were valid.

Beyond the potential pitfall of mere presence is the problem that the findings of researchers may be ethnocentric. That is, researchers may impose their own values — their own worldviews — on the subject matter of their study. How do we know, for example, that Rothe is depicting the truckers' point of view and not his own? One method of reducing personal bias is known as the "member test of validity" (Douglas, 1970: 21). For example, if the truckers Rothe studied did not recognize themselves in his account — that is, if they saw Rothe's account as inauthentic — then we would worry about bias or distortion. Rothe was careful to "test" his tentative observations and insights on his informants by asking them questions and checking for observations that would falsify his impressions. Again, this is a research problem that extends well beyond participant observation. In fact, participant observation can be seen as the method that takes most seriously the task of understanding the members of a group from the members' point of view, stressing in particular their definition of the situation.

A third problem beyond presence and ethnocentrism is this: How do researchers know that the "tools" of their inquiry (e.g., questions, instructions, requests) did not in fact "create" or "generate" the resulting "findings"? For example, did Rothe create a finding by focussing a good deal of his attention on the independence or individualism of truckers? Alternatively, did Lenton invent a relationship between social class and child discipline by asking questions that might be interpreted in different ways by the members of different classes? Again, this involves issues of reliability and validity. Lenton can be confident that she did not construct or create a pseudo-relationship between class and discipline to the extent that she shows that the basic pattern of findings is repeated across different questions about the disciplining of children. Rothe distinguished between (1) truckers' comments made in response to his questions and (2) statements his informants volunteered or that Rothe overheard during his fieldwork. In addition, he used information provided to him by police officers, motel managers, weigh-scale attendants, and others who regularly met truckers. These alternative sources of information helped him avoid the problem of "creating" meaning. If truckers volunteered information that corroborated Rothe's impressions, and if these impressions were further reinforced by other knowledgeable observers, his faith in the authenticity of his account increased.

Not all observation can involve participation. Stephen Richer (1984) believed that we could gain useful insights into sexual inequality by studying the play of girls and boys. Specifically, he wanted to investigate issues related to sex-segregated and cross-sex play among young children. Richer chose to observe play in two settings — one a summer camp where children ranged in age from 6 to 14, and the other, a day-care centre where 3- to 4-year-old chil-

dren were enrolled. Richer observed strikingly different patterns of play in the two settings. In the preschool, "boys and girls displayed no reluctance whatsoever to play with one another" (Richer, 1984: 172). Conversely, at the summer camp, cross-sex play was rarely seen and even then only within specific settings or times. This latter observation is particularly important in Richer's work because he discovered circumstances in which cross-sex play did occur among older children — namely, when formal adult supervision was not present and when one camp group competed in sports against another camp group.

The believability of Richer's research is enhanced by the fact that he observed events in their natural settings. He did not create a situation to see how people reacted (e.g., laboratory experiments) nor did he rely on people reporting on their own attitudes or behaviours (as in survey research). He was not a participant in the activity and so his involvement could not have distorted events (as may occur in participant observation). It is true that his presence as an observer may have influenced the activity patterns of others but this was easy for him to check (he asked camp counsellors and day-care supervisors whether outside observers changed patterns of play).

Direct observation is a very good research strategy, one that many people rely on in their own lives — "only believe it if you see it with your own eyes." The problem in much scientific research, in both the social and the natural sciences, is that we cannot see many things with "our own eyes." Natural scientists routinely use instruments such as electron microscopes and magnetic resonance imaging machines to "see" the natural world (e.g., electrons, cell membranes). Similarly, social scientists use a variety of techniques (e.g., surveys, experiments) to help them "see" the social world.

▲ OTHER METHODS OF RESEARCH

Historical Sociology

Some sociologists study social change. Max Weber, for example, attempted to explain the rise of capitalism by showing how Protestantism invigorated capitalist growth. Émile Durkheim was interested in how moral education helped to socially integrate a rapidly changing society. Both writers sought to answer sociological questions by examining historical change as evidence of significant social processes.

Sociologists are more likely than historians to use historical evidence to test theories of social change. Sociologists place less emphasis on history for history's sake.

Gordon Laxer's (1989) work shows how sociologists can also make effective use of comparative, historical methods. Laxer sought to explain why the Canadian economy has remained heavily tied to the production of resources (e.g., wood, oil, grain, minerals) with high levels of capital investment by foreigners. He wanted to test different theories about economic development, such as whether Canada's relatively late industrialization explains our present economic structure. To do this, he systematically compared Canadian economic patterns (e.g., levels of manufacturing activity, levels of foreign investment) with those of other countries, and in particular other late-developing countries such as Japan and Sweden. Laxer suggests that we can best understand Canada's relative position in the world economy, and especially our greater reliance on exporting raw materials as opposed to the sale of manufactured goods, on the internal politics of early Canadian development — principally, a weak farmers' movement around the turn of the twentieth century. In contrast to countries such as Sweden and Japan, Canada did not have a strong, ethnically united farming class that could push for domestic economic policies (such as the creation of banks willing to lend money for long-term investment) that ultimately facilitated strong industrial development.

The logic of Laxer's analysis is not unlike that of other sociological research. His key dependent variable is foreign investment and he measured how this investment changed historically in several different countries. Among his independent variables is the organizational strength of farmers (the agrarian class). By comparing an admittedly small number of cases, he sought to decide what was both similar and different in the cases. By comparing the historical record using a small number of variables across a set of different countries, he was able to sort out plausible causal factors that influenced Canada's position relative to other countries.

Sociologists like Laxer sometimes rely on other researchers' historical accounts. He relied primarily on economic histories that had already been written about each country he included in his analysis. Other sociologists go back to original sources to reconstruct a historical record pertinent to their focus. For example, Gillian Creese (1988) examined gender relations in the Vancouver labour force and labour movement early in this century. Her aim was to improve our understanding of the

historical dynamics leading to the segregated work of women and men. Included in the archival material that she used were the full proceedings of the Royal Commission on Labour Conditions in British Columbia, documents on strikes and lockouts between 1907 and 1939, the minutes of local labour unions, and press coverage from newspapers. Any single source could give only partial coverage of the events she wished to examine. By using a variety of sources, she was able to increase the reliability of her findings. Creese also relied on published data from the Canadian censuses for the decades in which she was interested.

Use of Official Statistics

Governments have a long history of collecting statistical data. Government bureaucracies first began to collect statistics to help rulers determine both the size of their taxation base and the number of fighting men they could put on the battlefield. Since then, the scope of government or official statistics has expanded and now includes information on births and deaths, unemployment rates, imports and exports, and so on. Sociologists have made good use of official statistics.

For example, Brym (1986) was interested in how support for social-democratic political parties was related to the resources on which different social classes could draw. His dependent variable, electoral support for leftist political parties, was measured as the percentage of voters casting ballots supporting social-democratic or communist parties in ten capitalist democracies, including Canada. He focussed on three key independent variables: a measure of the inequality of income in a country, the type of electoral system in a nation, and the percentage of the labour force that was unionized. His measures of these variables (except the type of electoral system) were derived from official statistics. Brym showed that, contrary to earlier research, class-based political activity was still strong in many countries he studied, especially if there were leftist political parties with the resources necessary to run effective campaigns.

McMullan and Swan (1989) used official statistics in their investigation of arson in Nova Scotia. They relied on police-reported arson for the period 1970–85. The data showed a substantial rise in both the actual number and the rate of reported arson (number of arsons per 1000 fires) between 1973 and 1981, with a modest decline in subsequent years. Arson, of course, is difficult to prove, and McMullan and Swan were careful to check with a second source to verify the pattern they had established. When they used fire-marshall data, as opposed to police-report data, they found similar trends. In accounting for the fluctuating arson rate (their dependent variable) they pointed to interest rates and unemployment rates as the variables affecting arson rates. On the basis of official reports, and from interviews that they conducted with enforcement and insurance officials, McMullan and Swan concluded that most arson involves the burning of one's own property, even though the criminal definition of arson continues to emphasize vandalism.

The arson example nicely illustrates a central problem with official statistics. These statistics are not objective facts on which everyone can agree. The very definition of arson makes it difficult to prove. Furthermore, different interest groups have a great deal at stake over whether a fire is officially reported as arson. More and more arsonists are property owners themselves, and their interests are typically opposed by those of insurance investigators, who wish to pay no settlements for illegal fires. Again, issues of validity are at stake: Do the official definitions used to generate, say, arrest statistics, arson rates, or strike statistics correspond to the theoretical concepts that sociologists wish to use? In addition, sociologists must be certain that official statistics reflect changes in the behaviours they are examining, rather than changes in the practices of the officials collecting the statistics.

■ THE ANALYSIS OF NUMERICAL DATA

As these research examples imply, sociological evidence frequently comes in numerical form — that is, as quantifiable evidence (e.g., number of disciplinarians, arsons, or voters). Finding and interpreting patterns in numerical data is complex. To help in summarizing numerical information, social scientists routinely rely on statistical techniques. In this section I briefly illustrate some key aspects of the process. I begin with a simple puzzle: Education affects income. In more formal terms, I begin with a hypothesis: The higher people's education is, the more they typically earn. Men and women have, on average, very similar levels of schooling. However, as a group, men earn higher wages or salaries in the labour market than do women. So, if education is a good predictor of income, and if women and men have similar amounts of schooling, why do men typically earn more than women?

There is a causal logic to what is being described here. Education is hypothesized to affect income. However, since women and men earn different wages in the labour market, yet have similar levels of schooling, maybe the causal link between education and income differs by sex. Although I can present only an elementary analysis here, issues of a wage gap between the sexes are part of the continuing debate over pay equity, comparable worth, and employment equity, all important policy questions.

To begin, we need to examine whether the basic facts, as I have just stated them, are accurate. I do this by using data from the 1994 General Social Survey, a survey conducted by Statistics Canada of a nationally representative sample of Canadians (11 876 randomly chosen Canadians, to be precise). Does education have a big effect on income? Table 21.1 gives us an answer. This table, called a contingency table or a cross-tabulation, shows the relationship between education and income. Education, the independent variable displayed across the top of the table, has three categories (low — twelve or fewer years of schooling; medium — thirteen or fourteen years of schooling; and high, more than fourteen years of schooling). For ease of presentation, annual personal income, the dependent variable, has been divided into two categories (low — personal income below $16 000 annually; and high — annual income at or above $16 000). The causal logic of the relationship, which underlies the construction of the table, is that education affects income (see Box 21.1 for the basic issues of causality).

Notice first how the table is arranged. The title describes the two variables being related. The independent variable (education) is placed on the top of the table and its values are clearly delineated. Below each value for education is a column of numbers. The dependent variable (income) is arrayed on the side of the table, again with the value labels clearly shown. Beside each value of the dependent variable is a row of numbers. The cross-classification of the two variables then creates a series of cells in the table. One cell contains people with both low education and income, and another contains people with medium education and high income. At the intersection of each column and row is a table cell. In this table there are six cells.

The concept of a contingency table comes from the idea that the category into which a person falls on the dependent variable is contingent on, or depends on, the category that a person occupies on the independent variable. If that hypothesis were true in this case, we would expect that, as we move across the education categories from low to high, the number of

◆ **Table 21.1** The Relationship between Level of Education and Personal Income for People Aged 25–34, Canada, 1994

	Level of education			
Income	Low	Medium	High	**Row totals**
Low	55%	56%	35%	51%
	(442)	(390)	(166)	(998)
High	45%	44%	65%	49%
	(360)	(309)	(308)	(977)
Column totals	100%	100%	100%	100%
	(802)	(699)	(474)	(1975)

SOURCE: Data from Statistics Canada, 1994 General Social Survey.

people receiving high incomes ought to rise. Does the data reveal this pattern? For people with low education, 360 had high incomes. For people with a high level of education, 308 had high incomes. These figures seem, at first glance, to run counter to our expectation. Notice, however, that because of how education was categorized, 802 people had what I defined as low education, while only 474 had high education. Comparing the actual number of people in each cell is therefore misleading, because there are different numbers of people in each column.

Rather than focussing on the raw numbers, we get a better understanding of the patterns when we standardize the data. We should ask not how many of the people in the low-education column had high incomes, but what *percentage* had high incomes. By expressing the numbers as percentages — that is, by standardizing the data — it is much easier to see the key patterns. So, 360 of 802 people in the low-education column had high incomes, or 45 percent (360 divided by 802 and then multiplied by 100). This tells us that for every 100 people with low education, 45 had high incomes. Making the same calculation for the high education column — (308/474) × 100 — we find that 65 percent of highly educated people earned high incomes (or 65 of every 100 people).

If you examine Table 21.1, you will see that the percentages are entered in the table. The actual number of people in each cell appears in parentheses. It is important to recognize that the percentages run down (or are calculated down) the columns, producing what are known as column percentages (i.e., 100 percent in each column). It is possible also to calculate row percentages, but these are not as useful in understanding the relationships appearing in contingency tables when the independent variable is placed across the top of the table.

So, do relatively more people with high education receive high income in comparison to people with low education? Yes. Of every 100 people in the high-education column, 65 receive high income (65 percent), compared with only 45 of every 100 in the low-education column (45 percent). The difference between these two percentages (20 percent) is one measure of the strength of the relationship between education and income. However, with no standard of comparison, it is difficult to say whether 20 percent signals a strong or a weak relationship. In a moment I will turn to a method of comparison that allows us to make such judgements.

In studying this table, some of you may have taken exception to my definitions of high and low incomes. Why should earning over $16 000 be considered a high income? What is defined as low and high income is arbitrary. However, when I define the lows and highs of income and education differently and produce several different tables, the basic patterns in the tables do not change. This replication gives me confidence that my decisions about how to categorize the variables does not affect the results.

The evidence in Table 21.1 corroborates the first part of the puzzle about the relationship between education and income that I hypothesized. But how does gender figure into the pattern? Table 21.2 contains two contingency tables. Here the question is how the link between education and income varies for women in comparison with men. Table 21.2 can be usefully thought of as Table 21.1, but with women and men separated into their own tables.

For women, the data patterns are not easily interpreted. Women with higher levels of schooling are more likely to earn high incomes (60 percent) than are women with low levels of schooling (55 percent), but the percentage difference is only 5 percent. Women with moderate levels of schooling are less likely than either of the other two groups to have high incomes (45 percent), a finding that at first glance is counterintuitive.

The second subtable in Table 21.2 contains the information for men. Men with higher levels of schooling are more likely to earn high incomes (70 percent) than are men with low levels of schooling (37 percent), a difference of 33 percent. Comparing the two percentage differences shows that the relationship between education and income is much stronger for men (33 percent) than for women (5 percent). Here, then, is an example of using percentage differences as a method of determining whether certain causal links are stronger than are other such links (a more complicated method for investigating these linkages relies on multiple regression — see Box 21.2).

What explains this finding of a difference between women and men in how education is related to income? There are a few possible reasons, all of which would have to be tested against the data to see whether they really help in making sense of the patterns displayed here. First, women and men could be working different numbers of hours per week, or weeks per year, and these differences could be related to both education and income. Second, women and men take different subjects at school and these fields of study may lead men into higher-paying jobs and women into lower-paying jobs. Third, men may be able to find jobs more closely related to their schooling than women. Fourth, many more women than men drop out of the labour force to start and raise a family, and these career interruptions may confound the causal links. Many other possible explanations exist, and further research is essential to sort them all out (see, e.g., Goyder, 1981; Wannell and Caron, 1995).

THE FUTURE OF SOCIAL RESEARCH

Social research involves the systematic study of the social world. The aim of such research activity is to develop explanations and understandings of social patterns so that we may improve the human condition. As we move into a new century, it is becoming increasingly obvious that we need to find innovative ways of organizing and running our human affairs. Starvation, environmental degradation, violence, and social injustice are among the many social problems we must confront. Solutions require adequate explanations and understandings for how these problems arise and persist.

Earlier in the chapter, I outlined several different sources of knowledge: common sense, religious faith, professional expertise, and science. Although these forms of knowledge share certain features (e.g., they are all imperfect), scientific reason encourages a set of practices, open review, and critical scepticism, which together work to reduce error.

Another way of emphasizing what is distinctive about the scientific method is to compare how social research differs from the work of other professionals who concentrate on similar social issues (e.g., the environment, gender relations). For example, what differentiates the work of documentary filmmakers, novelists, or journalists from that of social researchers? I have emphasized three features of scientific research that, in combination, separate it from the work of these other professionals. These three features of scientific work can be summarized as follows:

- research results are confronted by the critical scepticism of other scientists;

◆ **Table 21.2** The Relationship between Level of Education, Personal Income, and Gender for People Aged 25–34, Canada, 1994

| | Women | | | | Men | | | |
| | Level of education | | | | Level of education | | | |
Income	Low	Medium	High	**Total**	Low	Medium	High	**Total**
Low	45%	55%	40%	(463)	63%	56%	30%	(535)
High	55%	45%	60%	(513)	37%	44%	70%	(465)
Totals	100%	100%	100%		100%	100%	100%	
	(360)	(369)	(246)	(976)	(442)	(331)	(227)	(1000)

Note: Column and row totals are not equal for women due to rounding error.

SOURCE: Data from Statistics Canada, 1994 General Social Survey.

- social theory guides, either directly or indirectly, the evidence gathered; and
- evidence is systematically collected and analyzed.

Although some of these features are found in the work of other professionals, such as journalists, all three features are found in good social research. Replication and reproducibility have high currency in science as ways of encouraging scepticism. Good research contributes new ideas or evidence to our common stock of social theory. Finally, good research shows the careful collection and analysis of evidence.

These principles are a feature of all good research, but the methods that sociologists use to pursue their goal of explaining and understanding the social world take many forms. This diverse array of methods, including observing, questioning, and experimenting, offers sociologists many ways of inquiring about the social world. Each specific method has different strengths and weaknesses, which makes the choice of research strategy dependent on the sociological question.

Social-science research will continue to contribute to our sense of the world around us. Research on the environment, reproductive technology, multiculturalism, violence, and social-support networks all point to practical ways in which our human problems can be influenced by research findings. Effective policy solutions that benefit all people require sound social research. ■

Box 21.2
Introducing Statistical Ideas about Regression Analysis

In exploring the linkage between gender, education, and income, I introduced a series of alternative explanations. Testing each of these ideas using contingency tables would be extremely difficult because, with so many possible confounding variables, the tables we would have to generate would quickly become huge and unwieldy. An alternative to contingency-table analysis is regression analysis. The basic idea of regression, in summarizing the linkages between variables, can be explained most easily in graphic form.

Below is a graph with years of schooling arrayed along the horizontal axis (x-axis) and annual income levels displayed along the vertical axis (y-axis). Using these two lines as guides, we can then plot where each person in our sample falls. In other words, we can choose someone from our sample at random and move along the x-axis until we come to the level of education attained by our selected person. We can then proceed up from there, now using the y-axis as our guide, until we reach the level of the same person's annual income. The point that we reach is the intersection of two perpendicular lines, one drawn vertically from the x-axis (at the person's level of education) and the other drawn horizontally from the y-axis (at their annual income). For each person in our sample, we can locate exactly where these two lines fall in our graph, and place a mark or a dot at the appropriate spot. The result, similar to what I have depicted, is a scatterplot.

Notice that the scatterplot and the contingency table are related in important ways. First, as in the

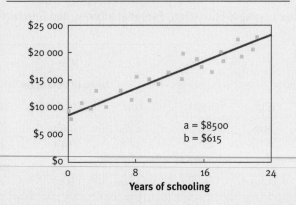

◆ Hypothetical Relationship between Employment Income and Years of Schooling

a = $8500
b = $615

Years of schooling

(continued)

Box 21.2
(continued)

contingency table, the independent variable (education) is arrayed horizontally. Second, note that the cells in the contingency table are analogous to the points on the graph, except, of course, that the cells are cruder categories (e.g., everyone with twelve or fewer years of schooling was in one cell whereas in the graph these people can be at different points). The key question, however, is what is analogous to the percentage difference?

A scatterplot can be summarized statistically using regression techniques. To summarize the relationship between education and income, a straight line can be drawn through the data points in such a way that the distance from each point to the line can be minimized. If all of the points lie exactly on the line, the fit of the line to the data will be perfect. The further the points are from the best-fitting line, the poorer is our ability to use a straight line to summarize the information and the weaker is the association between the two variables. The strength of association between two variables in a scatterplot is given by the *correlation coefficient* (r). The value of r can vary from -1 (a perfectly inverse relationship or negative association) to 0 (no association) to $+1$ (a perfectly proportionate relationship or positive association). The further r is from 0, the stronger the association. The correlation coefficient is, then, analogous to the percentage difference in tables.

With the education and income scatterplot, we can capture the central characteristics of our best-fitting line with two numbers. One number captures the slope of the line and tells us how much vertical increase (or decrease) occurs in the line for every unit of horizontal change along the x-axis. Using our example, for every additional year of schooling, how much does annual income increase? An easy way to remember this is to think of this number as the rise (income increase) over the run (change in years of schooling). A second number tells us at what point the line bisects the y-axis. If we have a perfectly fitting line, the equation for a straight line can be expressed as $y = a + bx$, where x and y are values on the two axes of the graph, "a" is the juncture at which the line crosses the y-axis, and "b" is the slope of the line.

What I have described here is a statistical technique known as simple linear regression, for one independent and one dependent variable. To explore the alternative interpretations for the link between education and income that I offered earlier, you would need to use multiple regression, where one dependent variable can be linked with a series of independent variables.

SUMMARY

1. Research methods are ways of getting evidence to test suppositions about the world around us. Behind the various techniques (e.g., experiments, interviews) we use to obtain evidence and expand our knowledge of the social world, we must recognize important assumptions about such things as facts, objectivity, and truth.

2. Science is one of several sources of knowledge. Like other kinds of knowledge, scientific knowledge can be wrong. However, unlike other ways of knowing, science incorporates explicit methods designed to reduce error in what is currently accepted as scientific knowledge. Evidence must be systematically collected and rigorously evaluated.

3. Good science integrates both good theory and good research. The latter two are inseparable. Theories are ideas about how the world works or claims about how to explain or understand the recurring, patterned nature of human activity.

4. Evidence is crucial to developing, revising, or discarding theoretical claims. In comparison with the evidence available in the natural sciences, the evidence available to social scientists presents added complexity because of the meaningful character of human social action. People, unlike molecules, assign meaning to their actions and to the actions of others.

5. Sociologists have devised many useful methods to obtain evidence about the social world. Observation and questioning are the two principal techniques, although each of them is conducted using a variety of formats, including experiments, surveys, participant observation, and interviews.

6. Good research adds to our knowledge of the world around us. Such knowledge expands our opportunities and options. Sociological knowledge helps either in solving social problems or by sensitizing us to our collective human condition, expanding our social horizons.

QUESTIONS TO CONSIDER

1. The teaching of faculty members in university and college departments could be evaluated in various ways. Suggest some different ways of doing such an evaluation and comment on the strengths and weaknesses of each approach.

2. Lenton chose to examine issues of child abuse by focussing more broadly on child discipline and by surveying parents about their disciplinary techniques. Suggest alternative designs for her study, commenting on the strengths and weaknesses of the various approaches.

3. Policy-makers frequently debate raising or lowering age restrictions on activities such as driving a car, drinking alcoholic beverages, or buying cigarettes. Suggest how you might design a study that could provide evidence about the possible consequences of either raising or lowering one of these age restrictions.

4. Immigration levels remain a contentious issue in Canada. Construct a short series of interview questions designed to assess people's knowledge of current immigration practices. Ask these questions of your friends and/or family. Ask how many immigrants enter Canada and from which countries they originate. Compare your findings with official statistics that are available in government publications at your college or university. How might you explain the patterns you discovered?

5. Discuss the claim that "facts speak for themselves." What problems exist in claiming that facts do "speak for themselves"? Conversely, what problems exist in claiming that facts do *not* "speak for themselves"? Consider especially the claim that we need firm standards against which to evaluate ideas or theoretical claims. Is it possible to establish such standards?

6. At parties, people are expected to be laid back, relaxed. Parties are times for having fun, for stepping outside the routines of school and/or work. However, phrases like "party pooper" suggest that parties too have rules and that violators of such rules can be ostracized. Others are glorified as "party animals," implying that some people take to partying better than others. How might you engage in a participant observation study to investigate these hunches systematically? Do categories such as "party animal" or "party pooper" exist, and, if so, how are they understood? Do "rules" exist at a party even though parties are in very important ways "escapist"? How might a sociologist seek to understand party life at your college or university?

GLOSSARY

causation A relationship between two variables where change or variation in one variable produces change or variation in a second variable. Four criteria are essential to establishing a causal relation between two variables: association, time ordering, nonspuriousness, and theoretical rationale.

dependent variable A variable that is assumed to depend on or be caused by one or more other variables (independent variables); the variable that is the effect, or outcome, in a cause–effect relationship.

ethnography The detailed description of a particular culture or way of life; the written results of a participant-observation study.

experiment A controlled test of the causal effects of a particular variable or set of variables on a dependent or outcome variable.

explanation An account of the causal logic that shows how and why variables influence one another.

external validity The generalizability of a particular finding from the study group to a larger population; the relevance of conclusions for a larger population; the ability to infer that the results of a study are representative of processes operating for a broader population.

Hawthorne effect The idea that people involved in a study may be influenced by the very process of being studied; the impact of a study on the subjects of the study.

hypothesis A knowledge claim or hunch about how the world works; a testable statement, derived from a theory, about the relationship between two variables.

independent variable Variable(s) presumed to affect or influence other variables; the causal variables.

interview A method of collecting information by asking people questions, either in person or over the telephone. Interviews range from highly structured (preset questions in a fixed order) to loosely structured (topic guidelines, but no prescribed question wording).

meaningful action Human action, as distinct from physical behaviour, occurs with specific intentions or reasons in mind. The uncontrollable tic in a person's eye is physical behaviour, which differs from a person who is winking at someone, where intention or purpose is central to understanding what is happening. Most human activity is meaningful action or social action.

measurement Procedures for assigning numbers to observations according to preset rules; the act of finding data or information relevant to theoretical concepts.

objectivity The attempt to minimize the effect of personal bias on research results; the idea of impartiality, of "fair hearings." Objectivity is an ideal enhanced by the work of any single researcher being open to the critical scrutiny of others. Objectivity as impartiality is a myth.

participant observation The study of social life involving the participation of the researcher, to varying degrees, in the activities of the group under investigation; an attempt to give an "insider's" account of a particular way of life or cultural system.

randomization A procedure used in experiments to assign test subjects to experimental conditions on the basis of chance.

reliability Consistency of measurements; the ability to reproduce the same measurements on repeated occasions.

sampling A process of selecting units from a larger population. Random sampling involves the selection of representative units (e.g., people, organizations) from a population (e.g., all Canadians, voluntary organizations in a city). Samples may be selected by probability (where every unit has a nonzero chance of selection) or nonprobability (where chance does not enter into the selection of sample units).

self-administered questionnaire A method of collecting information by having people record their own answers to preset questions.

spuriousness An incorrect inference about the causal relations between variables.

understanding The ability to provide a definition of the situation that members of a culture find authentic and valid.

validity The relevance or accuracy of measurement in relation to the theoretical concept that it is supposed to measure.

variable Something that varies; an attribute or event that can take on more than one value (e.g., unemployment rates, age, sex).

● SUGGESTED READING

Babbie, Earl. (1995). *The Practice of Social Research,* 7th ed. Belmont, CA: Wadsworth. Babbie provides the best general account of research methods that is available in sociology. He covers an array of methodologies with many illustrations and examples to emphasize key points.

Cresswell, John. (1994). *Research Design: Qualitative and Quantitative Appraoches.* Newbury Park, CA: Sage. A basic discussion of strategies for pursuing either qualitative or quantitative research.

Gray, George, and Neil Guppy. (1993). *Successful Surveys*. Toronto: Harcourt Brace. A practical guidebook to developing research designs and using effective survey-research techniques. This book covers only questionnaires and interviews.

Hammersley, Martyn, and Paul Akinson. (1995). *Ethnography: Principles in Practice*. London: Tavistock. One of the best books on the actual methods of participant observation, fieldwork, and ethnography, written by two researchers with extensive experience in their craft.

Kirby, Sandra, and Kate McKenna. (1989). *Experience, Research, Social Change: Methods from the Margins*. Toronto: Garamond. An approach to research methods that emphasizes the active involvement of the researcher in the research process. As the subtitle suggests, the book is aimed at research to aid those who suffer from exploitation, injustice, and inequality.

Miller, Delbert. (1991). *Handbook of Research Design and Social Measurement,* 5th ed. Newbury Park, CA: Sage. A resource book that provides a good source for ideas on research design, proposal writing, question items, and so on.

NOTES

1. Highlighting differences between the subject matter of the natural and the social sciences that have consequences for research is extremely complicated. For example, monkeys make friends with zoologists and, when studied, may react in similar ways to humans. It is important to consider in what ways the studying of people by people may add complexity to research, and how this in turn may stimulate us to think differently about how people study nonhumans. For example, issues of animal rights and environmental ethics raise questions about our traditionally human-centric view of the world.

2. Foschi and Buchan use the term "White" rather than English Canadian.

REFERENCES

Introduction

Bauman, Zygmunt. (1992). *Modernity and the Holocaust.* Ithaca, NY: Cornell University Press.

Mayer, J.P. (1944). *Max Weber and German Politics.* London: Faber and Faber.

Ossowski, Stanislaw. (1963). *Class Structure in the Social Consciousness.* Trans. S. Patterson. London: Routledge and Kegan Paul.

Weber, Max. (1946 [1922]). "Bureaucracy." In H. Gerth and C. Mills, eds. and trans., *From Max Weber: Essays in Sociology* (pp. 196–264). New York: Oxford University Press.

Chapter 1

Armstrong, Pat, and Hugh Armstrong. (1988). "Women, Family and Economy." In Nancy Mandell and Ann Duffy, eds., *Reconstructing the Canadian Family* (pp. 143–74). Toronto: Butterworths.

Babbie, Earl. (1986). *The Practice of Social Research,* 4th ed. Belmont, CA: Wadsworth.

Ball-Rokeach, S.J. (1980). "Normative and Deviant Violence from a Conflict Perspective." *Social Problems, 28,* 45–62.

Bell, Daniel. (1976). *The Coming of Post-industrial Society: A Venture in Social Forecasting.* New York: Basic Books.

Bottomore, Tom, and Robert J. Brym, eds. (1989). *The Capitalist Class: An International Study.* New York: New York University Press.

Brym, Robert J., and John Myles. (1989). "Social Science Intellectuals and Public Issues in English Canada." *University of Toronto Quarterly, 58,* 442–51.

Clark, Ronald W. (1971). *Einstein: The Life and Times.* New York: Avon.

DeKeseredy, Walter S., and Ronald Hinch. (1991). *Woman Abuse: Sociological Perspectives.* Toronto: Thompson Educational Publishing.

Durkheim, Émile. (1951 [1897]). *Suicide: A Study in Sociology.* Ed. G. Simpson; trans. J. Spaulding and G. Simpson. New York: Free Press.

Edel, Abraham. (1965). "Social Science and Value: A Study in Interrelations." In Irving Louis Horowitz, ed., *The New Sociology: Essays in Social Science and Social Theory in Honor of C. Wright Mills* (pp. 218–38). New York: Oxford University Press.

Fox, Bonnie J. (1986). "An Examination of 'the Longest Revolution': Women's Position in Canada, the 1960s to the 1980s." Paper presented at the Trends in Social Inequality conference, University of Western Ontario, London, ON.

Fox, Bonnie J., and John Fox. (1986). "Women in the Labour Market, 1931–81: Exclusion and Competition." *Canadian Review of Sociology and Anthropology, 23,* 1–21.

Giddens, Anthony. (1982). *Sociology: A Brief but Critical Introduction.* New York: Harcourt Brace Jovanovich.

Guppy, Neil, and R. Alan Hedley. (1993). *Opportunities in Sociology.* Montreal: Canadian Sociology and Anthropology Association.

Harvey, Andrew A., Katherine Marshall, and Judith A. Frederick. (1991). *Where Does Time Go?* Cat. no. 11-612E, no. 4. Ottawa: Statistics Canada.

Health Canada. (1994). *Suicide in Canada: Update of the Report of the Task Force on Suicide in Canada.* Ottawa: Mental Health Division, Health Services Directorate, Health Programs and Service Branch, Health Canada.

Johnson, Holly. (1996). *Dangerous Domains: Violence against Women in Canada.* Scarborough, ON: Nelson Canada.

Lukes, Steven. (1973). *Émile Durkheim, His Life and Work: A Historical and Critical Study.* London: Penguin.

Meissner, Martin. (1988). "The Domestic Economy — Half of Canada's Work: Now You See It, Now You Don't." In Lorne Tepperman and James Curtis, eds., *Readings in Sociology: An Introduction* (pp. 365–72). Toronto: McGraw-Hill Ryerson.

Mills, C. Wright. (1959). *The Sociological Imagination.* New York: Oxford University Press.

Myles, John. (1988). "The Expanding Middle: Some Canadian Evidence on the Deskilling Debate." *Canadian Review of Sociology and Anthropology, 25,* 335–64.

Myles, John, Garnett Picot, and Ted Wannell. (1993). "Does Post-industrialism Matter? Evidence from the Canadian Experience." In Gøsta Esping-Andersen, ed., *Changing Classes: Stratification and Mobility in Post-industrial Societies* (pp. 171–94). London: Sage.

Novek, Joel, and Karen Kampen. (1992). "Sustainable or Unsustainable Development? An Analysis of an Environmental Controversy." *Canadian Journal of Sociology, 17,* 249–73.

Ornstein, Michael D. (1983). "The Development of Class in Canada." In J. Paul Grayson, ed., *Introduction to Sociology: An Alternate Approach* (pp. 224–66). Toronto: Gage.

Reed, Christopher. (1986). "Today's Woman: Is Equality Enough?" *Globe and Mail.* November 7, p. A7.

Richardson, Jack. (1990). "Economic Concentration and Social Power in Contemporary Canada." In James Curtis and Lorne Tepperman, eds., *Images of Canada: The Sociological Tradition* (pp. 341–50). Scarborough, ON: Prentice Hall Canada.

Shalev, Michael. (1992). "The Resurgence of Labour Quiescence." In Marino Regini, ed., *The Future of Labour Movements* (pp. 102–32). London: Sage.

Statistics Canada. (1995). *Causes of Death 1993.* Cat. no. 84-208. Ottawa: Statistics Canada.

Strong-Boag, Veronica. (1986). " 'Ever a Crusader': Nellie McClung, First-wave Feminist." In Veronica Strong-Boag and Anita Clair Fellman, eds., *Rethinking Canada: The Promise of Women's History* (pp. 178–90). Toronto: Copp Clark Pitman.

Swinamer, J.L. (1990). "The Value of Household Work in Canada." In Craig McKie and Keith Thompson, eds., *Canadian Social Trends* (p. 166). Toronto: Thompson Educational Publishing.

Toffler, Alvin. (1990). *Powershift: Knowledge, Wealth, and Violence at the Edge of the 21st Century.* New York: Bantam.

Weber, Max. (1964 [1949]). " 'Objectivity' in Social Science and Social Policy." In Edward A. Shils and Henry A. Finch eds. and trans. *The Methodology of the Social Sciences* (pp. 49–112). New York: Free Press of Glencoe.

Yllo, Kersti A. and Murray A. Smith. (1990). "Patriarchy and Violence against Wives: The Impact of Structural and Normative Factors." In Murray A. Straus and Richard J. Gelles with the assistance of Christine Smith, eds., *Physical Violence in American Families: Risk Factors and Adaptations to Violence in 8,145 Families* (pp. 383–99). New Brunswick, NJ: Transaction Books.

Chapter 2

Archer, Joan. (1988). "Class, Gender, and the Relations of Distribution," *Signs, 13,* 473–97.

Aries, Philippe. (1981). *The Hour of Our Death.* New York: Knopf.

Baker, Maureen. (1985). *What Will Tomorrow Bring? A Study of the Aspirations of Adolescent Women.* Ottawa: Canadian Advisory Council on the Status of Women.

Baker, Maureen, ed. (1989). *Families: Changing Trends in Canada,* 2nd ed. Toronto: McGraw-Hill Ryerson.

Becker, Howard S., Blanche Geer, Everett C. Hughes, and Anselm L. Strauss (1961). *Boys in White: Student Culture in Medical School.* Chicago: University of Chicago Press.

Blau, Peter M., and Otis D. Duncan. (1967). *The American Occupational Structure.* New York: John Wiley.

Brim, Orville G., Jr. (1968). "Socialization through the Life Cycle." In Orville G. Brim, Jr. and Stanton Wheeler, eds., *Socialization after Childhood: Two Essays* (pp. 3–49). New York: John Wiley.

Bromberg, Heather. (1996). "Are MUDs Communities? Identity, Belonging and Consciousness in Virtual Worlds." In R. Shields, ed., *Cultures of Internet: Virtual Space, Real Histories, and Living Bodies* (pp. 143–52). London: Sage.

Burgess, R.L., and R.A. Richardson. (1984). "Child Abuse during Adolescence." In R.M. Lerner and N.L. Galambos, eds., *Experiencing Adolescents: A Sourcebook for Parents, Teachers and Teens* (pp. 119–52). New York: Garland.

Clausen, John A. (1986). *The Life Course.* Englewood Cliffs, NJ: Prentice Hall.

Coleman, John C., and Leo Hendry. (1990). *The Nature of Adolescence,* 2nd ed. New York: Routledge, Chapman, and Hall.

Cooley, Charles Horton. (1902). *Human Nature and the Social Order.* New York: Scribner's.

Coontz, Stephanie. (1992). *The Way We Never Were: American Families and the Nostalgia Trap.* New York: Basic Books.

Corsaro, William A. (1992). "Interpretive Reproduction in Children's Peer Cultures." *Social Psychology Quarterly, 55,* 160–77.

DeLoache, Judy S., Deborah J. Cassidy, and C. Jan Carpenter. (1987). "The Three Bears Are All Boys: Mother's Gender Labelling of Neutral Picture Book Characters." *Sex Roles, 17,* 163–78.

Dibbell, Julian. (1996). "A Rape in Cyberspace or How an Evil Clown, a Haitian Trickster Spirit, Two Wizards, and a Cast of Dozens Turned a Database into a Society." ftp://parcftp.xerox.com/pub/MOO/papers/Village Voice.txt.

Donahue, T., and J. Costar. (1977). "Counselor Discrimination against Young Women in Career Selection." *Journal of Counseling Psychology, 24,* 481–86.

Dweck, C.S., T.E. Goetz, and N.L. Strauss. (1980). "Sex Differences in Learned Helplessness: IV: An Experimental and Naturalistic Study of Failure Generalization and Its Mediators." *Journal of Personality and Social Psychology, 38,* 441–52.

Eliade, M. (1963). *Myth and Reality.* New York: Harper and Row.

Elkin, Frederick, and Gerald Handel. (1972). *The Child and Society: The Process of Socialization.* New York: Random House.

Erikson, Erik H. (1982). *The Life Cycle Completed.* New York: Norton.

Freud, Sigmund. (1962 [1930]). *Civilization and Its Discontents.* Trans. James Strachey. New York: W.W. Norton.

Friedenberg, Edgar Z. 1959. *The Vanishing Adolescent.* New York: Dell.

Garfinkel, Harold. (1956). "Conditions of Successful Degradation Ceremonies." *American Journal of Sociology, 61,* 420–24.

Gecas, Viktor. (1981). "Contexts of Socialization." In M. Rosenberg and Ralph H. Turner, eds., *Social Psychology: Sociological Perspectives* (pp. 165–99). New York: Basic Books.

Glaser, Barney, and Anselm L. Strauss. (1967). *The Discovery of Grounded Theory: Strategies for Qualitative Research.* Chicago: Aldine.

Goffman, Erving. (1959). *The Presentation of Self in Everyday Life.* New York: Anchor Doubleday.

Goffman, Erving. (1961). *Asylums.* New York: Anchor Books.

Goffman, Erving. (1963). *Behavior in Public Places*. New York: Free Press.

Goffman, Erving. (1971). *Relations in Public*. New York: Basic Books.

Greenglass, E. (1982). *A World of Difference*. Toronto: John Wiley.

Haas, Jack. (1989). "The Process of Apprenticeship: Ritual Ordeal and the Adoption of a Cloak of Competence." In M. Coy, ed., *Anthropological Perspectives on Apprenticeship: From Theory to Method and Back Again* (pp. 82–105). Albany, NY: SUNY Press.

Haas, Jack, and William Shaffir. (1987). *Becoming Doctors: The Adoption of a Cloak of Competence*. Greenwich, CT: JAI Press.

Hall, G. Stanley. (1904). *Adolescence*. New York: Appleton.

Handel, Gerald. (1990). "Revising Socialization Theory." *American Sociological Review, 55*, 463–66.

Harlow, Harry F., and Margaret Harlow. (1962). "Social Deprivation in Monkeys." *Scientific American, 207*, 137–46.

Harrison, Algea O., Melvin N. Wilson, Charles J. Pine, Samuel Q. Chan, and Raymond Buriel. (1990). "Family Ecologies of Ethnic Minority Children." *Child Development, 61*, 347–62.

Hendricks, Jon, and C. Davis Hendricks. (1986). *Aging in Mass Society: Myths and Realities,* 3rd ed. Boston: Little, Brown.

Hogan, Dennis P., and Nan Marie Astone. (1986). "Transition to Adulthood." *Annual Review of Sociology, 12*, 109–30.

Huston, A.C. (1983). "Sex-typing." In Paul H. Mussen, ed., *Handbook of Child Psychology*. Vol. 4, 4th ed. (pp. 387–467). New York: John Wiley.

Jensen, Arthur. (1969). "How Much Can We Boost IQ and Scholastic Achievement?" *Harvard Educational Review, 39*, 1–123.

Klapp, Orrin E. (1969). *A Collective Search for Identity*. New York: Holt, Rinehart and Winston.

Kohn, Melvin L., Atsushi Naoi, Carmi Schooler, and Kazimiercz M. Slomczynski. (1990). "Position in the Class Structure and Psychological Functioning in the United States, Japan, and Poland." *American Journal of Sociology, 95*, 964–1008.

Lawson, David. (1996). "The Brave New World of Work." *The Silhouette*, November 7.

Lewis, M. (1972). "State as an Infant–Environment Interaction." *Merrill-Palmer Quarterly, 18*, 95–121.

Light, Donald L., Jr. (1980) *Becoming Psychiatrists: The Professional Transformation of Self*. New York: W.W. Norton.

Maccoby, E.E., and C.N. Jacklin. (1974). *The Psychology of Sex Differences*. Stanford, CA: Stanford University Press.

Mead, George H. (1934). *Mind, Self and Society*. Chicago: University of Chicago Press.

O'Kelly, Charlotte G., and Larry S. Carney. (1986). *Women and Men in Society*, 2nd ed. Belmont, CA: Wadsworth.

Piaget, Jean. (1950). *The Psychology of Intelligence*. Boston: Routledge and Kegan Paul.

Piaget, Jean, and Barbel Inhelder. (1969). *The Psychology of the Child*. New York: Basic Books.

Richer, Stephen. (1988). "Equality to Benefit from Schooling: The Issue of Educational Opportunity." In D. Forcese and S. Richer, eds., *Social Issues: Sociological Views of Canada* (pp. 262–86). Toronto: Prentice Hall.

Riesman, David. (1950). *The Lonely Crowd*. New York: Basic Books.

Robinson, B.W., and E.D. Salamon. (1987). "Gender Role Socialization: A Review of the Literature." In B.W. Robinson and E.D. Salamon, eds., *Gender Roles: Doing What Comes Naturally?* (pp. 123–42). Toronto: Methuen.

Rosenthal, Robert, and Lenore Jacobson. (1968). *Pygmalion and the Classroom*. New York: Holt, Rinehart and Winston.

Rubin, J., F. Provenzano, and Z. Luria. (1974). "The Eye of the Beholder: Parents' Views on Sex of Newborns." *American Journal of Orthopsychiatry, 44*, 512–19.

Rushton, P., and A. Bogaert. (1987). "Race Differences in Sexual Behavior: Testing an Evolutionary Hypothesis." *Journal of Research on Personality, 21*, 529–51.

Sebald, Hans. (1986). "Adolescents' Shifting Orientation toward Parents and Peers: A Curvilinear Trend over Recent Decades." *Journal of Marriage and the Family, 48*, 5–13.

Shaffir, William. (1987). "Separation from the Mainstream in Canada: The Hassidic Community of Tash." *The Jewish Journal of Sociology, 29* (1), 19–35.

Shanas, Ethel, Peter Townsend, Dorothy Wedderburn, Henning Friis, Paul Milhøj, and Jan Stehouwer. (1972). *Old People in Three Industrial Societies*. New York: Atherton.

Shepard, Jon M. (1993). *Sociology,* 5th ed. New York: West.

Singh, J.A.L., and Robert M. Zingg. (1942). *Wolf Children and Feral Man*. New York: Harper and Row.

Skolnick, Arlene. (1991). *Embattled Paradise: The American Family in an Age of Uncertainty*. New York: Basic Books.

Sowell, Thomas. (1978). "Three Black Histories." In Thomas Sowell, ed., *Essays and Data on American Ethnic Groups* (pp. 7–64). Washington DC: The Urban Institute.

Spitz, Rene A. (1945). "Hospitalism: An Inquiry into the Genesis of Psychiatric Conditions in Early Childhood." *The Psychoanalytic Study of the Child, 1*, 53–74.

Stebbins, Robert A. (1990). *Sociology: The Study of Society,* 2nd ed. New York: Harper and Row.

Stryker, Sheldon. (1980). *Symbolic Interactionism*. Menlo Park, CA: Benjamin/Cummings.

Turkle, Sherry. (1996). "Who Am We?" http://www.wired.com/wired/4.01/features/turkle.html.

White, L., and D. Brinkerhoff. (1981). "The Sexual Division of Labor: Evidence from Childhood." *Social Forces, 60*, 170–81.

Chapter 3

Adorno, T. (1975). "Culture Industry Reconsidered." *New German Critique, 6*, 12–19.

Baudrillard, J. (1987). "Modernity." *Canadian Journal of Political and Social Theory, 11* (3), 63–71.

Bell, D. (1976). *The Cultural Contradictions of Capitalism.* London: Heinemann.

Berger, P., and T. Luckmann. (1966). *The Social Construction of Reality.* New York: Doubleday.

Berry, J., and J. Laponce. (1994). "Evaluating Research on Canada's Multiethnic and Multicultural Society." In J. Berry and J. Laponce, eds., *Ethnicity and Culture in Canada* (pp. 3–16). Toronto: University of Toronto Press.

Bibby, R. (1990). *Mosaic Madness.* Toronto: Stoddart.

Bourdieu, P. (1977). *Reproduction in Education, Society and Culture.* London: Sage.

Bourdieu, P. (1984). *Distinction.* Cambridge, MA: Harvard University Press.

Breton, R. (1984). "The Production and Allocation of Symbolic Resources." *Canadian Review of Sociology and Anthropology, 21* (2), 123–44.

Breton, R. (1988). "The Evolution of the Canadian Multicultural Society." In A.J. Fry and C. Forceville, eds., *Canadian Mosaic* (pp. 25–44). Amsterdam: Free University Press.

Cheal, D. (1979). "Hegemony, Ideology and Contradictory Consciousness." *Sociological Quarterly, 20* (1), 109–17.

Cheal, D. (1981). "Ontario Loyalism: A Socio-religious Ideology in Decline." *Canadian Ethnic Studies, 13* (2), 40–51.

Cheal, D. (1988). *The Gift Economy.* New York: Routledge.

Citizens' Forum on Canada's Future. (1991). *Citizens' Forum on Canada's Future: Report to the People and Government of Canada.* Ottawa: Supply and Services Canada.

Crook, S., J. Pakulski, and M. Waters. (1992). *Postmodernization.* London: Sage.

Dhruvarajan, V. (1989). *Hindu Women and the Power of Ideology.* Granby, MA: Bergin and Garvey.

Dunk, T. (1991). *It's a Working Man's Town.* Montreal and Kingston: McGill-Queen's University Press.

Durkheim, É. (1947 [1915]). *The Elementary Forms of the Religious Life.* Glencoe, IL: Free Press.

Featherstone, M., ed. (1990). *Global Culture.* London: Sage.

Featherstone, M. (1991). *Consumer Culture and Postmodernism.* London: Sage.

Finn, G. (1988). "Women, Fantasy and Popular Culture: The Wonderful World of Harlequin Romance." In R. Gruneau, ed., *Popular Cultures and Political Practices* (pp. 51–67). Toronto: Garamond.

Foucault, M. (1980). *Power/Knowledge.* New York: Pantheon.

Goffman, E. (1967). *Interaction Ritual.* New York: Doubleday.

Granzberg, G. (1979). "The Introduction of Television into a Northern Manitoba Cree Community." In J. Steinbring, G. Granzberg, C. Pereira, and C. Hanks, *The Impact and Meaning of Television among Native Communities in Northern Manitoba* (pp. 3–55). Winnipeg: University of Winnipeg.

Gruneau, R., and D. Whitson. (1993). *Hockey Night in Canada.* Toronto: Garamond.

Guindon, H. (1988). *Quebec Society.* Toronto: University of Toronto Press.

Habermas, J. (1987). *The Theory of Communicative Action.* Vol. 2. Boston: Beacon.

Harrison, T. (1995). *Of Passionate Intensity: Right-wing Populism and the Reform Party of Canada.* Toronto: University of Toronto Press.

Karim, K. (1993). "Constructions, Deconstructions, and Reconstructions: Competing Canadian Discourses on Ethnocultural Terminology." *Canadian Journal of Communication, 18* (2), 197–218.

Kelly, R. (1994). "The Cultural Tourist — Friend or Foe." *Focus on Culture, 6* (4), 1–3.

Kline, S. (1993). *Out of the Garden.* London: Verso.

Lipset, S.M. (1990). *Continental Divide.* New York: Routledge.

Marx, K. (1976). Speech on the question of free trade, delivered to the Democratic Association of Brussels at its public meeting of January 9, 1848. In K. Marx and F. Engels, *Karl Marx and Friedrich Engels: Collected Works.* Vol. 6 (pp. 450–65). New York: International Publishers.

Parsons, T. (1966). *Societies: Evolutionary and Comparative Perspectives.* Englewood Cliffs, NJ: Prentice Hall.

Simmel, Georg. (1971). *On Individuality and Social Forms.* Chicago: University of Chicago Press.

Smith, D. (1990). *Texts, Facts, and Femininity.* New York: Routledge.

Tepper, E. (1994). "Immigration Policy and Multiculturalism." In J. Berry and J. Laponce, eds., *Ethnicity and Culture in Canada* (pp. 95–123). Toronto: University of Toronto Press.

Vanderburgh, R. (1995). "Modernization and Aging in the Anicinabe Context." In R. Neugebauer-Visano, ed., *Aging and Inequality* (pp. 101–13). Toronto: Canadian Scholars' Press.

Walker, Gillian. (1995). "Violence and the Relations of Ruling: Lessons from the Battered Women's Movement." In M. Campbell and A. Manicom, eds., *Knowledge, Experience, and Ruling Relations: Studies in the Social Organization of Knowledge* (pp. 65–79). Toronto: University of Toronto Press.

Weber, M. (1968 [1922]). *Economy and Society.* Vol. 1. New York: Bedminster.

Whimster, S., and S. Lash, eds. (1987). *Max Weber, Rationality and Modernity.* London: Allen and Unwin.

Willis, P. (1977). *Learning to Labour.* Farnborough, UK: Saxon House.

Chapter 4

Bernheimer, C., and C. Kahane. (1985). *In Dora's Case: Freud–Hysteria–Feminism.* New York: Columbia University Press.

Boothby, William. (1990). *Death and Desire: Psychoanalytic Theory and Lacan's Return to Freud.* New York: Routledge.

Brownmiller, Susan. (1984). *Femininity.* New York: Simon and Schuster.

Busby, Karen. (1993). "LEAF and Pornography: Litigating on Equality and Sexual Representation." Unpublished paper, Faculty of Law, University of Manitoba.

Canada. (1984). Committee on Sexual Offences against Children and Youths in Canada. *Report.* [The Badgley Report]. Ottawa: Supply and Services Canada.

Canada. (1993). Royal Commission on New Reproductive Technologies. *Proceed with Care: Final Report.* Ottawa: Minister of Government Services.

Canadian Advisory Council on the Status of Women. (1991). *Brief to the Royal Commission on New Reproductive Technologies.*

Chodorow, Nancy. (1978). *The Reproduction of Mothering.* Berkeley, CA: University of California Press.

Connell, R.W. (1987). *Gender and Power.* Stanford, CA: University of California Press.

Cossman, Brenda, and Bruce Ryder. (1996). "Customs Censorship and the Charter: The Little Sisters Case." *Constitutional Forum,* 7, 4.

Darwin, Charles. (1871). *The Descent of Man.* London: J. Murray.

Elias, Norbert. (1978). *The Civilizing Process.* Trans. Edmund Jephcott. New York: Pantheon.

Foucault, Michel. (1978). *The History of Sexuality.* Vol. 1. Trans. Robert Hurley. New York: Pantheon.

Foucault, Michel. (1980). *Herculine Barbin: Being the Recently Discovered Memoirs of a Nineteenth-Century French Hermaphrodite.* Trans. Richard McDougall. New York: Pantheon.

Freud, Sigmund. (1955 [1920]). *Beyond the Pleasure Principle.* In James Strachey, ed. and trans., *The Standard Edition of the Complete Psychological Works of Sigmund Freud.* Vol. 18. London: Hogarth Press.

Freud, Sigmund. (1973 [1915–17]). *Introductory Lectures on Psychoanalysis.* Trans. James Strachey; ed. James Strachey and Angela Richards. Vol. 1 of the Pelican Freud Library [cited hereafter as PFL]. Harmondsworth, UK: Penguin Books.

Freud, Sigmund. (1976 [1900]). *The Interpretation of Dreams.* Trans. James Strachey; ed. James Strachey assisted by Alan Tyson and Angela Richards. Vol. 4 of PFL. Harmondsworth, UK: Penguin Books.

Freud, Sigmund. (1977a [1905]). *On Sexuality.* Trans. James Strachey; comp. and ed. Angela Richards. Vol. 7 of PFL. Harmondsworth, UK: Penguin Books.

Freud, Sigmund. (1977b [1905, 1909]). *Case Histories I.* Trans. Alix and James Strachey; ed. Angela Richards. Vol. 8 of PFL. Harmondsworth, UK: Penguin Books.

Freud, Sigmund. (1985 [1929]). *Civilization and Its Discontents.* Trans. and ed. James Strachey. Vol. 12 of PFL. Harmondsworth, UK: Penguin Books.

Freud, Sigmund, and Josef Breuer. (1974 [1895]). *Studies on Hysteria.* Trans. James Strachey; ed. James Strachey and Angela Richards. Vol. 3 of PFL. Harmondsworth, UK: Penguin Books.

Gilman, Sander. (1985). *Difference and Pathology: Stereotypes of Sex, Race and Madness.* Ithaca, NY: Cornell University Press.

Hite, Shere. (1976). *The Hite Report.* New York: Dell.

Hite, Shere. (1988). *Women and Love.* New York: Random House.

Kaufman, Michael. (1993). *Cracking the Armour: Power, Pain and the Lives of Men.* Toronto: Viking.

Kennedy, L., and M. Davis. (1993). *Boots of Leather, Slippers of Gold: The History of a Lesbian Community.* New York: Routledge.

Kinsey, Alfred, Wardell Pomeroy, and Clyde Martin. (1963). *Sexual Behavior in the Human Male.* Philadelphia: W.B. Saunders.

Laqueur, Thomas. (1990). *Making Sex: Body and Gender from the Greeks to Freud.* Cambridge, MA: Harvard University Press.

Ontario. (1985). Law Reform Commission. *Report on Human Artificial Reproduction and Related Matters.* Toronto: Ministry of the Attorney General.

Russett, Cynthia. (1989). *Sexual Science: The Victorian Construction of Womanhood.* Cambridge, MA: Harvard University Press.

Solinger, Rickie. (1992). *Wake Up Little Susie: Single Pregnancy and Race before Roe v. Wade.* New York: Routledge.

Staff of the Institute for Sex Research. (1953). *Sexual Behavior in the Human Female.* Philadelphia: W.B. Saunders.

Torgovnick, Marianne. (1990). *Gone Primitive: Savage Intellects, Modern Lives.* Chicago: University of Chicago Press.

Valverde, Mariana. (1985). *Sex, Power and Pleasure.* Toronto: Women's Press.

Valverde, Mariana. (1991). *The Age of Light, Soap and Water: Moral Reform in English Canada, 1885–1925.* Toronto: McClelland and Stewart.

Weeks, Jeffrey. (1986). *Sexuality.* London: Tavistock.

Wolf, Naomi. (1990). *The Beauty Myth: How Images of Beauty Are Used against Women.* London: Chatto and Windus.

Women's Legal Education and Action Fund. (1996). *Equality and the Charter: Ten Years of Feminist Advocacy before the Supreme Court of Canada* (pp. 201–21). Toronto: Emond Montgomery.

Zizek, Slavoj. (1993). "Enjoy Your Nation as Yourself!" In Slavoj Zizek, ed., *Tarrying with the Negative* (pp. 200–38). Durham, NC: Duke University Press.

Chapter 5

Andersen, R. (1995). *Consumer Culture and TV Programming*. Boulder, CO: Westview Press.

Ang, I. (1985). *Watching Dallas: Soap Opera and the Melodramatic Imagination*. London: Methuen.

Barthes, R. (1973). *Mythologies*. London: Paladin.

Boyd-Barrett, O. (1977). "Media Imperialism: Towards an International Framework for the Analysis of Media Systems." In J. Curren et al., eds., *Mass Communication and Society* (pp. 116–35). London: Edward Arnold.

Canada. (1986). Task Force on Broadcasting Policy. *Report*. Ottawa: Supply and Services Canada.

Canada. (1991). Task Force on the Economic Status of Canadian Television. *Report*. Ottawa: Supply and Services Canada.

Canada. (1993). House of Commons. Standing Committee on Communications and Culture. *Television Violence: Fraying Our Social Fabric*. Issue no. 6. Ottawa: Supply and Services Canada.

Canada. (1996). *Making Our Voices Heard: Canadian Broadcasting and Film for the 21st Century*. Ottawa: Supply and Services Canada.

CRTC (Canadian Radio-television and Telecommunications Commission). (1990). *The Portrayal of Gender in Canadian Broadcasting: Summary Report*. Ottawa: Supply and Services Canada.

Candussi, D., and J. Winters. (1988). "Monopoly and Contents in Winnipeg." In R. Picard et al., eds., *Press Concentration and Monopoly* (pp. 139–45). Norwood, NJ: Ablex.

Cohen, B. (1963). *The Press and Foreign Policy*. Princeton, NJ: Princeton University Press.

Collins, R. (1990). *Culture, Communication and National Identity: The Case of Canadian Television*. Toronto: University of Toronto Press.

Cooper, B. (1994). *Sins of Omission: Shaping the News at CBC TV*. Toronto: University of Toronto Press.

Dobbin, M. (1993). "Is Canada's Debt Crisis Really a Revenue Crisis?" *The Globe and Mail*, April 6.

Ellis, D. (1992). *Split Screens: Home Entertainment and the New Technologies*. Toronto: Friends of Canadian Broadcasting.

Ericson, R., P. Baranek, and J. Chan (1989). *Negotiating Control: A Study of News Sources*. Toronto: University of Toronto Press.

Felson, R. (1996) "Mass Media Effects on Violent Behaviour." In R. Hagan and K. Cook, eds., *Annual Review of Sociology, 22*, pp. 103–28.

Fiske, J. (1987). *Television Culture*. London: Methuen.

Flitterman, S. (1983). "The Real Soap Operas: TV Commercials." In E. Kaplan, ed., *Regarding Television* (pp. 84–96). Frederick, MD: University Publications of America.

Forman, H. (1933). *Our Movie-Made Children*. New York: Macmillan.

Freedman, J. (1984). "Effect of Television Violence on Aggressiveness." *Psychological Bulletin, 96*, 227–46.

Friedrich-Cofer, L., and A. Huston. (1986). "Television Violence and Aggression: The Debate Continues." *Psychological Bulletin, 100*, 364–71.

Gans, H. (1979). *Deciding What's News: A Study of CBS Evening News, NBC Nightly News, Newsweek and Time*. New York: Pantheon.

Geen, R., and S. Thomas. (1986). "The Immediate Effects of Media Violence on Behaviour." *Journal of Social Issues, 42* (3), 7–27.

Goffman, E. (1959). *The Presentation of Self in Everyday Life*, New York: Doubleday Anchor Books.

Hackett, R. (1991). *News and Dissent: The Press and the Politics of Peace in Canada*. Norwood, NJ: Ablex.

Hale, F. (1988). "Editorial Diversity and Concentration." In R. Picard, J. Winter, M. McCoombs, and S. Lacy, eds., *Press Concentration and Monopoly: New Perspectives on Newspaper Ownership and Operation* (pp. 161–76). Norwood, NJ: Ablex.

Hall, S. (1980). "Encoding/Decoding." In S. Hall, D. Hobson, A. Lowe, and P. Willis, eds., *Culture, Media, Language* (pp. 128–38). London: Hutchinson.

Hall, S., C. Critcher, T. Jefferson, J. Clarke, and B. Roberts. (1978). *Policing the Crisis: Mugging, the State and Law and Order*. London: Macmillan.

Hardin, H. (1985). *Closed Circuits: The Sellout of Canadian Television*. Vancouver: Douglas & McIntyre.

Herman, E., and N. Chomsky. (1988). *Manufacturing Consent: The Political Economy of the Mass Media*. New York: Pantheon.

Hobson, D. (1982). *Crossroads: The Drama of a Soap Opera*. London: Methuen.

Hodge, R., and D. Tripp. (1986). *Children and Television: A Semiotic Approach*. Cambridge, UK: Polity Press.

Horkheimer, M., and T. Adorno. (1982 [1947]). *Dialectic of Enlightenment*. New York: Continuum Books.

Huesmann, L., and N. Malamuth. (1986). "Media Violence and Anti-social Behaviour: An Overview." *Journal of Social Issues, 42* (3), 1–6.

Innis, H. (1951). *The Bias of Communication*. Toronto: University of Toronto Press.

Iyengar, S., and D. Kinder. (1987). *News that Matters: Agenda-Setting and Priming in a Television Age*. Chicago: University of Chicago Press.

Klapper, J. (1960). *The Effects of Mass Communication*. Glencoe, IL: Free Press.

Knight, G. (1982a). "News and Ideology." *Canadian Journal of Communication, 8* (4), 15–41.

Knight, G. (1982b). "Strike Talk: A Case Study of News." *Canadian Journal of Communication, 8* (3), 61–79.

Knight, G. (1988). "Stratified News: Media, Sources and the Politics of Representation." In P. Bruck, ed., *A Proxy for Knowledge: The News Media as Agents in Arms Control and Verification* (pp. 15–24). Ottawa: Carleton International Proceedings.

Knight, G., and J. O'Connor. (1995). "Social Democracy Meets the Press: Media Coverage of Industrial Relations Legislation." *Research in Political Sociology, 7,* 183–206.

Lang, K., and G. Lang. (1983). *The Battle for Public Opinion: The President, the Press and the Polls during Watergate.* New York: Columbia University Press.

Maclean's. (1996). "The Prince of Papers." November 11, 56–61.

McCoombs, M. (1988). "Concentration, Monopoly, and Content." In R. Picard, J. Winter, M. McCoombs, and S. Lacy, eds., *Press Concentration and Monopoly: New Perspectives on Newspaper Ownership and Operation* (pp. 129–37). Norwood, NJ: Ablex.

McCoombs, M., and D. Shaw (1972). "The Agenda-Setting Function of the Mass Media." *Public Opinion Quarterly, 36,* 176–85.

McCormack, T. (1994). "Codes, Ratings and Rights." *Institute for Social Research Newsletter* (York University, Toronto), *9* (1).

McLuhan, M. (1964). *Understanding Media: The Extensions of Man.* New York: Mentor Books.

McLuhan, M. (1969). *The Gutenberg Galaxy.* New York: Mentor Books.

McQuaig, L. (1995). *Shooting the Hippo: Death by Deficit and Other Canadian Myths.* Toronto: Viking.

Meyrowitz, J. (1985). *No Sense of Place: The Impact of Electronic Media on Social Behaviour.* Oxford: Oxford University Press.

Miller, M. (1987). *Turn Up the Contrast: CBC Television Drama since 1952.* Vancouver: University of British Columbia Press.

Modleski, T. (1983). "The Rhythms of Reception: Daytime Television and Women's Work." In E. Kaplan, ed., *Regarding Television: Critical Approaches — An Anthology* (pp. 67–74). Frederick, MD: University Publications of America.

Morley, D. (1986). *Family Television: Cultural Power and Domestic Leisure.* London: Comedia.

National Media Archive. (1989). "Priming Canadian Media Audiences." *On Balance, 2* (6), 1–8. Vancouver: Fraser Institute.

National Media Archive. (1993). "Immigration I: The Human Interest Story." *On Balance, 6* (3), 1–8. Vancouver: Fraser Institute.

Press, A. (1991). *Women Watching Television: Gender, Class and Generation in the American Television Experience.* Philadelphia: University of Pennsylvania Press.

Raboy, M. (1984). *Movements and Messages: Media and Radical Politics in Quebec.* Toronto: Between the Lines.

Raboy, M. (1990). *Missed Opportunities: The Story of Canada's Broadcasting Policy.* Montreal and Kingston: McGill-Queen's University Press.

Rosen, R. (1986). "Soap Operas: Search for Yesterday." In T. Gitlin, ed., *Watching Television* (pp. 42–67). New York: Pantheon.

Rutherford, P. (1982). *A Victorian Authority: The Daily Press in Late Nineteenth-Century Canada.* Toronto: University of Toronto Press.

Severin, W., and J. Tankard. (1992). *Communication Theories: Origins, Methods and Uses in the Mass Media.* New York: Longman.

Smythe, D. (1981). *Dependency Road: Communications, Capitalism, Consciousness and Canada.* Norwood, NJ: Ablex.

Statistics Canada. (1990). "Who Listens to Radio?" *Focus on Culture, 2* (4), 1.

Statistics Canada. (1994). *Television Viewing 1993.* Ottawa: Industry, Science and Technology Canada.

Stone, G., and M. McCoombs. (1981). "Tracing the Time Lag in Agenda-Setting." *Journalism Quarterly, 58,* 51–55.

Taras, D. (1990). *The Newsmakers: The Media's Influence on Canadian Politics.* Scarborough, ON: Nelson.

Trim, K., with G. Pizante and J. Yaraskavitch. (1983). "The Effects of Monopoly on the News: A Before and After Study of Two Canadian One-Newspaper Towns." *Canadian Journal of Communications, 9* (3), 33–56.

van Dijk, T. (1991). *Racism and the Press.* London: Routledge.

Variety. (1995). "Spotlight: Variety's Global 50." August 28–September 3, 28.

Varis, T. (1984). "The International Flow of Television Programs." *Journal of Communication, 34* (1), 143–52.

Wernick, A. (1991). *Promotional Culture: Advertising, Ideology and Symbolic Expression.* London: Sage.

White, M. (1992). *Tele-advising: Therapeutic Discourse in American Television.* Chapel Hill, NC: University of North Carolina Press.

Williams, R. (1976). *Keywords: A Vocabulary of Culture and Society.* London: Fontana.

Williams, T.M., ed. (1986). *The Impact of Television: A Natural Experiment in Three Communities.* Orlando, FL: Academic Press.

Wolfe, M. (1985). *Jolts: The TV Wasteland and the Canadian Oasis.* Toronto: Lorimer.

Wright, C. (1975). *Mass Communication: A Sociological Perspective.* New York: Random House.

Znaimer, M. (1996). "TVTV: The Television Revolution: A Rebuttal." *Canadian Journal of Communication, 21* (1), 67–73.

Chapter 6

Bellah, Robert. (1967). "Civil Religion in America." *Daedalus, 96,* 1–21.

Berger, Peter. (1961). *The Noise of Solemn Assemblies.* New York: Doubleday.

Bergin, Allan E. (1983). "Religiosity and Mental Health: A Critical Reevaluation and Meta-analysis." *Professional Psychology: Research and Practice, 14,* 170–84.

Beyer, Peter. (1993). "Roman Catholicism in Contemporary Quebec." In W.E. Hewitt, ed., *The Sociology of Religion: A Canadian Focus* (pp. 133–55). Toronto: Butterworths.

Beyer, Peter. (1997). "Religious Vitality in Canada: The Complementarity of Religious Market and Secularization Perspectives." *Journal for the Scientific Study of Religion, 36*, 272–88.

Bibby, Reginald W. (1987). *Fragmented Gods: The Poverty and Potential of Religion in Canada*. Toronto: Stoddart.

Bibby, Reginald W. (1993). *Unknown Gods: The Ongoing Story of Religion in Canada*. Toronto: Stoddart.

Bibby, Reginald W. (1994). *Unitrends*. Toronto: United Church of Canada, Department of Stewardship Services.

Bibby, Reginald W. (1995). *The Bibby Report: Social Trends Canadian Style*. Toronto: Stoddart.

Bibby, Reginald W. (1996). *Project Canada Consultation on Research and Ministry*. Lethbridge, AB: The University of Lethbridge.

Bibby, Reginald W. (1997). "Going, Going, Gone: The Impact of Geographical Mobility on Religious Involvement." *Review of Religious Research, 38*, in press.

Bibby, Reginald W., and Merlin B. Brinkerhoff. (1973). "The Circulation of the Saints: A Study of People who Join Conservative Churches." *Journal for the Scientific Study of Religion, 12*, 273–83.

Bibby, Reginald W., and Merlin B. Brinkerhoff. (1983). "Circulation of the Saints Revisited: A Longitudinal Look at Conservative Church Growth." *Journal for the Scientific Study of Religion, 22*, 253–62.

Bibby, Reginald W., and Merlin B. Brinkerhoff. (1994). "Circulation of the Saints: 1966–1990: New Data, New Reflections." *Journal for the Scientific Study of Religion, 33*, 273–80.

Bibby, Reginald W., and Armand Mauss. (1974). "Skidders and Their Servants: Variable Goals and Functions of the Skid Road Rescue Mission." *Journal for the Scientific Study of Religion, 13*, 421–36.

Bibby, Reginald W., and Donald C. Posterski. (1985). *The Emerging Generation: an Inside Look at Canada's Teenagers*. Toronto: Irwin.

Bibby, Reginald W., and Donald C. Posterski. (1992). *Teen Trends: A Nation in Motion*. Toronto: Stoddart.

Bibby, Reginald W., and Harold R. Weaver. (1985). "Cult Consumption in Canada: A Critique of Stark and Bainbridge." *Sociological Analysis, 46*, 445–60.

Bouma, Gary D. (1970). "Assessing the Impact of Religion: A Critical Review." *Sociological Analysis, 31*, 172–79.

Brady, Diane. (1991). "Saving the Boomers." *Maclean's*, June 3, 50–51.

Brannon, Robert. (1971). "Organizational Vulnerability in Modern Religious Organizations." *Journal for the Scientific Study of Religion, 10*, 27–32.

Campbell, Robert A., and James E. Curtis. (1994). "Religious Involvement across Societies." *Journal for the Scientific Study of Religion, 33*, 215–29.

Clark, S.D. (1948). *Church and Sect in Canada*. Toronto: University of Toronto Press.

Cogley, John. (1968). *Religion in a Secular Age*. New York: New American Library.

Crysdale, Stewart. (1961). *The Industrial Struggle and Protestant Ethics in Canada*. Toronto: Ryerson Press.

Demerath, N.J., III, and Phillip E. Hammond. (1969). *Religion in Social Context*. New York: Random House.

Dobbelaere, Karel. (1981). "Secularization: A Multi-Dimensional Concept." *Current Sociology, 29*, 201–16.

Durkheim, Émile. (1965 [1912]). *The Elementary Forms of the Religious Life*. New York: Free Press.

Fallding, Harold. (1978). "Mainline Protestantism in Canada and the United States: An Overview." *Canadian Journal of Sociology, 2*, 141–60.

Finke, Roger, and Rodney Stark. (1992). *The Churching of America, 1776–1990*. New Brunswick, NJ: Rutgers University Press.

Fledderus, Bill. (1997). "Evangelicals more Similar to Catholics, American Cousins than to Each Other: Angus Reid Poll." *Faith Today*, January–February, 18–19.

Frankel, B. Gail, and W.E. Hewitt. (1994). "Religion and Well-Being among Canadian University Students." *Journal for the Scientific Study of Religion, 33*, 62–73.

Freud, Sigmund. (1962 [1928]). *The Future of an Illusion*. New York: Doubleday.

Gee, Ellen M., and Jean E. Veevers. (1990). "Religious Involvement and Life Satisfaction in Canada." *Sociological Analysis, 51*, 387–94.

Geertz, Clifford. (1968). "Religion as a Cultural System." In Donald Cutler, ed., *The Religious Situation* (pp. 1–46). Boston: Beacon Press.

Gerth, H., and C. Wright Mills. (1958). *From Max Weber: Essays in Sociology*. New York: Oxford University Press.

Glock, Charles, Benjamin Ringer, and Earl Babbie. (1967). *To Comfort and to Challenge*. Berkeley, CA: University of California Press.

Glock, Charles Y., and Rodney Stark. (1965). *Religion and Society in Tension*. Chicago: Rand-McNally.

Gorsuch, Richard L. (1988). "Psychology of Religion." *Annual Review of Psychology, 39*, 201–21.

Gorsuch, Richard, and Daniel Aleshire. (1974). "Christian Faith and Ethnic Prejudice: A Review and Interpretation of Research." *Journal for the Scientific Study of Religion, 13*, 281–307.

Hadden, Jeffrey. (1969). *The Gathering Storm in the Churches*. Garden City, NJ: Doubleday.

Herberg, Will. (1960). *Protestant, Catholic, Jew*. Rev. ed. New York: Doubleday.

Hewitt, W.E. (1992). "The Social Justice Program of the Canadian Catholic Church: An International Case-Comparative Analysis." *Sociological Analysis, 53*, 141–58.

Hobart, Charles. (1974). "Church Involvement and the Comfort Thesis." *Journal for the Scientific Study of Religion, 13*, 463–70.

Hunsberger, Bruce. (1980). "A Reexamination of the Antecedents of Apostasy." *Review of Religious Research, 21*, 158–70.

Hunsberger, Bruce, and L.B. Brown. (1984). "Religious Socialization, Apostasy, and the Impact of Family Background." *Journal for the Scientific Study of Religion, 23,* 239–51.

Kanagy, Conrad L., and Leo Driedger. (1996). "Changing Mennonite Values." *Review of Religious Research, 37,* 342–53.

Kelley, Dean. (1972). *Why Conservative Churches Are Growing.* New York: Harper and Row.

Kirkpatrick, Clifford. (1949). "Religion and Humanitarianism: A Study of Institutional Implications." *Psychological Monographs, 63* (9).

Lee, Gary, and Robert Clyde. (1974). "Religion, Socioeconomic Status, and Anomie." *Journal for the Scientific Study of Religion, 13,* 35–47.

Levin, Jeffrey S., and Kyriakos S. Markides. (1986). "Religious Attendance and Subjective Health." *Journal for the Scientific Study of Religion, 25,* 31–40.

Lewis, David L. (1993). "Canada's Native Peoples and the Churches." In W.E. Hewitt, ed., *The Sociology of Religion: A Canadian Focus* (pp. 235–51). Toronto: Butterworths.

Luidens, Donald A., and Roger J. Nemeth. (1989). "After the Storm: Closing the Clergy–Laity Gap." *Review of Religious Research, 31,* 183–95.

Marx, Karl. (1970 [1843]). *Critique of Hegel's "Philosophy of Right."* Trans. Annette Jolin and Joseph O'Malley. Cambridge, MA: Harvard University Press.

Marx, Karl, and Friedrich Engels. (1964). *On Religion.* New York: Schocken Books.

Metz, Donald. (1967). *New Congregations: Security and Mission in Conflict.* Philadelphia: Westminster Press.

Mitchell, Robert. (1966). "Polity, Church Attractiveness, and Ministers' Careers." *Journal for the Scientific Study of Religion, 5,* 241–58.

Nelson, L.D., and Russell Dynes. (1976). "The Impact of Devotionalism and Attendance on Ordinary and Emergency Helping Behaviour." *Journal for the Scientific Study of Religion, 15,* 47–59.

Nemeth, Mary. (1993). "God Is Alive: The Religion Poll." *Maclean's,* April 12, 32–37.

O'Toole, Roger, Douglas F. Campbell, John A. Hannigan, Peter Beyer, and John H. Simpson. (1993). "The United Church in Crisis." In W.E. Hewitt, ed., *The Sociology of Religion: A Canadian Focus* (pp. 273–87). Toronto: Butterworths.

Rokeach, Milton. (1965). *Paradoxes of Religious Belief.* Information Service, National Council of Churches, February 13, 1–2.

Rokeach, Milton. (1969). "Religious Values and Social Compassion." *Review of Religious Research, 11,* 3–23.

Roof, Wade Clark, and Dean R. Hoge. (1980). "Church Involvement in America: Social Factors Affecting Membership and Participation." *Review of Religious Research, 21,* 405–26.

Roozen, David A., William McKinney, and Wayne Thompson. (1990). "The 'Big Chill' Generation Warms to Worship." *Review of Religious Research, 31,* 314–22.

Rouleau, Jean-Paul. (1977). "Religion in Quebec: Present and Future." *Pro Mundi Vita: Dossiers,* November–December, No. 3.

Rushby, William, and John Thrush. (1973). "Mennonites and Social Compassion." *Review of Religious Research, 15,* 16–28.

Srole, Leo. (1956). "Social Integration and Certain Corollaries." *American Sociological Review, 21,* 709–16.

Stahl, William. (1986). "The Land that God Gave Cain: Nature and Civil Religion in Canada." Presented at the annual meeting of the Society for the Scientific Study of Religion, Washington, DC, November.

Stark, Rodney, and William Sims Bainbridge. (1985). *The Future of Religion.* Berkeley, CA: University of California Press.

Stark, Rodney, and Charles Y. Glock. (1968). *American Piety.* Berkeley, CA: University of California Press.

Statistics Canada. (1993). *Religions in Canada.* 1991 Census of Canada. Cat. no. 93-319. Ottawa: Industry, Science and Technology Canada.

Stiller, Brian. (1997). *From the Tower of Babel to Parliament Hill.* Toronto: HarperCollins.

Weber, Max. (1958 [1904–5]). *The Protestant Ethic and the Spirit of Capitalism.* New York: Scribner's.

Weber, Max. (1963). *Sociology of Religion.* Boston: Beacon Press.

Whyte, Donald. (1966). "Religion and the Rural Church." In M.A. Tremblay and W.J. Anderson, eds. *Rural Canada in Transition* (pp. 79–92). Ottawa: Agricultural Economics Research Council of Canada.

Wilson, Bryan. (1975). "The Secularization Debate." *Encounter, 45,* 77–83.

Wimberley, Ronald C. (1971). "Mobility in Ministerial Career Patterns: An Exploration." *Journal for the Scientific Study of Religion, 10,* 249–53.

Wuthnow, Robert. (1973). "Religious Commitment and Conservatism: In Search of an Elusive Relationship." In Charles Glock, ed., *Religion in Sociological Perspective* (pp. 117–32). Belmont, CA: Wadsworth.

Chapter 7

Antoniou, Andreas, and Robin Rowley. (1986). "The Ownership Structure of the Largest Canadian Corporations, 1979." *Canadian Journal of Sociology, 11,* 253–68.

Bellin, Seymour S., and S.M. Miller. (1990). "The Split Society." In Kai Erikson and Steven Peter Vallas, eds., *The Nature of Work: Sociological Perspectives* (pp. 173–91). New Haven, CT: American Sociological Association and Yale University Press.

Black, Don, and John Myles. (1986). "Dependent Industrialization and the Canadian Class Structure: A Comparative Analysis." *The Canadian Review of Anthropology and Sociology, 23,* 157–81.

Boothby, Daniel. (1993). "Schooling, Literacy and the Labour Market: Towards a 'Literacy Shortage'?" *Canadian Public Policy, 19,* 29–35.

Box, Steven. (1987). *Recession, Crime and Punishment.* London: Macmillan.

Breen, Richard, and David B. Rottman. (1995). *Class Stratification: A Comparative Perspective.* London: Harvester Wheatsheaf.

Brown, Lester R. (1993). "What on Earth Is the World Coming To?" *Manchester Guardian Weekly*, August 8, p. 19. [Adapted from L.R. Brown, H. Kane, and E. Ayres. (1993). *Vital Signs 1993: The Trends that Are Shaping Our Future.* New York: W.W. Norton and the Worldwatch Institute.]

Brym, Robert J. (1979). "Political Conservatism in Atlantic Canada." In Robert J. Brym and R. James Sacouman, eds., *Underdevelopment and Social Movements in Atlantic Canada* (pp. 59–79). Toronto: New Hogtown Press.

Calliste, Agnes. (1987). "Sleeping Car Porters in Canada: An Ethnically Submerged Split Labour Market." *Canadian Ethnic Studies*, 19, 1–20.

Clark, Terry Nichols, and Seymour Martin Lipset. (1991). "Are Social Classes Dying?" *International Sociology*, 6, 397–410.

Creese, Gillian, Neil Guppy, and Martin Meissner. (1991). *Ups and Downs on the Ladder of Success: Social Mobility in Canada.* General Social Survey Analysis Series 5. Cat. no. 11–612E, no. 5. Ottawa: Statistics Canada.

Dahrendorf, Ralf. (1959). *Class and Class Conflict in Industrial Society.* London: Routledge and Kegan Paul.

Davis, Kingsley, and Wilbert E. Moore. (1945). "Some Principles of Stratification." *American Sociological Review*, 10, 242–49.

Economic Council of Canada. (1992). *The New Face of Poverty: Income Security Needs of Canadian Families.* Cat. no. EC22-186/1992E. Ottawa: Supply and Services Canada.

Esping-Andersen, Gøsta. (1990). *Three Worlds of Welfare Capitalism.* Princeton, NJ: Princeton University Press.

Grabb, Edward G. (1990). *Theories of Social Inequality: Classical and Contemporary Perspectives*, 2nd ed. Toronto: Holt, Rinehart and Winston.

Hughes, Karen. (1995). "Women in Non-traditional Occupations." *Perspectives on Labour and Income*, 7 (Autumn), 14–19.

Krahn, Harvey. (1992). *Quality of Work in the Service Sector.* General Social Survey Analysis Series 5. Cat. no. 11–612E, no. 6. Ottawa: Statistics Canada.

Krahn, Harvey. (1995). "Non-standard Work on the Rise." *Perspectives on Labour and Income*, 7 (Winter), 35–42.

Krahn, Harvey, and Graham S. Lowe. (1993). *Work, Industry, and Canadian Society*, 2nd ed. Toronto: Nelson Canada.

Krahn, H., G.S. Lowe, T.F. Hartnagel, and J. Tanner. (1987). "Explanations of Unemployment in Canada." *International Journal of Comparative Sociology*, 28, 228–36.

Krugman, Paul. (1994). "Long-term Riches, Short-term Pain." *The New York Times*, September 25, p. F9.

Krymkowski, Daniel H., and Tadeusz K. Krauze. (1992). "Occupational Mobility in the Year 2000: Projections for American Men and Women." *Social Forces*, 71, 145–57.

Lenski, Gerhard. (1966). *Power and Privilege: A Theory of Social Stratification.* New York: McGraw-Hill.

Li, Peter. (1982). "Chinese Immigrants on the Canadian Prairie, 1919–47." *Canadian Review of Sociology and Anthropology*, 19, 527–40.

Longman, Phillip. (1985). "Justice between Generations." *Atlantic Monthly*, June, pp. 73–81.

Love, Roger, and Susan Poulin. (1991). "Family Income Inequality in the 1980s." *Perspectives on Labour and Income*, 3 (Autumn), 51–57.

Morissette, René, John Myles, and Garnett Picot. (1994). "Earnings Inequality and the Distribution of Working Time in Canada." *Canadian Business Economics*, 2 (3), 3–16.

Myles, John. (1996). "Public Policy in a World of Market Failure." *Policy Options*, 17 (6), 14–19.

Myles, John, and Adnan Turegun. (1994). "Comparative Studies in Class Structure." *Annual Review of Sociology*, 20, 103–24.

National Council of Welfare. (1995). *Welfare Incomes, 1994.* Cat. no. H68-27/1994E. Ottawa: Supply and Services Canada.

National Council of Welfare. (1996). *Poverty Profile, 1994.* Cat. no. H67-1/4-1994E. Ottawa: Supply and Services Canada.

Oja, Gail. (1987). *Changes in the Distribution of Wealth in Canada, 1970–1984.* Income Analytic Report no. 1. Cat. no. 13-588, no. 1. Ottawa: Statistics Canada.

Osberg, Lars. (1981). *Economic Inequality in Canada.* Toronto: Butterworths.

Palmer, Bryan. (1986). *The Character of Class Struggle: Essays in Canadian Working Class History, 1850–1985.* Toronto: McClelland and Stewart.

Pentland, H. Clare. (1981). *Labour and Capital in Canada: 1650–1860.* Toronto: Lorimer.

Porter, John. (1968). "The Future of Upward Mobility." *American Sociological Review*, 33, 5–19.

Rashid, Abdul. (1993). "Seven Decades of Wage Changes." *Perspectives on Labour and Income*, 5 (Summer), 9–21.

Reich, Robert B. (1991). *The Work of Nations: Preparing Ourselves for 21st-Century Capitalism.* New York: Knopf.

Reiman, Jeffrey H. (1979). *The Rich Get Richer and the Poor Get Prison: Ideology, Class and Criminal Justice.* New York: John Wiley and Sons.

Richardson, R. Jack. (1990). "Economic Concentration and Social Power in Contemporary Canada." In J. Curtis and L. Tepperman, eds., *Images of Canada: The Sociological Tradition* (pp. 341–51). Scarborough, ON: Prentice Hall.

Roberge, Roger, Jean-Marie Berthelot, and Michael Wolfson. (1995). "Health and Socio-economic Inequalities." *Canadian Social Trends*, Summer, pp. 15–19.

Ryscavage, Paul. (1995). "A Surge in Growing Income Inequality?" *Monthly Labor Review*, August, pp. 51–61.

Statistics Canada. (1984). *Charting Canadian Incomes, 1951–1981*. Cat. no. 13-581E. Ottawa: Supply and Services Canada.

Statistics Canada. (1996). *Income Distributions by Size in Canada, 1995*. Cat. no. 13-207. Ottawa: Statistics Canada.

Tanner, Julian, Harvey Krahn, and Timothy F. Hartnagel. (1995). *Fractured Transitions from School to Work: Revisiting the Dropout Problem*. Toronto: Oxford University Press.

Wanner, Richard A. (1993). "Patterns and Trends in Occupational Mobility." In J. Curtis, E. Grabb, and N. Guppy, eds., *Social Inequality in Canada: Patterns, Problems, Policies*, 2nd ed. (pp. 153–78). Scarborough, ON: Prentice Hall.

Weber, Max. (1948 [1922]). *From Max Weber: Essays in Sociology*. Eds. and trans. H.H. Gerth and C.W. Mills. London: Routledge and Kegan Paul.

Westergaard, John. (1995). *Who Gets What? The Hardening of Class Inequality in the Late Twentieth Century*. Cambridge, UK: Polity Press.

Wilkinson, R.G. (1992). "Income Distributions and Life Expectancy." *British Medical Journal, 304*, 165–68.

Wolff, Edward N. (1991). "The Distribution of Household Wealth: Methodological Issues, Time Trends, and Cross-sectional Comparisons." In Lars Osberg, ed., *Economic Inequality and Poverty: International Perspectives* (pp. 92–133). Armonk, NY: M.E. Sharpe.

Wright, Erik Olin. (1985). *Classes*. London: Verso.

Wright, Erik Olin, and Bill Martin. (1987). "The Transformation of the American Class Structure, 1960–1980." *American Journal of Sociology, 93*, 1–29.

Zeitlin, Irving M., with Robert J. Brym. (1991). *The Social Condition of Humanity*, Cdn. ed. Toronto: Oxford University Press.

Chapter 8

Agocs, Carol, and Monica Boyd. (1993). "The Canadian Ethnic Mosaic Recast for the 1990s." In James Curtis, Edward Grabb, and Neil Guppy, eds., *Social Inequality in Canada: Patterns, Problems and Policies* (pp. 330–52). Scarborough, ON: Prentice Hall.

Agocs, Carol, Catherine Burr, and Felicity Somerset. (1992). *Employment Equity: Cooperative Strategies for Organizational Change*. Toronto: Prentice Hall Canada.

Arscott, Jane, and Linda Trimble. (1997). "Introduction — In the Presence of Women: Representation and Political Power." In Jane Arscott and Linda Trimble, eds., *In the Presence of Women: Representation in Canadian Governments* (pp. 1–17). Toronto: Harcourt Brace and Company, Canada.

Armstrong, Pat, and Hugh Armstrong. (1994). *The Double Ghetto: Canadian Women and Their Segregated Work*, 3rd ed. Toronto: McClelland and Stewart.

Bashevkin, Sylvia B. (1991). "Women's Participation in Political Parties." In Kathy Megyery, ed., *Women in Canadian Politics: Toward Equity in Representation* (pp. 61–79). Toronto: Dundurn Press.

Bashevkin, Sylvia B. (1993). *Toeing the Lines: Women and Party Politics in English Canada*, 2nd ed. Toronto: Oxford University Press.

Basow, Susan. (1986). *Gender Stereotypes: Traditions and Alternatives*, 2nd ed. Monterey, CA: Brooks/Cole.

Best, Pamela. (1995). "Women, Men and Work." *Canadian Social Trends, 36* (1), 30–33.

Boyd, Monica. (1990). "Sex Differences in Occupational Skill: Canada, 1961–1986." *Canadian Review of Sociology and Anthropology, 27*, 285–315.

Boyd, Monica. (1992). "Gender, Visible Minority and Immigrant Earnings Inequality: Reassessing an Employment Equity Premise." In Vic Satzewich, ed., *Deconstructing a Nation: Immigration, Multiculturalism and Racism in '90s Canada* (pp. 279–321). Halifax: Fernwood.

Boyd, Monica. (1996). "Female Migrant Labour in North America: Trends and Issues for the 1990s." In Alan Simmons, ed., *International Migration, Refugee Flows and Human Rights in North America: The Impact of Trade and Restructuring* (pp. 193–213). New York: Center for Migration Studies.

Boyd, Monica, Brenda Hughes, and Jamie Miller. (1997). "Power at Work: Women and Men in Management, Supervision and Workplace Planning." Unpublished paper. Department of Sociology, Florida State University.

Boyd, Monica, Maryann Mulvihill, and John Myles. (1991). "Gender, Power and Postindustrialism." *Canadian Review of Sociology and Anthropology, 28*, 407–36.

Brodie, Janine. (1991). "Women and the Electoral Process in Canada." In Kathy Megyery, ed., *Women in Canadian Politics: Toward Equity in Representation* (pp. 3–59). Toronto: Dundurn Press.

Broverman, I., S.R. Vogel, S.M. Broverman, F.E. Clarkson, and P.S. Rosenkranz. (1972). "Sex Role Stereotypes: A Current Appraisal." *Journal of Social Issues, 28* (2), 59–78.

Burt, Sandra. (1993). "The Changing Patterns of Public Policy." In Sandra Burt, Lorraine Code, and Lindsay Dorney, eds., *Changing Patterns: Women in Canada*, 2nd ed. (pp. 212–37). Toronto: McClelland and Stewart.

Canada. (1958). Department of Labour. Women's Bureau. *Women at Work in Canada*. Ottawa: Supply and Services Canada.

Canada. (1995). Laws. Statues of Canada. Employment Equity Act. 43–44 Elizabeth II, Vol. II, Chapter 44.

Connelly, Patricia. (1978). *Last Hired, First Fired: Women and the Canadian Work Force*. Toronto: Women's Press.

Crompton, Susan, and Leslie Geran. (1995). "Women as Main Wage-Earners." *Canadian Perspectives on Labour and Income, 7* (4), 26–29.

Devereaux, Mary Sue. (1993). "Time Use of Canadians in 1992." *Canadian Social Trends*, 8 (3), 13–16.

Duffy, Ann. (1986). "Reformulating Power for Women." *Canadian Review of Sociology and Anthropology*, 23, 22–46.

Duffy, Ann, and Norene Pupo. (1992). *Part-time Paradox: Connecting Gender, Work and Family*. Toronto: McClelland and Stewart.

Economic Council of Canada. (1991). *Employment in the Service Economy*. Ottawa: Supply and Services Canada.

England, Paula. (1993). *Comparable Worth: Theories and Evidence*. New York: Aldine de Gruyter.

Erickson, Lynda. (1991). "Women Candidates for the House of Commons." In Kathy Megyery, ed., *Women in Canadian Politics: Toward Equity in Representation* (pp. 101–25). Toronto: Dundurn Press.

Frederick, Judith. (1993). "Tempus Fugit: Are You Time Crunched?" *Canadian Social Trends*, 31 (Winter), 6–10.

Frederick, Judith. (1995). *As Time Goes By . . . : Time Use of Canadians*, Cat. no. 89-544E. Ottawa: Industry, Science and Technology Canada.

Gaskell, Jane. (1986). "Conceptions of Skill and the Work of Women: Some Historical and Political Issues." In Roberta Hamilton and Michele Barrett, eds., *The Politics of Diversity: Feminism, Marxism and Nationalism* (pp. 361–80). London: Verso.

Gaskell, Jane. (1991). "What Counts as Skill? Reflections on Pay Equity." In Judy Fudge and Patricia McDermott, eds., *Just Wages: A Feminist Assessment of Pay Equity* (pp. 141–59). Toronto: University of Toronto Press.

Ghalam, Nancy Zukewich. (1993). *Women in the Workplace*, 2nd ed. Statistics Canada. Cat. no. 71-534E. Ottawa: Industry, Science and Technology Canada.

Human Resources Development Canada. (1995). *Annual Report. Employment Equity Act, 1995*. Ottawa: Human Resources Development Canada.

Jackson, Chris. (1996). "Measuring and Valuing Households' Unpaid Work." *Canadian Social Trends*, 42 (4), 25–29.

Krahn, Harvey. (1995). "Non-standard Work on the Rise." *Perspectives on Labour and Income*, 7 (4), 35–42.

Lowe, Graham. (1987). *Women in the Administrative Revolution: The Feminization of Clerical Work*. Cambridge, UK: Polity Press.

Mackie, Marlene. (1980). "The Impact of Sex Stereotypes upon Adult Self-Imagery." *Social Psychology Quarterly*, 43, 121–25.

Maille, Chantal. (1990). *Primed for Power: Women in Canadian Politics*. Ottawa: Canadian Advisory Council on the Status of Women.

McCormack, Thelma. (1975). "Toward a Nonsexist Perspective on Social and Political Change." In Marcia Millman and Rosabeth Moss Kanter, eds., *Another Voice: Feminist Perspectives on Social Life and Social Science* (pp. 1–33). Garden City, NY: Anchor Books.

McDonald, Marci. (1994). "Rebel with a Cause: After Nine Years on the Attack, Sheila Copps Is Learning the Lessons of Power." *Maclean's*, April 4, 16–22.

Myles, John, and Gail Fawcett. (1990). *Job Skills and the Service Economy*. Working Paper no. 4. Ottawa: Economic Council of Canada.

Oderkirk, Jillian, and Clarence Lochhead. (1992). "Lone Parenthood: Gender Differences." *Canadian Social Trends*, 27 (4), 16–19.

Pal, Leslie. (1989). *Public Policy Analysis*. Toronto: Nelson Canada.

Pendakur, Krishna, and Ravi Pendakur. (1995). "Earnings Differentials among Ethnic Groups in Canada." Reference SRA-34. Ottawa: Department of Canadian Heritage, Corporate and Intergovernmental Affairs, Strategic Research and Analysis.

Phillips, Paul, and Erin Phillips. (1983). *Women and Work*. Toronto: Lorimer.

Pierson, Ruth. (1977). "Women's Emancipation and the Recruitment of Women into the Labour Force in World War II." In Susan Mann Trofimenkoff and Alison Prentice, eds., *The Neglected Majority* (pp. 125–45). Toronto: McClelland and Stewart.

Prentice, Alison. (1977). "The Feminization of Teaching." In Susan Mann Trofimenkoff and Alison Prentice, eds., *The Neglected Majority* (pp. 49–65). Toronto: McClelland and Stewart.

Robinson, Gertrude J., and Armande Saint-Jean, with the assistance of Christine Rioux. (1991). "Women Politicians and Their Media Coverage: A Generational Analysis." In Kathy Megyery, ed., *Women in Canadian Politics: Toward Equity in Representation* (pp. 127–69). Toronto: Dundurn Press.

Séguin, Rhéal. (1996). "Quebec Puts Brakes on Pay Equity." *The Globe and Mail*, November 8, p. A7.

Statistics Canada. (1993a). *The Daily*. Statistics Canada, Ottawa. March 2.

Statistics Canada. (1993b). *Employment Income by Occupation: The Nation*. 1991 Census of Canada. Cat. no. 93-332. Ottawa: Industry, Science and Technology Canada.

Statistics Canada. (1993c). *Labour Force Activity: The Nation*. 1991 Census of Canada. Cat. no. 93-324. Ottawa: Industry, Science and Technology Canada.

Statistics Canada. (1993d). *Occupation: The Nation*. 1991 Census of Canada. Cat. no. 93-327. Ottawa: Industry, Science and Technology Canada.

Steinberg, Ronnie J. (1990). "Social Construction of Skill." *Work and Occupations*, 17, 449–82.

Ursel, Jane. (1992). *Private Lives, Public Policy: 100 Years of State Intervention in the Family*. Toronto: Women's Press.

Vickers, Jill. (1997). "Toward a Feminist Understanding of Representation." In Jane Arscott and Linda Trimble, eds., *In the Presence of Women: Representation in Canadian Governments* (pp. 20–46). Toronto: Harcourt Brace.

Vickers, Jill, Pauline Rankin, and Christine Appelle. (1993). *Politics as if Women Mattered: A Political Analysis of the National Action Committee on the Status of Women*. Toronto: University of Toronto Press.

Weiner, Nan, and Morley Gunderson. (1990). *Pay Equity: Issues, Options and Experiences*. Toronto: Butterworths.

Young, Lisa. (1997). "Fulfilling the Mandate of Difference: Women in the Canadian House of Commons." In Jane Arscott and Linda Trimble, eds., *In the Presence of Women: Representation in Canadian Governments* (pp. 82–103). Toronto: Harcourt Brace.

Chapter 9

Abella, Irving, and Harold Troper. (1982). *None Is Too Many: Canada and the Jews of Europe, 1933–1948*. Toronto: Lester & Orpen Dennys.

Anderson, Benedict. (1983). *Imagined Communities: Reflections on the Origin and Spread of Nationalism*. London: Verso.

Angus Reid Group. (1991). *Multiculturalism and Canadians: National Attitude Study 1991*. Ottawa: Multiculturalism and Citizenship Canada.

Avery, Donald. (1995). *Reluctant Host: Canada's Response to Immigrant Workers*. Toronto: McClelland and Stewart.

Badets, Jane. (1993). "Canada's Immigrants: Recent Trends." *Canadian Social Trends*. Cat. no. 11-008E. Ottawa: Statistics Canada.

Balthazar, Louis. (1993). "The Faces of Quebec Nationalism." In Alain-G. Gagnon, ed., *Quebec: State and Society*, 2nd ed. (pp. 2–17). Scarborough, ON: Nelson.

Barkan, Elazar. (1992). *The Retreat of Scientific Racism*. Cambridge, UK: Cambridge University Press.

Barker, Martin. (1981). *The New Racism: Conservatives and the Ideology of the Tribe*. London: Junction Books.

Bissoondath, Neil. (1994). *Selling Illusions: The Cult of Multiculturalism*. Toronto: Stoddart.

Bolaria, B. Singh, and Peter Li. (1988). *Racial Oppression in Canada*. Toronto: Garamond.

Boldt, Menno. (1993). *Surviving as Indians: The Challenge of Self-government*. Toronto: University of Toronto Press.

Bonacich, Edna. (1972). "A Theory of Ethnic Antagonism: The Split Labor Market." *American Sociological Review*, 37, 547–59.

Bonacich, Edna. (1979). "The Past, Present and Future of Split Labor Market Theory." *Research in Race and Ethnic Relations*, 1, 17–64.

Bonacich, Edna. (1980). "Class Approaches to Ethnicity and Race." *Insurgent Sociologist*, 10, 9–23.

Bourgeault, Ron. (1988). "The South African Connection." *Canadian Dimension*, 21, 6–10.

Boyd, Monica. (1992). "Gender, Visible Minority and Immigrant Earnings Inequality: Reassessing an Employment Equity Premise." In Vic Satzewich, ed.

Deconstructing a Nation: Immigration, Multiculturalism and Racism in '90s Canada (pp. 279–321). Halifax: Fernwood.

Brym, Robert, with Bonnie Fox. (1989). *From Culture to Power: The Sociology of English Canada*. Toronto: Oxford University Press.

Brym, Robert, and Rhonda Lenton. (1993). "The Distribution of Anti-semitism in Canada in 1984." In Robert Brym, William Shaffir, and Morton Weinfeld, eds., *The Jews in Canada* (pp. 112–19). Toronto: Oxford University Press.

Cannon, Margaret. (1995). *The Invisible Empire: Racism in Canada*. Toronto: Random House.

Castles, Stephen, and Godula Kosack. (1984). *Immigrant Workers and Class Structure in Western Europe*. London: Oxford University Press.

Citizenship and Immigration Canada. (1996). *You Asked About . . . Immigration and Citizenship*. Ottawa: Supply and Services Canada.

Clement, Wallace. (1975). *The Canadian Corporate Elite*. Toronto: McClelland and Stewart.

Cole, Douglas, and Ira Chaikin. (1990). *An Iron Hand upon the People: The Law against the Potlatch on the Northwest Coast*. Vancouver: Douglas & McIntyre.

Collins, Jock. (1988). *Migrant Hands in a Distant Land: Australia's Post-war Immigration*. Sydney: Pluto Press.

Daenzer, Pat. (1993). *Regulating Class Privilege*. Toronto: Canadian Scholars Press.

Darroch, Gordon. (1979). "Another Look at Ethnicity, Stratification and Social Mobility in Canada." *Canadian Journal of Sociology*, 4, 1–25.

Doob, Christopher. (1996). *Racism: An American Cauldron*. New York: HarperCollins.

Economic Council of Canada. (1991). *Economic and Social Impacts of Immigration*. Ottawa: Supply and Services Canada.

Fiske, Jo-Anne. (1996). "The Womb Is to the Nation as the Heart Is to the Body: Ethnopolitical Discourses of the Canadian Indigenous Women's Movement." *Studies in Political Economy*, 51, 65–96.

Fleras, Augie, and Jean Elliot. (1996). *Unequal Relations: An Introduction to Race, Ethnic and Aboriginal Dynamics in Canada*. Scarborough, ON: Prentice Hall.

Fournier, Marcel, Michael Rosenberg, and Deena White. (1997). *Quebec Society: Critical Issues*. Scarborough, ON: Prentice Hall.

Frideres, James. (1993). *Native Peoples in Canada: Contemporary Conflicts*. Scarborough, ON: Prentice Hall.

Gerber, Linda. (1990). "Multiple Jeopardy: A Socio-economic Comparison of Men and Women among the Indian, Métis and Inuit Peoples of Canada." *Canadian Ethnic Studies*, 22, 69–84.

Geschwender, James. (1994). "Married Women's Wage Labor and Racial/Ethnic Stratification in Canada." *Canadian Ethnic Studies*, 26, 53–73.

Gibbins, Roger, and J. Rick Ponting. (1986). "Historical Background and Overview." In J. Rick Ponting, ed.,

Arduous Journey (pp. 18–56). Toronto: McClelland and Stewart.

GRES. (1997). "Immigration and Ethnic Relations in Quebec: Pluralism in the Making." In Marcel Fournier, Michael Rosenberg and Deena White, eds., *Quebec Society: Critical Issues* (pp. 95–112). Scarborough, ON: Prentice Hall.

Ha, Tu Thanh. (1995). "The PQ's Narrow Ethnic Vision." *The Globe and Mail*, November 11, p. D1.

Hawkins, Freda. (1989). *Critical Years in Immigration: Canada and Australia Compared*. Montreal and Kingston, ON: McGill-Queen's University Press.

Henry, Frances. (1989). "Who Gets the Work in 1989?" Background Paper. Ottawa: Economic Council of Canada.

Henry, Frances, and Effie Ginsberg. (1985). *Who Gets the Work: A Test of Racial Discrimination in Employment*. Toronto: Urban Alliance on Race Relations and the Social Planning Directorate.

Henry, Frances, Carol Tator, Winston Mattis, and Tim Rees. (1995). *The Colour of Democracy: Racism in Canadian Society*. Toronto: Harcourt Brace.

Herberg, Edward. (1990). "The Ethno-racial Socioeconomic Hierarchy in Canada: Theory and Analysis in the New Vertical Mosaic." *International Journal of Comparative Sociology, 31*, 206–21.

Holton, Robert, and Michael Lanphier. (1994). "Public Opinion, Immigration and Refugees." In Howard Adelman, Allan Borowski, Meyer Burstein, and Lois Foster, eds., *Immigration and Refugee Policy: Australia and Canada Compared*, vol. 1. Toronto: University of Toronto Press.

Hou, Feng, and T.R. Balakrishnan. (1996). "The Integration of Visible Minorities in Contemporary Canadian Society." *Canadian Journal of Sociology, 21*, 307–26.

Howard, Rhoda. (1996). "Ethnicity and Group Rights Claims," Paper presented to the annual meeting of the Canadian Sociology and Anthropological Society, St. Catherines, ON.

Iacovetta, Franca. (1992). *Such Hardworking People: Italian Immigrants in Postwar Toronto*. Montreal and Kingston, ON: McGill-Queen's University Press.

Isajiw, Wsevolod. (1977). "Olga in Wonderland: Ethnicity in Technological Society." *Canadian Ethnic Studies, 9*, 77–85.

Jenson, Jane (1993). "Naming Nations: Making Nationalist Claims in Canadian Public Discourse." *Canadian Review of Sociology and Anthropology, 30*, 337–58.

Krosenbrink-Gelissen, Ernestine. (1994). "The Native Women's Association of Canada." In James Frideres, ed., *Native Peoples in Canada* (pp. 335–64). Scarborough, ON: Prentice Hall.

Latouche, Daniel. (1993). " 'Quebec: See Under Canada': Quebec Nationalism in the New Global Age." In Alain-G. Gagnon, ed., *Quebec: State and Society*, 2nd ed. (pp. 40–51). Scarborough, ON: Nelson.

Lewis, Oscar. (1961). *The Children of Sanchez*. New York: Random House.

Li, Peter. (1988). *The Chinese in Canada*. Toronto: Oxford University Press.

Li, Peter. (1996). *The Making of Post-war Canada*. Toronto: Oxford University Press.

Lian, Jason, and David Ralph Matthews. (1995). "Does the Vertical Mosaic Still Exist?: Ethnicity and Income in Canada, 1991." Paper presented at the Canadian Ethnic Studies Association Biennial Meeting, Gimli, MB.

Lieberson, Stanley. (1991). "A New Ethnic Group in the United States," in Norman Yetman, ed., *Majority and Minority* (pp. 444–56). New York: Allyn and Bacon.

Marger, Martin. (1997). *Race and Ethnic Relations: American and Global Perspectives*, 4th ed. New York: Wadsworth.

Marx, Karl. (1967 [1867]). *Capital*, Vol. 1. New York: International Publishers.

Macmillan, David. (1985). "Scottish Enterprise and Influences in Canada, 1620–1900." In R.A. Cage, ed., *The Scots Abroad: Labour, Capital and Enterprise, 1750–1914* (pp. 46–79). London: Croon Helm.

McMillan, Alan. (1988). *Native Peoples and Cultures of Canada*. Vancouver: Douglas & McIntyre.

Métis National Council. (1983). *A Brief to the Standing Committee on Legal and Constitutional Affairs*. Ottawa, September 8.

Miles, Robert. (1982). *Racism and Migrant Labour*. London: Routledge.

Miles, Robert. (1989). *Racism*. London: Routledge.

Milner, Henry, and Sheilagh Hodgins Milner. (1973). *The Decolonization of Quebec*. Toronto: McClelland and Stewart.

Mitchell, Marybelle. (1996). *From Talking Chiefs to a Native Corporate Elite*. Montreal and Kingston, ON: McGill-Queen's University Press.

Montagu, Ashley. (1972). *Statement on Race*. London: Oxford University Press.

Nagler, Mark. (1972). "Minority Values and Economic Achievement: The Case of the North American Indian." In Mark Nagler, ed., *Perspectives on the North American Indian* (pp. 131–42). Toronto: McClelland and Stewart.

Nikolinakos, Marios. (1973). "Notes Towards an Economic Theory of Racism." *Race, 14*, 365–81.

Omi, Michael, and Howard Winant. (1986). *Racial Formation in the United States: From the 1960s to the 1980s*. New York: Routledge and Kegan Paul.

Pentland, H. Clare. (1981). *Labour and Capital in Canada, 1650–1860*. Toronto: Lorimer

Pettipas, Katherine. (1995). *Severing the Ties that Bind*. Winnipeg: University of Manitoba Press.

Pineo, Peter, and John Porter. (1985). "Ethnic Origin and Occupational Attainment." In Monica Boyd, John Goyder, Frank Jones, Hugh McRoberts, Peter Pineo, and John Porter, eds., *Ascription and Achievement: Studies in Mobility and Status Attainment in Canada* (pp. 357–93). Ottawa: Carleton University Press.

Porter, John. (1965). *The Vertical Mosaic*. Toronto: University of Toronto Press.

Ramirez, Bruno. (1991). *On the Move: French-Canadian and Italian Migrants in the North Atlantic Economy 1860–1914*. Toronto: McClelland and Stewart.

Reitz, Jeffrey and Raymond Breton. (1994). *The Illusion of Difference: Realities of Ethnicity in Canada and the United States*. Toronto: C.D. Howe Institute.

Rex, John, and David Mason, eds. (1986). *Theories of Race and Ethnic Relations*. Cambridge: Cambridge University Press.

Richmond, Anthony. (1994). *Global Apartheid: Refugees, Racism and the New World Order*. Toronto: Oxford University Press.

Roy, Patricia. (1989). *A White Man's Province*. Vancouver: University of British Columbia Press.

Royal Commission on Aboriginal Peoples. (1996). *Report*. Ottawa: Supply and Services Canada.

Satzewich, Vic. (1991). *Racism and the Incorporation of Foreign Labour*. London: Routledge.

Satzewich, Vic, and Linda Mahood. (1994). "Indian Affairs and Band Governance: Deposing Indian Chiefs in Western Canada, 1896–1911," *Canadian Ethnic Studies, 26*, 40–58.

Satzewich, Vic, and Terry Wotherspoon. (1993). *First Nations: Race, Class and Gender Relations*. Scarborough, ON: Nelson.

Scott, George. (1990). "A Resynthesis of the Primordial and Circumstantial Approaches to Ethnic Group Solidarity: Towards an Explanatory Model." *Ethnic and Racial Studies, 13*, 147–71.

Special Committee on the Participation of Visible Minorities in Canadian Society. (1984). *Equality Now!* Ottawa: Supply and Services Canada.

Statistics Canada. (1995). *Profile of Aboriginal Canadians*. Cat. no. 94-325. Ottawa: Supply and Services Canada.

Steinberg, Steven. (1981). *The Ethnic Myth*. Boston: Beacon Press.

Thomas, W.I., and Florian Znaniecki. (1918). *The Polish Peasant in Europe and America*. New York: Knopf.

Titley, Brian. (1986). *A Narrow Vision: Duncan Campbell Scott and the Administration of Indian Affairs in Canada*. Vancouver: University of British Columbia Press.

van den Berghe, Pierre. (1986). "Ethnicity and the Sociobiology Debate." In John Rex and David Mason, eds., *Theories of Race and Ethnic Relations* (pp. 246–63). Cambridge, UK: Cambridge University Press.

Whitaker, Reginald. (1987). *Double Standard: The Secret History of Canadian Immigration*. Toronto: Lester & Orpen Dennys.

Whitaker, Reginald. (1993). "From the Quebec Cauldron to the Canadian Cauldron." In Alain-G. Gagnon, ed., *Quebec: State and Society*, 2nd ed. (pp. 18–39). Scarborough, ON: Nelson.

White, Pamela. (1992). "Challenges in Measuring Canada's Ethnic Diversity." In Stella Hryniuk, ed., *20 Years of Multiculturalism: Success and Failure* (pp. 163–82). Winnipeg: St. John's College Press.

Wiley, Norbert. (1967). "Ethnic Mobility and Stratification Theory." *Social Problems, 15*, 147–59.

Williams, Eric. (1964). *Capitalism and Slavery*. London: Andre Deutsch.

Wilson, Edward. (1978). *On Human Nature*. New York: Vintage.

Wong, Lloyd, and Nancy Netting. (1992). "Business Immigration to Canada: Social Impact and Racism." In Vic Satzewich, ed., *Deconstructing a Nation: Immigration, Multiculturalism and Racism in '90s Canada* (pp. 93–121). Halifax: Fernwood.

Woodsworth, J.S. (1972). *Strangers within Our Gates*. Toronto: University of Toronto Press.

York, Geoffrey. (1989). *The Dispossessed*. Toronto: Lester & Orpen Dennys.

Zong, Li. (1994). "Structural and Psychological Dimensions of Racism: Towards an Alternative Perspective." *Canadian Ethnic Studies, 26*, 122–34.

Chapter 10

Adams, Patricia. (1991). *Odious Debts: Loose Lending, Corruption, and the Third World's Environmental Legacy*. Toronto: Earthscan.

Angeles, Gracia. (1993). "Building a Women's Union in the Philippines: Fighting for Women's Rights." Interview. *Multinational Monitor*, June, 16–20.

Armer, J. Michael, and John Katsillis. (1992). *Encyclopedia of Sociology*. New York: Macmillan.

Arrighi, Giovanni. (1993). "World Income Inequalities and the Future of Socialism." *Socialism of the Future, 1* (2), 195–208.

Bairoch, Paul. (1982). "International Industrialization Levels from 1750 to 1980." *Journal of European Economic History, 11* (2), 270–71.

Baran, Paul A. (1957). *The Political Economy of Growth*. New York: Monthly Review Press.

Barnet, Richard, and Richard Muller. (1974). *Global Reach: The Power of the Multinational Corporations*. New York: Simon and Schuster.

Block, Fred L. (1977). *The Origins of International Economic Disorder*. Berkeley, CA: University of California Press.

Burt, Martha R., and Barbara E. Cohen. (1989). *America's Homeless: Numbers, Characteristics, and Programs that Serve Them*. Washington, DC: Urban Institute Press.

Cardoso, Fernando, and Enzo Faletto. (1979). *Dependency and Development in Latin America*. Berkeley, CA: University of California Press.

Castaneda, Jorge. (1993). "Can NAFTA Change Mexico?" *Foreign Affairs, 72* (4), 66–80.

Deane, Phyllis. (1979). *The First Industrial Revolution*. Cambridge, UK: Cambridge University Press.

Delage, Denys. (1993). *Bitter Feast: Amerindians and Europeans in Northeastern North America, 1600–64*. Vancouver: University of British Columbia Press.

Dreidger, Leo. (1989). *The Ethnic Factor: Identity and Diversity*. Toronto: McGraw-Hill Ryerson.

Dunning, John H. (1993). *Multinational Enterprises and the Global Economy*. Wokingham, UK: Addison-Wesley.

Ecumenical Coalition for Economic Justice (ECEJ). (1990). *Recolonization or Liberation: The Bonds of Structural Adjustment and Struggles for Emancipation*. Toronto: Our Times.

Ehrensaft, Philip, and Warwick Armstrong. (1981). "The Formation of Dominion Capitalism: Economic Truncation and Class Structure." In Allan Moscovitch, ed., *Inequality: Essays on the Political Economy of Social Welfare*. Toronto: University of Toronto Press.

Esping-Andersen, Gøsta. (1985). *Politics against Markets: The Social Democratic Road to Power*. Princeton, NJ: Princeton University Press.

Evans, Peter. (1985). "After Dependency: Recent Studies of Class, State, and Industrialization," *Latin American Research Review*, 20, 149–60.

Evans, Peter. (1987). "Foreign Capital and the Third World State." In Myron Weiner and Samuel Huntington, eds., *Understanding Political Development* (pp. 319–52). Boston: Little, Brown.

Forbes. (1992). "Ranking Foreign Billionaire Fortunes." July 20, pp. 150–222.

Foster-Carter, Aidan. (1989). "The Myth of South Korea." *Far Eastern Economic Review*, 145 (31), 46–47.

Francis, Diane. (1987). *Controlling Interest: Who Owns Canada?* Toronto: Seal.

Franke, Richard W., and Barbara Chasin. (1991). "Kerala State, India: Radical Reform as Development". *Monthly Review*, 42 (8), 1–39.

Fukuyama, Francis. (1993). *The End of History and the Last Man*. New York: Avon.

Gasslander, Olle. (1962). *History of Stockholms Enskilda Bank to 1914*. Stockholm: Stockholms Enskilda Banken.

Gerschenkron, Alexander. (1962). *Economical Backwardness in Historical Perspective*. Cambridge, MA: Harvard University Press.

Goldthorpe, J.E. (1984 [1975]). *The Sociology of the Third World*, 2nd ed. Cambridge, UK: Cambridge University Press.

Gupta, Surinder Nath. (1979). *British: The Magnificent Exploiters of India*. New Delhi: S. Chand and Co.

Harrison, Paul. (1993). *Inside the Third World: The Anatomy of Poverty*, 3rd ed. Harmondsworth, UK: Penguin.

Herman, Edward S., and Noam Chomsky. (1988). *Manufacturing Consent*. New York: Pantheon.

Hobsbawm, Eric. (1968). *Industry and Empire*. Harmondsworth,: Penguin.

Hobsbawm, Eric. (1990). *Nations and Nationalism since 1780: Programme, Myth, Reality*. Cambridge, UK: Cambridge University Press.

Hoogvelt, Ankie M.M. (1982). *The Third World in Global Development*. London: Macmillan.

Howe, Gary, and David Goodman. (1992). *Small Holders and Structural Change in the Brazilian Economy: Opportunities in Rural Poverty Alleviation*. San José, Costa Rica: International Fund for Agricultural Development.

Innis, Harold. (1973 [1956]). *Essays in Canadian Economic History*. Toronto: University of Toronto Press.

Institute for Management Development (IMD). (1995). *The World Competitiveness Yearbook 1995*. Lausanne, Switzerland: IMD.

Institute for Management Development (IMD). (1996). *The World Competitiveness Yearbook 1996*. Lausanne, Switzerland: IMD.

International Monetary Fund (IMF). (1993). *World Economic Outlook — May 1993*. Washington, DC: IMF.

Invest in Sweden Agency (ISA). (1996). *Sweden in Fact 1996*. Stockholm: ISA.

Landes, David. (1969). *The Unbound Prometheus: Technological Change and Industrial Development in Western Europe from 1750 to the Present*. Cambridge, UK: Cambridge University Press.

League of Nations. (1945). *Industrialization and Foreign Trade*. New York: League of Nations.

Love, Joseph L. (1980). "Raúl Prebisch and the Origins of the Doctrine of Unequal Exchange." *Latin American Research Review*, 15 (3), 52–56.

Macdonald, Donald S. (1990). *The Koreans: Contemporary Politics and Society*, 2nd ed. Boulder, CO: Westview Press.

Marchak, Patricia. (1991). *The Integrated Circus: The New Right and the Restructuring of Global Markets*. Montreal and Kingston, ON: McGill-Queen's University Press.

Mardon, Russell. (1990). "The State and the Effective Control of Foreign Capital: The Case of South Korea." *World Politics*, 43 (1), 111–38.

Marx, Karl, and Friedrich Engels. (1986 [1848]). *The Communist Manifesto*. Moscow: Progress Publishers.

Meek, Ronald. (1976). *Social Science and the Ignoble Savage*. Cambridge, UK: Cambridge University Press.

Nelson, Joan M., ed. (1990). *Economic Crisis and Policy Choice: The Politics of Adjustment in the Third World*. Princeton, NJ: Princeton University Press.

Nordlund, Sven. (1989). *Upptackten Av Sverige* [Foreign Investment in Sweden]. Umea, Sweden: Umea University.

Norman, E.H. (1940). *Japan's Emergence as a Modern State*. New York: U.S. Institute of Pacific Relations.

O'Brien, Philip. (1976). "Was the United States Responsible for the Chilean Coup?" In P. O'Brien, ed., *Allende's Chile* (pp. 217–43). New York: Praeger.

Ostry, Sylvia. (1990). *Government and Corporations in a Shrinking World*. New York: Council on Foreign Relations Press.

Palma, Gabriel. (1981). "Dependency and Development: A Critical Overview." In D. Seers, ed., *Dependency Theory: A Critical Reassessment* (pp. 20–78). London: Frances Pinter.

Pastor, Manuel, Jr., and Gary Dymski. (1991). "Debt Crisis and Class Conflict in Latin America." *Capital and Class, 43*, 203–31.

Rostow, W.W. (1965). *The Stages of Economic Growth.* Cambridge, UK: Cambridge University Press.

Sampson, Anthony. (1973). *The Sovereign State of ITT.* New York: Stein and Day.

Seers, Dudley, ed. (1981). *Dependency Theory: A Critical Reassessment.* London: Frances Pinter.

Smith, Adam. (1976 [1776]). *An Inquiry into the Nature and Causes of the Wealth of Nations.* Chicago: University of Chicago Press.

Smith, Thomas C. (1955). *Political Change and Industrial Development in Japan: Government Enterprises, 1868–1880.* Stanford, CA: Stanford University Press.

Swedish Institute, The. (1992). "Sweden's Foreign Trade." *Fact Sheets on Sweden.* Stockholm, November.

United Nations. (1986). "World Comparison of Purchasing Power and Real Product for 1980." New York: United Nations.

United Nations. (1992). *Human Development Report 1992.* New York: Oxford University Press.

United Nations. (1995). *World Economic and Social Survey 1995.* New York: United Nations.

United Nations. (1996). *Human Development Report 1996.* New York: Oxford University Press.

United Nations Conference on Trade and Development (UNCTAD). (1989). *Trade and Development Report, 1989.* New York: United Nations.

United Nations Conference on Trade and Development (UNCTAD). (1993). *Trade and Development Report, 1993.* New York: United Nations.

Walker, Stuart. (1993). "This Passing Show." *Alternatives, 19* (2), 46–49.

Wolf, Eric R. (1982). *Europe and the People without History.* Berkeley, CA: University of California Press.

World Bank. (1992). *World Development Report 1992.* New York: Oxford University Press.

Chapter 11

Anderson, M. (1971). *Family Structure in Nineteenth-Century Lancashire.* Cambridge, UK: Cambridge University Press.

Arat-Koc, S. (1993). "The Politics of Family and Immigration in the Subordination of Domestic Workers in Canada." In B. Fox, ed., *Family Patterns, Gender Relations* (pp. 278–97). Toronto: Oxford University Press.

Baker, M. (1995). *Canadian Family Policies.* Toronto: University of Toronto Press.

Bernard, J. (1972). *The Future of Marriage.* New Haven, CT: Yale University Press.

Blumenstein, P., and P. Schwartz. (1983). *American Couples.* New York: William Morrow.

Boulton, M. (1983). *On Being a Mother: A Study of Women with Preschool Children.* London: Tavistock.

Bradbury, B. (1982). "The Fragmented Family: Family Strategies in the Face of Death, Illness and Poverty, Montreal, 1860–1885." In J. Parr, ed., *Childhood and Family.* (pp. 109–29). Toronto: McClelland and Stewart.

Brown, S., J. Lumley, R. Small, and J. Astbury. (1994). *Missing Voices: The Experiences of Motherhood.* Melbourne: Oxford University Press.

Collier, J., M. Rosaldo, and S. Yanagisako. (1982). "Is There a Family? New Anthropological Views." In B. Thorne with M. Yalom, eds., *Rethinking the Family* (pp. 25–40). New York: Longman.

Cott, N. (1977). *Bonds of Womanhood: "Women's Sphere" in New England, 1780–1835.* New Haven, CT: Yale University Press.

Crawford, M., and R. Gartner. (1992). *Woman Killing. A Report Prepared for the Women We Honor Action Committee, The Women's Directorate.* Toronto: The Women's Directorate.

Davidoff, L., and C. Hall. (1987). *Family Fortunes: Men and Women in the English Middle Class, 1780–1850.* Chicago: University of Chicago Press.

Eyer, D. (1996). *Motherguilt: How Our Culture Blames Mothers for What's Wrong with Society.* New York: Random House.

Fausto-Sterling, A. (1985). *Myths of Gender: Biological Theories about Women and Men.* New York: Basic Books.

Finch, J. (1989). *Family Obligations and Social Change.* Cambridge, UK: Polity Press.

Finnie, R. (1993). "Women, Men and the Economic Consequences of Divorce: Evidence from Canadian Longitudinal Data." *Canadian Review of Sociology and Anthropology, 30* (2), 205–41.

Flandrin, J. (1979). *Families in Former Times: Kinship, Household and Sexuality.* Cambridge, UK: Cambridge University Press.

Fox, B. (1997). "Reproducing Difference: Changes in the Lives of Partners Becoming Parents." In M. Luxton, ed., *Feminism and Families.* Halifax: Fernwood.

Furstenberg, F., and A. Cherlin. (1991). *Divided Families: What Happens to Children When Parents Part.* Cambridge, UK: Harvard University Press.

Gaskell, J. (1983). "The Reproduction of Family Life: Perspectives of Male and Female Adolescents." In J. Veevers, ed., *Continuity and Change in Marriage and Family* (pp. 219–34). Toronto: Holt, Rinehart and Winston.

Gerson, K. (1985). *Hard Choices: How Women Decide about Work, Career and Motherhood.* Berkeley, CA: University of California Press.

Goelman, H., A. Pence, D. Lero, L. Brockman, N. Glick, and J. Berkowitz. (1992). *Canadian National Child Care Study.* Statistics Canada, Cat. no. 89-527E. Ottawa: Health and Welfare Canada.

Graham, H. (1987). "Being Poor: Perceptions and Coping Strategies of Lone Mothers." In J. Brannen and G. Wilson, eds., *Give and Take in Families: Studies in Resource Distribution* (pp. 56–74) London: Allen and Unwin.

Greven, P. (1973). "Family Structure in Seventeenth-Century Andover, Massachusetts." In M. Gordon, ed., *The American Family in Social-Historical Perspective* (pp. 77–100). New York: St. Martin's Press.

Hanawalt, B. (1986). *The Ties that Bound: Peasant Families in Medieval England.* New York: Oxford University Press.

Hareven, T. (1982). *Family Time and Industrial Time: The Relationship between Family and Work in a New England Industrial Community.* Cambridge, UK: Cambridge University Press.

Hertz, R. (1986). *More Equal than Others: Women and Men in Dual-Career Marriages.* Berkeley, CA: University of California Press.

Hochschild, A. (1989). *The Second Shift: Working Parents and the Revolution at Home.* New York: Viking.

Iacovetta, F. (1992). *Such Hardworking People: Italian Immigrants in Postwar Toronto.* Montreal and Kingston, ON: McGill-Queen's University Press.

Lasch, C. (1977). *Haven in a Heartless World: The Family Beseiged.* New York: Basic Books.

Laslett, B., and J. Brenner. (1989). "Gender and Social Reproduction: Historical Perspectives." *Annual Review of Sociology, 15,* 381–404.

Laslett, P., and R. Wall, eds. (1972). *Household and Family in Past Time.* Cambridge, UK: Cambridge University Press.

Leacock, E.B. (1981). *Myths of Male Dominance: Collected Articles on Women Cross-Culturally.* New York: Monthly Review Press.

Lee, R.B. (1979). *The !Kung San: Men, Women and Work in a Foraging Society.* Cambridge, UK: Cambridge University Press.

Lewontin, R.C., S. Rose, and L. Kamin. (1984). *Not in Our Genes: Biology, Ideology and Human Nature.* New York: Pantheon.

Luxton, M. (1980). *More than a Labour of Love: Three Generations of Women's Work in the Home.* Toronto: Women's Press.

Marcil-Gratton, N. (1993). "Growing Up with a Single Parent: A Transitional Experience? Some Demographic Measurements." In J. Hudson and B. Galaway, eds., *Single Parent Families: Perspectives on Research and Policy* (pp. 73–90). Toronto: Thompson Educational Publishing.

Marshall, C. (1994). "Household Chores." In *Canadian Social Trends.* Vol. 2 (pp. 197–200) Toronto: Thompson Educational Publishing.

May, E. (1988). *Homeward Bound: American Families in the Cold War Era.* New York: Basic Books.

May, M. (1985). "Bread before Roses: American Workingmen, Labor Unions and the Family Wage." In R. Milkman, ed., *Women, Work and Protest: A Century of U.S. Women's Labor History* (pp. 1–22). Boston: Routledge and Kegan Paul.

McKie, C. (1993). "An Overview of Lone Parenthood in Canada." In J. Hudson and B. Galaway, eds., *Single Parent Families: Perspectives on Research and Policy* (pp. 53–72). Toronto: Thompson Educational Publishing.

McLanahan, S. (1985). "Family Structure and the Reproduction of Poverty." *American Journal of Sociology, 90* (4), 873–901.

McLanahan, S., and L. Bumpass. (1988). "Intergenerational Consequences of Family Disruption." *American Journal of Sociology, 94* (1), 130–52.

Mitterauer, M., and R. Sieder. (1982). *The European Family: Patriarchy to Partnership from the Middle Ages to the Present.* Oxford: Basil Blackwell.

Morton, M. (1988). "Dividing the Wealth, Sharing the Poverty: The (Re)formation of 'Family' in Law in Ontario." *Canadian Review of Sociology and Anthropology, 25* (2), 254–76.

National Council of Welfare. (1996). *Poverty Profile 1994.* Ottawa: Supply and Services Canada.

Oakley, A. (1980). *Women Confined: Towards a Sociology of Childbirth.* Oxford: Martin Robertson.

O'Brien, C.A., and L. Weir. (1995). "Lesbians and Gay Men Inside and Outside Families." In N. Mandell and A. Duffy, eds., *Canadian Families: Diversity, Conflict, and Change* (pp. 111–39). Toronto: Harcourt Brace.

Parsons, T., and R. Bales. (1955). *Family, Socialization and Interaction Process.* New York: Free Press.

Rapp, R., and E. Ross. (1986). "The 1920s: Feminism, Consumerism and Political Backlash in the U.S." In J. Friedlander, B. Cook, A. Kessler-Harris, and C. Smith-Rosenberg, eds., *Women in Culture and Politics* (pp. 52–62). Bloomington, IN: Indiana University Press.

Rosenberg, H. (1987). "Motherwork, Stress and Depression: The Costs of Privatized Social Reproduction." In H.J. Maroney and M. Luxton, eds., *Feminism and Political Economy: Women's Work, Women's Struggles* (pp. 181–97). Toronto: Methuen.

Russell, S. (1987). "The Hidden Curriculum of School: Reproducing Gender and Class Hierarchies." In H.J. Maroney and M. Luxton, eds., *Feminism and Political Economy: Women's Work, Women's Struggles* (pp. 229–45). Toronto: Methuen.

Rutter, M. (1981). "Social-Emotional Consequences of Day Care for Preschool Children." *American Journal of Orthopsychiatry, 51* (1), 374–98.

Smith-Rosenberg, C. (1975). "The Female World of Love and Ritual: Relations between Women in Nineteenth-Century America." *Signs, 1* (1), 1–31.

Stack, C. (1974). *All Our Kin: Strategies for Survival in a Black Community.* New York: Harper and Row.

Stansell, C. (1987). *City of Women: Sex and Class in New York, 1789–1860.* Urbana, IL: University of Illinois Press.

Statistics Canada. (1992a). *Families: Number, Type and Structure.* 1991 Census of Canada. Cat. no. 93-312, Table 3. Ottawa: Industry, Science and Technology Canada.

Statistics Canada. (1992b). *Lone Parent Families in Canada.* Cat. no. 89-522E, Occasional. Ottawa: Industry, Science and Technology Canada.

Statistics Canada. (1993a). *A Portrait of Families in Canada*. Cat. no. 89-523E, Occasional, Table 1.4. Ottawa: Industry, Science and Technology Canada.

Statistics Canada. (1993b). *Labour Force Activity of Women by Presence of Children*. 1991 Census of Canada. Cat. no. 93-325, Table 1. Ottawa: Industry, Science and Technology Canada.

Tilly, L., and J.W. Scott. (1978). *Women, Work and Family*. New York: Holt, Rinehart and Winston.

Turnbull, C. (1961). *The Forest People*. New York: Doubleday.

Weitzman, L. (1984). "Sex-Role Socialization: A Focus on Women." In J. Freeman, ed., *Women: A Feminist Perspective* (pp. 157–238). Palo Alto, CA: Mayfield.

Weston, K. (1991). *Families We Choose: Lesbians, Gays, Kinship*. New York: Columbia University Press.

Chapter 12

Althauser, Robert. (1989). "Internal Labor Markets." *Annual Review of Sociology*, 15, 143–61.

Andrew, Caroline, Céline Coderre, and Ann Denis. (1994). "Women in Management: The Canadian Experience." In Nancy J. Adler and Dafna N. Izraeli, eds., *Competitive Frontiers: Women Managers in a Global Economy* (pp. 377–87). Cambridge, MA: Oxford University Press.

Becker, Gary S. (1975). *Human Capital: A Theoretical and Empirical Analysis with Special Reference to Education*, 3rd ed. Chicago: University of Chicago Press.

Bell, Daniel. (1976). *The Coming of Post-industrial Society*. New York: Basic Books.

Bell, E.M. (1990). "The Bicultural Life Experiences of Career-Oriented Black Women." *Journal of Organizational Behavior*, 11, 459–77.

Bendix, Reinhard. (1974). *Work and Authority in Industry*. Berkeley, CA: University of California Press.

Blauner, Robert. (1964). *Alienation and Freedom*. Chicago: University of Chicago Press.

Braverman, Harry. (1974). *Labor and Monopoly Capital: The Degradation of Work in the Twentieth Century*. New York: Monthly Review Press.

Bridges, William. (1994). *Job Shift: How to Prosper in a Workplace without Jobs*. Don Mills, ON: Addison-Wesley.

Burawoy, Michael. (1979). *Manufacturing Consent: Changes in the Labour Process under Monopoly Capitalism*. Chicago: University of Chicago Press.

Calliste, Agnes. (1993). "Sleeping Car Porters in Canada: An Ethnically Submerged Split Labour Market." In Graham S. Lowe and Harvey Krahn, eds., *Work in Canada: Readings in the Sociology of Work and Industry* (pp. 139–53). Scarborough, ON: Nelson.

Campell, Andrew. (1996). "From Shop Floor to Computer Room." *The Globe and Mail*, December 30, pp. A1, A8.

Canadian Labour Congress. (1993). "Two Years under Free Trade: An Assessment." In Graham S. Lowe and Harvey Krahn, eds., *Work in Canada: Readings in the Sociology of Work and Industry* (pp. 115–19). Scarborough, ON: Nelson.

Carey, Alex. (1967). "The Hawthorne Studies: A Radical Criticism." *American Sociological Review*, 32, 403–16.

Chamberlain, Art. (1996). "Surprise! We're Happy in Our Work, Poll Shows." *The Toronto Sun*, October 8, p. A1.

Dassbach, Carl H.A. (1996). "Lean Production, Labor Control, and Post-Fordism in the Japanese Automobile Industry." In William C. Green and Ernest J. Yanarella, eds., *North American Auto Unions in Crisis: Lean Production as Contested Terrain* (pp. 19–40). Albany, NY: SUNY Press.

Economic Council of Canada. (1991). *Good Jobs, Bad Jobs: Employment in the Service Economy*. Ottawa: Supply and Services Canada.

Edwards, P.K., and Hugh Scullion. (1982). *The Social Organization of Industrial Conflict*. Oxford: Blackwell.

Edwards, Richard. (1979). *Contested Terrain: The Transformation of the Workplace in the Twentieth Century*. New York: Basic Books.

Friedson, Eliot. (1970). *The Profession of Medicine: A Study in the Sociology of Applied Knowledge*. New York: Harper and Row.

Galarneau, Diane. (1996). "Unionized Workers." *Perspectives on Labour and Income*, (Spring), 42–52.

Gibb-Clark, Margot. (1996). "Fewer People Work 'Normal' Week." *The Globe and Mail*, September 19, p. B11.

Graham, Laurie. (1995). *On the Line at Subaru-Isuzu: The Japanese Model and the American Worker*. Ithaca, NY: ILR Press and Cornell University Press.

Hall, Marny. (1993). "Private Experiences in the Public Domain: Lesbians in Organizations." In Jeffrey Hearn, Deborah L. Sheppard, Peta Tancred-Sheriff, and Gibson Burrell, eds., *The Sexuality of Organization* (pp. 125–38). Berkeley, CA: Sage.

Henson, Kevin D. (1996). *Just a Temp*. Philadelphia: Temple University Press.

Hodson, Randy, and Teresa Sullivan. (1985). "Totem or Tyrant? Monopoly, Regional and Local Sector Effects on Worker Commitment." *Social Forces*, 63 (3), 716–31.

Hodson, Randy, and Teresa Sullivan. (1990). *The Social Organization of Work*. Belmont, CA: Wadsworth.

Inglis, Sarah. (1994). "McDonald's Union Drive-Thru: Sarah Inglis Tells Her Story." *Our Times*, (June/July), 39–41.

Jones, Frank E. (1996). *Understanding Organizations: A Sociological Perspective*. Cooksville, ON: Copp Clark.

Kamata, Satoshi. (1982). *Japan in the Passing Lane: An Insider's Account of Life in a Japanese Auto Factory*. Trans. T. Akimoto. New York: Pantheon.

Kanter, Rosabeth Moss. (1977). *Men and Women of the Corporation*. New York: Basic Books.

Krahn, Harvey J. (1992). *Quality of Work in the Service Economy*. General Social Survey Analysis Series 6. Cat. no. 11-612E, no. 6. Ottawa: Statistics Canada.

Krahn, Harvey J., and Graham S. Lowe. (1993). *Work, Industry and Canadian Society*, 2nd ed. Scarborough, ON: Nelson.

Laxer, Gordon. (1989). *Open for Business: The Roots of Foreign Ownership in Canada*. Don Mills, ON: Oxford University Press.

Livingstone, D.W. (1993). "Conclusion: Aging Dinosaurs or All-Round Workers?" In June Corman, Meg Luxton, D.W. Livingstone, and Wally Secombe, eds., *Recasting Steel Labour: The Stelco Story* (pp. 145–55). Halifax: Fernwood.

Lowe, Graham S. (1987). *Women in the Administrative Revolution: The Feminization of Clerical Work*. Toronto: University of Toronto Press.

McKay, Shona. (1993). "Willing and Able." In Graham S. Lowe and Harvey Krahn, eds., *Work in Canada: Readings in the Sociology of Work and Industry* (pp. 166–71). Scarborough, ON: Nelson.

McLaughlin, D.B. (1983). "Electronics and the Future of Work: The Impact on Pink and White Collar Workers." *Annals of the American Academy of Political and Social Science*, 470, 152–62.

Miles, J. (1850). *Chapters in the Life of a Dundee Factory Boy*. Cited in Keith Grint. (1991). *The Sociology of Work: An Introduction*. Cambridge, UK: Blackwell.

Milkman, Ruth, and Cydney Pullman. (1991). "Technological Change in an Auto Assembly Plant: The Impact on Workers' Tasks and Skills." *Work and Occupations*, 18, 123–47.

Morissette, René. (1991). "Are Jobs in Large Firms Better?" *Perspectives on Labour and Income*, (Autumn), 40–50.

Morissette, René, and Deborah Sunter. (1993). *What Is Happening to Weekly Hours Worked in Canada?* Ottawa: Statistics Canada.

Myles, John. (1988). "The Expanding Middle: Some Canadian Evidence on the Deskilling Debate." *Canadian Review of Sociology and Anthropology*, 25 (3), 335–64.

Myles, John. (1991). "Post-industrialism and the Service Economy." In Graham S. Lowe and Harvey Krahn, eds., *Work in Canada: Readings in the Sociology of Work and Industry* (pp. 124–34). Scarborough, ON: Nelson.

Noreau, N. (1994). "Involuntary Part-Timers." *Perspectives on Labour and Income*, 6 (3), 25–30.

O'Reilly, Brian. (1990). "Is Your Company Asking Too Much?" *Fortune*, March 12, 38–43.

Osterman, Paul. (1995). "The Transformation of Work in the United States: What the Evidence Shows." In Bryan Downie and Mary Lou Coates, eds., *Managing Human Resources in the 1990s and Beyond* (pp. 71–92). Kingston, ON: Industrial Relations Centre Press.

Polanyi, Karl. (1957). *The Great Transformation*. Boston: Beacon Press.

Powell, Gary. (1990). "One More Time: Do Female and Male Managers Differ?" *Academy of Management Executive*, 4 (August), 68–75.

Rifkin, Jeremy. (1995). *The End of Work: The Decline of the Global Labor Force and the Dawn of the Post Market Era*. New York: G.P. Putnam.

Rinehart, James. (1986). "Improving the Quality of Working Life through Job Redesign: Work Humanization or Work Rationalization?" *Canadian Review of Sociology and Anthropology*, 23 (4), 507–30.

Rinehart, James. (1996). *The Tyranny of Work: Alienation and the Labour Process*, 3rd ed. Toronto: Harcourt Brace.

Rinehart, James, David Robertson, Chris Huxley, and Jeff Wareham. (1994). "Reunifying Conception and Execution of Work under Japanese Production Management? A Canadian Case Study." In Tony Elger and Chris Smith, eds., *Global Japanization? The Transnational Transformation of the Labour Process* (pp. 152–74). London: Routledge.

Robertson, David, James Rinehart, Christopher Huxley, Jeff Wareham, Herman Rosenfeld, Alan McGough, and Steve Benedict. (1993). *The CAMI Report: Lean Production in a Unionized Auto Plant*. North York, ON: CAW Research.

Robertson, David, and Jeff Wareham. (1990). *Technological Change: Air Canada Customer Sales and Service*. North York, ON: CAW Research.

Rosener, Judy B. (1990). "Ways Women Lead." *Harvard Business Review*, November/December, 119–25.

Shain, Alan. (1995). "Employment of People with Disabilities." *Canadian Social Trends*, (Autumn), 8–13.

Sheppard, Deborah L. (1993). "Women Managers' Perceptions of Gender and Organizational Life." In Jeffrey Hearn, Deborah L. Sheppard, Peta Tancred-Sheriff, and Gibson Burrell, eds., *The Sexuality of Organization* (pp. 151–66). Berkeley, CA: Sage.

Solo, Sally. (1990). "Stop Whining and Get Back to Work." *Fortune*, March 12, 49–50.

Spenner, Kenneth. (1983). "Deciphering Prometheus: Temporal Change in the Skill Level of Work." *American Sociological Review*, 48 (6), 824–37.

Toffler, Alvin. (1980). *The Third Wave*. New York: Bantam.

Wallace, Bruce. (1994). "Reward or Sacrifice?" *Maclean's*, March 14, 38–40.

Wallace, Michael. (1989). "Brave New Workplace: Technology and Work in the New Economy." *Work and Occupations*, 16 (4), 393–415.

White, Julie. (1993). "Patterns of Unionization." In Linda Briskin and Patricia McDermott, eds., *Women Challenging Unions: Feminism, Democracy and Militancy* (pp. 191–206). Toronto: University of Toronto Press.

Womack, J., D. Jones, and D. Roos. (1990). *The Machine that Changed the World*. New York: Rawson and Associates.

Zuboff, Shoshana. (1988). *In the Age of the Smart Machine: The Future of Work and Power*. New York: Basic Books.

Chapter 13

Apple, M. (1988). *Teachers and Texts.* New York: Routledge.

Axelrod, P. (1990). *Making a Middle Class: Student Life in English Canada During the Thirties.* Montreal and Kingston, ON: McGill-Queen's University Press.

Bellamy, L., and N. Guppy. (1992). "Opportunities and Obstacles for Women in Canadian Higher Education." In J. Gaskell and A. McLaren, eds., *Women and Education* (pp. 163–92). Calgary: Detselig.

Bernstein, B. (1977). *Class, Codes and Control.* Vol. 3: *Toward a Theory of Educational Transmission,* 2nd ed. London: Routledge and Kegan Paul.

Blau, P., and O. Duncan. (1967). *The American Occupational Structure.* New York: Wiley.

Bourdieu, P., and J.-C. Passeron. (1977). *Reproduction in Education, Society and Culture.* Beverly Hills, CA: Sage.

Bowles, S., and H. Gintis. (1976). *Schooling in Capitalist America.* New York: Basic Books.

Collins, R. (1979). *The Credential Society.* New York: Academic Press.

Cornbleth, C., and D. Walker. (1995). *The Great Speckled Bird: Multicultural Politics and Education Policy Making.* New York: St. Martin's Press.

Cummins, J., and M. Danesi. (1990). *Heritage Languages: The Development and Denial of Canada's Linguistic Resources.* Toronto: Ourschools/Ourselves.

Dreeben, R. (1968). *On What Is Learned in School.* Boston: Addison-Wesley.

Economic Council of Canada. (1964). *Annual Review.* Ottawa: Queen's Printer.

Economic Council of Canada. (1992). *A Lot to Learn: Education and Training in Canada.* Ottawa: Supply and Services Canada.

Eyre, L. (1992). "Gender Relations in the Classroom: A Fresh Look at Coeducation." In J. Gaskell and A. McLaren, eds., *Women and Education* (pp. 193–220). Calgary: Detselig.

Fleming, W.G. (1974). *The Individualized System: Findings from Five Studies.* Toronto, ON: OISE.

Gaskell, J. (1992). *Gender Matters from School to Work.* Milton Keynes, UK: Open University Press.

Gidney, B., and W. Millar. (1990). *Inventing Secondary Education: The Rise of the High School in Nineteenth Century Ontario.* Montreal and Kingston, ON: McGill-Queen's University Press.

Gilbert, S. (1993). *Leaving School: Results from a National Survey Comparing School Leavers and High School Graduates 18 to 20 Years of Age.* Ottawa: Human Resources and Development Canada.

Guppy, N. (1984). "Access to Higher Education in Canada." *Canadian Journal of Higher Education, 14* (3), 79–93.

Guppy, N., and K. Pendakur. (1989). "The Effects of Gender and Parental Education on Participation within Post-secondary Education in the 1970's and 1980's." *Canadian Journal of Higher Education, 19* (1), 49–62.

Hodgetts, A.B. (1964). *What Culture? What Heritage? A Study of Civic Education in Canada.* Toronto: OISE.

Jencks, C. (1972). *Inequality.* New York: Basic Books.

Kelly, D. (1995). *Balancing Diversity and Community: A Large Urban High School Adopts the Mini School Approach.* Toronto: Canadian Education Association.

Kerckhoff, A. (1990). *Getting Started: Transition to Adulthood in Great Britain.* Boulder, CO: Westview Press.

Knotterus, J. (1987). "Status Attainment Research and Its Image of Society." *American Sociological Review, 52* (1), 113–21.

Lareau, A. (1991). *Home Advantage: Social Class and Parental Intervention in Elementary Education.* Philadelphia: Falmer Press.

Lazerson, M., J. McLaughlin, B. McPherson, and S. Bailey. (1985). *An Education of Value.* Cambridge, UK: Cambridge University Press.

Marchak, P. (1975). *Ideological Perspectives on Canada.* Toronto: McGraw Hill.

McNeil, L. (1986). *Contradictions of Control, School Structures and School Knowledge.* New York: Routledge.

Olsen, P., and P. Burns. (1983). "Politics, Class and Happenstance: French Immersion in a Canadian Context." *Interchange, 14* (1), 1–17.

Ornstein, M. (1983). "Class Gender and Job Income in Canada." *Research in Social Stratification and Mobility, 2,* 41–75.

Osborne, K. (1980). *"Hard Working, Temperate and Peaceable": The Portrayal of Workers in Canadian History Textbooks.* Winnipeg: University of Manitoba.

Parsons, T. (1959). "The School Class as a Social System." *Harvard Educational Review, 29,* 297–318.

Pike, R. (1981). "Sociological Research on Higher Education in English Canada, 1970–1980: A Thematic Review." *Canadian Journal of Higher Education, 11* (2), 1–25.

Porter, J. (1965). *The Vertical Mosaic.* Toronto: University of Toronto Press.

Reich, R. (1991). *The Work of Nations: Preparing Ourselves for 21st Century Capitalism.* New York: Knopf.

Richer, S. (1979). "Sex Role Socialization and Early Schooling." *Canadian Review of Sociology and Anthropology, 16,* (2), 195–205.

Rumberger, R. (1981). *Overeducation in the U.S. Labor Market.* New York: Praeger.

Shepherd, J., and G. Vulliamy. (1983). "A Comparative Sociology of School Knowledge." *British Journal of Sociology of Education, 4* (1), 3–18.

Tomkins, G.S. (1986). *A Common Countenance: Stability and Change in the Canadian Curriculum.* Scarborough, ON: Prentice Hall.

Willis, P. (1977). *Learning to Labour.* Farnborough, UK: Saxon House Press.

Chapter 14

Abu-Lughod, Janet L. (1991). *Changing Cities: Urban Sociology*. New York: HarperCollins.

Bell, Wendell. (1968). "The City, the Suburbs and a Theory of Social Choice." In Scott Greer, Dennis McElrath, David W. Minar, and Peter Orleans, eds., *The New Urbanization* (pp. 132–68). New York: St. Martin's Press.

Berger, Bennett. (1960). *Working Class Suburb*. Berkeley, CA: University of California Press.

Brym, Robert J. (1986). "An Introduction to the Regional Question in Canada." In Robert J. Brym, ed., *Regionalism in Canada* (pp. 1–45). Toronto: Irwin.

Burgess, Ernest W. (1961). "The Growth of the City: An Introduction to a Research Project." In George A. Theodorson, ed., *Studies in Human Ecology* (pp. 37–44). Evanston, IL: Row, Peterson.

Castells, Manuel. (1989). *The Informational City: Information, Technology, Economic Restructuring and the Urban–Regional Process*. Oxford and Cambridge, MA: Blackwell.

Chandler, Tertius, and Gerald Fox. (1974). *3000 Years of Urban Growth*. New York and London: Academic Press.

Clairmont, Donald, and Dennis Magill. (1974). *Africville: The Life and Death of a Canadian Black Community*. Toronto: McClelland and Stewart.

Davis, Mike. (1990). *City of Quartz: Excavating the Future in Los Angeles*. London and New York: Verso.

Driedger, Leo. (1991). *The Urban Factor: Sociology of Canadian Cities*. Toronto: Oxford University Press.

Egan, Timothy. (1995). "The Serene Fortress: Many Seek Security behind Walls and Guards of Private Communities." *New York Times*, September 3, pp. 1, 10.

Fava, Sylvia Fleis. (1956). "Suburbanism as a Way of Life." *American Sociological Review*, 21, 34–37.

Filion, Pierre. (1991). "The Gentrification–Social Structure Dialectic: A Toronto Case Study." *International Journal of Urban and Regional Research*, 15, 553–74.

Firey, Walter. (1947). *Land Use in Central Boston*. Cambridge, MA: Harvard University Press.

Fishman, Robert. (1987). *Bourgeois Utopias: The Rise and Fall of Suburbia*. New York: Basic Books.

Fishman, Robert. (1990). "Megalopolis Unbound." *The Wilson Quarterly*, (Winter), 25–45.

Florence, Elinor. (1997). "A Happy Hoofer Gets On with Life." *The Globe and Mail*, January 7, p. A18.

Fowler, Edmund P. (1992). *Building Cities that Work*. Montreal and Kingston, ON: McGill-Queen's University Press.

Frieden, Bernard J., and Lynne B. Sagalyn. (1989). *Downtown, Inc.: How America Rebuilds Cities*. Cambridge, MA: The MIT Press.

Garrau, Joel. (1991). *Edge City: Life on the New Frontier*. New York: Doubleday.

Goldberger, Paul. (1996). "The Rise of the Private City." In Julia Vitullo Martin, ed., *Breaking Away: The Future of Cities* (pp. 135–47). New York: The Twentieth Century Fund Press.

Golden, Hilda H. (1981). *Urbanization and Cities*. Lexington, MA: D.C. Heath.

Goldsmith, Charles. (1996). "Prefab Irish Pubs Sell Pints World-Wide." *Wall Street Journal*, October 25, pp. B1 and B5.

Gordon, Ian, and Saskia Sassen. (1992). "Restructuring the Urban Labor Markets." In Susan S. Fainstein, Ian Gordon, and Michael Harloe, eds., *Divided Cities: New York and London in the Contemporary World* (pp. 105–28). Oxford and Cambridge, MA: Blackwell.

Hannigan, John A. (1995). "The Postmodern City: A New Urbanization?" *Current Sociology*, 43 (1), 152–217.

Harris, Chauncey, and Edward Ullman. (1945). "The Nature of Cities." *Annals of the American Academy of Political and Social Science*, 242 (November), 7–17.

Hauser, Philip M. (1965). "Urbanization: An Overview." In Philip M. Hauser and Leo F. Schnore, eds., *The Study of Urbanization*. New York: Wiley.

Hoyt, Homer. (1939). *The Structure and Growth of Residential Neighborhoods in American Cities*. Washington, DC: Federal Housing Authority.

Jackson, Kenneth T. (1985). *Crabgrass Frontier: The Suburbanization of the United States*. New York: Oxford University Press.

Jensen, Brigitte, Richard Mozoff, and Anthony H. Richmond. (1970). *Sociological Aspects of Urban Renewal in Toronto*. Toronto: York University, Institute for Behavioural Research.

Kleniewski, Nancy. (1997). *Cities, Change and Conflict: A Political Economy of Urban Life*. Belmont, CA: Wadsworth.

Leinberger, Christopher B., and Charles Lockwood. (1986). "How Business Is Reshaping America." *The Atlantic Monthly*, 258, (October), pp. 43–52.

Ley, David. (1991a). "Gentrification." In Kent Gerecke, ed., *The Canadian City* (pp. 181–96). Montreal: Black Rose Books.

Ley, David. (1991b). "The Inner City." In Trudi Bunting and Pierre Filion, eds., *Canadian Cities in Transition* (pp. 313–48). Toronto: Oxford University Press.

Logan, John R., and Harvey L. Molotch. (1987). *Urban Fortunes: The Political Economy of Place*. Berkeley, CA: University of California Press.

Lorimer, James. (1978). *The Developers*. Toronto: Lorimer.

Lorinc, John (1996). "Trespassers Will Be Prosecuted." *Toronto Life*, September, pp. 47–52.

McGahan, Peter. (1995). *Urban Sociology in Canada*, 3rd ed. Toronto: Harcourt Brace.

McKenzie, Evan. (1989). "Morning in Privatopia." *Dissent*, 36 (Spring), 257–60.

Michelson, William D. (1973). *Environmental Change*. Research Paper No. 60, Centre for Urban and Community Studies, University of Toronto.

Nader, George A. (1975). *Cities of Canada, Volume One: Theoretical, Historical and Planning Perspectives.* Toronto: Macmillan.

Palen, J. John. (1992). *The Urban World*, 4th ed. New York: McGraw Hill.

Palen, J. John. (1995). *The Suburbs.* New York: McGraw Hill.

Reid, Barton. (1991). "A Primer on the Corporate City." In Kent Gerecke, ed., *The Canadian City* (pp. 63–78). Montreal: Black Rose.

Reynolds, Malvina. (1964). *Little Boxes and Other Handmade Songs.* New York: Oak.

Rose, D. (1984). "Rethinking Gentrification: Beyond the Uneven Development of Marxist Urban Theory." *Environment and Planning D: Society and Space, 2* (1), 47–74.

Seeley, R.A. Sim, and E.W. Loosley. (1956). *Crestwood Heights: A Study of the Culture of Suburban Life.* New York: Wiley.

Sewell, John. (1993). *The Shape of the City: Toronto Struggles with Modern Planning.* Toronto: University of Toronto Press.

Simmel, Georg. (1950). "The Metropolis and Mental Life." In Kurt H. Wolff, ed. and trans., *The Sociology of Georg Simmel* (pp. 409–24). Glencoe, IL: The Free Press.

Smith, Neil. (1979). "Towards a Theory of Gentrification." *Journal of the American Planning Association, 45*, 538–48.

Smith, Neil, and Michael LeFaivre. (1984). "A Class Analysis of Gentrification." In John J. Palen and Brian London, eds., *Gentrification, Displacement and Neighborhood Revitalization* (pp. 43–64). Albany, NY: SUNY Press.

Social Planning Council of Hamilton and District. (1963). *The Social Costs of Urban Renewal.* Hamilton, ON: SPCHD.

Sorkin, Michael. (1992). "Introduction: Variations on a Theme Park." In Michael Sorkin, ed., *Variations on a Theme Park: The New American City and the End of Public Space* (pp. xi–xv). New York: The Noonday Press.

Stone, Leroy O. (1967). *Urban Development in Canada.* Ottawa: Dominion Bureau of Statistics.

Thomas, William I., and Florian Znaniecki. (1918–20). *The Polish Peasant in Europe and America*, 5 vols. Chicago: University of Chicago Press.

Tönnies, Ferdinand (1957 [1887]). *Community and Society.* Trans. Charles Loomis. East Lansing, MI: Michigan State University Press.

Warde, Alan. (1991). "Gentrification as Consumption: Issues of Class and Gender." *Environment and Planning D: Society and Space, 9* (2), 223–32.

Weber, A.F.(1963 [1899]). *The Growth of Cities in the Nineteenth Century.* Ithaca, NY: Cornell University Press.

Whyte, William H. (1956). *The Organization Man.* New York: Simon and Schuster.

Wilson, Elizabeth. (1991). *The Sphinx in the City: Urban Life, the Control of Disorder, and Women.* London: Virago Press.

Wirth, Louis. (1938). "Urbanism as a Way of Life." *American Journal of Sociology, 44*, 1–24.

Wittberg, Patricia. (1992). "Perspectives on Gentrification: A Comparative Review of the Literature." *Research in Urban Sociology, 2*, 17–46.

Zimmer, Basil G. (1964). *Rebuilding Cities: The Effects of Displacement and Relocation on Small Business.* Chicago: Quadrangle Books.

Zorbaugh, Harvey. (1929). *The Gold Coast and the Slum.* Chicago: University of Chicago Press.

Chapter 15

Adams, W.M. (1990). *Green Development: Environment and Sustainability in the Third World.* New York: Oxford University Press.

Bakvis, H., and N. Nevitte. (1992). "The Greening of the Canadian Electorate: Environmentalism, Ideology and Partisanship." In R. Boardman, ed., *Canadian Environmental Policy: Ecosystems, Politics and Process* (pp. 144–63). Toronto: Oxford University Press.

Blowers, A., D. Lowry, and B.D. Solomon. (1991). *The International Politics of Nuclear Waste.* London: Macmillan.

Bullard, R.D. (1990). *Dumping in Dixie: Race, Class and Environmental Quality.* Boulder, CO: Westview Press.

Buttel, F.H. (1975). "The Environmental Movement: Consensus, Conflict and Change." *Journal of Environmental Education, 7*, 53–63.

Buttel, F.H. (1987). "New Directions in Environmental Sociology." *Annual Review of Sociology, 13*, 465–88.

Cable, S., and M. Benson. (1993). "Acting Locally: Environmental Injustice and the Emergence of Grassroots Environmental Organizations." *Social Problems, 40*, 464–77.

Capek, S.M. (1993). "The Environmental Justice Frame: A Conceptual Discussion and an Application." *Social Problems, 40*, 5–24.

Clarke, L., and J.F. Short, Jr. (1993). "Social Organization and Risk: Some Current Controversies." *Annual Review of Sociology, 19*, 375–99.

Cotgrove, S. (1982). *Catastrophe or Cornucopia: The Environment, Politics, and the Future.* Chichester, UK: Wiley.

Cotgrove, S., and A. Duff. (1981). "Environmentalism, Values and Social Change." *British Journal of Sociology, 32*, 92–110.

Cylke, F.K., Jr. (1993). *The Environment.* New York: HarperCollins College.

Derksen, L., and J. Gartrell. (1993). "The Social Context of Recycling." *American Sociological Review, 58*, 434–42.

Devall, B., and G. Sessions. (1985). *Deep Ecology: Living As If Nature Mattered.* Salt Lake City, UT: Peregrine Smith Books.

Downs, A. (1972). "Up and Down with Ecology: The 'Issue-Attention Cycle.'" *The Public Interest, 28,* 38–55.

Duncan, O.D. (1959). "Human Ecology and Population Studies." In P.M. Hauser and O.D. Duncan, eds., *The Study of Population* (pp. 678–716). Chicago: University of Chicago Press.

Dunlap, R.E., and W.R. Catton Jr. (1979). "Environmental Sociology." *Annual Review of Sociology, 5,* 243–73.

Dunlap, R.E., and W.R. Catton Jr. (1983). "What Environmental Sociologists Have in Common (Whether Concerned with 'Built' or 'Natural' Environments)." *Sociological Inquiry, 53,* 113–35.

Dunlap, R.E., and K.D. Van Liere. (1978). "The New Environmental Paradigm: A Proposed Measuring Instrument and Preliminary Results." *Journal of Environmental Education, 9,* 10–19.

Dwyer, A. (1992). "The Trouble at Great Whale." *Equinox,* (January/February), 28–41.

d'Eaubonne, F. (1974). *La Feminisme ou la Mort.* Paris: P. Horay.

Eyerman, R., and A. Jamison. (1989). "Environmental Knowledge as an Organizational Weapon: The Case of Greenpeace." *Social Science Information, 28,* 99–119.

Fields, D.M. (1993). "We Can't Grow on Like This (Review of *Beyond the Limits*)." *The Futurist,* (January–February), 40–41.

Foster, J. (1978). *Working for Wildlife.* Toronto: University of Toronto Press.

Fowlkes, M., and P. Miller. (1987). "Chemicals and Community at Love Canal." In B.B. Johnson and V.T. Covello, eds., *The Social and Cultural Construction of Risk* (pp. 55–78). Dordrecht, Holland: D. Reidel.

Freudenburg, W.R. (1991). "Rural–Urban Differences in Environmental Concern: A Closer Look." *Sociological Inquiry, 61,* 167–98.

Freudenburg, W.R. (1993). "Risk and Recreancy: Weber, the Division of Labour and the Rationality of Risk Perceptions." *Social Forces, 71,* 909–32.

Gale, R.P. (1983). "The Environmental Movement and the Left: Antagonists or Allies?" *Sociological Inquiry, 53,* 179–99.

Gallopin, G.C., P. Gutman, and H. Maletta. (1989). "Global Impoverishment, Sustainable Development and the Environment: A Conceptual Approach." *International Social Science Journal, 41,* 375–97.

Gerhards, J., and D. Rucht. (1992). "Mesomobilization: Organizing and Framing in Two Protest Campaigns in West Germany." *American Journal of Sociology, 98,* 555–95.

Gidengil, E. (1990). "Centres and Peripheries: The Potential Culture of Dependencies." *Canadian Review of Sociology and Anthropology, 27,* 23–48.

Greenbaum, Alan. (1995). "Taking Stock of Two Decades of Research on the Social Bases of Environmental Concern." In Michael D. Mehta and Eric Ouellet, eds., *Environmental Sociology: Theory and Practice* (pp. 125–52). North York, ON: Captus Press.

Grossman, G.M., and H.R. Potter. (1977). "A Trend Analysis of Competing Models of Environmental Attitudes." Working Paper no. 127. Department of Sociology and Anthropology, Purdue University, West Lafayette, IN.

Hallman, W.K., and A. Wandersman. (1992). "Attribution of Responsibility and Individual and Collective Coping with Environmental Threats." *Journal of Social Issues, 48,* 101–18.

Hannigan, John A. (1995). *Environmental Sociology: A Social Constructionist Perspective.* London and New York: Routledge.

Harrison, K., and G. Hoberg. (1991). "Setting the Environmental Agendas in Canada and the United States: The Cases of Dioxin and Radon." *Canadian Journal of Political Science, 24,* 3–27.

Hays, S. (1959). *Conservation and the Gospel of Efficiency: The Progressive Conservation Movement.* Cambridge, MA: Harvard University Press.

Hines, J.M., H.R. Hungerford, and A.N. Tomera. (1986–87). "Analysis and Synthesis of Research on Responsible Environmental Behavior: A Meta-Analysis." *Journal of Environmental Education, 18,* 1–8.

Jones, R., and R.E. Dunlap. (1992). "The Social Bases of Environmental Concern: Have They Changed over Time?" *Rural Sociology, 57,* 28–47.

Koppes, C. (1988). "Efficiency, Equity, Esthetics: Shifting Themes in American Conservation." In D. Worster, ed., *The Ends of the Earth: Perspectives on Modern Environmental History* (pp. 230–51). Cambridge, UK: Cambridge University Press.

Kriesi, H. (1989). "New Social Movements and the New Class in the Netherlands." *American Journal of Sociology, 94,* 1078–1116.

Ladd, A.E., and S. Laska. (1991). "Opposition to Solid Waste Incineration: Pre-Implementation Anxieties Surrounding a New Environmental Controversy." *Sociological Inquiry, 61,* 299–313.

Lovelock. J. (1987). *Gaia: A New Look at Life on Earth.* Oxford: Oxford University Press.

Macdonald, D. (1991). *The Politics of Pollution: Why Canadians Are Failing Their Environment.* Toronto: McClelland and Stewart.

Maloney, M., and M. Ward. (1973). "Ecology: Let's Hear from the People: An Objective Scale for the Measurement of Ecological Attitudes and Knowledge." *American Psychologist, 28,* 583–86.

Meadows, D.H., D.L. Meadows, and J. Randers. (1992). *Beyond the Limits: Confronting Global Collapse, Envisioning a Sustainable Future.* Post Mills, VT: Chelsea Green.

Meadows, D.H., D.L. Meadows, J. Randers, and W.W. Behrens. (1972). *The Limits to Growth.* New York: Universe Books.

Milbrath, L.W. (1984). *Environmentalists: Vanguard for a New Society.* Albany, NY: SUNY Press.

Naess, A. (1973). "The Shallow and Deep Long-range Ecology Movement." *Inquiry, 16,* 95–100.

Novek, J., and K. Kampen. (1992). "Sustainable or Unsustainable Development? An Analysis of an Environmental Controversy." *Canadian Journal of Sociology, 17,* 249–73.

Perrow, C. (1984). *Normal Accidents*. New York: Basic Books.

Schnaiberg, A. (1980). *The Environment: From Surplus to Scarcity*. New York: Oxford University Press.

Schumacher, E.F. (1973). *Small Is Beautiful*. New York: Harper.

Shrivastava, P. (1987). *Bhopal: Anatomy of a Crisis*. Cambridge, MA: Ballinger.

Silvertown, J. (1989). "A Silent Spring in China." *New Scientists*, (July), 55–58.

Smith, C. (1992). *Media and Apocalypse: News Coverage of the Yellowstone Forest Fires, Exxon Valdez Oil Spill, and Loma Prieta Earthquake*. Westport, CT: Greenwood Press.

Stein, I.P. (1988). *Cities under Siege*. Toronto: Atlantic Press.

Tindall, D.B. (1994). "Collective Action in the Rainforest: Personal Networks, Collective Identity, and Participation in the Vancouver Island Wilderness Preservation Movement." Ph.D. thesis, Department of Sociology, University of Toronto.

Turner, J.H. (1981). *Sociology: Studying the Human System*, 2nd ed. Santa Monica, CA: Goodyear.

Ungar, S. (1992). "The Rise and (Relative) Decline of Global Warming as a Social Problem." *Sociological Quarterly*, 33, 483–501.

Uusitalo, L. (1990). "Are Environmental Attitudes and Behavior Inconsistent? Findings from a Finnish Study." *Scandinavian Political Studies*, 13, 211–26.

Van Liere, K.D., and R.E. Dunlap. (1980). "The Social Bases of Environmental Concern: A Review of Hypotheses, Explanations and Empirical Evidence." *Public Opinion Quarterly*, 44, 181–97.

Warren, K.J. (1990). "The Power and Promise of Ecological Feminism." *Environmental Ethics*, 12, 125–46.

Williams, G. (1992). "Greening the New Canadian Political Economy." *Studies in Political Economy*, 37, 5–30.

World Commission on Environment and Development [The Brundtland Commission]. (1987). *Our Common Future: Report to the United Nations General Assembly*. New York: Oxford University Press.

Wynne, B. (1992). "Risk and Social Learning: Reification to Engagement." In S. Krimsky and D. Golding, eds., *Social Theories of Risk* (pp. 275–97). Westport, CT: Praeger.

Yearley, S. (1991). *The Green Case: A Sociology of Environmental Issues, Arguments and Politics*. London: HarperCollins Academic.

Chapter 16

Abella, Irving, and Harold Troper. (1982). *None Is Too Many*. Toronto: Lester & Orpen Dennys.

Angus Reid Group. (1989). *Immigration to Canada: Aspects of Public Opinion*. Ottawa: Employment and Immigration Canada.

Avery, Don. (1979). *Dangerous Foreigners: European Immigrant Workers and Labour Radicalism in Canada, 1896–1932*. Toronto: McClelland and Stewart.

Beaujot, Roderic. (1996). "The Role of Immigration in Changing Demographic Structures." Paper presented at the National Symposium on Immigration and Integration, Winnipeg, October.

Beaujot, Roderic, and Kevin McQuillan. (1982). *Growth and Dualism: The Demographic Development of Canadian Society*. Toronto: Gage.

Canada. (1996). Citizenship and Immigration. *1997 Annual Immigration Plan*. Ottawa: Supply and Services Canada.

Careless, J.M.S. (1963). *Canada: A Story of Challenge*. Toronto: Macmillan.

Demeny, Paul. (1988). "Social Science and Population Policy." *Population and Development Review*, 14, 451–79.

Dionne, Claude. (1989). "Le choix d'avoir un enfant." Paper presented to Association des Economistes du Québec (ASDEQ) conference, Quebec, April.

Duchesne, Louis. (1993). "Evolution de la population au Québec et au Canada depuis un siècle et demi en l'absence de migrations." *Cahiers québécois de démographie*, 22 (1), 1–22.

Dumas, Jean. (1996). *Report on the Demographic Situation in Canada, 1995*. Statistics Canada. Cat. no. 91-209. Ottawa: Supply and Services Canada.

Economic Council of Canada. (1991). *Economic and Social Impacts of Immigration*. No. 22-176. Ottawa: Economic Council of Canada.

Ehrlich, Paul R., and Anne H. Ehrlich. (1990). *The Population Explosion*. New York: Simon and Schuster.

Fellegi, Ivan P. (1988). "Can We Afford an Aging Society?" *Canadian Economic Observer*, 1, (10), 4.1–4.34.

Howell, Nancy. (1979). *Demography of the Dobe !Kung*. New York: Academic Press.

McKeown, K., R.G. Brown, and R.G. Record. (1972). "An Interpretation of the Modern Rise of Population in Europe." *Population Studies*, 26, 345–82.

Malthus, T.R. (1798). *An Essay on the Principle of Population, as it Affects the Future Improvement of Society. With Remarks on the Speculations of Mr. Godwin, M. Condorcet and Other Writers*. London: J. Johnson.

Maslove, Allan, and David Hawkes. (1989). "The Northern Population." *Canadian Social Trends*, 15, 2–7.

Meek, Ronald L., ed. (1971). *Marx and Engels on the Population Bomb: Selections from the Writings of Marx and Engels Dealing with the Theories of Thomas Robert Malthus*. Trans. Dorothea L. Meek and Ronald L. Meek. Berkeley, CA: Ramparts Press.

Nagnur, Dhruva. (1986). *Longevity and Historical Life Tables*. Statistics Canada. Cat. no. 89-506. Ottawa: Supply and Services Canada.

Nash, Alan. (1989). "Can We Meet the Refugee Challenge?" *Policy Options*, 10 (7), 21–26.

Pacini, Marcello. (1992). Foreword to special issue, "The New Europe and International Migration." *International Migration Review*, 26 (2), 231–33.

Population Reference Bureau. (1996). *1996 World Population Data Sheet*. Washington, DC: Population Reference Bureau.

Richmond, Anthony H. (1988). *Immigration and Ethnic Conflict*. New York: St. Martin's Press.

Seward, Shirley, and Marc Tremblay. (1991). *Immigrants in Canada: Their Response to Structural Change (1981–1986)*. Discussion Paper 91.B.2. Ottawa: Institute for Research on Public Policy.

Simon, Julian L. (1990). *Population Matters*. New Brunswick, NJ: Transition Publishers.

Sinding, Steven. (1993). Panel presentation to the Plenary Session on the contribution IUSSP to the 1994 UN International Conference on Population and Development. Paper presented at the General Conference of the IUSSP, Montreal, August.

Statistics Canada. (1990). *Population Projections for Canada and the Provinces and Territories, 1989–2011*. Cat. no. 91-520. Ottawa: Supply and Services Canada.

Tepper, Elliot L. (1987). "Demographic Change and Pluralism." *Canadian Studies in Population, 14*, 223–35.

United Nations. (1989). *Review and Appraisal of the World Population Plan of Action*. New York: United Nations.

United Nations. (1993). *The Age and Sex Distribution of the World Population*. UN ST/ESA/Ser A/134. New York: United Nations.

United Nations. (1995) *Population and Development: Programme of Action adopted at the International Conference on Population and Development, Cairo, 5–13 September 1994*. UN ST/ESA/Ser. A/149. New York: United Nations.

Van de Kaa, Dirk. (1987). "Europe's Second Demographic Transition." *Population Bulletin, 42* (1), 1–58.

Van de Walle, Étienne, and John Knodel. (1980). "Europe's Fertility Transition: New Evidence and Lessons for Today's Developing World." *Population Bulletin, 34* (6), 1–34.

Wattenberg, Ben. (1987). *The Birth Dearth: What Happens When People in Free Countries Don't Have Enough Babies?* New York: Pharas Books.

Weinfeld, Morton. (1988). "Immigration and Canada's Population Future: A National Building Vision." Discussion paper, McGill University, Department of Sociology.

Ziegler, E. (1988). "Refugee Movements and Policy in Canada." Report for Review of Demography and Its Implications for Economic and Social Policy. Ottawa: Health and Welfare Canada.

Chapter 17

Albrow, M. (1990). Introduction. In M. Albrow and E. King, eds., *Globalization, Knowledge and Society* (pp. 3–13). London: Sage.

Albrow, M. (1993). "Globalization." In W. Outhwaite and T. Bottomore, eds., *The Blackwell Dictionary of Twentieth Century Social Thought* (pp. 248–49). Cambridge, MA: Blackwell.

Albrow, M. (1997). *The Global Age: State and Society Beyond Modernity*. Stanford, CA: Stanford University Press.

Albrow, M., J. Made, N. Washbourne, and J. Durrschmidt. (1994). "The Impact of Globalization on Sociological Concepts: Community, Culture and Milieu." *Innovation, 7*, 371–389.

Anderson, B. (1983). *Imagined Communities: Reflections on the Origin and Spread of Nationalism*. London: Verso.

Archer, M.S. (1991). "Sociology for One World: Unity and Diversity." *International Sociology, 6*, 131–47.

Basavarajappa, K.G., R.P. Beaujot, and T.J. Samuel. (1993). *Impact of Migration in the Receiving Countries: Canada*. Geneva: International Organization for Migration.

Bauman, Z. (1991). *Intimations of Postmodernity*. London: Routledge.

Beck, U. (1992). *The Risk Society: Towards a New Modernity*. Newbury Park, CA: Sage.

Bell, D. (1976). *The Coming of Post-Industrial Society: A Venture in Social Forecasting*. New York: Basic Books.

Bellah, R., R. Madsen, W.M. Sullivan, A. Swidler, and S.M. Tipton. (1985). *Habits of the Heart: Middle America Observed*. Berkeley, CA: University of California Press.

Best, M. (1990). *The New Competition*. Cambridge, MA: Harvard University Press.

Brown, L.R., H. Kane, and E. Ayres. (1993). *Vital Signs: The Trends That Shape Our Future*. New York: W.W. Norton.

Budd, L., and S. Whimster, eds. (1992). *Global Finance and Urban Living*. New York: Routledge.

Burton, J.W. (1972). *World Society*. New York: Cambridge University Press.

Cardoso, F.H., and E. Faletto. (1979). *Dependency and Development in Latin America*. Berkeley, CA: University of California Press.

Carnoy, M., M. Castells, S.S. Cohen, and F.H. Cardoso. (1993). *The New Global Economy in the Information Age: Reflections on Our Changing World*. Philadelphia: Pennsylvania State University Press.

Castles, S., and M.J. Miller. (1993). *The Age of Migration: International Population Movements in the Modern World*. New York: St. Martin's Press.

Coupland, D. (1991). *Generation X: Tales for an Accelerated Culture*. New York: St. Martin's Press.

Dahrendorf, R. (1975). *The New Liberty*. London: Routledge.

Dicken, P. (1992). *Global Shift: The Internationalization of Economic Activity*. London: Chapman.

Eade, J., ed. (1997). *Living the Global City: Globalization as a Local Process*. New York: Routledge.

Ekins, P. (1992). *A New World Order: Grassroots Movements for Global Change*. New York: Routledge.

Elias, N. (1978, 1982). *The Civilizing Process*. Vol. 1: *The History of Manners* (1978). Vol. 2: *State and Civilization* (1982). Oxford: Blackwell.

Etzioni, A. (1994). *The Spirit of Community: The Reinvention of American Society*. New York: Touchstone.

Falk, R. (1992). *Explorations at the Edge of Time: The Prospects for World Order*. Philadelphia: Temple University Press.

Featherstone, M. (1995). *Undoing Culture: Globalization, Postmodernism and Identity*. Thousand Oaks, CA: Sage.

Frank, A.G. (1967). *Capitalism and Under-Development in Latin America*. New York: Monthly Review Press.

Fröbel, F., J. Heinrichs, and O. Kreye. (1980). *The New International Division of Labour: Structural Unemployment in Industrialized Countries and Industrialization in Developing Countries*. Cambridge, UK: Cambridge University Press.

Fukuyama, F. (1992). *The End of History and the Last Man*. New York: Free Press.

Giddens, A. (1990). *The Consequences of Modernity*. Stanford, CA: Stanford University Press.

Giddens, A. (1991). *Modernity and Self-Identity: Self and Society in the Late Modern Age*. Cambridge, UK: Polity.

Gifford, D. (1990). *The Farther Shore: A Natural History of Perception*. New York: Atlantic Monthly Press.

Gore, A. (1992). *Earth in the Balance: Ecology and the Human Spirit*. Boston: Houghton Mifflin.

Hall, J.A. (1985). *Power and Liberties: The Causes and Consequences of the Rise of the West*. Oxford: Blackwell.

Hall, S. (1992). "The Question of Cultural Identity." In S. Hall, D. Held, and T. McGrew, eds., *Modernity and Its Futures* (pp. 274–313). Cambridge, UK: Polity and Open University Press.

Harvey, D. (1989). *The Condition of Postmodernity: An Enquiry into the Conditions of Cultural Change*. Cambridge, MA: Blackwell.

Held, D. (1991). "Democracy, the Nation State and the Global System." In D. Held, ed., *Political Theory Today* (pp. 197–235). Cambridge, UK: Polity.

Held, D. (1995). *Democracy and the Global Order*. Cambridge, UK: Polity.

Hirst, P., and G. Thompson. (1996). *Globalization in Question*. Cambridge, UK: Polity.

Inkeles, A. (1983). *Exploring Individual Modernity*. New York: Columbia University Press.

International Sociological Association. (1986–). *International Sociology*, Vol. 1– . London: Sage.

Jameson, F. (1991). *The Cultural Logic of Late Capitalism*. New York: Verso.

Janelle, D.G. (1991). "Global Interdependence and Its Consequences." In S.D. Brunn and T.R. Leinbach, eds., *Collapsing Space and Time: Geographic Aspects of Communications and Information* (pp. 49–81). London: HarperCollins.

Kennedy, P. (1988). *The Rise and Fall of the Great Powers*. New York: Random House.

Kerr, C., J.T. Dunlop, F.H. Harbison, and C.A. Myers. (1960). *Industrialism and Industrial Man*. Cambridge, MA: Harvard University Press.

King, A.D. (1990). *Global Cities: Post-Imperialism and the Internationalization of London*. London: Routledge.

Laszlo, E. (1989). *The Inner Limits of Mankind*. London: Oneworld.

Latour, B. (1993). *We Have Never Been Modern*. Hemel Hempstead, UK: Harvester Wheatsheaf.

Lenin, V.I. (1975 [1917]). "Imperialism: The Highest Stage of Capitalism." In R.C. Tucker, ed., *The Lenin Anthology* (pp. 204–74). New York: W.W. Norton.

Lyotard, J.-F. (1984). *The Postmodern Condition*. Minneapolis, MN: University of Minneapolis Press.

MacCannell, D. (1976). *The Tourist: A New Theory of the Leisure Class*. New York: Schocken.

McGrew, A. (1992). "A Global Society?" In S. Hall, D. Held, and T. McGrew, eds., *Modernity and Its Futures* (pp. 61–116). Cambridge, UK: Polity and Open University Press.

McLuhan, M. (1962). *The Gutenberg Galaxy*. Toronto: University of Toronto Press.

Mann, M. (1986). *The Sources of Social Power*. Vol. 1: *A History of Power from the Beginning to A.D. 1760*. Cambridge, UK: Cambridge University Press.

Marx, K. (1970 [1867]). *Capital*. Vol. 1. London: Lawrence and Wishart.

Meadows, D.H., D.L. Meadows, J. Randers, and W.W. Behrens. (1972). *The Limits to Growth*. New York: Universe Books.

Mills, C.W. (1956). *The Power Elite*. New York: Oxford University Press.

Morgan, R., ed. (1984). *Sisterhood Is Global*. New York: Anchor Press.

Nisbet, R. (1993). "Society." In W. Outhwaite and T. Bottomore, eds., *The Blackwell Dictionary of Twentieth Century Social Thought* (pp. 626–28). Cambridge, MA: Blackwell.

Oman, C. (1994). "Globalisation and Regionalisation: The Challenge for Developing Countries." OECD Development Centre Paper. Paris: OECD.

Perlmutter, T. (1993). "Distress Signals: A Canadian Story — An International Lesson." In T. Dowmunt, ed., *Channels of Resistance: Global Television and Local Empowerment* (pp. 16–26). London: British Film Institute Publishing.

Pettman, R. (1979). *State and Class: A Sociology of International Relations*. London: Croom Helm.

Putnam, T. (1993). "Beyond the Modern Home: Shifting the Parameters of Residence." In T. Bird, B. Curtis, T. Putnam, G. Robertson, and L. Tickner, eds., *Mapping the Futures: Local Cultures, Global Change* (pp. 150–68). New York: Routledge.

Ritzer, G. (1992). *The McDonaldization of Society*. Newbury Park, CA: Pine Forge.

Robertson, R. (1992). *Globalization: Social Theory and Global Culture*. Newbury Park, CA: Sage.

Rosenau, J. (1989). *Interdependence and Conflict in World Politics*. Lexington, MA: D.C. Heath.

Rousseau, J.J. (1968 [1762]). *The Social Contract*. New York: Penguin.

Sachs, W., ed. (1993). *Global Ecology: A New Arena of Political Conflict*. Halifax: Fernwood.

Sassen, S. (1991). *The Global City: New York, London, Tokyo*. Princeton, NJ: Princeton University Press.

Sieghart, P. (1985). *The Lawful Rights of Mankind*. New York: Oxford University Press.

Sklair, L. (1991). *Sociology of the Global System*. New York: Harvester Wheatsheaf.

Smith, A. (1910 [1776]). *The Wealth of Nations*. 2 vols. New York: E.P. Dutton.

Stehr, N. (1994). *Knowledge Societies*. Thousand Oaks, CA: Sage.

Thoreau, H.D. (1927 [1854]). *Walden, or Life in the Woods*. London: Chapman and Hall.

Touraine, A. (1971). *The Post-Industrial Society: Tomorrow's Social History: Classes, Conflicts and Culture in the Programmed Society*. New York: Random House.

Touraine, A. (1995). *Critique of Modernity*. Cambridge, MA: Blackwell.

Van der Pijl, K. (1989). "The International Level." In T. Bottomore and R.J. Brym, eds., *The Capitalist Class: An International Study* (pp. 237–66). Hemel Hempstead, UK: Harvester Wheatsheaf.

Wallerstein, I. (1974, 1980, 1989). *The Modern World-System*. 3 vols. New York and San Diego: Academic Press.

Waters, M. (1995). *Globalization*. London: Routledge.

Weber, M. (1976 [1904–5]). *The Protestant Ethic and the Spirit of Capitalism*. London: Allen and Unwin.

Willetts, P. (1982). *Pressure Groups in the Global System*. London: Pinter.

Yip, G.S. (1993). *Total Global Strategy: Managing for Worldwide Competitive Advantage*. Englewood Cliffs, NJ: Prentice Hall.

Chapter 18

Adler, Freda. (1975). *Sisters in Crime: The Rise of the New Female Criminal*. New York: McGraw Hill.

Becker, Howard, ed. (1964). *The Other Side*. New York: Free Press.

Becker, Howard. (1973). *Outsiders: Perspectives on Deviance*. New York: Free Press.

Braithwaite, John. (1981). "The Myth of Social Class and Criminality Revisited." *American Sociological Review*, 46, 36–57.

Canadian Centre for Justice Statistics. (1996a). *Adult Correctional Services in Canada, 1994–95*. Ottawa: Statistics Canada.

Canadian Centre for Justice Statistics. (1996b). *Canadian Crime Statistics: 1995*. Ottawa: Statistics Canada.

Cawsey, R.W. (1991). *Report of the Task Force on the Criminal Justice System and Its Impact on the Indian and Métis People of Alberta*. Edmonton: Province of Alberta.

Chambliss, William. (1973). "The Saints and the Roughnecks." *Society*, 11, 24–31.

Christie, Nils. (1993). *Crime Control as Industry*. London: Routledge.

Cloward, Richard, and Lloyd Ohlin. (1960). *Delinquency and Opportunity: A Theory of Delinquent Gangs*. New York: Free Press.

Cohen, Albert. (1955). *Delinquent Boys: The Subculture of the Gang*. New York: Free Press.

Cohen, Stanley. (1985). *Visions of Social Control*. Cambridge, UK: Polity.

Commission on Systemic Racism in the Ontario Criminal Justice System. (1995). *Report of the Commission on Systemic Racism in the Ontario Criminal Justice System*. Toronto: Queen's Printer.

Crane, David. (1996). "New 'Global Crimes' on Horizon for 21st Century," *The Toronto Star*, February 5, p. A12.

Doob, Anthony. (1991). *Workshop on Collecting Race and Ethnicity Statistics in the Criminal Justice System*. Toronto: Centre of Criminology, University of Toronto.

Durkheim, Émile. (1938 [1895]). *Rules of Sociological Method*. Trans. S. Solovay and J. Mueller; ed. G.E.G. Catlin. Chicago: University of Chicago Press.

Erickson, Patricia. (1996). "The Selective Control of Drugs." In B. Schissel and L. Mahood, eds., *Social Control in Canada* (pp. 59–77). Don Mills, ON: Oxford University Press.

Findlay, Deborah. (1996). "The Body Perfect: Appearance Norms, Medical Control, and Women." In B. Schissel and L. Mahood, eds., *Social Control in Canada* (pp. 174–200). Don Mills, ON: Oxford University Press.

Foucault, Michel. (1979). *Discipline and Punish: The Birth of the Prison*. New York: Vintage.

Frazier, Charles. (1976). *Theoretical Approaches to Deviance: An Evaluation*. Columbus, OH: Charles Merrill.

Frideres, Jim. (1996). "Native Canadian Deviance and the Social Control of Race." In B. Schissel and L. Mahood, eds., *Social Control in Canada* (pp. 288–319). Don Mills, ON: Oxford University Press.

Gartner, Rosemary, Kathryn Baker, and Fred Pampel. (1990). "Gender Stratification and the Gender Gap in Homicide Victimization." *Social Problems*, 37, 593–612.

Gartner, Rosemary, and Anthony Doob. (1994). "Trends in Criminal Victimization: 1988–1993." *Juristat*, 14 (13), 1–20.

Gottfredson, Michael, and Travis Hirschi. (1990). *A General Theory of Crime*. Stanford, CA: Stanford University Press.

Hagan, John, A.R. Gillis, and Janet Chan. (1978). "Explaining Official Delinquency: A Spatial Study of Class, Conflict, and Control." *Sociological Quarterly*, 19, 386–98.

Hagan, John, John Simpson, and A.R. Gillis. (1987). "Class in the Household: A Power-Control Theory of Gender and Delinquency." *American Journal of Sociology*, 92, 788–816.

Handelman, Stephen. (1995). *Comrade Criminal: Russia's New Mafiya*. New Haven, CT: Yale University Press.

Health and Welfare Canada. (1977, 1991, 1994). *Mental Health Statistics: Institutional Admissions and Separations*. Ottawa: Statistics Canada.

Hendrick, Dianne. (1996). "Canadian Crime Statistics, 1995." *Juristat*, 16 (10), 1–21.

Hirschi, Travis. (1969). *Causes of Delinquency*. Berkeley, CA: University of California Press.

Lemert, Edwin. (1967). *Human Deviance, Social Problems, and Social Control.* Englewood Cliffs, NJ: Prentice Hall.

Manitoba. (1991). *Report of the Aboriginal Justice Inquiry of Manitoba.* Winnipeg: Public Inquiry into the Administration of Justice and Aboriginal People.

Mann, W.E. (1968). *Deviant Behaviour in Canada.* Toronto: Social Science Publishers.

Martin, Sandra. (1996). "In Your Face." *Toronto Life,* July, pp. 70–77.

Marx, Gary. (1995). "The Engineering of Social Control: The Search for the Silver Bullet." In J. Hagan and R. Peterson, eds., *Crime and Inequality* (pp. 225–46). Stanford, CA: Stanford University Press.

Menzies, Robert. (1989). *Survival of the Sanest: Order and Disorder in a Pretrial Psychiatric Clinic.* Toronto: University of Toronto Press.

Merton, Robert. (1938). "Social Structure and Anomie." *American Sociological Review, 3,* 672–82.

Merton, Robert. (1957). *Social Theory and Social Structure.* New York: Free Press.

Myers, Linnet. (1996). "Flip Side of Freedom." *The Toronto Star,* January 2, p. A11.

Palmer, Stuart and John Humphrey. (1990). *Deviant Behavior: Patterns, Sources, and Control.* New York: Plenum.

Quinney, Richard. (1977). *Class, State, and Crime: On the Theory and Practice of Criminal Justice.* New York: McKay.

Reed, Micheline. (1996). "Adult Correctional Services in Canada: Highlights for 1994–95." *Juristat, 16* (7), 1–16.

R. v. Metcalfe. (1927). 49 C.C.C. 260–67 (Sask. Dist. Ct.).

Sampson, Robert, and Janet Lauritsen. (1994). "Violent Victimization and Offending: Individual- and Community-level Risk Factors." In A.J. Reiss and J. Roth, eds., *Understanding and Preventing Violence,* Vol. 3, (pp. 1–114). Washington, DC: National Academy Press.

Scott, Robert A. (1969). *The Making of Blind Men.* New York: Russell Sage.

Shearing, Clifford. (1992). "The Relation between Public and Private Policing." In M. Tonry and N. Morris, eds., *Crime and Justice: An Annual Review of Research,* Vol. 15 (pp. 399–434). Chicago: University of Chicago Press.

Spitzer, Steven. (1975). "Toward a Marxian Theory of Deviance." *Social Problems, 22,* 638–651.

Spradley, James. (1970). *You Owe Yourself a Drunk: An Ethnography of Urban Nomads.* New York: Little, Brown.

Steffensmeier, Darrell, and Emilie Allan. (1991). "Gender, Age, and Crime." In J. Sheley, ed., *Criminology* (pp. 67–94). Belmont, CA: Wadsworth.

Sutherland, Edwin. (1939). *Principles of Criminology.* Philadelphia: Lippincott.

Sutherland, Edwin. (1949). *White Collar Crime.* New York: Dryden.

Sykes, Gresham, and David Matza. (1957). "Techniques of Neutralization: A Theory of Delinquency." *American Sociological Review, 22,* 664–70.

Tanner, Julian. (1996). *Teenage Troubles: Youth and Deviance in Canada.* Scarborough, ON: Nelson.

Taylor, Ian, Paul Walton, and Jock Young. (1973). *The New Criminology: For a Social Theory of Deviance.* London: Routledge and Kegan Paul.

Turk, Austin. (1969). *Criminality and the Legal Order.* Chicago: Rand McNally.

Vold, George. (1958). *Theoretical Criminology.* New York: Oxford University Press.

Weis, Joseph G. (1987). "Social Class and Crime." In M. Gottfredson and T. Hirschi, eds., *Positive Criminology* (pp. 71–90). Beverly Hills, CA: Sage.

Wolfgang, Marvin, Robert Figlio, Paul Tracy, and Simon Singer. (1985). *The National Survey of Crime Severity.* Washington, DC: U.S. Government Printing Office.

Woodard, Joe. (1996). "Anything but Spanking." *Western Report, 11,* (July 15), 34–35.

Wortley, Scot. (1996). "Justice for All? Race and Perceptions of Bias in the Ontario Criminal Justice System — A Toronto Survey." *Canadian Journal of Criminology, 38,* 439–467.

Chapter 19

Barber, Benjamin R. (1996). "Jihad vs. McWorld." In Robert J. Brym, ed., *Society in Question: Sociological Readings for the 21st Century* (pp. 193–99). Toronto: Harcourt Brace.

Bashevkin, Sylvia. (1986). "Independence versus Partisanship: Dilemmas in the Political History of Women in English Canada." In V. Strong-Boag and A. Fellman, eds., *Rethinking Canada: The Promise of Women's History* (pp. 246–75). Toronto: Copp Clark.

Bierstedt, Robert. (1974). "An Analysis of Social Power." In *Power and Progress: Essays in Sociological Theory* (pp. 220–41). New York: McGraw Hill.

Brint, Stephen. (1984). "New Class and Cumulative Trend Explanations of the Liberal Political Attitudes of Professionals." *American Journal of Sociology, 90,* 30–71.

Brym, Robert J. (1979). "Political Conservatism in Atlantic Canada." In Robert J. Brym and R. James Sacouman, eds., *Underdevelopment and Social Movements in Atlantic Canada* (pp. 59–79). Toronto: New Hogtown Press.

Brym, Robert J. (1989). "Politics." In Robert J. Brym with Bonnie J. Fox. *From Culture to Power: The Sociology of English Canada* (pp. 57–79). Toronto: Oxford University Press.

Brym, Robert J. (1992). "Some Advantages of Canadian Disunity: How Quebec Sovereignty Might Aid Economic Development in English-Speaking Canada." *Canadian Review of Sociology and Anthropology, 29,* 210–26.

Brym, Robert J., Michael Gillespie, and Rhonda Lenton. (1989). "Class Power, Class Mobilization, and Class Voting: The Canadian Case." *Canadian Journal of Sociology, 14,* 25–44.

Clark, Terry Nichols, and Seymour Martin Lipset. (1991). "Are Social Classes Dying?" *International Sociology*, 6, 397–410.

Clarke, Harold D., Jane Jenson, Lawrence LeDuc, and Jon H. Pammett, eds. (1996). *Absent Mandate: Canadian Electoral Politics in an Era of Restructuring*, 3rd ed. Toronto: Gage.

Clement, Wallace. (1975). *The Canadian Corporate Elite: An Analysis of Economic Power*. Toronto: McClelland and Stewart.

Davies, James C. (1969). "Toward a Theory of Revolution." In Barry McLaughlin, ed., *Studies in Social Movements: A Social Psychological Perspective* (pp. 85–108). New York: Free Press.

Frank, Jeffrey. (1994). "Voting and Contributing: Political Participation in Canada." In *Canadian Social Trends* (pp. 333–37). Toronto: Thompson Educational Publishers.

Gamson, William. (1968). *Power and Discontent*. Homewood, IL: Dorsey Press.

Goffman, Erving. (1974). *Frame Analysis*. Cambridge, MA: Harvard University Press.

Gurr, Ted Robert. (1970). *Why Men Rebel*. Princeton, NJ: Princeton University Press.

Inglehart, Ronald. (1990). *Culture Shift in Advanced Industrial Society*. Princeton, NJ: Princeton University Press.

International Labour Organization. (1987). *Yearbook of Labour Statistics, 1986*. Geneva: ILO.

Jenkins, J. Craig. (1983). "Resource Mobilization Theory and the Study of Social Movements." *Annual Review of Sociology*, 9, 527–53.

Korpi, Walter. (1974). "Conflict, Power and Relative Deprivation." *American Political Science Review*, 68, 971–84.

Korpi, Walter. (1983). *The Democratic Class Struggle*. London: Routledge and Kegan Paul.

Lipset, Seymour Martin. (1968 [1951]). *Agrarian Socialism: The Cooperative Commonwealth Federation in Saskatchewan*, rev. ed. Berkeley, CA: University of California Press.

Lodhi, Abdul Qaiyum, and Charles Tilly. (1973). "Urbanization, Crime, and Collective Violence in 19th Century France." *American Journal of Sociology*, 79, 296–318.

McCarthy, John D., and Mayer N. Zald. (1977). "Resource Mobilization and Social Movements: A Partial Theory." *American Journal of Sociology*, 82, 1212–41.

Marshall, T.H. (1965). "Citizenship and Social Class." In T.H. Marshall, ed., *Class, Citizenship, and Social Development: Essays by T.H. Marshall* (pp. 71–134). Garden City, NY: Anchor.

Melucci, Alberto. (1980). "The New Social Movements: A Theoretical Approach." *Social Science Information*, 19, 199–226.

Melucci, Alberto. (1995). "The New Social Movements Revisited: Reflections on a Sociological Misunderstanding." In Louis Maheu, ed., *Social Classes and Social Movements: The Future of Collective Action* (pp. 107–19). London: Sage.

Myles, John. (1989 [1984]). *Old Age in the Welfare State: The Political Economy of Public Pensions*, rev. ed. Lawrence, KS: University Press of Kansas.

Myles, John. (1995). "When Markets Fail: Social Welfare in Canada and the United States." Discussion Paper 68. Geneva: United Nations Research Institute for Social Development.

Oberschall, Anthony. (1973). *Social Conflict and Social Movements*. Englewood Cliffs, NJ: Prentice Hall.

O'Connor, Julia S. (1996). "From Women in the Welfare State to Gendering Welfare State Regimes." *Current Sociology*, 44, (2), 1–130.

Olsen, Dennis. (1980). *The State Elite*. Toronto: McClelland and Stewart.

Porter, John. (1965). *The Vertical Mosaic: An Analysis of Social Class and Power in Canada*. Toronto: University of Toronto Press.

Roche, Maurice. (1995). "Rethinking Citizenship and Social Movements: Themes in Contemporary Sociology and Neoconservative Ideology." In Louis Maheu, ed., *Social Classes and Social Movements: The Future of Collective Action* (pp. 186–219). London: Sage.

Rootes, Chris. (1995). "A New Class? The Higher Educated and the New Politics." In Louis Maheu, ed., *Social Classes and Social Movements: The Future of Collective Action* (220–35). London: Sage.

Smelser, Neil. (1963). *Theory of Collective Behavior*. New York: Free Press.

Snow, David A., et al. (1986). "Frame Alignment Processes, Micromobilization, and Movement Participation." *American Sociological Review*, 51, 464–81.

Stackhouse, John. (1996). "What Is Poverty?" *The Globe and Mail*, October 12, pp. D1, D5.

Statistics Canada. (1996). "Federal Government Debt." http://www.statcan.ca/documents/english/pgdb/state/government/gov+03.htm.

Strong-Boag, Veronica. 1986. " 'Ever a Crusader': Nellie McClung, First-wave Feminist." In V. Strong-Boag and A. Fellman, eds., *Rethinking Canada: The Promise of Women's History* (pp. 178–90). Toronto: Copp Clark Pitman.

Tilly, Charles. (1978). *From Mobilization to Revolution*. Reading, MA: Addison-Wesley.

Tilly, Charles. (1979). "Collective Violence in European Perspective." In H. Graham and T. Gurr, eds., *Violence in America: Historical and Comparative Perspective*, 2nd ed. pp. 83–118). Beverly Hills, CA: Sage.

Tilly, Charles, Louise Tilly, and Richard Tilly. (1975). *The Rebellious Century, 1830–1930*. Cambridge, MA: Harvard University Press.

Turner, Bryan S. (1986). *Citizenship and Capitalism: The Debate over Reformism*. London: Allen and Unwin.

United Nations Development Program. (1995). *World Development Report 1995: Workers in an Integrated World*. New York: Oxford University Press.

Ward, Bruce. (1981). "Coyote Condition Makes Our Strikes Long, Spiteful Battles." *The Toronto Star,* August 5, p. 20.

Weber, Max. (1946 [1922]). "Class, Status, Party." In H.H. Gerth and C. Wright Mills, eds. and trans., *From Max Weber: Essays in Sociology* (pp. 180–95). New York: Oxford University Press.

Chapter 20

Bales, R. (1962). "Attitudes towards Drinking in the Irish Culture." In D. Pittman and C. Snyder, eds., *Society, Culture, and Drinking Patterns* (pp. 157–87). New York: Wiley.

Blumer, H. (1969). *Symbolic Interactionism: Perspective and Method.* Englewood Cliffs, NJ: Prentice Hall.

Broverman, I., D. Broverman, F. Clarkson, P. Rosenkrantz, and S. Vogel. (1970). "Sex-Role Stereotypes and Clinical Judgements of Mental Health." *Journal of Consulting and Clinical Psychology, 34,* 1–7.

Brown, C., and K. Jaspers, eds. (1993). *Consuming Passions: Feminist Approaches to Weight Preoccupation and Eating Disorders.* Toronto: Second Storey.

Collins, R. (1979). *The Credential Society: An Historical Sociology of Education and Stratification.* New York: Academic Press.

Dahrendorf, R. (1959). *Class and Class Conflict in Industrial Society.* Stanford, CA: Stanford University Press.

Daly, M. (1978) *Gyn/Ecology: The Metaethics of Radical Feminism.* Boston: Beacon Press.

Davis, K., and W. Moore. (1945). "Some Principles of Stratification." *American Sociological Review, 10,* 242–49.

Djilas, M. (1957). *The New Class: An Analysis of the Communist System.* New York: Praeger.

Douglas, J. (1967). *The Social Meanings of Suicide.* Princeton, NJ: Princeton University Press.

Durkheim, É. (1966 [1897]). *Suicide: A Study in Sociology.* Trans. J. Spaulding and G. Simpson. New York: Free Press.

Eichler, Margrit. (1987). *Nonsexist Research Methods: A Practical Guide.* Boston: Allen and Unwin.

Eichler, Margrit. (1988). *Families in Canada Today,* 2nd ed. Toronto: Gage.

Frank, A. (1969). *Latin America: Underdevelopment or Revolution: Essays on the Development of Underdevelopment and the Immediate Enemy.* New York: Monthly Review Press.

Garfinkel, H. (1967). *Studies in Ethnomethodology.* Englewood Cliffs, NJ: Prentice Hall.

Gibson, A. (1960). *The Logic of Social Enquiry.* London: Routledge and Kegan Paul.

Goffman, E. (1963). *Stigma: Notes on the Management of Spoiled Identity.* Englewood Cliffs, NJ: Prentice Hall.

Greene, J. (1959). *The Death of Adam: Evolution and Its Impact on Western Thought.* Ames, IA: Iowa State University Press.

Hartmann, H. (1984). "The Unhappy Marriage of Marxism and Feminism: Towards a More Progressive Union." In A. Jaggar and P. Rothenberg, eds., *Feminist Frameworks: Alternative Theoretical Accounts of the Relations between Women and Men* (pp. 172–89). New York: McGraw Hill.

Hertz, R. (1986). *More Equal than Others: Women and Men in Dual-Career Marriages.* Berkeley, CA: University of California Press.

Hoffman, L. (1989). "Effects of Maternal Employment in the Two Parent Family." *American Psychologist, 44,* 283–92.

Kasselbaum, G., D. Ward, and D. Wilner. (1971). *Prison Treatment and Parole Survival: An Empirical Assessment.* New York: Wiley.

Laslett, B., and C. Warren. (1975). "Losing Weight: The Organizational Promotion of Behavioural Change." *Social Problems, 23,* 69–80.

Lupri, E. (1991). "Fathers in Transition: The Case of Dual-Earner Families in Canada." In J. Veevers, ed., *Continuity and Change in Marriage and Family* (pp. 242–54). Toronto: Holt, Rinehart and Winston.

Luxton, M. (1986). "Two Hands for the Clock: Changing Patterns in the Gender Division of Labour in the Home." In M. Luxton and H. Rosenberg, eds., *Through the Kitchen Window: The Politics of Home and Family* (pp. 17–36). Toronto: Garamond.

Mahon, M. (1992). *The Persistent Prison? Rethinking Decarceration and Penal Reform.* Toronto: University of Toronto Press.

Martinson, R. (1974). "What Works? Questions and Answers about Prison Reform." *Public Interest, 35,* 22–54.

Marx, K. (1904 [1859]). *A Contribution to the Critique of Political Economy.* Trans. N. Stone. Chicago: Charles H. Kerr.

Marx, K. (1972 [1844]). "Contribution to the Critique of Hegel's *Philosophy of Right:* Introduction." In R. Tucker, ed., *The Marx–Engels Reader* (pp. 11–23). New York: W.W. Norton.

Merton, R. (1968 [1949]). *Social Theory and Social Structure.* New York: Free Press.

Moore, K., and I. Sawhill. (1984). "Implications of Women's Employment for Home and Family Life." In P. Voydanoff, ed., *Work and Family: Changing Roles of Men and Women* (pp. 153–71). Palo Alto, CA: Mayfield.

Nett, E. (1988). *Canadian Families: Past and Present.* Toronto: Butterworths.

Parsons, T. (1951). *The Social System.* Glencoe, IL: Free Press.

Phillips, A. (1992). "Universal Pretentions in Political Thought." In M. Barrett and A. Phillips, eds., *Destabilizing Theory: Contemporary Feminist Debates.* (pp. 10–30). Cambridge, UK: Polity.

Piven, F., and R. Cloward. (1971). *Regulating the Poor: The Functions of Public Welfare.* New York: Pantheon.

Solzhenitsyn, A. (1973–75). *The Gulag Archipelago.* London: Collins/Fontana.

Tong, R. (1989). *Feminist Thought: A Comprehensive Introduction*. Boulder, CO: Westview Press.

Ursel, J. (1992). *Private Lives, Public Policy: 100 Years of State Intervention in the Family*. Toronto: The Women's Press.

Weber, M. (1958 [1904–5]). *The Protestant Ethic and the Spirit of Capitalism*. New York: Scribner.

Weinberg, M. (1996). "The Nudist Management of Respectability." In E. Rubington and M. Weinberg, eds., *Deviance: The Interactionist Perspective*, 6th ed. (pp. 308–16). Boston: Allyn and Bacon.

Chapter 21

Brym, Robert. (1986). "Incorporation versus Power Models of Working Class Radicalism with Special Reference to North America." *Canadian Journal of Sociology*, 11, 227–51.

Burt, Sandra. (1990). "Canadian Women's Groups in the 1980s: Organizational Development and Policy Influences." *Canadian Public Policy*, 16, 17–28.

Creese, Gillian. (1988). "The Politics of Dependence: Women, Work and Unemployment in the Vancouver Labour Movement before World War II." *Canadian Journal of Sociology*, 13, 121–42.

Douglas, Jack. (1970). "Understanding Everyday Life." In J. Douglas, ed., *Understanding Everyday Life* (pp. 3–44). Chicago: Aldine.

Foschi, Martha, and Shari Buchan. (1990). "Ethnicity, Gender, and Perceptions of Task Competence." *Canadian Journal of Sociology*, 15, 1–18.

Giddens, Anthony. (1984). *The Constitution of Society*. Berkeley, CA: University of California Press.

Ginsberg, Effie, and Frances Henry. (1985). *Who Gets the Work?* Toronto: Urban Alliance on Race Relations and the Social Planning Council of Toronto.

Goffman, Erving. (1961). *Asylums: Essays on the Social Situations of Mental Patients and Other Inmates*. New York: Doubleday/Anchor.

Goyder, John. (1981). "Income Differences between the Sexes: Findings from a National Canadian Survey." *Canadian Review of Sociology and Anthropology*, 17, 176–83.

Gray, George, and Neil Guppy. (1993). *Successful Surveys*. Toronto: Harcourt Brace.

Laxer, Gordon. (1989). *Open for Business: The Roots of Foreign Ownership in Canada*. Toronto: Oxford University Press.

Lenton, Rhonda. (1990). "Techniques of Child Discipline and Abuse by Parents." *Canadian Review of Anthropology and Sociology*, 27, 157–85.

McMullan, John, and Peter Swan. (1989). "Social Economy and Arson in Nova Scotia." *Canadian Journal of Criminology*, 281–308.

Maybin, Fiona. (1993). *Gender Discrimination and the Recruitment Process: Matching People and Jobs*. Unpublished M.A. thesis. University of British Columbia.

Pineo, Peter, and John Porter. (1967). "Occupational Prestige in Canada." *Canadian Review of Anthropology and Sociology*, 4, 24–40.

Reitz, Jeffrey. (1993). "Statistics on Racial Discrimination in Canada." *Policy Options*, 14, 32–36.

Richer, Stephen. (1984). "Sexual Inequality and Children's Play." *Canadian Review of Anthropology and Sociology*, 21, 166–80.

Roethlisberger, F.J., and William Dickson. (1939). *Management and the Worker*. Cambridge, MA: Harvard University Press.

Rothe, Peter. (1991). *The Trucker's World: Risk, Safety, and Mobility*. New Brunswick, NY: Transaction Publishers.

Sudman, Seymour, and Norman Bradburn. (1982). *Asking Questions: A Practical Guide to Questionnaire Design*. San Francisco: Jossey-Bass.

Wannell, Ted, and Nathalie Caron. (1995) "Male–Female Earnings Gap among Recent Postsecondary Graduates." *Education Quarterly Review*, 2 (1), 20–34.

Waxler-Morrison, Nancy, Gregory Hislop, Bronwen Mears, and Lisa Kan. (1991). "Effects of Social Relationships on Survival for Women with Breast Cancer: A Prospective Study." *Social Science and Medicine*, 33, 177–83.

Weber, Max (1949 [1904, 1905, 1917]). *The Methodology of the Social Sciences*. Glencoe, IL: Free Press.

NAME INDEX

SUBJECT INDEX

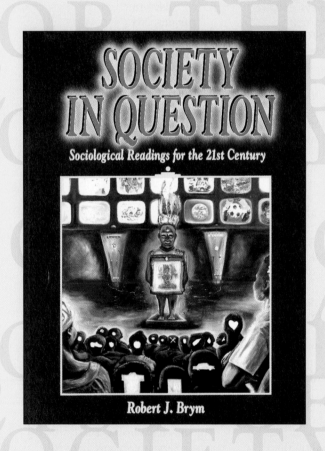

READER REPLY CARD

We are interested in your reaction to *New Society: Sociology for the 21st Century,* Second Edition, by Robert J. Brym. You can help us to improve this book in future editions by completing this questionnaire.

1. What was your reason for using this book?

   ❏ university course   ❏ college course
   ❏ continuing education course   ❏ professional development
   ❏ personal interest   ❏ other _____

2. If you are a student, please identify your school and the course in which you used this book.

3. Which chapters or parts of this book did you use? Which did you omit?

4. What did you like best about this book?

5. What did you like least about this book?

6. Please identify any topics you think should be added to future editions.

7. Please add any comments or suggestions.

8. May we contact you for further information?

Name: _____

Address: _____

_____

Phone: _____

(fold here and tape shut)

MAIL ⇒ POSTE

Canada Post Corporation / Société canadienne des postes

Postage paid
If mailed in Canada

Port payé
si posté au Canada

Business Reply

Réponse d'affaires

0116870399   01

0116870399-M8Z4X6-BR01

Larry Gillevet
Director of Product Development
HARCOURT BRACE & COMPANY, CANADA
55 HORNER AVENUE
TORONTO, ONTARIO
M8Z 9Z9